DOOM TO BOOM

DOOM
TO
BOOM

The explosive story behind the
most dramatic decade in the life
of Middlesbrough FC

DAVE ALLAN
AND
ADRIAN BEVINGTON

MAINSTREAM
PUBLISHING
EDINBURGH AND LONDON

Photo Credits

The authors and publishers are grateful to the following for permission to use photographs in this book: North News and Pictures; Highland Studios; ASP; Arthur Foreman; AirFotos Ltd; Mark Leech; Blades Sports Photography.

Every effort has been made to trace copyright owners but in some instances this has not been possible.

First published in Great Britain in 1996 by
MAINSTREAM PUBLISHING COMPANY (EDINBURGH) LTD
7 Albany Street
Edinburgh EH1 3UG

ISBN 1 85158 902 3

A catalogue record for this book is available from the British Library

Typeset in Sabon by Bibliocraft, Dundee

Printed and bound in Great Britain by Butler and Tanner Ltd, Frome, Somerset

CONTENTS

CHAPTER ONE

The First One Hundred and Ten Years

Although the Middlesbrough story moved into overdrive during the decade 1986–96, the club has a long history dating back one hundred and twenty years. Those were the days when multi-million pound transfer deals weren't even the stuff of fantasies. Indeed, the club was formed by a group of cricket enthusiasts keen to find a winter-time hobby.

Over the next one hundred and twenty years, the club was to achieve numerous highs and just as many lows. Although unable to win a major honour, the club was to boast many star players including such greats as George Camsell, Wilf Mannion, George Hardwick, Brian Clough and Graeme Souness.

The club was formed at a meeting of the town's amateur cricket club in the gym of the Albert Park Hotel on 18 February 1876. The friends frequently met in the gym at the back of the building, which still stands in the town's Linthorpe Village. For many years, it was believed that the club was formed at a tripe supper in the town's Talbot Hotel, but research by the club's official historian Harry Glasper unearthed the truth behind the formation of Middlesbrough Association.

The newly-formed football club was given permission to play games at the Old Archery Ground in Albert Park and their first ever match took place in February 1877 against a local rugby union side, Tees Wanderers. Jackson Ewbank struck Middlesbrough's first goal in a 1–1 draw. The Middlesbrough team for that historic match was: Harvey, Windross, Hardisty, Booth, Parkin, Lees, Ewbank, Greenwood, Jenkins, Harrison, Hildreth.

The first away game followed on 22 December that year when Middlesbrough lost 1–0 at Barnard Castle. However, home games soon began to attract crowds of some 200, resulting in the Parks Committee advising the club to find a new home as spectators were spilling on to the pitch and damaging the turf.

Although it was reported in 1878 that the club would play on a rented field in Grove Hill, Middlesbrough had moved to Breckon Hill Road by March 1879 where spectators were charged three pence admission. Average takings were under £3.

At this early stage, the club found games hard to come by as football was still in its formative years. However, it continued to grow as a spectator sport and when the club moved to an old cricket field on Linthorpe Road a first ever four-figure crowd saw Middlesbrough play Sheffield Exchange.

Regular competitive games were established with the formation of the Cleveland Association in 1881 and Middlesbrough took part in the FA Cup for the first time two years later. However, the formation of the Football League in 1888 led to a split in the club, with many players looking to join the league and turn professional. A break-away was inevitable and those supporting professionalism broke away to form a club called Ironopolis Football Company.

Although they did not attempt to join the Football League, the old club decided they would have to turn professional to avoid becoming the town's second-class club. Ironopolis – nicknamed 'The Washers' or 'The

Nops' – won three successive Northern League championships, leaving Middlesbrough – or The Scabs – in their wake.

While Ironopolis joined the Football League's extended Second Division in 1893, it was a short-lived league history. After just one season, the club folded after hitting financial problems, despite avoiding the re-election zone. During this time, Middlesbrough had reverted to amateur status and again went on to reassert themselves as the region's top club, clinching the Northern League championship in 1894, 1895 and 1897 and the FA Amateur Cup in both 1895 and 1898.

In 1895, Middlesbrough beat Old Carthusians 2–1 in front of a crowd of 4,000 in the FA Amateur Cup final at Headingley, thanks to strikes from Dave Mullen and 'Happy' Nelmes. Three years later they clinched the cup for a second time, beating Uxbridge 2–1 at Crystal Palace with Bishop and Kemplay on target.

Middlesbrough finally made the step up to the Football League in 1899, having been elected into the Second Division and played their first league match at Lincoln in 1899, a 3–0 defeat. A first league win followed by a 1–0 scoreline over Grimsby Town at the Linthorpe Road ground on 23 September. Although they failed to win a single away match all season, the club did enough to avoid the bottom positions, finishing fourteenth out of eighteen clubs.

With the club on a steady financial footing, efforts were made to progress and, in only their third season of league football, promotion to Division One was clinched when Middlesbrough finished second to West Bromwich Albion. After just one year of First Division football, the club left the Linthorpe Road ground for the newly-built Ayresome Park. Celtic were the first visitors for an official opening in September 1903. A first league game followed, with north-east rivals Sunderland winning 3–2.

Two years later, the club caused a football sensation and were accused of trying to buy their way out of relegation trouble when they signed centre-forward Alf Common for a

record transfer fee of £1,000. Even so, Common's arrival was a success and the club avoided the drop. That same year, goalkeeper Tim Williamson became the club's first England international.

Middlesbrough, whose nickname became 'Boro', were to stay in the top flight of the Football League until 1924, achieving a best ever position of third in 1913–14 when the great forward George Elliott was at his peak. After just three years in Division Two, First Division football returned in 1927 when the club won the Second Division championship in spectacular style. Centre forward George Camsell created a divisional record by netting 59 league goals.

Despite that success, relegation followed just one year later but Boro bounced back to clinch a second championship and another promotion in 1929. This time they were to stay in the top flight for twenty-five years. Although they were unable to mount a sustained title bid, they twice

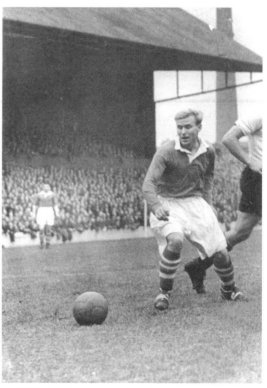

Wilf Mannion was perhaps the greatest player in Middlesbrough's history – until recent years.

Champions: John Hickton and Frank Spraggon lift the Second Division championship trophy at Ayresome Park in 1974.

reached the quarter-final of the FA Cup (in 1936 and 1947), as local-born stars Wilf Mannion and George Hardwick established themselves as England international heroes. In 1949, a club record 53,596 watched the team take on Newcastle United at Ayresome Park.

However, the good times couldn't last and relegation came in 1954. It was the start of twenty years outside the top flight. Despite having a hugely talented forward line – including England internationals Brian Clough, Alan Peacock and Eddie Holliday – they were unable to win promotion and by the time Ayresome Park was used to help host the 1966 World Cup finals they had been relegated to Division Three for the first time ever.

Fortunately, Boro won promotion at the first attempt, with stars like John O'Rourke, John Hickton and Arthur Horsfield all regular goalscorers. But there was more frustration when Stan Anderson's side narrowly failed time

after time to clinch promotion to the top flight.

It took the arrival of former England World Cup star Jack Charlton and the signing of ex-Scotland international Bobby Murdoch to turn the near misses into success. At the first attempt, Charlton inspired Boro to a record points haul as promotion was clinched long before the 1973–74 season had ended. Players such as Graeme Souness, Willie Maddren, Jim Platt and David Armstrong established themselves as household names over the next few years. An Anglo-Scottish Cup success was clinched in 1975, though real honours remained agonisingly out of reach.

Manchester City knocked Jack's lads out of the League Cup at the semi-final stage in 1976 and four times Boro reached the last eight of the FA Cup between 1975 and 1981. It was the 1981 run which ended in a fateful quarter-final replay defeat to Wolves at Molineux. That night's 3–1 defeat was seen by many pundits as

the start of a downward spiral which was to lead to the club's liquidation and near extinction five years later.

Frustrated by the club's lack of real success and ambition, many young stars left Boro for bigger clubs. Players such as David Armstrong, Craig Johnston, David Hodgson and Mark Proctor left for big fees and were replaced by far less talented players. Former player Bobby Murdoch, now in the manager's role, was unable to halve the downturn which ended in relegation in 1982.

Murdoch was sacked after a disastrous start to the 1982–83 campaign, to be replaced by Malcom Allison. Although he helped the club avoid relegation, Allison was not happy about the club's policy of selling their young stars to make ends meet and was sacked when he refused to do so.

For a short spell, former hero Jack Charlton stood in as caretaker manager and it was he who recommended that one of his former players, Willie Maddren, should be given the job as full-time manager. Alas, Maddren always had a mountain to climb. His talents as a coach were undeniable, but the club was facing a financial crisis and success on the pitch would not come overnight.

CHAPTER TWO

Doomed to Relegation – 1985–86

Having come frighteningly close to relegation to Division Three in 1984–85, Middlesbrough were hoping for a much brighter campaign in 1985–86. With a newly appointed chairman in Alf Duffield, manager Willie Maddren was in a more confident frame of mind for the start of the campaign.

Just before escaping relegation to the Third Division by the narrowest of margins at Shrewsbury in May, Maddren had been given money to develop a winning side, though £200,000 was hardly a king's ransom! He wasted no time in using his new found finance, quickly acquiring the services of Huddersfield's Brian Laws, a skillful defender, and target-man style centre-forward Archie Stephens from Bristol Rovers, two players who would go on to be firm favourites with the fans.

Two seasons earlier, former manager Malcolm Allison had twice taken Manchester United's reserve goalkeeper Stephen Pears on loan. Pears was an instant hit with Boro supporters. Unfortunately Allison was unable to raise the cash for Pears at the time, but with a small amount of money at his disposal, Maddren instantly snapped up the Brandon-born keeper for £80,000 – a signing which would prove to be one of the best in the club's history.

'Pearsey cost over a third of my budget but I think he was my best buy,' says Maddren. 'He was a little bit of an introvert but he was a good trainer. He was the crowd's choice, too, and we needed to try to boost the ticket sales. He was brave, agile and I thought he would improve the last line of the defence. He went on to become a great stalwart for the club.'

Another of his targets, the experienced midfielder Don O'Riordan, soon arrived at Ayresome from Carlisle United, while Maddren also arranged for former Sunderland striker Gary Rowell to return to his native north east in a bid to increase the team's goal power.

It proved to be a big setback for the club when player-coach David Mills was injured. Top scorer with fourteen goals the previous season he never appeared for Middlesbrough again.

Maddren gave four players their debuts as Boro opened the season with a trip to the capital for a game at Plough Lane with Dave Bassett's Wimbledon. Along with Rowell and O'Riordan, Maddren blooded young defenders Steve Corden and Gary Pallister. Corden had come up through the junior ranks, while Pallister had joined the club from Northern League outfit Billingham Town, a year after being overlooked by former boss Allison. The real quirk in Corden and Pallister making their debuts alongside one another was that Boro were only able to pay Pallister's wages when he first joined the club because Corden's father, club director Dick, was prepared to pay them personally.

'We were desperately short of players for that opening match,' recalls Maddren. 'Hamilton, Ward and Beagrie were all suspended, Nattrass was only half fit while Pallister and Corden were making their debuts because we were so short. I thought, "Here we go again."'

All the hope which the club took into that opening fixture rapidly evaporated as Boro were well and truly hammered 3–0; and that

wasn't the only disaster, because young Corden was carried off with a broken leg just before half-time.

The story seemed all too familiar as Boro travelled to Third Division Mansfield for a first-round first leg Milk Cup tie the following Tuesday evening. Boro were soundly beaten 2–0 and missed out on an important away goal when Rowell missed a penalty.

The shock cup defeat was 20-year-old Pallister's last first team appearance for Boro for three months. Maddren dropped the future England star, replacing him in defence with the experienced Tony McAndrew.

Recalls Pallister: 'Despite losing 3–0, the Wimbledon game went quite well for me. I got some favourable write-ups in the press and had generally impressed people. Against Mansfield, though, I was terrible. The whole team didn't play well but I had a really bad game and wasn't surprised to be dropped.'

Some hope was restored when Ayresome Park hosted its first game of the campaign with the visit of Fulham. A salmon-like leap from Archie Stephens enabled him to head home the game's only goal, and in doing so he clinched Boro's first points of the season. A worrying sign, however, was the paltry crowd of just 5,368.

From the next three league games Boro picked up only one point, a goalless draw at newly promoted Hull City, but what was even more concerning was that Boro had scored only one goal in the opening five fixtures.

Boro's exit from the Milk Cup at least allowed supporters some compensation in seeing Boro hit four goals for the first time in four years. Unfortunately, Mansfield equalled the feat in a 4–4 draw which saw the lower division club go through 6–4 on aggregate.

By this time, another two additions to the squad had arrived in the form of Pat Heard from Newcastle United and Mitch Cook from Scarborough. Heard was an experienced First Division performer and seemed to be just the player to bring some quality to the side – or so people thought! Cook was a midfielder who was totally unproven but had shown great promise with the Seasiders.

Maddren says: 'I brought Pat Heard in from Newcastle but he didn't do it for me. I think he was my worst buy. He had a poor attitude, in my opinion. People ask me why I persevered with him but what other alternative was there?'

David Mills, who was acting as assistant to Maddren while he was injured, reflects: 'Willie's record in the transfer market was very good. People were critical of Heard but it's important to remember he cost just £5,000. He had been a good player and had a good pedigree, having played for the likes of Villa, Everton, Sheffield Wednesday and Newcastle. Before people say he was a poor buy who didn't perform, they should consider how much we actually paid for him.'

Mills also reveals that he and Maddren came close to signing others who went on to become top players. 'We went for a lad called Neil Pointon at Scunthorpe. I think we offered £35,000 and they wanted another £5,000, but Alf Duffield wasn't prepared to pay more. He later played for Everton. Then there was Ian Baird, who played for Boro several years later. I think his club wanted £50,000 and Willie spoke to him, but the deal didn't come off for whatever reason.'

Back on the pitch, a slight improvement began in September. The team remained unbeaten, though they hardly set the world alight with four draws and a last minute 1–0 win at Sheffield United, thanks to a scrappy goal from Rowell.

Maddren recalls: 'We played Stoke City in September and we were winning 1–0. Gary Gill was playing in the middle of the park and we were starting to get good balance in the team and I could see us starting to climb the league. But in the last five minutes Gary Rowell was hacked down in the box by George Berry. It was a penalty. I couldn't believe the referee, Trelford Mills, didn't give the decision. From the goalkick, the ball bounced to a Stoke player who hit a shot from 35 yards. It dropped through Pearsy's hands and trickled over the line. At that point, I said to Steve Smelt, "It won't happen for me, here – I need that little bit of luck and I haven't got it."'

The win at Bramall Lane, however, moved

Boro into their highest position of the season when they reached fifteenth spot for one week only. David Currie was the only player apart from five-goal Rowell to find the net during September.

October began with the visit of Crystal Palace to Ayresome Park where a crowd of under 5,000 – very much the norm by now – witnessed Boro suffer a 2–0 defeat and another game without a home goal. The Palace game triggered a new problem, a very public disagreement between manager Maddren and young central defender Tony Mowbray.

Mowbray recalls: 'I played in the centre of defence alongside Irving Nattrass in the defeat by Crystal Palace on the Saturday. The following Monday morning, Willie just ignored me. I would pass him in the corridor and he would blank me. I didn't think I deserved to be treated like that, but I was pencilled in for a game against Bradford City two weeks later. I went in to see Willie and told him I wasn't in the right state of mind for a game and wouldn't be playing after the way I'd been treated. He was furious and said I would never play for the club again.'

But Maddren insists: 'We had a discussion with Tony and his father and they wanted a better deal for him. There was nothing we could do. He was wanting the sort of deal players in previous years had been on, but we were playing in front of crowds of 5,000. He had missed the boat in that respect. I offered Tony what I was able to. His father's advice was to go on the list. I recognised that Tony was Middlesbrough's future but I didn't have the relationship with him I would have liked.

'We'd had a practice match and looked at playing a sweeper system or flat back four. I don't think Tony played a part in the last twenty minutes of the game and I was possibly going to leave him out, but then Tony McAndrew got injured, so I named Mowbray in the team for the Bradford City game. But he came in and told me he wasn't in the right frame of mind to play. I told him he was presumptuous and then, in a fit of temper, I told him he would never play for the club again. I was disappointed in his attitude though I feel he was possibly being misled somewhat.

'Three weeks later, I was offered £30,000 for Tony by Joe Royle at Oldham. I refused to take it and he upped it to £35,000. I told him I wasn't going to sell him because he was still part of my long-term plans, so Joe bought Andy Linighan from Leeds.'

Alas, this was also a time which saw Ayresome Park sink to new depths when a crowd of just 2,177 attended a game with Carlisle in the newly launched Full Members Cup. It was the lowest attendance for a first team game in Ayresome Park's long history.

The following game saw Bernie Slaven make his debut in the Yorkshire derby with Leeds United at Elland Road. Slaven, a £25,000 bargain from Albion Rovers, had ended the previous season as the top scorer in Scotland. After watching him in a trial for Boro's reserves, Maddren knew he had to sign him. 'He was way beyond anything I had at the club,' he says. 'After the reserve game, I got the gateman to make sure the gates were locked and there was no scouts from other clubs hanging around. I got on the phone to Albion's chairman and got him to accept £15,000 down with £10,000 to follow later. Even that fee was too big for us and, in chairman Alf Duffield's absence, I got the go-ahead from director Steve Gibson.'

Slaven adds: 'It was a huge thrill to sign for a club like Middlesbrough. It was just the chance I'd been waiting for.'

Leeds were also going through a difficult period, having themselves been relegated from the First Division alongside Boro four years earlier. They were languishing towards the bottom of the table. Manager Eddie Gray had been dismissed the previous week, much to the annoyance of the supporters, and the game became a side show to their animated campaign to have him reinstated. Boro lost 1–0 and there was hardly any cause for the travelling fans to become too excited at the prospect of Slaven firing the team to glory.

One week later Boro took on the Third Division champions Bradford City at Ayresome Park and, this time, Slaven delivered his home debut goal in a 1–1 draw, chipping

Goalkeeper Stephen Pears clears the danger in a 1–1 home draw against Bradford City in October 1985, a game which saw Bernie Slaven score on his home debut.

the ball over goalkeeper Peter Litchfield.

Afterwards, Maddren was full of praise for his new striker, commenting: 'Slaven showed what he is capable of and he can get better, but I was disappointed with the service we gave him. He will be a crowd-pleaser because he has more than a flair for goals. He is creative in and around the box.'

Boro travelled to Roker Park the following Tuesday for the first Wear–Tees derby in four seasons. Sunderland had just been relegated but were now under the stewardship of high-profile manager Lawrie McMenemy, who was said to be on mega-bucks to get Sunderland promoted at the first attempt. McMenemy was, of course, doing his utmost to achieve this, but not in the manner in which his directors were expecting because they were struggling at the foot of the table.

Boro had Stephens sent off early in the game after two vicious assaults on Sunderland central defender Shaun Elliott, leaving big problems for

Maddren's men. In the end Boro were beaten by a first half goal from a shot deflected past Stephen Pears by Tony McAndrew at the Roker end.

By now Boro were in big relegation trouble, a situation which wasn't helped by another defeat at Grimsby Town, though at least the team managed a goal apiece from Laws and Stephens in a 3–2 reverse.

'Psychologically, players got into the habit of losing,' reflects Maddren. 'We would be hitting the bar while the game was goalless and end up wondering if we could hold on. The difference between success and failure was so slight.'

A week later Boro drew another blank but gained a point due to Blackburn's inability to force the ball home. Incredibly Boro's defensive record mirrored that of a promotion side at this stage of the season, but the injury to David Mills was proving very costly because there was a clear lack of goals at the other end.

'I was disappointed for Willie and for myself,' admits Mills. 'My Achilles problem alone kept me out for more than twelve months which was frustrating because I'm sure I could have made a contribution. I might have scored another ten goals – and that would have made a huge difference.'

On 16 November Maddren was finally rewarded with only his third win of the season when Boro beat Joe Royle's Oldham in a five-goal thriller at Ayresome Park in front of a crowd of just 4,234. Back in the side that day, in place of the injury-prone Irving Nattrass, was Gary Pallister, who had just returned from a loan spell with near neighbours Darlington.

'I remember Willie telling me that I would be back in the team,' he says. 'Playing competitive football with Darlington in the Fourth Division had been good experience and had toughened me up. I felt a lot more confident and went on from there.'

Rowell grabbed his sixth goal of the campaign in the last minute against Oldham, while David Currie and Pat Heard both opened their accounts.

Though Boro were struggling in terms of their league position, Pallister did not believe Boro would still be in a relegation position come the end of the season.

'With players like Heard and Rowell, I thought we had too much experience to go down. Now I know we had too many of what Tony Mowbray used to call journeymen footballers. They were there for their next pay-day and didn't have the club at heart.'

Though they suffered a 3–0 reverse at Millwall in their next game, Boro bounced back with another victory as they brushed aside the challenge of relegation rivals Shrewsbury on a snowbound Ayresome pitch. Rowell and Heard were again on the scoresheet, while veteran McAndrew got his first goal of the season against a Shrews defence which had a young Nigel Pearson at the heart of it.

Gary Rowell celebrates after scoring in a 3–1 home win over Shrewsbury in November 1985. It was only the fourth league win of the season.

Goal! Stalwart Tony McAndrew makes a point after scoring in a vital 2–0 derby win over Sunderland on 28 December 1985.

Boro's trip to Stoke should have seen them take all three points but after taking a two-goal lead through Stephens and O'Riordan they threw the game away.

Bernie Slaven believes the troubles could be put down to the poor attitude of some of the senior players. 'Although he was a nice guy, Willie Maddren wasn't a disciplinarian and some of the players tended to take advantage of that. There was a real lack of discipline during the training sessions – too much messing about and not enough serious work.'

Brian Laws agrees with Slaven, saying: 'Willie was such a nice fella and didn't have a ruthless streak in him. I feel a lot of the senior pros abused him at times. Some of them didn't appreciate what he was doing for the club.'

Gary Pallister goes further, insisting: 'You'd find some of the players missing come the tough games. There were players on the injury list that you couldn't help but wonder about.'

Promotion chasers Wimbledon were the next visitors to Ayresome Park for a game which saw Boro gain revenge for the opening day disaster. The game was a major success for the back-in-favour Tony Mowbray as he grabbed the only goal of the match.

Boro continued their improved form by thrashing bottom club Fulham 3–0 at Craven Cottage on the Saturday before Christmas with two goals from Rowell and one from Slaven (his first since his home debut two months earlier).

This left Boro clear of the relegation zone in eighteenth position as they entered the Christmas period, which must have given Maddren some hope that he might be turning the corner. Another favourable trip, to Carlisle on Boxing day, beckoned. But, again, it wasn't to be as Boro suffered another 1–0 defeat.

A crowd of 19,701 packed into a freezing Ayresome Park for the visit of Sunderland on 28 December, although the figure included a large travelling contingent, to see if Boro could get back to winning ways. By now Boro were

playing with a back five with O'Riordan dropping back from midfield to join Mowbray and Pallister in the centre of defence and McAndrew and Laws in the full-back positions.

The Sunderland game proved to be a real triumph for the defence as they performed outstandingly, offering no opportunity to the visitors, while it was Mowbray and McAndrew who hit the target in a 2–0 victory. It was Boros' fourth win in six games.

With only one goal conceded in the last four league games, Boro's tails were up again and it seemed the defence was improving all the time. One player, in particular, was coming on in leaps and bounds – Gary Pallister.

'Willie Maddren was fantastic for me,' he says. 'I always felt I could trust him. In fact, he showed me a lot of favouritism, taking me for extra training, especially in the very early days. Basically, he realised I was a lazy sod and that I needed a lot more stamina, so he got me on the weights.'

Maddren recalls: 'Mowbray and Pallister were always going to be the main two, though I had a long-term vision of having Colin Cooper as my sweeper because he read the game so well. I could see the nucleus of the team – we had a great foundation, if only I could buy a bit of time. I was a great advocate of getting it right down the middle and making yourself difficult to beat.

'It looked as if it was starting to turn for us when we won the derby game against Sunderland. We knew another win would take us just short of mid-table.'

Boro went into the New Year's day fixture with Huddersfield Town at Ayresome Park with great expectations, but controversially lost the game 1–0.

'We were atrocious,' admits Maddren. 'I couldn't believe two performances could be so different. Then, just before half-time Bernie played this one-two and toed the ball past the goalkeeper. It was a perfectly good goal and he couldn't possibly have been offside but the linesman gave it against him. If we'd gone in 1–0 up having played crap, I could have given them a complete bollocking, but at 0–0 I couldn't because it could have totally

demoralised them. Again, I got to to the point where I thought it just wasn't going to happen for me. Had we won that match, the players could have started to look at the league table and realise they weren't as bad as they thought they were, but we were always fifth or sixth from bottom.

'We needed a goalscorer because Bernie was still adjusting. I was a little bit disappointed with Archie Stephens because he had promised so much when I signed him but he had a poor season. He wasn't the aggressive Archie that I thought he was, though I don't know why.'

Boro travelled to high flying Norwich City and suffered another setback, a 2–0 defeat sending them spiralling back towards trouble. Two days later Boro faced Southampton in a rearranged FA Cup third round tie at Ayresome Park. At the time the Saints were one of the First Division's better sides, packed full of internationals, and it was no surprise to see them cruise past Boro with a 3–1 victory in front of a crowd of 12,730. Danny Wallace smashed an excellent hat-trick past Pears. However, it was a poor display by a Boro defence which included experienced defenders Tony McAndrew and Irving Nattrass.

'Tony had joined the club as part of the deal which took Darren Wood to Chelsea the previous season,' says Maddren. 'I wanted him to be on the pitch and shake his fist, to be a leader on the park, but he wasn't the same player he was when he left Middlesbrough. Meanwhile, Irving was struggling with injuries, which meant that two of my most experienced players were performing at 75 per cent of their total capabilities. The likes of Mowbray, Pallister and Cooper were going to be the salvation of the club, but even Mowbray was still quite green at the time. He was going through a big learning curve, having been converted from left-back.'

By then, Bruce Rioch had teamed up with Maddren as assistant manager. The 1–0 defeat at Portsmouth increased the pressure on Maddren and he was sacked after a 3–1 home defeat by Charlton. Almost immediately Rioch was given the job, with thirteen games to save the club from relegation. Meanwhile, the

RIOCH TAKES OVER THE REINS

While Boro's ever-worsening plight was coming to a head in the boardroom, the effect on the playing side was considerable. It resulted in the sacking of Willie Maddren and the appointment of Bruce Rioch.

In January 1986, Boro had advertised in *The Times* for a first-team coach and interviewed several candidates for the job.

'I'd been working with John Coddington as a part-time coach, but I advertised the position of first-team coach,' explains Maddren. 'Bruce was on the shortlist, with John Pickering, Peter Morris and Stan Ternant.

'If I'm honest, I liked John more – I thought he would be honest and loyal – but it was the first time I compromised with the chairman, Alf Duffield. He fancied Bruce and I had no dislike of him. Everyone was saying Bruce was a big threat to me but I didn't give two hoots who got my job if I got the sack. I got on very well with Bruce but knew he might not be content with the number two job.'

Rioch recalls: 'I'd been in America working with Seattle for a year. I'd twice been a player with Seattle in the NASL. I saw the job advertised in one of the national newspapers and met with Willie Maddren and Alf Duffield at Ayresome Park for the interview, which I was sure had gone well.

'I actually remember leaving the boardroom with the chairman and his secretary asked me to pop next door to claim my expenses. My reply was that I'd collect them when I came back, which could be described as pompous, but I was confident I could do the job.

'It was on the following Monday or Tuesday that I received a call from Willie offering me the job.'

Rioch recalls a conversation he had with Maddren soon after taking up the role. 'Willie had explained to me in the interview that he was under pressure from the club to get results, adding he had three games to get them, starting the following Saturday at Portsmouth and followed by further tough games at home to Charlton and Leeds.

'Travelling back from Portsmouth after a 1–0 defeat, I recall him saying that if we didn't get good results he might have to step down. I said he didn't need to do that and told him to dig his heels in and battle it out.'

Within a week, however, Maddren had gone following another defeat, to Lennie Lawrence's promotion-chasing Charlton Athletic.

David Mills believes his former team-mate had done all he could for the club and was not to blame for the team's plight.

'No-one knew how difficult that job was,' says Mills. 'Resources were so limited and there were virtually no staff whatsoever. We knew we had some great young players coming through – the likes of Colin Cooper, Stuart Ripley, Lee Turnbull and Peter Duffield – but they were still babies really and we didn't feel it was right to throw them in at the deep end.

'The first team, which we had largely inherited, had a lot of mediocrity. Willie had tried to strengthen it and had got several bargains – Pears for £80,000, Slaven for £25,000 and Laws for £30,000, while Archie Stephens gave terrific service to the club.'

Maddren himself recalls: 'I gave myself a tough three or four games for things to improve. The Charlton game was a pretty inept performance, with Mowbray far and away our best player. I was almost hoping the chairman might make me an offer to leave that I couldn't refuse. Instead, he said that he wanted me to resign. I told him I couldn't afford to resign because I had eighteen months of my contract left and wanted compensating. I would go for half of what my contract was worth and he agreed to that.

'It took me a long time to get over leaving the club, but I eventually looked back and realised how little I'd had to work with. It gave me pride to see the players I'd developed do well for the club but I think I'd taken them as far as I could. I honestly don't think I could have sorted things out because I'd given it my all and was mentally exhausted.'

Rioch vividly remembers Maddren's departure.

'We were asked to go upstairs to see the chairman after the home defeat by Charlton. After speaking to us both, the chairman asked to speak to Willie on his own. It transpired Willie was to leave the club and I was given the opportunity to take the job.'

Despite Maddren's time in charge ending the way it did, Mills believes Maddren made the right decision to take on the task.

'It was always going to be difficult and Willie knew that, but those kind of chances don't come round very often. Willie didn't do it for money – his salary must have been the worst in the Second Division by a mile. He just wanted to make the club a success.'

Given the desperate situation the club was in, Mills believes Maddren worked wonders.

'I've never experienced a situation like it in all my years in football. It was the hardest time of my football career. I was in charge of the youth team and I remember we couldn't even make a cup of tea for the opposition at half-time because we couldn't afford the tea-bags. We didn't even have soap or towels at the ground. Of course, I couldn't burden Willie with problems like that – he had enough on his plate as it was.'

In financial terms, the club was not much better off under Rioch, but things were set to take a rapid upturn over the next two seasons.

In charge: Bruce Rioch succeeded Willie Maddren as Boro manager.

weather took a turn for the worse with a real cold spell settling in.

Rioch says of this period: 'The poor weather allowed us to spend time with the players on the training ground. I remember we spent some time in Scotland. Indeed, we played a friendly match with Celtic and really it was a case of finding the best players for the best positions, round pegs in round holes. We had to get them playing to a pattern, understanding their role in the team and get them to feel confident on the ball, and to do this we played a lot of shadow football.'

Boro's physio at the time, Steve Smelt, has very clear memories of those early training sessions under Rioch. He recalls: 'I'll never forget his first training session – it was a freezing cold morning and Bruce had the first eleven playing a game of shadow football which entailed them moving around on a full size pitch without a ball, listening to his instructions. It was very regimented the way he walked the players through every move, from goalkeeper

to full-back and so on, but that was the way he got them to perform the way he did.'

At this point, David Mills had returned to fitness but a freak training accident ruled him out for another six months. 'I'd got over the Achilles injury by February but then I crashed into a five-a-side goal and broke my arm,' he reveals.

Pallister, who did not get on well with Rioch, remembers the day he took charge of the squad for the first time.

For his first training season, he took us up to Hall Drive and ran the bollocks off us,' he reveals. 'We finished, came back to Ayresome and then he took us back and ran the b******s off us again!'

Although he made Pallister a first team regular, Rioch wanted the gangly centre-back to alter his style.

'I remember him pulling in Tony Mowbray and I one day to tell us he wanted us to be the solid rocks on which the team could be built. I could understand him asking that of Mogga,

but I just wasn't that sort of player.'

Rioch's first game in charge was a rearranged fixture at home to mid-table Grimsby. With only a few changes to the team, Boro tore the Mariners apart in a comprehensive 3–1 victory, Slaven scoring with two headers and Mowbray also on target.

Another good display – with 18-year-old Colin Cooper making his first team debut as substitute – followed as they unluckily went down 2–1 at Crystal Palace, having led for much of the game. They turned on some real style against Leeds United, only to draw the game 2–2 – although Currie's gem of a free-kick gave great hope for the future.

The crowds were gradually starting to increase. Rioch was giving everyone hope through his team's much improved displays which continued a few days later against Sheffield United. Almost incredibly, however, the result was a 2–1 defeat.

After that game, chairman Alf Duffield shared his disappointment with the fans but said he was convinced Boro were in very capable hands with Bruce Rioch.

Teenagers Colin Cooper and Stuart Ripley had both been given a regular place in the side, at the expense of Heard and Rowell, as the battle heated up. Cooper, who was playing in midfield, admits he did not feel any pressure on him.

'I don't think I realised what it was all about,' he says. 'I was a young lad and desperate to take my chance but I can't remember feeling any pressure over the relegation issue.'

Results certainly improved during the run-in, as Boro were victorious at Huddersfield (3–0) and Blackburn (1–0) and at home to Portsmouth (1–0) and Millwall (3–0). However, while performances were improving on the pitch, things took a turn for the worse off it with the shock resignation of chairman Alf Duffield on the eve of a 1–0 defeat at Oldham.

At a press conference before the game, Duffield explained: 'I'm no longer prepared to pour money into the club. I don't want Middlesbrough to be a one-man band and it

was time for Teesside business people to rally round.'

Reports at the time suggested Duffield had made a massive £700,000 contribution to the club and that he was responsible for paying the players' wages for the current season. Duffield added: 'I can do no more, I feel very sad but with me out of the way the club may benefit.'

When asked if he would ask the club for his money back, he answered wryly: 'Do you think they can pay me?'

The chairman's regular column for the home game with Millwall was written by the club's young director Steve Gibson – later to become chairman – who discussed the club's new share proposal for the summer.

The Millwall clash came in the penultimate game of the season, and the magnificent 3–0 scoreline gave Boro a great deal of confidence as they went into the final match, at Shrewsbury for the second year in succession, needing a win to guarantee safety. Unfortunately, an over-zealous tackle by Millwall's Les Briley ruled Cooper out of the final showdown so another 18-year-old, Lee Turnbull, was brought in to replace him.

Recalls Turnbull: 'Until the Millwall game, my only first-team experience was in the Full Members Cup against Hull City. Then I got on for Coops after twenty minutes at Millwall for my league debut. Having been a Boro fan all my life, it was brilliant to play for the club.

'Then, the day before the Shrewsbury game, we were at Lilleshall when Bruce told me I was in the team. It was such an important game for the club, I didn't expect to play until I was named in the side. The truth is that if I hadn't been playing I'd have been stood with my mates in the terraces, watching the game.'

The Shrews themselves were not totally clear of the mire; Boro had no reason to doubt their ability to save themselves again. Steve Smelt recalls the build up to the game by saying: 'We felt the game was ours as we'd been there before and done it and we weren't in a bad state.

'As part of the pre-match build-up we'd spent a few days at Lilleshall and the mood in the camp was excellent. I remember Lee Turnbull was selected for the game and

Despite this photograph, Archie Stephens did not score a bag-full of goals during the 1985–86 season. He was to make a bigger impact the following year.

although he was very young, he was a livewire striker and we expected to win.'

The game was played in a very hostile atmosphere. There was a large contingent of travelling Boro fans and a heavy police presence to maintain order. There had been crowd trouble a year earlier when Boro had won at Gay Meadow, but this time things did not go so smoothly. A food kiosk inside the ground was set on fire.

After early sparring on the pitch, Shrewsbury began to get on top and took the lead in sixteen minutes when Colin Robertson scored in front of the Boro supporters. This resulted in a pitch invasion from so-called Middlesbrough fans, who also ripped the stanchion off the goalposts. Riot police eventually cleared the pitch and the game continued, though there was no further scoring during the first forty-five minutes.

In the second period, Stephens struck the equaliser with a close-range volley to spark another mini pitch invasion. Things turned sour for Boro when Pallister was sent off on the hour and ten-man Boro's resistance ended when Hughes snatched the winner for Shrewsbury with just six minutes remaining. Boro were down and faced only their second ever season in the Third Division.

It is no surprise that Pallister has painful memories of that fateful day – and his dismissal, in particular.

'There was a hostile atmosphere, made worse when the fans rioted after Shrewsbury went ahead. Then, from a free-kick, I got a flick on for Archie to score. Then a lad broke through and I was chasing him and slid in to make a tackle. I don't think I committed a foul in the game – and I still say I won the ball before I caught the man. As far as I was concerned, it was a fair tackle but the referee saw it differently.

'I remember hearing the cheer of the Shrewsbury fans after their second goal while I was sat in the dressing room. I was uncontrollable at the time. I felt I'd let everyone down. There were no tears – I just felt so guilty.'

Brian Laws recalls: 'We didn't go into the match thinking it was useless, that we were down, but our time had come. Afterwards, the dressing room was like a morgue. There were a few tears shed – but that was good because it showed how much the club meant to the players.'

Even Turnbull cannot look back on his full debut with any satisfaction.

'It was a tense day,' he says. 'We didn't perform, the game seemed to pass us by. Afterwards, those of us who had supported Boro as kids were in tears. Bruce came into the dressing room and told us we would bounce back, but it was a terrible day.'

It truly was a terrible day. But there were more, far more terrible days to come in the weeks ahead. Boro faced the prospect of only their second season in Division Three, but if people thought that was bad, they hadn't realised the nightmare had just begun. The club was in dire straits.

The bottom of the table looked like this:

	P	W	D	L	F	A	Pts
Shrewsbury	42	14	9	19	52	64	51
Sunderland	42	13	11	18	47	61	50
Blackburn	42	12	13	17	53	62	49
Carlisle	42	13	7	22	47	71	46
Boro	42	12	9	21	44	53	45
Fulham	42	10	6	26	45	69	36

CHAPTER THREE

Liquidation: How Disaster was Averted – The True Story

Middlesbrough's future as a professional football club was on the line during the summer of 1986.

The club had been in financial difficulties for several seasons but by the time they were relegated from Division Two at Shrewsbury in May that year, the crippling debts which had been allowed to mount up over the previous years had become a real threat to the club's continuing existence.

The club had been without a chairman since the resignation of Alf Duffield towards the end of the season. Duffield, a self-made businessman, was the fourth supremo of the club in five years, his predecessors being Mike McCullagh, George Kitchen and Charles Amer. Amer had led the club throughout the successful period of the 1970s but relinquished his position amid speculation and rumours surrounding his financial dealings relating to the club in the press.

Kitchen, a strong ally of Amer on the board, took over responsibility and presided over the club as it tumbled out of Division One in 1982, but it was not long before the reins were passed to McCullagh. The bad times continued with the club running on a shoestring budget and hovering above the relegation trapdoor to Division Three until the inevitable happened in the summer of 1986.

It was a far cry from Jack Charlton's tenureship when Middlesbrough attracted crowds of 30,000 and from the time when John Neal's multi-talented young squad was tipped for trophies in the early 1980s. Supporters generally feel that the club's free-fall began on 10 March 1981, when Neal's team lost an FA Cup sixth round replay in extra time to Wolves at Molineux. The result appeared to hang over the club like a black cloud as the team Neal had built and developed was allowed to disintegrate, with the cream of the crop being sold off for big fees.

Managers came and went, as did players, although it must be said of a lesser quality, and the club just kept spiralling downwards. It appeared that Middlesbrough Football Club had little hope of being successful while the long-serving board retained power.

Steve Gibson, aged just 26, became the club's youngest ever board member in 1984. He was earning recognition with his developing shipping business, Bulkhaul. Gibson, Middlesbrough born and bred, was also a diehard Boro fan. He had suffered at the club's demise with everyone else.

Gibson recalls: 'I joined the club in November 1984 after getting involved through my links with local football. I'd always had season tickets but I was approached to sponsor Middlesbrough and I agreed to put up an advertising board.

'A club director, Keith Varley, came to see me at my office. He told me the club were looking for new ideas and asked me if I would be prepared to meet with the chairman, Mike McCullagh, which I agreed to do.

'After several meetings, Mike asked me if I would be interested in joining the board. I liked both Mike and his finacial advisor, Miles Middleton. Miles was a very honest guy who told me the financial problems the club had.'

It was not a good time to be a Middlesbrough supporter during the 1984–85 season as Boro were in the Second Division relegation zone with ever-decreasing gates.

However, Gibson was not put off by what he saw from the outside: 'The gates were down

to about 5,000 and the club was losing £5,000 or £6,000 a week but I decided to join the board because I wanted to find out about the club. This was an excellent opportunity. I was just as frustrated as every fan at the decline of the club from the late '70s, when the club was in the First Division and challenging for honours. It had been a massive decline within the space of five or six years.'

The board of Middlesbrough Football Club had been held in the utmost contempt by the frustrated supporters. Middlesbrough were renowned as a selling club, but nobody could ever work out why that had to be. Gates had always been relatively high, yet there never appeared to be any ambition from the top. Even when managers developed good players, there seemed to be little effort made to strengthen what was already there. The team's own fans used to describe Boro as a second-rate club with a second-rate team. It was a real bone of contention.

Gibson cared deeply about the club and seized his opportunity.

'I was disappointed and very curious to find out what was behind the decline,' he reveals.

'On joining the board, I began to appreciate where the problem lay. It was in the boardroom.

'Within a short period of time, I became disenchanted with my board colleagues and realised that Mike McCullagh didn't have the resources to change things. It was obvious that there was no substance or ability in the boardroom. Further decline was inevitable.'

The new board member recognised that the club needed radical change – and fast.

'It needed a massive influx of cash. The management accounts were something you just didn't see and everything, right the way through the club, was rotten. The place was depressing. Ayresome Park and its offices were dirty and there was no spark among the people. If these people had been employed in any other business, that business would have ended up in decline.'

Gibson began to dig deeper and he soon became aware of the boardroom politics and personality clashes.

'McCullagh recognised the inadequacies of the club,' he says. 'He was very bitter against the previous leading shareholder, Charles Amer. Amer had presided over the club during the major part of its decline and during the time the controversial sports hall was built.'

The sports hall that Gibson refers to was built at the rear of the North stand at Ayresome Park and was regarded as a white elephant which was a factor in the club's financial ruin.

'When I arrived it was very difficult to find out what the debts were. It was a hand-to-mouth existence. Whoever shouted the loudest got paid; if you didn't shout, you didn't get paid.'

At this stage, McCullagh had already entered into discussion with Alf Duffield, who at that time was seen on Teesside as very successful with his engineering business, ITM.

'Alf was very flamboyant,' remembers Gibson. 'He wasn't shy of publicity and it was easy to read about or listen to what Alf had to say, and, he claimed to be a very wealthy man with a very successful business.'

Supporters saw Duffield as the messiah who could lift the club from the murky depths and lead it to the promised land. With that in mind, Gibson, too, was happy to have him on board.

'I felt that it was a very good move for the football club and that Alf would take the club forward. I sat down and had a long chat with him and he said everything I wanted to hear. He'd stabilise the club financially and he was going to support the manager, Willie Maddren, by making funds available.

'By this time Mike McCullagh had already planned his exit route, and I was disappointed because he'd brought me into the club.'

Within months of Duffield taking over, former chairman McCullagh resigned as a director.

Boro fought a relegation battle throughout the 1984–85 campaign, with manager Maddren allowed only minimal resources. It was a hard baptism into the world of management for 33-year-old Maddren, a Boro legend as a player, whose career had been cruelly cut short by injury. Somehow, he kept the club up in 1985, thanks to a 2–0 victory at

Shrewsbury on the final day of the season, and Gibson had great belief in him.

'Willie was a great judge of players, but he could only do so much with what he had. He couldn't turn water into wine, but he kept the club up.

'So at the end of that season there was some optimism. We hadn't been relegated which was a success story in itself. Alf Duffield was installed as chairman, the club's finances appeared to be stabilised and Alf had gone public in saying money would be made available for players.

'Alf was true to his word. Willie knew who he wanted – Stephen Pears, Bernie Slaven, Archie Stephens, Brian Laws and Don O'Riordan. He topped that up with free transfers.'

Duffield may have been making all the right noises, but little things about him left Gibson unsure.

'I was disappointed in Duffield. I expected him to clear out the board but he didn't do that. All the old guys were still there – and gradually I began to understand why.

'Alf had taken over the club but he didn't have control over the shareholders – and in the background was Charles Amer.

'At this time, there was some suspicion of Amer within the boardroom. During the period of decline Parkway Estates had undertaken a considerable amount of work for Middlesbrough Football Club. The commitment to this work was a huge amount of money for the football club to find in its difficult financial situation.'

Gibson reveals: 'Amer was the chairman of Middlesbrough Football Club and Parkway Estates did internal work for the club, including the building of the contoversial sports complex.

'I've actually seen a letter that was written by Graham Kelly, then secretary of the Football League, to Charles Amer, asking how he was going to finance the sports complex because he was applying for grant aid. Amer replied that it would be with the sale of players, Armstrong, Proctor, Johnston and Hodgson. That letter is still in the possession of Middlesbrough Football Club.'

Unfortunately for everyone concerned, the season got off to a disastrous start and despite the occasional good performance, it became another long struggle to keep the wolves from the door. Again Maddren did everything that was humanly possible, but in some quarters it was felt that he wasn't being supported 100 per cent by certain parties, as Steve Gibson remembers.

'The season went on and it was a struggle. Part of the problem was that Willie was stretched. He was still doing everything, but players who he brought in didn't have time to settle and one or two of the senior pros let him down badly.'

Maddren found himself in something of a catch 22 position. The club needed instant results, which left him no time to wait for the developing kids who were coming through. He had people in the wings in the reserves who were doing very well like Ripley and Cooper, but Maddren felt it would be too early for them.

'He brought in Pallister, who he was getting very excited about, Cooper and all the other good youngsters, but decided that the old pros could get us through.'

Results on the field weren't the only problem though, as Gibson was about to find out . . .

'As the season progressed it became apparent to me that Duffield's business was in financial difficulty. Alf had the football club at heart, there's no doubt about that, but what he didn't have was the experience. He wanted instant results and they weren't forthcoming.'

This was to prove the downfall of Maddren.

'Alf wanted somebody else alongside Willie and he brought in Bruce Rioch. That was Alf's appointment and perhaps the best thing he did for the football club while he was there. It made Willie very uneasy because it wasn't his appointment. Within about six weeks of Bruce joining us, Willie was fired and Bruce, who realised the senior pros were running amok, immediately clamped down on them.

'We started to see he wasn't frightened of putting the kids in. He would rather go down fighting than have one or two senior pros not giving their all for the cause. Bruce's attitude

was absolutely refreshing and we started getting results. Before he took over, we'd all got used to the idea of relegation, but with Bruce results came and we were perhaps unfortunate to go down.

'Problems arose approximately four weeks before the end of the season. Bruce was very precise and disciplined in his own approach and he was not at all frightened of speaking his mind. It was obvious there was growing conflict between Duffield and Rioch.

'I was becoming increasingly aware that cash we had expected to go into the football club had dried up, and there were rumours around town that other people weren't getting paid by ITM. At a dinner at the Billingham Arms Hotel, there was an almighty argument between Rioch and Duffield. The next morning, I got a call at 8 a.m. from the club secretary David Thorne, who said: "We have a problem, I have a letter from Alf Duffield resigning as chairman."

'I was bitterly disappointed because I felt Duffield would have at least telephoned to inform me. I told David Thorne to sit on it until I got down to the club. I thought it through and took legal advice. I spoke to Alf in the next few days and became aware that he had financial difficulties himself and was no longer in a position to help the club.

'I came to understand that Duffield had leant money himself or arranged for the bank to lend money to the club which he had secured. I thought the club was getting more financial stability but what had actually happened was that instead of putting capital into the club, all he'd done was arrange for bigger loans.'

Such was their scale, that trying to quantify the loans was a virtually impossible task. Eventually, Gibson called a board meeting to share some of the detail of the debt with other directors.

'I asked them to keep it absolutely quiet because we needed to get through the season,' he recalls. 'But within 24 hours somebody from the board – I've never found out who, though I have my suspicions – went public with the news.'

Enraged and naturally suspicious, Gibson made attempts to find out more about exactly what was going on at the club. He found increasing difficulty in obtaining details of the club's accounts.

'Things were going missing all over the place.'

While such revelations were becoming public knowledge, Rioch was trying desperately to keep the team in the Second Division. It was Gibson who kept the manager updated with events.

'I guessed the debt at that stage, in April 1986, at around £1.4–£1.5 million and I told Bruce what was going on. During that time, Bruce and I became very close. I told him I would find a way of getting us through to the end of the season.

'While Bruce was busy trying to keep morale high among the lads and to avoid relegation, I was trying to keep the creditors at bay,' continues Gibson. 'If we had forfeited any fixtures then the club would have been disqualified by the Football League.'

Eventually, the club got through to the end of the season, though it ended, disastrously, in relegation to Division Three. There was worse news off the pitch. It was now evident that the club's debts were far higher than Gibson had initially anticipated.

'I still couldn't quantify the figure because there were still matters which I didn't fully understand.'

While the debts were numerous, it was clear that one major debt was down to the building of the ill-fated sports complex.

'Amer still had an outstanding bill to the club of £100,000, which he hadn't paid himself when he was chairman,' reveals Gibson. 'This bill went back to around 1978 and he was prepared to take action against the club for non-payment of it.

'The club had counter-sued Amer because the sports complex was an absolute disaster, a shambles. The squash courts were different sizes; you could put a ball on the left-hand side of the complex and it would roll quicker than it would on the right-hand side. There were doors which opened on to a six-foot drop and others which opened up to a brick wall.'

Not surprisingly, Middlesbrough's new director was furious and held several meetings with Amer, who refused to accept any responsibility.

There could be little doubt that time was running out for Middlesbrough Football Club. Therein, lay a dilemma for Gibson.

'The problem I had was that if I saved the football club who would I be saving it for? The answer, unfortunately, was that it would be for the existing shareholders, who had already failed.

'ICI and British Steel were downgrading on Teesside and the shipbuilding had died. There was something like 28 per cent male unemployment in certain areas of the town and the end of the club would be another nail in the coffin of Middlesbrough.'

In a desperate attempt to salvage something from the situation, Gibson held a meeting with Middlesbrough Borough Council's chief executive John Foster and council leader Mike Carr.

Gibson outlined the club's grave situation in a no-holds-barred discussion. 'It needs a vast input of cash, we've been relegated and we need to pay the wages,' he said.

Explaining his approach to the council, Gibson says: 'My business was growing and doing well but I lacked big time credibility as an individual. I went to Middlesbrough Council in the hope that they could supply that credibility. Thankfully, they agreed to lead an attempt to build a consortium to save the football club.'

Gibson was also introduced to Graham Fordy, Cleveland sales executive for Scottish and Newcastle Breweries. He asked Fordy, a lifelong Middlesbrough supporter, if S&N would be interested in forming part of a consortium to save the club.

It was eventually agreed that Gibson would approach S&N, while Middlesbrough Council would approach ICI. At the same time, an advert would be placed in *The Times* newspaper asking for any other interested parties to come forward.

Fordy remembers this period very well, although he admits his first meeting with

Gibson seemed unlikely to herald a harmonious relationship.

'I'd been a Boro supporter all my life, and in the mid '80s I became a shareholder. At the final AGM, it became clear the club was in great difficulty, and that was the first time I met Steve Gibson. There wasn't what you would call an instant relationship formed because he bullishly asked me why, if I wanted to help the club, did I not get some money out of my pocket and put it into the club.'

The relationship may have got off to a bad start, but it wasn't long before the two became strong allies.

'Steve was desperately looking for people to help, and he knew I was very friendly with Mark Page, then of Radio One fame. He asked Mark to find out if I could get interest from Newcastle Breweries, which resulted in me contacting Steve. I told him that although I doubted any interest from the brewery, I would be happy to assist.'

Eventually, after several discussions and a presentation by the club, S&N began to show an interest. Fordy recalls being questioned on the benefits of the brewery joining the consortium at their head office in Newcastle.

'I supported it strongly and said there was the possibility of trade improvements,' he says.

Meanwhile, Gibson was doing everything possible to enlist support, but it was far from plain sailing.

'People from all over came forward, but there were a lot of time-wasters.

'We needed money to raise £1.5 million and, at that stage, we were planning to pay previous creditors 50p in the pound but the next fight was with the Football League. I had a belief we would win, especially as Middlesbrough Council, S&N and ICI had a real interest, along with my company, Bulkhaul. It was fantastic to have support, because I'd carried the burden from Alf Duffield quitting through to about the May of that year.'

Undeterred, an ever-more determined Gibson continued to make progress with the new consortium.

'We put the advert in *The Times*, which took up a huge amount of time because I was

speaking to people morning, noon and night about the football club.'

The consortium was about to come across a man who appeared to be a potential saviour, a man who would become synonymous with the liquidation period and a key player in the club's finances for the next seven years.

Gibson explains: 'One of the replies we had was from a guy called Henry Moszkowicz, who had helped the club previously, prior to my involvement, so he had some credibility. I flew down to Heathrow with John Foster and spoke to Henry. John explained how we were trying to set up a consortium of five or six members to put in £200,000 each, which would be used to negotiate with our creditors.'

What the consortium became increasingly sure about was that it did not want to save the existing football club because its existing shareholders would be the ones to benefit, remaining on the board. So they concluded that the old club would have to die.

'After careful consideration, I felt that the club had no chance of survival whilst it was operating under its present structure, with authority with the board as a whole,' says Gibson. 'I felt that the only way that the club had a chance was if I took total control. Therefore, I called a board meeting and asked for total executive powers.

'After a long and heated meeting, and thanks to the support of Dick Corden and Keith Varley, I was given full authorisation to run the club, with the board's previous authority ceasing. If that had not been forthcoming, I would have resigned immediately as I did not believe that the club had any future if it did not follow that path that gave me the authority to start approaching people.

'Now at this stage my relationship with Duffield had gone right down because he was in financial trouble while I was asking people to take 40p in the pound on their debts. If they took more than 40p then the club was dead, but if they accepted 40p or 50p in the pound we had a chance. Most of the debt was owed to the previous directors. There was over £500,000 to Duffield and £100,000 to Amer, who were seeking full payment.

'The other problem we had was the Midland Bank, with whom we had an overdraft. The Midland had a charge on the assets which were Ayresome Park and the Hutton Road training ground and we entered into negotiations with them.'

Meanwhile, with the interest of Henry Moszkowicz, there was much anticipation. Gibson continues: 'I went down to London with John Foster to meet Henry again. John told him we planned to kill the old club while trying to have a friendly arrangement with the creditors. Within ten minutes, Henry offered us a £200,000 cheque. I said, "Henry, we don't need that, your word is good enough. We haven't yet got a proper structure to cope with that." We then had five members capable of raising £900,000.'

The consortium was officially formed in John Foster's office at Middlesbrough Council.

'We then had agreement with Duffield that he would wind up the company and we were quite happy for that to progress,' reveals Steve Gibson. 'But we had to get agreement with the Football League and they needed a scapegoat.'

At the time, the game in England was at a low ebb, with football hooliganism at its peak. The Bradford City fire and Heysel disaster added to the feeling of mourning. Middlesbrough weren't the only club in financial trouble either. Other clubs were finding that frivolous spending in the late '70s and early '80s had left them in dire straits. Several clubs had used the liquidation process as a path to survival, leaving huge unpaid debts behind them, but the Football League, concerned for the image of the game, had decided enough was enough.

In Boro's case, liquidation was a necessity. The club was on its last legs and in real danger of folding. But previous misdemeanours of other clubs resulted in a lack of support from the league, as Gibson recalls.

'There was Wolves, Swansea and about six or seven clubs right on the brink, but they were going to pick Middlesbrough as a scapegoat.

The rules changed from day to day. We thought we had a deal and then they would

Boro players leave Ayresome Park for their final training session before liquidation. Left to right: *Gary Pallister, Bernie Slaven, Don O'Riordan and Archie Stephens.*

'I asked him which player he was referring to and he told me, "Gary Pallister – I'll give you £35,000 for him."'

'No player at this football club was for sale – we were trying to keep the club together.'

As the season drew closer, the consortium pooled money to pay the players' wages, but some players had no intentions of staying with the club.

Gibson recalls: 'One player, Don O'Riordan, took advantage of us not paying their wages on only one occasion. We weren't happy with his conduct. O'Riordan had only joined the club a year earlier and he was one of the senior pros who we felt had not done enough for the club. Once the opportunity to leave the club came, because he was in effect on a free transfer, he was able to boost his own personal income at the cost of Middlesbrough Football Club.

'All the other players were fantastic. Bruce got them tuned in and we carried on pre-season training anywhere we could, whether it was Billingham Synthonia or Stewart Park. Bruce got all the senior pros out of the club and we were left with a very small squad. They were training but we didn't know whether the club would be saved.

"There was a crescendo building as we got closer to the new season.'

Gibson took the opportunity to take his wife for a week's break in Italy. Three days into the holiday, Gibson heard from John Foster the sort of news he had dreaded.

'We've got a problem,' said Foster, on the line from Middlesbrough. 'The council has been rate-capped and Mike Carr is on holiday.'

'What are you telling me, John?' asked Gibson.

'I don't know what I'm telling you, but we've got a problem,' replied Foster.

'I took the next flight home and a taxi picked me up from Teesside airport,' continues Gibson. 'It was the taxi driver who told me the council had announced that they were withdrawing their £200,000 from the consortium.

'Although the officers of Middlesbrough Council worked very hard, I don't think that

change their minds. We got no help from the Football League – they had a hidden agenda, which was to crucify a football club, and this small club in the north-east was the one they picked on.'

Apart from the club being targeted as an example, certain individuals appeared to have a conflict of interests with regards to Middlesbrough's survival hopes.

Gibson reveals: 'One of the members of that committee, Ron Noades, telephoned me several months before the consortium was set up, and his conversation went along the lines of, "I understand you've got terrible financial difficulties down at Middlesbrough. Is there any way I can help?"

'I said I would welcome any help and he said, "We have a fantastic lottery department here and you should get in on it." I told him I needed help now and he said, "Well, I might be able to help by taking a player off your hands."'

Still smiling despite the tension: the players during their final training session before the club's liquidation.

the councillors involved came out with any credit whatsoever. The message we got was that although they couldn't help us financially, they would do everything in their power to help.'

A meeting followed in which it was suggested that the remaining members of the consortium 'chipped in' to make up the loss of the council's £200,000 contribution.

'Scottish and Newcastle Breweries felt they were unable to do so and ICI felt the same, but Henry Moszkowicz offered an extra £150,000 to make his contribution £350,000 and I stuck in a further £25,000,' says Gibson. 'So the £900,000 became £825,000 and that's all we had.

'We still felt that would be enough but with three days to the start of the season, the Football League came up with their ruling. We were told that unless we came up with a bond which was open-ended, paid all creditors 100p in the £1 and proved we had £350,000 working capital, we would not be allowed to play our first game against Port Vale.'

That evening Gibson was stunned to see Tyne-Tees Television announce the death of Middlesbrough Football Club. Later the same evening, he was entertaining Dutch guests at the Cleveland Tontine restaurant when Bruce Rioch walked in. Over a drink, the two became

evermore determined that all was not lost.

'There was an underlying spirit there which said all's not dead,' recalls Gibson. 'Out of necessity, we had split into two camps. There were ICI's representative, Colin Henderson, and myself living in the town hall in John Foster's office, while Charles Wellington, an ICI legal representative, Graham Fordy and Reg Corbidge, also of Scottish and Newcastle Breweries, were down in London.

'That Thursday before the opening game was a very hard day,' continues Gibson. 'We were trying to define the set of rules we'd been given by the Football League. We felt the most important word was "proper" on the debt of the creditors. The Football League were asking us to do things which were unreasonable and we found out around this time, that Ron Noades had our players, Gary Pallister and Brian Laws, at Selhurst Park in the event that if Middlesbrough Football Club went out of business, they'd be interested in signing them. Talk about self-interest!'

Gibson has his own forthright views on the actions of Noades. 'It was not what I expected from a member of the Football League management committee.

'He later wrote in *Four Four Two* magazine how he'd been offered Gary Pallister by the

receivers for £35,000 but he'd refused because he didn't want to do any damage to Middlesbrough Football Club. That is not the way it happened.'

With two days to go to the big kick-off, however, the consortium still didn't have the money. Gibson recalls arriving at the town hall at 8 a.m. on the Thursday to find Colin Henderson in a surprisingly upbeat mood.

'At this time, what we were doing was planning for the fact that if the club was saved we would still need a ground, we still needed referees etcetera. We were buying studs and the like; we didn't have a ground. We were busy getting the police, fire brigade and ambulance service sorted out.'

In London, the party arrived at the offices of Norton Rose, ICI's solicitors, late on Thursday, in preparation for an early meeting with the Football League the following morning.

Graham Fordy vividly remembers the time leading up to the deadline.

'We arrived at Norton Rose in Westminster at about 10 p.m. We met Henry Moszkowicz and his solicitor, Mr Teacher, there to try to formulate a plan for our meeting with the Football League.

'This pre-meeting was opened with advice from the Norton Rose solicitor, basically saying he didn't understand what we were trying to achieve because it had been proved we had over £2 million of debts and the consortium only had £825,000, which in principle made the club insolvent and everything a waste of time.

'We had our guidelines of what each member of the consortium required and we went through this. The meeting finished at 2 a.m.'

After catching up on some sleep for a few hours, the meeting re-commenced over breakfast at 6.30 before the meeting with the Football League.

'Friday, 23 August was a very frustrating day. We thought we'd be sitting around a big table and everybody would discuss their views,' says Fordy. 'What actually happened was that we were in one room with our legal advisors and the Football League were in another room with theirs. It was a case of notes being passed from one room to another. Every time we actually felt we'd broken the back of a problem, the Football League would throw up another one.'

Unfortunately, Henry Moszkowicz was now becoming a problem to the other members of the consortium. Fordy recalls: 'He was to discuss the drafting of certain articles of the new company to favour himself because he felt that the two corporate companies were getting too powerful. His fear of Scottish and Newcastle Breweries and ICI was that, although he had got to know Reg Corbidge and myself and Colin Henderson of ICI, if we were to be replaced by different people from our organisations it could present problems to him.

'He insisted that any change of representatives could only be accepted by a unanimous vote by the existing board. There were numerous clauses that he wanted implementing, such as if any member of the consortium wanted to sell their shares at any time, those shares had to be placed on the table and each existing member had the right to buy in their existing percentage. This would mean Henry Moszkowicz's shares would continue to grow as he had the biggest percentage anyway.'

It was already clear to everyone concerned that Moszkowicz might present problems in the future, and many people couldn't understand why he wanted to be involved with Middlesbrough, when he had no obvious ties with the area.

Fordy describes his early perceptions of the man: 'Henry was a complex character, who in the initial stages mystified us. We all wanted to find out his connection with Middlesbrough Football Club. He didn't appear to be a strong supporter of any club, but he told us that during his childhood he had once witnessed Middlesbrough giving Derby a thrashing and Boro became his team from that day forward. How true this was no one will ever know, but it became apparent at a later stage that Henry just saw the opportunity of becoming involved with a football club. As the major shareholder, I believe he felt he could actually control the club. It didn't turn out that way because there were stronger characters on the board than he expected.

'I came to view Henry as a man who changed his views constantly. He could be so dogmatic over which way he wanted us to go at one meeting; then, in the next, his views had changed.'

The deadline came closer and closer and the Football League said that unless all the documents were completed by 5.30 p.m., they would announce to the world that Middlesbrough Football Club's fixture list for the following season was null and void.

Back in Middlesbrough, Steve Gibson had an inkling on the Thursday evening that all might not be lost. 'Colin Henderson winked at me as we left that night, and on the Friday morning he told me that ICI had agreed to a bond whereby they picked up a major part of any subsequent debt, in the belief that we could convince the Football League that a lot of the creditors were not exactly honourable. We'd also have to put in the £825,000.

'The bond meant ICI paid a substantial amount first, then any further debt would be shared among the remaining members pro-rata. That bond allowed the legal people at the Football League to, in effect, go into the bank account or any consortium member's and take out the money for any claimant.'

Back in London, the initial documents were signed by Graham Fordy, Reg Corbidge and Henry Moszkowicz with just ten minutes to spare before the Football League's deadline.

'That the club had been saved was undoubtedly down to the final planning and contribution of Colin Henderson,' admits Gibson. 'I'm still not sure how Colin was able to deliver the bond with all it's liability and risk, in a format that was acceptable to all the consortium members. But, in doing so, he had saved the future of Middlesbrough Football Club.'

Indeed, during the final days of the negotiations with the Football League, the club considered the way in which the club should be structured. It was felt that, in recognition of Henderson's leadership during the previous months, he would be the natural choice as chairman and that the board would also consist of Gibson, Fordy, Corbidge and Moszkowicz.

At a press conference in Middlesbrough Town Hall, Colin Henderson and Steve Gibson announced the news that every Boro fan had been praying for. Middlesbrough Football Club had been saved.

They went on to explain that Middlesbrough would play their opening game at the Victoria Ground the following evening, after Hartlepool had played their own game.

So Middlesbrough Football & Athletic Company (1986) Limited was formed, after the consortium had purchased a 'dead' company, Blackplay Limited, 'off the shelf'.

Henry Moszkowicz had wanted to call the newly formed organisation Sporting Club Middlesbrough, but that was against the wishes of the rest of the consortium.

CHAPTER FOUR

The Only Way is Up – 1986–87

This was to be the season for a phoenix-like rise from the ashes for the newly formed Middlesbrough Football. While the financial disputes raged on throughout the summer, manager Bruce Rioch and his assistant Colin Todd remained totally committed to the club and they set about getting the playing side back on track.

Rioch recalls: 'I think I let twenty players go at the end of the 1985–86 season, give or take a few. I can recall Steve Gibson coming into the room with the provisional liquidator and saying the club was in serious debt, around £1.4 to £1.5 million. A few days later it was up to £1.9 million, then up to £2.2 million and suddenly I thought, "Hello! There's a few skeletons in the cupboard here."

'I was looking at the problems from the club's point of view and my own – I had no contract, no agreement and I was living in digs while my family was in Birmingham. I decided to stick tight with the club and that's how it was when I went off on my summer holiday to Spain.

'There, I received a call from a gentleman who was in charge of the financial affairs at the club who said he had some news for me. I was standing in the hotel reception with a glass of beer and he said: "I'm sorry to say it's not good news – we have terminated your employment with the club and we've stopped your salary. If you wish to continue working for the club without salary you can do so."

'I was about four days into a fortnight's vacation and I took a sip of my San Miguel and thought, "Well, it can't hurt me here." So I said: "I can't do any worse, I'm on holiday for

fourteen days – yes, I'll carry on working for you."

'When I got back to the club, there were one or two players adamant they were going to leave, but the players who held fast were the magnificent ones.'

Departures during the summer included Don O'Riordan, David Currie, Peter Beagrie, David Mills and Tony McAndrew, while Irving Nattrass retired through injury.

Mills, in particular, was disappointed to be released.

'The relationship between Bruce and I wasn't particularly amiable. We weren't best pals, let's put it that way,' he admits. 'We had a fall-out and it was clear I was of no value to him while I was injured. It's fair to say we weren't two of a kind. You were never confident of interpreting Bruce, he was very unpredictable. He was totally different from Willie Maddren.'

Rioch adds: 'I recall saying to Colin Todd that this was probably going to be the most difficult time of his career. We had to be very positive with the players – no down sides. If we had a downer, it would be in private.

'What we were looking for were players with a great desire and determination – a will to compete and ability to play. I found it in abundance with some of the younger lads and while we were short in numbers, we had fourteen players with real guts and quality who lived, ate, slept and drank football with Middlesbrough.

'We had to juggle them around, and that's why Colin Cooper ended up as a left-back. We didn't have anyone for that position in practice

THE 'DEBTS' MOUNT UP

Unremitted joy at the success of Bruce Rioch's young team during the 1986–87 season helped deflect the bitter taste of the ensuing legal wrangles off the pitch.

The business consortium, the club's saviours throughout the liquidation saga, were forced to pay certain debtors they firmly believed were dishonourable.

Club chairman Colin Henderson and secretary Charles Wellington represented the board in negotiations with the club's liquidators, Peat Marwick. Henderson's job was to ensure that the club only paid creditable debtors and that any disputed or fraudulent claims were fully investigated and resolved in a fair and satisfactory manner.

Colin Henderson became the new club's first chairman.

But, despite the honest endeavours of Henderson and Wellington, the club felt that several disputed creditors acted badly by insisting on payment.

Steve Gibson, who was the only member of the pre-1986 board to remain part of the reformed club, has particularly bitter memories of the time.

These actions meant that initial debts of £825,000 quickly increased to £2.5 million as people with previous involvement with the club came forward to claim old debts, some going back as many as seven years.

One of those who came forward was former chairman Charles Amer. The club insisted that Peats should only pay proveable debts. After much discussion, against the views of some board members, Peat Marwick agreed to pay Amer.

'I felt very disappointed when we had to pay £100,000 of the club's money to Charles Amer,' says Gibson.

'His "debt" dated back to the days when he was chairman of the club. The club had made a counter-claim against his company but Parkway Estates went into liquidation before the club's counter claim against the company could be heard.'

The consortium had no choice but to pay other debtors and ultimately some £2.5 million was paid.

From the consortium, a new board had been formed comprising new chairman Colin Henderson (representing ICI), Steve Gibson (Bulkhaul), Reg Corbidge and Graham Fordy (both Scottish & Newcastle Breweries) and Henry Moszkowicz.

But they faced an uphill struggle in the fight against financial strife. The club were hit with another bill when the Football League decided to recover all of its costs from its negotiations with the club from the previous months. 'Their legal costs were substantial,' recalls Gibson. 'They stopped their normal distribution of cash between member clubs coming to Middlesbrough until we had settled the debt, so we were financially strapped from day one. They even forced us to pay some of the grant which Charles Amer had secured years earlier for the sports complex. It came to many hundreds of thousands of pounds. On top of this, the Football Trust wanted its money back.'

There were others, too. Alf Duffield, another former chairman, and the Midland Bank were among those demanding money from old debts.

Amid the mayhem, there was a shining light that kept everyone smiling. 'We were under some pressure,' says Gibson. 'But what eased some of it were the achievements of Bruce Rioch and Colin Todd. They marshalled their troops and had the players believing they could climb mountains. Rioch was magnificent. He had some good players but he gave them belief, skills and discipline.'

matches, so in training we decided to play him against Stuart Ripley and he never gave Rippers a kick. I thought we've got a player here. We'd seen him play as a centre-back or sweeper the year before but thought he might do us at left-back. Blimey – not half he did!'

So, despite the off-the-field wrangling, Boro finally kicked off their Third Division campaign against Port Vale at Hartlepool's Victoria Ground just over an hour-and-a-half after Hartlepool had finished their opening fixture.

The 2–2 draw gave everyone a huge boost of confidence after the trauma of the previous season and summer of concern. One player who had noticed a real change at the club since Bruce Rioch's arrival was Gary Gill who was given a midfield role by the new boss.

He says: 'I felt sorry for Willie Maddren who was building a side, he always stood by me and showed faith in my ability. But it wasn't a good

1986–87 Match of the Season

23 August 1986

MIDDLESBROUGH 2 PORT VALE 2

This was the historic clash which saw Boro banish the worries of the traumatic summer and make the short trip across the River Tees to Hartlepool's Victoria Ground to take on Port Vale – a game most people had doubted would ever actually happen.

On a warm, sunny evening, the match followed on from Hartlepool's own game with Cardiff City earlier that afternoon. Despite all the public support shown for Middlesbrough throughout the turmoil of the previous months, only 3,456 made the short trip to witness the rebirth of the club.

Bruce Rioch fielded a Boro side with an average age of just 21 years and five months for the clash, with 18-year-old debutant Gary Parkinson at right-back. Only five of the team were over the age of 22. Absent from the action was the suspended Gary Pallister, who was replaced by Alan Kernaghan.

Boro led 2–0 at half-time with both goals coming from Archie Stephens, the second a stunning 25-yard drive which the veteran striker described as 'the best of my career'.

Alas, after completely dominating the first hour, their lack of preparation and overall fitness finally caught up with them. Port Vale grabbed two second half goals through Richard O'Kelly and Paul Maguire, the equaliser coming just five minutes from time to rob Boro of maximum points.

Despite slipping up, the performance was to be admired, coming out of such adversity, and was certainly a platform to build on. Afterwards, Rioch said: 'We ran out of steam but it was the first ninety minutes we've had against a league side. We'll learn from it.'

Brian Laws, who was switched from his normal full-back slot to midfield, recalls: 'It was strange to play a home game at Hartlepool but stranger still to play out of position like that. I told Bruce that I wasn't a midfield player but he obviously saw something I didn't. I knew I could score goals but I really didn't see myself as a midfielder.'

Alan Kernaghan felt the result was a very positive one for the team. 'It gave us an extra jolt of confidence because even though a draw was not the best result possible, it was still a good display and a nice relief to get a game under our belt.'

time to be playing football in front of small crowds who could be very harsh on the players.

'As soon as Bruce arrived he got us playing attractive football, and tactically Bruce was the best manager I ever played under.'

The Littlewoods Cup draw had thrown up an intriguing fixture in the first round with Boro having to face temporary landlords Hartlepool United. A disappointing crowd of just over 2,000 watched the side play a hard fought 1–1 draw in torrential rain at the Victoria Ground, with Bernie Slaven netting Boro's goal.

By this time Boro had lost their physio Steve Smelt to Sunderland. He had felt the need of security for his family when the club went into liquidation and the job at Roker Park was instantly offered to him. Boro were using Hartlepool physio Tommy Johnson on loan, a move which would soon become permanent.

Johnson explains: 'Boro's chief scout, Barry Geldart, and I had played football together for Stockton in the North Eastern League and he asked me if I'd like to join Middlesbrough. At the same time, Bruce Rioch told me that he knew all about my record and that he wanted me to join. It took me over a week to make up my mind. I'd been at Hartlepool for twenty-seven years and it was a big wrench to leave but, at 59, it was an honour to take up such a job.'

Wigan provided the opposition for the second league game when Boro made their first ever visit to Springfield Park but on the eve of the game there was another departure from Boro's ranks.

The previous season's top scorer, Gary Rowell, joined Second Division Brighton on a free transfer. Rioch said of his departure: 'He was not going to be part of the plans this year. There's no point having players who form no part of your plans. He was on a good contract – a very good contract – which has now been cancelled.'

Against Wigan, Boro were under heavy pressure for the majority of the first half and appeared to be struggling, but Rioch worked some of his psychology on the players at half-time, so much so that they came back to win

2–0 through strikes from Turnbull and Mowbray.

'If we had started off badly, we could have been relegated again,' reflects Turnbull. 'Fortunately, in Bruce, we had just the man for the job. It needed a strong character to drag the club back from the brink and he did it.'

Rioch recalls the win at Wigan, commenting: 'I remember crossing the pitch at half-time, heading for the tunnel, and their left-back was saying to one of his mates, "This team's rubbish, we can beat these." I went into the dressing room and said, "Fellas, they've just thrown everything they've got at us and they still haven't got a goal and they think we're rubbish! So let's go out there and beat them" – and we did. We had spirit, a great spirit.

'I always liked to keep them guessing off the field, but on it they had to know exactly what they were doing. That's why the pattern of play was so evident. They were a young group so they could be influenced. Colin and I shaped them for the future.'

Boro finally returned to Ayresome Park after all the trials and tribulations for the return leg of the Littlewoods Cup tie with Hartlepool. The game was watched by nearly 8,000 supporters who witnessed Boro sail past their neighbours with a goal apiece from Stuart Ripley – his first for the club – and Gary Hamilton.

It wasn't until early October that Boro were finally defeated and that was in their thirteenth game, a League Cup tie at Birmingham, when they were edged out by the odd goal in five during extra-time. By this time, former Leeds United and Scotland star Eddie Gray had joined Boro to take charge of the youth and reserve team, while Todd was promoted to first team coach.

Before the defeat at St Andrews, Boro extended their lead at the top of the table to three points following an emphatic 4–1 win at Norman Hunter's Rotherham. Scoring goals was no longer a problem for a team which was receiving praise from up and down the country for its attractive, free-flowing football. Stephens and Laws hit two goals apiece in the mauling of Rotherham.

Laws proved to be a revelation in his new

Holding aloft the padlocks for Ayresome Park ready to reopen the ground are club directors Steve Gibson and Graham Fordy with David Storey.

midfield role and cracked eight goals in a run of just ten appearances early in the campaign.

'I had the belief to shoot from distance with power,' he says. 'Maybe I was a bit greedy because I annoyed my fellow players at times but I was always confident of scoring.'

Prior to a top-of-the-table clash with Blackpool at Ayresome Park, Rioch received a Manager of the Month award in front of a very healthy crowd of 11,470 – Boro's biggest for a league game in two-and-a-half years.

Assistant manager Colin Todd recalls that both he and Bruce were very confident after pre-season that they had a good season ahead of them.

'We always felt that given that little bit of luck you need, and if we could stay clear of injuries, we could win promotion. We had a back four of Parkinson, Mowbray, Pallister and Cooper, with Stephen Pears in goal, who've all done well, and they were the cornerstone of the team.

'Little Gary Hamilton had tremendous

ability and along with Brian Laws and Gary Gill in midfield they got goals, while Archie Stephens and Bernie Slaven were natural goalscorers.

'The squad was very easy to manage because they had no experience, as such, and they just accepted what we said – but the more success they had the more it benefited them.

'Bruce was a disciplinarian – very strict. With the younger players you could get away with it, but man-management plays a big part in football and that's where I came in with the handling of the players. If Bruce had been a bit severe, I put my arm around them.'

Incredibly, after steering Boro to the top of the table, Rioch still hadn't been offered a contract with the club.

He recalls: 'I remember the chairman, Colin Henderson, saying the board had discussed the issue and what they were offering was a three-month agreement which would take me up to Christmas to see how it went.

'I'd just gone right through the summer since

May without wages and I just said, "No, I'm not doing that." My family was in Birmingham and I was living in digs in the north east. I'd paid lodgings for all the youngsters, I'd paid the kit manager's car repairs because they were getting no income. To be fair, they eventually came back and offered me a contract which gave me some substance.'

Against Blackpool, Boro let themselves down for the first time in the season with a 3–1 defeat. Most of the damage was done by a young Paul Stewart. Shortly after the game Rioch openly criticised both Pallister and Slaven in the *Evening Gazette,* again one of his psychology games.

Neither Slaven nor Pallister have forgotten that public rollicking.

'It's true, I wasn't at my best that day but the whole team played badly,' insists Slaven. 'He reckoned it was time I showed what I got paid for – and that hurt. But I also saw it as a case of him throwing down the gauntlet and I was always one to meet a challenge like that head-on. It had the desired effect of making me pick up my game.'

Pallister, on the other hand, insists he found such public humiliation demotivating.

'I gave the ball away with a silly pass and Paul Stewart scored,' he recalls. 'Bruce blamed me for that goal and another one, I think. I wasn't happy about it. It was disappointing to see your manager slag players off like that. I didn't like being ridiculed in public and, as a mark of respect, I don't think you should wash your dirty linen in public.'

Boro's new management team: manager Bruce Rioch (left) *with reserve team coach Eddie Gray* (centre) *and first team coach Colin Todd.*

Rioch certainly got his message across as Boro stormed to a 3–1 victory over lowly Walsall (wearing Boro's away kit) the following week, although 3,000 fans had been lost from the gate. Stephens was on target again with another brace of goals, taking his total to ten by 11 October, though he had a warning for supporters.

He said: 'It's great to reach ten goals so quickly, but I hope everyone doesn't think I will keep scoring at this rate!'

The victory over Walsall left Boro with a two-point cushion over Blackpool at the top. However, Bruce's babes suffered a 1–0 setback in a midweek game at Notts County, when Ian McParland turned Pallister before firing home from an angle. Next came a 2–2 draw at Bristol City, a game which saw Boro slip behind Bournemouth, their next opponents.

Just under 11,000 turned up to see Boro take on Bournemouth after Rioch had pleaded with supporters to 'roar the team on'. That's exactly what they did as Boro went on the rampage with goals from Stephens, Slaven, Hamilton and Ripley in a memorable 4–0 win.

Following a disappointing home draw with Bolton, Boro prepared for one of the biggest games of the season – the north east derby with Darlington at Feethams. The game was played in a very tense atmosphere, and was marred by crowd violence which resulted in the police making eighty-eight arrests. Boro worked hard for a 1–0 victory, the goal coming courtesy of Stephens. The violence was not confined to the spectators, with former Boro star David Currie sent off for retaliation after thirty minutes. The goal itself was controversial with Stephens firing home after skipper Tony Mowbray had won a strong challenge with Darlington goalkeeper Kevin Carr.

The FA Cup gave Boro an opportunity to exact some revenge on Blackpool for the 3–1 hammering a month earlier. Boro crushed the Seasiders 3–0 with Slaven, who had earlier been criticised by Rioch, scoring the club's first hat-trick for six years.

After the game, he said: 'I had something to prove against Blackpool and I think I made my point. After the last game against Blackpool the

Bang! Bernie Slaven puts the record straight with one of his three goals in an FA Cup win over Blackpool in November 1986. Slaven had been criticised by Bruce Rioch after an earlier game with the Seasiders.

boss had a bit of a go at me in the press. It was the worst write-up of my career and I didn't think it was fair at the time. I was aware I had to prove I could play against Blackpool and that the previous performance was just an off-day.

'This time, everything was great. The team played really well and kept giving me the ball to my feet. That's the way I like it.'

Ironically, Slaven revealed that he had still not fully settled into his role as a front runner, adding: 'When I was with Albion Rovers I had a free role, coming in behind the strikers, it's a wee bit strange to me where I'm playing now and I'm still learning.'

A further victory followed at Newport with Mowbray grabbing a last-gasp winner.

Through the Freight Rover Trophy, a competition for lower division clubs, Boro were given a good opportunity of reaching Wembley and they won their first game of the season by comprehensively defeating Doncaster 3–0. Recently acquired striker Paul Proudlock grabbed two goals on his debut only to find

himself dropped for the next league game with Chester City.

Chester upset the form book with a 2–1 victory but Boro bounced back with an impressive run in the league, collecting ten points from the next twelve. Three successive clean sheets, against Doncaster, Brentford and Carlisle, were ample evidence of an ever-strengthening defence.

Colin Cooper, an ever-present at left-back, reflects: 'We were an incredibly young side and it speaks volumes for Bruce, in particular, that we did so well. He was a stickler for rules and regulations and kept us on the straight and narrow. He was harsh but he was spot on, too. With so many teenagers and lads in their early twenties, it was easy for him to manipulate us the way he wanted, while Mogga always backed him all the way.

'But it was easy for him in a way because all any of us wanted to do was play football for Middlesbrough. We were all young lads, most of us local, and we were great mates off the

pitch as well as on it. I've never known a closeness like it in all my time in football. It was very special. In fact, I'll be very surprised if any of the lads don't count themselves as mates with everyone else.'

December also saw Boro make progress in the FA Cup when they earned a creditable 1–0 victory at Notts County, with a Hamilton goal. Despite the win, Rioch and Pallister were at loggerheads after the tie.

'I gave away a free-kick from which they scored, though it was disallowed,' recalls Pallister. 'Afterwards, I had a run-in with Bruce. He wanted to have a go at me in front of the other lads. I don't know what it was that caused the friction between us, though it's safe to say I didn't live my life as intensely as he would have liked me to. I think I was just too laid back and maybe he felt I lacked discipline.

'Bruce was very regimented and I rebelled against him. I would argue back – and I wasn't the only one – though he was an intimidating figure. I don't think he treated me fairly so I always felt more comfortable dealing with Colin Todd, who I had a lot of respect for; he was a genuinely nice guy. Of course, every club needs discipline, otherwise people would run amok, but you can't make people be something they're not. You've got to handle different people in different ways and Bruce didn't do that.'

Rioch strengthened his squad with the arrival of 25-year-old Ronnie Coyle on loan from Celtic. December saw hard-working midfielder Gary Gill score his first goal for the club in a 1–0 win over Carlisle on Boxing day. It was a great feeling for the local born star.

'Bruce had us playing a 4–4–2 system and I had a very professional role, breaking down the opposition attacks,' he explains. 'I used to get through a lot of defensive work but I always felt I had a lot more to offer. But I never got the opportunity to score goals because I was always sitting in for Brian Laws who did a lot more attacking.'

Mansfield were Boro's next opponents over the Christmas period for a tough game at Field Mill. Proudlock grabbed his third goal in three starts since his arrival at the club when he tapped home the rebound from a Parkinson piledriver, but a rare error from goalkeeper Pears allowed the Stags a share of the spoils.

On Proudlock, Gary Gill says: 'Paul was another player who was easygoing but never really made it. He was never really given a chance by Bruce.'

On New Year's Eve, former Wolves manager Brian Little arrived at the club to take over as team coach from the recently departed Eddie Gray, who had left to manage lowly Rochdale. Little had been considered very unfortunate to lose his job at Molineux and Bruce Rioch was 'delighted' to be working with his former Aston Villa team mate once again.

Chairman Colin Henderson was also happy with the first half of the season, commenting that, 'Supporters can look forward to 1987 with confidence, though, at the same time, I don't want everybody to get carried away.'

Top of table at the end of 1986, Boro travelled to York City for a New Year's day derby clash at Bootham Crescent without the injured Proudlock who was replaced by a less than fully fit Stephens. The pitch was only passed fit ninety minutes before kick-off by referee Colin Seel, after hours of heavy rain. Boro never adapted to the conditions and found themselves 2–0 down at half-time due to a deflected Martin Butler shot and a mistake by Pears. Tony Mowbray replied with a header a minute into the second half to give some hope but despite heavy pressure it was York's Tony Canham who sealed the Minstermen's victory in the eighty-sixth minute with another deflected goal in front of a crowd of 8,620.

After the game, Rioch admitted: 'Stuart Ripley didn't play very well – he has done better for us. The front men also might have done better, but then you can't do much about two deflected goals.'

A steady 2–0 victory over lowly Newport County, with one of the goals coming from Gill – his second in consecutive home games – set Boro back on winning ways for the forthcoming FA Cup third round clash with Fourth Division Preston North End.

Prior to the cup tie, Rioch made Aston Villa's reserve team striker Paul Kerr the club's

first signing since liquidation. Although the fee was just £50,000, this was considered big money at the time and Kerr was expected to produce the goods. However, his arrival at Ayresome Park was a bit of a culture shock, as he admits: 'I took a long time to settle at Middlesbrough. I'd come from a massive club to one with virtually no facilities whatsoever. It was all a bit of a shock and it affected my form. But I'd been in and out of the first team at Villa and was desperate to make a regular breakthrough.'

Kerr went straight into the line-up, on the left side of midfield, for the Preston game which turned out to be an anti-climax in front of the first crowd of over 15,000 all season. On a frozen pitch, Boro never got going and worse followed when Preston's 5 foot 2 inch midfielder Ronnie Hildersley struck home a spectacular 25-yard drive just before the break. Things got worse when Brian Laws picked up a knee injury just after half-time and, despite sustained pressure on former Boro keeper

David Brown's goal, they just couldn't break the deadlock.

A week later Boro, who had been one of the few clubs in the league without shirt sponsorship, signed a deal with local DIY store Dickens. The debut for the new shirts came in the Freight Rover Trophy against Halifax Town, a game which saw Boro just sneak a 2–1 victory with goals from Kernaghan and Ripley.

Back in league action, a further two victories followed, the first a 3–0 win at Bury. Kerr recalls: 'I had an outstanding game that day – but that was it for about two months. I began to get stick from the fans and eventually Rioch pulled me into his office. He told me that he knew I had ability but that if I wanted to win over the fans I had to get out there and get stuck in. Putting my foot in didn't come naturally to me but I made myself do it and slowly my confidence started to come back.'

A 1–0 home victory over Bristol Rovers followed. Unfortunately, though, it was soured by a serious knee injury to Brian Laws which

Gary Hamilton scores a sensational goal in a 3–0 home win over Fulham in February 1986.

kept him out for the rest of the season.

'It was my cruciate ligaments,' explains Laws. 'For a while, I wondered if my career was over. My time out made me open my eyes and realise that football doesn't last forever. For the first time, I began to think long-term.'

Rioch and Todd were welcomed to Rochdale by former coach Eddie Gray for the second round proper of the Freight Rover Trophy. Boro scraped through by the narrowest of margins on penalties.

The next eight games, one of them a Freight Rover Trophy quarter-final defeat at the hands of Mansfield, saw Boro stutter with four defeats and only two wins.

This was the stage of the season when Gary Gill struggled to keep his place and he recalls: 'We were chasing results and I began to take a bit of stick off the crowd and didn't really feel appreciated. It resulted in Lee Turnbull being selected ahead of me for several games.'

Former Holgate idol David Hodgson returned to Teesside on loan. He had been a big name during the days of John Neal's management, but had become something of a journeyman since leaving Ayresome for Liverpool five years earlier. Moving on to Sunderland and Norwich failed to help him recapture his best form.

His first game on his return came in a crunch top-of-the-table clash at Bournemouth's Dean Court, crammed full for a match which saw Boro humbled 3–1. Pallister received six stitches after suffering a headwound in a collision with Cherries striker Trevor Aylott and was forced to miss the following game.

'There was nothing malicious about the challenge but I got a very nasty cut,' says Pallister.

With Kernaghan replacing Pallister in defence the following Saturday, a goal from Mowbray secured a 1–0 success over Bristol City. Ronnie Coyle made his home league debut, but the biggest cheer was saved for Hodgson's appearance. Sadly, it all ended in dismay for Hodgy who was dismissed during the second half of a very heated game.

Although he was delighted to be in the side for that game, Kernaghan well remembers how

tough it could be under Rioch's regime.

'Bruce could be frightening to a young lad,' he admits. 'He came to the club with a reputation, due to stories that had come from his time at Torquay. From time to time, he did let his temper go and tea was thrown everywhere, but it was nothing really.

'He was always up to mind games with the players. Sometimes he would speak to you and then other times he would pin the team sheet up while we were out training and then disappear. This meant that you'd have calmed down by the time you saw him again if you were out of the team!'

Before Boro's home game with Notts County with the side dropping to its lowest position of the season Rioch delivered a call to

Put it there, partner! Strikers Bernie Slaven and Archie Stevens celebrate another goal as Gary Parkinson races in to join them.

arms and demanded the side remain unbeaten for the rest of the season. How prophetic those well-chosen words proved to be!

Rioch's youngsters responded with ten wins and three draws from the final thirteen games. Nine of the players appeared in every one of those games. Those players who played such a big part in the club's final run-in were Pears, Cooper, Mowbray, Parkinson, Slaven, Stephens, Hamilton, Ripley and Pallister, while Kerr missed only one.

First, Boro swept aside fellow promotion-chasers Notts County by a 2–0 scoreline – the strike partnership of Slaven and Stephens again coming up trumps – before an impressive 1–0 success at Blackpool's Bloomfield Road,

secured by another Stephens strike.

Following a goalless draw at home to Rotherham, a crowd of almost 12,000 turned out for the home derby with Darlington to see Steve Spriggs – signed on a month-to-month contract – make his debut. Slaven's eighteenth goal of the season earned Boro a share of the spoils, though former Boro player Alan Roberts netted for Darlington to become the first opponent to score at Ayresome for more than four months.

Now the young Boro side was to move into overdrive. Slaven was on target again in a 1–0 victory at Bolton before revenge was exacted for that 3–1 New Year's day defeat at York. The scores were turned around with Boro running out 3–1 winners at Ayresome Park through strikes by Ripley, Stephens and substitute Turnbull, playing his first game for over five months. With Spriggs out, Rioch reshuffled his pack to bring Turnbull into the starting line-up for a 1–0 win away at Carlisle, Pallister scoring his first goal for the club.

'I used to get ribbed mercilessly about not scoring,' admits Pallister. 'But I was the decoy for set-pieces. I'd be at the near post. But, for a change, Bernie Slaven took the corner instead of Gary Hamilton and I glanced the ball in, though Bernie insists it was his goal.'

Meanwhile, Turnbull responded with the second goal in a 2–0 home victory over Brentford after Slaven had netted goal number twenty-one. Gillingham were the next victims – assuring Boro of at least a play-off spot – as Stephens scored his sixteenth league goal of the campaign to set the ball rolling towards a 3–0 success. The Gills were one of the division's top sides but they were steamrollered by a Boro side whose thirst for success now matched its manager's. Top scorer Slaven again found the net while Turnbull scored his third in four games. With Gillingham now out of the running and Bournemouth looking certain of the championship, it was a straight race for second place between Boro and Lou Macari's Swindon Town.

A sixth straight win came at Chester, courtesy of strikes from Mowbray and Hamilton. In the next game, Hamilton kept his

cool from the penalty spot to make it seven successive wins, a run bettered only once in the club's long history, by Jack Charlton's side of 1973–74.

With Swindon slipping up at home to Gillingham, Boro now needed just two points from their final two games to secure automatic promotion.

The first of those games was against Wigan Athletic at Ayresome Park. It ended goalless but was a match that will forever live in the memory of all who witnessed it. On a glorious summer's evening nearly 19,000 fans packed into Ayresome Park in the hope of seeing Boro win promotion. Wigan got caught up in traffic and made the kick-off by the skin of their teeth. The

This was the defence which conceded only three goals in the final 13 league games of the 1986–87 season to clinch promotion. Goalkeeper Stephen Pears is pictured with from left to right Gary Parkinson, Tony Mowbray, Gary Pallister and Colin Cooper.

action saw one-way traffic in the direction of Wigan's goal, but the goal just wouldn't come. Still, Boro only needed a point if Swindon failed to pick up all three points from their game the same evening, Swindon slipped up and the great news soon spread like wildfire around the terraces.

In the dying moments, Stephens rose typically to meet a Ripley cross and powered a header goalwards which was somehow kept out by Wigan's veteran goalkeeper Roy Tunks. Many of the crowd believed the ball had crossed the line, which caused a celebratory pitch invasion. The referee re-started the game but, in his wisdom, he waited for the action to move towards the players' tunnel before

Stuart Ripley rides the challenge during a goalless draw with Wigan in May 1987 which saw Boro clinch promotion to Division Two.

blowing the final whistle.

This result meant that, to all intents and purposes, Boro were promoted as runners-up behind Harry Redknapp's Bournemouth side. Scenes of jubilation followed the whistle with thousands of fans celebrating on the pitch and calling for the new messiah, Bruce Rioch. In the end the players and Rioch himself made an appearance in the directors' box to mass approval from their ranks of supporters.

'That night was the best of my life at Boro,' reflects Gary Pallister. 'I'll never forget going up to the directors' box after the game to see thousands of supporters on the pitch. It was just an incredible achievement to win promotion so soon after liquidation.'

The final game of the season saw Boro travel to Doncaster Rovers. The promotion party was tempered slightly due to crowd restrictions at Doncaster's dilapidated Belle Vue ground. Many fans were unable to travel.

Even so, a 2–0 victory with goals from Hamilton and Ripley, sparked off another party. The players left the field without most of their clothing, which had gone to the fans in the crowd as mementoes of the great season.

The final league table showed Boro in second place:

	P	W	D	L	F	A	Pts
Bournemouth	46	29	10	7	76	40	97
Boro	46	28	10	8	67	30	94
Swindon	46	25	12	9	77	47	87

Stuart Ripley gives much of the credit for Boro's promotion to Rioch. 'I think people underestimate the effect Bruce had. I believe that we would have gone in the opposite direction with virtually any other manager. He dominated young lads and bullied them into becoming good players.

'While Bruce instilled discipline, Colin Todd was more of a calming influence. They were good foils for each other.'

CHAPTER FIVE

Up, Up and Away! – 1987–88

After the incredible success story of the previous season, it would perhaps have been realistic for Boro to aim for consolidation in their first season back in Division Two. But Bruce Rioch and his team were far too ambitious for that and immediately set their sights on another promotion challenge. And what a season it was to be.

Rioch's only buy during the summer of 1987 was tough-tackling Dean Glover from Aston Villa for £25,000. At Villa, Glover had always played in a defensive role, but Rioch brought him in as a central midfield partner for Gary Hamilton.

Rioch didn't feel the need to change things too much. 'I set about improving the side,' he explains. 'We knew we had good players, we knew we didn't have too much changing to do, because the players understood the way we were playing and they understood the system

Celebration time in the opening game of the 1987–88 season as goalscorer Archie Stephens (left) *is congragulated by debutant Dean Glover* (centre) *and Stuart Ripley.*

and their roles in it. 'The chairman had always said to me that any revenue left over could be spent on team-building, so to keep the continuity going I went and picked up new players from Villa.

'Deano – or Spamhead, as he was known to the rest of the lads – was a great pro, a great character whose make-up I knew very well when he joined the club. He didn't mess around on the pitch.'

Glover's arrival, however, came as a bitter blow for Gary Gill who was to make only three league appearances all season.

'I was injured in pre-season and Dean got settled in my midfield role,' he remembers. 'It was a bit hard to take. I didn't feel a part of the success that season.'

Millwall, managed by John Docherty, were Boro's first opponents on their return to Division Two and a crowd of 11,471 saw Archie Stephens score a spectacular diving header in a hard-fought 1–1 draw.

Glover's second game in a Boro shirt saw him walk straight into the heat of a Wear–Tees derby at Roker Park in the first round first leg of the Littlewoods Cup. Despite Sunderland having just been relegated to Division Three for the first time in their history, they still managed to take a 1–0 advantage into the second leg at Ayresome Park. More disappointing than the result was the first half dismissal of Glover for elbowing Sunderland's central defender Gary Bennett.

A day later, talented young striker Lee Turnbull was involved in a surprise move to Aston Villa, with 24-year-old goalkeeper Kevin Poole travelling in the opposite direction to understudy Stephen Pears.

Looking back on the move, Turnbull says: 'Bruce had told me that he wanted me to go on and become a good player. Then, on the team bus after we'd lost at Sunderland, he said he wanted to have a word with me. He explained that Graham Taylor had been in touch from Aston Villa. I asked him what he wanted me to do and he told me to go and have a chat. I was miffed that he was even considering letting me go but I realised he wanted to sign Poole and I decided to leave.'

Rioch's team, meanwhile, were finding goals hard to come by, and this continued when they drew another blank in a 1–0 defeat at Stoke City, although in controversial circumstances.

The Potters goal came from a penalty after Pallister had brought down Carl Saunders, but the big central defender almost rectified his mistake by forcing the ball home in the dying moments.

Unfortunately for Pally, referee David Elleray disallowed the goal, claiming Stoke's George Berry had been fouled on the goalline, although it was clear to anybody watching he had collided with a team-mate!

Boro finally got back on the goals trail in the return leg of the Littlewoods Cup, beating Sunderland 2–0 in front of a crowd of over 15,000. Slaven got his first goal of the season with a spectacular bicycle kick, while skipper Mowbray sealed the victory with a second half header.

After the game, Sunderland's Mark Proctor – formerly with Middlesbrough – said: 'I have no complaints, they deserved to win.'

Rioch was also delighted with the result, saying: 'It meant a great deal to them beating Sunderland, and they worked very hard to achieve it.'

It was at this time that Boro's young defenders were starting to attract the attention of the First Division's big guns, with Manchester United, Liverpool, Tottenham and Glasgow Rangers all watching their progress, though Rioch was quick to point out that he was under no pressure to sell any of his young stars.

Boro squeezed home a late winner from Slaven in the next game at home to a defensive-minded Oldham but the team was still struggling to hit top form. A midweek 3–1 reverse at Crystal Palace at least saw Slaven finding his old goalscoring form, while Boro at last put in a decent performance, passing the ball in the style everyone had become acquainted with.

Boro slipped to fourth from bottom following a 3–2 home defeat by Swindon, causing concern among supporters, though

Slaven grabbed his fourth goal in as many games.

With what looked like troubled times ahead, Boro travelled to Villa Park for what seemed likely to be one of the toughest games of the season. To add extra spice to the proceedings, Paul Kerr, Dean Glover, Kevin Poole and manager Bruce Rioch were all making a return to their former club. It was Kerr who had a glorious night. By his own admission, the diminutive star had struggled since arriving at Middlesbrough and was without a goal in thirty-one games. Back on his old stamping ground, however, he earned Boro three points with a clever flick over Nigel Spink in the seventy-second minute.

'One thing I had stopped doing since joining Boro was scoring goals,' reflects Kerr. 'I'd been a prolific scorer for Villa's reserves so it was great to go back and get one over on them like that.'

After the win, Tony Mowbray sounded the rallying call by stating: 'Now we've got to try to put a good run together. We know we've let everybody down and we want to put the record straight.' Prophetic words!

Boro followed up their return to winning ways with another victory, this time a resounding 3–0 win over Bournemouth with two goals from Hamilton and another from Slaven.

Revelling in his success after the game, Hamilton said: 'I love playing in my new role as a front man; I believe in my ability to score goals.'

Billy Bremner's Leeds United were next to suffer at the hands of Boro's new-found self-belief when they were comprehensively beaten 2–0 at Ayresome Park. Pallister and Kerr got the goals in a game in which Boro were never in any real danger. The result moved Boro up to seventh in the Second Division table, which caused the bookmakers to slash their odds on Rioch's team winning promotion from 33–1 to 14–1. Pallister shared in the increased optimism by remarking: 'We need fear nobody in this division.'

Boro's three-game winning streak came to an end when Villa gained revenge for their earlier defeat, with a 1–0 Littlewoods Cup victory at Ayresome Park, but it was only a temporary blip as they returned to winning ways in the next league game at Ewood Park, Blackburn, and moved into fourth place. Kerr was again on the scoresheet, as was Alan Kernaghan in his first game of the season.

Boro won many new admirers through this performance, including the *Sunday Express* who said: 'Manager Bruce Rioch seems to have welded a side with pace, flair and lots of application, and the present occupants of the Second Division leadership should keep an eye on Middlesbrough.'

Coach Colin Todd saluted the performance by adding: 'We have watched a lot of teams in the Second Division and there is nothing to be frightened of.'

Despite being held to a disappointing goalless draw by lowly Reading at Ayresome, Boro retained fourth place for the crunch clash with league leaders Bradford City at Valley Parade. A great deal of media attention surrounded the Bradford game, which was selected as the live commentary match on Radio 2. A near capacity crowd of 14,222 attended the game, but Boro failed to capitalise on Bradford's mini injury crisis.

The score remained goalless at half-time. Bradford began to find holes in Boro's armoury as the game wore on, and it was no surprise when they went ahead through a Mark Leonard header from John Hendrie's cross. The Yorkshire side increased their lead in the sixty-third minute through Leigh Palin, following a great run by Stuart McCall, which left Boro with a great deal to do. A flicker of hope was rekindled four minutes later when Hamilton was fouled by City goalkeeper Peter Litchfield in the penalty area.

Hammy took it upon himself to take the kick, which unluckily hit the foot of the post before being scrambled away by Litchfield, taking Boro's last hopes of a comeback with it.

Following the defeat, Boro slipped to eighth place, but nobody was despondent. Rioch warned: 'Don't write us off. We'll be back. We can go on to even better things after a tough outing like this.'

Meanwhile, Pallister had been very impressed with Bradford: 'On the day, Bradford were by far the best side we've played, though I'm already looking forward to the return game at Ayresome Park against them.'

A few days later Boro were back in Littlewoods Cup action in the second leg of the tie with Aston Villa at Villa Park, but a first-minute Paul Birch goal sent Boro out of the competition on a 2–0 aggregate score. One high point of the game was the return of Brian Laws who had been out of action for eight months through injury, when he made an appearance as a second half substitute.

Brian Laws was on target in a 4–1 win over Huddersfield in October 1987 after a long injury lay-off.

Boro got back to winning ways a few days later when they made another trip to West Yorkshire, this time to face bottom-of-the-table Huddersfield Town. A superb Slaven hat-trick and a brilliant 30-yard volley from Laws in the last minute moved Boro into fifth place in the table, though nine points behind leaders Bradford.

After the game, Slaven revealed how he had reverted back to his favourite position. He said: 'I had been out on the left wing for six games and I was starting to go off the boil. But before the game the boss took me to one side in the hotel and gave me a vote of confidence. He told me he was putting me back up front and that's where I want to be. I thought I'd go out there

and show the boss that I was grateful, so those goals were for him.'

They were also an answer to team-mate Paul Kerr who had wound up Slaven before the match, mocking his poor goalscoring record of late.

'I knew "Nookie" was a bit of a joker but that really got to me,' admits Slaven. 'I don't know whether it was a serious dig but I was determined to prove him wrong.'

In response, Kerr laughs: 'I used to wind Bernie up all the time, but it was all in jest. He was the most frustrating player and could drive you up the wall. Unlike the rest of us, he had come into the professional game late and had not been taught tactics and teamwork in quite the same way. But rather than let that bother us, Bruce told us he was a free spirit and we should just put up with it. Most of us had no problem with that – especially given the cash his goals earned us in win bonuses.'

Ron Atkinson's improving West Brom side were beaten 2–1 at Ayresome Park a week later when Boro came from a goal down in the final ten minutes with Slaven and Cooper (his first career goal) hitting the mark.

Boro were now in third position as they went into action against Ipswich Town at Ayresome Park; again they had to come from behind. Boro grabbed three second half goals through Pallister, Slaven and man-of-the-match Kernaghan.

At the time Rioch was being connected with a move for Crystal Palace's future England international Andy Gray, who was valued at £200,000, though Aston Villa were reported to have already made a bid of £125,000.

Meanwhile, both Bruce Rioch and Colin Todd pledged their own futures to the club by agreeing new three-year contracts.

A drab goalless draw away to Birmingham City was quickly followed by an outstanding 4–0 home victory over Shrewsbury Town. Slaven grabbed another hat-trick, while Kernaghan was again on the scoresheet.

However, Kernaghan recalls: 'It was frustrating under Bruce because I was in and out of the team. The reason for that was because I was playing at centre-forward and not

scoring enough goals, particularly when I was alongside Bernie Slaven who was banging in thirty goals a season!'

The 4–0 result sent Boro into second place, only six points behind Bradford at the top of the table, but Rioch was quick to bring his players back down to earth. He said: 'The going will get tougher, and although I was pleased with the performance against Shrewsbury, it's important to remember we face a different proposition at Maine Road in our next game against Manchester City.'

Mowbray achieved a milestone against Shrewsbury when he made his two hundredth appearance for the club, but it was a disappointing time for Archie Stephens. The 33-year-old striker went on the transfer list just prior to the game against the Shrews after losing his place a few months earlier to Kernaghan.

Boro travelled to Maine Road the following Wednesday and showed great character in coming away with a 1–1 draw in front of a crowd of 18,434. Glover broke his Boro duck with a stunning 22-yard low drive which put Boro ahead and only an Andy Hinchcliffe goal in the second half prevented another victory.

Referring to his goal, Glover said: 'I'm absolutely delighted. It was great to get the first out of the way and now I'm looking for more.'

Nottingham Forest boss Brian Clough was an interested spectator at the game, apparently watching Gary Pallister.

Another tough game at Sheffield United followed, but Rioch's youngsters, ever-growing in confidence, produced one of their most clinical performances to date; a very impressive 2–0 victory with goals from Slaven and Ripley.

After the game, Sheffield United's former Boro coach Danny Bergara couldn't hide his admiration for his former club. 'Boro were brilliant and must have every chance of promotion. They are going to go a long, long way. There are so many good players there.'

A poor midweek display saw Boro slip out of the Simod Cup 1–0 at Ipswich which really got to Rioch. He publicly lashed his players on the eve of Saturday's top-of-the table clash with third-placed Hull City by saying: 'The passing against Ipswich was diabolical and so was the commitment. Only Mowbray and Glover were making contact out there.'

Boro reacted to Rioch's blast by producing a battling performance against Hull, winning the game through a Ripley piledriver. A week later Boro squeezed out another 1–0 win at Plymouth, despite having Parkinson sent off for the first time in his career. The performance left Rioch promising: 'The best is yet to come.'

Barnsley travelled to Ayresome Park a week later where they suffered a 2–0 defeat thanks to goals from Slaven, his fifteenth of the season, and Kernaghan. The result sent Boro into first place for the first time, on goal difference from Terry Dolan's Bradford.

Boro drew a blank in their next game at Leicester, but the point increased their lead at the top. Archie Stephens came on as a second half substitute for Kernaghan, his final appearance in a Boro shirt before a £12,000 move to Carlisle United.

After the game Steve Spriggs, who had made three appearances the previous season, signed a month's contract with Boro after a spell in Cyprus, although he failed to make an appearance on his return, walking out after only a few days.

Stoke City were soundly beaten a week later as Boro made it six clean sheets in a row, with Slaven and Hamilton on target in a 2–0 win for the table-toppers.

Steve Pears set an all-time club record a week later in the 0–0 draw at Bournemouth – his seventh consecutive clean sheet. The ace shot-stopper, ever modest, praised his team-mates saying: 'It's not just me, it's the whole team who deserve the credit. We have such a good understanding now that we can almost read each other's minds.'

As a result, Boro moved two points clear of Bradford at the top. In that game, another former Aston Villa player was introduced to their ranks – Mark Burke, who went on for Slaven in the second half.

On his signings from Villa, Rioch recalls: 'I was trying to keep the continuity going by picking up my first four buys from Villa. Paul Kerr, Dean Glover, Kevin Poole and Mark Burke were all the right age, so able to integrate

1987–88 Match of the Season

30 January 1988
EVERTON 1 BORO 1

3 February 1988
BORO 2 EVERTON 2 (aet)

9 February 1988
EVERTON 2 BORO 1

The FA Cup ties with reigning league champions Everton in 1988 will live forever in the memory of those who were fortunate enough to see them. Boro's indifferent form prior to the first game meant that although hopes were high, realistically Everton were expected to overcome any challenge Rioch's boys could offer.

Colin Harvey's Everton side had finally overcome Sheffield Wednesday after a marathon series of cup ties, and they were expected to knock Boro out of the cup at Goodison Park . . . but Rioch's rookies had other ideas.

Around 5,000 Teessiders made the trip across the Pennines to give their full backing to the players and they weren't disappointed. Boro started the game very strongly, though chances were at a premium. It remained goalless until just before the interval when Graeme Sharp gave the Toffeemen the lead after a sliced Mowbray clearance. To his credit, Rioch used half-time to rally his troops and they equalised early in the second half when Kerr slid home a Hamilton through-ball. Everton pressed for the remainder of the half but they could not penetrate Boro's defence with Steve Pears in outstanding form.

Passions were high at Ayresome Park for the replay, particularly following the fifth-round draw which had paired the winners with Liverpool who were running away with the First Division.

A crowd of over 25,000 crammed into the old ground to be entertained by some exhilarating football. The midfield battle between Dean Glover and Peter Reid was a war with no quarter given as the ball moved from end to end. Boro lost Pallister midway through the first half with concussion and he was replaced by Kernaghan. Hearts sank in the sixty-sixth minute when Everton's Dave Watson headed home at the East end of the ground and despite a monumental assault on goal, Boro's dreams looked shattered as the game moved into the final minute.

Step forward Boro's captain fantastic Tony Mowbray who threw himself at a corner to fire a header into the Holgate end goal, sending the crowd delirious. With extra-time beckoning, Rioch's youngsters surrounded their mentor to hear more words of encouragement. Rioch, a former Everton player, was delighted with his team's response. It was Kernaghan who scrambled the ball over the line in the ninety-ninth minute to give Boro the lead for the first time in the tie.

The noise was overwhelming. Boro were controlling proceedings and as the clock ticked on, thoughts turned to facing Liverpool in the next round. With the crowd whistling for the match to end, the home side continued to attack. Kerr had the ball near the Everton by-line and Rioch recalls: 'He tried to play it off the defender's legs, aiming to earn a corner, but it went out for a goal kick. Neville Southall sent a long punt downfield which bounced in our box, Colin Cooper challenged for the ball with Trevor Steven and it bounced past Pearsy into the net. It was a big disappointment.'

The crowd went silent in disbelief. So near and yet so far. Recalls Kerr: 'I was gutted when Steven scored. The players raised their game for that match but it was a terrible way to miss out.'

Tony Mowbray adds: 'I can still see that header as Steven and Coops leaped up; how the ball stuck in the mud and seemed to take forever to cross the line, despite Pearsy's despairing dive.'

Even so, there would be another chance a week later, though Rioch lost the toss which meant another trip to Merseyside. It was after that 2–2 draw, however, that Rioch spoke the immortal words that inspired a fanzine which is published to this day: 'If I was going to the moon, the one man I would like to take with me would be Tony Mowbray.'

Before the replay, Brian Laws said: 'We have nothing to fear, we can go to Goodison Park and win the game.'

The conditions, however, were not suited to Boro's stylish passing game, with a gale blowing and heavy rain, though it didn't dampen the spirits of the travelling army of supporters. BBC television's Bob Wilson stated: 'Boro's 5,000 supporters sounded more like 50,000 as they cheered their team on.'

Everton took an early lead but Boro – resilient as ever – fought back in the second half to equalise through an excellent goal from Ripley following great work on the left wing from Kerr.

It looked like the game was heading for extra-time once again until Mowbray deflected a shot into his own net and the dream was over.

'I got more national recognition from that game than any other,' reveals Mowbray. 'People wrote to me from all over the country telling me about how I could overcome such adversity. But that series of cup ties is part of Middlesbrough folklore now.'

Still Boro could hold their heads up high after outstanding displays of skill and desire to win, in front of over 94,000 supporters over the three games.

into another group of young players and it gave the squad strength.

'I knew we couldn't afford First Division players, so I'd go and watch a lot of the big clubs' reserve games. 'I remember going to Villa's training ground three or four times, popping my head round the door to speak to the manager and coach who I knew from my days there. Not only did I watch them play, but I went over and watched them on the training ground so I could get a good picture of what their temperament and character was like, and I could get them at the right value.'

A crowd of 23,536 packed into Ayresome Park for the Boxing day clash with Blackburn Rovers who, like Boro, were on a thirteen–game unbeaten run, while also fielding on-loan Barcelona striker Steve Archibald in their side. Slaven struck home from close range on the half hour, but the prolific Simon Garner equalised nine minutes later. The game finished 1–1, but it was Rovers who had produced the better football, which disappointed Rioch who admitted: 'We weren't good enough.'

Two days later Boro travelled to Elland Road to face in-form Leeds United in front of a massive crowd of 34,186. Sadly for Boro, they never got going in a white-hot atmosphere and were soundly beaten 2–0. Added to the disappointment of suffering their first defeat since early October was the bitter blow of having Stuart Ripley sent off with Leeds' Glynn Snodin for throwing a couple of right hooks at each other.

Still Boro topped the table at the end of 1987 which must rank as one of the brightest year-ends in the club's history.

Boss Bruce Rioch was delighted with his team and he publicly applauded them by telling them to: 'Take a bow, you've been brilliant.'

The Christmas hangover continued with a very disappointing 3–1 defeat at Oldham on New Year's day which meant Boro dropped to third in the table behind Aston Villa and Crystal Palace.

With form slipping, Bruce's boys faced a stern test in the FA Cup third round when they travelled to non-league Sutton United.

Despite controlling most of the game on a

Full-back Colin Cooper takes over in goal from the injured Stephen Pears during a promotion clash with Aston Villa in February 1988.

heavily sanded pitch, Boro didn't take the lead until the sixty-eighth minute when Pallister headed home a Hamilton corner. Still Sutton wouldn't lie down and equalised with only eight minutes remaining through Mark Golley.

Boro went into the replay knowing they would face First Division opposition in the fourth round in league champions Everton or Sheffield Wednesday should they overcome Sutton.

Kevin Poole replaced the injured Stephen Pears in goal, but it was at the other end that the problems were occurring as the goals appeared to have dried up. The game went into extra-time, but only just as Sutton's Nigel Golley – brother of Mark – headed against the crossbar with only two minutes of normal time remaining.

It was Paul Kerr who broke the deadlock when he forced the ball home from a Glover cross, much to the relief of the 17,000 crowd, who sportingly applauded the part-timers off the field at the final whistle. Looking back, Kerr has far from fond memories of the win. 'I wasn't even excited about scoring,' he insists. 'All it did was avoid further embarrassment. We were all relieved to have come through it.'

The following Saturday, Boro slipped down

to fifth in the table after conceding a late Teddy Sheringham goal in a 2–1 defeat at fellow promotion-chasers, Millwall. However, Rioch saw only a positive side to the defeat, insisting: 'We are on the right track. I enjoyed the way we played and Bernie Slaven's performance was first class.'

The manager's post-match analysis proved correct when high-flying Crystal Palace travelled to Ayresome Park for another 'six-pointer'. Without hitting their best form, Boro won 2–1 through goals by Mowbray and Glover to set the team back on the right path, while putting them in a positive frame of mind for the forthcoming cup tie at Everton.

Following two successive draws with the Goodison club, Boro earned a league point with a 1–1 draw at Swindon, Mowbray grabbing the goal.

There was no time for a hangover from the defeat by Everton in the second replay, as Boro were quickly back in action for a Valentine's day match with Aston Villa, covered live on national television. Villa were sitting on top of the table with Boro lying in sixth place and eight points behind the leaders.

The game was packed with incident, the first occurring when Pears left the field for treatment to a head wound after colliding with Garry Thompson's elbow. Colin Cooper took temporary charge of the number one shirt and the crowd were kept amused by his quick kit change in the middle of the pitch.

On thirty-five minutes, Mowbray was caught out by Thompson's pace which resulted in the striker supplying the cross for Tony Daley to slam the ball past the temporarily repaired Pears. Boro needed to win the game to retain any realistic chance of automatic promotion and the pressure was on. Midway through the second half, Rioch replaced Kerr and Ripley with Kernaghan and Burke and the game instantly changed.

Slaven's shot was only parried by Nigel Spink and Kernaghan pounced to prod the ball home for Boro's equaliser.

A flying header from captain Tony Mowbray clinches a vital 2–1 win over Aston Villa in February 1988.

The near 17,000 crowd were creating an electric atmosphere as Boro pressed for the winner. With only six minutes remaining Laws hoisted a high ball into the Villa box which found the unmarked Mowbray, who powered an unstoppable header past Spink to give Boro a glorious victory.

It was a great tonic for the captain who picked up Jack Charlton's award for the man-of-the-match bottle of champagne. Boro moved up into third place, hot on the heels of Bradford and Villa.

Reading held Rioch's team to a goalless draw at Elm Park before Bradford made the return trip to Ayresome. John Hendrie, chief tormentor in the earlier fixture, again proved a thorn in Boro's side as Terry Dolan's team dictated the pace of the game, running out comfortable 2–1 winners.

'I used to hate playing against Hendrie,' admits Colin Cooper. 'He had terrific pace. He was a strong, awkward little bugger.'

With every game crucial, Boro fought out another goalless draw, this time at West Brom.

Goals were proving very difficult to come by with no natural strike partner for Bernie Slaven and this was concerning Rioch.

'We were looking for a centre-forward, and the type I was looking for was a player who could not only score goals in his own right, but could also create chances in the box for other people,' he recalls. 'We only had £150,000 to spend so we were searching everywhere. I kept looking through *Rothmans Football Yearbook* at players' records!'

Boro got back to winning ways thanks to a Glover penalty and a Kerr goal in a sluggish 2–0 win over lowly Huddersfield, then followed up with a 1–0 win at Shrewsbury, thanks to another penalty by Glover.

With transfer deadline day looming, Rioch began a frantic search of the transfer market. He recalls: 'The scouts had already been to Watford to look at Trevor Senior but they came back and said, "No, not Trevor". I looked up his goal record in *Rothmans* again; it was

Gary Pallister outjumps Bradford City's John Hendrie at Ayresome Park in February 1988.

A determined Alan Kernaghan heads home Boro's second in a 3–1 win over Plymouth in April 1988.

phenomenal. I thought okay, he might not be the left-footer, he might not be the perfect player we are looking for, but he's a goalscorer. If we're going to try and get up with the money we have, if his character's right – and it was – then let's go for him.'

Senior did have a fantastic goalscoring record from his days at Reading, but since his move to First Division Watford the previous summer he had dried up.

The new striker made his debut in a drab 1–1 draw at home to Birmingham City which left Boro with a lot of work to do.

Rioch called for the team to produce a quality performance in the Easter Saturday clash with Sheffield United and it came straight out of the top drawer.

Stuart Ripley gave the Blades the complete runaround, scoring the first hat-trick of his career, Senior scored his first goal for the club and Slaven was not left out, grabbing a brace to make it a resounding 6–0.

Modest Ripley reflects: 'I was just feeling

confident at the time.'

On Easter Monday only a tremendous display by Hull City goalkeeper Tony Norman kept Boro out in a goalless draw.

Goals from Ripley and Hamilton sent Manchester City packing as the countdown to promotion really began.

With only two teams gaining automatic promotion it was imperative for Boro to keep their form, but nobody was prepared for the next game at Ipswich. Boro were renowned throughout the country for their defensive qualities, but the Suffolk club's young striker Dalian Atkinson showed scant regard for reputations, firing an unstoppable hat-trick as Boro crashed to a 4–0 defeat. The day was also marred by the sending off of Cooper which would cause him to miss vital games in the run-in.

The following Saturday Rioch's troops returned to winning ways with a resounding victory over Plymouth Argyle. Kernaghan replaced Senior, who was struggling to find his

1986–87 Match of the Season

30 January 1988
BORO 2 CHELSEA 0

3 February 1988
CHELSEA 1 BORO 0

A passionate crowd of 25,531 crammed into Ayresome for the first leg and watched Boro set about building a lead from the first whistle.

Glover let the Blues know he meant business when he put in a strong early challenge on striker Gordon Durie which left the Scotland star requiring treatment. On the half-hour Boro finally broke the deadlock when Slaven chipped over a cross for Senior to head over the hesitant Kevin Hitchcock.

Eight minutes into the second half, Senior repaid the compliment by sending Slaven clear towards the Holgate end. Slaven elected to shoot for goal from the narrowest of angles, and he would have been in for some severe criticism had he not pounced on the rebound from Hitchcock's initial save to hammer the ball into the net before leaping on to the fencing behind the goal in celebration. The game ended 2–0, a good solid platform to build on.

It was only halfway, though, and Chelsea were confident to say the least that they could wipe the floor with Middlesbrough in the return game. Comments were made by several of Bobby Campbell's players in national newspapers in the build-up to the game. Steve Wickes, in particular, belittled Boro, while Ron Atkinson had Chelsea down as clear winners, as did Bobby Charlton on BBC television.

With 40,500 fans in Stamford Bridge the atmosphere was more than hostile, even though Boro supporters made up nearly one quarter of the gate. Tony Mowbray described how 'You couldn't hear yourself think; the noise level was so high you could not hear your mate from five yards away.'

A typical shot of Bernie Slaven on the Holgate fence after scoring against Chelsea in the 1988 promotion play-offs.

Bruce Rioch recalls the morning of the game in particular: 'There'd been a lot of talk about the second leg with Chelsea, and one article more than any other stands out. It was in the Daily Telegraph on the morning of the game, comparing the teams' strengths and weaknesses.

'The journalist wrote that the greatest difficulty that Chelsea face today is the team spirit within Middlesbrough Football Club and its dressing room; it is without doubt the greatest spirit in any league club in the country.

'When I read that I knew exactly what he meant because that was the case. Chelsea were going to have to overcome not only the team, but the spirit and togetherness and I put a heavy emphasis on the need for great spirit. It moves mountains, it comes to your rescue, it comes to the fore when you need it.'

Boro were under early siege from Chelsea and Pears was forced into making a brilliant save from Pat Nevin. Boro's response came from Cooper whose long-range effort came off the inside of the post to present Slaven with a great chance, only for the leading goalscorer to head the ball over the bar from six yards.

Nevin was causing Boro real problems and it was no surprise when he found the unmarked Gordon Durie in the nineteenth minute who fired Chelsea ahead. From this point until half-time it was one-way traffic from Chelsea, but somehow the Boro youngsters held on to go in only 1–0 down.

Chelsea began the second half in the same manner and it looked unlikely that Boro would hang on, until midway through the half the pace dropped and they became more comfortable.

On the final whistle the players had to dash for the tunnel as a constant stream of marauding Chelsea thugs ran on to the pitch and towards the Boro contingent at the other end of the ground. Scenes were very ugly and many Middlesbrough fans were attacked while the players were forced to put their celebrations on hold until the Police took control of proceedings, making ninety-nine arrests.

In the dressing-room Bruce Rioch described the result as: 'The proudest, sweetest moment in my twenty-five years in the game.

'A year ago I was delighted at our promotion from the Third Division. but this is a really special day, one I will never forget. It's a good feeling to know you have helped make people proud.'

(continued)

(*continued*)

Chairman Colin Henderson was another delighted man: 'I have to keep pinching myself to make sure the dream has come true.

'I cannot speak too highly of what Bruce Rioch, his staff and the players have done. It was a truly remarkable story.'

After half an hour the players returned to the pitch to share their jubilation with the fans. Tony Mowbray walked along the front of the terracing to shake hands with as many of them as possible while he said: 'I want this day and night to go on for ever and ever!'

For 20-year-old Gary Parkinson it went too fast: 'I can't remember much about the game, just the incredible noise and the way I felt when Chelsea scored.

'I feel a wee bit sorry for them, they've got some good players and it's a big club, but we've been through a lot in the last two years and we deserve promotion.'

Chelsea's controversial chairman Ken Bates remained philosophical despite relegation, saying: 'It was a very good game of football. I went into the Middlesbrough dressing room after the game and told them they will be a credit to the First Division and will have nothing to worry about.'

form, while Glover was also a casualty of the defeat.

Ripley was again in red-hot form, firing Boro in front from a very acute angle, while Kernaghan responded to Rioch's reward of a shirt with a very hard-working display which was capped by a superb header. The goal of the game, however, came from Hamilton, who thundered a volley into the goal at the Holgate end. Unfortunately for Boro, a lapse by Pallister gave the Devon side a consolation goal, and how crucial it was to prove.

Two days later Boro travelled to Barnsley for a bank holiday game, backed by around 8,000 supporters. The game was only a few minutes old when both Ripley and Bernie Slaven scored to send the fans wild. A further Slaven goal in the second half gave Boro a tremendous 3–0 win which left them requiring a victory over mid-table Leicester in the final game of the season to secure promotion.

Ayresome Park was like a carnival for the visit of David Pleat's side who weren't expected to show a great deal of resistance. With over 27,645 packing into the ground, Boro took to the field without the suspended Cooper.

Unfortunately, Boro completely froze as they were overrun by a Leicester side which included Gary McAllister and Mike Newell in its ranks, finding themselves 2–0 down in the second half. Slaven responded to give Boro hope with a tap-in which even he admits was clearly offside, but the second goal would not come.

At the end of the game there were scenes of

massive confusion as players and fans alike tried to calculate who had won promotion. Millwall had gone up as champions, but Aston Villa and Boro were level on points and goal difference. There were rumours that it had been confirmed that Boro were up, but they were red herrings as it turned out Villa had won more games over the season to guarantee their promotion.

The final league table was:

	P	W	D	L	F	A	Pts
Millwall	44	25	7	12	72	52	82
Aston Villa	44	22	12	10	68	41	78
Boro	44	22	12	10	63	36	78
Bradford	44	22	11	11	74	54	77
Blackburn	44	21	14	9	68	52	77

The ground was like a morgue as supporters left, facing the prospect of the play-offs against Bradford City, who had already done the double over them.

'We learned a lot that day,' insists Stuart Ripley. 'We'd taken things for granted and we allowed the party mood to affect us. Gary McAllister ran the show.'

So it was to Valley Parade, with Cooper still suspended, though Senior was back in place of Kernaghan. A capacity crowd of 16,017 saw Boro take to the field in their all-white strip for a high-noon kick-off in brilliant sunshine.

At half-time the score remained goalless. The fireworks started on sixty-seven minutes when Bradford went ahead. Senior gave Boro the perfect response when he levelled two

minutes later, only for City's captain, Stuart McCall, to restore the lead within a minute. So Boro had been defeated for a third time by the Yorkshire side and many supporters were beginning to think Boro were jinxed against them.

However, the Boro management team were confident that Senior's goal would prove crucial and that was how it turned out. With just under 26,000 expectant fans in Ayresome Park, Boro produced a tremendous display in the return leg, yet they could only manage one goal, from Slaven, in normal time. This levelled the ties at 2–2 with Boro having the crucial away goal as they kicked off extra time. In that added half hour, Hamilton fired home at the Holgate end to win the tie.

Rioch recalls: 'It was a bit low on the coach on the way home after the defeat at Valley Parade so I got on the mike to liven things up and we started having a bit of fun.

'In the home game we brought Paul Kerr off the flank a little and left room for Parky to come down the other side, and he ran past Ormondroyd all night. Deano came back in midfield and he didn't mess around.'

In the play-off final, Boro faced Chelsea over two legs, with the first at Ayresome Park. Chelsea had been dragged into the relegation zone at the foot of the First Division, but they had destroyed Blackburn in the play-off semi-final.

Colin Cooper recalls: 'We were on a high and Bruce told us that no matter what we thought, Chelsea wouldn't be able to raise their game after their relegation battle.'

Rioch was proved right, as Boro won 2–1 over two legs.

A week later, a civic reception was held for players and officials at Middlesbrough Town Hall which saw the whole area come to a complete standstill. Supporters climbed up lamp-posts, shinned up drain pipes and stood on each other's shoulders to salute their victorious heroes, for providing what had been a quite remarkable season.

CHAPTER SIX

The Rioch Revolution Stumbles – 1988–89

This season the Boro bandwagon completed a whirlwind return to the top flight less than two years after liquidation – but Bruce Rioch's young players were to find this challenge their toughest yet.

During the summer of 1988, Boro prepared for their first season in Division One for seven years, with Rioch compiling a list of transfer targets. Top of the list was Ipswich Town's highly rated England Under-21 international Mark Brennan. Much to everyone's surprise, however, the first transfer activity at Ayresome Park was the departure of Brian Laws to Nottingham Forest.

Laws was one of the most experienced players in the squad and he was expected to sign a new contract with the club. Rioch was asking for £250,000 for the 26-year-old, while Forest were offering just under £100,000. A league tribunal set the fee at £120,000, a bargain for Forest considering the sterling service he gave them in the following years.

Boro would never have lost the player but for a bust-up between Laws and Rioch. Recalls Laws: 'Bruce had signed a lot of the other players up on long-term contracts before the transfer deadline the previous season. We couldn't formally finalise a deal in time but we eventually shook hands on a two-year deal and the club announced it to the press.

'When we won promotion, we went on tour to America, but I travelled out there on my own because I'd just lost my mam. When I got there, I found Bruce had reneged on the agreement and was offering me a one-year contract instead. I didn't feel I could play for him after that. I felt sick that he could do that. I rang my wife back in England and told her to send letters to all Premiership clubs informing them of my availability. I was sad to leave Middlesbrough but I was determined to get away from him.'

Looking back on the incident, Rioch admits: 'I might have made an error at the end of the season with Brian Laws. His contract was up, he'd been recovering from a major knee injury and I probably made an error in not working hard enough to keep him.'

The summer of '88 also saw a new appointment in the management support staff, with the arrival of former Derby and England star defender David Nish as Boro's youth team coach. Nish was brought in to reduce Brian Little's heavy workload, as he had become reserve team coach.

Midfielder Brennan eventually signed for Boro on 22 July for a fee of £350,000 and a

Mark Brennan was Boro's only signing at the start of the 1988–89 season.

delighted Rioch, who had beaten off the challenge of Norwich, Southampton and Sheffield Wednesday, announced: 'Brennan is a talented midfield player who can be a great asset to the team if he maximises his ability. He has all the necessary strengths. He has two good feet and I'm sure he will fit into our style of play.'

Other players who were linked with Boro during the summer were Liverpool's Jan Molby and Gary Ablett, Everton's Wayne Clarke, Kevin Sheedy and Adrian Heath, Motherwell's Fraser Wishart and Ireland international Frank Stapleton, though none of these players joined the club.

So Boro went into their first game of the season at Derby County with only one new addition to their squad but in a confident frame of mind. Skipper Tony Mowbray revealed: 'We are buzzing and ready for the First Division. We've had a good build-up and everybody is chirpy, we are all tremendously looking forward to it.'

The game itself proved to be a typical opening day affair, played at 100 miles per hour with little creativity. Derby's Paul Goddard scored the game's only goal five minutes after the interval when Stephen Pears mis-punched a Nigel Callaghan cross to the oncoming striker, who looped a header back over him. Boro pressed in the second half and should have equalised through Trevor Senior, though they

CHANGE – ON AND OFF THE PITCH

The shape of Middlesbrough F.C. of 1986 was slowly transforming both on and off the pitch. As the club made managerial and player changes, the board and shareholders were also undergoing change.

The first major change came with the resignation from the board of Henry Moszkowicz, though he stayed on as a shareholder for some years. Another change came when Scottish & Newcastle Breweries sold their shares in the club to the other existing shareholders.

Steve Gibson recalls: 'It took me about a year before I began to understand Henry Moszkowicz's motivation towards being involved with Middlesbrough Football Club. I felt he was motivated by a need to be loved. Being a director gave him a status which he enjoyed in the town. He used it as a platform for his own politics. He was writing articles in newspapers and signing them "Henry Moszkowicz, Director, Middlesbrough F.C." It was totally against what we were trying to do. We told him that as a non-executive director this was wrong. Only the chairman should be dealing with the press.'

At the same time, Moszkowicz began to fall out with the other board members. 'He didn't understand football or how it worked,' explains Gibson. 'I found myself in constant confrontation with the man and his ideas. He couldn't take pressure. When you questioned him and asked him to explain his actions, he would physically shake. I fed on that. I would bring pressure to the board meetings.'

Unlike the other board members, Moszkowicz was keen to see the board's voting system restructured from the 'one shareholder, one vote' principle to reflect more clearly the number of shares each shareholder had. Moszkowicz had 48 per cent of the club's shares so such a restructure would clearly be of benefit to him. But his fellow board members refused to budge.

Finally, he threatened to quit the board. Gibson asked him to put his resignation in writing and Moszkowicz obliged. It was a decision he would come to regret. 'Once Henry had quit as a director, he had very little input into the board,' explains Gibson. 'It was the board that was running the club, rather than the shareholders, so he had cut himself out of the decision-making process.'

What was more, only on a unanimous vote by all of the board members could he ever be reinstated. With Gibson on the board, such an event was never likely to occur – and never did. 'Henry tried to get back on the board but I was determined not to let him,' admits Gibson. 'At the same time, he had about £700,000 in the club and couldn't afford to pull out.'

Meanwhile, after just two years as shareholders, Scottish & Newcastle Breweries demanded a dividend on their investment. It was a non-starter and they were soon at loggerheads, both with the club and their representatives on the board, Graham Fordy and Reg Corbidge.

Fordy and Corbidge emerged from the ensuing saga with a great deal of credit. Gibson explains: 'S&N had their eyes on investing in Newcastle United so they wanted out. But first they put pressure on Graham and Reg to get the club to accept liability for the bond. S&N felt their employees should act on behalf of the company but Graham and Reg, as board members, instead acted in the interests of Middlesbrough F.C. It eventually cost them their jobs with S&N. If they had not stood firm, it could have caused the collapse of the football club.'

Eventually, S&N sold their shares to Gibson, ICI and Moszkowicz. Gibson now owned 20 per cent of the shares, ICI 32 per cent and Moszkowicz 48 per cent.

Blasting a sensational goal against Norwich City in the opening home match of the 1988–89 season is Tony Mowbray. Alas, Boro lost the game 3–2.

were unlucky when Peter Shilton denied Brennan a debut goal with a brilliant save from a free-kick.

Rioch's response to his team's defeat was to step up his search for new talent, and he was linked with the Arsenal trio of Perry Groves, Kevin Richardson and Martin Hayes. He admitted: 'We know we need a couple of new faces in our team, but it is an injection of quality we want and that takes time.'

Gary Pallister, who had missed the opening clash through injury, returned to the team for the first home game against Norwich City, amid speculation that Liverpool had tabled a £1.3 million bid for him. Having been capped by England while still in the Second Division, the classy centre-back was now considered hot property.

A crowd of just over 18,000 attended a sun-drenched Ayresome Park for Boro's home return to top flight, but they were disappointed when Robert Rosario poked Norwich in front

in the second minute. It was Tony Mowbray who led the fight-back, equalising with a sizzling strike from fully 35 yards six minutes later. Boro then had a twenty-minute spell of complete dominance without finding the target, only for Robert Fleck to force the ball home to give Norwich a 2–1 half-time lead. Brennan put Norwich 3–1 up with an unfortunate own goal on his home debut, before Mark Burke reduced the arrears on the hour. Even so, Norwich weren't prepared to wilt and they returned to Norfolk with all three points.

Rioch wasn't too despondent after the game, saying: 'We have a lot of work to do but we will get there in the end.' Norwich boss Dave Stringer was full of praise for Boro, adding: 'I feel that many teams will come to Ayresome Park this season and find it very hard to get a result.'

A few days after the game, Boro beat off competition from Nottingham Forest, Arsenal and Derby to sign 14-year-old England

1988–89 Match of the Season

1 October 1988

COVENTRY CITY 3 MIDDLESBROUGH 4

As a clash between two of the top flight's less glamorous clubs, this didn't look the most exciting of the day's fixtures. But anyone fortunate enough to have been at Highfield Road that day will never forget it.

Boro went into the match lying from third bottom of the First Division, while Coventry, enjoying one of the best periods in their history, were placed sixth before kick-off.

Despite the league standings, Sky Blues boss John Sillett fired out an eve-of-the-game warning to his players after receiving glowing reports of Boro's performance at Tottenham a week earlier.

Sillett said: 'They are a superb footballing side and knock the ball about. We will have to work hard if we want to win. If Middlesbrough come to attack us, we will be in for a great game of football.'

How right Sillett was. Boro lit the blue touch paper against a Coventry side which hadn't conceded a goal for four-and-half hours, after David Speedie had given the home team an early lead.

Tony Mowbray had been the victim of a stomach upset on the eve of the game, and Speedie took advantage of his absence to outjump the Boro defence and head home on seven minutes.

Within sixty seconds, Boro were level. Bernie Slaven netted the first goal of a wondrous thirty-minute hat-trick which fired his side into a 3–1 half-time lead. All of Slaven's goals were of the highest order – the first a shot from the edge of the box into the top corner, his second a volley from a Ripley cross and the third followed a Burke cross which he hooked home, again on the volley.

'It was just one of those days when everything went in,' reflects Slaven. 'When the third goal hit the net, I was asking the lads whose boots I had on! There's no doubt it was the best hat-trick of my career.'

Mark Burke appeared to have sealed Boro's victory when he added a fourth on fifty-five minutes. Paul Kerr played a Brazilian-style backheel to send Stuart Ripley away down the left wing; Ripley crossed for Burke to finish off the move of the match.

The game was still not over, however, as never-say-die Speedie responded with the second hat-trick of the game. His third, with seventeen minutes of the game still remaining, made the scoreline 4–3 and caused Boro to live on their nerve ends for the remainder of the match.

Incredibly, Speedie's treble consisted of three headers, which was all the more remarkable considering his height of just 5 feet 6 inches.

Afterwards, Bruce Rioch saluted his side by saying: 'When we get going like that, we are as good as anyone in the First Division.'

Colin Cooper, who captained the side in Mowbray's absence, recalls: 'Bruce said a lot of nice things about me after that match, but I'm not sure how the other lads felt about it. At the time, it was by far my proudest moment in football.'

schoolboy triallist Jamie Pollock.

Prior to Boro's trip to Manchester United, Pallister was recalled to the England squad, after missing out on the European Championship disaster, for the game with Denmark, while Stuart Ripley and Colin Cooper were included in the Under-21 squad.

Over 40,000 were at Old Trafford as Boro tried in vain to break their First Division duck. In a hard-fought game, it was the class finishing of United's inspirational captain Bryan Robson which separated the sides following his 20-yard drive in the seventieth minute after an unfortunate slip from Pallister. However, the United skipper was lucky to be on the field after his awful foul on Boro's young left-back Cooper fifteen minutes earlier, which only earned a lecture from referee Roger Milford.

A first victory was finally achieved a week later at Ayresome Park when a solitary Gary Hamilton goal was enough to beat Wimbledon. Hamilton was delighted with the win, saying: 'I thought we played our best football of the season in the first half.'

Meanwhile rumours were rife on Teesside that Trevor Senior would soon be on his way out of the club after a disappointing start to the season, and that he could well be replaced by Coventry City's Middlesbrough-born striker Keith Houchen.

Three further points should have been forthcoming a week later when Boro travelled to Spurs for a glamorous game with the North London aristocrats. Bernie Slaven put Boro ahead with his first goal of the season on twenty-seven minutes, only for Chris Waddle to equalise just before the break. Mowbray responded early in the second half when he stabbed home Hamilton's free-kick and that was how the score remained until the eighty-fifth minute. Substitute David Howells equalised in controversial circumstances when he charged into Pears to head home and this was followed by a remarkable penalty decision two minutes into injury time. Referee John Martin adjudged that Pallister had hauled Paul Moran down when he had clearly won the ball, and awarded Spurs the penalty.

England star Waddle was on the mark again,

leaving Boro to travel back to Teesside pointless and cursing their luck.

'We were a little bit hard done by that day,' remembers Colin Cooper. 'In the tunnel after the game, we were having a go at anybody and everybody. We were furious with the late penalty decision, though, looking back, it was fair enough.'

In the week following the Tottenham defeat, Bruce Rioch tied up seven of his young stars on long-term contracts. Colin Cooper, Gary Hamilton, Tony Mowbray, Gary Pallister, Gary Parkinson, Stuart Ripley and Bernie Slaven all committed their futures to the club – a huge boost for the fans who knew there was enough talent there for years to come.

A delighted Rioch said: 'It's a good sign. The club recognises that these players have a role to play in the future of the club and the players want to be part of it.'

Tranmere Rovers provided the opposition for the Littlewoods Cup second round and it proved to be a disappointing evening as Rioch's men failed to hit the target again in a 0–0 draw.

By this time, Senior had become a target for the boo-boys in the crowd, and it reached a peak against Tranmere. Rioch substituted the striker during the game and then revealed he would be chatting to the player over his situation. Within days he had rejoined Reading in a cut-price deal.

Senior recalls: 'I can honestly say I enjoyed my stay with the club, and my only regret is that it didn't last longer. I recall being booed off the field before leaving the club, when my mate turned round to me and said: "This crowd are right behind you, they can't wait to see the back of you!" Seriously though, I still have a lot of friends in the area. I settled very easily and found the people very friendly.'

Senior didn't travel with the squad to Coventry after being put on the transfer list by Rioch, who said: 'Senior gave us a big boost when he joined the club in March, and scored some important goals. But he faces an impossible battle to come back from the present situation and if the right offer comes along it will be accepted, providing the player is happy.'

Stuart Ripley has fond memories of Senior.

'Trevor was one of the nicest blokes. He had a fantastic goalscoring record at Reading but he knew his own limitations. In truth, I think he knew he wasn't good enough for the top flight.'

Tony Mowbray adds: 'Señor Senior could laugh at himself – which was fortunate because everyone else did! I'll never forget the first day he joined the club when we had some shooting practice in training. His shots were bouncing off his knees or flying over the bar, everywhere but the target. You'd have thought his legs were tied together. In fact, he was so bad, he made me look like Rivelino!'

But Mowbray adds: 'Above all else, Trevor was a smashing lad.'

Meanwhile, Rioch was linked with an interest in Oxford's Dean Saunders and Ian Wright of Crystal Palace – two strikers who would go on to achieve great things in the game. Unfortunately, neither player joined Middlesbrough.

A week after a 4–3 win at Coventry, Gary Hamilton, aged just 22, made his two hundredth league appearance against West Ham, while Pallister was being watched by England coach Mike Kelly with a view to England's World Cup qualifying game with Sweden. The clash with the Hammers also marked the return to Ayresome Park of the maverick Malcolm Allison, his first visit to the ground since being sacked almost five years earlier.

The Hammers were adrift at the bottom of the table despite adding Liam Brady to their ranks. Pallister couldn't have failed to impress Kelly as he played a key role in a defensive shut-out, while scoring the only goal of the game just before the break to secure a further three points. He was duly selected for the squad to face the Swedes.

Boro came back down to earth three days later when they came a cropper against Fourth Division Tranmere Rovers in the Littlewoods Cup. A goal from Mark Hughes in the forty-fourth minute sent Boro out of the competition, but it was exactly what they deserved for such a lack-lustre performance. It was obvious that Rioch was seething because he fielded Pallister, Ripley, Kerr, Slaven and Burke in the reserve side the next night at Stoke!

However, Rioch denied he had argued with Pallister after the Tranmere game, insisting: 'It's not true that I had harsh words with Gary Pallister or any of the players and banished them to the reserves. I never spoke to any player in that way after the Tranmere game, as they will tell you.'

At the same time, Gary Gill, who had rarely figured in the first team over the past eighteen months, turned down a new two-year contract.

In the build-up to Boro's home game with Luton, Rioch publicly stated that Gary Parkinson would be next in line for England recognition following Gary Pallister's selection at full level, while Cooper and Ripley had received Under-21 caps.

On the eve of the Luton game, Manchester United revealed that Boro had submitted a written offer in the region of £750,000 for striker Peter Davenport. Aston Villa were also reported to be bidding for the player.

Boro continued their improved league form against Luton with a convincing 2–1 victory, the goals coming from Slaven and a 25-yard piledriver from Cooper. The result saw Boro move up into eighth place in the league and, with Newcastle lying bottom, the scene was set for a red victory in the midweek Tyne-Tees derby.

However, it wasn't to be as McFaul's side controlled the game with Brazilian international Mirandinha causing untold problems for the Boro defence as the Geordies ran out 3–0 winners. After the game Rioch complained: 'We were second best on too many occasions.'

Meanwhile, Peter Davenport had indicated that he would make his decision on Boro or Villa that weekend. Boro faced Millwall at Ayresome Park on 29 October, and before kick-off the club announced to the crowd that they had smashed their transfer record to secure the signature of Davenport. A fee of £700,000 had been agreed with Manchester United for the former England and Nottingham Forest striker and he was given a standing ovation.

Davenport reveals: 'I'd already been up to Middlesbrough to meet Bruce and been very

impressed. They really made a play for me, but my wife-to-be Julie, hadn't been able to make the trip. Anyway, I'd promised Villa I would go and speak to them, and on this occasion I took Julie with me. Villa weren't half as keen as Boro, giving me a take-it or leave-it feeling, so I returned to Middlesbrough to show her how much better they'd treat me.

'Another of my reasons for signing was Bruce's promise that I'd be playing as a central striker, a role I preferred to the wide position I'd been playing for Manchester United. Added to that, Bruce assured me he would be bringing in half a dozen more new players during the season to strengthen the squad, something which never materialised.'

Boro beat Millwall 4–2 in a thrilling encounter which saw Slaven open the scoring with an astonishing strike after only two minutes, as if he had a point to prove. Millwall hit back with goals from Cascarino and Sheringham. Ripley equalised immediately after the re-start, and further goals from Burke and Parkinson ensured victory.

Slaven admits that his goal was an answer to suggestions from some quarters that Davenport would be his replacement.

'Bruce had made it clear that he saw Dav as a strike partner for me but there were some who thought otherwise,' he says. 'That was just the sort of challenge I always thrived on – as was proved by that opening goal.'

A delighted Davenport assured Boro fans: 'My best is yet to come. I'm looking forward to playing with the Boro team. I really enjoyed the Millwall game and I know now that Boro's style will suit mine. I like to play football and so do they. I'll be used as a target man and that's where I like to be best, just as I was at Forest. I want to do well for Boro and my target is to get back into the England squad. I think I can do it because my best years are still to come.'

Boro also completed the signing of another former England international in Mark Barham, who had been freed by Huddersfield Town.

Davenport's debut came in the cauldron atmosphere against Liverpool at Anfield in front of a sell-out crowd. On the day of the game there was further good news when reserve team captain Gary Gill had a change of heart and signed a new two-year contract. Boro gave a gallant display at Anfield, threatening to tear the Reds apart on several occasions. Indeed, only the magnificent form of Mike Hooper in the Liverpool goal prevented it from happening.

Ian Rush broke the deadlock on the stroke of half-time after a goalmouth scramble, but it still looked as if a draw was on the cards. Davenport went ever so close to a debut goal when his stunning drive was tipped over the bar by Hooper, who described the save as: 'The best of my whole career.' Liverpool made further inroads as the game progressed and added two more goals through Aldridge and Beardsley.

After the game Aldridge admitted: 'I thought the scoreline flattered us.' Bruce Rioch was far from displeased, adding: 'The dressing room is absolutely bubbling, we could have got something out of the game with a bit of luck in front of goal.'

Speaking about his new signing, he said: 'He could have had a couple. Once the rest of the team gets used to the way he plays, his threat to defenders and his ability to turn and commit people, then we will see more benefits.'

Boro players were beginning to earn a lot more international recognition at this time, with Gary Pallister about to win his second England cap after the home game with QPR, while Colin Cooper was named Barclays Young Player of the Month, an award nominated by full England boss Bobby Robson.

The QPR match was a milestone for Mark Brennan as he scored his first goal for the club in a hard-fought 1–0 win which moved Boro into seventh spot. However, Davenport had a quiet game, rarely threatening in front of a crowd of over 20,000.

'We were looking pretty healthy and felt we belonged in the top league,' says Colin Cooper. 'But then everything seemed to start catching up with us.'

A week after the win over QPR, Boro travelled to the capital for a clash with second-placed Arsenal and they were given a footballing lesson by George Graham's side, going down 3–0. A cruel 1–0 defeat at the hands

of an ultra-defensive Sheffield Wednesday side at Ayresome saw Boro slip to eleventh in the table, but it was the lack of goals that were a concern. In the three games leading up to Christmas Boro remained unbeaten, yet they weren't decisive enough to win a game, drawing at home to Villa in a 3–3 classic, finishing level in a goalless draw with Charlton, while grabbing a 2–2 draw at Forest.

After seven games, record signing Davenport still hadn't found the net and people were wondering if he would ever score.

Rioch hit back by saying: 'Peter Davenport has been our sharpest forward since he came here. His overall contribution around the penalty box has been good and that's one of the things we expected from him. At the moment we are still getting used to Peter and he is getting to know us. These things take time. I am not concerned about him at all.'

A Dean Glover penalty was all Boro could muster on Boxing day in a 2–1 defeat at Goodison Park to leave Boro without a win in six games. The festive fixture list had not been kind to Bruce Rioch and his team, offering the long trip to championship contenders Norwich on New Year's Eve. After some poor performances, Boro pulled rank and forced a hard-earned 1–1 goalless draw at Carrow Road.

Davenport finally broke his duck during the opening game of 1989 – and how fitting that the opposition were his former side, Manchester United!

A near-capacity Ayresome crowd saw Boro return to some of the early season champagne style of football, creating chance after chance. Brennan and Hamilton dictated the game in midfield against a United side which had comprehensively beaten Liverpool only two days earlier. It was midway through the second-half when the Birkenhead-born Davenport forced home his first goal for the club, much to the relief of both himself and the fans.

Davenport recalls: 'It was a big relief to get the goal against United because the pressure was beginning to build up. I'd already had a couple of goals disallowed due to Bernie being offside, and I'd hit the post too.'

The comment regarding Slaven reveals the frustration Davenport felt with his striking partner. At the time, it was clear to the fans that their partnership was not taking off.

'In all the time I was with Boro, I don't think I ever got a chance laid on for me by Bernie,' insists Davenport. 'But that's just the sort of player he was.

'I considered myself both a goalscorer and somebody who could provide and I did find it frustrating at times not to get anything back. But it was just a case of it not working out on the pitch. There were certainly no problems off it, despite what rumour-mongers said.'

Slaven agrees that he got on with Davenport off the pitch, but disagrees with any suggestion that he refused to pass to his strike partner.

It's there! Peter Davenport ends his goal drought by scoring his first goal for Boro against his former club Manchester United on 2 January 1989.

'It's a ridiculous accusation,' he insists. 'I prided myself on being a good passer but, apart from a very few exceptions, I passed to no one once I was in the box. I always felt that passing to someone else when you had a chance of scoring yourself was a crime.'

By this time Davenport had already experienced the harsh way in which Rioch spoke to his players. 'I was made PFA representative soon after my arrival because Pearsy didn't want it any more and I quickly realised that Bruce lacked man-management skills. I remember playing a reserve game just after arriving – a 1–1 draw at York, I think – and Bruce just walked in at the end and said, "You're all fined £50 for not trying." I couldn't believe it. You can't do that – not even my worst

critic could use that against me.

'After a few weeks I went in to see Bruce to ask when the new players would be coming, because I felt we could be in danger of slipping down the league. Bruce and Colin laughed me out of court, mocking: "Who are you? What do you know?"'

A welcome break from their league battle arrived the following Saturday when Grimsby Town, a side fifth from bottom of the Fourth Division arrived to face Boro, thirteenth in the First Division, in the third round of the FA Cup. A good crowd of over 19,000 saw Slaven put Boro in front on thirty-nine minutes through a header from a Hamilton corner. The game appeared to be in Boro's pocket as the second half progressed, until the Mariners brought on substitute Andy North, who equalised with his first kick in the seventy-first minute.

Pallister responded with a header against the crossbar in the seventy-eighth minute, but the real agony came three minutes from time when Grimsby's giant striker, Keith Alexander, flicked the ball on for North to head home his second goal of the game, creating one of the biggest shocks of the day.

It was at this point that Rioch revealed he was interested in signing Newcastle United's John Hendrie, who he had missed out on during the summer when the winger had joined the Geordies from Bradford City.

Boro responded to the cup shock with a scintillating display at Southampton a week later when they trounced the south coast side 3–1 at The Dell. Kerr, Slaven and Burke scored goals of outstanding quality to lift Boro back into the top half of the table, but the downside of the game was the sending off of Davenport, following a bad challenge on Ray Wallace.

Of the game, Kerr says: 'My family are from Portsmouth so they all went along to the Dell to watch that match – and, for some reason, I always seemed to play well in front of my family. I seemed to be able to raise my game.'

While Boro were beating Saints, there was sadness concerning the death of former Boro star Mick Baxter who had lost his battle with cancer at just 32 years of age.

Tottenham arrived at Ayresome with their galaxy of stars for the next clash, and the near 24,000 crowd were treated to a marvellous game. Paul Gascoigne suffered the 'Mars Bar treatment' – having several hurled at him from the crowd – and he was guilty of giving the ball away to Colin Cooper in the forty-first minute for the left-back to unleash a 35-yard piledriver past Erik Thorstvedt. Even so, the goal had come against the run of play, so it was no surprise when Paul Stewart equalised before the break following a great ball from man-of-the-match Chris Waddle.

Four minutes after the restart, Waddle again supplied Stewart to put Terry Venables' side 2–1 up. Boro appeared to be in trouble, they could not cope with Waddle who was picking the ball up in his own penalty area before making telling runs or pinpoint passes. Ripley was another who was having a tremendous game, playing in a central striking role, and it was a fitting reward for him when he levelled the scores after sixty-four minutes. The game then swung from end-to-end without any further goals which left Boro in tenth position, two places above Spurs at the end of January.

Boro missed out on Wembley yet again a week later when Second Division Crystal Palace ran out 3–2 winners in a Simod Cup quarter-final. Cooper put Boro 2–1 up with a brilliant low drive with only ninety seconds of the game remaining, yet Palace still managed to win the game. Phil Barber and Ian Wright both found the net in the remaining seconds.

It was in the week after the Palace game that reserve team coach Brian Little suddenly left the club to 'have a crack at management', which he soon did at Darlington.

Another hasty exit was made that week, when fans' favourite Dean Glover moved to Port Vale in a whirlwind £200,000 deal, amid rumours around the town that the player had seriously fallen out with the management. Glover denies such talk, insisting his departure was purely for football reasons.

'I wanted to see how far I could go as a player,' he says. 'Midfield wasn't my position and Port Vale offered me the chance to revert to my favoured role in central defence. I felt I could play at the highest level but not in the

role I was being asked to fill. Things might have been different if I'd been given a chance at centre-back, but I told Toddy that I wasn't happy with reserve team football.'

There were suggestions that Glover had stuck up for Mark Burke during a bust-up with the management team but Glover says simply: 'I always stuck up for Burkey. He was a quiet, shy lad and I looked after him.'

At the time, Rioch remarked: 'Port Vale originally offered £100,000 at the start of the week but I turned it down. They came back with the new offer and I decided to accept it. We had to evaluate the situation and decide if we could get a much bigger fee outside of the First Division. In many respects I am disappointed to see Dean go because he is a terrific character who has worked hard for us, but he has only been on the fringe of the first team this season and naturally he is keen for regular football.'

Rioch gave a debut to local-born defender Nicky Mohan in the home game with third-placed Coventry City, while Kevin Poole made his first appearance of the season in place of the injured Stephen Pears. In a disappointing game, Cyrille Regis put the Sky Blues ahead on thirty-five minutes, only for Slaven to equalise before half-time with his thirteenth goal of the season.

'I played with two great goalscorers in my career,' says Paul Kerr. 'One of them was Gary Shaw at Aston Villa the other was Bernie Slaven.'

It was clear by this time, however, that a number of players were suffering a loss of form, either through injury or lack of confidence, but with only a wafer-thin squad Bruce Rioch had to make do.

At Luton, he was reported to have blown up after a 1–0 defeat on the astro-turf pitch with a series of rows and tantrums in the dressing room. The harmony of the club appeared to be breaking down amidst personality clashes.

Mark Burke recalls: 'The problems arose as new players came into the club. We had been used to having a team drawn from local lads, while others like Paul Kerr, Dean Glover, and myself, who were all from Birmingham, had played our role in the building process. We all loved the place and cared deeply about it, but to new players Middlesbrough was just another club.

'Added to that, these players were coming into the club on much better contracts than the rest of us.'

Gary Gill was just returning to the first team picture after some outstanding performances in the reserves, but all was not well between him and the manager.

'Bruce was very strict but I always felt that his personal management skills let him down,' says Gill. 'Once he had an altercation with you, it meant you had to do something really special to get back in the team. I had been playing ever so well for Brian Little in the reserves, and was actually top scorer. Brian showed real faith in me and I always responded to that from a manager, while Bruce would never say anything to me in training. Brian and Colin Todd always gave me encouragement, telling me I would get a first team chance.

'I could have moved to another club in the division below and been much better off financially, but I was happy to stay. I'd played in the games at Southampton and Luton, where, despite losing, I was pleased with the way I'd performed. We went to Millwall the following Tuesday night and I was dropped from the squad completely. Bruce said nothing, so the next day I went to see him and told him I should be in the first team. His response was that he'd needed to change things tactically.

'The next thing I knew, it was in the newspaper that we'd had a fall-out and I wanted to leave the club.'

Yet in the press after the Luton game, while lambasting most of his team, Rioch said: 'Gary Gill and Paul Kerr worked hard.'

Boro lost the Millwall game 2–0 to slide further down the table, though relegation hadn't even been considered. Peter Davenport was coming under increasing pressure after being recalled for the defeat. He'd still only managed the one goal, while the rest of his game was failing to impress supporters.

Colin Todd spoke up for the record signing, explaining: 'Peter gives the team another dimension with his all-round game.' It was at

this time that Boro were said to be on the verge of signing Shrewsbury Town's Northern Ireland international midfielder Bernard McNally for around £400,000. Rioch was also being linked with Tottenham youngster Shaun Murray, though a ludicrous fee of £500,000 was being quoted for the midfielder, and with Middlesbrough-born Paul Dalton, a triallist and Manchester United reserve, who was said to be homesick.

A capacity crowd filled Ayresome Park for the first top flight Tees-Tyne derby for almost twelve years on 26 February, hoping to see Boro return to winning ways against second from bottom Newcastle. Jim Smith's side looked very average as Boro attacked them, but it was the Geordies' Liam O'Brien who shocked the crowd with a stunning goal on the half-hour.

It took the introduction of substitute Burke to get Boro back on level terms on sixty-three minutes when he sent over a fine cross for Slaven to head home. The final twenty-five minutes saw intense Boro pressure, but Tommy Wright in Newcastle's goal earned the visitors a crucial point.

The visit of title chasers Liverpool at the beginning of March saw another Ayresome sell-out, as Boro returned to England from a mid-season tour of Bermuda. Liverpool produced one of the most clinical displays ever seen at Ayresome Park giving Boro a footballing lesson as they beat them 4–0.

The result sent nerves jangling around the ground, as the prospect of a relegation dogfight suddenly became the topic of conversation. Despite not winning a game since mid-January, Boro remained in twelfth position, but the worrying thing was that Sheffield Wednesday, lying third from bottom, were only four points behind.

The series of bad results left Rioch frantically trying to bring new players into his squad in the week building up to the third successive home game with Derby County. The most likely target appeared to be QPR's bad-boy defender Mark Dennis. Dennis, despite his poor disciplinary record, was as a recognised quality left-back who would be able to step into the side in place of Colin Cooper, a player obviously suffering with injury. Dennis was valued at around £225,000, while another target was said to be Leicester City's Gary McAllister.

Rioch's frustrations began to show when he hit a broadside at the fans who had jeered Mark Brennan off the field after he had dislocated his shoulder in a reserve game at Ayresome Park.

Rioch held talks with Dennis prior to the home game with Derby, where, once again, Boro drew a blank in a dreadful 1–0 defeat. The goal itself was a disaster as Pears palmed a swerving Ted McMinn corner into his net. Boro slipped to thirteenth in the table after the defeat and Dennis returned to London to consider the move.

Rioch tabled a £200,000 bid for Luton Town's England midfielder Steve Williams and the deal was accepted by the Hatters. The stumbling block, however, was the player's flourishing business in Southampton. Eventually both deals broke down due to personal reasons, but Rioch did manage to snap up former Boro star Mark Proctor for £300,000 from Sheffield Wednesday.

Proctor, who had left the club for Nottingham Forest more than seven years earlier, remembers receiving a call from Boro's assistant manager, Colin Todd.

'He asked me if I would be prepared to come back,' recalls Proctor. 'Ron Atkinson had been in charge at Wednesday for only five or six weeks but I'd never missed a game under him. I think they were hoping for Gordon Strachan to replace me, though he was also a target for Middlesbrough.

'I always hoped I'd come back to Boro and when I re-joined the club I thought I would finish my career there. Boro had had a reasonable season until then but Bruce wanted a bit of experience in the midfield. He told me he wanted to bring in a few other new faces – Strachan and Dennis were mentioned – but they never materialised.'

Rioch pursued a second deal, his target believed to be Manchester United's Strachan, but he also made an audacious bid to snatch Newcastle United's Brazilian international Mirandinha from St James' Park. Newcastle

After being linked with many top players, Boro re-signed Mark Proctor during the 1988–89 campaign.

boss Jim Smith appeared keen to part with the Brazilian, but Rioch was once again foiled, over a work permit on this occasion. Sadly for Boro, he also missed out on Strachan, who opted for Second Division Leeds United.

The club's chief executive Keith Lamb reveals: 'Gordon was all set to meet up with us at Ayresome Park for talks. Unfortunately, before he set off from Manchester, he received a call from Leeds United, asking him to pop in to Elland Road on the way over. He signed for Leeds that afternoon without speaking to us. Who knows what might have happened if we'd signed Strachan?'

So the transfer deadline passed with Proctor being the only new arrival, as Boro prepared for their trip to Wimbledon. Rioch realised the responsibility on the 28-year-old's shoulders saying: 'We are hoping his experience will help the team in general and also help some of the players. He can lift other people in the side.'

With Proctor making his debut alongside winger Mark Barham – signed on a short-term contract – Boro achieved a hard-earned 1–1 draw against Wimbledon at Plough Lane, which provided a solid platform for the home game with league champions Everton. Proctor went into the clash sporting five stitches above his left eye, courtesy of a wildly swung elbow from a certain Vinny Jones.

Over 23,000 witnessed the Easter Monday clash with the Merseysiders and they were treated to another thriller, and yet another draw. Gill had his finest game in a Boro shirt, leaving Everton's England internationals in the shade, while Barham also enjoyed a fine home debut. Gill's shot came back off the post for Slaven to put Boro in front, only for Everton to hit back with two goals before half-time.

A Parkinson penalty put the home side back on level terms, until Pat Nevin put the Blues back in front. Boro refused to give up though, and Davenport volleyed home Gill's cushioned header for a share of the spoils in a 3–3 draw.

Gill clearly recalls the game: 'That game was a big challenge for me because although I was playing well away from home, there was still a lot of doubt in the crowd about my ability. It seemed half the crowd wanted me to have a bad time and I heard a lot of comments before the game.

'But from the word go I was winning challenges, I was having one of those days where it was all going right. I felt I'd turned the corner, I could sense something new and I was so proud that I was doing it in the First Division.'

Rioch was delighted with the performances of Gill and Proctor in the Boro engine room, commenting: 'Proctor had a good game on his home debut, while Gilly was so competitive. He is Boro through and through and he loves to compete. The two of them toiled and sweated for the club and that's just what we are looking for.'

The downside, of course, was that while Boro had scored three goals they had still failed to win the game.

'It was typical of us,' admits Proctor. 'We were shipping goals in left, right and centre at the time. The defence had lost a bit of confidence and were obviously feeling the pressure.'

The point left Boro eighth from bottom with eight games to go, though only four points above Southampton in third from bottom slot.

A disastrous 2–0 defeat at relegation-threatened Charlton left Boro fifth from bottom, and for the first time seriously in danger of going down. They were three points

ahead of third-bottom Luton with one game in hand.

Fourth-bottom Southampton were next to arrive at Ayresome for a real six-pointer, and Rioch called for the players to: 'Pull together for a mammoth effort; you are playing for your future.'

Meanwhile, Kerr publicly spoke about his dismay at being out of the team.

'I don't know why I've been left out, but I think the side needs me back in it. However, I'll have to wait and see what happens.'

The game against Southampton proved to be a disaster for Gill. The midfielder broke his leg in an unfortunate collision with Saints goalkeeper John Burridge, just as he was recapturing his best form.

'After the Everton game Bruce's attitude towards me changed,' reflects Gill. 'He suddenly thought he had a footballer on his hands and he respected me a bit more. When I ran out on the pitch against Southampton, the crowd were cheering my name which allowed me to enjoy myself.

'In the first ten minutes I hardly got a pass and ended up going for a stupid challenge because I was so hungry for the ball. Unfortunately, my leg got caught and John Burridge accidentally rolled on it. I heard a click in my leg. I got up and tried to run but fell down straight away.

'Physio Tommy Johnson came on to the pitch, put his arm around me and said: "It's a battle son – run it off!" Saying that, I wasn't really giving him any help with his diagnosis because I was so desperate to continue. Anyway, I eventually came off and the club doctor, Dr Dunn, sent me for an x-ray which showed a break in my leg.'

The game looked lost for Boro as they trailed 3–1 with only thirteen minutes remaining before Slaven hammered home a stunning 25-yard drive and substitute Burke headed an eighty-ninth minute equaliser. The result saw Boro move up one place in the table to sixth from bottom.

However, it was clear that the rock-solid defence of the previous two seasons was now a pale shadow of its former self.

'It was a shock to the system to concede so many goals,' admits Tony Mowbray. 'We had done so well initially, but when your confidence goes it becomes hard to see where the next win is coming from.'

His central defensive partner Gary Pallister adds: 'The defence had been the cornerstone of the side, but we were now playing against the best teams every week and we just didn't get to grips with it. The truth is we didn't know how to handle good teams. We didn't have the maturity or nous to handle it. There was a massive gulf between the top flight and lower divisions and we were too young and naive to bridge the gap.'

Rock-bottom West Ham provided Boro's next opposition for a midweek game at Upton Park and things looked like going from bad to worse when Boro fell behind. It was Slaven who was once again on the spot, twice on this occasion, as Boro grabbed their first victory for three months.

'After beating West Ham, we thought we were more or less safe,' admits Mark Proctor. 'We looked at the table and thought we would be okay and probably relaxed a bit.'

A missed opportunity by Proctor cost Boro victory at Queens Park Rangers a week later, but the team seemed to be turning the corner, unbeaten in three with only one goal conceded.

Proctor admits: 'I missed a sitter in the goalless draw at QPR, but that was the day of the Hillsborough disaster. News filtered through about all the fatalities as we travelled home and football no longer seemed so important. It was especially painful for me because I was still living in the Sheffield area at the time.'

In-form Nottingham Forest were the next visitors to Ayresome Park, for the victims of the Hillsborough disaster where a minute's silence was totally respected by a crowd of almost 21,000. Brian Clough's side responded to Hamilton's first half goal by cruising into a 4–1 lead. One of the most embarrassing sights of the day was the performance of Cooper, who was carrying an injury so bad that he could hardly run.

'I had broken my foot in a 50–50 challenge

against Coventry,' he reveals. 'I didn't want to miss any games so when I was asked if I was okay to play, I kept saying yes when I should have said no. The closer it got towards the end of the season, the more desperate I became not to miss a game. The only reason I got that far was because I was doing no training.

'I had to come off at half-time during the Forest game. I was in so much pain that I suffered a muscle spasm. I'd gone on for far too long.'

Slaven and Davenport hit back for Boro late in the game against Forest, but they were only consolation goals in a 4–3 defeat.

'We were dominating games, scoring three goals and still not winning,' grimaces Stuart Ripley. 'At that level, if teams have a weakness, the opposition find it and our weakness was that we were so cavalier in the way we attacked. It's okay to attack with flair as long as you temper it with defensive nouse – and we never did that. We played some great football and enjoyed it while it lasted but, looking back, it was obvious what would happen.'

Colin Cooper goes along with that, remarking: 'I'm not sure we could have played it any other way. The players were comfortable with that style and we enjoyed it. Bruce didn't insist on us playing football at all costs but that was how we played it.'

However, Gary Pallister says even the enjoyment factor had gone out of the club by this time.

'We got into a rut in the second half of the season and it got to the point where it felt like the wheels had come off the club. It wasn't a happy club any more. There was no enjoyment in training and it was then that I made my mind up that I wanted to leave.'

However, Pallister did not reveal his plans until the summer and Boro went into their final three games in seventh-bottom place, six points ahead of third-bottom Luton Town, though the Bedfordshire club had a game in hand.

Graham Taylor's Aston Villa, a side level on points with Boro, provided the opposition for the next game at Villa Park.

Kevin Poole was in magnificent form in the Boro goal and this gave the rest of the team

confidence to attack the home defence, which led to Davenport squeezing the ball home in the sixty-fourth minute. With a minute to go, it looked as if Boro would pick up the three points which would surely send them to safety, only for Stuart Gray to rise and head home a Nigel Callaghan cross for a share of the spoils.

Davenport couldn't believe the actions of Burke in the final minute just before Villa equalised.

'We were cruising 1–0, our fans were singing "we're staying up", and with a minute to go we got into an attacking position with a four-on-two situation. Mark had the ball and then for some reason that only he knows, he turned round and tried to knock a 60-yard pass back to Kevin Poole. The pass was cut out and they equalised.

'If we'd won that game we'd have stayed up. Villa stayed up instead, and went on to finish runners-up a year later. Who knows what we'd have done?'

Ripley believes he knows the answer to that question.

'If we'd stayed up – and we would have had we won that game – then we'd have gone on to become an excellent Middlesbrough team.'

The point left Boro in seventh-bottom slot as they went into their final home game of the season with league leaders Arsenal.

Another crowd of over 21,000 saw Boro toil hard in the hot sun, comfortably keeping the champions-elect at bay. Gunners' boss George Graham replaced Paul Merson with Martin Hayes in the seventieth minute and he responded by running on to a long kick from goalkeeper John Lukic, which had been flicked on by Alan Smith, to slot the ball past Poole.

Boro slipped into fourth from bottom position in the league with only one game to go – a tough trip to fellow relegation candidates, Sheffield Wednesday, Mark Proctor's former club.

'I couldn't believe it,' says Proctor. 'Both clubs were in the bottom half of the table when I joined Boro and I noticed that the last game was between the two sides. But I was sure it wouldn't go to the last game – I thought we'd both be safe by then. I could not believe it when

it came down to a straight clash between the two sides, with one of us destined to go down.'

Boro went behind to a Steve Whitton goal and, despite several chances, there was something about the display which seemed to indicate that the players were resigned to defeat. Burke was the chief culprit on the day when he missed a golden opportunity during the second half.

The 1–0 defeat meant that Boro slipped into a relegation position for the first time on the final day of the season, cruelly costing them their place among football's élite.

'For one of the few times in my entire career, I really felt pressure that day,' admits Proctor. 'Afterwards, it was awful. There were a few tears shed. Bruce and Toddy tried to rally us but everyone was just so dejected. It was probably the worst day of my career.'

It was hard to take for the players and supporters alike, after all the good work which had taken the club from liquidation and the Third Division to the top half of the First Division.

Following the disappointment, people looked for a scapegoat and fingers were pointed. Most of the blame was aimed at the signing of Davenport. Up until his arrival, Boro had been playing superb football and had begun to find the net with regularity. In addition, his arrival had led to unrest in the dressing room and the splits with Bruce Rioch which followed.

However, Rioch refutes any allegations that Davenport was to blame for the club's spiral down the table.

'Peter Davenport was brought to the club because he'd played First Division football with Manchester United and Nottingham Forest, and we thought he would be successful with us. He was a player who had lots of ability, lots of talent, but sometimes it's a case of right place wrong time.

'We were doing okay and we thought it would be a good signing. I'm not sure the balance and rapport of the front two was right. I think that's the best way to analyse it – they come in pairs and I'm not sure Davenport and Slaven were a partnership.

Bruce Rioch struggled to continue his initial success as Middlesbrough manager.

'We were playing the Liverpools and Manchester Uniteds and although we beat some of them, they weren't easy games. We had climbed very quickly and managers in the division said to me on our travels that we may have gone just a bit too quick. It was a major blow personally because we'd had two seasons of going forward.'

Rioch's number two, Colin Todd, supports the manager's sentiments: 'In terms of targets at the start of the season, we would have been happy to finish fourth from bottom, but we were relegated. You can't put the slide down to one player. Davenport had a tremendous career at Forest and Manchester United. We monitored him, we brought him in and it can happen with a lot of players, it just didn't happen for Peter. He probably didn't have the right partner and I think it's wrong to say that Peter was a bad signing, it just didn't work out.

'That can happen with signings in general – everything is a gamble. We spent a lot of money

on Peter thinking it would work and it didn't work as one would have liked. But there was no blame on Peter whatsoever for our relegation.'

Tony Mowbray, who joined Gary Pallister in the England B squad at the end of the season, reflects: 'The club had to be seen to be going forward. We were all young lads together and perhaps two, three or even four new players were needed. Bernie Slaven was a goalscoring machine but we needed another goalscorer. As it was, Peter Davenport was brought in and he probably wasn't the player we needed. We needed an Archie Stephens type to win balls in the air.'

Meanwhile, Slaven comments: 'All season long, people told us we were too good to go down and perhaps we believed it ourselves. Unfortunately, we weren't winners.'

Whatever the reason for the downfall, Boro were heading back into the Second Division after only one year in the top flight. Now the character of many of the players would truly be tested to the full.

The final league table showed how close it was at the bottom:

	P	W	D	L	F	A	Pts
Sheffield W	38	10	12	16	34	51	42
Luton	38	10	11	17	42	52	41
Aston Villa	38	9	13	16	45	56	40
Boro	38	9	12	17	44	61	39
West Ham	38	10	8	20	37	62	38
Newcastle	38	7	10	21	32	63	31

CHAPTER SEVEN

The Downward Spiral Continues – 1989–90

Despite Middlesbrough starting out as promotion favourites and ending up battling against a second successive relegation, the 1989–90 season still turned out to be a truly memorable year. Boro played at Wembley for the first time in the club's one hundred and thirteen-year history.

Boro began the season with all of the players who had come so close to staving off the drop the previous year, while Bruce Rioch moved into the transfer market to further strengthen the squad. In came experienced midfielder Trevor Putney, £300,000 from Norwich City, and talented winger Alan Comfort, £175,000 from Third Division Leyton Orient and an accomplished goalscorer.

Explaining his decision to join Boro, Putney says: 'My contract was up at Norwich and they had offered me a bad deal, so I decided to move. Howard Wilkinson at Leeds had made an offer for me and I was all set to go there when it suddenly fell through. Then I received a call from Colin Todd, asking me to join him and Bruce Rioch at Middlesbrough. I must admit my first reaction was that it was further north than I wanted to move; but Colin invited my wife and I up for the weekend to have a look around and we were impressed, so much so that I signed for the club.'

Both new signings made their Boro debuts in the opening day clash against newly promoted Wolves, whose twin strike-force of Steve Bull and Andy Mutch had caused nightmares for opposition defences in the Third Division. But Wolves were to find Division Two much tougher and Boro always looked a class above Graham Turner's boys at Ayresome Park.

Bernie Slaven scored twice, while Mark Proctor and Peter Davenport were also on target as Boro ran out 4–2 winners to send home happy a crowd of almost 22,000.

The one setback from that opening day victory was an injury to Paul Kerr. It turned out to be stress fractures in five places which sidelined the midfielder for over four months. It was a devastating blow for Kerr who was so fired up for the new campaign that he had decided to give up alcohol for a full season in a bid to improve his fitness.

'I vividly remember standing with a pint in my hand on 1 July and saying, "This is my last drink until the end of the season,"' he says. 'I ate all the right food and trained extremely hard as well. I wanted to see if it would improve my performance. Bruce Rioch admitted he had never seen me in such good shape and I started that first game on fire. The injury put me back to square one, it was very disappointing. In fact, if I hadn't been injured then I might still be at Middlesbrough now.'

Four days later, a battling display against Leeds United at Elland Road, and Comfort's first goal for his new club, looked set to clinch a point. Unfortunately, a horrific error by goalkeeper Kevin Poole resulted in the ball slipping past him and into the net from Gary Parkinson's back-pass – and handed Leeds all three points.

'That was my most embarrassing moment in football,' admits Poole. 'Parky turned the ball back to me but as I went to pick the ball up it hit a divot and bounced over my shoulder. I can't deny that it hit my confidence and affected my game in the weeks after that.'

There was more heartache when north-east rivals Sunderland ran out 2–1 winners at Roker Park the following Sunday. That match proved to be Gary Pallister's swansong before joining Manchester United and Alan Kernaghan was called up for a thrilling 3–3 draw against another of the newly promoted clubs, Sheffield United, at Ayresome Park. The impressive Comfort was again on target while Slaven hit two more – one of them a sensational long-range effort, but there were question marks over a defence which had now conceded nine goals in just four league fixtures.

Afterwards, Rioch suggested Slaven was Boro's bargain buy of all-time, while Tony Mowbray admitted: 'We are all thankful to Bernie – his finishing was absolutely brilliant. I've never seen him strike shots from outside the box before like he has been doing.'

Rioch admits that he was unhappy but not surprised at Pallister's departure: 'We were sad to be losing a player of Pallister's quality because we had always said that if you want to go straight back up you've got to hang on to your best players. I'd always said to the players, "If the club can't match your ambitions then there may well be an entitlement to leave." I just felt that coming down was always going to affect one or two players, and Pally had got himself into the England side so he was tied up with agents and First Division players. There was a likelihood he was going to be the first to leave and so it transpired.

'He had a long-term contract with us so we had to get the best deal we could. Manchester United's first offer was about £1.5 million and Fergie thought he had him with that. I sat down with Colin Henderson and we discussed it. We set our tactics out accordingly and ended up with £2.3 million. Still, I didn't like losing good players, just as any manager doesn't, because you can't replace them.'

Steve Gibson comments: 'The relationship between Bruce and the players deteriorated once we got relegated and Pallister began to get tapped and eventually wanted to be away. Bruce recommended we accept an offer from Manchester United for Pally. The board didn't want to accept. We agreed we would not sell Pally for less than £2.3 million and that the money would be made available for new players.'

Substitute Mark Burke scored the goal in a 1–1 draw at Barnsley and was unfortunate to remain on the bench as Ayresome Park played host to Bournemouth, the prolific Slaven and midfielder Proctor scoring in a 2–1 success.

There was reason to believe Boro were moving into top gear when Fourth Division Halifax Town were easily defeated 4–0 in the second round first leg of the Rumbelows Cup, but Slaven's ninth goal in eight games was no more than a consolation as Portsmouth ran out easy 3–1 winners in one following match at Fratton Park. With only two wins in their opening seven league games, Boro were struggling to make the expected impact and a 1–0 win over Hull City, courtesy of Proctor's third goal of the season, failed to convince anyone that the tide had turned.

There was more misery with a 1–0 defeat by Watford at Vicarage Road, though the formality of beating Halifax was completed with yet another Slaven goal in the second leg of the Rumbelows Cup tie. Gary Gill made his first start of the season and, surprisingly, captained the side that night.

New signing Simon Coleman, a £500,000 buy from Mansfield Town, made his first start in an unaccustomed role at right-back against Plymouth in mid-October. Naturally a centre-back, Coleman was played out of position in an experimental defensive formation against Argyle. Coleman was one of the few players who emerged from the game with any credit. Davenport, who had been recalled for the match, was out again for a home clash against Brighton, while Gill was never to play for the club again.

It still hurts Gill that his time with his home-town club ended the way it did.

'We'd not been getting on, but one day Bruce came in and apologised to me and Dav, who had also been treated badly. The next thing I knew I was captain for the trip to Halifax and would have been for a league game at Blackburn. Unfortunately, the gods were against me because, despite it being September,

the game was postponed and I never got in the team again.'

By this point Rioch knew he had problems.

'It's possible that the club suffered a relegation hangover,' he reflects. 'We had good training facilities at Maiden Castle but one or two of the players were unhappy about them, though initially they'd never voiced their opinion. Once such nit-picking started, I knew there were problems.

'Our form suffered, though it's hard to give a reason why that was. Obviously it's to do with the people at the top, primarily the manager. I'd gone as far as I could with some of the players, though not all of them. We'd lost Gary Hamilton with a knee injury, while Cooper, Mowbray and Pears had plenty left in them and Ripley was fantastic. But sometimes you've got to rebuild a side and I sometimes wonder if I should have brought other people in quicker.'

Mark Proctor has his own theory on what had gone wrong.

'I thought we would go straight back up. We were the promotion favourites and a big scalp for every team we played. Teams seemed to raise their game against us. People used to ask me what the problem was but I didn't know. Bruce had tried to strengthen the squad but it didn't work out. Alan Comfort was talented but picked up a serious injury, while Trevor Putney had a good pedigree but didn't show it at times.'

Stuart Ripley was one of the players criticised for showing a marked downturn in his form compared to the previous season, but he explains: 'I had been injured throughout the pre-season and lacked a lot of match fitness. It's true I didn't play well that season but I was picking up hamstring injuries time after time. I crashed my car through a fence while travelling back from our training ground at Maiden Castle and dislodged the base of my back. After that, there were days when I would get up and could hardly walk.

'One thing that did disappoint me was that I didn't feel I got the proper medical treatment. My problem was actually easy to put right but it was never sorted until Lennie Lawrence joined the club and sent me to the Bimal Clinic. Obviously, all the fans saw were my performances on a Saturday afternoon and rightly wondered what was going on. There was a bit of finger-pointing which did hurt me.'

Rioch made more wholesale changes for the Brighton game. Mohan, Kernaghan, Davenport and Gill were replaced by Cooper, Brennan, Ripley and Parkinson, with Coleman reverting to centre-back. It was a move to revitalise the side and it appeared to have worked with Boro coasting at 2–0 ahead. But Rioch was left fuming when the visitors hit back to grab a 2–2 draw.

Burke was named in the starting line-up for the first time since the previous May for a visit to Oldham, while Kernaghan was recalled, though this time he reverted to centre-forward alongside Slaven. It was another ploy which failed to work as the Latics scored twice without reply.

In normal circumstances, the Rumbelows Cup would have provided a welcome relief from the disastrous league form, but visitors Wimbledon were anything but entertaining as they did their utmost to kill the game as a spectator sport after going a goal up. Fortunately, Boro got a second bite of the cherry when Slaven's eleventh goal of the season clinched a replay.

Boro failed to score for the fourth time in five league games as West Bromwich Albion held out for a goalless stalemate at Ayresome, followed by a 1–1 draw at Port Vale, Kernaghan, now back in defence, on the scoresheet. Things got worse with a 1–0 cup replay defeat by Wimbledon, though spirits were momentarily lifted by a fighting 2–2 draw against Newcastle at St James' Park. Proctor and Brennan were both on target for Boro.

Boro's joy at winning a priceless point was tempered, however, by a freak knee injury to Alan Comfort. As it turned out, the winger had played his last game in league football and would eventually be forced to retire from the professional game aged just 26.

Physio Tommy Johnson remembers the incident vividly.

'It was incredibly unfortunate because Alan wasn't even in a tackle. He was trying to retrieve the ball out on the wing, twisted and

The career of Alan Comfort, pictured in action against WBA, came to an end with an injury at Newcastle in November 1989.

went down. I raced over to him and Dr Dunn, the club doctor, came over. We eventually got him to the treatment room and packed his knee with ice but there was no way of telling how serious the injury was at the time. Later, Dr Dunn called the specialist, Mr Muckle, and Alan was put into plaster at Middlesbrough General Hospital.

'Somehow he just never got over it, though he tried and tried. People were sure he would be back but it wasn't to be. It was terribly sad because he was such a nice fella. He stood out from most players in that not once did I ever hear him swear.'

There was more gloom when Swindon won 2–0 at Ayresome Park and West Ham scored twice without reply at Upton Park. Rioch's pre-season promotion favourites had now gone a disastrous nine league games without a win – losing five of them – and it was self-evident that Boro faced a crisis if the corner could not be turned soon. On his part, Rioch believed a

striker was now a must as the next signing.

There seemed little reason to believe Boro would get any change from their visit to Ewood Park to take on Blackburn Rovers but Kernaghan, recalled as a striker in place of Burke, was on fire on a night he will never forget. The 22-year-old crashed home an incredible hat-trick in a 4–2 victory – a perfectly timed response to Rioch's suggestion that he needed a new striker.

'Everything Alan hit went in the net that night,' smiles Mark Proctor. 'He certainly shook a few people with that performance. For some reason, he had been a target of the boo-boys though I could never understand why they picked him out. I had it for a short spell and it's awful, but I thought Kerny was a talented player and was very hard done by.'

Not surprisingly, the team showed no changes when Oxford visited Ayresome Park on 25 November and were duly beaten by a single strike from Slaven. Four days later, Kernaghan

1989–90 Season

FANS' HERO RIOCH SACKED

Just weeks before Boro's first ever appearance at Wembley, the fans were shaken by the sacking of manager Bruce Rioch. It was the end of an era and fans and players alike were split on the wisdom of the decision.

The night before, a home defeat to Watford had seen Boro fall still further and the horrific prospect of a second successive relegation was becoming a real possibility. Despite the run to the ZDS Cup final, the board felt it was time to act.

Looking back, Steve Gibson acknowledges that it was not an easy decision to make but explains: 'The relationship between Bruce and the players had deteriorated. Although they still respected him, he was no longer able to get a quart out of a pint pot. We were in very grave danger of relegation to the Third Division.

'It was a very hard decision for Colin Henderson, as chairman, to make because he was very close to Bruce. But we thought long and hard about it and felt we needed a change.'

Another concern of the board was that Rioch did not appear to be checking out prospective targets with the necessary detail. 'We felt he wasn't researching players in the way he should,' says Gibson. 'He wanted to buy a left winger, Nigel Callaghan, from Aston Villa, but it seemed too easy. Davenport hadn't been a success, Brennan wasn't a success and the way the whole thing with Callaghan happened left us feeling like it would be another mistake.

'Callaghan had been recommended by a friend of a friend of Bruce's, but when we asked him who had watched him, there wasn't a response. Although we never actually said "don't do it", we were able to change Bruce's mind.'

The board's scepticism about Callaghan proved to be spot on. Within months, he had given up the professional game to become a DJ on a holiday island.

Colin Todd was the new man in charge in March 1990.

Such concerns, combined with a run of disastrous league results, left the board with no option but to sack the club's former Messiah, but Rioch took it all in his stride

Gibson recalls: 'The day we sacked Bruce, he accepted it with great dignity. It wasn't change for the sake of change. The message from around the club was that some of the players were not as committed to Bruce as they should have been.'

On his part, Rioch reflects: 'That season our form suffered. It's hard to give a reason for why that was, though obviously it's to do with the people at the top and particularly the manager. I think I'd just gone as far as I could with some of the players. Perhaps I should have brought in new people more quickly but you can never tell.'

Rioch prefers not to dwell on his departure from the club, preferring to remember the happier times. 'I remember the good times more than anything because they were fantastic. They

(continued)

(continued)

were four super years, where we raised people's expectations. It brought renewed enthusiasm into the town and its people. The rapport and friendship I have with Middlesbrough and its people is excellent – and it always will be. That doesn't often happen to managers.'

However, he admits: 'At one stage, I actually thought I might be at Middlesbrough forever. It hurt me to miss out on the cup final. But you don't ask for any time in this industry. You know the job – if they cut it short, they cut it short.'

Rioch's replacement was his former sidekick, assistant manager Colin Todd. It was an obvious progression with Gibson commenting: 'I don't think Colin ever lost the respect of the players. He was well away from the bullying that had gone on at the club. We decided we'd give Toddy the job.'

was injured as Port Vale were sent reeling out of the Zenith Data Systems Cup at the first round stage. Slaven fired in two more while Coleman scored his first for the club, though less than 7,000 attended Ayresome for the game.

Kernaghan returned for a visit to Molineux the following Saturday though, somewhat surprisingly, it was as a central defender. Boro showed little bite as they ended a run of three straight wins with a 2–0 defeat by Wolves and then predictably lost at home to promotion favourites Leeds United by the same scoreline.

Colin Cooper, who, at the time, was struggling to regain his excellent form of old, comments: 'That season was hard. If we'd got off to a decent start, things might have been different but then the gremlins seemed to creep into the mind. Eventually, even our football started to suffer, which had never been a problem even in relegation from the First Division.'

That match was to be Kevin Poole's last league appearance for the club. He was dropped for a home clash against Leicester City to make way for the fit-again Stephen Pears who had been sidelined for nine months.

On an astonishing afternoon, Pears devoted one of the great goalkeeping performances to his recently deceased father, as he denied City's on-loan striker Kevin Campbell a hat-trick. Pears' stunning saves inspired Boro to a 4–1 victory, full-back Cooper firing in two of the goals.

Incredibly, there was more to come as Boro finally delivered the goals and performances the fans had believed them capable of. Ron Atkinson's First Division Sheffield Wednesday – the side who had condemned Boro to relegation eight months earlier – were taken apart in the second round of the Zenith Data Systems Cup. Slaven took his season's tally to nineteen in twenty-eight games, firing a hat-trick as strike partner Kernaghan completed a second successive 4–1 rout. Boro were now on the crest of a wave and Slaven hit goal number 20 to clinch a 1–0 Boxing day success over struggling Bradford City at Valley Parade.

If the supporters thought the only way was up, however, they were wrong. The year ended with a 3–0 mauling at Ipswich Town and the 1990s got underway with an instantly forgettable 1–0 home defeat to Stoke City.

Typically, Boro lifted themselves to hold First Division Everton to a goalless draw at Ayresome in the third round of the FA Cup. Four days later, the replay at Goodison ended 1–1 when Parkinson hit an astonishing long-range effort.

The Jekyll and Hyde displays continued with a 3–0 derby demolition of promotion-chasing Sunderland at Ayresome Park. Perhaps this was just another show of Boro's age-old knack of lifting their game for the big games, but the Roker men were sent packing with goals from Davenport, Slaven and another long-range belter from Parkinson.

Kerr made his first start since the opening day in the second replay against Everton, again at Goodison, as Boro finally succumbed by a single goal. However, Mowbray picked up an injury at this time and Rioch considered

1989–90 Match of the Season – 1

25 March 1990

CHELSEA 1 MIDDLESBROUGH 0 – ZDS CUP FINAL

After one hundred and fourteen years, the dream finally became reality on a Sunday afternoon in March 1990 when Boro faced Chelsea at Wembley stadium.

The competition may have been the unglamorous Zenith Data Systems Cup, but that didn't prevent 35,000 Boro supporters making the trip to the twin towers.Indeed, there would have been many more but for ticket restrictions.

Although he had taken over the managerial reins from Bruce Rioch, Colin Todd awarded injured skipper Tony Mowbray the honour of leading the team out on to the field.

The crowd of 76,369 made a deafening noise from the moment the sides entered the arena, and it was First Division Chelsea who made the brighter start.

However, every time they attacked the Boro defence, they found Alan Kernaghan in fantastic form, winning tackles and blocking shots.Boro retorted with a shot from acting captain Mark Proctor, while Kernaghan almost forced Peter Nicholas into scoring an own goal.

The breakthrough eventually came in the twenty-sixth minute when Simon Coleman needlessly fouled Kerry Dixon on the edge of the penalty area to give Bobby Campbell's side a free-kick in a dangerous area. Long range specialist Tony Dorigo stepped forward to take the kick, bending the ball around the wall and just past the out-stretched arms of Stephen Pears into the top right-hand corner.

Pears responded moments later with a save from another Dorigo free-kick, before Boro began to stamp some authority on the game.

At half-time Boro trailed 1–0, but they came out looking like a different side in the second half, completely dominating proceedings.Yet, despite holding 90 per cent of the possession, they failed to force Chelsea keeper Dave Beasant into making a save.

Peter Davenport appeared to pose most problems to the opposition with his tricky runs down the left wing, although he didn't receive enough of the ball to be a real menace.

In the final ten minutes, Boro threw everything into attack without ever really threatening to equalise. This was part of the side's problem at the time – a lot of pretty football without any penetration.

Smiles from Mark Proctor despite the 1–0 defeat to Chelsea in the Zenith Data Systems Cup final. Boro fans had turned one end of Wembley into a sea of red and white.

After the final whistle, the supporters applauded Boro's courageous display with a heart-rending rendition of *You'll Never Walk Alone*, while the Chelsea fans responded by spitting on the Boro players as they climbed the steps to receive their medals in the Royal box.

To Peter Davenport it was one of the best days of his career: 'The supporters were fantastic, creating an incredible atmosphere. People say it was only the Zenith Data Systems Cup Final, but the atmosphere was at least a match for that of the FA Cup Final I appeared in for Sunderland in 1992.'

Chelsea skipper Peter Nicholas received the man of the match award, but most Boro fans agree the award should have gone to Alan Kernaghan for his impeccable display.

After the game, Kernaghan said: 'We've always been taught to be patient and we were, we never panicked and if the chance had come along we would have taken it. Chelsea caused us few problems. Perhaps it sounds big headed, but I found it very easy. We are used to a big match atmosphere and we went out there and played. I enjoyed the game, but not the result.'

Mark Proctor, captain for the day, was very positive about the performance saying: 'We gave it our best shot and our fans were magnificent, they tried to will us a goal, but it wasn't to be. I only hope it's not another hundred years before we come back again.'

Young midfielder Owen McGee, who ran his socks off on the energy-sapping Wembley pitch, felt the result went the wrong way: 'We deserved to win on possession and play. I'm very disappointed with the result, but the day was everything I thought it would be.'

(continued)

(continued)

Bobby Campbell was mystified at Middlesbrough's lowly league standing after watching the game: 'When you look at the way Middlesbrough played against us, and Aston Villa in the semi-final, you can't understand why they are where they are.'

Looking back Alan Kernaghan recalls: 'I remember the coach journey, then when we walked out on to the Wembley pitch. The stadium just seemed to be awash with red and white.

'David Nish got me out on to the pitch early so that I could get warmed out and run my nerves out of my system.

'I thought we played all right during the game itself though Cheslea weren't anything special, but the atmosphere was brilliant, it meant a great deal to the players to be playing in a cup final at Wembley, regardless of it being the Zenith Data Systems Cup. It was a wonderful day.'

switching full-back Cooper to centre-back – a position in which he was to win a full England cap with Nottingham Forest some years later.

'Simon Coleman had come in and was expected to be the new Gary Pallister,' recalls Cooper. 'But there were a couple of injuries just after Christmas and Bruce asked me if I had ever played centre-back. I had actually played there for the club's youth team and we discussed the possibility of me playing there for the first

team but nothing ever came of it.'

Surprise table-toppers Sheffield United proved too strong for Boro at Bramall Lane. However, Boro were now just two steps from Wembley, albeit in the much-maligned Zenith Data Systems Cup. The next tie, the northern semi-final, saw them meet their deadly rivals Newcastle United, another of the division's top sides. In a closely fought contest, Cooper lashed home the game's only goal to clinch a northern

How about that? Paul Kerr is ecstatic after scoring Boro's second goal against his former club Aston Villa to send Middlesbrough to Wembley for the first time.

1989–90 Match of the Season – 2

5 May 1990

MIDDLESBROUGH 4 NEWCASTLE UNITED 1

This was the ultimate end-of-season clash, with both sides needing victory in the Tees-Tyne derby, but for starkly differing reasons. To say this match was balanced on a knife edge would be a gross understatement. The game was crucial to both teams as their seasons hung in the balance.

Both sides had suffered the trauma of relegation from the top flight the previous May, but Newcastle's response to the disappointment was poles apart from Boro's.

Jim Smith's side went into the clash on the back of an impressive nine-match unbeaten run, searching for a win as they attempted to bounce back into the top flight at the first attempt. For Boro, however, it was a case of three points or bust. Anything less would mean automatic relegation to Division Three.

Boro also had their eyes on fellow strugglers Bournemouth who were at home to newly promoted Leeds United, while Sheffield United's display at Leicester was on the minds of Newcastle.

The atmosphere was electric as the teams raced from the tunnel on to the pitch to be welcomed by just under 19,000 partisan fans. Newcastle had received only 1,000 tickets for the game, but many more attended St James' Park to watch it on a big screen.

In the dramatic end-of-season game against north-east rivals Newcastle United in 1990, Ian Baird outjumps Mark Stimson.

A tense first half ended goalless, but there was bad news from Filbert Street, if you were a Geordie, where Sheffield United were leading the home side 4–2.

The second half at Ayresome was an entirely different story, with Boro taking the lead on the hour after news of a Leeds goal at Dean Court. It was Bernie Slaven who delivered the goods, connecting sweetly with a left wing cross from Paul Kerr.

Six minutes later, Slaven turned provider when he pounced on a John Anderson mistake to give Ian Baird a simple tap-in.

Newcastle pulled one back three minutes later in very unfortunate circumstances for young Boro defender Owen McGee, who deflected the ball past Stephen Pears from a Kevin Brock header.

With the game back in the balance, Boro put their foot on the gas. Baird, who had struggled for goals since joining the club some months earlier, struck a superb angled shot to put Boro 3–1 up. Then, in the final minute, Mark Proctor's shot rebounded off a post into the path of the onrushing Slaven who joyously slammed in his second and Boro's fourth.

Of course, the 4–1 success would have meant nothing had Bournemouth beaten Leeds United. But confirmation of Leeds' 1–0 win at Dean Court meant Boro had escaped a second successive relegation. Newcastle were forced into the promotion play-offs in which they later lost to Sunderland.

(continued)

(continued)

Baird's celebrations that day were particularly noticeable, as he appeared to be taunting Newcastle's defender Bjorn Kristensen. Baird remembers: 'I'd had a few run-ins on the pitch with Kristensen prior to that game. There was a lot at stake, but it was nothing personal. There was a lot of tension out there that day and it would have been terrible for Middlesbrough had they been relegated.'

On his partnership with Slaven, the big striker says: 'Bernie never worked too hard, but he was always good for a goal, and he's certainly the best finisher I ever played with.'

area final tie against Aston Villa.

A week later, Boro made the trip to Villa Park for the first leg as rank outsiders against a Villa side who were second in the top flight. Twenty-year-old local lad Owen McGee made his first start as Boro rocked the favourites with a scrambled goal from Slaven and a superb free-kick from Brennan to take a 2–1 lead into the second leg. Boro had never been this close to Wembley.

It would have been understandable had the players had their minds on Wembley when they returned to league action against Portsmouth at Ayresome Park – but they kept their concentration to take all three points, thanks to goals from Kerr and Slaven, as new £500,000 striker Ian Baird made his debut. However, it was fortunate that Slaven was even on the pitch, having taken his boots off in the dressing room at half-time and announced that he would not be taking to the field for the second half. His gripe was that he had not had a touch while being played wide on the left in order to accommodate target man Baird.

'We were 1–0 up at half-time but I'd played no part in the game,' recalls Slaven. 'I told Bruce he could get a dummy to play out there because there was no way I was going to. I was seeing absolutely nothing of the ball and was totally frustrated. The only reason I went back on was because the other lads persuaded me to. But I proved my point because I scored my goal after Bruce had moved me back into the centre during the second half.'

Baird, meanwhile, was the man who Rioch believed could score the goals to pull Boro out of the mire. Not since Archie Stephens four years earlier had Boro had a successful target

man to link up with Slaven in attack.

With Baird cup-tied, however, Kernaghan was again in attack for the nail-biting second leg of the ZDS Cup northern area final, with the mouth-watering prize of that first ever Wembley appearance if Boro could hold their nerve. The celebrations as Boro finally reached the twin towers – through goals from Slaven and Kerr – went long into the night, though the game spelt disaster for midfielder Trevor Putney, who was stretchered off the pitch suffering from a broken leg after a crunching tackle from Villa's Gordon Cowans.

Putney did not play again for eight months, an unavoidable setback which he says Bruce Rioch struggled to come to terms with.

'Bruce got annoyed when I broke my leg,' insists Putney. 'I don't think he had a lot of time for players with injuries but, after all, I didn't break my leg on purpose. And yet he never once phoned me or came to see me after it happened. It was clear he loved his football but he appeared to be feeling the pressure a bit at the time – results weren't going well and he seemed to be turning people against him.'

Rioch knew that there was still much work to be done in the league. Unfortunately, the knowledge that they were Wembley-bound seemed to distract the players from the important work of collecting league points. Mowbray and Slaven both found the net at Bournemouth in a 2–2 draw but the 3–1 defeat at Oxford which followed was something close to the disastrous early season form. Alas, it was just the first of four straight league defeats which were to cost Rioch his job.

When Rioch was sacked, the bottom of the table looked like this:

	P	W	D	L	F	A	Pts
Boro	33	9	7	17	38	49	34
Bradford	33	6	12	15	34	51	30
Barnsley	31	7	9	15	31	56	30
Stoke	33	5	13	15	26	49	28

Injury meant skipper Tony Mowbray played his last game of the campaign in the Manor Ground defeat, which was followed by 1–0 defeats against Brighton and West Ham. What proved to be Rioch's last game in charge was a 2–1 home loss to Watford as Boro seemed more than ever destined for a relegation battle.

Rioch's replacement, his former assistant Colin Todd, made only one change to the side which had lost to Watford, bringing in Mohan for Kernaghan in a goalless draw at Hull. During the following week, he moved to strengthen the squad by signing two players. Left-back Jimmy Phillips left Oxford United in a deal worth £250,000 while Irish B international Martin Russell made a £175,000 switch from Scarborough.

Although Russell was to play no part in the first team that season, Phillips stepped straight in for his Boro debut in place of the inexperienced McGee. There was to be no dream start, however, with Blackburn gaining revenge for the Ewood embarrassment by running up a 3–0 win at Ayresome Park.

After nine games without a goal, striker Baird finally got off the mark with the opening strike in a 2–1 win at Plymouth – the first victory under Todd and the first league success for six weeks. It left Boro in good spirits for the Zenith Data Systems Cup final against Chelsea, and another league win followed when Slaven struck the only goal of the match against Oldham, watched by an impressive Ayresome crowd of over 17,000.

There was now genuine hope that Boro would move away from the drop zone and a valuable point from a goalless draw at WBA did little to alter that view. However, a kamikaze-style performance at home to Port Vale saw a 2–0 lead transformed into a 3–2 defeat, former player Dean Glover scoring from the penalty spot for Vale.

'It was a battle to survive and sometimes we shot ourselves in the foot,' admits Todd. 'Losing to Port Vale after being 2–0 up really knocked us back but we picked ourselves up.'

Despite that shock, there were definite signs that Todd was now sorting out the defensive problems and Boro secured a goalless draw at Stoke before defeating fellow strugglers Bradford City 2–0 on Teesside.

That win appeared to have alleviated fears of a second relegation but there were more twists to come. A 2–1 defeat at Leicester was followed by a 2–1 home loss to Ipswich. Slaven's thirtieth goal of the season clinched a vital point at Swindon in a 1–1 draw but Boro were left staring relegation in the face four days later when Barnsley won 1–0 at Ayresome Park.

Suddenly, Boro were in a relegation position and no longer in control of their own destiny. Only one game remained – at home to north-east rivals Newcastle United . . .

Going into that final game, the bottom of the table looked like this:

	P	W	D	L	F	A	Pts
Bournemouth	45	12	12	21	57	75	48
Boro	45	12	11	22	48	62	47
Bradford	44	9	13	22	43	66	40
Stoke	45	6	18	21	34	62	36

CHAPTER EIGHT

Stability at Last! – 1990–91

Compared to the trials and tribulations of the previous season, 1990–91 was to be relatively successful. Indeed, for the first half of the season Boro's form was every bit as good as the team promoted under Bruce Rioch three years earlier.

Having avoided relegation by the narrowest of margins, it was no surprise when manager Colin Todd moved to strengthen the squad, though he insists promotion was never the number one objective.

'There was a board meeting during the close season and I was asked by the chairman, Colin Henderson, to consolidate,' recalls Todd. 'That made me think that if I finished half-way up the table they would be satisfied with that, but that's not how it turned out.'

Before the season got underway, two of the players signed by Bruce Rioch for the top flight season two years earlier left the club. Midfielder Mark Brennan joined First Division Manchester City for £500,000, while Peter Davenport was transferred to neighbours Sunderland for £300,000.

To replace them, in came John Hendrie, John Wark and Robbie Mustoe. Although 33-year-old Wark was only to spend one season with the club, Hendrie and Mustoe were to make big impacts and stay on Teesside for some years.

Hendrie, a £500,000 buy who had just helped Leeds United clinch the Second Division championship, linked up with his former Elland Road team-mate Ian Baird. Hendrie recalls: 'A lot of people doubted my wisdom in leaving a go-ahead club for one which could have gone down the previous season, but Colin Todd sold

the club to me. It was clear Howard Wilkinson didn't want me at Leeds anymore, though he never bothered telling me to my face.

'I got home one day to find a note on the kitchen table saying Colin Todd had phoned and wanted to speak to me. When I called him, he said the two clubs had agreed a fee. I couldn't believe it. Leeds hadn't even told me I was available. Even so, I went along to meet him and decided to join Boro after thinking about the move over the weekend.'

Meanwhile, £375,000 midfielder Mustoe was following Jimmy Phillips from Oxford United, though he was not as big a name as Hendrie at the time. Although signed on a free transfer from Ipswich Town, Wark boasted an outstanding goalscoring record as an attacking midfielder, but, in his twilight years, Todd chose to play him in a more defensive role just in front of the back four.

With Jimmy Phillips and Martin Russell having been signed late the previous season, Todd had now stamped his mark on the side with five of his own players in the squad. Looking back, he remarks: 'Russell didn't really hit it off but I must say that Mustoe, Hendrie and Phillips were excellent buys for the club.'

Hendrie, Mustoe and Wark made their Boro debuts in the opening league match against much-fancied West Ham United at Ayresome Park, but a dull goalless draw ensued in front of an excellent crowd of over 20,000. Although instantly forgettable for most, the game is still vividly remembered by Mark Proctor for all the wrong reasons.

He recalls: 'I'd had a good 1989–90 season but had undergone hernia and cartilage

operations during the summer and had had no pre-season to get myself fit. But Toddy told me that he wanted me to play the first game and insisted I shouldn't worry. I wasn't convinced but he talked me into it. It was ridiculous. I actually got through the game but didn't play well and was dropped. After that, I was left out for months and yet it was hardly my fault that I didn't play well.'

Next came the first leg of a League Cup clash with Third Division Tranmere, with Russell making his first start for the club five months after joining Boro from Scarborough.

New signing John Wark's first goal for the club clinched a 1–0 win over Notts County in September 1990.

Rovers centre-back Steve Vickers – later to play for Boro – stunned Stephen Pears with a cracking long-range goal before Mowbray equalised for shocked Boro.

The following Saturday, at Plymouth, Stuart Ripley replaced the injured Baird. The game ended 1–1, Slaven the goalscorer, though the striker missed at least two other chances set up by the impressive Hendrie. However, Slaven made up for his misses with the winner in a 2–1 League Cup success at Tranmere in midweek.

A first league win of the season came against newly promoted Notts County at Ayresome Park. The powerful, surging runs of Ripley tore the heart out of the hapless visitors, though it was Wark who scored his first goal for the club, sliding the ball home after a goal-mouth scramble. Notts County were to get their revenge much later.

The players took great confidence from that performance and, a week later, stunned promotion favourites Swindon Town – who had only been denied promotion a year earlier as a punishment for financial irregularities – with an exciting 3–1 victory. Slaven was back to his typical goalscoring, notching two, while new boy Mustoe grabbed the other.

Two days later, there was disappointment when the defence displayed frailties in a 3–1 defeat at Port Vale, while a 1–0 home loss to a very strong Oldham side followed, despite a recall for Baird. It was no surprise when Todd wielded the axe, dropping Slaven and Russell for Ripley and Paul Kerr for the first leg of the Rumbelows Cup third round tie with north-east neighbours Newcastle United. It was a glorious night for 22-year-old Mustoe, who was unknown to many Boro fans before joining the club. The midfielder netted both excellent goals in a memorable 2–0 success. 'That was one of the highlights of my career,' recalls Mustoe. 'It was fantastic to do so well so early in my Boro career.'

Kerr marked his return the following Saturday against struggling Leicester City. With just three minutes of the first half remaining, Boro led by a single goal – scored by Phillips – but Hendrie slammed in a stunning second, sub Slaven a sensational third and Kerr the fourth before half-time. Kerr notched another, while Baird also found the target in the second half to complete a 6–0 rout.

Hendrie has fond memories of the match and remarks: 'That was one of my best games for the club – I had a blinder – but the whole team played ever so well.'

Kerr adds: 'It was great to get two after

1990–91 Match of the Season – 1

29 September 1990

MIDDLESBROUGH 6 LEICESTER CITY 0

Boro recorded their biggest victory for three years when they completely outclassed a sorry Leicester side at Ayresome Park in 1990.

Colin Todd's side had made an indifferent start to the season, but went into the game on the back of a solid 2–0 League Cup victory over Newcastle.

Not surprisingly, Todd named an unchanged side, preferring to leave fit-again Bernie Slaven on the bench, allowing Ian Baird and Stuart Ripley the opportunity to continue as strike partners.

Baird hammered the ball past Mike Hooper after just three minutes, only to have his effort ruled out for off-side. It was an ominous sign for the east midlands side, because on six minutes Jimmy Phillips headed home a John Hendrie cross from the edge of the six-yard box to fire Boro in front.

After twelve minutes, Todd had to re-shuffle his pack when Ripley pulled a hamstring while in full flight. This resulted in Slaven entering the game earlier than anticipated.

Leicester's Ally Mauchlen gave Boro a scare on the half hour when he crashed a 30-yard drive against Stephen Pears' right-hand post, only to see the ball rebound to safety.

Worse was to follow for David Pleat's side in the thirty-eighth minute when central defender Steve Walsh hauled down the on-rushing Robbie Mustoe. Referee William Burns of Scarborough had no option but to dismiss Walsh and reduce Leicester to ten men.

Boro took advantage of this, first through John Hendrie, who received a long ball, skipped past Paul Ramsey and fired past Hooper, making it 2–0.

Paul Kerr was next on the goals' trail, catching the defence flat-footed and blasting a low, hard drive that beat Hooper. Leicester were shell-shocked at 3–0 down, but Slaven showed no mercy, scoring a sensational goal twenty-two seconds into injury time. The Scot cleverly controlled a high ball before spinning round and, in one movement, volleying the ball home.

So Boro led 4–0 at half-time, which caused Pleat to replace David Oldfield with the experienced Ricky Hill. It didn't stem the tide though, as Colin Cooper played a quickly-taken free-kick to Baird, who grabbed his second of the game when he drilled the ball home from the edge of the area.

In the seventy-third minute Hendrie, in scintillating form, flew down the left wing then unselfishly squared the ball to Kerr, who made it 6–0 with a tap-in from the edge of the six-yard box.

Three minutes later it was almost seven when Hendrie sent in a curling shot which Hooper could only tip on to the bar. As the ball came down, it was bundled over the line, but Mr Burns disallowed the goal for a foul on the goalkeeper.

being out for the first few games. I was in good goalscoring form for a while – in fact, that season was probably the best I played for Middlesbrough.'

In a warm-up for their cup tie at St James' Park, Boro visited Newcastle in the league and returned home with a well-earned goalless draw, and then gave warning of their forthcoming surge of away form with an excellent 3–0 mauling of Watford at Vicarage Road, Mowbray and Baird (2) the goalscorers. More cup progress was made when a stormy match at St James' Park – the third game against Newcastle in two weeks – saw the Geordies win 1–0 but Boro hold on for a 2–1 aggregate success.

Next came the return of Bruce Rioch with his Millwall team and a 2–1 success had Todd's boys on a high. After a rapturous welcome for Rioch from the adoring Teesside public, still thankful for what he had done for the club, Boro got down to business and forced Alex Rae to turn the ball into his own net. It was the second goal, however, which will remain forever in the memories of all who saw it. Picking up the ball just outside his own penalty area, Hendrie raced forward along the right side of the pitch. He admitted later that he was simply aiming to 'make up ground', but found the Millwall defence back-peddling to the point where he felt he had no option but to go for goal. In all, the winger left five players trailing in a 70-yard run before stroking the ball home to complete what was arguably the greatest ever goal by a Boro player.

'Every time I'm out people ask me about that goal,' smiles Hendrie. 'At first I was simply trying to take the pressure off the back four by taking the ball forward, but everything just opened up for me. By the time I was on the edge of the 18-yard box, there was only one place I was going – straight for goal! There's no doubt it was my best ever goal.'

Hendrie says much of the credit for the goal belonged to Colin Todd.

'My strongest asset was my ability to run at defences and Colin encouraged me to go for it. He felt Howard Wilkinson had knocked the confidence out of me at Leeds, which was probably true. Colin gave me that confidence again by telling the other lads: "Give John the ball and let him get on with it."'

The team, unchanged for a fifth successive league match, went in search of another win at Bristol Rovers and promptly fell flat on their faces with a desperately disappointing 2–1 defeat.

Even so, the only change for a visit to Molineux was Russell replacing the injured Wark. The result was a 1–0 defeat by Wolves. Wark returned as Slaven regained his best form, the striker netting a hat-trick in a 4–2 win at Brighton with Baird also on target. Wark was missing again as Boro earned another excellent result when First Division Norwich City visited Ayresome Park in the Rumbelows Cup at the end of October. Kerr fired Boro ahead before Hendrie sealed a 2–0 win with another sensational goal, this time cutting in from the right wing before unleashing an astonishing long-range shot into the top corner of the net.

With Wark again sidelined, Trevor Putney started a game for the first time since suffering a broken leg in the ZDS Cup against Aston Villa nine months earlier. After so long out, Putney was understandably raring to go, but he has fond memories of the way he was looked after during his time on the sidelines.

'Colin Todd was great with me while I was out,' he explains. 'He showed a lot of interest in me and made me feel part of the squad by doing things like inviting me on weekends away with the team.'

Putney made a happy return as Kerr notched the only goal of the game against Barnsley to keep Boro on the promotion trail. A fourth consecutive victory came through a lone Slaven strike at WBA.

Despite the winning run, home form was still sadly lacking and the third Ayresome defeat of the season came against Lennie Lawrence's Charlton Athletic in a game which saw Slaven taken off at half-time. Slaven was furious with the decision and walked out of Ayresome Park's gates while the second half was underway. That brought him into conflict with Colin Todd.

'I couldn't believe I was taken off,' explains Slaven. 'We were 1–0 down at half-time and

Striker Ian Baird was in superb goalscoring form during the first half of the 1990–91 campaign.

needed goals. Surely, therefore, you don't take off your top scorer. I hadn't played well but neither had anyone else. My blood was boiling because I really wondered if there was more to his decision than tactics. I ended up walking out and driving home. The game was still going on while I was taking my dogs for a walk.'

Todd's thoughts on the incident and Slaven, in general, reveal something of why the two did not get on.

'Bernie was a very temperamental boy,' insists Todd. 'You don't mind players going to the press as long as they conduct themselves in the right manner. But as soon as he knew he was left out, Bernie would go straight to the press, which was wrong.'

John Wark feels Todd has a point.

'Everyone knew that Bernie and Toddy didn't get on. But if Bernie didn't agree with things, he tended to lose it a bit. You can't storm off like he did. The players did think it was concerning.'

The players were no doubt thankful that

Boro now had three successive away fixtures. Certainly, the results suggested that was the case. Baird, returning to Portsmouth where he had spent an unhappy year of his career, scored a cracking goal in a 3–0 hammering of Pompey.

Then came a 3–1 win over Hull City in the first round of the Zenith Data Systems Cup at Ayresome, but Boro again struggled to make an impact on home soil, needing extra time to take the tie.

On the Saturday Boro hit five goals away from home for the first time in almost ten years. Oxford United were beaten to the tune of 5–2 at the Manor Ground as Baird netted his first hat-trick for the club – two of them penalties – while Slaven and Mustoe also found the net. Oxford may not have been the most glamorous team but they were nobody's fools either. Make no mistake, this was an outstanding result.

The game stands out in the memory of John Wark, who says: 'Beating Oxford by that scoreline was really special. Teams were scared of us by that point.'

However, that win and other good away performances only served to emphasise the disappointing home form, a frustrating area which always threatened to de-rail the promotion challenge. The explanation, says John Hendrie, was down to the influential but ageing Wark's lack of fitness.

'We were more effective away from home on the counter-attack, with Rippers, Bernie and myself up front. We would let teams come at us and John Wark would sit in front of the back four and soak things up. Then he'd hit great passes forward to set us up. At home, it was up to us to have a go and attack the visiting teams. We couldn't just sit back in the same way but John didn't have the legs to get up and down the pitch, so we tended to struggle.'

Slaven fired in another two in the dying minutes of a Rumbelows Cup fifth round tie at Villa Park, but it was not enough to stop Aston Villa going through with a 3–2 scoreline.

The tie saw Kernaghan substituted and dropped – a decision which did not help the player to see eye-to-eye with the manager.

'The problem with Colin was that he was never really sure what he wanted us to do and would often change his direction,' says Kernaghan. 'Over the years I had taken stick from the crowd, as had many others during the relegation seasons, but Colin substituted me against Aston Villa after I'd received some abuse. I told him that I thought he was letting the fans pick the team by bowing to their pressure. Because of that I was out of the team for six or seven weeks until being loaned out to Charlton.'

With Kernaghan's replacement, Simon Coleman, starting a game for the first time all season, a sixth win in seven league games followed with one of the more convincing home performances, 3–0 against struggling Hull City. Baird's strike was his seventh in six games, while Slaven had now notched nine in his last ten outings. Their prolific partnership, combined with Boro's classic counter-attacking, was becoming the scourge of defences up and down the country.

At this stage, the league table looked like this:

	P	W	D	L	F	A	Pts
West Ham	19	12	7	0	32	12	43
Oldham	19	12	5	2	38	18	41
Boro	19	11	3	5	36	16	36
Sheffield W.	18	10	6	2	37	19	36
Wolves	19	7	8	4	29	20	29

With Owen McGee making his first start of the season, unbeaten fellow leaders West Ham United were held to a goalless draw at Upton Park, but First Division Manchester City proved too strong in the Zenith Cup at Maine Road, where Boro lost 2–1. Then there was more Ayresome frustration when Blackburn stole all three points with a 1–0 scoreline.

Colin Cooper, who had not missed a game at that point, was not happy with his new role at right-back. Cooper's dilemma was whether he owed his loyalty to the club or to his close friends within the squad.

'I had my ups and downs with Colin Todd over whether I should play right-back or left-back,' he reveals. 'I preferred left-back because that was where I'd enjoyed all my success. But Jimmy Phillips was the regular left-back under Colin and I played right-back, which I wasn't happy about because that meant I was keeping one of my mates, Gary Parkinson, out of the team. I found myself apologising to Parky – "Sorry mate, it's not my fault."

'At the time, it did matter to me because so many of the lads from Bruce's team had gone through so much together. To be honest, we found it hard to believe that anyone could come in and do a better job than we could. We didn't like outsiders coming in and taking the places of our mates.'

With the pressure on to ensure they remained in the promotion race, Boro pulled off an outstanding 1–0 win at Ipswich on Boxing day, thanks to Baird's strike, but it was the end of the Christmas cheer. Having won four of their previous five away games in the league, Todd's team surprisingly crumbled to a 3–0 defeat by Bristol City and then looked out classed in a 2–0 home defeat to Sheffield Wednesday on New Year's day. That win saw the Owls increase the gap between Boro and the top three clubs.

Four days later, Boro were held to a goalless draw by Plymouth at Ayresome Park, though there was confidence that excellent away form would see them through at the second time of asking. Before the replay, however, came a home league game against . . . Plymouth! For the second time in a week, Argyle held Boro to a goalless draw. Gary Parkinson played his first game in eight months in place of Cooper at right-back as goals from Baird and Kerr sealed a hard-fought 2–1 win.

There was more controversy when Slaven, who had played on the left wing before being taken off, blasted: 'If the manager is not going to play me down the middle, then he should drop me.'

Todd was furious with his player's comments and blasted him behind closed doors before publicly snapping back: 'Every player must be prepared to play wherever the manager wants them to play. It should be much more important to a professional that he is named in the first team. Other players get on with it and don't complain. I'm very annoyed.'

Now Boro paid a visit to Meadow Lane to take on the fast-improving Notts County. Ripley, a sub in eleven of the previous twelve league games, returned in place of Slaven but Boro slipped to a 3–2 defeat, though Baird had the consolation of netting his fourteenth goal of the season, while Ripley scored the other. With only one win in the last seven league games, Boro's season was disintegrating and all hopes of automatic promotion would be lost if the slide could not be arrested.

Looking back, John Hendrie says he wasn't surprised to see Boro slip up.

'I never felt we were one of the top two or three teams. We always looked a wee bit short, the squad lacked strength in depth. But Bairdy, who I'd played with at Leeds United, was in a different class that season and he was probably at the peak of his form.'

Mark Proctor begs to differ with Hendrie on this point.

'The fans liked Bairdy because he was blood and thunder. The Middlesbrough public have always taken to players with commitment. That's why Dean Glover was such a favourite during his time with the club.'

There was more reason for despondency in the FA Cup when Boro fell to a shock 2–0 defeat at the hands of Third Division Cambridge United at the Abbey Stadium. Dropped from the side for the cup defeat was Paul Kerr, who admits: 'I remember the Notts County match vividly and I was awful. If I'm honest, I've got to say I was predictable in my unpredictability. The fans used to give me stick for that but that was just me. I wanted to do well and used to take a lot of responsibility on the ball but I did have some bad games. But to play badly, you have to see the ball a lot. It was never a case of me hiding away and letting the game pass me by.'

Slaven returned in place of Ripley, and loan signing Colin Walsh, an attacking midfielder, made his first start at home to Swindon Town. Winning ways returned as Mustoe and Slaven netted for a 2–0 win. There was no game for another seventeen days, during which time goalkeeper Stephen Pears was ruled out for the rest of the season through injury. Andy Dibble was brought in on loan from Manchester City and there followed two more victories, the first a 3–2 win over relegation threatened WBA at Ayresome Park, thanks to a late error by Albion keeper Mel Rees. Then Slaven's seventeenth of the season clinched a 1–0 win at Charlton.

Boro had their tails up but the Ayresome curse struck yet again with a 2–1 home defeat to Portsmouth – a reverse which angered the supporters who booed the team off the pitch at half-time. Given the innocuous display they had just witnessed, it seemed fair enough, but Slaven did not agree and hit back at them in the press.

'I couldn't believe they were booing us when there was still half of the game left to play,' he explains. 'We had some of the best fans in the country but they had this tendency to turn on us when things weren't going well. I felt they should get behind us during the match and keep their criticism for the end if we had lost. I know my comments upset some of the punters but I was simply trying to remind them that we all wanted success for Middlesbrough Football Club.'

Two goalless draws, at Hull and at home to Oxford, emphasised the challenge ahead but there was still time to win automatic promotion if the players could return to their early season form. There was every reason to be positive after a memorable 3–0 mauling of north-east rivals Newcastle United at Ayresome Park, Slaven scoring twice and Walsh crashing home an excellent first goal for the club. Eighteen-year-old striker Ian Arnold made his first team debut as a late substitute in that match.

But the ever-worsening relationship between Todd and Mark Proctor had now reached a low point. Proctor reveals: 'I had a big fall-out with Toddy and we didn't actually speak to each other for weeks on end. After forcing me to play in the first game when I wasn't fit, he had left me out for three months, even when I was fit. Too often I was totally overlooked and it got on my nerves. I had expected to play against Oxford but stormed off home when I realised I wasn't in the team.

'But it backfired on him because we only drew 0–0. The day before the Newcastle match, he told me he wanted me to play but I told him where to stick it. I wasn't prepared to dig him out of a hole when I felt he had done nothing for me. He even threatened to tell the *Gazette* about my attitude but I didn't care, I was totally gone. I felt like I'd been used. After that, we didn't speak to each other again until Jim Smith joined and he made us shake hands. Incredibly, I was then made captain of the team!'

While the likes of Proctor and Slaven did not get on way with Todd, John Hendrie was on good terms with him.

'I got on very well with Toddy,' he says. 'A lot of the players had known him as a coach where he had tended to be very much one of the lads, so they didn't seem to have quite the respect for him they should have had. He wasn't one to rant and rave and I always held him in very high respect.'

Two days after the derby win, Mark Burke – Ayresome's forgotten man, having played his last first team game fourteen months earlier – was allowed to join Wolves for a bargain £25,000. Although he never got the opportunity at Middlesbrough to fulfil his massive potential, Burke retains fond memories of the club.

'I loved the fans and the whole place. In fact, I still come back to the area regularly and get copies of the *Evening Gazette* sent to me to stay in touch.'

Four days after the derby win, Boro scored three more goals but still lost as Leicester ran out 4–3 winners at Filbert Street. McGee scored his one and only first team goal for the club but was still criticised by Todd for his naive defending.

Also on target in the defeat at Leicester was Trevor Putney, who believes one of the factors in Boro's struggle was the age-old tendency to under-achieve against the so-called minnows and raise their game against the bigger sides.

'We did really well against the good teams but dropped blobs against the teams we should have beaten,' he recalls. 'To be fair, the side never really clicked. Colin probably got the manager's job too soon. Part of his problem was that he and his assistant, David Nish, were very much alike, maybe a little too soft. Every team needs a taskmaster.'

In comparison, John Wark believes the team was good enough but simply lacked consistency.

'We had a good squad, with players like Cooper, Mowbray, Slaven, Baird and Proctor. Up to Christmas we were there or thereabouts but we died off and just couldn't get going again. Mowbray, in particular, stood out. He was Mr Boro and I wouldn't be surprised to see him go back one day as the manager.'

Mowbray scored, along with Kerr, in a 2–2 draw at Millwall before two more poor home results, a 2–1 defeat by Watford and a 1–1 draw with Ipswich. Wark was dropped from the team to play Watford and he recalls: 'Toddy left me out after saying I wasn't talking to the players enough in the dressing room, geeing them up and so on. But I was never that type. I told him: "Surely that's your job." Colin wasn't strong as a manager and couldn't motivate players in the same way others can.'

While Wark was to start just one more game in a Middlesbrough shirt, Kerr had played his last in the Watford defeat.

'The truth of the matter is that I was up in the air and no longer knew if I was in or out of the team, while I had off-the-pitch troubles too, so I decided to cut my losses and leave,' he explains. 'Bruce Rioch asked me to join Millwall but only made me an offer two hours before the transfer deadline. I was due a loyalty bonus from Middlesbrough but was given a take-it-or-leave-it offer and had to make my mind up there and then. I decided to go for it and was very popular with the Millwall fans. Unfortunately, I hated London.'

With Kerr joining Millwall for £125,000, Walsh returning to Charlton and Wark and Putney dropped, Hendrie and Proctor were recalled to the team which lost 1–0 against Blackburn at Ewood Park. One win in nine league games was the sort of form usually associated with relegation candidates, rather than the promotion hopefuls Boro were supposed to be. It was evident by now that even a play-off place might not be achieved.

But two goals from Ripley clinched a 2–1 home win over Bristol City and that was followed by a crushing 4–0 success over Port Vale at Ayresome Park, with Boro at last playing to their best form. Russell – in for the dropped Slaven – scored only his second Boro goal (the first having also come against Port Vale). Although out of form and at loggerheads with Todd, Slaven was not happy about being left out. Todd recalls: 'I'd named the side on the pitch and Bernie reacted in front of everyone, showing a total lack of respect for myself. I think the players looked at me as if to say they felt he was totally out of order. They didn't like what Bernie had been doing. At the end of the day, every player thinks he should be in the side but, in football, you've got to accept the manager's decisions.'

Bernie agrees he over-reacted. 'Toddy intended playing John Hendrie in my place up front and I couldn't believe he was going to play a winger instead of me. I told him that it was a joke. Looking back, I was hot-headed. I should have held my tongue and had a quiet word with him later. I don't regret what I said but Toddy wasn't a bad guy and didn't deserve that type of hassle from me.'

Alas, the inconsistencies continued with successive 2–0 away defeats, at Sheffield Wednesday and Bristol Rovers, before successive 2–0 home wins, against Wolves and Brighton. Local-born 17-year-old Jamie Pollock made his debut as substitute in the success over Wolves, while Ripley took his tally to five in six games playing as a striker against Brighton.

Those victories had all but sealed a play-off place but Boro still needed to make sure. They should have done so against champions Oldham Athletic at Boundary Park in the penultimate match but failed to take their chances in a game they dominated and the Latics ran out 2–0 winners.

'We battered Oldham and should really have won but it just didn't happen,' admits Mark Proctor.

Boro went into the final league match knowing that Barnsley would need to beat them by four clear goals to deny them a play-off spot. Mel Machin's Barnsley out-fought Boro but the four-goal win was never really on. Boro lost by a single goal. Poor Barnsley still believed they had reached the play-offs, but a late goal by Brighton against Ipswich Town had in fact denied them.

The final league table looked like this:

	P	W	D	L	F	A	Pts
Oldham	46	25	13	8	83	53	88
West Ham	46	24	15	7	60	34	87
Sheffield W.	46	22	16	8	80	51	82
Notts Co.	46	23	11	12	76	55	80
Millwall	46	20	13	13	70	51	73
Brighton	46	21	7	18	63	69	70
Boro	46	20	9	17	66	47	69

Now it was the play-offs, with Boro finishing well short of a top-three place which had once appeared a real possibility. Having finished seventh, Boro faced the division's form team, Notts County, in the play-off semi-final. In the first leg at Ayresome Park, County, always the better side, looked set for a 1–0 win until Phillips slid home a late equaliser for Boro.

There was still belief that County could be overcome in the second leg, but Boro were

Left-back Jimmy Phillips scores a late equaliser against Notts County in the home leg of the 1990 play-off semi-finals. Unfortunately, Boro lost the second leg.

denied the services of the excellent Ripley through injury. Without him, they fell to a 1–0 defeat and it was Notts County who went on to the Wembley final where they clinched promotion with a 4–0 destruction of Brighton.

The loss of Ripley, says Jim Smith, who had joined as first-team coach during the end of season run-in, was the key to the defeat.

'Ripley's injury was a huge blow,' he reflects. 'If we'd had Ripley for that second leg, we'd have won – that's how important he was.'

With or without Ripley, John Hendrie still believes Boro could have won the tie if he had been played down the middle.

'Notts County were the form team at the time but they were only average. I remember looking at their centre-halves and thinking how I would have loved to have been up against them. Instead, Bernie played down the middle but he had had a big fall-out with Toddy and

that day he just wasn't at the races. It wasn't one of Bernie's better games.

'I played out wide and was starved of the ball. It was so frustrating because if Toddy had played me down the middle it might have been a different story. I'd played there against Port Vale and we'd tortured them that night and I'm sure my pace would have given Notts County's centre-backs a lot of trouble.'

Slaven adds further credence to Hendrie's argument when he says: 'My form was poor because my mind simply wasn't right. I was pretty sure Toddy wanted rid of me and would sell me during the summer so it was difficult to perform to the best of my ability.'

While Notts County marched on to the top flight, for Boro all that was left was an unhappy squad of players and a manager determined to begin a wholesale clear-out.

CHAPTER NINE

Lennie's Lions Head for the Top – 1991–92

If the 1990–91 campaign was a huge anti-climax, the 1991–92 season was its exact opposite. Boro fans could hardly have dreamed of a more exciting season as the club strove for honours on three fronts.

New manager Lennie Lawrence had been set a challenge of winning promotion within two years but almost from day one it looked achievable at the first time of asking. It was, however, by no means a straight forward transformation from play-off also-rans to genuine championship challengers. First of all, Lawrence had to sort the wheat from the chaff and those devoted to the Boro cause from those committed to leaving.

On his first day in charge, he saw each player individually to ask them about their futures. Recalls Lawrence: 'I asked them if they wanted to stay or go. Half of them had had enough and wanted to get out, while others who had fallen out with Colin Todd – Slaven, Parkinson and others – agreed to stay.

'Having been close to signing Alan Kernaghan for Charlton, I now had to persuade him to stay with Boro. Fortunately I was successful.'

Of those who left, Simon Coleman joined Derby County for £350,000, Ian Baird went to Hearts for £300,000, Colin Cooper joined Millwall for a similar fee, Kevin Poole moved to Leicester, Trevor Putney joined Watford and John Wark was given a free transfer and eventually rejoined Ipswich Town.

Lawrence admits he made a mistake on two of the players he shipped out.

'I paid up John Wark because I thought he was finished,' he says. 'But he proved me wrong by enjoying several more good years at Ipswich. I hardly knew Cooper and for his first year at Millwall he didn't look too good. Then they switched him to centre-back and I was left to regret letting him go.'

Cooper, however, insists his heart was set on leaving no matter what Lawrence said.

'Lennie made it clear he didn't want me to leave,' he recalls. 'But I felt it was a case of now or never. I'd spoken to Bruce Rioch about a move to Millwall on transfer deadline day in March but had decided not to go. The time was wrong, I just wasn't sure if I wanted to leave Middlesbrough and everything it meant to me. But it made the decision easier when Lennie replaced Toddy. It was just another link with the team of '86 and '87 being broken and I knew the time was now right.'

Putney was also pleased to leave as he had struggled to sell his house in East Anglia.

'I had a year left on my contract but Lennie spoke my language – he was like a breath of fresh air – and he agreed to let me join Watford. But I loved Middlesbrough and couldn't believe the fans, who were so friendly. We used to get 16,000 when we were having a bad time. It was a fabulous place.'

John Hendrie admits he could easily have left the club too.

'There had been a few problems at the end of the previous season when the chairman, Colin Henderson, publicly criticised some of the players for living out of the area. I was living in the Leeds district while Bairdy and Warky were also based outside the Teesside area. Bairdy wasn't happy about it and, if I'd taken it the same way, I would have left too. But I

decided to ignore it because the chairman never bothered to say anything to me personally.

'Then Lennie took over and he didn't know anything about me and vice-versa. He looked at my record and saw that I'd been with four different clubs over the past four seasons and

thought I'd always be on the go. But that couldn't have been further from the truth. I was happy at Middlesbrough and wanted to stay.'

In the meantime, there were only three new faces among the playing staff. Talented full-back Curtis Fleming completed a £50,000

CHANGE AT THE TOP

The summer of 1991 saw the surprise departure of Colin Todd, the manager leaving the club 'by mutual agreement', though it was clear there was some bitterness. His successor was Lennie Lawrence, a relatively unknown quantity in north-east soccer after almost a decade in London with Charlton Athletic.

Todd's departure was a surprise because, in his only full season in charge, he had led the club to the Second Division promotion play-offs just a year after Boro had come frighteningly close to relegation. It seemed to supporters that he had put the club back on track but the board felt otherwise.

Steve Gibson remembers: 'Colin did brilliantly with the money we made available to him. But, at the end of the season, we were disappointed that, having made the play-offs, our performances against Notts County were sub-standard. We hadn't achieved what we felt we were good enough to achieve. We thought we should have beaten Notts County.

'We felt that perhaps there had to be some change in the structure of the club and that the manager needed some help – perhaps more coaching staff to change the club's youth development policy. At that stage, I approached our former manager Willie Maddren but I don't think Colin was happy about it. Willie was offered a top job of youth development director. Colin Todd and Colin Henderson had a very difficult discussion which resulted in the manager resigning.'

One of the first tasks for new manager Lennie Lawrence was to persuade Alan Kernaghan to stay with Middlesbrough. Lawrence had previously been set to sign Kernaghan for Charlton.

Following his departure, an understandably disappointed Todd – who was to be reunited with Bruce Rioch at Bolton – said he would have signed new players for the new season. He had placed twelve players on the transfer list and aimed to replace them with the likes of Hartlepool striker Joe Allon, Coventry winger Dave Smith and midfielders Ray Attevald, of Everton, and Robbie Dennison, of Wolves.

Meanwhile, the club turned its attentions to finding Todd's successor. A short list of potential targets was drawn up. The list included Barnsley boss Mel Machin but Lennie Lawrence was always the prime target.

Colin Henderson flew out to Italy where Machin was enjoying a family holiday but 'went cold' on him and decided to pull out all the stops for Lawrence.

Alan Kernaghan provided the connection which was to lead to Lawrence moving to Teesside. 'I'd had Alan on loan, he went back and then I was quite close to buying him when Colin Todd suddenly resigned,' recalls Lawrence. 'Keith Lamb came on the phone. He seemed interested in me and asked if I was always going to be at Charlton, so I said: "Look, if this is serious, you're going to have to speak to my chairman."'

Gibson vividly recalls his first meeting with Lawrence at Crathorne Hall Hotel. 'Lennie was well up for it. He knew a lot about us and he knew the players he wanted, including Paul Wilkinson and Willie Falconer.'

Like Gibson, Henderson was impressed with Lawrence and a deal was quickly struck, with the club announcing to the world that its new manager was Lennie Lawrence.

Goal! Robbie Mustoe scores the only goal of the game against Millwall on the opening day of the 1991–92 season to get Lennie Lawrence's managerial reign off to the perfect start.

move from Irish side St Patrick's Athletic, while striker Paul Wilkinson and midfielder Willie Falconer came from Watford in a deal eventually valued at £800,000 with Trevor Putney going in the opposite direction.

While Lawrence knew he had a good set of players to work with, he felt there was plenty of room for improvement.

'I'd seen Middlesbrough in the play-offs the previous season,' he explains. 'They passed the ball for the sake of passing it. They needed a more definite pattern of play.'

New boys Wilkinson and Falconer made their Boro debuts in a 1–0 opening day win over Millwall – Colin Cooper's new club – at Ayresome Park. Slaven, the club's top scorer for the previous five seasons, was left on the subs bench as Boro lost their next two fixtures, at Derby and Ipswich, but things clicked into place for the Tees-Tyne derby against Newcastle United. Although the game attracted less than 17,000 supporters, goals from Wilkinson, Proctor and Falconer completed a

rousing 3–0 win and began a run of six successive league victories.

Super-sub Slaven set up Falconer's opener and then netted a late second himself in a 2–0 home win over Portsmouth before scoring two more in the final four minutes of a 2–1 win against Oxford United at the Manor Ground. With in-form Ripley injured, Slaven made his first start in a 2–1 victory at Watford. Wilkinson and Falconer, described by Lawrence as 'absolute bargains', were both on target against their former club. On paper, the home clash against fellow promotion-chasers Leicester City looked the toughest game so far, but substitute Ripley's pin-point crossing resulted in two second half goals for Wilkinson and another for Slaven.

'Ripley has all the makings of a great player,' crowed Wilko.

Falconer took his popularity among the fans to cult status by scoring his fourth goal in six games, the only goal of the match at home to Tranmere, as Boro moved five points clear at

The team photograph that nearly didn't happen – Middlesbrough Football Club 1986-87, about to embark on a most dramatic decade.

Young guns having some fun! Gary Parkinson and Colin Cooper celebrate winning promotion from Division Three in 1987 following Boro's goalless draw with Wigan.

It's more than a feeling! Bruce Rioch's Babes show their delight after their aggregate victory over Chelsea in the Second Division promotion play-offs in 1988.

Middlesbrough FC were the number one club in the North-East for two seasons following the arrival of Lennie Lawrence in August 1991.

A victorious Boro are cheered on by thousands of fans as they receive a civic reception following their promotion from Division Two in 1992.

The man behind the revolution – Steve Gibson.

It's all change at Ayresome Park with Bryan Robson and his assistant Viv Anderson at the helm in 1994.

It's party time! Robbo's Boro celebrate promotion to the Premier League at the first attempt as Endsleigh League First Division Champions after the final game of the 1994–95 campaign at Tranmere.

The end of an era – supporters leave Ayresome Park for the final time after 92 years at the old ground.

£5.25 million signing Nick Barmby celebrates firing Boro into the lead against champions Blackburn as they head for the higher echelons of the Premier League in 1995.

From Doom – Ayresome Park as it was during its final year . . .

. . . and during its demolition a few months later.

To Boom – the Cellnet Riverside Stadium under construction in early 1995 . . .

. . . and in its completed splendour in August 1995.

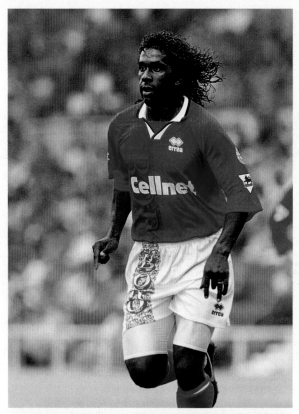

Boro continued to dance the Samba with the arrival of their third Brazilian, Emerson, a £4 million buy from Portuguese champions FC Porto during the close season of 1996.

Bryan Robson sent shudders around the football globe when he splashed out £7 million on Italian ace striker Fabrizio Ravanelli from Juventus in 1996.

the top of the Second Division table.

Meanwhile, injury-blighted midfielder Gary Hamilton started a loan spell with Darlington and played his first league football for almost two-and-a-half years. During that time he had undergone three knee operations.

After stuttering for the first time in seven games in a 1–1 draw at Plymouth Argyle, the twin strike force of Slaven and Wilkinson grabbed the goals that clinched a seventh win in eight league games in a 2–1 success over Sunderland. Slaven's simple strike came just eighteen seconds into the match after an awful mix-up between Sunderland defender Kevin Ball and goalkeeper Tony Norman. Unfortunately, Hendrie and Sunderland's Paul Hardyman were both sent off after the Boro winger reacted to a wild elbow from the Roker defender.

Although not entirely convincing, Boro's form had been good enough to leave their opponents trailing in their wake, but the bubble burst in October. A 1–0 half-time lead at Bristol Rovers became a 2–1 defeat by the final whistle, made worse by the dismissal of Ripley for aiming a head-butt towards Rovers defender David Mehew. That began a run of just one win in seven league matches. Missing from this run, significantly, was the influential Falconer who had gone on the long-term injury list with serious knee trouble.

A wafer-thin squad was already being stretched to the limit, however, and Lawrence tried to plug the gaps with the loan signings of Rab Shannon (from Dundee), John Hewitt (from Celtic) and Brian Marwood (from Sheffield United), while he also gave first team chances to young pro's Jamie Pollock, Ian Arnold and Michael Young. Midfielder Pollock, a 17-year-old local lad with the heart of a lion, was rarely out of the first team picture again but the others struggled to make an impact.

Although there were some less-than-inspiring results, Lennie Lawrence was determined not to panic and John Hendrie remarks: 'One thing about Lennie was that he didn't make mountains out of molehills when we had blips in our form. He would simply tell

Teenager Jamie Pollock, pictured with a Young Eagle of the Month award, made a big impact when he came into the side during the 1991–92 season.

us that we would get it right on Saturday.'

A 1–0 Ayresome Park win over Port Vale – Kernaghan the scorer – was sandwiched between a goalless home draw with Wolves, a 1–0 defeat at Grimsby, a 1–1 draw at home to Southend and a 2–1 defeat at Barnsley. Ripley was the face-saver against Southend, scoring a sensational second half equaliser from 25 yards.

Despite a man-of-the-match performance by Stephen Pears at Blundell Park, he was finally beaten with just eight minutes remaining as Boro turned in an abysmal display against a very average Grimsby side. 'We just can't defend from set pieces,' groaned Lawrence, after Neil Woods' winner came from a corner. 'I've never seen anything like it.'

Meanwhile, the Barnsley defeat on Bonfire Night marked the end of an era as club captain Tony Mowbray played his last Middlesbrough game after dedicating a decade of his life to the Boro cause. Mowbray, the club's captain fantastic and veteran of over 400 games, joined Scottish giants Celtic in a £1 million deal.

The inspirational 27-year-old made the decision to leave his beloved Boro after much soul-searching, but explained he was desperate for a new challenge.

'Motivation had become so difficult for me at Middlesbrough,' he says. 'It was the everyday

routine of the same place, same faces. It wasn't good for me, the club or the supporters because I wasn't enjoying it anymore.

'I'll always feel a special affinity with my home-town club and would have loved to have spent my entire career with Middlesbrough, but it wasn't to be.'

Lennie Lawrence, the man who let Mogga leave, revealed: 'Tony told me he was thinking about leaving at the start of the season but decided to see how it went. He needed to move but he hadn't come crashing at my door or gone to the newspapers. He was very sensible about it.

'Originally Celtic offered £800,000 and I jacked them up to £1 million. Despite his obvious abilities, that was good money for him.'

In a twist to the tale, fellow centre-back Nicky Mohan became Mogga's replacement after turning down a proposed £175,000 move to Plymouth Argyle on the same day.

After rejecting the switch, Mohan insisted: 'I'm a Middlesbrough lad and all I've ever wanted to do was play for my home-town club.'

Lawrence kept faith with Mohan, despite having been linked with Millwall's Alan McLeary and Ipswich Town's Hartlepool-born David Linighan.

Lawrence decided two players should now share the responsibilities of skipper. Kernaghan was made team captain and Proctor club captain. The choice of Kernaghan, once the victim of the boo-boys, was no surprise.

'Lennie gave me a great deal of confidence,' he recalls. 'He showed faith in me in a similar way to Bruce Rioch with Tony Mowbray. It made me feel good and I felt much more relaxed when playing. It resulted in my best spell for the club. When Lennie offered me the captaincy, I didn't really fancy it at first but decided to give it a go. I didn't have to change much because I was already a moaner and a groaner on the pitch.'

Lawrence clearly held Kernaghan in high esteem, and the player was a big fan of the manager too.

'I always found Lennie to be the total opposite of Bruce Rioch,' he says. 'He was so laid back and there weren't many tantrums, unlike Bruce.'

Nicky Mohan played at the heart of Boro's defence for a visit to Brighton, but Lawrence swung the axe in response to several below-par performances. Slaven, Proctor and Parkinson were all dropped as the manager insisted: 'I have been fair and I have been patient. I don't like sweeping changes but there's an attitude problem.' Even so, it was sub Slaven who stroked home a second half penalty to grab a 1–1 draw.

Just days later, the man who many believed would be Slaven's replacement signed for the club. Hull City's prolific striker Andy Payton joined Boro in a club record £750,000 deal, half Hull's original valuation.

Payton signed too late to play in the home game against Charlton Athletic and Slaven responded to the rumours of his impending departure by netting for the third successive game. Lawrence's former club, Charlton, were just off the promotion pace but fell to a 2–0 defeat, thanks to goals from Slaven and the recalled Mohan.

Even so, there was much speculation that Slaven would make way for Payton for the following match, against Bristol City at Ayresome Park. Typically forthright, Slaven blasted: 'I won't play second fiddle to anyone. I'm happy to stay if I'm wanted, and I'm happy to go if I'm not.'

Lawrence dismissed as 'cobblers' suggestions that Slaven had played his last game for the club and put him in the starting line-up against City, alongside Payton! The new signing, due to be substitute, was called upon to replace the injured Hendrie. In a dramatic debut, he scored after only four minutes and was stretchered off with an ankle ligament injury at half-time. Watched by a disappointing crowd of less than 13,000, Payton latched on to Curtis Fleming's excellent pass before rounding goalkeeper Andy Leaning for a dream start. But with Boro leading 2–1 at half-time, the new striker failed to appear for the second half and under pressure Slaven took full advantage. Having earlier scored Boro's second, the 31-year-old scored again early in

What a start for £750,000 record signing Andy Payton as he slides home a goal just four minutes into his Boro debut against Bristol City.

the second half after Wilkinson's header had rebounded off the post.

Clearly Slaven was determined to make it as difficult as possible for Lawrence to drop him, but he wondered if he would get a fair chance.

'I was quite happy to fight for my place,' he says. 'But Lennie had already dropped me and suggested I wasn't a team player. Now he'd signed another striker at a time when I didn't think I had his full support.'

But Lawrence insists he did not see it that way.

'People saw Andy as a replacement for Bernie. That wasn't the case but it didn't make him the most popular man in the dressing room. It was his first big move and it made things difficult for him. He was given a hard time. He didn't attempt to mix with the players but I knew when I bought him that he wasn't a social mixer. I bought him to score goals but it never worked out that way.'

Before another ball was kicked, Boro again moved into the transfer market to sign Andy Peake for £150,000. Peake, 30, had impressed Lawrence when he had played under him at Charlton.

'I bought Peake because we didn't have an anchor player like him,' explains Lawrence. 'Proctor had injury problems. We'd also lost Falconer through injury which was a shame because he didn't half look a player when he first came.'

Proctor admits his relationship with the manager was not a happy one.

'I was never a great lover of Lennie,' Proctor says. 'He had done a reasonable job at Charlton on a limited budget but he obviously thought I was past my sell-by date. One of his favourite sayings was, "the axe will fall," and it invariably fell on either myself, Bernie Slaven or Gary Parkinson. He tried to keep me quiet by giving me the club captaincy when Tony Mowbray left. I shouldn't have accepted it because from then on it was difficult to vent my

frustrations in the same way.'

With Payton injured but Peake making his debut, Boro slipped to a 2–1 top-of-the-table defeat at Blackburn before Swindon grabbed a 2–2 draw on 7 December, despite goals from Wilkinson and Slaven. Although it was Wilko's first league goal in more than two months, it took his overall tally to thirteen. Strike partner Slaven had now netted in six successive league games.

Having defeated Bournemouth and Barnsley in the earlier rounds, Boro played host to First Division Manchester City in the Rumbelows Cup. They out-fought their glamorous rivals in a game played in such thick fog it was impossible to see from one end of the pitch to the other. Mustoe and Wilkinson scored the goals that clinched a quarter-final tie with Second Division Peterborough.

After a three-week lay-off, competitive football returned with the Tyne-Tees derby on Boxing day. It was battling Boro who grabbed a famous victory as Wilkinson ran half the length of the pitch before scoring the only goal of the match. The 1–0 success, which took Boro to joint second in the table, was also Boro's first clean sheet away from home in nine months!

But there was a shock in store for buoyant Boro as they crashed to their heaviest defeat for two-and-a-half years, 4–0 at rampant Portsmouth. A stunned Lawrence conceded: 'Portsmouth astonished me. I was staggered by their passing and movement. I would have given you 1,000–1 against that result happening. Normally, only Manchester United or Liverpool could have walloped us like that.' But the defeat was particularly badly timed for goalkeeper Pears who had been nominated for an England B call-up by Lawrence. Watched by England's assistant manager, Lawrie McMenemy, Pears was not at his brilliant best and admitted afterwards: 'Any international chance I had has gone out of the window. I'd hoped there might be a chance of England recognition but I won't be losing any sleep over it.'

Winger Ripley returned for the New Year's day home clash against Derby County, the team Boro had already beaten 4–2 in the Zenith Cup.

Ripley had lost 10lb during a bout of the flu over Christmas. Fleming and Payton were both dropped as Proctor won a recall, but a scrappy 1–1 draw failed to excite a crowd of just over 16,000.

While Boro had now won only four out of their last fourteen league fixtures, they continued to turn it on in the cup tournaments. On 4 January they came face-to-face with Manchester City for the second time in a month, and again shocked their more illustrious rivals by the same scoreline, 2–1. Wilkinson was again one of their tormentors, despite missing one chance he described as the worst miss of his career. This time he was joined on the scoresheet by team captain Kernaghan.

It was a time for celebration for Boro but, behind the scenes, the game had marked the end of the road for loyal club servant Gary Hamilton. The 25-year-old had returned from a three-month loan spell with Darlington, disappointed that the Quakers had failed to offer him a permanent move. Hamilton reveals: 'Lennie named me as fifteenth man for the Manchester City game, but the knee went again in the reserve match at Notts County a few days earlier. I'd spent twenty-seven months trying to regain my fitness but that's when I realised it was never going to be right and I had to retire from the professional game.'

Having played more than 250 games for the club by the time he was 23, Hamilton could well have gone on to become one of Middlesbrough's all-time greats. The sad end to his career touched the hearts of everyone at the club, but Stuart Ripley had particular reason for feeling real sorrow. For almost two seasons Ripley had carried a niggling injury which affected his back. It was having an adverse affect on his form and fitness so when Lawrence took over as manager the player expressed his concerns.

'I wasn't happy with the treatment I'd been getting and was worried how long I could go on like that,' explains Ripley. 'The first thing Lennie did was get me sorted out with a good specialist and it took only a few weeks to get it right. Having had this niggling injury for so long, it was a huge weight off my shoulders.

1991–92 Match of the Season – 1

4 March 1992

MIDDLESBROUGH 0 MANCHESTER UNITED 0

11 March 1992

MANCHESTER UNITED 2 MIDDLESBROUGH 1 (aet)

It was, says Lennie Lawrence, 'a phenomenal performance'. In fact, it was two phenomenal performances. In the space of seven days, rank outsiders Boro twice went agonisingly close to causing a huge upset in the semi-final of the Rumbelows Cup.

Hailed by Lawrence as the best team in England, United's all-star line-up included internationals like Ryan Giggs, Andrei Kanchelskis, former Boro star Gary Pallister, and Bryan Robson – 'one of the great inspirational players of the modern game,' said Lawrence.

Second Division Boro were determined to give it all they had in their attempt to take the club into a major cup final for the first time in their history, and they lifted their game way beyond even their promotion-chasing form.

Ayresome Park's biggest crowd for four years – 25,572 – saw Boro throw everything at United, only to be denied by the impressive Peter Schmeichel who made several saves after the excellent Paul Wilkinson had calved out the openings, while Gary Parkinson came desperately close with a superb long-range effort.

United had their chances too but the first leg ended goalless.

It had been thirteen years since a club from outside the top flight had won at Old Trafford. That was the measure of Boro's task for the second leg and yet the players still believed they could pull off a win.

Watched by over 45,000 spectators, United went in front on the half hour when Robson, McClair and Webb moved the ball across for Lee Sharpe to crash a lovely drive into the far corner.

Bernie Slaven holds off a challenge from Manchester United's Bryan Robson during the first leg of the Rumbelows Cup semi-final at Ayresome Park.

Boro held out against great pressure for the remainder of the first half but blew the game wide open on fifty minutes when Slaven lost his marker, Pallister, and fired home an equaliser from Ripley's accurate cross.

That goal seemed to lift the Teessiders and could so easily have proved the launchpad for victory. Pallister hacked the ball off the line ten minutes from time after Hendrie's goal-bound chip looped over Schmeichel.

Then, twelve minutes into extra-time, substitute Falconer appeared to have clinched the tie in his first match for over five months. He met Hendrie's right-wing cross with precision and power and the ball looked destined for the top right-hand corner. But Schmeichel threw himself across the goal to make a stunning save that broke the hearts of Boro's fans.

Instead of Boro, it was United who clinched a place in the final. In the opening minute of the second half, Robson's header set up Giggs for a clinical volley into the net and United were Wembley-bound.

Looking back on the match, Lawrence insists: 'If Falconer's header had gone in, we were going to Wembley because, while United were good at the time, they weren't the team they have become in the mid-'90s. The Boro supporters were absolutely stupendous that night.'

(continued)

(continued)

John Hendrie agrees it was 'a fantastic game' but adds: 'We had our chances and I thought my shot was on its way in until Pallister knocked it off the line. It was a hell of a disappointment to lose after we'd come so close.'

However, Jimmy Phillips feels it was the game at Ayresome which was crucial. 'I truly believe that if we'd grabbed a goal in the first leg to take to Old Trafford we'd have gone through, but Schmeichel's magnificent save in the second leg was obviously the key,' he remarks.

Despite the cup exit, Boro's players drew strength from the fact they had come so close and directed that new found self-belief into the promotion campaign.

But it really got to me when Hammy was forced to quit the game. He was a great player, one of the best I played with, and it was terrible to see him finished so young.'

Mark Burke agrees with those sentiments.

'Hammy was very under-rated,' he says. 'He was technically gifted as well as being a battler. It was a terrible shame that he had to retire so early, but he had been allowed to play on with what was a terrible knee injury.'

Next came the Rumbelows Cup quarter-final at Peterborough, giant-killers over Liverpool in the previous round. Posh should have been dead and buried but the woodwork denied Boro on three occasions and a replay was set for the start of February.

There was a return to winning ways in a crunch table-topper against Ipswich Town at Ayresome Park on 11 January. Payton's luck finally took an upturn when he came off the bench to net the only goal of the match. The record buy acknowledged his feelings of frustration at being pushed into the regular role of substitute.

'I can only play down the middle,' he said. 'It's no use putting me on the wing. So it looks as though it's a straight choice between me and Bernie Slaven. That's nothing personal, but we're clearly in the same boat.'

The same old inconsistencies continued with a 2–0 defeat at Millwall. Lawrence responded by blasting: 'Our aversion to travel has become a psychological problem. Pollock and Mustoe were unrecognisable from the pair who played so well against Ipswich.'

Boro's players rose to the challenge once again, however, when they took on Sheffield Wednesday at Hillsborough in the fourth round

of the FA Cup. After falling behind to a superb David Hirst strike early on, Boro hit back to grab a shock win through great goals from Hendrie and Wilkinson.

'We deserved that win,' insists Hendrie. 'A lot of our supporters went down to see the game and there was a fantastic atmosphere. I played on the wing that night and came in off the the line to score the goal.'

That success was followed by an excellent 2–1 win at Port Vale. Two quality goals, the first from the outstanding Hendrie and the second from Mustoe, ensured all three points went to the Teessiders.

Four days later came the quarter-final replay against Peterborough, but the minnows were no push-over. Dogged Posh frustrated Boro for most of the match and it became clear the breakthrough would only come through a flash of inspiration. It came from crowd favourite Ripley who, in the eightieth minute, went on a twisting run before launching an unstoppable 20-yard drive into the far corner of the net. Raved Lawrence: 'Stuart doesn't score many but when he does they tend to be special.'

There was more cup joy for Boro three days later as they fought out a 1–1 FA Cup fifth round draw at Portsmouth, thanks to a last-gasp equaliser from Kernaghan, one of the outstanding performers all season long. Lennie's battlers were now the only club in the league still in with a chance of honours in the league, FA Cup and Rumbelows Cup. Unfortunately, they came back to earth with a bump in the replay as they conceded four goals to Portsmouth for the second time in two months. Lawrence was forced to admit that his team had been 'humiliated' despite twice

1991–92 Match of the Season – 2

2 May 1992

WOLVERHAMPTON WANDERERS 1 MIDDLESBROUGH 2

One of the most dramatic games in Boro's history on 2 May 1992 culminated in promotion to the inaugural Premier League.

For the eighth successive season, the club had entered the final week of the season still not knowing what division they would be playing in the following year. Four wins from the previous five games had pushed Boro into second place behind champions Ipswich Town, but with one match remaining three teams – Derby, Leicester and Boro – were all still in with a chance of snatching the second promotion slot.

Boro's destiny would be decided at Molineux, home of Wolverhampton Wanderers. Mid-table Wolves had nothing but pride to play for but they were hell-bent on ruining any promotion party. Lennie Lawrence's side knew exactly what they had to do – win and they were up. Any other result and their future would be in the hands of the gods.

In a surreal build-up to the game, there was a fire in one of the stands, while gun cartridges were found on the pitch. The game was, nevertheless, given the go-ahead. Goalkeeper Ian Ironside made his Boro debut in place of the injured Stephen Pears. Andy Payton was also ruled out through injury, though the experienced Bernie Slaven was an able replacement in attack.

Boro battled throughout the first half without making the vital breakthrough, while news filtered through that Derby were beating Swindon Town 2–0. If the scores remained the same, Derby would pip Boro to promotion. Inspiration was needed to turn things around.

Instead things got worse. First, Wolves went ahead midway through the second half. Then, Nicky Mohan was dismissed for attempting to break up a fracas. It seemed luck was not on Boro's side.

We're going up: Andy Payton and Andy Peake are ecstatic after the 2–1 win at Molineux had clinched promotion to the inaugural Premier League.

But the game took another twist when Jon Gittens scrambled home an equaliser and Boro – urged on by many travelling fans in the ground and many more perched on a nearby fly-over – surged forward in search of the winner.

The dramatic goal came when Wilkinson met Jamie Pollock's cross with a header he described as 'the worst of my career'. The ball crept in at the far post and Boro were 2–1 ahead.

Boro held on for scenes of joyous celebration, with Lawrence carried around the pitch shoulder-high by jubilant fans and players. Boro were up!

Recalling that momentous day, Lawrence says: 'The final twenty-five minutes were quite unreal. It was as if there was a collective will power from all the players to give it one more shot. Wilko scored with the worst header of all-time but the day ranks as one of the best of my life. The scenes afterwards were fantastic.'

And he makes the startling admission: 'Wilko's goal was crucial because if we had gone into the play-offs we wouldn't have won. We'd played over sixty games and were at the end of our tether.'

It's not surprising that debutant Ironside cites the match as 'the most memorable of my career'. He was told five days before the game that he would be playing and recalls: 'Because I had so long to prepare, I wasn't too nervous on the day. But the press had hounded me during the week and I'd begun to feel the pressure until Lennie put a protective shield around me.

'The story about the fire and the gun cartridges was all a bit off-putting. In fact, the lads joked that I'd set it all up to get the game called off!

'But even when we were 1–0 down I never thought we'd lose. And my abiding memory of the celebrations afterwards is of being covered in champagne and lucozade.'

Looking back on the campaign, Stuart Ripley says: 'I really enjoyed that season and I rated Lennie very highly. John Hendrie and I kept swapping wings and it worked a treat, while I always knew where Wilko would be. I didn't even need to look up, I'd just hit my crosses to the back post and nine times out of ten he'd win the ball.'

Delight on the face of Paul Wilkinson after scoring in a 1–1 FA Cup draw at Portsmouth in February 1992.

having led in the first half through Wilkinson.

The FA Cup defeat came just four days after a goalless home draw with Second Division leaders Blackburn Rovers. Lawrence played a psychological game by insisting after the match that he had abandoned hopes of catching Kenny Dalglish's side.

By now, Southampton central defender Jon Gittens had joined the club on loan to cover for injuries to Kernaghan and Mohan. Although Lawrence admitted the 28-year-old wasn't the most gifted player on the ball, he said he had pace and was a strong, natural defender. Gittens had almost joined Newcastle for £325,000 but the deal had fallen through and the player made his Boro debut against Blackburn.

A headed winner from Kernaghan clinched a vital three points at Swindon and ended February on a high note. The thoughts of most Boro fans had already turned to the mouth-watering clash against mighty Manchester United in the first leg of the Rumbelows Cup semi-final on 4 March. The hard-fought goalless draw was followed by another draw during which the players displayed their ability

to adapt to two completely different games. Cambridge United may have been alongside Boro in the chase for promotion but their uncompromising long-ball style and unglamorous image must have made it difficult for Boro to motivate themselves. However, honours were even as Wilkinson's eighteenth goal of the season clinched a deserved point.

The heartbreaking 2–1 semi-final second-leg defeat by Manchester United at Old Trafford must have left Boro deflated but they showed great character in lifting themselves for a 1–0 win at Southend United. Slaven's penalty was the only goal of the game. Lawrence remembers it as 'a dreadful game', during which Phillips received his marching orders. With Boro now out of the cup competitions, they were left with a huge fixture backlog and it was clear it would take a special effort to close the gap on the teams above them.

But there was a tremendous spirit within the squad and they continued to surpass themselves. A goalless draw at Cambridge, with Scotland boss Andy Roxburgh watching fit-again Willie Falconer in action, was followed

by an impressive 4–0 mauling of Brighton. Slaven scored a hat-trick against the Seagulls for the second successive season and Hendrie scored with a breathtaking 20-yard chip. However, the Cambridge match spelt heartbreak for Pears who suffered a fractured cheekbone in an incident with striker Dion Dublin. Pears, outstanding all season, had deservedly been named in the England B squad for the forthcoming match against Czechoslovakia but was forced to pull out of the game.

Lingering hopes of automatic promotion took another blow when a 2–1 defeat at Leicester City was followed by a desperately disappointing 2–1 loss at home to Watford. Boro now faced a daunting task if they were to push for a top-two spot and it seemed the fans had given up hope too. Less than 14,000 turned up to see Boro fall to Watford at Ayresome Park.

The anti-climax continued with a 1–1 draw against Bristol City at Ashton Gate. Following the defeats by Leicester and Watford, changes were made and both Ripley and Slaven were dropped, with the latter not even on the bench. The decision pushed the manager's already rocky relationship with Slaven to breaking point.

Recalls Slaven: 'In seven years at the club, I'd never once been left out of the first fourteen except when I'd been injured. I was deeply hurt, but Lennie didn't even try to explain to me why he was leaving me out. Eventually the two of us had a blazing row over it on the pitch before the match. Being left out was one thing, but what made me angry was the fact he made no effort to cushion the blow. My blood was boiling. I told him I'd done it on Teesside while he'd proved nothing yet. We didn't get on well anyway and I felt he was letting personal grudges get in the way of his team selection.'

Not surprisingly perhaps, Slaven began only two of the final nine league games but a superb last minute free-kick by Phillips snatched all three points the following Friday night against Tranmere at Prenton Park. Loan star Gittens, a sub that night, believes it was a crucial win.

'It was a great team performance. We were really buzzing and everyone was brilliant' he says. It was also the start of seven successive games for Gittens, who stepped in for the injured Kernaghan, ruled out for the rest of the season after undergoing a knee operation. However, the huge backlog of fixtures was beginning to catch up with the players. When Boro faced Barnsley at Ayresome in mid-April it was their sixth game in just two weeks, and the resulting 1–0 defeat appeared to have finally ended hopes of automatic promotion.

'If we don't improve on that performance around the penalty area, we will not finish in the top six, never mind the top two,' said Lawrence, who called for more ruthlessness from his players.

At this point, the league table looked like this:

	P	W	D	L	F	A	Pts
Ipswich	42	23	10	9	65	46	79
Cambridge	42	18	15	9	56	39	69
Leicester	41	20	8	13	57	50	68
Blackburn	42	19	9	13	61	46	66
Derby	42	19	9	14	59	47	66
Charlton	41	19	9	13	50	44	66
Boro	40	18	11	11	48	36	65

The Ayresome attendance against Oxford United two days later dropped below the 12,000 mark. With six games remaining, Boro needed a miracle to make the top two, but Lawrence insisted it was still possible if his shattered players could lift themselves to win five of their final six fixtures.

A late strike by Payton – only his third in five months with the club – clinched a 2–1 victory over Oxford. Ripley netted for the second successive game against Plymouth before Falconer secured a 2–1 win. It would have been more decisive but Plymouth player-manager Peter Shilton saved Payton's spot-kick to top a stunning performance. Suddenly, however, the impossible dream seemed to be possible again.

Then came another blow. Peter Davenport, who had suffered such a disappointing spell with the club, cast off his 'Boro reject' tag in style with a stunning goal as Sunderland

inflicted a devastating defeat at Roker Park. It was a cruel defeat but, says Jon Gittens, Lawrence was furious.

'Lennie could be over-emotional after a game and he would often criticise the players to the press when it would have been better to wait until the Monday when he had calmed down.

'I'll never forget the Sunderland defeat when Davenport scored a spectacular goal from 25 yards. There was nothing Nicky Mohan nor I could have done about the goal and yet Lennie suggested he could have driven a bus through the defence. It didn't do a great deal for our confidence.'

The night after the Roker defeat, Leicester City beat fellow promotion candidates Cambridge 2–1 at Filbert Street and it looked odds-on that Brian Little's men would now clinch the second automatic promotion slot behind Ipswich, leaving Boro in the play-offs.

The latest league table looked like this:

	P	W	D	L	F	A	Pts
Ipswich	44	23	11	10	66	48	80
Leicester	44	23	8	13	61	51	77
Derby	44	21	9	14	64	49	72
Boro	43	20	11	12	52	39	71
Cambridge	44	18	16	10	59	43	70
Charlton	43	19	11	13	52	46	68

Now Boro faced three games in a week and everyone knew it was imperative to win the successive home games against Bristol Rovers and Grimsby Town. That would still leave the door open if they could pull off a good result against Wolves at Molineux on the final Saturday of the season.

Another lowly crowd, just 14,000, for the Rovers match suggested the supporters still thought the odds were stacked against catching Leicester. But the Ayresome Park stars, and top scorer Wilkinson, in particular, performed heroics against all the odds. Wilko netted both goals – though Rovers insisted he used his hands, not his head, for the second – in a nerve-racking 2–1 win to get off to the perfect start in this vital week.

Then came his old club Grimsby and Wilkinson obliged yet again, this time with the second, killer goal after Phillips had coolly slotted home the opener from the penalty spot. That success clinched a place in the play-offs at the very least, with the league table like this:

	P	W	D	L	F	A	Pts
Ipswich	45	23	12	10	67	49	81
Boro	45	22	11	12	56	40	77
Leicester	45	23	8	14	61	53	77
Derby	45	22	9	14	66	50	75
Cambridge	45	19	16	10	63	45	73
Charlton	45	20	11	14	54	47	71

Now the pressure was really on. The final day clash with mid-table Wolves would decide the club's future.

The 2–1 win at Molineux clinched promotion and resulted in fantastic scenes of jubilation, culminating in an open-topped bus journey through the town watched by thousands of supporters.

'This is just the start,' said a delighted Lawrence.

The final league table looked like this:

	P	W	D	L	F	A	Pts
Ipswich	46	24	12	10	70	50	84
Boro	46	23	11	12	58	41	80
Derby	46	23	9	14	69	51	78
Leicester	46	23	8	15	62	55	77
Cambridge	46	19	17	10	65	47	74
Blackburn	46	21	11	14	70	53	74

CHAPTER TEN

Up With the Big Boys . . . For Now! – 1992–93

Middlesbrough began the first ever Premier League season like a house on fire, but the flames had been well and truly extinguished long before the campaign had ended.

Manager Lennie Lawrence began the campaign refusing to talk of simply surviving in the top flight. He believed real success was there for the taking and several of the players suggested qualification for a UEFA Cup place was a possibility. There was a general feeling that this squad was far better equipped to compete at this level than the young, inexperienced set of players who had struggled so badly four years earlier under Bruce Rioch. But, as the season progressed, such positive talk was to prove misguided.

Lawrence was determined to keep faith with the players who had won promotion, though two senior members of the squad had moved on by the time Boro kicked off the new campaign against Coventry City at Highfield Road on 15 August.

After seven years with the club, Stuart Ripley joined Blackburn Rovers for £1.3 million in July. The manager was disappointed to lose him but felt there was little point in making him stay.

'About six weeks before the end of the promotion season, Stuart told me, "Look, I don't want to make a song and dance about it, but whether or not we go up, I feel it's time for me to leave." He felt it made sense to leave while he was still enjoying himself. I told him if he still felt the same way at the end of the season, then I would see what I could do.'

When the summer came, Ripley restated his need for a new challenge and the deal with Blackburn was struck. He recalls: 'I just felt it was time to move on after so long with the club. I was also a bit wary about the club's ambitions. We'd already been in the top flight once and come straight back down and there didn't seem to be the resources to keep us up this time either. You've got to throw money at it to ensure you stay in the top flight and Middlesbrough weren't prepared to do that.'

At the time, Ripley upset many Boro fans when he said: 'I honestly believe Middlesbrough will always live in the shadows of Newcastle and Sunderland and that annoys me. Boro have got the best team in the north-east but the lack of exposure is ridiculous.'

Ripley's replacement was 26-year-old Tommy Wright, a winger who had scored twenty-two goals for Leicester City the previous year. Wright cost the club £650,000 – half the price of Ripley – but believed he would prove to be a better player than his predecessor.

He almost joined Newcastle but explained: 'Newcastle didn't have the money and wanted a cash and player deal. Then, when Middlesbrough came in, I didn't have any hesitation about signing.'

Speaking at the time, Lawrence said: 'It's now or never for Tommy at 26 years old. I've got good vibes about this deal. I'll be very surprised if he doesn't fit in.'

Meanwhile, Jon Gittens' loan deal was made permanent with Boro paying Southampton £200,000 for the central defender. But his purchase seemed surprising when Lawrence moved into the transfer market again a week before the season began to bring in defenders Derek Whyte and Chris Morris

Defenders Derek Whyte (above) and Chris Morris try on Boro scarves after signing for Middlesbrough shortly before the start of the 1992–93 campaign.

he wasn't good enough for the Premier League. I signed him out of sympathy and because he had done well for us.'

Not surprisingly, the deal for Whyte in particular upset Gittens who recalls: 'During the coach journey home after our last day win at Molineux, I asked Lennie where I stood with regards to a permanent deal. He told me he would have to wait and see what money was available. Eventually I was offered a one-year contract but I think he only signed me because he felt obliged to after my goal against Wolves. I don't think many people expected me to do well but I had a good pre-season and Lennie told me I'd be in the starting line-up for the opening game. You can imagine how gutted I was when, a couple of days before the first game, Lennie went out and signed Whyte and Morris for big fees and on long contracts.

'Then, when Lennie named the team the night before the game, he named Derek and Chris but not me, without having said a word to me beforehand to explain. When I asked him about it, he said the situation had changed. From that moment on, things were always going to be difficult.'

The departure of Payton, however, was the biggest surprise. Although he had struggled to find his goalscoring touch, he had never been given a long run in the first team and there seemed every reason to believe the goals would come given the chance.

Looking back, he believes the awful 5–1 friendly defeat at Lincoln City was the catalyst.

John Gittens' world was turned upside down when he was left out of the side during 1992–93.

from Celtic, with Andy Payton travelling in the opposite direction. Whyte was valued at £900,000 – a new club record – while £600,000-rated Morris and Payton were seen as direct swaps. Scotland international Whyte was, like Gittens and club captain Alan Kernaghan, a central defender, while Republic of Ireland star Morris was a right-back.

Explaining the swoop, Lawrence says he knew he had to make a move after a disappointing pre-season draw at York and a humiliating 5–1 hammering at lowly Lincoln.

'Our pre-season was awful and I felt we couldn't go on like that,' he explains. 'Payton was having a recurring nightmare and Celtic were interested in him. At the same time, we were short defensively so I took Whyte and Morris, and put Payton into the deal. People can value each player how they like.'

Of the Gittens deal, he admits: 'Jon was a good lad and had done a good job but we knew

1992–93 Match of the Season

22 August 1992

MIDDLESBROUGH 4 LEEDS UNITED 1

This victory and performance against the reigning champions looked certain to go down as the greatest in Middlesbrough's modern history. It still ranks as special but United's disappointing season, which saw them fail to win a single away game, subdues the success with hindsight.

United made the trip to Ayresome Park as proud champions of England, but Boro's newly promoted lions ripped the heart out of Howard Wilkinson's shell-shocked stars.

From the very start, Boro looked head and shoulders above the Elland Road side and it was the Teessiders who looked more like championship material, going two goals up inside ten minutes.

Despite a disappointing crowd of just 18,649, this was a truly glorious day for the supporters and players alike and raised premature hopes that Boro could be a success in the Premiership.

The opening goal came on eight minutes when new signing Tommy Wright, playing against one of his old clubs, found Paul Wilkinson with a low cross which evaded Leeds centre-back Chris Fairclough. Wilkinson did the rest, poking the ball home past John Lukic.

Paul Wilkinson scores one of his two goals in the 4–1 win over champions Leeds United at Ayresome Park.

Just sixty seconds later it was 2–0 with the same partnership again combining with deadly effect. This time Wilkinson met Wright's long cross with a brave, diving header to stun a Leeds side which included stars like Eric Cantona, David Batty and Gary McAllister.

Boro' keeper Ironside twice denied Cantona before the outstanding Wright notched a third goal two minutes into the second half, nodding home from Jimmy Phillips' deep corner.

Quite incredibly, it was 4–0 on fifty-nine minutes, another former Leeds player, John Hendrie, crashing home a fierce drive after beating Fairclough and Chris Whyte to Wright's pinpoint pass.

A lone goal from Cantona twenty minutes from the end was United's only consolation on a day they were taught a football lesson.

While the game was memorable for every Boro player, it was particularly special for Hendrie, who had left Leeds under a cloud two years earlier.

'It was the first time I'd played against Leeds since leaving Elland Road and I was fired up,' he admits. 'On the day, we battered them but they didn't play like champions all season. It's fair to say, however, that I enjoyed my post-match pint that day!'

'The defence was looking ropy and Lennie obviously had his eye on Whyte and Morris. But I was looking forward to playing in the Premier League and had no intention of leaving. Then Lennie told me, "Celtic have been in touch; it's entirely up to you if you want to go." Celtic were a massive club, while Mogga was already there, so I thought it was a great move, especially as Lennie was willing to let me go.'

Wright, Whyte and Morris duly made their Boro debuts at Highfield Road, but the team performance was well below par as they fell two goals behind, with the normally dependable Pears looking shaky in goal. It emerged later that he was suffering a recurrence of a rib injury and he missed the next eleven games. Two goals behind, Boro finally began to play and pulled a goal back through Wilkinson's clever lob just after the hour. But sub Slaven's 'equaliser' was ruled out for offside and Coventry held on for all three points.

Ironside replaced Pears against Manchester City four days later when Ayresome Park hosted its first Premier League match, while Slaven was in the starting line-up for Mustoe. Slaven celebrated his call-up in style with a two-goal blast, the second a rare header from Hendrie's pinpoint cross, to give Boro all three points.

'I'm not totally familiar with Bernie scoring goals like that,' admitted Lawrence afterwards. 'I got quite a surprise with the way he rose at the near post for the second goal.'

Meanwhile, Slaven smiles as he remembers: 'We tore City's defence to shreds that night and I couldn't have written a better script for my comeback. It was fantastic, especially as it was against a Premier League team.'

Next came a barn-storming 4–1 crushing of champions Leeds United as Boro forced the national press to reconsider their pre-season verdict of making the club relegation favourites. However, a 2–1 defeat at unfancied Southampton, thanks to two late goals, brought everyone back down to earth, with Lawrence announcing: 'We totally surrendered in the worst Middlesbrough fashion. Our lack of concentration is like a cancer.'

The prolific Wilkinson, holding off John Wark, scored his fifth goal in five games, to help rescue a point at home to Ipswich Town. It could and should have been three points, but Slaven fired his last-minute penalty wide of the mark. Another disappointing Ayresome crowd of just 15,000 watched a 2–0 win over Sheffield United before Boro moved into sixth spot with a tremendous 1–0 success at Manchester City, thanks to an own goal from youngster Garry Flitcroft. City had now lost to Boro four times in the last ten months.

Such a successful start was all the more remarkable given the 'keeper crisis the club was suffering. With first choice Pears ruled out and his replacement, Ironside, also injured, Brian Horne had been brought in on loan from Millwall and had kept clean sheets in his first two full games. That short run came to an end at Loftus Road but Boro still led 3–2 in the dying seconds. A tremendous attacking display had resulted in goals from Kernaghan, Wright and Falconer but a reckless challenge by Morris on QPR's Andy Sinton gave the home side a last minute penalty which was converted by Sinton to make the final score 3–3.

Lawrence recalls that day with a wry smile.

'Two things happened which made an excellent start into a very good start. First, we missed a last minute penalty against Ipswich when Bernie and Parky argued over who should take it. That cost us two points. Then, we conceded a last minute penalty at QPR, which was a harsh decision, but nevertheless cost us another two points. When I look back on it now, I don't know if it would have made a difference in the end but it would have kept us in the hunt a bit longer.'

Having lost only two of the opening eight league games, attentions were then turned to the Coca-Cola Cup and a north-east derby against Kevin Keegan's rejuvenated Newcastle United. The Geordies were wiping the floor with First Division teams but found Boro's defence – and Ironside in particular – far tougher with Boro holding out for a goalless draw in the first leg at St James' Park.

Back in the league, title-chasing Aston Villa proved far too good though Lennie's lions did well to lose by only the single goal, 3–2. Then

Willie Falconer is all smiles after scoring the first of Boro's two goals against Sheffield United in September 1992.

came the visit of Manchester United, who were to finish the season as champions. It was a replay of the previous season's cup semi-final and Boro again lifted their game to fight out a 1–1 draw, with Slaven scoring what proved to be his last goal for the club.

He recalls: 'My old mate, Gary Pallister, and I enjoyed our own personal battle in that match. I was determined to get one over on him and was ecstatic when I got past him and beat Peter Schmeichel. I only wish I had known at the time that it would be my last goal for Middlesbrough. If I had known, I'd have spent even longer celebrating on the Holgate fence!'

Even at this early stage, however, there was trouble brewing among the players. Jon Gittens, who played against United in place of the injured Kernaghan, reveals: 'The defence were obviously letting in too many goals and Lawrence wasn't happy. I recall one of our forwards turning round and saying, "Well, we're doing our bit." He was inferring that other areas of the team weren't, which didn't

go down too well. And yet this was at a time when we needed to be strong as a unit.'

The forward in question, it seems, was Hendrie. He recalls: 'I was stitched up in an interview with a tabloid newspaper. I said we need to tighten up at the back but it was taken out of context. Some of the lads weren't very happy about it so I explained how it happened. But I had nothing to apologise about and eventually told them to take it how they wanted. If they couldn't accept my explanation, I wasn't going to lose any sleep over it.

'If we'd kept more clean sheets we'd have been okay. The previous season the defence had taken all the praise but some of them didn't like the criticism when things went wrong.'

There was a shock to the system when Wilkinson's goal against Newcastle at Ayresome Park proved to be no more than a consolation in a 3–1 Coca-Cola Cup defeat. With Pears recalled in goal and Proctor making his first start of the season, Boro returned from White Hart Lane with a point after a 2–2 draw,

while 19-year-old Graham Kavanagh made his first team debut in a disappointing 1–0 home defeat by Nottingham Forest. Kavanagh was again in the team for a 1–1 draw against Sheffield Wednesday and hit the post in a game that saw Wilkinson score his eighth of the season.

Wilkinson scored the goal which almost clinched a win at Carrow Road over surprise Premiership leaders Norwich City, only for a late goal by Darren Sutch to ruin the party. Hendrie and Falconer returned from injury against Norwich but few players emerged from a 4–1 mauling at Liverpool with any credit. With Israeli international Ronny Rosenthal in sensational form, Boro's defence was left in tatters and their only reply came when Phillips converted a penalty shortly before half-time.

That week Bernie Slaven's name went on the transfer list after Lawrence accused him of being disruptive. But the two remain at loggerheads over whose decision it was for the striker's name to be circulated. Lawrence's version of the story is this:

'Bernie came to see me and said he wanted to go. I told him I would see what I could do but asked him not to go public about it. But Bernie being Bernie, he was determined to go to the press. So he ran to the papers and got the fans behind him. Meanwhile, I persevered with trying to get some money for him. Lots of people came in for him on a free but most of them were offering him a contract until the end of that season so it dragged on for two or three months, which didn't help matters at all.'

Slaven begs to differ, insisting: 'I felt I had no choice but to ask to be put on the transfer list. Although my heart wasn't in it, I felt I had to go on the list. If the manager was so determined to see me leave, I saw little point in staying. What's more, I only went public with my grievances when Lennie forced me to train with the trainees after another of our bust-ups. The way he treated me was a disgrace so I saw no reason to keep quiet about it.'

A first win in eleven attempts came thanks to strikes from Hendrie and Morris against Wimbledon at Ayresome but it was sandwiched between two 4–1 defeats, as struggling Oldham

Athletic repeated the Anfield scoreline at Boundary Park. New £500,000 signing Craig Hignett made his Boro debut in that game. Hignett, 21, had been a prolific goalscorer from midfield for Crewe Alexandra but was making a big step up. He remembers how excited he was to join the club.

'Other clubs had been sniffing but I made my mind up to speak to Middlesbrough because they were the first club to offer Crewe the right money. The club seemed to be on the up and Lennie told me that we weren't far off being one of the top eight clubs. He was hoping to make two or three more signings which he thought could push us into Europe.'

Despite the increasingly poor performances, Boro were still in mid-table and looking fairly comfortable. They seemed determined to prove a point when big-spending Blackburn Rovers visited Teesside. Falconer, Gittens, Parkinson and Proctor were all dropped for the match as Lawrence made wholesale changes to the side which had showed so little heart against Oldham.

Gittens remembers feeling that he was on his way out after the Oldham débâcle.

'I wasn't even called into the squad until the Manchester United match and only got in when Kernaghan was injured. But I thought I played quite well with the exception of the Liverpool defeat when the first goal was my fault. I made a weak backpass and Rosenthal ran on to it to score from an acute angle. But I was only dropped after the Oldham defeat and I remember thinking, "This is the end of me." I actually played a few more games but I was eventually left out.'

Gittens wasn't the only player whose relationship with the manager was on a downward spiral. Mark Proctor had been in the side throughout October and November but admits he was 'p***ed off' to be omitted after the game at Anfield. He was taken off during the match and well remembers a conversation he had with Lawrence the following week.

'I've probably been your best player for the last month,' he told the manager.

'Yes, you're probably right,' replied Lawrence.

'And now you're going to tell me that I'm not in the team, aren't you?' was Proctor's knowing response.

'Yes,' admitted the manager.

'I can't remember exactly how he explained leaving me out but it was probably some tactical rubbish,' says Proctor. 'After that, I was basically disregarded. I didn't get anything like the number of chances he gave to other players and that seemed completely unfair.'

Looking back, Lawrence feels Proctor has a point.

'To be fair to Proc, he was the only one who could say I never gave him a chance in the Premier League. I didn't think he had the legs, while he was very similar to Peakey who did very well. But, yes, I've got to hold my hands up and say Proc never got a fair chance.'

For the Blackburn fixture, in came Nicky Mohan for his first game since the memorable win at Wolves seven months earlier, together with the fit-again Andy Peake, one of the most impressive players so far. It was Stuart Ripley's first return to the club but the flying winger, who had enjoyed superb early form for Rovers, was far from his best and admitted later that the occasion had got to him. But it was a memorable day for Ripley's former wing partner, Hendrie. Playing in a new central striking role, Hendrie netted an incredible fifteen–minute hat-trick to turn a 1–0 lead for Blackburn into a 3–1 cruise for Boro. A late own goal ensured an exciting finish but it was Hendrie's day.

'It was a fantastic match – possibly the game of my life,' reflects Hendrie. 'We all thought things were starting to go right again but it didn't work out like that.'

That memorable win was also a home debut for Hignett but his abiding memory of the match is starkly different from anyone else's.

'I was about to score but John Hendrie pushed me out of the way and he scored instead!' he recalls.

Boro then embarked on a morale-sapping run of twelve league games with only one win, and it began to look as though they were in trouble long before the end of the season. A goalless home draw with Chelsea was, for

Hignett, his best match of the season.

'I was involved in everything that day,' he says. 'Their keeper, Kevin Hitchcock, made some good saves while I hit the bar with a free-kick. In fact, I think I hit the bar or post in five of the next six games after that.'

That was followed by a hard-earned 1–1 draw at Arsenal, when Boro led for a long period, while chances galore – most notably from Wilkinson – went begging in a 2–2 draw against Everton at Goodison Park on Boxing day. But Hignett showed what he was capable of by scoring both Boro goals against the club he supported as a youngster.

Craig Hignett was the new face around Ayresome Park in December 1992 after joining the club from Crewe Alexandra. His signing was a last roll of the dice for under-pressure manager Lennie Lawrence.

Lawrence comments: 'Hignett is one of the best players to have come from the bottom division in the last ten to fifteen years. He was young and inexperienced to come into a struggling side but he was a good player and well worth the money.'

Two days later Crystal Palace clinched a 1–0 win at Ayresome, with the result that 6,000 fewer fans witnessed a defeat by the same scoreline at home to QPR on 4 January. By this time, Lawrence admits he was a worried man.

'October and November had seen a gradual slide,' he explains. 'We kept conceding goals late on. At the time we put it down to tiredness but I think it was a lack of concentration. We rallied in December and finished up with 27 points on Boxing day. But then I got terribly worried. We lost 1–0 to Palace despite laying siege to their goal and found Nigel Martyn in

inspired form. Then QPR showed us how to do it on the break and I knew we wouldn't be able to battle our way out of it because we didn't have that type of player. I was hoping we could play our way out of it but it wasn't to be . . .'

Jimmy Phillips has good reason to remember Lawrence's despondent mood after the defeat by QPR.

'We lost the game but we were still in a relatively good league position, but Lennie had a negative sense of looking at a relegation battle. In the dressing room after the match, he announced, "Relegation, you lot, I can see it coming." A much more positive approach would have had a far better effect.'

Though some of the players criticise Lawrence, others believe he should have been given more cash to spend on new players. Alan Kernaghan insists: 'We merited our good early position in the Premier League but the problems arose due to our lack of depth in the squad. The finances weren't there to strengthen. I remember speaking to John Hendrie and Stephen Pears about our frustration with it all.'

Hendrie adds: 'Some of the lads felt Lennie became negative about our chances too early. Maybe they had a point because we probably needed him to be bubbly and encouraging. We were lacking concentration and conceding late goals. In fact, things were so bad we started to think we were going down by December.'

Attentions were turned to the FA Cup and a third round draw against Chelsea. It was an uninspired game but Boro grafted out a 2–1 win to clinch a fourth round draw at Nottingham Forest.

Next came an away match at Aston Villa, screened live on Sky Television. In front of the nation's football fans, Boro fell to an embarrassing 5–1 defeat. Only the supporters emerged from the game with any credit. After hearing Villa fans chant 'We want six, we want six . . .', the Teesside faithful responded with 'We want two, we want two'!

Boro were thankful to get away from league action and took on Nottingham Forest at the City Ground in the FA cup. Falconer got the goal that clinched a 1–1 draw and a replay back at Ayresome Park. Three days later,

Southampton were beaten 2–1 in the Premiership to end a run of three successive league defeats.

But things were about to get substantially worse. It began with a thumping 3–0 defeat at Elland Road as Leeds exacted revenge for their early season mauling. But Jimmy Phillips again criticises the manager's man-management. He recalls: 'At half-time it was 0–0 and we'd been much the better team in the first forty-five minutes. We'd had a goal disallowed and had two good penalty appeals turned down. But Lennie came into the dressing room and blasted us. He said we had to improve in the second half because Leeds would never play as badly as that again.'

The score was the same when Brian Clough's relegation-haunted Forest swept aside Boro's defence in the Cup replay, though there was a welcome return to action, as substitute, for Slaven who many thought had played his last game for the club. Indeed, Slaven was in from the start when high-flying Coventry visited for a league game but a 2–0 defeat further increased concerns.

Whilst he agrees the defeat was a disaster for the team, Slaven has fond memories of the game against the Sky Blues.

'To play again for Boro completed an incredible turn-around because only a month earlier Lennie had insisted I would never play for the club again. Even I had resigned myself to leaving. But I'll never forget the great reception I got from the fans when I ran on to the pitch before the game got underway. That was a special moment.'

A visit to fellow strugglers Sheffield United became a fourth successive game without a goal, as the Blades scored twice without reply, and rock-bottom Forest then beat Boro for the third time that season, 2–1 at Ayresome, as Middlesbrough-born 35-year-old Chris Kamara made his Boro debut on loan from First Division Luton Town. Four successive league defeats, and the next game was against Manchester United at Old Trafford!

Despite a sensational display from Pears, United won 3–0 and Boro had now lost eight of their last nine Premier League fixtures. Craig

Hignett was far from happy about being dropped from the team.

'I kept getting left out and I couldn't work out why,' he says. 'I was young and inexperienced but Lennie never tried to explain. It was frustrating because I wanted to show what I could do.'

There was a brief respite when a determined display against Ipswich at Portman Road saw a lone goal from Wilkinson secure all three points. There were some who believed the corner had now been turned but, similar to the victory at West Ham four years earlier, it was a false dawn. A 2–0 defeat at Wimbledon

CHAIRMAN QUITS IN POWER STRUGGLE

A series of behind-the-scenes events led to the shock resignation of chairman Colin Henderson in the second half of the 1992–93 season, resulting in what the press labelled 'a power struggle'.

According to Steve Gibson, the actions of Henderson, chairman since 1986, had begun to lead to friction between Henderson and other board members.

Gibson reveals: 'My first disillusionment with Colin surfaced when we were in the Premier League. I felt he'd done a very good job for the club but he was very conservative in his views. I was finding it very difficult to get any information from the club. Colin was telling us very little.'

Gibson's concern increased as board meetings became increasingly infrequent. 'I was aware that people were being fired from their jobs on Colin's instruction while others were getting jobs at the club for reasons I didn't understand.'

Gibson became further disillusioned when he discovered Henderson had attended a meeting with local bodies to explore the possibility of the club moving to a new stadium without informing his fellow board members. During the meeting, Henderson had apparently been negative towards the prospect of Middlesbrough leaving Ayresome Park. 'He had dismissed the proposals out of hand without even discussing the matter with the rest of the board,' reveals Gibson.

'I felt that we didn't receive any clear leadership from Colin on what to do over Ayresome Park,' says Gibson. 'It felt to me that he wanted to virtually ignore the big issues, leaving the problems of team relations to Lennie Lawrence and the restructuring of the ground to Keith Lamb.'

At the same time, Gibson felt the chairman was not lending enough support to manager Lennie Lawrence in his bid to keep the club in the Premier League. 'We should have been going the extra mile to help keep us in the top flight but Colin, with the liquidation saga in his mind, wanted to remain prudent and careful. I fully understood that but felt that some risk-taking was needed to progress the club and secure our place in the Premier League. I felt that if we could get the right results then the base was there to look at the economics. Lennie needed to know that if players weren't producing he could bomb them out, that he had full authority to use whatever discipline he felt necessary, but he didn't have that.

'The chairman was running the club as though it was his own, with little or no involvement from the other directors, and yet he didn't have a single share in it.'

Although the pair were no longer socialising together, Gibson says that was not always the way. 'Initially I had an excellent relationship with him but we were starting to niggle at each other.'

A number of meetings followed during which proposals were put forward designed to restrict Henderson's powers and restructure the board. The proposals were supported by all but Henderson.

'We had a very ugly board meeting when he was told that we felt he was abusing his authority and that some of the control had to come back to the board,' says Gibson. 'Verbally, the meeting ended very violently,' recalls Gibson. 'Colin quit as chairman and issued a far-reaching press statement airing in public our substantial problems. He told the press that I wanted all the power and wanted to be chairman. This was done against my wishes.'

In fact, the club was to struggle on for some months without a chairman, during which time the fans would suffer another relegation. But Henderson's statements encouraged former director Henry Moszkowicz, who still held a significant number of shares in the club, to present himself as a viable new chairman.

Henderson and Moszkowicz suddenly became allies at a time when Gibson had opened discussions with ICI's George Cooke on ways in which the club could progress. Cooke and ICI's legal representative Nigel Payton were keen to act as a medium between the two different parties but soon realised they faced an impossible task.

Gibson outlined his plans for the club to Cooke and it soon became evident that the two were on a similar wavelength and that they could do business together. However, in the meantime, they would explore every avenue to find a way to include Henry Moszkowicz in the club.

MISSED OPPORTUNITIES

Three failures by Lennie Lawrence in vital transfer dealings sowed the seeds of doubt in the mind of Steve Gibson that he did not hold the necessary influence.

Gibson recalls: 'Lennie set out three clear targets. First, he wanted to persuade Stuart Ripley to stay with Middlesbrough. Then he aimed to convince both Gavin Peacock and Robert Lee that their futures lay on Teesside. His failure in all three cases raised major question-marks in my mind over his ability to take us forward.'

With Ripley convinced that his future lay elsewhere, Lawrence was still hopeful of signing Newcastle star Peacock and talented Charlton winger Lee, who had played under him for many years at The Valley. Both players were exciting talents and the prospect of seeing them in Boro shirts excited the fans. Peacock had scored twenty-two goals in a struggling United side the previous season while Lee, 25, had hit thirteen while setting up many more.

Lawrence recalls: 'I tried to sign Peacock first because he looked set to leave Newcastle. He came to speak to us but he wanted to hang on and see what happened. I knew his dad very well from my days at Charlton but I think they had resolved that his next move would be back to London. Kevin Keegan persuaded him to stay there because, unfortunately, Gavin viewed joining Middlesbrough as a sideways move even though we were a division higher than United.'

In fact, Peacock stayed on at St James' Park for another year, scoring twenty goals as United won the First Division championship.

If missing out on Peacock was a blow, it was nothing in comparison to the fiasco over Robert Lee.

In the opening weeks of the Premier League season, with Boro still doing well, Lawrence tried to tempt Lee into a move to Ayresome Park, and, for a while, looked almost certain to be successful.

Lawrence still feels bitter about the way things went.

'I'd had word from people who knew Robert that he was deadly serious about his interest in coming up to Middlesbrough,' he says. 'I tried to buy him for £400,000, which was a mistake on my part. I started too low, though my directors were keen to avoid starting my bidding at a high price. I eventually worked the offer up to £700,000, which Charlton accepted, but it took two or three weeks to get there, one of which our chairman Colin Henderson spent trying to get the bank to make the money available.

'Eventually, Robert came up to speak to us and we made him a very generous offer – top money for Middlesbrough at the time. But something wasn't quite right. He wanted to go away and think about it. In the meantime, West Ham tapped him up but didn't have the money for the transfer fee.

'Meanwhile, Kevin Keegan looked at this and must have thought, "Oh, Lennie's not a bad judge of a player." I don't think they knew too much about him but they came in at the last minute and Robert's head was turned by Keegan, who was one of his childhood idols, and he signed for Newcastle.'

Lee, of course, went on to establish himself as one of the game's most influential midfielders, winning full England caps, but Lawrence feels Boro's failure to sign him was not completely his fault.

'We took too long to get our bid sorted out,' he reflects. 'I remember saying to someone in the Middlesbrough hierarchy that I should have offered £700,000 and then gone to £1 million. They replied that the club might not have wanted to go over £700,000. Jesus Christ – £2.7 million would have been cheap!'

Steve Gibson's recollection of the Lee débâcle, however, differs from Lawrence's version.

Gibson recalls: 'Robert's father was in the same business as me and rang me to say he wanted his son in the Premier League with Boro and Lennie.

'Lennie's view was that because they had approached us, we had the player, so we should offer Charlton £400,000. I asked Lennie what his value was and he told me it was £700,000. I told him that if that was what he was worth then that was what we should offer. Instead, Lennie offered £400,000, then £500,000 and eventually £700,000. It dragged on for weeks until everyone knew about it.'

With the news of Boro's interest out of the bag and Charlton annoyed by Boro's cut-price bids, Lee joined Newcastle.

followed a week later. Then came the visit of Liverpool, themselves surprise contenders for the drop after a very disappointing season. Despite an own goal from Steve Nicol, however, Liverpool ran out 2–1 winners. There followed a 1–1 draw at Blackburn before a crunch match that Lawrence built up as the one which would decide the club's future.

Meanwhile, Bernie Slaven, scorer of almost 150 Boro goals, finally left the club. He was one of Middlesbrough's goalscoring legends and the decision to release a player who had done so much for the club during an eight-year stay on Teesside, incensed many fans.

The relationship between Lawrence and Slaven had been stormy from the very start and had not been helped by the manager's tendency to drop his 31-year-old striker for Premier League away games.

After going on the transfer list early in the season, Slaven spoke to a whole host of clubs including WBA, Bolton, Stockport, Motherwell, Wolves, Hearts and Port Vale, while Premier League sides like Blackburn and Aston Villa also showed an interest. But Slaven couldn't agree the long-term contract he wanted so stayed on at Ayresome.

Things became increasingly more strained between manager and player and the pair fell out a number of times, with the result that Slaven was eventually forced to train with the club's youth trainees. Finally, he joined Second Division promotion hopefuls Port Vale, after turning down Bruce Rioch's Bolton, and scored in their first ever appearance at Wembley, in the Auto Glass Trophy Final against Stockport two months later.

'There was always friction between us,' admits Slaven. 'Eventually Lennie gave me a free transfer because he felt I was a problem personality. Leaving Middlesbrough was the hardest decision I ever made but I wasn't made to feel welcome at the club. The fans were special to me but I knew it was time to leave.'

Given the conflict between the two, it is no surprise to find that Lawrence had few regrets about Slaven's departure.

'It was my fault that Bernie didn't go in September or October, or even the previous summer, but I persevered with trying to get some money for him,' he says. 'I respect the goals he scored when we won promotion but I never got on with him, never saw eye-to-eye.'

Fellow strugglers Oldham Athletic were the visitors to Ayresome Park in a real six-pointer, though the attendance dipped to just 12,000. But Boro made them look like AC Milan as the Boundary Park club ran up a three-goal lead before Mohan and Hignett gave the final scoreline some respectability at 3–2. The game was a disaster for Boro and confirmed in the minds of many supporters that the team were doomed to another relegation.

All of those fears were substantially increased a week-and-a-half later with a four-goal crushing against Chelsea at Stamford Bridge when Lennie's once proud lions looked more like tame pussycats. It was an unfortunate game for striker Dwight Marshall, on loan from Second Division Plymouth, to make his debut as substitute.

The defeat so enraged Lawrence that he made wholesale changes for the visit to Teesside of Arsenal on 6 April. This would be a chance for the kids, he said. In came teenagers Pollock and Kavanagh among five changes from the Stamford Bridge catastrophe. And the changes saw some much-needed pride return to the performance as all three points were won for only the third time since the turn of the year, Hendrie's goal clinching a 1–0 win.

Although the odds were no longer good, there was still hope of escaping the drop through a good run of results. An unchanged team gave their all against Everton at Ayresome but lost 2–1 and then fell to another embarrassing defeat, 4–1 at Crystal Palace. Now it was all over bar the shouting – and there wasn't much of that from Boro's disconsolate fans.

Yet the final three games provided a grandstand finish and the sort of goalscoring spree which, if it had come sooner, could well have kept the club in the Premiership.

The first of the three games came against Tottenham at Ayresome Park. Tommy Wright, who had suffered from loss of form and injuries after a good start for the club, was recalled to

the action and took a starring role with two of the goals, while Wilkinson netted for the thirteenth time in the league to complete a surprise 3–0 rout.

By now Boro were relying on other teams to slip up if they were to have even a remote chance of avoiding relegation. A display of pride and passion saw them overpower a stunned Sheffield Wednesday at Hillsborough. Goals from Falconer, Pollock and Hendrie opened a three-goal lead before the Owls put two past goalkeeper Andy Collett, making his first team debut. Collett was one of the heroes of this performance but, alas, it was all too late for Boro. Results elsewhere made the result irrelevant and Boro were relegated after only one season in the top flight.

The final game, at home against Norwich City, was a formality for Boro, though it was important to the Canaries who needed a point to be assured of a place in Europe for the first time. In a ding-dong battle, both attacks ran riot as the game ended in a 3–3 draw. Top scorer Wilkinson took his overall tally for the season to fifteen, while Hendrie again proved that he could be a potent force in a central striking role, grabbing his ninth of the campaign. Falconer was Boro's other scorer as Boro ended the season unbeaten in three games for the first time since December and having scored nine goals.

The reality, however, was that they now faced a return to First Division football with even less funding to mount a promotion campaign. The way ahead looked anything but bright.

The bottom of the table on the final day looked like this:

	P	W	D	L	F	A	Pts
Oldham	42	13	10	19	63	74	49
Crystal P.	42	11	16	15	48	61	49
Boro	42	11	11	20	54	75	44
Notts F.	42	10	10	22	41	62	40

Looking back on the relegation, Jimmy Phillips reflects: 'Before the Premier League season began, we thought we were in with a good chance of staying up. We made a great start and did well up until Christmas, but the squad wasn't strong enough. We needed another three or four experienced players, while Lennie's attitude changed from the positive one he had shown during the promotion season. The fact he had previously struggled with Charlton tended to give him a bit of a negative outlook.'

For his part, Lawrence admits Boro simply weren't up to the task.

'We were ill-equipped for the Premier League on and off the field,' he says. 'We'd have needed every ounce of luck to have gone our way to have stayed up. There was a massive boardroom battle going on. The only thing I've got against Middlesbrough is that between October and March there wasn't a board meeting and no assistance was forthcoming.

'I asked for some money for a striker just before the transfer deadline but I was refused. My only criticism is that they didn't support me enough. They could have said to me, "You're hopeless, you're sacked,"' but, instead, they did nothing.

'Colin Henderson said he wasn't happy with some of my staff. He felt they weren't working right with me, a suggestion which I refuted. I felt it was a matter of players, rather than the coaches. In fact, all of my staff are still at the club, apart from George Shipley who I took with me to Bradford City.'

Despite the obvious regrets, Lawrence still feels there were positive points.

'The spirit in the dressing-room was quite good, even towards the end of the season. I remember John Hendrie saying the spirit was much better than the one he had experienced in Newcastle's relegation side. We never lost it completely. It was just that so many players were out of their depth.'

CHAPTER ELEVEN

Boro at the Crossroads – 1993–94

The task of returning to the Premier League at the first attempt was never going to be easy. Without half a dozen of the experienced players who had battled throughout the previous season, it was nigh on impossible.

Lennie Lawrence, having survived pressure from many fans, continued as manager, but his task was made that much harder when the board told him they needed to raise funds by selling players. According to Lawrence, they demanded he raise £750,000 through sales.

'With that in mind, I knew the first offer I got, I would have to accept,' he explains. 'The first offer was for Jimmy Phillips and the second was for Willie Falconer, and we accepted both, bringing in £650,000.

'Everyone knew Alan Kernaghan wanted to leave and early in the season Manchester City boss Brian Horton made it known he fancied Alan. So off he went to City for £1.6 million, which was a master-stroke, if I say so myself.'

Kernaghan, who had recently won his first international cap for the Republic of Ireland, felt he needed to stay in the Premier League to increase his chances of playing in the 1994 World Cup finals. He says: 'I felt that if I signed another contract I'd probably remain with Boro for the rest of my career. I didn't want to turn around at 35 and regret not having had a go with another club. I think it was a good deal for Middlesbrough and me. They got £1.6 million for a player who had cost them nothing while I was getting the big challenge I desired.'

Phillips, however, remembers his departure from the club with a degree of regret.

'It was a bit of a disappointment because I was happy to stay,' he reveals. 'My contract was up for renewal but the club only offered me half of what I had previously been on. Then Lennie told me Bolton had made an offer for me and that I should talk to them. After speaking to Bolton, I went back to Lennie and asked him if he could improve his offer. He told me he couldn't and advised me to join Bolton.'

Falconer, however, was happier to leave and says: 'I moved to Sheffield United for differing reasons. Personally, it was the attraction of the Premiership. Boro were also trying to generate some income and Lennie told me I was the first player they had received a firm offer for.'

Jimmy Phillips was disappointed to leave Middlesbrough following relegation from the Premier League.

Meanwhile, Jon Gittens joined Portsmouth on a free transfer – just a year after being signed for £200,000 – while Mark Proctor and Ian Ironside were also allowed to leave the club for Tranmere and Stockport respectively. Gary

1993–94 Match of the Season

24 August 1993

BARNSLEY 1 BORO 4

Following this devastating win, Middlesbrough were made clear promotion favourites by many pundits as they challenged for an immediate return to the Premiership.

Lennie Lawrence's side had plummeted to relegation in their first season in the top flight but this result took their First Division start to three wins out of three, scoring ten goals in the process.

The new kid on the block was 18-year-old winger Alan Moore, who had opened his account with two stunning goals on his full debut in the opening 3–2 win at Notts County. And Moore did not disappoint this time around, earning rave reviews as he scored twice and set up the other two for striker John Hendrie.

Boro had expected a tough match and looked set to get it when Barnsley's player-manager Viv Anderson headed the home side ahead in a crowded penalty box.

However, cheered on by a large Teesside contingent, Boro bounced back to equalise shortly before half-time when Moore turned in a shot from close-range on the back post.

Teenage sensation Alan Moore was in breath-taking form early in the 1993–94 campaign.

If the first half had been tough, the second forty-five minutes was quite the opposite. Boro simply ripped apart a beleaguered Barnsley defence, with even the vastly experienced Anderson helpless to halt the rout.

The architect of the five-star performance was teenage sensation Moore whose tricky skills resulted in the fans chanting his name and comparing him to Manchester United's wing wonder Ryan Giggs.

Hendrie, the club's player of the year in the previous season, was the thankful recipient of Moore's skills, scoring twice in the second half after magnificent trickery by his young team-mate. First Hendrie slid the ball home to put Boro ahead before later wrapping up the marvellous win by heading home the fourth goal from Moore's cross.

In between, Moore netted a quite awesome goal, skipping through the outstretched legs of defenders before lashing a low shot into the far corner of the net.

This was a night to remember for Moore – and one to forget for Viv Anderson, who ruefully recounted the tale of this 4–1 defeat ten months later when he became Middlesbrough's assistant manager.

Parkinson had been reunited with Bruce Rioch at Bolton Wanderers the previous April.

Although he acknowledges he didn't make the impression he had hoped during his short stay with the club, Gittens blasts: 'What really hurt me was when Lennie spoke to the press and suggested I hadn't shown commitment to Middlesbrough. Yet I'd moved from the south coast to a new house in the north-east.'

Like Gittens, Ironside's contract had also come to an end. He would have been delighted to stay with the club but says: 'Lennie took me aside and explained. I'd appeared on the team-sheet thirty-nine times; if I was named again, even as a non-playing substitute, it would mean Middlesbrough would have to pay Scarborough another £30,000. He said the money wasn't available so he would have to let me go.'

Meanwhile, Craig Hignett admits he thought his short career with the club would come to an end.

'I really thought I would go because Lennie was selling other players who had been regulars while I had been in and out of the team,' he explains. 'But I was quite happy to stay because I was confident I'd do well at that level.'

To compensate for the wholesale departures, Lawrence had no option but to give a number of youngsters a chance to shine in the first team; cash for new signings was not forthcoming. Teenagers Philip Stamp, Michael Barron, Ian Johnson, Andy Todd and Neil Illman were all handed their league debuts, while fellow youngsters Paul Norton, Michael Oliver and Mark Taylor all won run-outs in the much-maligned Anglo-Italian Cup.

But three youngsters stood out above all the rest. The fast-maturing Jamie Pollock played his one hundredth game for the club shortly after his twentieth birthday, and he was joined in the first team on a regular basis by left-winger Alan Moore and left-back Richard Liburd. Moore, a precocious talent with superb skills, starred from day one after progressing through the ranks while Liburd made his mark after stepping up from non-league football with Eastwood Town.

With no new signings in the squad, success

Young Richard Liburd was a big hit with supporters during his one season as a first team regular.

was always going to be a tall order, and yet Boro made a sensational start. They won their opening four league games, scoring thirteen goals into the bargain. In fact, counting the final three games of the Premier League season, they scored three or more goals in seven consecutive league games.

The season opened with a potentially tricky fixture at Notts County, with Liburd making his league debut and Moore in the starting line-up for the first time. Wilkinson, looking for a third successive season as the club's top scorer, was on target but the real star of the match was 18-year-old Moore. He cracked in two sensational, long-range goals to crown a supreme full debut as Boro ran out 3–2 winners.

The following game was expected to be far tougher. Big-spending Derby County, the pre-season promotion favourites, had annihilated Sunderland 5–0 in their opening match but they were brought back down to earth at Ayresome Park. Boro oozed confidence in every department as goals from Kernaghan, Hendrie

and Wilkinson completed a 3–0 win that could easily have turned into a rout.

On the Tuesday came another away trip, this time to Viv Anderson's Barnsley. Barnsley took an early lead through their player-manager but it was soon transformed into another Alan Moore super show. The youngster lashed home two goals and set up another two for the in-form Hendrie.

Of Moore's sensational start, Hendrie says: 'Alan was one of the most laid back lads you could meet. He had always had the talent but sometimes you felt like he needed a rocket up his backside. Then he came in and did wonders. He made an astonishing start but he was only young and we knew he couldn't play like that every week.'

There was another stiff test the following Saturday as another of the big spenders, Wolves, played host to Boro at Molineux. A crowd of over 21,000 witnessed a tremendous battle, with Boro twice leading through Hendrie, only to be pegged back each time. A 2–2 draw was on the cards until Pollock let fly with a hopeful long-ranger which slipped under goalkeeper Mike Stowell's body to make it twelve points out of twelve for table-topping Boro.

With six goals in the opening four games, Hendrie was the division's top scorer but

SHOULD WE STAY OR SHOULD WE GO?

As the team struggled on the pitch during the 1993–94 campaign, exciting plans were being put into place that would form the basis of a bright new future for Middlesbrough F.C.

Although the club was still without a chairman, since the resignation of Colin Henderson the previous season, discussions were already well underway towards planning a move from Ayresome Park, the club's home of the previous ninety years.

Keith Lamb, the club's chief executive, accompanied Steve Gibson to a meeting with the Teesside Development Corporation regarding the potential for the building of a new stadium on the outskirts of the town.

'I was very excited by the discussion,' says Gibson. 'Certain powerful individuals on Teesside didn't think the club had the ability or the resource to deliver its end, but we were determined that we could deliver.'

Gibson's plans had the backing of ICI (between them, Gibson and ICI had a 52 per cent shareholding) but Henry Moszkowicz (who held the remaining shares) was wary. 'It emerged that a lot of dialogue had taken place between Henry and Colin Henderson. Henry thought my plans were too ambitious and would lead the club into financial ruin. His preference was to refurbish Ayresome Park and make it into a 20,000 all-seater ground.

'That was totally against my views and I was determined to oppose it with all my might. I don't think Colin Henderson had a clue how to make the club anything more than an average First Division team and Henry was coming from the same direction as Colin. I knew it needed a big cash input to take the club to the top of the Premiership with a new stadium and a new manager. It was like a jigsaw but, to be completed, it needed unity in the boardroom. We didn't have that unity because of self-interest.'

Although he had the support of directors Graham Fordy and Reg Corbidge, Gibson knew he needed ICI on his side and it was clear they were now seeing things his way. 'ICI had been badly bitten over the bond following liquidation but one of their representatives was George Cooke, who began to share my vision for the club.'

With ICI's support, Gibson's vision of a new Middlesbrough Football Club, in a fantastic new stadium, was emerging as a real possibility.

always felt that the bubble would burst.

'I signed a new contract with the club immediately after the home game with Norwich when we'd just been relegated,' says the winger-turned-striker. 'Lennie had promised to play me down the middle and it was a case of better the devil you know. We had a strong team but we needed more troops in the camp so I was surprised we didn't bring in one or two players over the summer.

'But I was delighted to be playing as a striker, instead of out wide. I was like a big kid with a new toy.'

Full-back Anthony Barness, on loan from Chelsea, made his Boro debut in place of the rested Liburd in a disappointing but ultimately meaningless 2–1 Anglo-Italian Cup defeat at Grimsby Town, before the Ayresome boys bounced back to their best form with a rout of Barnsley, this time by 3–0 in the Anglo-Italian Cup. Wilkinson scored two of those goals, but it was Hendrie – with seven goals in six games – who was setting the pace on the goals front. That match also saw 17-year-old midfielder Philip Stamp go on as substitute for his first team debut.

Things were going very smoothly; too smoothly, as it turned out. Boro dropped to third after a shock 1–0 defeat at unglamorous Southend United. Then came a simply awful 2–1 home defeat to Stoke City, a game which marked the end of Alan Kernaghan's Middlesbrough career. Now, for the first time, Lawrence was forced to change his starting line-up for a league game, Nicky Mohan stepping in alongside Derek Whyte at the heart of the defence, for an instantly forgettable goalless draw with Luton Town at Ayresome.

Just 5,651 fans turned up three days later for a Coca-Cola Cup second round first leg tie with Brighton. Those who didn't bother to go missed a treat, as Hignett turned it on scoring four goals in a 5–0 demolition. Hignett was the first player to score four goals for the club since Micky Burns in a 7–2 win over Chelsea sixteen years earlier.

'Scoring four goals was great,' reflects Hignett, 'but it would have been nicer if there had been a few more fans to see it.'

Curtis Fleming made his first start of the season, in place of the injured Hendrie, in a 1–1 draw against WBA at the Hawthorns, Whyte scoring his first goal for the club. Boro were now fifth but leaped back to the top with a 2–0 home win over Leicester City, thanks, yet again, to goals from Wilkinson and Hendrie.

However, Boro were made to look ordinary by struggling Birmingham City on 2 October, when Hendrie and Moore found the net in a 2–2 draw at Ayresome.

The second leg of the tie with Brighton resulted in an 8–1 aggregate win, and Stamp made his first start. He retained his place in midfield instead of the injured Pollock in a disappointing 2–0 defeat at Watford. Fringe players Collett, Todd, Kavanagh and Illman all played from the start in a 3–1 Anglo-Italian Cup defeat in Pisa, though it was clear Lawrence was unwilling to play a full-strength side.

Next came the Tees-Wear derby against Sunderland. Less than 13,000 supporters – the lowest post-war attendance for the fixture – turned out to see Boro display the sort of passion and killer instinct that could yet make it a successful season. Wilkinson scored twice to take his tally to eight, while Hignett netted his seventh and Hendrie his twelfth.

Boro were now third and held that position through a 1–1 draw against Millwall at the Den, before the prolific Hendrie netted his fourteenth in his last seventeen appearances in a hard-fought 1–1 draw against Premier League Sheffield Wednesday in the Coca-Cola Cup at Ayresome Park.

Mustoe's goal grabbed a home point against Peterborough but a 2–0 defeat at Portsmouth signalled the start of the rot which was to transform a promotion challenge into a relegation battle. Boro had maintained a top five position thanks to an immense effort and good fortune with injuries. But the wafer-thin squad cracked as an injury crisis enveloped the club. The biggest blow was the loss of top scorer Hendrie, whose appearance against Peterborough was to be his last for four months. Centre-back Michael Barron and winger Ian Johnson were called up from the

reserves to make their league debuts against Pompey, while Kavanagh also made his first league start of the campaign.

'Looking back, it's incredible how many kids were given their debuts that season,' says Craig Hignett. 'Moorsey and Stampy are the only two to establish themselves so the others must look back and wonder what it was all about. Most of them have normal jobs now and yet they must have been thinking they had a future in the game at that point. Basically, we didn't have a squad as such, we were down to the bare bones and as soon as injuries happened we were in trouble.'

To ease the stretched squad, midfielder John Gannon was brought in on loan from Sheffield United but made little impact in a 1–0 home defeat that saw Boro plummet to tenth. Andy Peake made a welcome return from injury in the Coca-Cola Cup replay at Sheffield

Wednesday and the team with five teenagers were only beaten by a late, late super strike from Carlton Palmer after Mustoe had equalised for Boro.

Less than 3,000 Teessiders bothered to turn up for a goalless Anglo-Italian Cup draw against Ancona. The game was relatively meaningless but the poor crowd was indicative of the way supporters were becoming disenchanted with the lack of quality in the team and the lack of ambition within the club.

Things came to a head when just 6,800 turned out for a live televised league game against Bolton Wanderers at Ayresome Park on 21 November. Beleaguered Boro lost the match in terrible weather conditions and it was easy to understand the stay-away fans. Craig Hignett who played in the match, recalls: 'The game was on TV and it was snowing but that was still an incredibly poor crowd. Ayresome

GIBSON TAKES OVER THE REINS

Steve Gibson emerged from another power struggle at boardroom level to take the reins finally in February 1994. The behind-the-scenes wrangle led to the end of Henry Moszkowicz's involvement with the club and put the wheels in motion for the club's move to a new stadium.

The series of events began with a meeting between Gibson and Moszkowicz at the Royal York Hotel in York, organised by ICI who wanted to see if there was any way of accommodating Moszkowicz on the board.

'I was willing to accommodate him but only if it was in the best interests of the club,' says Gibson. 'Within ten minutes he had told me everything he wanted – and we were poles apart. He wanted 40 per cent of the votes. He said I was too ambitious. That we would be better off in the First Division than in the top league and that we should stay at Ayresome Park.'

Gibson says: 'I told Henry that I was fully supportive of the plans to build a new stadium and to build a team capable of competing at the highest level in the English game. I explained that I felt I had the support of George Cooke and ICI, while I already knew I had the support of Graham Fordy and Reg Corbidge.

'I highlighted the financial costs of achieving our ambitions and explained how it could be done. I told Henry I would purchase his shares if he felt he couldn't be involved.

'I was disappointed, therefore, when Henry held a press conference outlining how he saw the club's future. His plans were totally opposed to what I had outlined to him and I felt it was no longer possible to negotiate with Henry. He had to be removed from the club.'

Within 48 hours of the press conference, however, Moszkowicz had disposed of his shares to Gibson, while Colin Henderson was removed from the board. Now the more constructive work of building the club to the vision of Gibson and Cooke could commence.

Park was a terrible place that season but the club was showing no ambition and the fans were fed up. I'm not surprised they stayed away.'

Lawrence agrees that the low crowds were a blow to the club but explains his philosophy over why he utilised so many young and inexperienced players. 'I aimed to consolidate that year.

'I thought we'd bring some young players through without spending any silly money, then we'd be ready placed to challenge for promotion the following season. But they won't have that on Teesside.'

Meanwhile, Lawrence attempted to strengthen the squad by bringing Tony Mowbray back to the club. Mowbray was struggling to hold down a regular place at Celtic and was more than willing to return.

'It was my big ambition to return to Boro – and, in many ways, it still is,' reveals Mowbray. 'Apparently there was a clause which stated Boro had first refusal if Celtic decided to sell me. I was all set to re-sign but somehow it all fell through.

'But I'm at the stage in my life where I feel that football management is where I'll find my niche. As a footballer, I'm a grafter and admit I don't have the talent of some players. There are no guarantees, but I believe I will succeed as a manager because I love studying the systems, tactics and motivational side of the game. Ideally, I'd love to manage Middlesbrough and Celtic at some point, though I may have to start off at a smaller club to prove myself first.'

Lawrence confirms he was interested in the former club captain but, with hindsight, does not regret that negotiations with Celtic broke down.

'I'm not sure whether he could have reproduced his old form again. Going back to a former club isn't always a good idea.' As it turned out, the two clubs could not agree terms and the deal fell through.

Back on the pitch, a weakened line-up fell to a 3–0 Anglo-Italian Cup defeat by Ascoli in Italy, before completing their fourth successive game without a goal in a 0–0 draw at Bristol

City. Another poor, disheartened performance at Stoke City resulted in a 3–1 defeat, despite Peake's first goal for the club. It was also an unhappy start for new signing Steve Vickers, a £700,000 buy from Tranmere Rovers.

Explaining his decision to bring the defender to Teesside, Lawrence says: 'We had scouted around and although we were all right for centre-backs, I thought Vickers was quality. I felt £700,000 was a good investment of the club's money.'

Vickers was to become one of Boro's stars over the next few years, but he missed the next four games through injury. Stand-in striker Kavanagh gave the club reason for hope with a two-goal blast as Notts County were beaten 3–0 but the win did little to ignite the imagination of the fans. In fact, only 1,600 of them attended Ayresome Park for a 1–0 defeat by Brescia in the Anglo-Italian Cup.

High-flying Nottingham Forest, who had been relegated with Boro the previous season, attracted a crowd of almost 27,000 to the City Ground two days after Christmas. Boro stepped up on recent performances as Moore scored a wonder goal – his seventh of the season – to grab a point in a 1–1 draw. A goalless home draw with Tranmere ensured that the year ended on the low note which had become the norm.

The New Year began with a return from injury for Vickers as Boro drew 1–1 against Oxford United at the Manor Ground, Pollock scoring his second of the season. The centre-back made his home debut as Wilkinson ended his ten-week blank by notching the only goal of the match against Grimsby Town.

The striker found the net again, as did Moore, in a 2–2 FA Cup third round draw at Cardiff, but more disappointment was in store before Boro began a recovery. Lennie's boys were left lingering in sixteenth place, just above the relegation zone, after a 2–1 defeat against Sunderland at Roker Park. Vickers' goal was the one bright spot in the game. Three days later, Boro were dumped out of the FA Cup after an embarrassing 2–1 home replay defeat by Cardiff City. Midfielder-cum-striker Kavanagh grabbed the goal but numerous other chances

went begging as the season went from bad to worse.

Things couldn't really get worse – and they didn't. Moore, one of the few bright spots in an otherwise forgettable season, scored to clinch a home point against Watford, before a 4–2 hammering of Millwall was watched by another embarrassingly low crowd of less than 7,000. Hignett struck two, while Wilkinson and Vickers also scored in the club's second win in ten attempts.

Long-term injury victim Tommy Wright returned to the side against Millwall but neither he nor his team-mates emerged with any credit in a 1–0 defeat at Peterborough. It seemed Boro could lift themselves against the better teams but lacked motivation when it came to the less glamorous clubs. This theory was given further credence when they completed a league double over Derby, Vickers' third goal in six games clinching a shock 1–0 win at the County Ground as Hendrie made his return after a four-month absence.

March began with a 1–0 home win over Wolves, before Mustoe's goal grabbed a point in a 1–1 draw at Luton Town. Out of the team by this time was Hignett, who felt he did not deserve to be left out.

'I wasn't happy,' he says. 'I was making runs and doing things off the ball that I felt Lennie didn't notice. I think he thought I was doing nothing.

'Usually I'd only find out that I wasn't playing when I read Eric Paylor's report in the *Evening Gazette*. Lennie would never tell me why I was being dropped and it got to the stage where I felt sure he would offload me. Nowadays, I'm more sure of myself but at the time I was a bit naive and couldn't always tell if someone was being straight with me. Dario Gradio, my boss at Crewe, was always up front with me and I appreciated that, but I never knew where I stood with Lennie.'

Although Boro fell to a 2–0 defeat against Leicester at Filbert Street, they bounced back when Wilkinson scored his thirteenth goal of the season to clinch all three points against Southend at Ayresome.

Boro moved back into the top ten for the first time in more than four months when Hendrie was among the scorers in a 3–0 victory over WBA. Although it was his first goal for five months, Hendrie was still top scorer on fifteen.

Suddenly Boro were within sight of the play-offs and moved into seventh place with a magnificent 1–0 win over runaway leaders Crystal Palace at Selhurst Park. Hignett struck the goal which condemned Palace to only their second home defeat of the season.

Top scorer John Hendrie returned from injury to score in a 3–0 win over WBA.

Now, with the team back to full strength, there was real hope that the roller-coaster season could end on a high. Three days after shocking the league leaders, however, Boro once again let themselves down against lesser opposition, losing 1–0 to relegation-threatened Birmingham City at St Andrews.

Pollock's fourth goal of the season collected a point against Grimsby at Blundell Park and the new-found belief on the pitch and among the supporters was reflected in an Ayresome gate of over 17,000 when promotion-chasing

Nottingham Forest visited Teesside. This was a game in which the fast-improving Pollock displayed power, passion and attacking flair to grab two goals in a 2–2 draw. However, Boro knew they should have won three points rather than one.

Two days later came a crushing 4–0 defeat at the hands of Tranmere Rovers at Prenton Park in a game that left Boro five points adrift of a play-off place. Lawrence described the display as the worst of the season and it was to prove a first and last game for the club for full-back David Winnie, on loan from Aberdeen.

Once again, the players lifted themselves to beat Oxford United 2–1, thanks to goals from Wilkinson and Moore. That was the first of three successive home games – a real opportunity to get back in the promotion race. Instead, raised expectations proved unfounded as Portsmouth cruised to a 2–0 win at Ayresome. Afterwards a bemused Lawrence admitted he was struggling to understand such a lack-lustre performance.

'It seems that the greater the expectation of victory, the more problems we have as a team coping with the pressure that expectation creates. Until we can conquer this somewhat baffling and frustrating problem we will not be able to move forward with any consistency.'

Supporters were understandably down-hearted about Boro's inconsistency and the attendance when Charlton were the visitors three days later fell below the 7,000 mark. Typically, fellow play-off hopefuls Charlton were brushed aside as Hendrie's sixteenth of the season and Moore's twelfth sealed all three points for the Teessiders.

More typically, but all the more infuriating,

a humbling 4–1 defeat at Bolton Wanderers followed with the consequence that a play-off place was no longer a realistic aim. Ayresome Park's smallest league crowd of the season, just 6,368, turned up three days later – and Boro ran Barnsley ragged to the tune of 5–0 to show what they were capable of when they turned it on. Pollock took his season's tally to eight with two goals while Wilkinson also hit two.

The final home game of the season saw champions Crystal Palace exact revenge for their earlier defeat, winning 3–2 in an exciting, end-to-end game. Immediately after the game, Lennie Lawrence learned that his future lay away from Ayresome Park.

Although he liked Lawrence, John Hendrie admits it wasn't a shock to the players when the manager was sacked.

'By the end of the season, the club was dead,' he reflects. 'It was flat and we needed something big to happen to kick-start everyone into action.'

Hignett, however, was not so disappointed to see the manager leave.

'I remember Lennie telling the players, "Don't back the wrong horse," as if he would still be there the following season but within a week he had gone. When you look at the state the club was in, it was no surprise to see him sacked. We weren't a team of winners and that had to change.'

So Boro went into their final match at Charlton with first team coach John Pickering as caretaker manager. To complete a topsy-turvy campaign, Boro went out on a high. Hendrie's hat-trick inspired a 5–2 rout of Lawrence's old club.

CHAPTER TWELVE

Up Where we Belong – 1994–95

After all the hype and hysteria surrounding the arrival of Bryan Robson, the new manager finally got down to planning his side for the new season in the Endsleigh League First Division.

Robson says: 'I knew a few of the players because I'd played against them. I knew Jamie Pollock, Robbie Mustoe, John Hendrie and Paul Wilkinson, who were all up to the standard of the First Division.

'I looked at us on video and we'd conceded fifty-four goals the season before. I thought there's definitely something wrong with the defence and that's why I went straight out and bought Nigel Pearson and Neil Cox. You can't win anything without a good solid base. That was the plan Viv and I had from the minute we arrived at the club.'

Pearson, who was immediately made club captain, was delighted with the move after two injury-blighted years with Sheffield Wednesday. He recalls: 'I had no hesitation in moving to the club. Obviously my respect for Bryan Robson and Viv Anderson was a major influence. I knew how passionate the fans were from my visits to Teesside as an opposition player. I promised them from the start that I'd give them 100 per cent commitment and I'd like to think I always gave them it.'

Neil Cox became the club's first ever £1 million signing when he made the move from Aston Villa. The 22-year-old says: 'I'd never have joined the club if I hadn't thought we'd win promotion. For that reason combined with the fact I was being offered regular first team football, I didn't see leaving Villa as a step down. Bryan Robson impressed me with his

plans for the club but no-one could have imagined what we would achieve over the next two years.'

Another new arrival was Robson's former Manchester United team-mate Clayton Blackmore on a free transfer. Despite his glittering Old Trafford career, he was excited about his new start. 'I had a few options but it was clear Middlesbrough were making huge strides forward. I was confident that we could win promotion at first attempt and it was quickly evident that that was the general feeling among the players. But the main factor in my decision to join Boro was Robbo. He has always had big ambitions – and he always carries them out.'

The only departures on Robson's arrival were defenders Nicky Mohan and Richard Liburd to Bradford City, and Andy Peake who retired to become a policeman.

Robson explains his reasons for their departures: 'I watched pre-season training and I thought a few players weren't up to it. Mohan was already going anyway because he was a free agent. For Liburd, I was offered what I thought was a lot of money for the player I thought he was. He was a good athlete but I didn't think he was great on the ball. That was my opinion and you can be proved wrong as a manager but you use your own judgement.

'I called Andy Peake in. I already knew I had Pollock and Mustoe and I knew what type of players they were. I also intended to play myself. I brought in Clayton Blackmore from Manchester United on a free, so I knew I was covered in the central midfield positions and you can't keep everybody happy.

THE ARRIVAL OF BRYAN ROBSON . . .

Bryan Robson's arrival as player-manager of Middlesbrough in May 1994 heralded what was probably the biggest coup in the club's history. But, as chairman Steve Gibson reveals, it was no knee-jerk reaction to the dismissal of Lennie Lawrence.

Gibson explains: 'I'd worked much closer with Lennie since becoming chairman. He was a smashing fella who I thought the world of. But I had to decide if he was the man to deliver the vision I had for the club.

'He'd been at the club for three years and I had to ask myself if I was prepared to make masses of cash available to him to invest in players. After much thought and consideration, the answer was "no." There was no point in achieving eighth or ninth in Division One, so even at Christmas time we were looking for a new manager. But there was nothing to be gained by appointing someone at that stage. The supporters wanted it, the press wanted it, but there was nothing to be gained. Timing was key.'

Gibson held a meeting with chief executive Keith Lamb and director George Cooke, where it was agreed that Lennie Lawrence was not the man to take the club forward. 'He'd lost the crowd,' recalls Gibson. 'We were getting 8,000 or 9,000 and we were hearing them chant "Lennie out." The club wasn't thriving.'

He reveals: 'Our next move was to discuss a new manager and we came up with six names. Three were existing managers and three were players who were coming to the end of their careers. We did some homework on them and made some discreet enquiries, then made a list of who we felt our competition would be, basically trying to forecast who would be getting the sack at the end of the season.

'We felt we could compete with them all, though the biggest threat at that stage was likely to come from Wolves and Manchester City. We made up our minds that Bryan Robson was head and shoulders above everyone else.

'One of our targets was to achieve promotion in that first season, but we knew Bryan was, at that time, going for the treble with Manchester United, so rather than make an instant approach we just got on with the end of the season, although we knew Wolves had made an approach for him.

'Lennie had always been totally honest and 100 per cent with us so there was no way we were going to compromise him by going behind his back. After the Crystal Palace defeat, which was the penultimate game of the season, we decided the timing for approaching Bryan was vital.

Viv Anderson joined Boro as Bryan Robson's assistant during the summer of 1994.

'Most managers get sacked at the end of the season. If you've got a month to go, you tend to let the manager see the season out. We felt that to get a start, we needed to move before the end of the season, and we were actually going to do it before the Palace game until we realised it was going to be screened live on television. We didn't want the embarrassment of going into that game having just fired the manager.

'Immediately after the Palace game, however, we called Lennie in and told him we were terminating his employment. He said he understood the reasons why, there was no bitterness and he'd enjoyed his time on Teesside. He was superb.'

Looking back, Lennie is philosophical about his departure, which he admits he was not expecting. 'With retrospect, I understand it, but at the time it took me by surprise. I thought they'd let me start the next season, having battled through. If I hadn't done it, then they'd have bombed me.

'Steve Gibson looked at it and thought "If we have an iffy season next year, we'll have wasted another season and, with the new stadium coming, we'll be under pressure before we start there."

'He felt he couldn't risk it with me. I never lost it with the players but I lost it with a percentage of the fans, though I think a lot of them look back on it now and realise it wasn't so bad.

'They wheeled me in after the game when Keith Lamb asked me to come upstairs. I didn't think anything of it. Steve Gibson was in there. He can't help it – he's blunt, there's no kindness about him, but I like and respect him greatly. He said "We're terminating your contract", to which I replied "Oh well, what are you going to do now?"'

(continued)

(continued)

. . . THE ARRIVAL OF BRYAN ROBSON

Gibson asked Lawrence for his views on who the club should go for as his replacement. One of the names Lawrence came up with was Bryan Robson. Despite being sacked, Lennie had a great affection and feeling of loyalty towards the club and he says: 'I cared a lot about the club. I put a lot into it. I remember staying back until six or seven o'clock waiting for parents to come along so they could sign schoolboy forms. I'd taken an interest in everything and I didn't want it to be wasted. Steve was aware that Alex Ferguson was a good friend of mine and he asked if I would be prepared to help. I said they'd been fine with me over my contract so I would speak to Alex Ferguson for the club, but I had to do it my way.'

'I contacted Fergie and went over to see United play Southampton on a Wednesday night. I was in Manchester for three days. I actually went to a pre-match meal with Fergie, who asked what I wanted to do. I ended up borrowing his office where I met Bryan.'

'I told him I'd just left Boro and that they were very interested in him.'

With Robson listening intently, Lawrence went on: 'I've left the place in an excellent state and you'll have money to spend – they'll have to give you two or three million. There's some good young players and no bad lads, nobody you need to clear out. You'll never have a better chance in management, you're never stronger than when you start.'

As you would expect with somebody of Bryan Robson's stature, Boro weren't the only club interested in securing his services.

Robbo himself reveals: 'I spoke to Coventry and Wolves about the manager's job, while Ron Atkinson and Trevor Francis, at Aston Villa and Sheffield Wednesday, approached me about a role as player-assistant manager.

'If Wolves hadn't demanded I join them at the transfer deadline I probably would have been Wolves manager, apart from the chairman stating in the press that I was too greedy with my personal demands.

'Lennie Lawrence played a big part in me joining the club by explaining about the new stadium and what Steve was like. He was very complimentary about the club.'

Robson admits: 'At first I thought Middlesbrough . . . I'm not so sure. I knew quite a bit about Middlesbrough from when I was a kid as a Newcastle supporter and at first it didn't really appeal to me. But when Lennie told me of the chairman's plans, I admit I started to change my mind.'

Lawrence met Robson again the following Friday at Wetherby and took him to meet Keith Lamb at the Little Chef on the A19. Gibson was determined Robson was going to be impressed with what he found.

'Having been bitten by taking people to Ayresome Park, we arranged for Bryan to be taken to Wilton Castle, where we had an artist's impression and model of the new stadium,' explains Gibson.

'We spent the day praying for sunshine and we got it. Everything looked excellent. George Cooke, Keith Lamb and I had a discussion with Bryan and my first impression was that he was coming over more out of politeness and he didn't really think his future was at Middlesbrough.

'After two hours, a very good dinner and a few drinks, I felt he would be very good for us and we would be very good for him. I felt Bryan's position was that the meeting had moved very well. He asked the kind of questions only an interested person would ask.

'We'd done our homework by talking to Wolves to find out what kind of questions Bryan asked, and they gave him a fabulous reference. My judgement, after two hours, was that it would work, and I also had a feeling it was Bryan's judgement as well. We had to discuss all the personal details, and he went away to sleep on it.'

Gibson was right. Robson had been impressed.

'I was pleasantly surprised with the way the chairman wanted to go,' he says. 'From the moment I spoke to him, I decided I wanted the job. He was very forthright and with the way he and George Cooke spoke and about the plan of the new stadium, he seemed honest. Once I found out the club's plans, I said to the chairman that I wanted to bring my own men into the job and he was fine with that.

'After the meeting at Wilton Castle, I went home to speak to my wife, Denise, and told her everything, and we came back over a few days later for dinner, this time with all the wives present. I wanted assurances on bringing my own staff in and that there would be money to go into the transfer market to strengthen the squad, which were agreed to.'

(continued)

(continued)

Gibson recalls the moment Robson agreed to come on board. 'Before dinner we sat down and talked football. After about half an hour Bryan put his hand across the table and said "You've got a deal" and we shook hands.

'George organised champagne, while I said "Excuse me", before going outside the room where I screamed the place down with joy!'

When the news broke, hundreds of fans turned up at Ayresome Park for the press conference, where the new manager spoke to the crowd via a megaphone informing them how pleased he was to be at the club, while impressing them all with his ball-juggling skills.

'Andy was a good servant to the club, but with Clayton and me coming in, I had to tell him I wasn't going to be doing him any favours by leaving him in the reserves. It surprised me that he decided to retire because I thought he would have moved to another club.

'I pulled individual players aside and told them what I expected of them if they wanted to stay with the club. I knew we would be a difficult team to beat once I'd assessed Coxy, Nigel Pearson, Steve Vickers, Derek Whyte, Curtis Fleming and Chris Morris along with our midfield players. But being difficult to beat doesn't mean you are going to win games.'

So Boro kicked off the season amid much hype and expectation, but with much to live up to. Record season ticket sales topped 9,500 for the final season at Ayresome Park,

Scottish Premier side Heart of Midlothian were the visitors for Boro's final pre-season friendly and the fans' first real opportunity to see their new signings in action. They impressed as Boro ran out comprehensive 3–0 winners.

The game also featured the introduction of Boro's new mascot, Roary the Lion, who was to prove a massive hit with the fans.

Meanwhile, the final piece in Robson's jigsaw was the arrival of Arsenal reserve goalkeeper Alan Miller for a fee of £425,000. Long-serving goalkeeper Stephen Pears missed the start of the season through injury, so Miller started the first game of the new campaign against Burnley as number one choice. At the time Robson said he believed Miller could go on to play for England.

Robson was never in much doubt as to who his first choice goalkeeper would be, recalling

'I'd decided early on that Alan was my number one goalkeeper because Pearsy was having a lot of problems with his calf, he was getting on and I thought I needed to pick my first team keeper.

'Alan had been in the situation at Arsenal where he had been number two behind David Seaman and I felt he needed to play all the time to get the best out of him. That's what made my mind up. I also knew at that point I would be releasing Pearsy at the end of the season because of his injury problems and his age.'

Over 23,000 packed into Ayresome for the Burnley game on a glorious afternoon, hoping to see the dawn of a golden era of football for Middlesbrough. Robson kept faith with the backbone of Lennie Lawrence's side and it was fitting that long-serving John Hendrie struck both goals as Boro cruised to a 2–0 victory.

'Neither I nor the team could have wished for a better start,' says Hendrie. 'The whole place was still buzzing because of Bryan Robson. Personally, I couldn't believe that he had come to Middlesbrough but Lennie had left him a good nucleus of players.'

Intriguingly, Hendrie reveals: 'I remember speaking to the chairman, Steve Gibson, at the end of the previous season after Lennie had gone. The players were flat but the chairman told me to mark his words that he would get the right man in.'

After the opening game, new skipper Nigel Pearson spoke about his new club.

'It's clear this club is going in the right direction and I can only see good times ahead as long as the team consistently produces the football we are capable of.'

However, he cautioned: 'With only one

promotion spot, it's going to be very difficult, but I'm sure we'll be one of the strongest teams in the First Division this season.'

Following the Burnley game, the visit of Premier League champions Manchester United for Clayton Blackmore's testimonial attracted a crowd of 20,000, who were privileged to witness some breathtaking goals from United striker Mark Hughes.

Blackmore was delighted with the response shown by the Teesside public, commenting: 'The fans have been absolutely fantastic and they have an important part to play by staying behind the team. The supporters haven't seen the best of this Middlesbrough side yet.'

Back in the league, Boro faced the long trip south to Southend United, where once again Hendrie was on the spot with another brace to sink the Shrimpers 2–0. Robson was pleased with the attitude shown by his players in the opening games: 'The club has had the habit in the past of failing to get the best results against the less glamorous sides but we have put that right here.'

Robson also played down speculation surrounding the possible signing of his former England team-mate Gary Lineker.

'I told Gary's agent to keep me in touch if he fancied another challenge when his contract with Grampus Eight was up in December. But that was about three months ago and I've heard nothing since.'

Robbo added: 'There's no reason why we shouldn't bring the world's biggest names to this club. With our new stadium we will be in a position to offer players as much as any other club. You've got to think big to be big.'

Former boss Bruce Rioch brought his highly-rated Bolton Wanderers side to Ayresome Park on the final Saturday in August for what many pundits were describing as a probable promotion clash. Prior to the Bolton game Boro had played a goalless draw with Italian side Piacenza in the Anglo-Italian Cup at Ayresome Park, and Robson blasted the whole concept of the competition.

'The game was disheartening for me, not because of the scoreline but for what I felt was a farcical performance by the Italian referee.'

Striker Paul Wilkinson was sent off for retaliation during the game.

Robbo added: 'I was advised the competition would be a waste of time, but I felt we had a good chance of winning it, while it would give me the opportunity to look at the fringe players. I am taking the competition seriously but what I've seen so far has been close to a farce.'

A diving Wilkinson header gave Boro all three points against Bolton, but it was a far from convincing display, though Robson's theory on building a sound base had already been proved right, as his defence was yet to be breached.

Derby County were another club which had set its stall out to win promotion to the lucrative Premier League, so Boro's mid-week clash with the Rams was certain to provide another very difficult game. Once again, the defence, marshalled impeccably by Pearson, proved too strong for Derby's attack, and it was Blackmore's first goal for his new club which left Boro sitting proudly on top of the table with a maximum twelve points.

Nothing emphasised the spirit in the dressing room more than the public show of strength and determination between manager and captain on the Baseball Ground pitch at the end of the game.

One of the chief beneficiaries of Robson's influence on and off the pitch was his fellow midfielder Jamie Pollock. Right from the start, he was delighted with Robson's appointment though he has words of consolation for Lawrence. 'Robbo coming to Middlesbrough was absolutely brilliant. To find someone like Bryan Robson was coming here confirmed that the club was going to go somewhere. It was a shame to see Lennie leave because he built the team but you can't argue this was a step up.'

Although some players were concerned for their futures, Pollock insists he was not.

'I'm not the type of player to worry about my place. If a player is better than me, then he's better than me and it's up to me to improve.

'Both Lennie and Bryan are very good at man-management, neither of them rant and rave. The little things don't matter, what's

Heading for victory: Paul Wilkinson dives between Bolton's former Boro defenders Alan Kernaghan (left) and Jimmy Phillips to score the only goal of the game against Bruce Rioch's Bolton in the 1994–95 season.

important is that you go out and perform on a Saturday. Where they differed, perhaps, was that Bryan wanted us to play more football, but then he had the players to do that while Lennie was often struggling for a team.'

Despite his good form in the early part of the season, Pollock admits his new, more defensive role alongside Robson did not come easily. 'I was used to playing with Robbie so it was strange getting used to playing with the gaffer. We were playing a very tight game which wasn't natural for me but the results showed that it worked.'

Alan Miller was finally beaten for the first time at Watford the following Saturday, when a deflected shot mid-way through the second half equalised Blackmore's first half strike, which left Boro with only a share of the spoils. Still, the point left Boro three points clear of the second-placed Swindon at the top of the table.

The game everyone had been waiting for

took place on 11 September, when mid-table Sunderland arrived at Ayresome Park for a 'live' televised derby game.

Before the game, Boro paraded to the fans their latest acquisition, Bolivian international Jaime Moreno. The 20-year-old cost Boro £250,000 after impressing on his debut in a pre-season friendly with Darlington when he scored two goals in a 3–0 victory. Robbo said: 'It will take Jaime a couple of weeks to settle in but I'm sure he will be of great, long-term benefit to the club.'

Meanwhile, the manager denied rumours that he was on the verge of signing Paul Gascoigne from Italian giants Lazio, despite the England international being at Boro's game with Watford.

'I can tell everyone now that it is all simply speculation,' he insisted. Robbo added that he was enjoying his combined career as player/manager: 'There's been nothing yet to suggest I change my view that I can

combine managing the team with playing.'

Mick Buxton's Sunderland side shocked everyone by going into a comfortable 2–0 lead at Ayresome Park, with both goals from Craig Russell, and it looked like Boro were about to suffer their first defeat of the season. That was until young Alan Moore showed a touch of a genius with twelve minutes remaining to reduce the arrears, before Pearson scored his first goal for the club two minutes later. There was still time for Hendrie to miss an amazing opportunity to turn the game on its head and give Boro all three points.

After the 2–2 draw, Robbo said: 'The game served as a timely reminder that, no matter what people say, Boro have no divine right to win every game. Our first half performance was our worst so far, but the lads showed great character in coming back, and I'm sure Sunderland were more relieved than us to hear the final whistle.'

After forty minutes of the next game against West Brom, it looked as if the bubble may have truly burst, when a stunning strike from the Baggies' Lee Ashcroft put Keith Burkinshaw's side ahead. Added to the goal, Boro had already suffered the trauma of losing Robbo through injury on thirteen minutes.

Robbie Mustoe replaced the manager and, three minutes before half-time, he drilled home a shot from the edge of the box to level the scores. On seventy-six minutes Pearson suffered a knee ligament injury which was to keep him out for several games.

Boro seemed to be heading for their third successive draw when, in the final minute, they were awarded a penalty which was competently converted by Craig Hignett, making his first appearance of the season.

Recalling the match, Hignett says: 'I was desperate to play by then. I'd had a really good pre-season and felt I should have been in the team from the start. It was very frustrating to be left out but when I got my chance I felt sharp, quick and enthusiastic. I'd changed from the previous season when I'd began to lose it a bit.'

Bolivian international Jaime Moreno, pictured after a reserve game with Sheffield Wednesday, brought his South American skills to Ayresome Park.

Pearson and Robson, two of the most influential players, were both missing for the trip to Port Vale but it didn't appear to be a problem as Boro took an early lead through Pollock, but despite dominating the game, they suffered their first defeat of the season due to two very unfortunate Vale goals. Alan Miller had also picked up an injury against West Brom and so Stephen Pears came in for his first game at Vale Park.

Scarborough provided the next opposition as Boro swapped the intensity of the league for a Coca-Cola Cup tie. The Seasiders were given an early exit from the competition, as Boro hammered them 8–2 over two legs, with Paul Wilkinson grabbing a hat-trick in the second.

Wilkinson had been leading scorer for the past few seasons, but was struggling to find the net with any regularity so he was pleased to see them go in against Scarborough. He recalls: 'It was nice to see them go in that night because I'd not been scoring too many. That was one of the few bright spots for me all season.'

Back in the league, Hendrie scored the only goal of the game as Boro inflicted a 1–0 defeat on Bristol City at Ashton Gate. Robson was delighted his side had got back to winning ways: 'We turned in a truly good team performance in the second half when we were solid defensively and created plenty of opportunities at the other end.'

Boro destroyed Mick McCarthy's highly rated Millwall side 3–0 with goals from Wilkinson, Hendrie and an own goal. Robbo was full of praise for his strikers: 'I believe Wilko's partnership with Hendrie gives us one of the best strike forces in the division.'

By now, Boro were flying and Jamie Pollock reflects: 'The confidence was sky-high. We had four or five new players in the squad and that had given everyone a boost so we were still on the crest of a wave.'

Boro followed up this game with a 1–1 draw with Cesena in the Anglo-Italian Cup with Jaime Moreno scoring his first goal for the club.

The win over Millwall gave Boro their best ever start to a season. They won seven and drew two of their opening ten league games, making them joint top of the division with Wolves,

many people's favourites for the one automatic promotion spot.

Tranmere provided the next hurdle and Boro really took the game to their fellow promotion-chasers at Ayresome Park. They constantly pressured the Birkenhead side, only to fall to a late sucker punch from Tranmere's mercurial striker, John Aldridge. John Hendrie was stunned by the defeat: 'We went in at the end of the game and thought "How did we lose that one?" but like any job you think to yourself it was just one of those days.'

After the hiccup against Tranmere, Boro travelled to Kenilworth Road to tackle David Pleat's Luton Town, where they were hammered 5–1 in a display that did nothing for the side's championship aspirations.

Robbo remains philosophical about the defeat: 'You get games like that when you look at the performance and you just know everybody had a bad day at the same time. You can't say too much because you know the players don't mean to play badly, so I don't tend to lose my temper, as there is nothing I can say to improve it. I get more annoyed when you draw a game you should have won and somebody gives a goal away. That's when I pinpoint them and lose my temper.'

After another draw in the Anglo-Italian Cup at Udinese, Boro were back in league action with the long trip to Portsmouth. The game was being played in front of a live television audience on a Sunday afternoon. Robbo made only three changes with Pears, Hignett and Wright being replaced by Miller, Todd and Moreno.

Hignett recalls: 'I wasn't happy about being dropped. I didn't play any worse than anyone else against Luton and, in fact, I'd been ill in bed the night before the game. But I got up in the morning, took some tablets and played.'

Boro tightened up at the back, but missed opportunities by Blackmore and Moreno meant Boro left Fratton Park with only one point.

They drew another blank at Aston Villa in the third round of the Coca-Cola Cup a few nights later as they suffered a 1–0 defeat when an Andy Townsend shot was deflected past Miller. However, it was a much improved

performance and the *Daily Express* wrote: 'The football that Robson has coached into Middlesbrough in his few months in charge at times outplayed Premiership Villa.'

Looking back at the Villa game Robbo said: 'In retrospect, we played some very good football and I was pleased with our overall performance. I certainly think we deserved to bring them back to Ayresome Park for a replay.'

It was at this time that the first sod was cut on the site of the club's yet-to-be-named new stadium.

Andy Collett joined Bristol Rovers on loan, while Robson looked forward to Boro's home clash with struggling Swindon with a warning for centre-backs Steve Vickers and Derek Whyte.

'Swindon are a good side, with Norwegian striker Jan-Aage Fjortoft the man who stands out. He did well in the Premiership last season and has made a good start this time around, so Steve Vickers and Derek Whyte will need to keep an eye on him.'

Boro saw off Swindon in a 3–1 victory with Neil Cox scoring his first goal for the club. They followed this with a 2–1 win over Oldham a few nights later which lifted Boro into second position behind Wolves.

A week later, Boro threw away a golden opportunity to go top of the table when they turned in a gutless display at Grimsby, going down 2–1. Robbo is very frank about the game: 'We were absolutely shocking in the first half and then to play the way we did in the second half showed that the lads' attitude wasn't right at the start of the game.

'They went into the game all slack, they under-rated the opposition and thought that, as we were going well, we'd win this game easily. They got a doing-and-a-half, Grimsby could have been four or five up at half-time, but what annoyed me more than anything was that in the second half we absolutely murdered Grimsby; it showed it was their attitude.

'If we're getting out-played by a better team I hold my hands up, but if we lose because of lack of application, I lose my temper. I wasn't very pleased with the performance at Grimsby and the table in the dressing room didn't think

it was very good either!'

Robbo fielded a young side for the trip to Ancona in the Anglo-Italian Cup, which saw them lose the game 3–1.

Alan Moore and Graham Kavanagh starred for the Republic of Ireland Under-21 side at St James' Park, Newcastle, with Pollock making a substitute appearance for England. November also saw the arrival of England goalkeeping coach Mike Kelly as full-time specialist coach to Boro's men between the posts.

On 20 November, Graham Taylor's Wolves visited Ayresome Park for a game that was billed as a clash of the titans. A packed Ayresome Park and mass TV audience saw Boro completely dominate and outplay the Black Country side in a thrilling 1–0 victory for the home side. Surprisingly, the only goal came from a Hendrie shot which took a wicked deflection to beat Mike Stowell in the Wolves goal, because Boro just kept opening up the Wolves defence at will to go back to the top of the table.

Central defender Steve Vickers remembers: 'Before the game there was a lot of apprehension but, at the end of the day, Wolves were lucky to get away with a 1–0 defeat.'

Craig Hignett, who hit the post and enjoyed an excellent game, adds: '1–0 didn't reflect the match, we could have had four or five.'

Jamie Pollock adds: 'It was a stunning performance. Having said that, Wolves were never in our class that year. We dictated the game from the first minute.'

Boro had hit a rich vein of form and confidence was sky high following the Wolves result as they made the trip to Charlton.

This game marked the return of skipper Pearson to the side, but it was top-scorer Hendrie and midfielder Pollock who were the heroes as the Boro ran out convincing 2–0 winners.

All the time, Robson was on the look out for new talent to add to his squad.

'I'd tried to buy Nick Barmby after I heard there was a bit of unrest at Tottenham. I just kept persevering with Nick all the time, saying that. I never really thought we would get him while we were in the First Division.'

One player who did join the ranks was non-league Arnold Town's hot-shot striker Chris Freestone, who was spotted by first team coach John Pickering.

Robbo was annoyed with press reports of a £500,000 bid from Ipswich Town for Vickers The boss said: 'It's an insult, the figure quoted may be enough for his right leg!'

Boro hit top form a week later against fourth from bottom Portsmouth, who were hammered 4–0 with two goals each from Wilkinson and Hignett. The *Sunday Express* wrote: 'In a one-sided match, Hignett scored two and set up one of Wilkinson's goals as Middlesbrough made themselves the team to catch in the Premiership race.'

Reading provided the mid-week opposition following the game with Portsmouth, and Boro came away with an excellent point against Mark McGhee's bright young side, though it could so easily have been three. Boro suffered their first sending off under Robson's tenure with the dismissal of Mustoe, though it didn't stop Wilkinson opening the scoring, only for the Royals to equalise in the final minute.

Peter Taylor's mid-table Southend side arrived at Ayresome Park in mid-December and a near 17,000 crowd expected to see them despatched in the same manner as Portsmouth. On this occasion, Southend showed a resilient spirit and shocked Boro with a 2–1 win, only the second home defeat of the season.

Manager Robson returned to the side for the trip to lowly Burnley and Boro were at full strength for the live televised game. In the previous two successful away performances, Robson had played with a back five, Pearson, Vickers and Whyte forming a central defensive trio. Boro were in outstanding form against a niggling Burnley side, with Robson enjoying his best game in a Boro shirt to date, completely dominating proceedings in the midfield while also supplying inch-perfect passes.

Robson's midfield partner Pollock recalls: 'You just need to look at the results when the gaffer played – I don't think we ever got beat – to know what his influence was like on the pitch. He put fear into the opposition players and gave confidence to our players. He was

always able to steady the boat when needed it.'

It was Hendrie who stole the headlines with an excellent hat-trick, taking his total for the campaign to thirteen.

On Boxing day, another tough away trip awaited Boro, in the shape of Dave Bassett's Sheffield United for a game which was predictably a ferocious battle.

Boro coped admirably with the Blades' physical style, yet fell behind to an unfortunate goal in the sixty-eighth minute. Hignett, who had been introduced as a forty-ninth minute substitute for the injured Hendrie fired Boro back on level terms in the seventy-third minute, and, had Wilkinson made sure of his last minute opportunity, all three points would have been Boro's.

Two nights later, Boro got out of jail against bottom-of-the-table Notts County after Gary McSwegan gave the Magpies an early lead. A recalled Hignett levelled again for Boro and skipper Pearson's glancing header put Boro in front. A far from convincing performance, it left Boro four points clear of Bolton Wanderers going into the game with Stoke City on New Year's Eve.

The downside of the Notts County win was the fractured collar-bone Neil Cox sustained which would keep him out for six weeks.

Vickers' headed goal earned Boro a point at the Victoria Ground to cap a fine first half of the season for Boro which satisfied the manager, who said: 'I've been pleased with the response of the players, fans and the whole area. Hopefully, 1995 will see us playing our football in the Premiership. If we were to miss out on promotion it would be disappointing but the new stadium gives us all plenty more to look forward to in 1995.'

The year began with an abandoned game against Barnsley due to a frozen pitch. It proved to be a particularly frustrating afternoon as the game was called off at half-time with Boro leading 2–1, as the conditions were no worse than at three o'clock.

Memories of Boro's famous 5–0 victory over Swansea City at the Vetch field in 1981 were evoked the following Saturday when Boro made the trip to South Wales for a tricky FA

Cup third round tie. It resulted in a 1–1 draw, thanks to a rare Moore header.

Before the replay, Boro were in action in another live televised Sunday game in Wiltshire against Swindon Town. A spectacular Hignett strike opened the scoring before a great Moore solo effort hit the post as Boro cruised through the early stages. They conceded a sloppy equaliser to the league's leading marksman Jan Fjortoft. Curtis Fleming needlessly got involved with Swindon's Luc Nijholt in the forty-first minute which resulted in the Republic of Ireland B international being dismissed. Swindon pressed harder in the second period and made sure of all three points with a goal from Kevin Taylor.

On the incident involving Fleming, a player who had greatly impressed the manager since his arrival at the club, Robson said: 'It was a bit harsh because Luc Nijholt made a meal of the incident, but Curtis should have known not to push him.

'Losing him meant we had to reorganise and play four across the back and the middle. That left us with a man short up front so we were always going to be up against it.'

Swansea arrived at Ayresome Park for the cup replay the following Wednesday. Only 13,940 fans turned up to witness Boro's poor cup record continue with a 2–1 defeat, therefore missing out on a glamour derby tie away to Newcastle United.

Going into Boro's home game with Brian Laws' Grimsby, Robson denied increased press speculation surrounding a move for Jan Fjortoft, while also ruling out any possibility of Pollock leaving for Premiership title-chasers Blackburn.

Boro were struggling for form and after Hignett missed a penalty, only a Mustoe goal four minutes from time gave Boro a share of the spoils, leaving them just two points clear of second-placed Wolves.

The lack of form was overshadowed by the post-match announcement of the arrival of former German under-21 international, Uwe Fuchs, on loan from Kaiserslautern until the end of the season.

Robbo recalls: 'I'd brought in Jaime from Bolivia and he was only a young lad who needed time to settle in. So Uwe came recommended by Tony Woodcock as he'd scored goals in the Bundesliga. We thought for a lease deal which would take him to the end of the season, he was worth the money, and we won the pools.'

Uwe was delighted with his new opportunity: 'It was a very exciting proposition, a new situation to me. With Jürgen Klinsmann doing so well at Tottenham, there was a lot of coverage on the English game in Germany.

'Anyway, I'd never been to England before, so I flew over for talks and I took in the Boro versus Grimsby match, where my first impressions were that the team was playing without a great deal of confidence after losing their top-of-the-table-position.'

Fuchs came on as a late substitute in a 1–0 home defeat by Reading a week later, without any time to stamp his authority on the game. TV's Gladiator Jet (Diane Youdale) made a half-time appearance, the first of many by the local-born Boro fan.

Still, Boro's odds were cut to 4/7 to win the league, while defender Derek Whyte said: 'We've spoken about our recent run of results in the dressing room and realise it can't go smoothly all of the time. We need a break like an own goal.

'Uwe Fuchs' reputation suggests he's a good player.'

The Reading result caused Boro to slip down to fifth position, though only one point behind the leaders. It was at this time that Robbo thought he'd added another foreigner to his ranks.

'I tried to sign Glenn Helder after going to watch him play. At the time I was getting lots of videos of foreign players sent to me, one of them Helder. I went to watch Arnhem play and I was quite impressed with the lad. He had good pace and quality, but Arsenal got on the trail. With all players abroad, you try to keep it quiet, but all the clubs get to know because the agents band them about.

'You can't blame anybody if a deal doesn't work because it is up to the player at the end

of the day, though he was very close to coming.'

There was good news for Pollock who celebrated his 21st birthday with his performance in the Football League's 3–2 success over their Italian counterparts in Southern Italy.

Fuchs made his full debut in a home game with Charlton Athletic, as Boro desperately tried to get back to winning ways. He didn't waste any time in endearing himself to the supporters, scoring a clever goal after only fifteen minutes for a 1–0 win.

Fuchs remembers: 'I struck up a great relationship with the crowd at Middlesbrough, and I think the main reason was that I scored in my first full game against Charlton. It helped give the team its confidence back, while it made me believe in myself.'

In the build-up to the Charlton game, top scorer Hendrie pledged his future to the club by signing a two-year extension to his contract taking him to the summer of 1997. The Scot said: 'You never know what's around the

corner, but I'd be happy to end my playing days with Boro.'

Boro went to Wolves three days later requiring nothing less than a victory from the highly charged atmosphere at Molineux.

The game provided a milestone for assistant manager Viv Anderson, who, at 38 years old, was named as a substitute.

Anderson didn't get the call at Wolves. He wasn't required as Boro kept up their fabulous record against the Black Country side with second half goals from Vickers and another from Fuchs, who had instantly established himself as a cult figure with Boro fans.

Playing in a new attacking role that night was Jamie Pollock, as Robson looked to cover for injuries. Pollock enjoyed an outstanding game and says: 'The role was very similar to the one Lennie Lawrence had me playing in front of Andy Peake and Robbie Mustoe the previous season. I absolutely loved it, playing just behind Uwe.'

Fuchs drew a blank in the next game, yet

Before Boro's vital 2–0 win at Wolves in February 1995, TV presenter Jimmy Greaves poses with mascots Roary (right) and Wolfie.

another live televised clash, this time at Millwall. Once again, Boro held firm at the back, making it three in succession, but they were unable to make the most of the attacking opportunities offered to them.

The big talking point of the game, however, was the gashed forehead manager Robson suffered, which needed several stitches. Rather than lose the impetus of their recent form, Robbo refused to withdraw himself from the home game with Bristol City. He wore a protective headband, as Boro attempted to close the gap on leaders Tranmere.

Before kick-off Boro found themselves in second place, three points behind John King's side but with two games in hand. Before the game, Miller received his Wilkinson Sword Goalkeeper Protector of the Month award from Gladiator Jet.

'It was great to win an award but it was an accolade for the whole defence,' says Miller. 'I felt I'd done well but the whole defence had been outstanding apart from the occasional blip.'

Fuchs was a man inspired against Bristol City, scoring a clinical hat-trick to take his total to five goals in three starts, though praise also had to be given to Moreno who had fed Fuchs superbly.

There were fears growing amongst fans that they may lose their new hero if Robbo didn't make Fuchs' move to the club permanent. Robbo said: 'I know that fans are concerned that by delaying a decision on Uwe we might miss out on him, but there is no chance of that happening, we can't lose him. There is no way his fee will become inflated by the goals he scores. We've already agreed a £500,000 fee and it's down in writing.

'There is no need for us to make a decision on Uwe until the end of the season. That is good for the club and for the player, because we want him to be sure he will be happy here.'

Robbo also denied growing speculation that he'd had a £1.5 million bid for Manchester United's Lee Sharpe turned down. 'If I thought I could get Sharpe for £2 million, I'd be on the phone to Alex Ferguson right now,' he said. 'His value is more like £4 million.'

Fuchs was back on the goal trail a few nights later as Boro brushed aside a resolute Watford side 2–0 at Ayresome Park, though Mustoe grabbed the headlines with a sensational long-range strike which he has since described as: 'the best of my career'.

Robson changed the team for the crunch game at Bolton, recalling fit again Hendrie, but the plan never worked. Finnish striker Mixu Paatelainen scored the only goal of the game in the fourteenth minute.

The result left Boro in second place, still three points behind Tranmere, but the mid-week rearranged game with Barnsley offered the opportunity of pole position. Moreno was recalled to the attack in place of Hendrie, and he obliged with his first league goal for the club. A goal from former Boro misfit Andy Payton on the hour gave Barnsley a share of the spoils.

Eighteen-year-old Keith O'Halloran was given a shock call-up to the first team for a home game with Derby County four days later after a series of excellent performances in the reserves. It turned out to be a rough debut for O'Halloran, playing at right-back, up against the Rams' experienced winger Paul Simpson.

Derby ran Boro ragged in the first half, with recently signed striker Lee Mills doing most of the damage, grabbing two goals as a shell-shocked Boro went into the dressing room at half-time 3–0 down. O'Halloran was substituted at half-time as Boro went in search of goals, which, to their credit, they got within ten minutes of the restart. Fuchs and Pollock put Boro right back in the picture. Referee Philip Wright turned down a strong penalty appeal, only for Marco Gabbiadini to hit straight back with a fourth for Derby. This left Boro's championship aspirations on a knife-edge with ten games remaining.

Robbo remembers the match vividly: 'The Derby game was well before the run-in. In a season you get a couple of games where you have a bad time and I'd class that as one of those.

'We were 3–0 down at half-time and just plain hopeless; then we came out for the second half and we deserved to have a penalty when it

was 3–2. If we'd got that penalty decision we'd have gone on to win the game.'

Jamie Pollock too has bitter memories of the defeat: 'We started the game poorly but at half-time we wondered what we were doing. We went in at half-time and the gaffer told us we had to pick ourselves up and go for it in the second half. Once we were back at 3–2, we were back in it, but we were punished heavily for mistakes that day.'

Sunderland presented the ideal opportunity to get back on track with the return derby match at Roker Park on an arctic Tuesday night. Robbo certainly had his men fired up, because they fought like tigers for every scrap. Mustoe even played on with a fractured cheekbone following a clash with Richard Ord.

It was fitting that the game's only goal came from the only Teessider in the Boro line-up, Pollock, a battling goal which epitomised his all-action style. Pollock celebrated joyously with Boro fans behind the goal. The promotion show was back on the road as they moved back to the top. For the unlucky Mustoe, it meant that the remainder of the season would be spent in the wings, thanks to the cheekbone injury.

Goal hero Pollock has joyous memories of the win, saying: 'Scoring the winner was great, especially as their fans had absolutely hammered me all night. It was up there with the highlights of my career. Robbie epitomised the spirit in the team in the way he carried on despite his eye injury.'

Mustoe reflects: 'Maybe my injury was a lucky omen because last time Boro had won promotion, I had been ruled out of the run-in too.'

In the build-up to transfer deadline day, there was increased speculation surrounding the arrival of new players at Ayresome Park. As the day dawned, it looked as if there would be no new arrivals for the run-in, but Bryan Robson's office was a hive of activity, which the manager described afterwards.

'It was my first experience of transfer deadline day as a manager and I can tell you it was a real eye-opener. My telephone is only just cooling down now – and I've had it in the fridge overnight!'

It proved to be a successful day's business for the manager. He broke Boro's transfer record when signing Swindon Town's Jan Fjortoft for £1.3 million and Phil Whelan from Ipswich Town for £300,000.

Looking back, Robbo describes the Fjortoft deal like this: 'I brought Jan Fjortoft in on deadline day because I thought he had that little bit of quality for the Premier League, while I also thought he would score us some important goals to get us promoted and give us a push at the end of the season.

'I'd made enquiries about Jan a month before the transfer deadline, but I'd given up on him at certain points after speaking to Steve McMahon, who just wasn't interested in doing business while they were still in the Coca-Cola Cup.

'Once I got to speak to Jan, it was a simple deal because he doesn't have an agent.'

One player who Robson missed out on was one of the Premier League's brightest young talents.

'I also offered £2 million for QPR's Trevor Sinclair, but Ray Wilkins said we could only have him for £3 million. I like Trevor, but I only had £2 million to spend and QPR were adamant they wanted three, so that was that.'

One player leaving Ayresome Park on deadline day was Boro's young goalkeeper, Andy Collett, who moved to Bristol Rovers in a permanent deal, after a successful loan spell, for £50,000.

While the season was developing, the new stadium was going up at a rapid pace. In March, former England captain Gary Lineker, in his role as presenter for BBC's *Grandstand*, attended the hugely popular visitors centre which had attracted thousands of fans a day to view 3D visuals of the stadium.

Fjortoft was on international duty with Norway when Port Vale visited Ayresome for another live televised Sunday game. Robbo broke his Boro duck with a stunning drive from outside the box to fire Boro into a fourteenth minute lead. Vickers increased the lead four minutes later, and a Fuchs goal in the second half gave Boro a 3–0 win.

Phil Whelan was also missing from the game

with Vale, due to a technicality with his transfer on deadline day which made him ineligible for the remainder of the campaign.

Fjortoft made his much anticipated debut on April Fool's day at West Bromwich's Hawthorns ground, but even bigger news was that of assistant manager, Viv Anderson, coming in as a replacement for the suspended Pearson, to make his debut. Hendrie made way for Fjortoft as Robson decided to pair the Norwegian captain with the in-form Fuchs to spearhead the attack.

In front of a large travelling support, Boro's first half display could only be described as disappointing, as they turned round 1–0 down. Robbo was desperate for victory against the club he began his career with and wasn't happy with the performance he was witnessing from his midfield berth.

'I decided to pull Alan Moore off when he did something which really annoyed me, so I shouted to John Pickering to get him off. Then a minute later he did this bit of magic, and set-up Jamie Pollock for the equaliser. I said "hold on a minute, leave him on", and he went on to score one and forced a defender into an own goal.'

Whyte was also picked out for special praise in the media after the game for his outstanding performance in his new role at left-back.

A trip to Oldham's Boundary Park for a rearranged mid-week game followed, and Fjortoft showed why he was the league's leading scorer when he unleashed a piledriver which flew against Paul Gerrard's bar.

Robson suffered a calf strain which was a bitter blow to the side, but not as much as a sickening cross-cum-shot which looped over Alan Miller in the final minute to give Oldham all three points.

Boro remained top of the table despite the defeat, with a four-point lead over Tranmere and Bolton, although the Birkenhead side had a game in hand, while Bruce Rioch's side would go top if they won their two games in reserve.

Paul Peschisolido gave Boro a fright when Stoke City visited Ayresome on 8 April. He equalised Pearson's early goal on the half-hour, and looked dangerous every time he moved into the penalty area. Moore, though, had found a rich vein of form, and it was he who showed another piece of genius in the seventieth minute to make sure of all three points.

Fuchs missed the Stoke game through injury, then found himself on the bench for the trip to bottom-of-the-table Notts County.

Thousands of Boro fans made the trip, filling one of the stands behind the goal, but it was Howard Kendall's side which seized the initiative, taking a second half lead. The travelling hordes were, by this time, in full voice and with their now infamous chant of "Uwe . . . Uwe . . .", demanding to see the introduction of their German hero.

Fuchs eventually replaced Bolivian international Moreno, and within minutes of entering the fray he latched on to a loose ball and slammed home a drive into the roof of the net. Incredible scenes of celebration followed with supporters and players mobbing Fuchs on the touchline.

In the end, a point couldn't be considered a successful return from a trip to the bottom club, though Boro retained top spot.

Fuchs and Fjortoft were teamed up for the arrival of in-form Sheffield United on Easter Monday, a clash which was over-publicised for all the wrong reasons.

Fjortoft gave Boro the lead with his first goal for the club in front of 23,225 fans, but United

The look says it all as Jamie Pollock points the way after scoring in a 3–1 win at WBA in April 1995.

1994–95 Match of the Season

30 April 1995

MIDDLESBROUGH 2 LUTON TOWN 1

Boro's penultimate game of the season – a crucial promotion match – also happened to be the final game in the ninety-two-year history of Ayresome Park.

There was intense publicity surrounding the game which was a complete sell-out, but Bryan Robson did his damndest to make sure the players were not caught up in the hype.

Boro went into the game with a three-point lead over second-placed Bolton, who had a game in hand, as did Tranmere and Wolves who were four and five points in arrears respectively. Boro were keen to avoid having to go to Tranmere on the final day of the season still requiring a point.

Robbo says: 'I remember speaking to Keith Lamb and saying I didn't want any of the lads caught up in the hype surrounding the game, and that's what happened.'

Sunday, 30 April turned out to be a barnstorming sunny afternoon with the majority of the crowd decked out in red and white to say farewell to the ground. Before the match, local-born soprano Suzannah Clarke gave a heart-thumping rendition of *You'll Never Walk Alone* with tremendous support from the crowd.

A trip into yesteryear followed when sixty Boro greats of the past paraded in front of the crowd, including Wilf Mannion, George Hardwick, Alan Peacock, Stuart Boam, Willie Maddren, Tony Mowbray and Bernie Slaven, who all received a fantastic reception.

Fans show their own way of congragulating Bryan Robson after the vital win against Luton Town that all but clinched promotion to the Premiership.

In the weeks building up to the game, supporters had been given the opportunity to vote for the name of the new stadium. They had been offered four choices after an initial poll of fans, and the choices were Erimus, Middlehaven, Teesside and Riverside. A giant envelope containing the name of the new stadium was torn open by the former players to unveil the name of Riverside to a crescendo of noise.

The first half proved to be a rather tense affair with Neil Cox missing a penalty. Just when it looked as if it was going to be one of those days, John Hendrie struck right on half-time to send the crowd wild with delight.

Luton were a different proposition in the second half and equalised through striker John Taylor – a Boro target during Lennie Lawrence's time in charge – mid-way through it, after some sloppy defending by Boro.

You could see the apprehension on the faces of the Boro supporters, but the players found a second wind and it was Hendrie who added a second, the last at Ayresome, following sterling work from Derek Whyte down the right hand side of the penalty area.

From that point on it was constant Boro as they carved out chance after chance, each of which went begging. But the day was Boro's and a 2–1 win was to all but clinch the First Division championship and promotion to the Premiership. Confirmation after the match of Tranmere's 5–1 away defeat gave another reason to celebrate.

Recalling the match, Robbo says: 'We had all our experienced players back for the game and that's why we won it.'

Goalscorer Hendrie adds: 'It was a fantastic feeling to score those two goals in such an important
(continued)

(continued)

match, especially because I hadn't been scoring for some time before that game. But we were well worth the win. As one of the longest-serving players in the team, the last match at Ayresome meant a lot to me but everyone concentrated on putting that out of their mind until after the game.'

Extremely emotional scenes followed after the final whistle. As the team did a lap of honour, fans celebrated with them, cheering them all the way. Some supporters stayed behind after the team had left the field, to cherish every last moment of their spiritual home.

soon equalised. The game degenerated into an ill-tempered affair with a series of bad tackles and off-the-ball tussles, which led to Fuchs being sent off for retaliation.

Another 1–1 draw was a disappointing outcome but the result was only of secondary importance, as Bryan Robson recalls: 'After the Sheffield United game, Dave Bassett called Jan and Uwe cheats, but that's what you expect from people like Dave who always come out with outrageous comments. It's just the way they are and it doesn't wind me up.

'Sheffield United were dirty on the day, and that's why Uwe took retribution. It's all part and parcel of the game. If people are knocking you about, you've got to stand up for yourself and that's what Uwe did.

'If you think you can intimidate players that's what you do, that's what Vinny Jones and Wimbledon have been doing for years. If you're weak enough to accept that, they'll intimidate you.

'You find people saying the First Division is harder than the Premier League. That's a load of rubbish, the Premier League is far harder. I found the First Division easier, with quickness

Queues snaked around Ayresome Park as fans clamoured for tickets for the last ever league game at the ground.

of thought and passing much easier.'

At this point Fuchs was unaware that he had made his final appearance for Boro in a competitive match, though he did admit that his partnership with Fjortoft hadn't really taken off.

'The signing of Jan Fjortoft didn't fill me with any apprehension as I'd been scoring goals and I felt my position was safe. In the end it wasn't easy for me to play alongside Jan because we were similar players. After his arrival, I scored just one more goal, but this didn't affect our relationship, which was fine.'

Torrential rain awaited the Boro hordes at Barnsley's Oakwell Ground where the away fans were massed on an open embankment. It provided a fascinating sight to see thousands of men huddled together in plastic raincoats which had been on sale outside the ground.

Fjortoft put Boro in front with a sensational curling shot, though again Robbo's men could not hold on to their lead and the game finished 1–1. Pollock was very unlucky not to add a goal when he slid in to force his shot against the underside of the bar.

After the game, Pollock was far from despondent with three successive draws: 'Barnsley is a hard place to go to, but we came back with a hard-earned point. Other teams are dropping points and we're feeling very confident. I'm sure the Luton game will be the one to look forward to.'

With hindsight, Pollock gives much of the credit to manager Robson, saying: 'We had led the league for so long but our nerves were starting to jangle as the other teams closed the gap. The gaffer steadied the boat and we picked up results. It was a strange feeling because we were drawing games and coming off the pitch feeling downhearted, but the gaffer was lifting our spirits and reminding us that it was a point gained not a point lost. He was always so calm.'

Despite the jubilant scenes after the final whistle against Luton a week later, the

Fans celebrate outside Ayresome Park after gathering to listen to radio reports of Bolton's draw at Stoke City. Bolton's failure to win the game meant Boro was promoted.

A beer-soaked Bryan Robson with celebrating Boro stars, John Hendrie, Neil Cox, Derek Whyte and Nigel Pearson.

championship still hung in the balance. Boro had one game at Tranmere remaining, but, should Bolton win their two remaining games, they would go up as champions if Boro slipped up.

Stoke provided Bolton's opposition at the Victoria Ground for a mid-week game, with thousands of Teessiders glued to their radios. The early news was good when Bolton's goalkeeper, Keith Branagan, was sent off for a professional foul, to be replaced by England great, Peter Shilton. Shilton's first job was to pick the ball out of the net from Toddy Orlygsson's resulting penalty kick. Bruce Rioch's side responded with an equaliser but that was all they could manage and Boro were champions!

The same evening, Tranmere were in action against Wolves, which was where Robson was, studying his next opponents. He remembers: 'I went to the Tranmere game with Steve Bruce and Viv. When I heard we'd gone up it was good stuff, Brucie was delighted for us. We had a great night in my local celebrating with our wives and a lot of people came back to my house.

'We continued the next day when we bought champagne for everyone at the club, but that's what all the hard work was about. I believe in the philosophy that you work hard and play hard.

'There were a few experienced managers

who criticised Middlesbrough when they took me on. A few people were waiting for me to fall flat on my face, so winning the championship at the first attempt gave me great satisfaction.'

Against Tranmere, Robson decided to blood some new talent from the reserve side which had done so well under Gordon McQueen in the Pontins League. Craig Liddle played the full game in midfield, while the reserves' goal machine, Chris Freestone, went on as a second half substitute. Boro fell behind on the stroke of half-time but they kept their shape and were rewarded with a second half goal from Fjortoft. More celebratory scenes followed to cap another excellent day in the club's progression.

The final league table was:

	P	W	D	L	F	A	Pts
Boro	46	23	13	10	67	40	82
Reading	46	23	10	13	58	44	79
Bolton	46	21	14	11	67	45	77
Wolves	46	21	13	12	77	61	76
Tranmere	46	22	10	14	67	58	76

The trip to Tranmere brings back good memories for Uwe Fuchs: 'I was sat in the main stand with Jamie Pollock and Alan Moore. There must have been around 5,000 Boro fans inside the ground, making a lot of noise. At half-time, as I was going to the toilet, I turned round to see a large group of supporters who began chanting my name when they recognised me – a really good memory.'

Two days after the Tranmere game, Robson asked Fuchs to call in his office at 5.00 p.m. the next day. Uwe recalls the situation graphically:

Supporters acknowledge Boro's promotion success during the final game at Tranmere's Prenton Park.

Cult hero Uwe Fuchs bids farewell to Middlesbrough fans after Stephen Pears' testimonial game.

'When I got there, Bryan told me to take a seat and began saying: "Uwe you've done a great job". That's when I knew I wasn't going to be signed by the club.

'He continued by saying: "I want to build a team here, spend a lot of money on players who have played at top European level."

'That's the way it was, I wasn't angry, and I still feel I could work with Bryan without any problems.

'However, I do believe I could have helped the team after they signed Nick Barmby and Juninho, though obviously my thoughts are hypothetical. Bryan didn't believe in me at Premier League level.'

On releasing Fuchs, Robson offers this theory: 'The fans turned round and asked what I was doing letting him go, but I think it was Uwe's level. I think he would have struggled in the Premier League, but that's only my opinion.

'It was a difficult decision because Uwe thought he could do it in the Premier League. He got on really well with all the boys and he's even been to see some of our games in the Premier League.

'He's a lovely lad but you can't let sentiment rule you in this game. I'm the manager and I've got to make decisions which are best for the club. It makes it a harder decision when fans write and tell you to sign him, but you've got to stick to your principles.

'He scored nine goals in thirteen games, which was a great strike record, but, at Millwall, he struggled to score a handful of goals in that league.

'I speak to my staff a lot, I don't like to make snap decisions, but I always felt that Uwe wouldn't be good enough for the Premier League and all my staff agreed with me.

'If we'd stayed in the First Division, I probably would have kept him for the challenge the following season.'

Long-serving goalkeeper Stephen Pears had been given a free transfer, but, before he departed, he was rewarded with a testimonial for his ten years of sterling service to the club.

Photographers surround captain Nigel Pearson as he holds aloft the Football League championship trophy.

The Endsleigh League First Division trophy was presented in front of almost 20,000 supporters before Pears' game against a Boro past side which included Bernie Slaven, Colin Cooper and Peter Beardsley as a guest. Pears had the pleasure of scoring the final goal ever at Ayresome Park, when he beat Alan Miller from the penalty spot, a fitting end for perhaps Boro's finest ever goalkeeper.

It was also an emotional night for Fuchs, as he received a standing ovation from the fans, who knew it would be the last time they would see him in a Boro shirt.

Fuchs says: 'I was fighting back the tears as the crowd were celebrating with all the players.

'Suddenly, though, they all began to shout my name which was a little embarrassing, but a marvellous way to say goodbye.'

Memories of that evening will live forever with those who attended the game. The most pleasing sight of the evening was that of skipper Nigel Pearson, arms aloft, with the trophy!

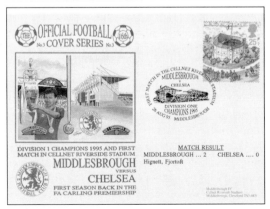

A first day cover envelope marking the First Division championship success and the move to the Cellnet Riverside Stadium.

CHAPTER THIRTEEN

Transforming Dreams into Reality – 1995–96

Stories abounded during the summer of 1995 that newly promoted Middlesbrough had £10 million available to spend on new players. It seemed an incredible sum of money for a club which had never spent more than £1.3 million on one player. But, within months, manager Bryan Robson was to spend the full £10 million on just two highly talented players.

Keen to ensure Boro had the class to compete with the very best in the Premier League, Robson drew up a list of top quality players who he believed may be available and who he felt would be a big asset to the club. It included Andrei Kanchelskis, Nick Barmby, Juninho and Ruud Gullit.

The prospect of Dutch superstar Gullit – a former European Footballer of the Year – joining Middlesbrough was an exciting one to say the least, but Robson admits it never got past the initial enquiry stage.

'When I heard that Gullit was available, I contacted his solicitor and enquired if he would be interested in coming to Middlesbrough,' he explains. 'I was given the message that, if he came to England, he would want to play in London. It didn't matter how big a club we were, he wanted to be based in London and that's why he signed for Chelsea.'

Boro's chase for Manchester United winger Kanchelskis, however, went way past that stage. Indeed, at one point, Robson was confident that the Russian international was on his way to Boro, having agreed to pay his former club £5 million.

'We came very close to signing Andrei,' he says. 'At one stage, I think it was even-Steven between ourselves and Everton, who he eventually joined. He is probably the best winger in Europe. He would have been a great buy so it was disappointing to miss out on him.

'I think his final decision was down to the fact that he didn't want to have to move house. Manchester's ice-hockey team has several Russian players, good friends of Andrei's, and he didn't really want to move away from the Manchester area. That's the way it goes sometimes.'

Kanchelskis wasn't his only target and, just four weeks before the season kicked off, Robson signed Tottenham's young England star Nick Barmby for £5.25 million. Barmby and goalkeeper Gary Walsh were the only new additions to the promotion-winning squad. Walsh signed from Manchester United for £250,000, with another £250,000 payable once he had made fifty appearances for the club. Behind the scenes, however, Robson was working hard to entice Brazilian star Juninho to the Cellnet Riverside Stadium.

Meanwhile, two players ended their spells with Middlesbrough – Stephen Pears and Andy Todd. Long-serving goalkeeper Pears joined Liverpool on a free transfer after enjoying his testimonial to mark ten years of loyal service with the club.

Explaining his decision to release Pears, Robson says: 'I felt Stephen was having a lot of injury problems and I knew Walsh was available. I wanted to build for the future and knew all about Walshy. His contract was up at United and I knew I had a good chance of signing him. He's a good goalkeeper but I made it quite clear that there was no guarantee of a first team place.' Initially reserve to Alan Miller,

BORO SMASH THEIR TRANSFER RECORD –
FOUR TIMES OVER!

The summer of 1995 saw Bryan Robson smash Boro's transfer record four times over with the £5.25 million signing of England international Nick Barmby from Tottenham.

Robson and Spurs chairman Alan Sugar had ran a public war of words in the press during negotiations for the player but Boro were the winners when the talented striker signed on the dotted line.

It was the first time in ninety years that Boro had signed a current England star – Steve Bloomer had been the last – and it finally proved the club was determined to reverse the trend of seeing top players leaving Teesside.

Boro's previous record transfer stood at £1.3 million for Jan Fjortoft but Robson was determined to get his man – even if it meant paying more than he thought Barmby was worth. 'It's my opinion that no player is worth that type of money,' says Robson. 'But the transfers of Andy Cole and Stan Collymore a few months earlier had pushed everyone's prices up. Although the fee was more than I wanted to pay, who's to say Barmby won't be worth twice that much in a few years.'

Of the signing, Robson says: 'Nick had impressed me when I saw him play for Tottenham's youth team a few years earlier and he looked very intelligent in the Spurs first team. I rate him among the top five young English players in the country, along with Jamie Redknapp, Steve McManaman, Robbie Fowler and Darren Anderton. In fact, he's probably in the top two of those.'

Hull-born Barmby was keen to return north after several years in London but insisted: 'The reason I joined Middlesbrough was because of Bryan Robson and the club's ambition. I knew the gaffer was a winner, always had been, and I knew he would be good for me. I didn't really have to think twice about the move.'

Walsh cost £500,000 from Robson's former club, Manchester United. 'I had no hesitation in signing,' he says. 'Robbo is the top man.'

Meanwhile, Todd made his extended loan spell with Bolton a permanent move when the two clubs agreed a fee of £500,000.

'Todd was a good young player but I was well covered for centre-backs and I felt Bolton made us a very good offer,' says Robson.

While striker Paul Wilkinson continued to look for a new club, midfielder Craig Hignett came off the transfer list after accepting a cut in his salary package. He was determined to earn a new deal with the club and Robson was willing to give him a chance.

'Craig wanted to prove that he could do it in the Premiership and showed just the sort of attitude I was looking for from my players,' adds Robson. 'All credit to him, he had a great start to the season after scoring a lot of goals in pre-season.'

Hignett still believed he had a lot to offer Boro and admits: 'I decided to stay because I wanted to prove the gaffer wrong. I told him that I didn't want to leave and would accept reduced terms to prove to him that I was good enough.'

Tipped as one of the pre-season relegation favourites by the London-based press, Robbo's boys opened their Premiership campaign at Highbury where former Boro manager Bruce Rioch paraded £13 million-worth of new talent in Dutch international Dennis Bergkamp and England captain David Platt. Boro were expected to be canon fodder for their more illustrious opponents but shook them by taking

the lead during the first half. Barmby, wearing Bryan Robson's favoured number seven shirt, started to pay back his huge transfer fee with a debut strike, coolly slotting the ball past David Seaman after great play by Robbie Mustoe and Jan Fjortoft.

Unfortunately, Boro held on to the lead for only a matter of minutes before Ian Wright headed home an equaliser. However, Alan Miller, making a return to his former club, was in outstanding form behind a rock-solid defence as Boro hung on for a 1–1 draw.

Afterwards, Robson said: 'That display is ample evidence that we are capable of finishing in mid-table this season, though achieving a European place would be the icing on the cake.'

Looking back on the match, he reflects: 'It was great for Nick to score in his first game, but the performance of the whole team was a confidence-booster. The nation's press had been

tipping us to go down but I was always confident we would do okay.'

A week later, Boro played their first game at the new Cellnet Riverside Stadium and the 2–0 success against Chelsea provided the perfect start at the club's new home. Next came the Tyne-Tees derby against Newcastle United – one of the big title favourites – and the defence hit new heights as it held out against a constant tide of attacks inspired by French winger David Ginola. Only minutes remained when United scored the game's only goal, Les Ferdinand heading in Ginola's left-wing cross.

However, Boro were denied what looked a certain penalty by referee Robbie Hart when Darren Peacock appeared to foul Jamie Pollock inside the penalty box in the final minute. Recalling the incident, Pollock says: 'It was a definite penalty. To be honest, there was no certainty of a goal if Peacock hadn't tackled me, but it was a foul – end of story.'

Far from downhearted, Boro were satisfied with their start and Nigel Pearson recalls: 'Those opening games boosted our confidence as the lads realised they had the ability to cope in the Premiership.'

With Miller ruled out through injury, Gary Walsh made his Boro debut between the sticks against Bolton Wanderers at Burnden Park on 9 September. However, Walsh was beaten by a superb long-distance chip from John McGinlay before Boro hit back to dominate the match. Bolton keeper Keith Branaghan made several astonishing saves before Hignett hit a deserved equaliser.

Jan Fjortoft remembers the spectacular effort that so nearly gave him a wonder goal that day but says: 'I was adapting to a new role where I was more of a provider than a goalscorer. But I felt my overall game was improving. Unfortunately, after a good start, things didn't go so well.'

Walsh kept a clean sheet on his home debut but Boro could not penetrate Southampton's defence in a goalless draw. The same ten outfield players took to the pitch for the sixth successive match to defeat Coventry 2–1 at the Riverside – Fjortoft and Vickers on target after Isiais had given the Sky Blues a shock lead.

Derek Whyte tussles with Arsenal's Denis Bergkamp in the opening day 1–1 draw at Highbury.

Flying high to head his first Premiership goal is Steve Vickers in the 2–1 win over Coventry City in September 1995.

Phil Whelan made his first Boro start six months after joining the club when Second Division Rotherham paid a visit to Teesside in the Coca-Cola Cup. Jaime Moreno was also in the starting line-up. However, Boro struggled to stamp their authority on the game and eventually scraped a 2–1 win, with the away leg still to play. Back to full strength in the league, Barmby netted the only goal of the match to clinch a first away win at rock-bottom Manchester City and send Boro into seventh spot.

Robbie Mustoe comments: 'At that point we were flying, though City were poor on the day. I hit the underside of the crossbar at Maine Road, so we could easily have won more comfortably.'

Then came a memorable 2–0 success over Premiership champions Blackburn Rovers at the Cellnet Riverside Stadium. Lookalikes Barmby and Hignett, nicknamed the Terrible Twins as a result of the excellent partnership

they were forging, were both on target in front of a crowd of 29,462, the biggest so far at the new stadium.

Robson recalls: 'That was a dominant performance. We stamped our authority on the whole game. At that point, some of the stuff Nick Barmby, Craig Hignett and Jan Fjortoft were playing was very exciting.'

Centre-back Vickers' second goal of the season sealed a 3–1 aggregate Coca-Cola Cup success over Rotherham, before a sixth straight win came courtesy of Hignett's penalty against Sheffield Wednesday at Hillsborough. Cock-a-hoop Boro were now in fourth place in the Premiership. Brazilian Footballer of the Year Juninho was all set to reinforce their challenge after agreeing to join them from Sao Paulo in a £4.75 million deal.

Despite the excellent team form, Jamie Pollock looks back on those opening games with mixed feelings. 'To be honest, Robbie Mustoe and myself found it very difficult

1995–96 Match of the Season

26 August 1995

MIDDLESBROUGH 2 CHELSEA 0

This was the first ever match at the Cellnet Riverside Stadium and those fans lucky enough to witness it will never forget it. On an emotional afternoon, Ayresome Park was forgotten as the club opened its doors on a new era at the state-of-the-art stadium.

In the days leading up to the game, there were still huge doubts over the safety certificate being awarded so the match could go ahead. Indeed, the green light was finally given only a day before at noon, much to the relief of everybody concerned.

Tickets were like gold dust on Teesside, as a crowd of 28,286 (Boro's highest home attendance for fourteen years) packed into the largest new stadium to be built in England for over fifty years. Chelsea's lack of support was the only reason for the game not being completely sold out.

On paper, it looked like a tough test for Robbo and his men, as Glenn Hoddle had added the international expertise of Ruud Gullit and Mark Hughes to his side during the summer.

The atmosphere was electric with excitement and anticipation as both sides walked out on to the immaculate pitch. Robson kept faith with the side which had played so well to earn a point at Highbury in the opening game, sticking with a back five formation.

Craig Hignett was the scorer of the first ever goal at the Cellnet Riverside Stadium.

From the start Boro showed they were really fired up for the encounter, with Nick Barmby and Hignett, buzzing around the pitch, and Robbie Mustoe winning almost every tackle in midfield.

Gullit was also to be admired. Playing in his role as sweeper, he majestically strolled forward to hit pin-point passes of unnerving accuracy.

On thirty-nine minutes, Barmby was sent clear on the left from a clever Jan Fjortoft flick. Barmby made his way into the Chelsea penalty area before unselfishly squaring the ball to the oncoming Craig Hignett who drove the ball into the top left-hand corner. Hignett had rubber-stamped his name into the record books by scoring the first ever goal at the new stadium.

The second half saw Chelsea go close on several occasions, with Hughes giving Boro supporters the biggest scare when he headed on to the bar.

However, Boro surged down the opposite end of the field on seventy-four minutes with more superb, free-flowing football. Again it was Barmby in the thick of the action, pulling the ball back across the face of the box for Fjortoft to cleverly steer the ball into the bottom left corner past the helpless Kharine.

That was the last of the goals, giving Boro a more than satisfactory start to their first season in their new home – a 2–0 win.

Goalscorer Hignett says: 'I told the press after the game that I closed my eyes and just hit the ball. I didn't close my eyes but the ball did take a bobble. It's good to know that I was the first ever goalscorer at the stadium. No matter what happens, no-one can ever take that away from me.'

After the game, midfield dynamo Robbie Mustoe said: 'The atmosphere at the Cellnet Riverside Stadium was excellent, it was very loud, particularly from the horseshoe.'

Chairman Steve Gibson was another who was delighted: 'We always felt the Teesside public would support an ambitious club, and it's been absolutely beyond our expectations.'

(continued)

(continued)

Of course, one of the major reasons Bryan Robson joined the club was the plans of the stadium, and he wasn't disappointed: 'Middlesbrough Football Club now has one of the best football stadiums in the whole country. One thing that struck me, was the way the structure of the stadium appeared to create a tremendous atmosphere. Certainly the players love it because that extra atmosphere can drive them on.'

Skipper Nigel Pearson admitted to having doubts about the game being played, but was extremely impressed with what he found: 'I think it's a fantastic stadium. Everyone was fairly surprised to see it was ready, considering how much work appeared to be outstanding when we made our first visit to the stadium a few days earlier. Without doubt, the atmosphere was tremendous.'

playing as a two-man midfield. Although there was a five-man defence behind us, the opposition were going straight past us. We were sacrificed for the team, which didn't exactly help our game, but we just got on with it.'

Hignett's penalty made it seven consecutive victories – five in the Premiership – at home to struggling QPR, though it could and should have been 2–0 as Fjortoft struck the bar with a second-half spot-kick. Even so, there was now real belief that Boro could challenge for a UEFA Cup spot, such was the confidence running throughout the club.

However, the wheels seemed to have fallen off the Boro bandwagon when they trailed 2–0 after only ten minutes against First Division Crystal Palace in the Coca-Cola Cup third round at Selhurst Park. Thankfully, two well-worked goals by Hignett – his fourth in five games – and Barmby clinched a 2–2 draw and a replay back on Teesside.

On that game, Gary Walsh reflects: 'I'm sure it was our magnificent team spirit which enabled us to claw our way back into that match. The spirit we had was very similar to Manchester United's.'

A visit to Old Trafford to take on Alex Ferguson's Manchester United saw Robson forced into his first outfield change for a league match. Whelan, who had also played against Palace, stepped in for the injured Whyte alongside Pearson and Vickers at the centre of the defence as 8,000 Middlesbrough fans, unable to buy a ticket for Old Trafford, watched the game on a big screen erected on the pitch at the Riverside. Alas, United appeared to lift their game after the dismissal of Roy Keane and went on to win 2–0, though

Boro had two good penalty claims turned down after apparent fouls on sub Moreno.

But Craig Hignett insists: 'I'm sure that if Boro's 8,000 had been at Old Trafford instead of 100 miles away, one of those penalty decisions would have gone our way.'

On 4 November, Juninho mania reached fever pitch. The little Brazilian made his Boro debut at home to Leeds United and took only minutes to set up Fjortoft for the opening goal. Juninho's superb run left several Leeds players in his wake before he unleashed an inch-perfect

Brazilian ace Juninho takes on a Leeds United defender on his Middlesbrough debut.

A TALE OF TWO STADIA

Just a year after the headline-grabbing arrival on Teesside of Bryan Robson came an even more incredible event in the history of Middlesbrough Football Club. After ninety-two years at Ayresome Park, the club moved to a fantastic new home on the outskirts of town. The Cellnet Riverside Stadium was born.

Though it took less than a year to build, the stadium only became reality after many months of negotiations, discussions and planning.

It was the Hillsborough Disaster during the 1989 FA Cup semi-final which was the catalyst to the dramatic move. In his resulting report, Lord Justice Taylor ruled that many of the lives lost on that fateful day could have been avoided if Hillsborough had been an all-seater stadium. Therefore, it was decided that all clubs in the top two divisions should have all-seater stadia in time for the start of the 1994–95 season.

Like every other club, Middlesbrough invested a great deal of time considering their options following the ruling. The obvious way forward was to develop Ayresome Park but it quickly became clear that a number of hurdles would need to be overcome to do so.

The club's chief executive Keith Lamb takes up the story. 'It became apparent that to turn Ayresome Park into a 30,000 capacity all-seater stadium would be expensive – about £9 million – and fraught with difficulties. Because of the way the ground was hemmed in by terraced housing, we would probably have had to double the height of the stands to re-develop it the way we wanted.

'In truth, to have any hope of gaining planning permission, we would have had to limit ourselves to a 20,000 capacity. It was plain that that would condemn Middlesbrough to the role of second class football club forever.'

Although a limited capacity was something former chairman Colin Henderson believed could work, his view was not shared by new chairman Steve Gibson, director George Cooke or Keith Lamb. Instead, they turned their attentions to the possibility of moving to a new home and opened discussions with Middlesbrough Council, who they had previously spoken to about developing Ayresome Park.

Research proved that an initial idea to develop an area close to Newport Bridge, known as Riverside Park, was not viable. Lamb recalls: 'We did discuss the possibility with the Teesside Development Corporation but it was a non-starter because it would have required the building of another bridge over the River Tees as the Newport Bridge already had traffic flow problems. The TDC then offered us Middlehaven.'

Middlehaven was largely an area of industrial wasteland close to the old Middlesbrough Docks. It was the TDC's

(continued)

An artist's impression of how Ayresome Park would have looked after a £9 million re-development.

Boro would have combined the old with the new if they had re-developed Ayresome Park.

(continued)

aim to develop it into an attractive leisure and retail park, including a centre for the Tall Ships, with the docks as the centre-piece. 'It was a chance to place the club at the centre of an attractive, up market environment,' says Lamb. 'It seemed to be a viable and attractive option for us.'

Lamb reflects: 'At the outset, there were sceptics at the TDC and the council who doubted that the football club could deliver its promise to build the sort of stadium we were talking about. Ironically, with the passage of time, it was to turn full circle and the other two parties were to become those who failed to deliver their promises.'

With the location agreed, the TDC helped to put the club in touch with a team of contractors. 'It was the role of the contractors to transform our "wish list" into reality,' says Lamb. At that stage, the contractors included Drivers Jonas as project managers, Ove Arup as structural engineers and Fletcher-Joseph as architects.

'We asked them to come up with a stadium design to hold 30,000 spectators to a budget of about £9 million,' reveals Lamb. 'They put the project out to tender to five different companies, asking them to price the project and produce any alternative proposals they had.'

'From those five tenders, we received fourteen alternative designs. One of them, from construction contractors Tilbury Douglas, architects the Miller Partnership and structural engineers Thorburn Colhoun was particularly attractive to us in terms of design and price. It was perfect, it seemed to capture exactly what we had in our minds.'

It was agreed that the club would go for this innovative design but, at the eleventh hour, the construction team demanded financial guarantees that the club was not prepared to make. Contractors Taylor Woodrow and engineers Ove Arup were invited to replace Tilbury Douglas and Thorburn and they immediately agreed to start work to the Miller Partnership's design.

Lamb reflects: 'The day I appointed Taylor Woodrow to build the stadium was the best day's work I have ever done. They were superb throughout and built the stadium astonishingly quickly.'

Due to alterations and improvements by the club to the stadium's concourses, bars and kiosks, the final cost of the stadium rose to £12 million. The work was funded by an £8 million medium term loan from the Dutch bank, ING, who later bought the collapsed Barings Bank, while the Football Trust provided another £3.25 million (the majority of which came as a grant).

The stadium itself, the biggest football stadium built in the UK for more than sixty years, was completed in time for the opening home game of the 1995–96 season against Chelsea.

By then it had been named the Cellnet Riverside Stadium, derived from the club's new sponsors, the mobile communications company Cellnet, and the name chosen by Middlesbrough supporters.

pass for Fjortoft to race on to and chip 'keeper John Lukic for what was later voted the club's goal of the season. Unfortunately, Boro seemed to run out of steam and were forced to settle for a 1–1 draw.

Robson recalls: 'It was a great through-ball for the goal from Juninho, but Jan still did well with his finish. Unfortunately, that game was also the start of all the injuries. We already had Whyte out while Robbie Mustoe picked up an injury against Leeds which kept him out for four months.'

With Juninho on international duty and Cox, Whyte, Barmby and Mustoe all injured, Robson was forced into wholesale changes for the replay against Crystal Palace at the Riverside. In came Moreno, Alan Moore and Robson himself – his first game of the season – while Craig Liddle continued to deputise for Cox at right-back. Although below strength, Boro proved too powerful for Palace, as Hignett and Fjortoft both found the net in a 2–0 win.

Neil Cox scored an early goal to send Boro on their way to a famous win over Liverpool in November 1995.

Full-back Chris Morris says: 'That was an important win at the time, because we'd let ourselves down with some sloppy defending in the original match. For once, the defence had the strikers to thank for getting them out of a hole.'

The versatile Liddle – a Northern League player with Blyth Spartans until a year earlier – was switched to midfield for a trip to Wimbledon, while 19-year-old Philip Stamp was called into action to replace the injured Hignett. However, the biggest talking point during a forgettable goalless draw was the midfield tussle between Juninho and the Dons' infamous hardman, Vinny Jones.

Boro dropped to ninth in the Premiership with a disappointing 1–0 home defeat by Tottenham, however they were back to set the Cellnet Riverside Stadium alight with a superb 2–1 victory over Liverpool four days later.

With Juninho in inspired form, Boro stormed into an early lead when Cox scored and went on to dominate the first half. Neil Ruddock equalised in the second half but within a minute Barmby had fired in a stunning winner to raise the roof of the Cellnet Riverside Stadium. Beating Liverpool was a special moment for me,' says Juninho. 'I had seen a lot of them on cable television and I admired them. That was a very good performance by Middlesbrough. I think English football is excellent and I knew then that I would enjoy myself.'

Unfortunately, they were unable to repeat their scintillating form in the Coca-Cola Cup fourth round against First Division Birmingham City. Juninho came closest to a goal in the 0–0 draw, striking the underside of the crossbar with a stunning free-kick.

An incredible start to a Premiership away game against QPR saw the home side miss an early penalty, and Barmby do likewise for Boro minutes later. However, Morris turned in the rebound to shoot Boro ahead with only his second goal for the club. Rangers hit back within minutes to grab a 1–1 draw.

Manchester City's brilliant Georgian star, Gheorge Kinkladze, lit up the Riverside on 9

TEESSIDE ROCKS TO A SAMBA BEAT

The date of 6 October 1995 is one which should go down in the history of Middlesbrough Football Club. It was the day the club completed the signing of Brazilian super star Juninho.

There was little doubt that it was the most audacious signing in the club's long history, even overshadowing the purchase of England star Nick Barmby some months earlier. But it took persistence and determination to ensure the club got its man.

Manager Bryan Robson first became aware of the little samba star – real name Oswaldo Giroldo Junior – during the 1995 Umbro Cup when Juninho shone for Brazil in games against Sweden, Japan and England. Robson, then Terry Venables' assistant with the England squad, was lost in admiration when the 22-year-old netted an astonishing free-kick in the 3–1 win over England at Wembley.

'I felt he would be a great acquisition for Middlesbrough,' says Robson. 'He had so much natural ability while it was clear he had great acceleration from a standing start.'

The Boro boss was already a fan of Brazilian football. Indeed, he had studied videos of Brazil's 1994 World Cup winners to see if any of their stars could fit into the Middlesbrough team. But it was Juninho, who had broken into the side only after the World Cup, who stood out.

Within weeks of seeing him play, Robson and Boro's chief executive Keith Lamb flew out to Brazil to open talks with Juninho's club, Sao Paulo.

'We arrived unannounced at the doors of their stadium,' recalls Lamb. 'We hadn't even told them we were going. We just jumped on a 'plane and set off to try and sign this player that, until a couple of weeks earlier, no-one had heard of.'

Robson and Lamb met representatives of the club and Juninho to establish an initial relationship. 'We had heard they might be interested in selling the player and we wanted to convince them we were serious,' explains Lamb. 'At first, they said there was no way they would sell him but they didn't want to upset us because they knew they might want to sell him one day. They were always very courteous to us.'

After three days, Robson flew home to England but Lamb remained in Sao Paulo and submitted a written offer for Juninho of $4.8 million (£3 million) on 29 June. Within hours, Sao Paulo replied in writing that they were not interested in selling their prize asset.

Undeterred, Lamb upped the bid on his return to England to $5 million. Six days later, on 13 July, Sao Paulo again replied in writing, insisting they were 'not interested' in selling Juninho and adding 'please don't insist any more'.

Things were put on hold as Juninho starred in the South America Championships but, in early October, the club heard that Sao Paulo had had a change of heart and were now ready to sell.

Once again, Robson and Lamb flew out to Brazil and began five days of negotiations, culminating in Juninho's transfer to Middlesbrough for $7.5 million (£4.75 million).

Lamb recalls: 'We clinched the deal in spite of the fact that Arsenal had said they were prepared to beat any offer by Middlesbrough.'

It was sweet revenge for Boro who been gazumped by Arsenal the previous season when the Gunners had signed Dutch international Glenn Helder after Boro had agreed terms with the player.

December when he opened the scoring with a stunning individual effort, but City were eventually beaten 4–1 by an inspired onslaught. Barmby scored twice and Juninho netted his first for the club. The best strike was scored by Stamp – just turned 20 – who netted a marvellous individual goal.

Says Stamp: 'That was a fantastic match for me. It was one of those goals which you dream of but, in truth, I was just happy to play.'

Whyte was dismissed for a second bookable offence in a 1–0 defeat against Blackburn at Ewood Park – Curtis Fleming making his first start. A big setback came with a shock 2–0 Coca-Cola Cup replay defeat against Birmingham at St Andrews, Kevin Francis netting both first half goals after Boro had given the ball away.

That disappointment was overcome by an excellent 4–2 hammering of West Ham United at the Riverside two days before Christmas. Juninho, playing his finest game for the club, was the inspiration. He played a part in three first half goals scored by Fjortoft, Cox and Morris, while fit again John Hendrie scored his first of the season in the second half.

'It's exciting to play with Juninho when he's in that form,' remarks Hendrie. 'But it was great for me just to play after all my injuries. I injured my groin pre-season in Norway and was filling the role that Craig Hignett ended up filling. It was terribly disappointing to miss the first game at the Riverside and it was stop-start from then on.'

Although fifth in the table, Boro knew they could go second if they won at Goodison Park on Boxing day. A disastrous 4–0 mauling ended such thoughts. It was the first time the defence had been run ragged in the Premiership, but there was worse to come. This was the start of a crippling injury crisis that completely over-stretched the first team squad.

'That was the start of our run of defeats but the scoreline itself was a one-off,' insists Robson. 'Our preparation for the match was far from ideal because we forgot to bring our kit and had to have it sent specially. That certainly didn't help our performance that day.'

Whyte, Fjortoft and Morris were all ruled

Jan Fjortoft was one of the many players sidelined during the club's injury crisis.

out of the visit to Nottingham Forest, where a Stuart Pearce penalty resulted in a 1–0 defeat, while five of the first choice players were missing for a 2–0 home defeat by Aston Villa on New Year's day.

The FA Cup campaign got underway at Notts County as Robson became the oldest player to appear for the club, aged 39. The tie also saw striker Paul Wilkinson make a surprise return to the side twelve months after starting his last first-team game. Available for transfer, Wilkinson was recalled to help out during the injury crisis and played a part in goals for Pollock and Barmby in a 2–1 victory.

Meanwhile, the tabloid press were running stories suggesting Juninho and his family were struggling to settle on Teesside. Looking back, Juninho reflects: 'Some of the things which were written were rubbish, they were not true, and I was upset by what was said. They said I was shocked by the cold and that it got dark at four o'clock in winter. I couldn't believe that

people would want to write such things and I was concerned that Middlesbrough fans might believe the stories. Of course I missed Brazil, but I had my family with me and friends came to visit. At the same time, Middlesbrough supporters made me feel very welcome.'

There were more injuries for a home clash against Arsenal but Boro let a 2–1 lead slip and eventually lost 3–2 despite some excellent first half play. Juninho scored his second for the club while Stamp asserted his increasing stature as a player of great potential with another excellent goal.

A fifth straight league defeat came at Southampton, despite an opening strike from Barmby, his ninth of the season. The 2–1 loss could easily have been far worse but for some outstanding goalkeeping from Walsh. However, things did get far worse with a visit to Stamford Bridge to take on Ruud Gullit and co, as a fired-up Chelsea side crashed in five goals without reply. It was certainly an unfortunate game for Keith O'Halloran to make his first appearance of the season.

Robson was naturally disappointed with such a heavy defeat but says he refused to be too downhearted.

'I knew it was down to injuries. The squad was at full stretch and we were down to only four or five of the first choice players. The injuries we suffered were incredible. I've never known anything like it in all my time in football. It was strange because one week we'd have four or five defenders injured, the next they'd be fit but four or five midfielders would be out. No club could cope with that week in and week out. We kept thinking everyone would be back soon but it just went on and on.'

Turning their attentions to the FA Cup, Boro were unable to find a way past Wimbledon's resolute defence at the Riverside, though it was clearly a relief to keep a clean sheet after conceding ten goals in the previous three games. Watching from the stands that evening was Brazilian World Cup winner, Branco, who was in talks with the club over a possible move to Teesside.

Despite the bad run, young Boro players Phil Stamp, Craig Liddle and Ben Roberts all signed new contracts with the club, with Robson explaining: 'In the past this club has lost too many of its top young players, but we are determined to keep them here from now on.'

Boro tried to stop the rot against Premiership leaders Newcastle United on 10 February and appeared to be heading for a famous win when John Beresford turned Juninho's cross into his own net in the first half. Alas, despite dominating the game, Boro's injury-blighted line-up was unable to hold on to the lead and eventually succumbed 2–1 when Walsh allowed a tame Ferdinand shot to trickle under his body.

On the run of defeats, Jamie Pollock says: 'We just weren't performing well at the time. We had the injuries but things clearly weren't right.

'Against Wimbledon, we played well but still lost. That was worse because we tortured them and still didn't win.'

There was yet another defeat as Wimbledon won the FA Cup replay by a 1–0 scoreline, but supporters were confident that the losing run would end with the visit of rock-bottom Bolton Wanderers to the Cellnet Riverside Stadium. They were wrong. Colin Todd's side, without an away win all season, ran riot to win 4–1 and Bolton fans sang the mocking question: 'Can we play you every week?'

Robbo grimaces when he remembers that game.

'We got off to a slack start, got back in it, then gave away a schoolboy goal before making another error. It was a bit of a shambles but we got punished for making the sort of mistakes you just can't afford to make.'

The run of eight straight league defeats had now equalled the club's worst ever run, set under Bob Dennison's management more than forty years earlier. Despite more injuries, however, a ninth defeat was avoided with a battling goalless draw at Coventry as Graham Kavanagh made his first start of the season after a terrible run of injuries.

In a bid to stem the tide, Robson signed Branco – full name Claudio Ibraim Vaz Leal – a Brazilian international, who had played more

than eighty times for Brazil including the 1994 World Cup final win. Branco, who owned his own contract and was a free transfer, lacked fitness but Robson was confident he would prove an excellent asset to the first team squad.

He says: 'I receive faxes all the time about players who are available or who might be interested in playing in England. As soon as his agent let me know that Branco was available, I was interested, especially on a free transfer. He could have gone to Japan or America and made a lot more money but he wanted to come to Middlesbrough.'

Supporters and players alike drew a huge sigh of relief that the run of defeats had ended, but there was more misery to come. First, Everton were 2–0 winners on Teesside; defender Michael Barron played his first league game for more than two years, while new signing Branco came off the substitutes bench to come agonisingly close to netting a debut goal with a rocket-like shot. Before then, however, Moore had been dismissed.

Next, a first minute error by Walsh let Ian Dowie in to set West Ham United on the way to a 2–0 win at Upton Park. Juninho, just back from helping Brazil qualify for the forthcoming Olympics, was a substitute along with his compatriot Branco but neither could swing the game Boro's way. Boro had now lost ten of their last eleven Premiership games, dropping from a potential second to thirteenth along the way over a three-month period. There were even concerns among the fans that relegation could follow.

'I didn't need to say anything to Gary about his mistake,' admits Robson. 'He knew what he had done – and I think it's fair to say he won't do it again!'

A welcome point came when Mustoe's equaliser secured a 1–1 home draw with Nottingham Forest. In that game, Boro became the first English team to play two Brazilians in their starting line-up. Another point followed in a goalless stalemate against Aston Villa, who were preparing to take part in the Coca-Cola

Despite a downturn in form, supporters were determind to enjoy the 1995–96 campaign, with Cellnet Happy Hands one of the features of the season.

Cup final against Leeds United.

'It was a relief to break the sequence against Forest,' says Robson. 'It would have been nice to get out there myself but I thought Branco helped us with his composure on the ball in the centre of the midfield. The lads had become a bit anxious and, in some ways, were trying too hard to get a result and were running into daft positions.'

By now, however, there were rumours circulating that Nick Barmby was wanting to leave the club less than a year after his £5.25 million move to Teesside. The rumours proved to be true when Barmby moved to Everton for a fee of £5.75 million only fourteen months after joining Boro. The move followed a frustrating start to the season for the England International who had struggled to link-up with Boro's international superstars.

Out of the team for the Forest match was Craig Hignett, who remarks: 'I was really sick to be out of the team because I felt I deserved to be in it. Sometimes it felt like I was being made to blame for the defeats. But it was clear that Juninho and Nick Barmby were the gaffer's choices ahead of me.'

A first league win in more than three months, and the first of any sort in just less than three months, came with a battling 1–0 win at beaten Coca-Cola Cup finalists Leeds United. Graham Kavanagh kept his cool from the spot after Barmby had been brought down by Lucas Radebe. Boro were let off the hook by a penalty miss from United's Gary McAllister and should have won more comfortably as defender Radebe spent the whole of the second half in goal in place of the injured John Lukic.

John Hendrie, who played against his old club at Elland Road just a day after his wife had given birth to a baby boy, remarks: 'After such a forgettable season on a personal level, it was great to go to Leeds and get one over on Howard Wilkinson who had released me. I was voted Boro's player of the month for March and it was great to know that Bryan Robson had picked me for the award.'

Looking back on the horrendous run of results, Robson says: 'Sometimes you do get depressed when result after result is going against you, but one thing that bad run did was show me the character and resilience of some of the lads. It was a good learning process for me, too. You've got to work hard for what you get out of this game and perhaps it all came a bit too easy at the start of the season.

'But for the injuries, though, I'm sure we could have kept up our early season form and it's quite possible that we could have qualified for the UEFA Cup.'

A second straight success followed a week later, on 5 April, when Sheffield Wednesday were comfortably beaten 3–1 at the Riverside. Miller returned in goal for the injured Walsh and the recalled Fjortoft struck twice – his first goals of 1996 – while reserve team striker Chris Freestone also netted in his first start. Freestone, a bargain £15,000 signing from Arnold Town, had been a prolific goalscorer for the club's reserve team for the last two seasons. He was a popular debutant among the fans but the real shock of the day came with the substitute appearance of youth team striker

Defender Curtis Fleming scored his long-awaited first goal for the club against Wimbledon late in the 1995–96 season.

Andrew Campbell, two weeks short of his seventeenth birthday!

Campbell, a star of the future, recalls: 'Playing for Boro was a dream come true. I've been a Boro fan all my life so it was just brilliant.'

Goalscorer Freestone added: 'It was the best day of my life. Scoring the goal crowned a brilliant day, a day I'd been waiting so long for.'

The following Saturday, Whelan scored his first goal for the club in a 1–1 draw at Tottenham, as yet another youngster, midfielder Mark Summerbell, enjoyed an excellent first team debut as an early substitute for the injured Mustoe.

Summerbell says: 'I was disappointed not to score, but it was unforgettable to play in such a big game.'

Curtis Fleming was celebrating on 13 April when he scored his first first team goal for Boro, after more than 150 appearances for the club. It was all in vain as Wimbledon ran out 2–1 winners.

In the final away match, Ian Rush bade farewell to Anfield as Stan Collymore's goal gave Liverpool a 1–0 win, though Cox was unlucky to see his late attempt come back off the post. It was a game which saw Campbell, now seventeen, make his first full start.

All that was left was one last match at the Cellnet Riverside Stadium, and it would decide who won the Premiership title. Robson's former club, Manchester United, needed only a draw to clinch the championship but a Boro victory would open the door for neighbours Newcastle if they could defeat Tottenham at St James' Park. Walsh returned in goal to face his former club but he was beaten three times by a powerful United side which ran out comfortable 3–0 winners to clinch the title in style.

So the Premiership trophy was presented at the Cellnet Riverside Stadium in the ground's first season – but it was Manchester United who received it. Perhaps, one day, it may be Middlesbrough.

CHAPTER FOURTEEN

Where do we go from Here?

In ten quite remarkable years, Middlesbrough Football Club has risen from the ashes of liquidation to the pinnacle of British football – from Doom to Boom. And yet, there is still so much further the club can go. With chairman Steve Gibson and manager Bryan Robson at the helm, there is little that Boro cannot achieve.

The feeling about the club's mid-table placing on their return to the Premiership was one of satisfaction rather than delight. It is time Middlesbrough won a major honour – and Gibson and Robson believe that will happen soon.

'The first honour will come. It is just a matter of when, not if,' insists Gibson. 'In

Chief executive Keith Lamb pictured with Nigel Pearson has been with the club throughout the majority of the last 10 years.

football, much depends on luck but we are putting together a team that will enable us to compete with the very best clubs in this country and, ultimately, Europe.'

Chief executive Keith Lamb goes further, saying: 'Something Colin Henderson once said to me sticks in my mind. He said that every football club has four vital ingredients – the fans, the players, the manager and the chairman. Well, throughout its history Middlesbrough Football Club has never been able to get all four right at the same time but, if ever we did, we would really take off. I think that for the last two years we have seen that to be the case.'

Since the end of the 1995–96 campaign, the club has continued to take huge strides forward. While the previous years of mediocrity have finally been left behind with the physical demolition of Ayresome Park, Bryan Robson has continued to strengthen the club's playing staff with the arrival of three top internationals. Fabrizio Ravanelli, Emerson and Mikkel Beck could all be stars of Middlesbrough's first trophy-winning team.

Emerson was the first of the trio to sign for the club, making a £4 million switch from Portuguese giants Porto shortly after the season had ended in May 1996. A Brazilian by birth, midfielder Emerson was an unknown quantity among English football fans but was soon to make a huge impact in the Premiership. The 24-year-old had been chased by many top clubs including Sampdoria, Fiorentina, Roma and Inter Milan but he chose Middlesbrough.

'I did not know anything about Middlesbrough before they came in for me but

Brazilian Emerson made an immediate impact in English Football.

signings. There were stories linking the club with Jürgen Klinsmann, Dion Dublin, Gabriel Batistuta and Gianluca Vialli. Indeed, Robson insisted he was interested in any top player who was available. The club met Vialli and his agent but the Italian star chose to sign for Chelsea instead. Batistuta's club, Fiorentina, were also contacted but insisted the Argentinian striker was not for sale.

But the breakthrough eventually came, and it followed months of negotiations by Robson and Lamb. The new player was Italian striker Fabrizio Ravanelli, who had scored for Juventus in the European Champions Cup final against Ajax in May. He cost Boro a new club record £7 million but Robson insisted he had got a bargain.

'I could have looked at Alan Shearer or Robbie Fowler but, even if their clubs had been willing to sell, how much would we have had to pay? Certainly a lot more than £7 million,' he explains. 'Just look how much Newcastle paid for Shearer. I'm confident Fabrizio will prove to be a real bargain.'

The club had opened talks with Juventus the previous Christmas when they had been told in no uncertain terms that Ravanelli was not for sale. But Robson persevered and, with Lamb, kept in regular contact with the Italian giants.

Steve Gibson reveals: 'Ravanelli was always our first choice striker, though Bryan short-listed others who would fit the bill. When we finally got Juventus to quote a figure, it was £12 million. We had no intention of paying that sort

as soon as I spoke to Bryan Robson I knew how ambitious he was,' explains Emerson, whose full name is Emerson Moises Costa. 'It was an exciting prospect to help them win a major honour, something they have never done before. At the same time, I spoke to Branco in Rio and it was clear how promising things are at Middlesbrough. We can go a long way.'

Robson was delighted to get Emerson, especially as the player's manager at Porto, former England boss Bobby Robson, did not want to sell the player. 'Bobby wasn't happy about losing Emerson,' admits the Boro manager. 'That will come as no surprise to anyone who has seen him play. Emerson has added real class to the team. He is a great ball winner, has strength and can pass the ball well. He wants to win a place in the Brazil squad and he has every chance of doing so while playing alongside Juninho.'

Robson promised Boro fans more top

Pictured at the press conference to announce his signing, Italian striker Fabrizio Ravanelli joined the club for £7 million.

With the arrival of Emerson and Ravanelli, Juninho's form early in the 1996–97 season was better than ever.

of money but the very fact they quoted a fee told us they would sell if we could agree on a price. Bryan persevered and his efforts finally paid off when we managed to agree a fee of £7 million. We were delighted with that.'

Ravanelli, initially upset that Juventus had agreed to sell him, soon changed his mind. 'There was a time when I thought I would always be with Juventus but it was not to be. Now I realise what a good move coming to Middlesbrough is for me. The ambitions and dreams of the club were a big selling point for me when I met Bryan Robson. They are determined to go forward, as is proved by signing players like Emerson and Juninho.

'I have been set the challenge of helping Middlesbrough win its first major honour. That is something which excites me. The club is aching for success. Of course, I feel pressure but that is something I am used to. Every year at Juventus we were expected to win trophies. But if I can play a part in helping Middlesbrough win something, I think that will be even more

Mikkel Beck was Boro's third signing during the summer of 1996.

rewarding. The flavour of the win will be more tasty!'

Boro signed a third international when Denmark striker Mikkel Beck joined the club from German Second Division side Fortuna Cologne. A complicated legal wrangle meant he was not available to play in Boro's early Premiership games but he is seen as an important player of the future.

Boro fans took all three players to their hearts immediately, with both Ravanelli and Emerson excelling on the Premiership stage at the start of the 1996–97 campaign. The Italian star hit a stunning hat-trick on his debut in a 3–3 draw with Liverpool at the Cellnet Riverside Stadium. No wonder he says: 'I think I will enjoy English football.'

The stage is set for another quite incredible decade in the life of Middlesbrough Football Club. Supporters will hope that the next ten years will be just as exciting as the last ten, but hopefully the ride will be more Boom than Doom.

APPENDIX 1
FIXTURES AUGUST 1985– MAY 1996
1985–86
Division 2

Date	Opposition		Result	Scorers	1	2	3	4	5
17. 8.85	Wimbledon	(a)	0 3		Pears	Laws	Corden*	Pallister	Mowbray
24. 8.85	Fulham	(h)	1 0	Stephens	Pears	Laws	Ward	McAndrew	Mowbray
27. 8.85	Charlton A	(a)	0 2		Pears	Laws	Ward	McAndrew	Mowbray
31. 8.85	Brighton & HA	(h)	0 1		Pears	Laws	Ward*	McAndrew	Mowbray
7. 9.85	Hull City	(a)	0 0		Pears	Laws	Heard	McAndrew	Mowbray
10. 9.85	Stoke City	(h)	1 1	Rowell	Pears	Laws	Heard	McAndrew	Mowbray
14. 9.85	Norwich City	(h)	1 1	Rowell (pen)	Pears	Laws	Heard	McAndrew	Mowbray
21. 9.85	Sheff Utd	(a)	1 0	Rowell	Pears	Laws	Heard	McAndrew	Mowbray
28. 9.85	Barnsley	(h)	0 0		Pears	Laws	Heard	McAndrew	Mowbray
5.10.85	Crystal Palace	(h)	0 2		Pears	Laws	Heard	McAndrew	Mowbray*
12.10.85	Leeds Utd	(a)	0 1		Pears	Laws	Heard	McAndrew	Mowbray
19.10.85	Bradford City	(h)	1 1	Slaven	Pears	Laws	Heard	McAndrew	O'Riordan
22.10.85	Sunderland	(a)	0 1		Pears	Laws	Heard	McAndrew	O'Riordan
26.10.85	Grimsby Town	(a)	2 3	Stephens, Laws	Pears	Laws	Heard	McAndrew	O'Riordan
2.11.85	Blackburn Rov	(h)	0 0		Pears	Laws	Heard	McAndrew	O'Riordan
16.11.85	Oldham A	(h)	3 2	Currie, Heard, Rowell	Pears	Laws	Heard	McAndrew	O'Riordan
23.11.85	Millwall	(a)	0 3		Pears	Laws	Heard	McAndrew	O'Riordan
30.11.85	Shrewsbury	(h)	3 1	Rowell, Heard, McAndrew	Pears	Laws	McAndrew	Mowbray	O'Riordan
7.12.85	Stoke City	(a)	2 3	Stephens, O'Riordan	Pears	Laws	McAndrew	Mowbray	O'Riordan
14.12.85	Wimbledon	(h)	1 0	Mowbray	Pears	Laws	McAndrew	Mowbray	O'Riordan
21.12.85	Fulham	(a)	3 0	Slaven, Rowell 2	Pears	Laws	McAndrew	Mowbray	O'Riordan
26.12.85	Carlisle Utd	(a)	0 1		Pears	Laws	McAndrew	Mowbray	O'Riordan
28.12.85	Sunderland	(h)	2 0	Mowbray, McAndrew	Pears	Laws	McAndrew	Mowbray	O'Riordan
1. 1.86	Huddersfield	(h)	0 1		Pears	Laws	McAndrew	Mowbray	O'Riordan
11. 1.86	Norwich City	(a)	0 2		Pears	Laws	McAndrew	Mowbray	O'Riordan
18. 1.86	Brighton & HA	(a)	3 3	Rowell 2, Slaven	McManus	Laws	McAndrew	Nattrass	O'Riordan
25. 1.86	Portsmouth	(a)	0 1		McManus	Laws	McAndrew	Mowbray	O'Riordan
1. 2.86	Charlton A	(h)	1 3	Rowell (pen)	Pears	Laws	McAndrew	Mowbray	O'Riordan
4. 3.86	Grimsby Town	(h)	3 1	Slaven 2, Mowbray	Pears	Laws	Nattrass	Mowbray	O'Riordan
8. 3.86	Crystal Palace	(a)	1 2	Slaven	Pears	Laws	Nattrass	Mowbray	O'Riordan*
15. 3.86	Leeds Utd	(h)	2 2	Currie 2	Pears	Laws	Nattrass	Mowbray	O'Riordan
18. 3.86	Sheff Utd	(h)	1 2	O'Riordan	Pears	Laws	Nattrass	Mowbray	O'Riordan
22. 3.86	Hull City	(h)	1 2	Currie	Pears	Laws	Nattrass	Mowbray	O'Riordan
25. 3.86	Barnsley	(a)	0 0		Pears	Laws	Nattrass	Mowbray	O'Riordan
29. 3.86	Huddersfield T	(a)	3 0	Hamilton 2, Slaven	Pears	Laws	Nattrass	Mowbray	O'Riordan
31. 3.86	Carlisle Utd	(h)	1 3	Hamilton	Pears	Laws	Nattrass	Mowbray	O'Riordan
5. 4.86	Blackburn Rov	(a)	1 0	Hamilton	Pears	Laws	McAndrew	Mowbray	O'Riordan
12. 4.86	Portsmouth	(h)	1 0	Mowbray	Pears	Laws	McAndrew	Mowbray	O'Riordan
19. 4.86	Oldham A	(a)	0 1		Kite	Laws	McAndrew	Mowbray	O'Riordan*
23. 4.86	Bradford	(a)*	1 2	Oliver (og)	Kite	Laws	McAndrew	Mowbray	Gill
26. 4.86	Millwall	(h)	3 0	Beagrie, Slaven (pen), Laws	Pears	Laws	McAndrew	Mowbray	O'Riordan
3. 5.86	Shrewsbury	(a)	1 2	Stephens	Pears	Laws	McAndrew	Mowbray	O'Riordan

Played at Leeds Road, Huddersfield, due to fire damage at Valley Parade

1985–86
Division 2

6	7	8	9	10	11	12	Crowd
Nattrass	Roberts	O'Riordan	Stephens	McAndrew	Rowell	Currie	2,844
Beagrie	**Hamilton**	**O'Riordan**	**Stephens**	**Rowell**	**Currie***	**Kernaghan**	5,368
Beagrie	Hamilton	O'Riordan	Stephens	Rowell	Kernaghan*	Currie	4,045
Heard	**Hamilton**	**O'Riordan**	**Stephens**	**Rowell**	**Beagrie**	**Kernaghan**	5,520
Beagrie	Gill	O'Riordan	Stephens	Rowell	Currie*	Kernaghan	7,710
Beagrie	**Gill**	**O'Riordan**	**Stephens**	**Rowell**	**Currie**		4,189
Nattrass	**Gill***	**O'Riordan**	**Stephens**	**Rowell**	**Beagrie**	**Cook**	5,462
Nattrass	Hamilton	O'Riordan	Stephens	Rowell	Beagrie		10,535
Nattrass	**Hamilton**	**O'Riordan**	**Stephens**	**Rowell**	**Beagrie***	**Cook**	5,572
Nattrass	**Hamilton**	**O'Riordan**	**Kernaghan**	**Rowell**	**Beagrie**	**Cook**	4,991
Nattrass	Hamilton	O'Riordan	Slaven	Stephens	Beagrie*	Currie	14,095
Nattrass	**Hamilton**	**Cook**	**Slaven**	**Currie**	**Beagrie**		6,130
Nattrass	Hamilton	Cook*	Slaven	Stephens	Currie	Beagrie	20,541
Nattrass	Hamilton	Cook*	Slaven	Stephens	Currie	Beagrie	4,378
Nattrass	Hamilton	Beagrie	Slaven	Stephens	Currie		5,140
Pallister	**Beagrie***	**Hamilton**	**Slaven**	**Rowell**	**Currie**		4,234
Pallister	Beagrie	Hamilton	Slaven	Rowell	Currie	Stephens	3,188
Pallister	**Hamilton**	**Heard**	**Slaven**	**Stephens**	**Rowell**		4,061
Pallister	Hamilton	Heard	Slaven	Stephens	Rowell*	Currie	7,646
Pallister	**Hamilton**	**Heard**	**Slaven**	**Stephens**	**Rowell**		4,531
Pallister	Hamilton	Heard	Slaven	Stephens	Rowell		3,513
Pallister	Hamilton	Heard	Slaven	Stephens	Rowell		4,238
Pallister	**Hamilton**	**Heard**	**Slaven**	**Stephens**	**Rowell**		19,701
Pallister	**Hamilton**	**Heard**	**Slaven**	**Stephens**	**Rowell**		8,487
Pallister	Hamilton	Heard	Slaven	Stephens	Rowell		13,050
Pallister	Hamilton	Heard	Slaven	Stephens	Rowell		10,098
Pallister	Hamilton	Heard	Slaven	Stephens	Rowell		10,768
Pallister*	Hamilton	Heard	Slaven	Stephens	Rowell	Beagrie	4,465
Pallister	**Slaven**	**Gill**	**Currie**	**Rowell**	**Beagrie**		4,412
Pallister	Slaven	Gill	Currie	Rowell	Beagrie	Cooper	4,863
Pallister	**Slaven**	**Gill**	**Currie**	**Rowell**	**Beagrie**		6,899
Pallister	**Slaven**	**Gill***	**Currie**	**Rowell**	**Beagrie**	**Cooper**	5,736
Pallister	**Slaven**	**Gill**	**Currie**	**Cooper***	**Beagrie**	**Ripley**	6,227
Pallister	Slaven	Ripley	Currie	Cooper	Hamilton		3,827
Pallister	Slaven	Cooper	Currie	Hamilton	Ripley		5,585
Pallister	**Slaven***	**Cooper**	**Currie**	**Hamilton**	**Ripley**	**Beagrie**	7,603
Pallister	Slaven	Ripley	Currie	Cooper	Hamilton		4,049
Pallister	**Ripley**	**Cooper**	**Slaven**	**Currie**	**Hamilton**		7,188
Pallister	Ripley	Cooper	Slaven	Currie	Hamilton	Kernaghan	4,193
Pallister	Slaven	Cooper	Hamilton	Currie	Ripley*	Stephens	3,426
Pallister	**Slaven**	**Cooper***	**Stephens**	**Hamilton**	**Beagrie**	**Turnbull**	5,484
Pallister	Slaven	Turnbull*	Stephens	Hamilton	Beagrie	Currie	6,695

1985–86

FA Cup

Date	Opposition		Result	Scorers	1	2	3	4	5
13. 1.86	Southampton	(h)	1 3	O'Riordan	Pears	Laws	McAndrew	Nattrass	O'Riordan

League Cup

20. 8.85	Mansfield	(a)	0 2		Pears	Laws	Ward	McAndrew	Mowbray
3. 9.85	Mansfield	(h)	4 4	Pollard (og), Currie, Rowell 2 (1 pen)	Pears	Laws	Ward	McAndrew	Mowbray

Full Members Cup

8.10.85	Carlisle United	(h)	2 0	O'Riordan, Saunders (og)	Pears	Laws	Heard	McAndrew	Mowbray
5.11.85	Hull City	(a)	1 3*	Slaven	Pears	Laws	Heard	McAndrew*	O'Riordan

*After extra time

1986–87
Division 3

Date	Opposition		Result	Scorers	1	2	3	4	5
23. 8.86	Port Vale	(h)*	2 2	Stephens 2	Pears	Laws	Cooper	Mowbray	Gill
30. 8.86	Wigan A	(a)	2 0	Turnbull, Mowbray	Pears	Laws	Cooper	Mowbray	Parkinson
6. 9.86	Bury	(h)	3 1	Stephens 2, Slaven	Pears	Laws	Cooper	Mowbray	Parkinson
13. 9.86	Gillingham	(a)	0 0		Pears	Laws	Cooper	Mowbray	Parkinson
17. 9.86	Bristol Rov	(a)	2 1	Slaven 2	Pears	Laws	Cooper	Mowbray	Parkinson
20. 9.86	Chesterfield	(h)	2 0	Mowbray, Laws	Pears	Laws	Cooper	Mowbray	Parkinson
27. 9.86	Fulham	(a)	2 2	Laws, Hamilton	Pears	Laws	Cooper	Mowbray	Parkinson
30. 9.86	Swindon T	(h)	1 0	Laws	Pears	Laws	Cooper	Mowbray	Parkinson
4.10.86	Rotherham	(a)	4 1	Stephens 2, Laws 2	Pears	Laws	Cooper	Mowbray	Parkinson
11.10.86	Blackpool	(h)	1 3	Stephens	Pears	Laws	Cooper	Mowbray	Parkinson
18.10.86	Walsall	(h)	3 1	Stephens 2, Laws	Pears	Laws	Cooper	Mowbray	Parkinson
21.10.86	Notts County	(a)	0 1		Pears	Laws	Cooper	Mowbray	Parkinson
25.10.86	Bristol City	(a)	2 2	Slaven, Laws	Pears	Laws	Cooper	Mowbray	Parkinson
1.11.86	Bournemouth	(h)	4 0	Stephens, Slaven, Hamilton, Ripley	Pears	Laws	Cooper	Mowbray	Parkinson
4.11.86	Bolton Wand	(h)	0 0		Pears	Laws	Cooper	Mowbray	Parkinson
8.11.86	Darlington	(a)	1 0	Stephens	Pears	Laws	Cooper	Mowbray	Parkinson
22.11.86	Newport County	(a)	1 0	Mowbray	Pears	Laws	Cooper	Mowbray	Parkinson
29.11.86	Chester C	(h)	1 2	Slaven	Pears	Laws	Cooper	Mowbray	Parkinson
13.12.86	Doncaster Rov	(h)	1 0	Mowbray	Pears	Laws	Cooper	Mowbray	Parkinson
21.12.86	Brentford	(a)	1 0	Slaven	Pears	Laws	Cooper	Mowbray	Parkinson
26.12.86	Carlisle Utd	(h)	1 0	Gill	Pears	Laws	Cooper	Mowbray	Parkinson
27.12.86	Mansfield T	(a)	1 1	Proudlock	Pears	Laws	Cooper	Mowbray	Parkinson
1. 1.87	York City	(a)	1 3	Mowbray	Pears	Laws	Cooper	Mowbray	Parkinson
3. 1.87	Newport County	(h)	2 0	Gill, Stephens	Pears	Laws	Cooper	Mowbray	Parkinson
24. 1.87	Bury	(a)	3 0	Slaven 2, Laws (pen)	Pears	Laws	Cooper	Mowbray	Parkinson
7. 2.87	Bristol Rov	(h)	1 0	Ripley	Pears	Laws*	Cooper	Mowbray	Parkinson
14. 2.87	Chesterfield	(a)	1 2	Slaven	Pears	Hamilton	Cooper	Mowbray	Parkinson
17. 2.87	Port Vale	(a)	0 0		Pears	Hamilton	Cooper	Mowbray	Parkinson
21. 2.87	Fulham	(h)	3 0	Slaven, Hamilton 2	Pears	Hamilton	Cooper	Mowbray	Parkinson
28. 2.87	Swindon T	(a)	0 1		Pears	Hamilton	Cooper	Mowbray	Parkinson
3. 3.87	Bournemouth	(a)	1 3	Slaven	Pears	Hamilton	Cooper	Mowbray	Parkinson

1985–86

FA Cup

6	7	8	9	10	11	12	Crowd	
Pallister	Hamilton	Heard	Slaven	Stephens*	Rowell	Currie	12,703	Round 3

League Cup

Pallister	Roberts*	O'Riordan	Stephens	Rowell	Currie	Kernaghan	3,179	Round 1/1
Beagrie	Hamilton*	O'Riordan	Kernaghan	Rowell	Currie	Stephens	4,051	Round 1/2

Full Members Cup

Nattrass	Hamilton	O'Riordan	Currie	Rowell*	Beagrie	Cook	2,177	
Hamilton	Turnbull**	Currie	Slaven	Kernaghan	Cook	Cooper,Beagrie	3,637	Northern Area s/f

1986–87
Division 3

Parkinson	Slaven	Stephens	Hamilton	Kernaghan*	Ripley	Turnbull	3,690	
Pallister	Slaven	Turnbull	Hamilton	Gill	Ripley		2,904	
Pallister	Slaven	Stephens	Hamilton	Gill	Ripley		6,499	
Pallister	Slaven	Stephens	Hamilton	Gill	Ripley		4,888	
Pallister	Slaven	Stephens	Hamilton	Gill	Ripley		3,768	
Pallister	Slaven*	Stephens	Hamilton	Gill	Ripley	Turnbull	7,633	
Pallister	Slaven	Stephens	Hamilton	Gill	Ripley		3,852	
Pallister	Slaven	Stephens	Hamilton	Gill	Ripley		9,221	
Pallister	Slaven	Stephens	Hamilton	Gill	Ripley		4,321	
Pallister	Slaven*	Stephens	Hamilton	Gill	Ripley	Kernaghan	11,470	
Pallister	Slaven	Stephens	Hamilton	Gill	Ripley		8,349	
Pallister	Slaven	Stephens	Hamilton	Gill	Ripley*	Turnbull	4,405	
Pallister	Slaven	Stephens	Hamilton	Gill	Ripley		8,800	
Pallister	Slaven	Stephens	Hamilton	Gill*	Ripley	Turnbull	10,702	
Pallister	Slaven	Stephens	Hamilton*	Gill	Ripley	Turnbull	10,092	
Pallister	Slaven	Stephens	Kernaghan	Gill	Ripley		9,947	
Pallister	Slaven	Stephens	Kernaghan*	Gill	Ripley	Hamilton	2,788	
Pallister	Slaven	Stephens	Kernaghan	Gill*	Ripley	Hamilton	9,376	
Pallister	Slaven	Stephens	Hamilton	Gill	Proudlock		8,100	
Pallister	Slaven	Stephens*	Hamilton	Gill	Ripley	Proudlock	5,504	
Pallister	Slaven	Stephens	Hamilton	Gill	Ripley		14,216	
Pallister	Slaven	Proudlock*	Hamilton	Gill	Ripley	Coyle	5,042	
Pallister	Slaven	Stephens	Hamilton	Gill	Ripley		8,611	
Pallister	Slaven	Stephens	Hamilton	Gill	Ripley		9,595	
Pallister	Slaven	Stephens	Kerr	Gill	Ripley		3,485	
Pallister	Slaven	Stephens	Kerr	Gill	Ripley	Kernaghan	9,610	
Pallister	Slaven	Stephens	Kerr	Gill	Ripley		4,085	
Pallister	Slaven	Stephens	Kerr	Gill	Ripley		3,263	
Pallister	Slaven	Stephens	Kerr	Gill	Ripley		9,361	
Pallister	Slaven	Stephens	Kerr	Kernaghan	Ripley		11,341	
Pallister*	Slaven	Stephens	Kerr	Kernaghan	Hodgson	Ripley	13,835	

1986–87

Division 3

Date	Opposition		Result	Scorers	1	2	3	4	5
7. 3.87	Bristol City	(h)	1 0	Mowbray	Pears	Coyle	Cooper	Mowbray	Parkinson
14. 3.87	Walsall	(a)	0 1		Pears	Hamilton	Cooper	Mowbray	Parkinson
17. 3.87	Notts County	(h)	2 0	Stephens, Slaven	Pears	Kernaghan	Cooper	Mowbray	Parkinson
21. 3.87	Blackpool	(a)	1 0	Stephens	Pears	Kernaghan*	Cooper	Mowbray	Parkinson
28. 3.87	Rotherham	(h)	0 0		Pears	Kernaghan*	Cooper	Mowbray	Parkinson
5. 4.87	Darlington	(h)	1 1	Slaven	Pears	Spriggs	Cooper	Mowbray	Parkinson
11. 4.87	Bolton Wand.	(a)	1 0	Slaven	Pears	Spriggs	Cooper	Mowbray	Parkinson
18. 4.87	York City	(h)	3 1	Ripley, Stephens, Turnbull	Pears	Spriggs*	Cooper	Mowbray	Parkinson
20. 4.87	Carlisle Utd	(h)	1 0	Pallister	Pears	Hamilton	Cooper	Mowbray	Parkinson
25. 4.87	Brentford	(h)	2 0	Slaven, Turnbull	Pears	Hamilton	Cooper	Mowbray	Parkinson
28. 4.87	Gillingham	(h)	3 0	Stephens, Slaven, Turnbull	Pears	Hamilton	Cooper	Mowbray	Parkinson
2. 5.87	Chester City	(a)	2 1	Mowbray, Hamilton	Pears	Hamilton	Cooper	Mowbray	Parkinson
4. 5.87	Mansfield T	(h)	1 0	Hamilton (pen)	Pears	Hamilton	Cooper	Mowbray	Parkinson
6. 5.87	Wigan A	(h)	0 0		Pears	Hamilton	Cooper	Mowbray	Parkinson
9. 5.87	Doncaster Rov	(a)	2 0	Hamilton, Ripley	Pears	Gill	Cooper	Mowbray	Parkinson

* Played at Victoria Ground, Hartlepool

FA Cup

15.11.86	Blackpool	(h)	3 0	Slaven 3	Pears	Laws	Cooper	Mowbray	Parkinson
7.12.86	Notts County	(a)	1 0	Hamilton	Pears	Laws	Cooper	Mowbray	Parkinson
10. 1.87	Preston NE	(h)	0 1		Pears	Laws*	Cooper	Mowbray	Parkinson

League Cup

26. 8.86	Hartlepool Utd	(a)	1 1	Slaven	Pears	Laws	Cooper	Mowbray	Parkinson
2. 9.86	Hartlepool Utd	(h)	2 0	Ripley, Hamilton	Pears	Laws	Cooper	Mowbray	Parkinson
23. 9.86	Birmingham C	(h)	2 2	Stephens, Ripley	Pears	Laws	Cooper	Mowbray	Parkinson
7.10.86	Birmingham C	(a)*	2 3	Laws 2 (1 pen)	Pears	Laws	Cooper	Mowbray	Parkinson

*After extra-time

Freight Rover Trophy

24.11.86	Doncaster Rov	(h)	3 0	Proudlock 2, Turnbull	Pears	Laws	Cooper	Mowbray	Parkinson
2.12.86	Chesterfield	(a)	1 2	Stephens	Pears	Laws	Cooper	Mowbray	Parkinson
21. 1.87	Halifax Town	(a)	2 1	Kernaghan, Ripley	Pears	Kernaghan	Cooper	Mowbray	Parkinson
10. 3.87	Rochdale	(a)	0 0*		Pears	Kernaghan*	Cooper	Mowbray	Parkinson
10. 3.87	Mansfield Town	(h)	0 1		Pears	Coyle*	Cooper	Mowbray	Parkinson

*Middlesbrough won 4 3 on penalties from Stephens, Cooper, Slaven, Hamilton

1987–88

Division 2

15. 8.87	Millwall	(h)	1 1	Stephens	Pears	Glover	Cooper	Mowbray	Parkinson
22. 8.87	Stoke City	(a)	0 1		Pears	Glover	Cooper	Mowbray	Parkinson
29. 8.87	Oldham A	(h)	1 0	Slaven	Pears	Glover	Cooper	Mowbray	Parkinson
1. 9.87	Crystal Palace	(a)	1 3	Slaven	Pears	Gill	Cooper	Mowbray	Parkinson
5. 9.87	Swindon T	(h)	2 3	Stephens, Slaven	Pears	Gill*	Cooper	Mowbray	Parkinson

1986–87

Division 3

6	7	8	9	10	11	12	Crowd	
Kernaghan	Slaven	Stephens	Hamilton	Gill	Hodgson		10,220	
Pallister	Slaven	Stephens*	Kerr	Gill	Ripley	Kernaghan	7,332	
Pallister	Slaven	Stephens	Kerr	Hamilton	Ripley		9,845	
Pallister	Slaven	Stephens	Kerr	Hamilton	Ripley	Gill	7,132	
Pallister	Slaven	Stephens	Kerr	Hamilton	Ripley	Gill	9,569	
Pallister	Slaven	Stephens	Hamilton	Gill	Ripley		11,969	
Pallister	Slaven	Stephens	Hamilton	Kerr	Ripley		5,858	
Pallister	Slaven	Stephens	Hamilton	Kerr	Ripley	Turnbull	10,546	
Pallister	Slaven	Stephens	Turnbull	Kerr	Ripley		5,993	
Pallister	Slaven	Stephens	Turnbull	Kerr	Ripley		9,942	
Pallister	Slaven*	Stephens	Turnbull	Kerr	Ripley	Coyle	11,937	
Pallister	Slaven	Stephens	Turnbull	Kerr	Ripley		3,788	
Pallister	Slaven	Stephens	Turnbull*	Kerr	Ripley	Gill	13,545	
Pallister	Slaven	Stephens	Turnbull	Kerr	Ripley		18,523	
Pallister	Slaven	Stephens	Hamilton*	Kerr	Ripley	Turnbull	3,556	

FA Cup

6	7	8	9	10	11	12	Crowd	
Pallister	Slaven	Stephens	Kernaghan	Gill	Ripley		11,205	Round 1
Pallister	Slaven	Stephens	Hamilton	Gill	Ripley		7,415	Round 2
Pallister	Slaven	Kerr**	Hamilton	Gill	Ripley	Coyle*/Kernaghan*	15,458	Round 3

League Cup

6	7	8	9	10	11	12	Crowd	
Gill	Slaven	Stephens	Hamilton	Rowell*	Ripley	Kernaghan	2,356	Round 1/1
Pallister	Slaven	Stephens*	Hamilton	Gill	Ripley	Turnbull	7,735	Round 1/2
Pallister	Slaven	Stephens	Hamilton	Gill	Ripley		9,412	Round 2/1
Pallister	Slaven	Stephens	Hamilton	Gill*	Ripley	Kernaghan	4,978	Round 2/2

Freight Rover Trophy

6	7	8	9	10	11	12	Crowd	
Pallister	Slaven*	Proudlock	Hamilton**	Gill	Ripley	Turnbull*/ Kernaghan**	3,977	prelim round
Pallister	Slaven	Stephens	Hamilton	Gill	Ripley		1,764	prelim round
Pallister	Slaven	Kerr	Hamilton	Gill	Ripley		1,411	round 1
Pallister	Slaven	Stephens	Kerr	Gill	Ripley**	Coyle**/ Hamilton**	2,615	round 2
Kernaghan	Slaven	Stephens	Hamilton	Gill	Hodgson**	Kerr*/Ripley*	11,754	area semi-final

1987–88

Division 2

6	7	8	9	10	11	12	Crowd
Pallister	Slaven	Stephens	Hamilton	Kerr	Ripley		11,471
Pallister	Slaven	Stephens	Hamilton*	Kerr	Ripley	Kernaghan	9,345
Pallister	Slaven	Stephens	Hamilton	Kerr	Ripley*	Kernaghan	10,551
Pallister	Slaven	Stephens	Hamilton	Kerr	Ripley		6,671
Pallister	Slaven	Stephens	Hamilton	Kerr	Ripley**	Kernaghan*/Proudlock**	9,344

1987–88

Division 2

Date	Opposition		Result	Scorers	1	2	3	4	5
8. 9.87	Aston Villa	(a)	1 0	Kerr	Pears	Glover	Cooper	Mowbray	Parkinson
15. 9.87	Bournemouth	(h)	3 0	Hamilton 2, Slaven	Pears	Glover	Cooper	Mowbray	Parkinson
19. 9.87	Leeds Utd	(h)	2 0	Pallister, Kerr	Pears	Glover	Cooper	Mowbray	Parkinson
26. 9.87	Blackburn	(a)	2 0	Kernaghan, Kerr	Pears	Glover	Cooper	Mowbray	Parkinson
29. 9.87	Reading	(h)	0 0		Pears	Glover	Cooper	Mowbray	Parkinson
3.10.87	Bradford City	(a)	0 2		Pears	Glover	Cooper	Mowbray	Parkinson
10.10.87	Huddersfield T	(a)	4 1	Slaven 3, Laws	Pears	Glover	Cooper	Mowbray	Parkinson
17.10.87	West Brom	(h)	2 1	Slaven, Cooper	Pears	Glover	Cooper	Mowbray	Parkinson
20.10.87	Ipswich Town	(h)	3 1	Pallister, Slaven Kernaghan	Pears	Glover	Cooper	Mowbray	Parkinson
24.10.87	Birmingham	(a)	0 0		Pears	Glover	Cooper	Mowbray	Parkinson
31.10.87	Shrewsbury	(h)	4 0	Slaven 3, Kernaghan	Pears	Glover	Cooper	Mowbray	Parkinson
4.11.87	Manchester C	(a)	1 1	Glover	Pears	Glover	Cooper	Mowbray	Parkinson
7.11.87	Sheffield Utd	(a)	2 0	Slaven, Ripley	Pears	Glover	Cooper	Mowbray	Parkinson
14.11.87	Hull City	(h)	1 0	Ripley	Pears	Glover	Cooper	Mowbray	Parkinson
21.11.87	Plymouth A	(a)	1 0	Hamilton	Pears	Glover	Cooper	Mowbray	Parkinson
28.11.87	Barnsley	(h)	2 0	Slaven, Kernaghan	Pears	Glover	Cooper	Mowbray	Parkinson
5.12.87	Leicester City	(a)	0 0		Pears	Glover	Cooper	Mowbray	Laws
12.12.87	Stoke City	(h)	2 0	Hamilton, Slaven	Pears	Glover	Cooper	Mowbray	Laws
19.12.87	Bournemouth	(a)	0 0		Pears	Glover	Cooper	Mowbray	Laws
26.12.87	Blackburn Rov	(h)	1 1	Slaven	Pears	Glover*	Cooper	Mowbray	Laws**
28.12.87	Leeds United	(a)	0 2		Pears	Burke	Cooper	Mowbray	Laws*
1. 1.88	Oldham Ath	(a)	1 3	Kerr	Pears	Laws*	Cooper	Mowbray	Parkinson
16. 1.88	Millwall	(a)	1 2	Slaven	Poole	Glover	Cooper	Mowbray	Parkinson
23. 1.88	Crystal Palace	(h)	2 1	Mowbray, Glover (pen)	Pears	Glover	Cooper	Mowbray	Parkinson
6. 2.88	Swindon Town	(a)	1 1	Mowbray	Pears	Glover	Cooper	Mowbray	Parkinson
14. 2.88	Aston Villa	(h)	2 1	Kernaghan, Mowbray	Pears	Glover	Cooper	Mowbray	Parkinson
20. 2.88	Reading	(a)	0 0		Pears	Glover	Cooper	Mowbray	Parkinson
27. 2.88	Bradford City	(h)	1 2	Cooper	Pears	Glover	Cooper	Mowbray	Parkinson
5. 3.88	West Brom	(a)	0 0		Pears	Glover	Cooper	Mowbray	Parkinson*
12. 3.88	Huddersfield	(h)	2 0	Glover (pen), Kerr	Pears	Glover	Cooper	Mowbray	Parkinson
19. 3.88	Shrewsbury T	(a)	1 0	Glover (pen)	Pears	Glover	Cooper	Mowbray	Parkinson
26. 3.88	Birmingham C	(h)	1 1	Pallister	Pears	Glover	Cooper	Mowbray	Parkinson
2. 4.88	Sheffield United	(h)	6 0	Senior 2, Ripley 3, Slaven	Pears	Glover	Cooper	Mowbray	Laws
4. 6.88	Hull City	(a)	0 0		Pears	Glover	Cooper	Mowbray	Laws
9. 4.88	Manchester C	(h)	2 1	Ripley, Hamilton	Pears	Hamilton	Cooper	Mowbray	Laws
23. 4.88	Ipswich Town	(a)	0 4		Pears	Glover*	Cooper	Mowbray	Laws
30. 4.88	Plymouth A	(h)	3 1	Ripley, Kernaghan, Hamilton	Pears	Parkinson	Cooper	Mowbray	Hamilton
2. 5.88	Barnsley	(a)	3 0	Ripley, Slaven 2	Pears	Parkinson	Cooper	Mowbray	Hamilton
7. 5.88	Leicester City	(h)	1 2	Slaven	Pears	Parkinson	Laws	Mowbray	Hamilton

1987–88

Division 2

6	7	8	9	10	11	12	Crowd
Pallister	Slaven	Stephens	Hamilton	Kerr	Ripley		12,665
Pallister	Slaven	Stephens*	Hamilton	Kerr	Ripley	Kernaghan	9,660
Pallister	Slaven	Stephens*	Hamilton	Kerr	Ripley	Kernaghan	12,051
Pallister	Slaven	Kernaghan	Hamilton	Kerr	Ripley		6,879
Pallister	Slaven	Kernaghan	Hamilton	Kerr	Ripley		10,093
Pallister	Slaven	Kernaghan	Hamilton*	Kerr	Ripley	Stephens	14,114
Pallister	Slaven	Kernaghan*	Hamilton	Kerr	Laws	Ripley	6,169
Pallister	Slaven	Kernaghan*	Hamilton	Kerr	Laws	Ripley	10,684
Pallister	Slaven	Kernaghan	Hamilton	Kerr	Laws*	Ripley	10,491
Pallister	Slaven	Kernaghan*	Hamilton	Kerr	Ripley	Laws	7,404
Pallister*	Slaven	Kernaghan	Hamilton	Kerr	Ripley	Laws	10,183
Pallister*	Slaven	Kernaghan	Hamilton	Kerr	Ripley	Laws	18,434
Pallister	Slaven	Kernaghan	Hamilton	Kerr	Ripley		11,278
Pallister	Slaven	Kernaghan*	Hamilton	Kerr	Ripley	Stephens	15,709
Pallister	Slaven	Kernaghan	Hamilton	Kerr	Ripley		9,428
Pallister*	Slaven	Kernaghan	Hamilton	Kerr	Ripley	Laws	12,732
Pallister	Slaven	Kernaghan*	Hamilton	Kerr	Ripley	Stephens	9,411
Pallister	Slaven	Kernaghan	Hamilton	Kerr	Ripley*	Parkinson	12,289
Pallister	Slaven*	Kernaghan	Hamilton	Kerr	Ripley	Burke	6,792
Pallister	Slaven	Kernaghan	Hamilton	Kerr	Ripley	Parkinson*/Burke**	23,536
Pallister	Slaven	Kernaghan	Hamilton	Kerr	Ripley	Parkinson	34,186
Pallister	Slaven	Kernaghan	Hamilton	Kerr	Ripley**	Gill*/Burke**	8,181
Pallister	Slaven	Kernaghan	Hamilton	Kerr	Laws		8,617
Pallister	Slaven	Ripley	Hamilton	Kerr	Laws		12,597
Pallister	Slaven*	Ripley	Hamilton	Kerr	Laws	Kernaghan	9,941
Pallister	Slaven	Ripley*	Hamilton	Kerr*	Laws	Burke/Kernaghan	16,957
Pallister	Slaven	Ripley*	Hamilton	Kerr*	Laws	Burke/Kernaghan	6,446
Pallister	Slaven*	Ripley	Hamilton	Kerr	Laws	Kernaghan/Burke	21,079
Pallister	Slaven	Ripley*	Hamilton	Kerr	Kernaghan	Laws/Burke	8,316
Pallister	Slaven	Ripley	Burke	Kerr	Laws		13,866
Pallister	Slaven	Ripley	Hamilton	Kerr*	Laws	Kernaghan	5,603
Pallister	Slaven	Ripley	Senior	Hamilton	Laws	Kerr	15,465
Pallister	Slaven	Ripley*	Senior	Kerr	Burke	Kernaghan	17,340
Pallister	Slaven	Ripley	Senior	Kerr	Burke		10,758
Pallister	Slaven	Ripley	Senior	Kerr	Burke		19,443
Pallister	Slaven	Ripley	Senior	Kerr	Burke	Hamilton	12,773
Pallister	Slaven	Ripley	Kernaghan	Kerr	Burke*	Glover	16,615
Pallister	Slaven	Ripley*	Kernaghan	Kerr	Laws	Burke	13,240
Pallister	Slaven	Ripley*	Kernaghan*	Kerr	Burke	Glover/Senior	27,645

1987–88

Play Offs

Date	Opposition		Result	Scorers	1	2	3	4	5
15. 5.88	Bradford City	(a)	1 2	Senior	Pears	Parkinson	Laws	Mowbray	Hamilton
18. 5.88	Bradford City	(h)	2 0*	Slaven, Hamilton	Pears	Parkinson	Cooper	Mowbray	Hamilton
25. 5.88	Chelsea	(h)	2 0	Senior, Slaven	Pears	Parkinson	Cooper	Mowbray	Hamilton
28. 5.88	Chelsea	(a)	0 1		Pears	Parkinson	Cooper	Mowbray	Hamilton

* After extra-time

FA Cup

Date	Opposition		Result	Scorers	1	2	3	4	5
9. 1.88	Sutton Utd	(a)	1 1	Pallister	Pears	Laws	Cooper	Mowbray	Parkinson
12. 1.88	Sutton Utd	(h)	1 0*	Kerr	Poole	Glover	Cooper	Mowbray	Parkinson
30. 1.88	Everton	(a)	1 1	Kerr	Pears	Glover	Cooper	Mowbray	Parkinson
3. 2.88	Everton	(h)	2 2*	Mowbray, Kernaghan	Pears	Glover	Cooper	Mowbray	Parkinson
9. 2.88	Everton	(a)	1 2*	Ripley	Pears	Glover*	Cooper	Mowbray	Parkinson

* After extra-time

League Cup

Date	Opposition		Result	Scorers	1	2	3	4	5
18. 8.88	Sunderland	(a)	0 1		Pears	Glover	Cooper	Mowbray	Parkinson
25. 8.88	Sunderland	(h)	2 0	Slaven, Mowbray	Pears	Glover	Cooper	Mowbray	Parkinson
23. 9.88	Aston Villa	(h)	0 1		Pears	Glover	Cooper	Mowbray	Parkinson
7.10.88	Aston Villa	(a)	0 1		Pears	Glover	Cooper	Mowbray	Parkinson

1988–89

Division 1

Date	Opposition		Result	Scorers	1	2	3	4	5
27. 8.88	Derby County	(a)	0 1		Pears	Parkinson	Cooper	Mowbray	Hamilton*
3. 9.88	Norwich City	(h)	2 3	Mowbray, Burke	Pears	Parkinson	Cooper	Mowbray	Hamilton
10. 9.88	Manchester Utd	(a)	0 1		Pears	Parkinson	Cooper	Mowbray	Hamilton
17. 9.88	Wimbledon	(h)	1 0	Hamilton	Pears	Parkinson	Cooper	Mowbray	Hamilton
24. 9.88	Tottenham	(a)	2 3	Slaven, Mowbray	Pears	Parkinson	Cooper	Mowbray	Hamilton
1.10.88	Coventry City	(a)	4 3	Slaven 3, Burke	Pears	Parkinson	Cooper	Kernaghan	Hamilton
8.10.88	West Ham Utd	(h)	1 0	Pallister	Pears	Parkinson	Cooper	Mowbray	Hamilton
22.10.88	Luton Town	(h)	2 1	Slaven, Cooper	Pears	Parkinson	Cooper	Mowbray	Hamilton
26.10.88	Newcastle Utd	(a)	0 3		Pears	Parkinson	Cooper	Mowbray	Hamilton
29.10.88	Millwall	(h)	4 2	Slaven, Ripley, Burke, Parkinson (pen)	Pears	Parkinson	Cooper	Mowbray	Hamilton
5.11.88	Liverpool	(a)	0 3		Pears	Parkinson	Cooper	Mowbray	Hamilton
12.11.88	QPR	(h)	1 0	Brennan	Pears	Parkinson	Cooper	Mowbray	Hamilton
19.11.88	Arsenal	(a)	0 3		Pears	Parkinson	Cooper	Mowbray	Hamilton*
26.11.88	Sheffield Wed	(h)	0 1		Pears	Parkinson	Cooper	Mowbray	Hamilton*
3.12.88	Nottingham For	(a)	2 2	Brennan, Ripley	Pears	Parkinson	Cooper	Mowbray	Hamilton
10.12.88	Aston Villa	(h)	3 3	Brennan, Hamilton, Mowbray	Pears	Parkinson	Cooper	Mowbray	Hamilton
17.12.88	Charlton Ath	(h)	0 0		Pears	Parkinson	Cooper	Mowbray	Hamilton
26.12.88	Everton	(a)	1 2	Glover (pen)	Pears	Parkinson	Cooper	Mowbray	Hamilton
31.12.88	Norwich City	(a)	0 0		Pears	Parkinson	Cooper	Mowbray	Hamilton
2. 1.89	Manchester Utd	(h)	1 0	Davenport	Pears	Parkinson*	Cooper	Mowbray	Hamilton
14. 1.89	Southampton	(a)	3 1	Kerr, Slaven, Burke	Pears	Mohan	Cooper	Mowbray	Hamilton
21. 1.89	Tottenham	(h)	2 2	Cooper, Ripley	Pears	Parkinson	Cooper	Mowbray	Hamilton

1987–88

Play Offs

6	7	8	9	10	11	12	Crowd	
Pallister	Slaven	Ripley	Senior	Kerr	Glover		16,017	SF/1
Pallister	**Slaven**	**Ripley***	**Senior***	**Kerr**	**Glover**	**Kernaghan/Laws**	**25,868**	**SF/2**
Pallister	**Slaven**	**Ripley**	**Senior**	**Kerr**	**Glover**		**25,531**	**F/1**
Pallister	Slaven	Ripley	Senior	Kerr	Glover		40,550	F/2

FA Cup

Pallister	Slaven	Gill	Hamilton	Kerr	Ripley		5,600	round 3
Pallister	**Slaven**	**Kernaghan**	**Hamilton***	**Kerr***	**Burke**	**Gill/Laws**	**17,932**	**round 3r**
Pallister	Slaven	Ripley	Hamilton	Kerr	Laws		36,564	round 4
Pallister*	**Slaven**	**Ripley**	**Hamilton**	**Kerr**	**Laws**	**Kernaghan**	**25,235**	**round 4r**
Pallister	Slaven*	Ripley	Hamilton	Kerr	Laws	Kernaghan/Burke	32,222	round4/2r

League Cup

Pallister*	Slaven	Stephens	Hamilton	Kerr	Ripley	Kernaghan	15,770	round 1/1
Pallister	**Slaven**	**Stephens**	**Hamilton**	**Kerr***	**Ripley**	**Gill**	**15,570**	**round 1/2**
Pallister	**Slaven**	**Stephens***	**Hamilton**	**Kerr**	**Ripley**	**Kernaghan**	**11,424**	**round 2/1**
Pallister	Slaven	Kernaghan*	Hamilton	Kerr	Ripley	Laws	11,702	round 2/2

1988–89

Division 1

Kernaghan	Slaven	Brennan	Senior**	Ripley	Glover	Gill/Burke	19,432
Pallister	**Slaven**	**Brennan**	**Senior***	**Ripley**	**Burke**	**Kernaghan**	**18,595**
Pallister	Slaven	Brennan	Ripley	Kerr*	Burke	Kernaghan	40,442
Pallister	**Slaven**	**Brennan**	**Senior**	**Kerr**	**Ripley**		**17,709**
Pallister	Slaven	Brennan	Senior	Kerr	Ripley		23,427
Pallister	Slaven	Brennan	Burke	Kerr	Ripley		14,527
Pallister	**Slaven**	**Brennan**	**Burke***	**Kerr***	**Ripley**	**Kernaghan/Glover**	**19,608**
Pallister	**Slaven**	**Brennan**	**Burke***	**Kerr**	**Ripley**	**Kernaghan**	**17,792**
Pallister	Slaven	Brennan	Burke	Kerr*	Ripley*	Kernaghan/Glover	23,927
Pallister	**Slaven**	**Brennan**	**Burke**	**Kerr***	**Ripley**	**Kernaghan**	**19,788**
Pallister	Slaven	Brennan	Burke	Davenport	Ripley		39,489
Pallister	**Slaven**	**Brennan**	**Burke***	**Davenport**	**Ripley**	**Kernaghan/Glover**	**20,565**
Pallister	Slaven	Brennan	Burke**	Davenport	Ripley	Kernaghan/Glover	32,294
Pallister	**Slaven**	**Brennan**	**Glover**	**Davenport**	**Ripley**	**Burke**	**19,310**
Pallister	Ripley	Brennan	Glover	Davenport	Burke		17,742
Pallister	**Ripley***	**Brennan**	**Glover**	**Davenport**	**Burke***	**Slaven/Kernaghan**	**18,096**
Pallister	**Slaven**	**Brennan**	**Glover**	**Davenport***	**Burke**	**Kernaghan**	**16,065**
Pallister	Slaven	Brennan	Glover**	Davenport	Ripley*	Kernaghan/Kerr	32,651
Pallister	Slaven	Brennan	Glover	Davenport	Ripley		16,021
Pallister	**Slaven**	**Brennan**	**Glover**	**Davenport**	**Ripley**	**Burke**	**24,411**
Pallister	Slaven	Gill*	Kerr	Davenport	Ripley	Burke	13,157
Pallister	**Slaven**	**Brennan***	**Kerr**	**Davenport**	**Ripley**	**Burke**	**23,692**

1988–89

Division 1

Date	Opposition		Result	Scorers	1	2	3	4	5
4. 2.89	Coventry City	(h)	1 1	Slaven	Poole	Mohan	Cooper	Mowbray	Hamilton
18. 2.89	Luton Town	(a)	0 1		Poole	Parkinson	Cooper	Mowbray	Hamilton
21. 2.89	Millwall	(a)	0 2		Poole	Parkinson	Cooper	Mowbray	Hamilton
26. 2.89	Newcastle Utd	(h)	1 1	Slaven	Poole	Parkinson	Cooper	Mowbray	Hamilton
11. 3.89	Liverpool	(h)	0 4		Pears	Parkinson	Cooper	Mowbray	Hamilton
18. 3.89	Derby County	(h)	0 1		Pears	Parkinson	Cooper	Mowbray	Hamilton
25. 3.89	Wimbledon	(a)	1 1	Slaven	Pears	Parkinson	Cooper	Mowbray	Proctor
27. 3.89	Everton	(h)	3 3	Slaven, Parkinson (pen), Davenport	Pears	Parkinson	Cooper	Mowbray	Proctor
1. 4.89	Charlton Ath	(a)	0 2		Poole	Parkinson	Cooper	Mowbray	Proctor
8. 4.89	Southampton	(h)	3 3	Hamilton, Slaven, Burke	Poole	Parkinson	Cooper	Mowbray	Proctor
11. 4.89	West Ham Utd	(a)	2 1	Slaven 2	Poole	Parkinson	Cooper	Mowbray	Proctor
15. 4.89	QPR	(a)	0 0		Poole	Parkinson	Cooper	Mowbray	Proctor
22. 4.89	Nottingham For	(h)	3 4	Ripley, Slaven, Davenport	Poole	Parkinson	Cooper*	Mowbray	Proctor
29. 4.89	Aston Villa	(a)	1 1	Davenport	Poole	Parkinson	Mohan	Mowbray	Proctor
6. 5.89	Arsenal	(h)	0 1		Poole	Parkinson	Mohan	Mowbray	Proctor
13. 5.89	Sheffield Wed	(a)	0 1		Poole	Parkinson	Mohan	Mowbray	Proctor

FA Cup

Date	Opposition		Result	Scorers	1	2	3	4	5
7. 1.89	Grimsby Town	(h)	1 2	Slaven	Pears	Burke	Cooper	Mowbray	Hamilton

League Cup

Date	Opposition		Result	Scorers	1	2	3	4	5
28. 9.88	Tranmere Rov	(h)	0 0		Pears	Parkinson	Cooper	Mowbray	Hamilton
11.10.88	Tranmere Rov	(a)	0 1		Pears	Parkinson	Cooper	Mowbray	Hamilton

Simod Cup

Date	Opposition		Result	Scorers	1	2	3	4	5
14.12.88	Oldham Ath	(h)	1 0	Glover (pen)	Pears	Parkinson	Cooper	Mowbray	Hamilton
21.12.88	Portsmouth	(h)	2 1*	Slaven, Glover	Pears	Parkinson	Cooper	Mowbray	Hamilton
11. 1.89	Coventry City	(h)	1 0	Davenport	Pears	Mohan	Cooper	Mowbray	Hamilton
28. 1.89	Crystal Palace	(h)	2 3	Slaven, Cooper	Pears	Parkinson	Cooper	Mowbray	Hamilton

1989–90

Division 2

Date	Opposition		Result	Scorers	1	2	3	4	5
19. 8.89	Wolves	(h)	4 2	Slaven 2, Proctor, Davenport	Poole	Parkinson	Mohan	Mowbray	Putney
23. 8.89	Leeds Utd	(a)	1 2	Comfort	Poole	Parkinson	Mohan	Mowbray	Putney
27. 8.89	Sunderland	(a)	1 2	Slaven	Poole	Parkinson	Mohan	Mowbray	Putney
2. 9.89	Sheffield Utd	(h)	3 3	Slaven 2, Comfort	Poole	Parkinson	Mohan	Mowbray	Kernaghan
9. 9.89	Barnsley	(a)	1 1	Burke	Poole	Parkinson	Mohan	Mowbray	Kernaghan
16. 9.89	Bournemouth	(h)	2 1	Slaven, Proctor	Poole	Parkinson	Mohan	Mowbray	Kernaghan
23. 9.89	Portsmouth	(a)	1 3	Slaven	Poole	Parkinson	Mohan	Mowbray	Kernaghan
27. 9.89	Hull City	(h)	1 0	Proctor	Poole	Parkinson	Mohan	Mowbray	Kernaghan
30. 9.89	Watford	(a)	0 1		Poole	Parkinson	Mohan	Mowbray	Kernaghan
14.10.89	Plymouth A	(h)	0 2		Poole	Coleman	Mohan	Mowbray	Kernaghan

1988–89

Division 1

6	7	8	9	10	11	12	Crowd	
Pallister	Slaven	Brennan	Burke	Kerr*	Ripley	Gill	17,532	
Pallister	Slaven	Brennan*	Gill**	Kerr	Ripley	Burke/Kernaghan	8,187	
Pallister	Slaven	Kerr	Kernaghan	Davenport	Ripley		11,396	
Pallister	Slaven	Brennan	Kerr*	Davenport	Ripley	Burke	24,385	
Pallister	Slaven	Brennan*	Ripley	Davenport	Kerr	Proudlock	25,197	
Pallister	Slaven	Kerr	Ripley	Davenport	Burke		16,580	
Pallister	Slaven	Gill	Ripley	Davenport	Barham		5,275	
Pallister	Slaven	Gill	Ripley*	Davenport	Barham	Kernaghan	23,151	
Pallister	Slaven*	Gill	Ripley*	Davenport	Barham*	Kernaghan/Hamilton	6,696	
Pallister	Slaven	Gill*	Hamilton	Davenport**	Ripley	Kernaghan/Burke	16,983	
Pallister	Slaven	Kernaghan	Ripley*	Burke	Hamilton	Kerr	16,217	
Pallister	Slaven	Kernaghan	Ripley	Burke	Hamilton		10,347	
Pallister	Slaven	Kerr	Ripley	Burke	Hamilton**	Davenport/Mohan	20,778	
Pallister	Slaven	Ripley	Hamilton	Davenport	Burke*	Kernaghan	18,590	
Pallister	Slaven	Ripley*	Hamilton	Davenport	Burke**	Kernaghan/Barham	21,803	
Pallister	Slaven	Kerr	Hamilton	Davenport	Burke*	Kernaghan	20,582	

FA Cup

6	7	8	9	10	11	12	Crowd	
Pallister	Slaven*	Brennan	Glover	Davenport	Ripley	Mohan	19,190	round 3

League Cup

6	7	8	9	10	11	12	Crowd	
Pallister	Slaven	Brennan	Senior*	Kerr	Ripley	Kernaghan	12,084	round 2/1
Pallister	Slaven	Brennan	Burke	Kerr	Ripley*	Kernaghan	8,617	round 2/2

Simod Cup

6	7	8	9	10	11	12	Crowd	
Pallister	Slaven	Brennan	Glover	Davenport	Burke		7,439	round 1
Pallister	Slaven	Brennan	Glover	Davenport	Ripley*	Kerr	6,853	round 2
Pallister	Slaven	Gill	Kerr	Davenport	Ripley		9,910	round 3
Pallister	Slaven	Brennan	Burke	Kernaghan	Ripley		16,314	round 4

1989–90

Division 2

6	7	8	9	10	11	12	Crowd
Pallister	Slaven	Proctor	Davenport	Kerr*	Comfort	Ripley	21,727
Pallister	Slaven	Proctor	Davenport	Ripley	Comfort		25,004
Pallister	Slaven	Proctor	Davenport	Ripley*	Comfort	Brennan	21,569
Putney	Slaven	Proctor	Davenport*	Brennan	Comfort	Ripley	17,897
Putney*	Slaven	Proctor	Ripley*	Brennan	Comfort	Davenport/Burke	10,535
Putney	Slaven	Proctor	Ripley*	Brennan*	Comfort	Davenport/Burke	16,077
Putney	Slaven	Proctor	Ripley*	Brennan*	Comfort	Davenport/Burke	7,305
Putney	Slaven	Proctor	Ripley	Brennan	Comfort		16,382
Putney	Slaven	Proctor	Ripley*	Brennan*	Comfort	Burke/Coleman	10,102
Putney	Slaven	Proctor	Davenport*	Gill*	Comfort	Ripley/Cooper	15,003

1989–90

Division 2

Date	Opposition		Result	Scorers	1	2	3	4	5
18.10.89	Brighton & HA	(h)	2 2	Mowbray, Parkinson (pen)	Poole	Parkinson	Cooper	Mowbray	Coleman
21.10.89	Oldham Ath	(a)	0 2		Poole	Parkinson	Cooper	Mowbray	Coleman
28.10.89	West Brom	(h)	0 0		Poole	Parkinson	Cooper	Mowbray	Kernaghan
30.10.89	Port Vale	(a)	1 1	Kernaghan	Poole	Parkinson	Cooper	Mowbray	Kernaghan
4.11.89	Newcastle Utd	(a)	2 2	Proctor, Brennan	Poole	Parkinson	Cooper	Mowbray	Kernaghan
11.11.89	Swindon Town	(h)	0 2		Poole	Parkinson	Cooper*	Mowbray	Kernaghan
18.11.89	West Ham Utd	(a)	0 2		Poole	Parkinson	Mohan	Mowbray	Coleman
21.11.89	Blackburn Rov	(a)	4 2	Kernaghan 3, Slaven	Poole	Parkinson	Mohan	Mowbray	Coleman
25.11.89	Oxford United	(h)	1 0	Slaven	Poole	Parkinson	Mohan	Mowbray	Coleman
2.12.89	Wolves	(a)	0 2		Poole	Mohan*	Cooper	Mowbray	Coleman
9.12.89	Leeds United	(h)	0 2		Poole	Parkinson	Cooper	Mowbray	Coleman
16.12.89	Leicester City	(h)	4 1	Cooper 2, Slaven, Ripley	Pears	Parkinson	Cooper	Mowbray	Coleman
26.12.89	Bradford City	(a)	1 0	Slaven	Pears	Parkinson	Cooper	Mowbray	Coleman
30.12.89	Ipswich Town	(a)	0 3		Pears	Parkinson	Cooper	Mowbray	Coleman
1. 1.90	Stoke City	(h)	0 1		Pears	Parkinson	Cooper	Mowbray	Coleman
14. 1.90	Sunderland	(h)	3 0	Davenport, Slaven, Parkinson	Pears	Parkinson	Cooper	Mowbray	Coleman
20. 1.90	Sheffield United	(a)	0 1		Pears	Parkinson	Cooper	Mohan	Coleman
3. 2.90	Portsmouth	(h)	2 0	Kerr, Slaven	Pears	Parkinson	McGee	Mohan	Coleman
10. 2.90	Bournemouth	(a)	2 2	Mowbray, Slaven	Pears	Parkinson	Mohan	Mowbray	Coleman
24. 2.90	Oxford United	(a)	1 3	Brennan	Pears	Parkinson	Mohan	Mowbray	Coleman
28. 2.90	Brighton &HA	(a)	0 1		Pears	Parkinson	Mohan	McGee	Coleman
3. 3.90	West Ham Utd	(h)	0 1		Pears	Parkinson	McGee	Kernaghan	Coleman
7. 3.90	Watford	(h)	1 2	Coleman	Pears	Parkinson	McGee	Kernaghan	Coleman
10. 3.90	Hull City	(a)	0 0		Pears	Parkinson	McGee	Mohan	Coleman
17. 3.90	Blackburn Rov	(h)	0 3		Pears	Cooper	Phillips	Mohan*	Coleman
20. 3.90	Plymouth A	(a)	2 1	Baird, Brennan	Pears	Parkinson	Phillips	Kernaghan	Coleman
31. 3.90	Oldham A	(h)	1 0	Slaven	Pears	Parkinson	Phillips	Kernaghan	Coleman
7. 4.90	West Brom	(a)	0 0		Pears	Parkinson	Phillips	Kernaghan	Coleman
11. 4.90	Port Vale	(h)	2 3	Slaven, Davenport	Pears	Parkinson	Phillips	Kernaghan	Coleman
14. 4.90	Stoke City	(a)	0 0		Pears	Parkinson	Phillips	Kernaghan	Coleman
16. 4.90	Bradford City	(h)	2 0	Slaven, Baird	Pears	Parkinson	Phillips	Kernaghan	Coleman
21. 4.90	Leicester City	(a)	1 2	Slaven	Pears	Parkinson	Phillips	Kernaghan	Coleman
25. 4.90	Ipswich Town	(h)	1 2	Baird	Pears	Parkinson	Phillips	Kernaghan	Coleman
28. 4.90	Swindon Town	(a)	1 1	Slaven	Pears	Cooper	Phillips	Kernaghan	Coleman
2. 5.90	Barnsley	(h)	0 1		Pears	Cooper	Phillips	Kernaghan	Coleman*
5. 5.90	Newcastle Utd	(h)	4 1	Slaven 2, Baird 2	Pears	Cooper	Phillips	Kernaghan	Coleman

FA Cup

Date	Opposition		Result	Scorers	1	2	3	4	5
6. 1.90	Everton	(h)	0 0		Pears	Parkinson	Cooper	Mowbray	Coleman
10. 1.90	Everton	(a)	1 1	Parkinson	Pears	Parkinson	Cooper	Mowbray	Coleman
17. 1.90	Everton	(a)	0 1		Pears	Parkinson	Cooper	Mowbray	Coleman

1989–90

Division 2

6	7	8	9	10	11	12	Crowd	
Putney	**Slaven***	**Proctor**	**Ripley**	**Brennan**	**Comfort**	**Kernaghan**	13,551	
Putney	Slaven	Proctor	Kernaghan	Burke	Comfort		6,835	
Putney	**Slaven**	**Proctor**	**Ripley**	**Brennan***	**Comfort**	Burke	14,076	
Putney	Slaven	Proctor	Ripley	Brennan	Comfort		7,708	
Putney	Slaven	Proctor	Ripley*	Brennan	Comfort**	Coleman/Burke	23,349	
Putney	**Slaven**	**Proctor**	Burke**	**Brennan**	Davenport	Mohan/Coleman	13,720	
Putney	Slaven	Proctor	Burke*	Brennan	Davenport	Kernaghan	18,720	
Putney	Slaven	Proctor	Kernaghan	Brennan	Davenport		8,317	
Putney	**Slaven**	**Proctor**	**Kernaghan**	**Brennan**	**Davenport**		13,756	
Kernaghan	Slaven	Proctor	Ripley*	Brennan	Davenport	Burke/Parkinson	12,357	
Kernaghan*	**Slaven**	**Proctor**	**Ripley**	**Putney**	Davenport	Brennan	19,686	
Putney	Slaven	Proctor	Kernaghan*	Brennan	Davenport	Ripley/Burke	11,428	
Putney	Slaven	Proctor	Kernaghan*	Brennan	Davenport	Ripley	10,008	
Putney*	Slaven	Proctor	Kernaghan	Brennan	Davenport	Ripley	14,290	
Ripley	**Slaven**	**Proctor**	**Kernaghan***	**Brennan**	**Davenport**	Burke	16,238	
Ripley	**Slaven**	**Proctor**	**Putney***	**Brennan**	**Davenport**	Kerr	17,698	
Ripley	Slaven	Proctor	Kernaghan	Brennan*	Kerr	McGee	15,950	
Ripley*	**Slaven**	**Proctor**	**Baird**	**Putney**	**Kerr**	Davenport	15,295	
McGee	Slaven	Kerr	Baird	Brennan	Davenport*	Ripley	7,360	
Proctor	Slaven	Kerr	Baird	Brennan	Davenport*	Ripley	5,949	
Proctor	Slaven	Kerr*	Baird	Brennan	Davenport	Ripley	5,504	
Proctor	**Slaven**	Kerr*	**Baird**	**Brennan**	**Ripley**	Davenport	23,617	
Proctor	**Slaven**	**Kerr**	**Baird**	**Brennan**	**Ripley**		14,008	
Proctor	Slaven	Kerr	Baird	Brennan	Ripley		6,602	
Ripley	**Slaven**	**Proctor**	**Baird**	Kerr*	**Davenport**	Kernaghan/Brennan	15,259	
McGee	Slaven*	Proctor	Baird	Brennan	Davenport	Ripley	7,185	
McGee*	**Slaven**	**Proctor**	Baird*	**Brennan**	**Davenport**	Ripley/Cooper	17,238	
McGee	Slaven	Proctor	Baird	Brennan	Davenport	Cooper	9,458	
McGee	**Slaven**	**Proctor**	Baird*	**Brennan**	**Davenport**	Ripley	14,973	
McGee*	Slaven	Proctor	Baird	Brennan*	Davenport	Ripley	8,636	
Ripley	**Slaven**	**Proctor**	**Baird**	Brennan*	**Davenport**	Kerr	16,376	
Ripley	Slaven	Proctor	Baird	Brennan*	Davenport	Kerr	9,203	
Ripley	**Slaven***	**Proctor**	**Baird**	**Brennan**	**Davenport**	Kerr	15,232	
Ripley	Slaven	Proctor	Baird	Kerr	Davenport		9,532	
Ripley	**Slaven**	**Proctor**	**Baird**	**Kerr**	**Davenport**	Brennan	17,015	
McGee	Slaven	Proctor	Baird	Kerr	Brennan		18,484	

FA Cup

6	7	8	9	10	11	12	Crowd	
Ripley	**Slaven**	Proctor*	**Kernaghan**	**Brennan**	**Davenport**	Kerr	20,075	round 3
Ripley	Slaven	Proctor	Kernaghan*	Brennan	Davenport	Kerr	24,352	round 3r
Ripley	Slaven	Proctor	Brennan	Kerr	Davenport*	Kernaghan	23,866	round 3r2

1989–90

League Cup

Date	Opposition		Result	Scorers	1	2	3	4	5
20. 9.89	Halifax Town	(h)	4 0	Comfort, Slaven 2, Kernaghan	Poole	Parkinson	Mohan	Mowbray	Kernaghan
3.10.89	Halifax Town	(a)	1 0	Slaven	Poole	Parkinson	Mohan	Gill	Kernaghan
25.10.89	Wimbledon	(h)	1 1	Slaven	Poole	Parkinson	Cooper	Mowbray	Kernaghan
1.11.89	Wimbledon	(a)	0 1		Poole	Parkinson	Cooper	Mowbray	Kernaghan

ZDS Cup

Date	Opposition		Result	Scorers	1	2	3	4	5
29.11.89	Port Vale	(h)	3 1	Slaven 2, Coleman	Poole	Mohan	Cooper	Mowbray	Coleman
20.11.89	Sheffield Wed	(h)	4 1	Slaven 3, Kernaghan	Pears	Parkinson	Cooper	Mowbray	Coleman
23. 1.90	Newcastle Utd	(h)	1 0	Cooper	Pears	Parkinson	Cooper	Mowbray	Coleman
30. 1.90	Aston Villa	(a)	2 1	Slaven, Brennan	Pears	Parkinson	Mohan	Kerr	Coleman
6. 2.90	Aston Villa	(h)	2 1*	Slaven, Kerr	Pears	Parkinson	Mohan	Mowbray	Coleman
25. 3.90	Chelsea		0 1		Pears	Parkinson	Cooper	Kernaghan	Coleman

After extra-time

1990–91

Division 2

Date	Opposition		Result	Scorers	1	2	3	4	5
25. 8.90	West Ham Utd	(h)	0 0		Pears	Cooper	Phillips	Mowbray	Kernaghan
1. 9.90	Plymouth A	(a)	1 1	Slaven	Pears	Cooper	Phillips	Mowbray	Kernaghan
8. 9.90	Notts County	(h)	1 0	Wark	Pears	Cooper	Phillips	Mowbray	Kernaghan
15. 9.90	Swindon Town	(a)	3 1	Slaven 2, Mustoe	Pears	Cooper	Phillips	Mowbray	Kernaghan
17. 9.90	Port Vale	(a)	1 3	Russell	Pears	Cooper	Phillips	Mowbray	Kernaghan
22. 9.90	Oldham A	(h)	0 1		Pears	Cooper	Phillips	Mowbray	Kernaghan
29. 9.90	Leicester City	(h)	6 0	Phillips, Hendrie, Kerr 2, Slaven, Baird	Pears	Cooper	Phillips	Mowbray	Kernaghan*
3.10.90	Newcastle Utd	(a)	0 0		Pears	Cooper	Phillips	Mowbray	Kernaghan
6.10.90	Watford	(a)	3 0	Mowbray, Baird 2.	Pears	Cooper	Phillips	Mowbray	Kernaghan
13.10.90	Millwall	(h)	2 1	Rae (og), Hendrie	Pears	Cooper	Phillips	Mowbray	Kernaghan
20.10.90	Bristol Rovers	(h)	1 2	Kerr	Pears	Cooper	Phillips	Mowbray	Kernaghan
23.10.90	Wolves	(a)	0 1		Pears	Cooper	Phillips	Mowbray	Kernaghan
27.10.90	Brighton & HA	(a)	4 2	Slaven 3, Baird	Pears	Cooper	Phillips	Mowbray	Kernaghan
3.11.90	Barnsley	(h)	1 0	Kerr	Pears	Cooper	Phillips	Mowbray	Kernaghan
6.11.90	West Brom	(a)	1 0	Slaven	Pears	Cooper	Phillips	Mowbray	Kernaghan*
10.11.90	Charlton A	(h)	1 2	Baird	Pears	Cooper	Phillips	Mowbray	Kernaghan
17.11.90	Portsmouth	(a)	3 0	Slaven, Baird, Stevens (og)	Pears	Cooper	Phillips	Mowbray	Kernaghan
24.11.90	Oxford United	(a)	5 2	Baird 3 (2 pens), Slaven, Mustoe	Pears	Cooper	Phillips	Mowbray	Kernaghan*
1.12.90	Hull City	(h)	3 0	Baird, Slaven, Kerr	Pears	Cooper	Phillips	Mowbray	Coleman
15.12.90	West Ham Utd	(a)	0 0		Pears	Cooper	McGee	Mowbray	Coleman
22.12.90	Blackburn Rov	(h)	0 1		Pears	Cooper	Phillips	Mowbray	Coleman
26.12.90	Ipswich Town	(a)	1 0	Baird	Pears	Cooper	Phillips	Mowbray	Coleman
29.12.90	Bristol City	(a)	0 3		Pears	Cooper	Phillips	Mowbray	Coleman
1. 1.91	Sheffield Wed	(h)	0 2		Pears	Cooper	Phillips	Mowbray	Coleman
12. 1.91	Plymouth A	(h)	0 0		Pears	Cooper*	Phillips	Mowbray	Coleman
19. 1.91	Notts County	(a)	2 3	Baird, Ripley	Pears	Parkinson	Phillips	Mowbray	Coleman

1989–90

League Cup

6	7	8	9	10	11	12	Crowd	
Putney	Slaven	Proctor	Ripley	Brennan	Comfort		10,613	round 2/1
Putney*	Slaven	Davenport	Burke	Brennan	Comfort	McGee	1,641	round 2/2
Putney	Slaven	Proctor	Ripley	Brennan	Comfort		12,933	round 3
Putney	Slaven	Proctor	Burke	Brennan	Davenport		3,554	round 3r

ZDS Cup

6	7	8	9	10	11	12	Crowd	
Putney*	Slaven	Proctor	Ripley	Brennan	Davenport	Burke	6,691	round 1
Ripley	Slaven	Proctor	Kernaghan	Brennan*	Davenport	Kerr	8,716	round 2
Ripley	Slaven	Proctor	Kerr	Brennan	Davenport*	McGee	16,948	northern s/f
Kernaghan	Slaven	Proctor	Ripley	Brennan	McGee		16,547	northern final 1
Ripley*	Slaven	Proctor	Kernaghan	Putney**	Kerr	McGee, Davenport	20,806	northern final 2
McGee	Slaven	Proctor	Ripley	Brennan	Davenport		76,369	final at Wembley

1990–91

Division 2

6	7	8	9	10	11	12	Crowd
Wark	Slaven	Mustoe	Baird	Proctor	Hendrie		20,680
Wark	Slaven	Mustoe	Ripley	Russell	Hendrie		6,266
Wark	Slaven*	Mustoe	Ripley	Russell	Hendrie	Baird	17,380
Wark	Slaven	Mustoe	Ripley	Russell*	Hendrie	Baird	9,127
Wark	Slaven*	Mustoe	Ripley	Russell	Hendrie	Baird	7,880
Wark	Slaven	Mustoe	Baird	Russell*	Hendrie	Ripley	19,363
Wark	Ripley*	Mustoe	Baird	Kerr	Hendrie	Slaven/McGee	16,174
Wark	Slaven	Mustoe	Baird	Kerr	Hendrie		17,023
Wark	Slaven	Mustoe	Baird	Kerr	Hendrie		8.057
Wark	Slaven	Mustoe	Baird	Kerr	Hendrie		20,277
Wark*	Slaven	Mustoe	Baird	Kerr	Hendrie	Putney	18,589
Russell*	Slaven	Mustoe	Baird	Kerr	Hendrie	Putney	17,285
Wark	Slaven	Mustoe	Baird	Kerr*	Hendrie**	Putney/Ripley	7,532
Putney	Slaven	Mustoe	Baird*	Kerr	Hendrie	Ripley	18,470
Putney**	Slaven	Mustoe	Baird	Kerr	Hendrie	Ripley/Coleman	10,521
Putney	Slaven*	Mustoe	Baird	Kerr	Hendrie	Ripley	17,998
Wark	Slaven	Mustoe*	Baird	Kerr	Hendrie**	Ripley/Proctor	8,433
Wark	Slaven	Mustoe	Baird	Kerr*	Hendrie	Ripley/Proctor	5,262
Wark*	Slaven	Mustoe	Baird**	Kerr	Hendrie	Ripley/Proctor	17,024
Wark	Slaven	Mustoe	Baird	Kerr	Hendrie*	Ripley	23,705
Wark	Slaven	Mustoe	Baird	Kerr*	Hendrie	Ripley	17,206
Proctor	Slaven	Wark	Baird	Kerr*	Hendrie	Ripley	12,508
Proctor	Slaven	Mustoe	Baird	Russell	Hendrie		14,023
Proctor*	Slaven	Wark	Baird	Kerr	Hendrie	Ripley	22,869
Putney	Slaven	Mustoe*	Baird	Kerr	Hendrie	Ripley/McGee	14,198
Putney	Hendrie	Wark	Baird	Kerr*	Ripley**	Slaven/Walsh	9,316

1990–91

Division 2

Date	Opposition		Result	Scorers	1	2	3	4	5
2. 2.91	Swindon Town	(h)	2 0	Mustoe, Slaven	Pears	Parkinson	Phillips	Mowbray	Walsh
19. 2.91	West Brom A	(h)	3 2	Slaven, Mustoe, Rees (og)	Dibble	Parkinson	Phillips	Mowbray	Walsh
23. 2.91	Charlton A	(a)	1 0	Slaven	Dibble	Parkinson	Phillips	Mowbray	Walsh
26. 2.91	Portsmouth	(h)	1 2	Parkinson (pen)	Dibble	Parkinson	Phillips	Mowbray	Walsh
2. 3.91	Hull City	(a)	0 0		Dibble	Parkinson	Phillips	Mowbray	Walsh
9. 3.91	Oxford United	(h)	0 0		Dibble	McGee	Cooper	Mowbray	Walsh
12. 3.91	Newcastle Utd	(h)	3 0	Slaven 2, Walsh	Dibble	McGee	Phillips	Mowbray	Walsh*
16. 3.91	Leicester City	(a)	3 4	Putney, Phillips, McGee	Dibble	McGee	Phillips	Mowbray	Walsh
20. 3.91	Millwall	(a)	2 2	Kerr, Mowbray	Dibble	McGee	Phillips	Mowbray	Walsh
23. 3.91	Watford	(h)	1 2	Baird	Dibble	McGee	Phillips	Mowbray	Kerr
30. 3.91	Ipswich Town	(h)	1 1	Mowbray	Dibble	Cooper	Phillips	Mowbray	Coleman
1. 4.91	Blackburn Rov	(a)	0 1		Dibble	Cooper	Phillips	Mowbray	Coleman
6. 4.91	Bristol City	(h)	2 1	Ripley 2	Dibble	Parkinson	Phillips	Kernaghan	Coleman
9. 4.91	Port Vale	(h)	4 0	Baird, Ripley, Russell, Wark	Dibble	Parkinson	Phillips	Mowbray	Coleman
13. 4.91	Sheffield Wed	(a)	0 2		Dibble	Parkinson	Phillips	Mowbray	Coleman
20. 4.91	Bristol Rovers	(a)	0 2		Dibble	Parkinson	Phillips	Wark	Coleman
27. 4.91	Wolves	(h)	2 0	Ripley, Hendrie	Dibble	Cooper	Phillips	Kernaghan	Coleman
4. 5.91	Brighton	(h)	2 0	Coleman, Ripley	Dibble	Cooper	Phillips	Kernaghan*	Coleman
7. 5.91	Oldham A	(a)	0 2		Dibble	Cooper	Phillips	Kernaghan	Coleman
11. 5.91	Barnsley	(a)	0 1		Dibble	Cooper	Phillips	Kernaghan	Coleman

Play-Offs

Date	Opposition		Result	Scorers	1	2	3	4	5
19. 5.91	Notts County	(h)	1 1	Phillips	Dibble	Cooper**	Phillips	Kernaghan	Coleman
22. 5.91	Notts County	(a)	0 1		Dibble	Kernaghan	Phillips	Mowbray	Coleman

FA Cup

Date	Opposition		Result	Scorers	1	2	3	4	5
5. 1.91	Plymouth	(h)	0 0		Pears	Cooper	Phillips**	Mowbray	Coleman
14. 1.91	Plymouth	(a)	2 1	Baird, Kerr	Pears	Parkinson	Phillips	Mowbray	Coleman
26. 1.96	Cambridge Utd	(a)	0 2		Poole	Parkinson	Phillips	Mowbray	Ripley

League Cup

Date	Opposition		Result	Scorers	1	2	3	4	5
28. 8.90	Tranmere Rov	(h)	1 1	Mowbray	Pears	Cooper	Phillips	Mowbray	Kernaghan
3. 9.90	Tranmere Rov	(a)	2 1	Mustoe, Slaven	Pears	Cooper	Phillips	Mowbray	Kernaghan
25. 9.90	Newcastle Utd	(h)	2 0	Mustoe 2	Pears	Cooper	Phillips	Mowbray	Kernaghan
10.10.90	Newcastle Utd	(a)	0 1		Pears	Cooper	Phillips	Mowbray	Kernaghan
30.10.90	Norwich City	(h)	2 0	Kerr, Hendrie	Pears	Cooper	Phillips	Mowbray	Kernaghan
28.11.90	Aston Villa	(a)	2 3	Slaven 2	Pears	Cooper	Phillips	Mowbray	Kernaghan*

ZDS Cup

Date	Opposition		Result	Scorers	1	2	3	4	5
20.11.90	Hull City	(h)	3 1*	Baird, Kerr, Ripley	Pears	Cooper*	Phillips	Mowbray	Coleman
19.12.90	Manchester City	(a)	1 2	Hendrie	Pears	Cooper	McGee	Mowbray	Coleman

* After extra-time

1990–91

Division 2

6	7	8	9	10	11	12	Crowd	
Putney	Slaven	Wark	Baird	Mustoe	Hendrie*	Ripley	14,588	
Putney	Slaven	Wark	Baird	Mustoe	Hendrie		15,334	
Putney	Slaven	Wark	Baird	Mustoe**	Hendrie*	Ripley/Proctor	5,510	
Putney	Slaven	Wark	Baird	Mustoe	Hendrie*	Ripley	15,922	
Putney	Slaven	Wark	Baird	Mustoe	Hendrie*	Ripley	6,828	
Putney*	Slaven	Wark	Baird	Mustoe	Ripley	Kerr	14,029	
Putney	Slaven	Wark*	Baird	Mustoe	Ripley	Kerr/Arnold	18,250	
Putney	Slaven	Wark	Baird	Mustoe*	Ripley	Kerr	8,324	
Putney	Slaven	Wark	Baird	Mustoe	Ripley	Kerr	10,371	
Putney	Slaven	Wark*	Baird	Mustoe	Ripley*	Arnold/Walsh	14,583	
Putney*	Slaven	Walsh	Baird	Mustoe	Ripley	Hendrie/Proctor	15,140	
Hendrie	Slaven	Proctor	Baird	Mustoe	Ripley		8,925	
Hendrie	Slaven	Proctor	Baird	Mustoe	Ripley	Walsh	13,846	
Hendrie*	Russell	Proctor	Baird	Mustoe**	Ripley	Slaven/Wark	15,053	
Hendrie*	Russell	Proctor	Baird	Mustoe	Ripley	Slaven	30,598	
Hendrie	Russell*	Proctor	Baird	Mustoe**	Ripley	Slaven/Kernaghan	5,722	
Russell*	Slaven	Proctor	Hendrie	Putney**	Ripley	Mustoe/Pollock	16,447	
Putney	Slaven	Proctor	Baird	Hendrie**	Ripley	Mustoe/Russell	18,054	
Putney	Slaven	Proctor	Baird	Hendrie	Ripley		14,213	
Putney	Slaven	Proctor	Baird	Hendrie	Ripley		14,494	

Play-Offs

6	7	8	9	10	11	12	Crowd	
Putney	Slaven	Proctor	Baird	Hendrie	Ripley*	Mowbray/Mustoe	22,343	
Putney	Slaven*	Proctor	Baird	Mustoe	Hendrie	Russell	18,249	

FA Cup

6	7	8	9	10	11	12	Crowd	
Proctor*	Slaven	Mustoe	Baird	Kerr	Hendrie	Ripley/McGee	13,042	round 3
Putney	Slaven*	Wark	Baird	Kerr	Ripley	Hendrie	6,956	round 3r
Putney	Hendrie	Wark	Baird	Mustoe	Walsh*	Slaven	9,531	round 4

League Cup

6	7	8	9	10	11	12	Crowd	
Wark	Slaven*	Mustoe	Baird	Russell	Hendrie	Ripley	10,667	round 1/1
Wark	Slaven	Mustoe	Ripley*	Russell	Hendrie	Baird	6,135	round 1/2
Wark	Ripley	Mustoe	Baird	Kerr	Hendrie		15,042	round 2/1
Wark	Slaven	Mustoe	Baird	Kerr	Hendrie		12,778	round 2/2
Putney	Slaven	Mustoe	Baird	Kerr	Hendrie		17,024	round 3
Wark	Slaven	Mustoe	Baird	Kerr	Hendrie	Ripley	17,317	round 4

ZDS Cup

6	7	8	9	10	11	12	Crowd	
Proctor	Slaven	Mustoe	Baird	Kerr	Ripley	McGee	8,926	round 1
Proctor	Slaven	Mustoe	Baird	Kerr	Ripley		6,406	round 2

1991–92

Division 2

Date	Opposition		Result	Scorers	1	2	3	4	5
17. 8.91	Millwall	(h)	1 0	Mustoe	Pears	Parkinson	Phillips	Mowbray	Kernaghan
21. 8.91	Derby County	(a)	0 2		Pears	Parkinson	Phillips	Mowbray	Kernaghan
24. 8.91	Ipswich Town	(a)	1 2	Wilkinson	Pears	Parkinson**	Phillips	Mowbray	Kernaghan
27. 8.91	Newcastle Utd	(h)	3 0	Wilkinson, Proctor, Falconer	Pears	Parkinson	Phillips	Mowbray	Kernaghan
31. 8.91	Portsmouth	(h)	2 0	Falconer, Slaven	Pears	Parkinson	Phillips	Mowbray	Kernaghan
4. 9.91	Oxford Utd	(a)	2 1	Slaven 2	Pears	Parkinson	Phillips	Mowbray	Kernaghan
7. 9.91	Watford	(a)	2 1	Wilkinson, Falconer	Pears	Parkinson	Phillips	Mowbray	Kernaghan
14. 9.91	Leicester City	(h)	3 0	Slaven, Wilkinson 2	Pears	Parkinson	Phillips	Mowbray	Kernaghan
17. 9.91	Tranmere Rov	(h)	1 0	Falconer	Pears	Parkinson	Phillips	Mowbray	Kernaghan
21. 9.91	Plymouth Argyle	(a)	1 1	Wilkinson	Pears	Parkinson**	Phillips	Mowbray	Kernaghan
28. 9.82	Sunderland	(h)	2 1	Slaven, Wilkinson	Pears	Parkinson	Phillips	Mowbray	Kernaghan
5.10.92	Bristol Rovers	(a)	1 2	Yates (og)	Pears	Parkinson	Phillips	Mowbray	Kernaghan
12.10.92	Wolves	(h)	0 0		Pears	Parkinson	Phillips	Mowbray	Kernaghan
19.10.92	Grimsby Town	(a)	0 1		Pears	Parkinson	Phillips	Mowbray	Kernaghan
26.10.92	Port Vale	(h)	1 0	Kernaghan	Pears	Parkinson	Phillips	Mowbray	Kernaghan
2.11.91	Southend Utd	(h)	1 1	Ripley	Pears	Parkinson*	Phillips	Mowbray	Kernaghan
5.11.91	Barnsley	(a)	1 2	Slaven	Pears	Parkinson*	Phillips	Mowbray	Kernaghan
9.11.91	Brighton	(a)	1 1	Slaven (pen)	Pears	Fleming	Phillips	Kernaghan	Mohan
16.11.91	Charlton	(h)	2 0	Mohan, Slaven	Pears	Fleming	Phillips	Kernaghan	Mohan
23.11.91	Bristol City	(h)	3 1	Payton, Slaven 2	Pears	Fleming	Phillips	Kernaghan	Mohan
30.11.91	Blackburn Rov	(a)	1 2	Slaven (pen)	Pears	Fleming**	Phillips	Kernaghan	Mohan
7.12.91	Swindon Town	(h)	2 2	Wilkinson, Slaven	Pears	Fleming	Phillips	Kernaghan	Mohan
26.12.91	Newcastle Utd	(a)	0 1	Wilkinson	Pears	Fleming	Phillips	Kernaghan	Mohan
28.12.91	Portsmouth	(a)	0 4		Pears	Fleming	Phillips	Kernaghan	Mohan
1. 1.92	Derby County	(h)	1 1	Mohan	Pears	Parkinson	Phillips	Kernaghan	Mohan
11. 1.92	Ipswich Town	(h)	1 0	Payton	Pears	Parkinson	Phillips	Kernaghan	Mohan
18. 1.92	Millwall	(a)	0 2		Pears	Parkinson	Phillips	Kernaghan	Mohan
8. 2.92	Port Vale	(a)	2 1	Hendrie, Mustoe	Pears	Parkinson	Phillips	Kernaghan	Mohan
22. 2.92	Blackburn Rov	(h)	0 0		Pears	Parkinson	Phillips	Gittens	Mohan
29. 2.92	Swindon Town	(a)	1 0	Kernaghan	Pears	Fleming	Phillips	Kernaghan	Gittens
7. 3.92	Cambridge Utd	(h)	1 1	Wilkinson	Pears	Parkinson**	Phillips	Kernaghan	Mohan
14. 3.92	Southend Utd	(a)	1 0	Slaven (pen)	Pears	Fleming	Phillips	Kernaghan	Mohan
17. 3.92	Cambridge Utd	(a)	0 0		Pears	Fleming	Phillips	Kernaghan	Mohan
21. 3.92	Brighton & HA	(h)	4 0	Slaven 3 (1 pen), Hendrie	Pears	Fleming	Phillips	Kernaghan	Mohan
28. 3.92	Charlton Ath	(a)	0 0		Pears	Fleming	Falconer	Kernaghan	Mohan
1. 4.92	Leicester City	(a)	1 2	Pollock	Pears	Fleming	Falconer	Kernaghan	Mohan
4. 4.92	Watford	(h)	1 2	Wilkinson	Pears	Fleming	Falconer	Kernaghan	Mohan**
7. 4.92	Bristol City	(a)	1 1	Hendrie	Pears	Fleming	Phillips	Kernaghan	Mohan
10. 4.92	Tranmere Rov	(a)	2 1	Proctor, Phillips	Pears	Fleming	Phillips	Kernaghan**	Mohan
13. 4.92	Barnsley	(h)	0 1		Pears	Fleming**	Phillips	Proctor	Gittens
15. 4.92	Oxford United	(h)	2 1	Ripley, Payton	Pears	Fleming	Phillips	Gittens	Mohan
18. 4.92	Plymouth Argyle	(h)	2 1	Ripley, Falconer	Pears	Fleming	Phillips	Gittens	Mohan
20. 4.92	Sunderland	(a)	0 1		Pears	Fleming	Phillips	Gittens	Mohan*
25. 4.92	Bristol Rovers	(h)	2 1	Wilkinson 2	Pears	Fleming	Phillips	Gittens	Mohan

1991–92

Division 2

6	7	8	9	10	11	12	Crowd
Falconer	Mustoe	Proctor	Wilkinson	Ripley	Hendrie		16,234
Falconer	Mustoe*	Proctor	Wilkinson	Ripley	Hendrie	Slaven	12,805
Falconer	Mustoe	Proctor*	Wilkinson	Ripley	Hendrie	Slaven/Fleming	9,822
Falconer	Mustoe	Proctor	Wilkinson	Ripley	Hendrie		16,970
Falconer	Mustoe*	Proctor	Wilkinson	Ripley	Hendrie	Slaven	12,320
Falconer	Mustoe	Proctor	Wilkinson	Ripley*	Hendrie	Slaven	4,229
Falconer	Slaven	Proctor	Wilkinson	Mustoe	Hendrie		8,715
Falconer	Slaven	Proctor	Wilkinson	Mustoe*	Hendrie	Ripley	16,633
Falconer	Slaven	Proctor	Wilkinson	Ripley	Hendrie*	Mustoe	16,550
Falconer	Slaven	Proctor*	Wilkinson	Ripley	Hendrie	Mustoe/Fleming	5,280
Mustoe	Slaven	Proctor	Wilkinson	Ripley	Hendrie		19.424
Mustoe**	Slaven*	Proctor	Wilkinson	Ripley	Hendrie	Shannon/Hewitt	4,936
Mustoe	Slaven	Proctor	Wilkinson	Ripley**	Pollock*	Fleming/Arnold	15,253
Mustoe	Slaven	Proctor	Wilkinson	Pollock	Marwood		10,265
Mustoe	Slaven	Proctor*	Wilkinson	Marwood	Hendrie	Pollock	11,403
Mustoe	Slaven	Pollock	Wilkinson	Ripley*	Hendrie	Fleming/Young	9,664
Mustoe	Slaven	Proctor	Wilkinson	Ripley	Hendrie	Fleming	6,525
Mustoe	Marwood*	Pollock**	Wilkinson	Ripley	Hendrie	Slaven/Proctor	8,270
Mustoe	Slaven	Proctor	Wilkinson	Ripley*	Hendrie	Hewitt	13,093
Mustoe	Slaven	Proctor	Wilkinson	Payton*	Ripley	Pollock	12,928
Mustoe*	Slaven	Proctor	Wilkinson	Peake	Ripley	Pollock/Parkinson	15,541
Mustoe	Slaven	Proctor	Wilkinson	Ripley	Pollock*	Peake	13,300
Mustoe	Slaven	Proctor	Wilkinson	Peake	Pollock*	Payton	26,563
Mustoe	Slaven	Payton	Wilkinson	Pollock*	Peake	Proctor	12,324
Mustoe*	Slaven	Peake	Wilkinson	Ripley	Proctor**	Payton/Pollock	16,288
Mustoe	Slaven	Pollock	Wilkinson	Hendrie*	Ripley	Payton	15,104
Mustoe	Pollock**	Payton*	Wilkinson	Hendrie	Ripley	Proctor/Peake	8,125
Mustoe	Pollock*	Peake	Wilkinson	Hendrie	Ripley	Proctor	7,019
Mustoe*	Peake	Payton	Wilkinson	Hendrie**	Ripley	Proctor/Slaven	19,353
Mustoe	Hendrie	Peake	Wilkinson	Pollock	Ripley		10,379
Peake	Slaven	Pollock*	Wilkinson	Hendrie	Ripley	Proctor/Gittens	14,686
Peake	Slaven	Pollock	Wilkinson	Hendrie	Falconer		7,272
Peake	Slaven	Pollock*	Wilkinson	Hendrie	Falconer	Gittens	7,318
Peake	Slaven	Pollock	Wilkinson*	Hendrie**	Falconer	Payton/Ripley	13,054
Peake	Slaven	Proctor	Wilkinson	Hendrie	Ripley*	Payton	8,250
Peake	Slaven	Pollock*	Wilkinson	Hendrie	Ripley**	Payton/Proctor	19,352
Peake	Slaven*	Pollock	Wilkinson	Hendrie	Ripley	Payton/Proctor	13,669
Peake	Pollock	Payton*	Wilkinson	Hendrie	Falconer	Ripley	12,814
Peake	Proctor	Falconer	Wilkinson	Hendrie	Ripley*	Payton/Gittens	8,842
Peake	Falconer	Pollock*	Wilkinson	Hendrie	Ripley	Slaven/Parkinson	12,743
Peake**	Slaven	Falconer	Wilkinson	Hendrie*	Ripley	Payton/Proctor	11,928
Proctor	Hendrie**	Falconer	Wilkinson	Payton	Ripley*	Slaven/Parkinson	15,086
Peake	Proctor**	Falconer	Wilkinson	Hendrie	Ripley	Slaven/Payton	25,093
Peake**	Hendrie	Falconer	Wilkinson	Payton	Ripley*	Slaven/Pollock	14,057

1991–92

Division 2

Date	Opposition		Result	Scorers	1	2	3	4	5
28. 4.92	Grimsby Town	(h)	2 0	Phillips (pen), Wilkinson	Pears	Fleming	Phillips	Gittens	Mohan
2. 5.92	Wolves	(a)	2 1	Gittens, Wilkinson	Ironside	Fleming	Phillips	Gittens	Mohan

FA Cup

Date	Opposition		Result	Scorers	1	2	3	4	5
4. 1.92	Manchester City	(h)	2 1	Kernaghan, Wilkinson	Pears	Parkinson	Phillips	Kernaghan	Mohan
4. 2.92	Sheffield Wed	(a)	2 1	Hendrie, Wilkinson	Pears	Parkinson	Phillips	Kernaghan	Mohan
15. 2.92	Portsmouth	(a)	1 1	Kernaghan	Pears	Parkinson	Phillips	Kernaghan	Mohan
26. 2.92	Portsmouth	(h)	2 4	Wilkinson 2	Pears	Parkinson	Phillips	Pollock	Mohan

League Cup

Date	Opposition		Result	Scorers	1	2	3	4	5
24. 9.91	Bournemouth	(h)	1 1	Wilkinson	Pears	Parkinson	Phillips	Mowbray	Kernaghan
8.10.91	Bournemouth	(a)	2 1*	Hendrie, Parkinson (pen)	Pears	Parkinson	Phillips	Mowbray	Kernaghan
29.10.91	Barnsley	(h)	1 0	Wilkinson	Pears	Parkinson	Phillips	Mowbray	Kernaghan
3.12.91	Manchester City	(h)	2 1	Mustoe, Wilkinson	Pears	Fleming	Phillips	Kernaghan	Mohan
8. 1.92	Peterborough	(a)	0 0		Pears	Parkinson	Phillips	Kernaghan	Mohan
12. 2.92	Peterborough	(h)	1 0	Ripley	Pears	Parkinson	Phillips	Kernaghan	Mohan
4. 3.92	Manchester Utd	(h)	0 0		Pears	Parkinson	Phillips	Kernaghan	Mohan
11. 3.92	Manchester Utd	(a)	1 2*	Slaven	Pears	Fleming	Phillips	Kernaghan	Mohan

*After extra time

ZDS Cup

Date	Opposition		Result	Scorers	1	2	3	4	5
22.10.91	Derby County	(h)	4 2*	Wilkinson 2, Phillips, Slaven	Pears	Parkinson*	Phillips	Mowbray	Kernaghan
26.11.91	Tranmere Rov	(h)	0 1		Pears	Fleming	Phillips	Kernaghan	Mohan

*After extra time

1992–93

Premier

Date	Opposition		Result	Scorers	1	2	3	4	5
15. 8.92	Coventry City	(a)	1 2	Wilkinson	Pears	Morris	Phillips	Kernaghan	Whyte
19. 8.92	Manchester City	(h)	2 0	Slaven 2	Ironside	Morris	Phillips	Kernaghan	Whyte
22. 8.92	Leeds United	(h)	4 1	Wilkinson 2, Wright, Hendrie	Ironside	Morris	Phillips	Kernaghan	Whyte
29. 8.92	Southampton	(a)	1 2	Wilkinson	Ironside	Morris	Phillips	Kernaghan	Whyte
1. 9.92	Ipswich Town	(h)	2 2	Kernaghan, Wilkinson	Ironside*	Parkinson	Phillips	Kernaghan	Whyte
5. 9.92	Sheffield United	(h)	2 0	Falconer, Wright	Horne	Morris	Phillips	Kernaghan	Whyte
12. 9.92	Manchester City	(a)	1 0	Flitcroft (og)	Horne	Morris	Phillips	Kernaghan	Whyte
19. 9.92	Q.P.R.	(a)	3 3	Kernaghan, Wright, Falconer	Horne	Morris	Phillips	Kernaghan	Whyte
26. 9.92	Aston Villa	(h)	2 3	Slaven, McGrath (og)	Ironside	Morris	Phillips	Kernaghan	Whyte
3.10.92	Manchester Utd	(h)	1 1	Slaven	Ironside	Morris	Phillips	Gittens	Whyte
17.10.92	Tottenham Hot	(a)	2 2	Mustoe, Wilkinson	Pears	Morris	Phillips	Kernaghan	Whyte
21.10.92	Nottingham For	(a)	0 1		Pears	Morris	Phillips	Kernaghan	Whyte

1991–92

Division 2

6	7	8	9	10	11	12	Crowd	
Pollock	Hendrie	Falconer	Wilkinson	Payton	Ripley		18,570	
Pollock	Slaven**	Falconer	Wilkinson	Hendrie	Ripley	Payton/Peake	19,123	

FA Cup

Mustoe*	Slaven**	Pollock	Wilkinson	Peake	Ripley	Hendrie/Payton	21,174	round 3
Mustoe	Pollock*	Peake	Wilkinson	Hendrie	Ripley**	Proctor/Payton	29,772	round 4
Mustoe	Pollock**	Peake	Wilkinson	Hendrie*	Ripley	Proctor/Payton	18,138	round 5
Mustoe	Peake	Payton*	Wilkinson	Hendrie	Ripley	Slaven	19,479	round 5r

League Cup

Falconer*	Slaven	Proctor	Wilkinson	Ripley	Hendrie	Mustoe	10,577	round 2/1
Mustoe	Shannon**	Proctor	Wilkinson	Ripley*	Hendrie	Slaven/Pollock	5,528	round 2/2
Mustoe	Slaven	Pollock	Wilkinson	Marwood*	Hendrie	Fleming	9,381	round 3
Mustoe	Slaven	Proctor	Wilkinson	Ripley	Pollock		17,286	round 4
Mustoe	Slaven	Hendrie	Wilkinson	Pollock	Ripley		15,302	round 5
Mustoe	Proctor	Pollock	Wilkinson	Hendrie	Ripley		21,973	round 5r
Mustoe*	Slaven	Pollock	Wilkinson	Hendrie	Ripley	Proctor	25,572	s/f 1
Mustoe*	Slaven	Pollock	Wilkinson	Hendrie	Ripley**	Proctor/Falconer	45,875	s/f 2

ZDS Cup

Mustoe	Slaven	Proctor	Wilkinson	Marwood	Pollock**	Fleming/Arnold	6,385	round 1
Mustoe	Slaven	Proctor	Wilkinson	Ripley	Pollock*	Young	6,952	round 2

1992–93

Premier

Peake	Wright	Mustoe*	Wilkinson	Hendrie	Falconer	Slaven	12,681	
Peake	Slaven	Falconer	Wilkinson	Wright*	Hendrie	Mustoe	15,369	
Peake	Slaven*	Falconer	Wilkinson**	Wright	Hendrie	Pollock/Mustoe	18,649	
Peake	Slaven	Falconer	Wilkinson	Wright	Mustoe		13,003	
Peake	Slaven	Falconer	Wilkinson	Wright	Mustoe	Horne	14,255	
Peake	Slaven	Falconer	Wilkinson	Wright	Mustoe		15,179	
Peake	Mustoe	Falconer	Wilkinson	Wright	Hendrie		25,244	
Pollock*	Hendrie	Falconer	Wilkinson	Wright	Mustoe	Slaven	12,272	
Peake	Slaven	Mustoe	Wilkinson	Pollock	Wright		20,905	
Peake	Slaven	Mustoe	Wilkinson	Wright	Pollock*	Hendrie	24,172	
Gittens	Slaven*	Mustoe	Wilkinson	Wright	Proctor	Fleming	24,735	
Gittens	Slaven	Kavanagh*	Wilkinson	Wright	Proctor	Fleming	17,846	

1992–93

Premier

Date	Opposition		Result	Scorers	1	2	3	4	5
24.10.92	Sheffield Wed	(h)	1 1	Wilkinson	Pears	Morris	Phillips	Kernaghan	Fleming
31.10.92	Norwich City	(a)	1 1	Wilkinson	Pears	Fleming	Phillips	Kernaghan	Whyte
7.11.92	Liverpool	(a)	1 4	Phillips (pen)	Pears	Fleming	Phillips	Kernaghan*	Whyte
21.11.92	Wimbledon	(h)	2 0	Hendrie, Morris	Pears	Fleming	Phillips**	Gittens	Whyte
28.11.92	Oldham Ath	(a)	1 4	Falconer	Pears	Fleming	Parkinson	Mustoe	Whyte
5.12.92	Blackburn Rov	(h)	3 2	Hendrie 3	Pears	Fleming	Phillips	Mohan	Whyte
11.12.92	Chelsea	(h)	0 0		Pears	Fleming	Phillips	Mohan	Whyte
19.12.92	Arsenal	(a)	1 1	Seaman (og)	Pears	Fleming	Phillips	Mohan	Whyte
26.12.92	Everton	(a)	2 2	Hignett 2	Pears	Fleming	Phillips	Mohan	Whyte
28.12.92	Crystal Palace	(h)	0 1		Pears	Fleming**	Phillips	Mohan	Whyte
4. 1.93	QPR	(h)	0 1		Pears	Fleming	Phillips	Mohan	Gittens
17. 1.93	Aston Villa	(a)	1 5	Hignett	Pears	Mohan	Phillips	Whyte**	Gittens
26. 1.93	Southampton	(h)	2 1	Mohan, Wilkinson	Pears	Fleming	Phillips	Morris	Mohan
30. 1.93	Leeds Utd	(a)	0 3		Pears	Fleming	Phillips	Morris	Mohan
6. 2.93	Coventry City	(h)	0 2		Pears	Morris**	Phillips	Mohan	Gittens
9. 2.93	Sheffield United	(a)	0 2		Pears*	Fleming	Parkinson	Whyte	Mohan
20. 2.93	Nottingham For	(h)	1 2	Phillips	Pears	Parkinson*	Phillips	Whyte	Gittens
27. 2.93	Manchester Utd	(a)	0 3		Pears	Morris	Phillips	Whyte	Mohan
2. 3.93	Ipswich Town	(a)	1 0	Wilkinson	Ironside	Morris	Phillips	Kernaghan	Peake
9. 3.93	Wimbledon	(a)	0 2		Pears	Morris	Phillips	Kernaghan	Peake
13. 3.93	Liverpool	(h)	1 2	Nicol (og)	Ironside	Morris	Phillips	Mohan	Peake*
20. 3.93	Blackburn Rov	(a)	1 1	Hendrie	Ironside	Morris*	Phillips	Mohan	Peake
22. 3.93	Oldham Ath	(h)	2 3	Mohan, Hignett	Ironside	Fleming	Phillips	Mohan	Peake
3. 4.93	Chelsea	(a)	0 4		Ironside	Fleming	Phillips	Hignett*	Kernaghan
6. 4.93	Arsenal	(h)	1 0	Hendrie	Pears	Fleming	Phillips	Kernaghan	Mohan
10. 4.93	Everton	(h)	1 2	Wilkinson	Pears	Fleming	Phillips	Kernaghan	Mohan
12. 4.93	Crystal Palace	(a)	1 4	Wilkinson	Pears	Fleming	Phillips	Kernaghan	Mohan
20. 4.93	Tottenham Hot	(h)	3 0	Wright 2, Wilkinson	Pears	Fleming	Phillips	Kernaghan	Whyte
1. 5.93	Sheffield Wed	(a)	3 2	Falconer, Pollock, Hendrie	Collett	Fleming	Phillips	Hignett	Morris
8. 5.93	Norwich City	(h)	3 3	Falconer, Wilkinson, Hendrie	Collett	Fleming	Phillips*	Kernaghan	Whyte

FA Cup

Date	Opposition		Result	Scorers	1	2	3	4	5
13. 1.93	Chelsea	(h)	2 1	Wright, Falconer	Pears	Fleming*	Phillips	Mohan	Gittens
23. 1.93	Nottingham For	(a)	1 1	Falconer	Pears	Fleming	Phillips	Morris	Mohan
3. 2.93	Nottingham For	(h)	0 3		Pears	Fleming	Phillips	Morris	Mohan

League Cup

Date	Opposition		Result	Scorers	1	2	3	4	5
23. 9.92	Newcastle Utd	(a)	0 0		Ironside	Morris	Phillips	Kernaghan	Whyte
7.10.92	Newcastle Utd	(h)	1 3	Wilkinson	Ironside	Morris	Phillips	Kernaghan	Whyte

1992–93

Premier

6	7	8	9	10	11	12	Crowd
Gittens	Slaven	Proctor	Wilkinson	Kavanagh	Wright		18,414
Gittens	Wright*	Falconer	Wilkinson	Proctor	Hendrie	Morris	14,449
Gittens	Mustoe	Falconer	Wilkinson	Proctor**	Hendrie	Morris/Slaven	34,974
Mustoe	Falconer	Pollock*	Wilkinson	Hendrie	Morris	Proctor/Kavanagh	14,524
Gittens	Falconer	Hignett*	Wilkinson	Proctor**	Wright	Pollock/Kavanagh	12,401
Mustoe*	Hendrie	Peake	Wilkinson	Hignett**	Wright	Pollock/Proctor	20,096
Pollock*	Hendrie	Peake	Wilkinson	Hignett	Wright	Kavanagh	15,599
Pollock	Hendrie	Peake	Wilkinson	Hignett*	Wright**	Falconer/Proctor	23,197
Pollock*	Hendrie	Peake	Wilkinson	Hignett	Wright	Falconer	24,391
Pollock*	Hendrie	Peake	Wilkinson	Hignett	Wright	Falconer/Proctor	21,123
Pollock	Hignett	Peake	Wilkinson	Wright*	Hendrie	Falconer	15,616
Falconer	Kavanagh*	Peake	Wilkinson	Wright	Hendrie	Pollock/Hignett	19,977
Falconer	Wright	Pollock	Wilkinson	Peake	Hendrie		13,921
Falconer	Wright*	Pollock	Wilkinson	Peake	Hendrie	Hignett	30,344
Falconer	Slaven	Hignett	Wilkinson	Peake	Hendrie*	Wright/Pollock	14,008
Gittens	Slaven	Pollock	Wright	Peake*	Hignett	Proctor/Ironside	15,184
Peake	Slaven	Hignett**	Wilkinson	Kamara	Wright	Morris/Kavanagh	15,639
Peake	Hendrie	Mustoe*	Wilkinson	Kamara	Wright	Slaven	36,251
Whyte	Hendrie	Mustoe	Wilkinson	Kamara*	Wright	Falconer	15,430
Whyte	Hendrie	Mustoe	Wilkinson	Falconer	Wright*	Slaven	5,821
Whyte	Hendrie	Mustoe	Wilkinson	Falconer	Hignett	Wright	22,463
Whyte	Wright	Mustoe	Wilkinson	Falconer	Hendrie	Kamara	14,041
Whyte*	Hendrie	Mustoe**	Wilkinson	Falconer	Wright	Kamara/Hignett	12,290
Whyte	Hendrie	Mustoe	Wilkinson	Falconer	Wright	Marshall	13,034
Peake	Hendrie	Kavanagh	Wilkinson	Pollock	Hignett		12,726
Peake	Hendrie	Kavanagh*	Wilkinson	Pollock	Hignett**	Whyte/Moore	16,627
Peake	Hendrie	Kavanagh	Wilkinson	Pollock	Hignett		15,123
Peake	Hendrie	Wright	Wilkinson	Pollock	Hignett		14,472
Whyte	Hendrie	Pollock*	Wilkinson	Peake	Wright**	Marshall/Falconer	25,949
Peake	Hendrie	Falconer	Wilkinson	Hignett**	Mustoe	Moore/Marshall	15,155

FA Cup

6	7	8	9	10	11	12	Crowd	
Kavanagh**	Hendrie	Peake	Wilkinson	Falconer	Wright	Pollock/Proctor	16,766	round 3
Falconer	Wright	Pollock	Wilkinson	Peake	Hendrie		22,296	round 4
Falconer	Wright	Pollock*	Wilkinson	Peake**	Hendrie	Kavanagh/Slaven	20,514	round 4r

League Cup

6	7	8	9	10	11	12	Crowd	
Pollock	Hendrie	Falconer*	Wilkinson	Wright	Mustoe	Slaven	25,814	round 2/1
Peake**	Slaven	Mustoe	Wilkinson	Wright	Hendrie*	Pollock/Gittens	24,390	round 2/2

1993–94
Division 1

Date	Opposition		Result	Scorers	1	2	3	4	5
14. 8.93	Notts County	(a)	3 2	Wilkinson, Moore 2	Pears	Morris	Liburd	Pollock	Kernaghan
21. 8.93	Derby County	(h)	3 0	Kernaghan, Short (og), Hendrie	Pears	Morris	Liburd	Pollock	Kernaghan
24. 8.93	Barnsley	(a)	4 1	Moore 2, Hendrie 2	Pears	Morris*	Liburd	Pollock	Kernaghan
28. 8.93	Wolves	(a)	3 2	Hendrie 2, Pollock	Pears	Morris	Liburd	Pollock	Kernaghan
11. 9.93	Southend Utd	(a)	0 1		Pears	Morris	Liburd	Pollock	Kernaghan
14. 9.93	Stoke City	(h)	1 2	Hignett	Pears	Morris	Liburd	Pollock	Kernaghan
18. 9.93	Luton Town	(h)	0 0		Pears	Morris*	Liburd	Pollock	Mohan
25. 9.93	West Brom	(a)	1 1	Whyte	Pears	Morris	Liburd	Pollock	Mohan
29. 9.93	Leicester City	(h)	2 0	Wilkinson, Hendrie	Pears	Morris	Liburd	Pollock	Mohan
2.10.93	Birmingham City	(h)	2 2	Hendrie, Moore	Pears	Morris	Liburd	Pollock	Mohan
10.10.93	Watford	(a)	0 2		Pears	Morris	Liburd	Stamp	Mohan
17.10.93	Sunderland	(h)	4 1	Hignett, Hendrie, Wilkinson 2	Pears	Morris	Liburd	Pollock	Mohan
24.10.93	Millwall	(a)	1 1	Barber (og)	Pears	Morris*	Liburd	Fleming	Mohan
30.10.93	Peterborough	(h)	1 1	Mustoe	Pears	Morris	Liburd	Fleming	Mohan
2.11.93	Portsmouth	(a)	0 2		Pears	Barron	Liburd	Mustoe	Mohan
6.11.93	Bristol City	(h)	0 1		Pears	Fleming	Liburd	Gannon	Mohan
21.11.93	Bolton Wand	(h)	0 1		Pears	Fleming	Liburd	Mustoe	Mohan
4.12.93	Bristol City	(a)	0 0		Pears	Fleming	Liburd*	Mustoe	Mohan
11.12.93	Stoke City	(a)	1 3	Peake	Pears	Fleming*	Liburd	Vickers**	Mohan
18.12.93	Notts County	(h)	3 0	Moore, Kavanagh 2	Pears	Fleming	Liburd	Mustoe	Mohan
27.12.93	Nottingham For	(a)	1 1	Moore	Pears	Fleming	Liburd	Mustoe	Mohan
29.12.93	Tranmere Rov	(h)	0 0		Pears	Fleming	Liburd	Mustoe	Mohan
1. 1.94	Oxford United	(a)	1 1	Pollock	Pears	Fleming	Liburd	Mustoe	Mohan
3. 1.94	Grimsby Town	(h)	1 0	Wilkinson	Pears	Fleming	Liburd	Pollock	Mohan
16. 1.94	Sunderland	(a)	1 2	Vickers	Pears	Fleming	Liburd	Pollock	Mohan
22. 1.94	Watford	(h)	1 1	Moore	Pears	Fleming	Whyte	Pollock	Mohan
6. 2.94	Millwall	(h)	4 2	Hignett 2, Vickers, Wilkinson	Pears	Fleming	Liburd	Peake	Vickers
12. 2.94	Peterborough	(a)	0 1		Pears	Fleming	Liburd	Peake	Vickers
22. 2.94	Derby County	(a)	1 0	Vickers	Pears	Fleming	Liburd	Peake	Vickers
5. 3.94	Wolves	(h)	1 0	Wilkinson	Pears	Fleming	Liburd*	Pollock*	Vickers
8. 3.94	Luton Town	(a)	1 1	Mustoe	Pears	Fleming	Mohan	Pollock	Vickers
12. 3.94	Leicester City	(a)	0 2		Pears	Fleming	Mohan	Pollock	Vickers
15. 3.94	Southend Utd	(h)	1 0	Wilkinson	Pears	Fleming	Liburd	Pollock	Vickers
19. 3.94	WBA	(h)	3 0	Wilkinson, Pollock, Hendrie	Pears	Fleming	Liburd	Pollock	Vickers
23. 3.94	Crystal Palace	(a)	1 0	Hignett	Pears	Fleming	Liburd	Mustoe	Vickers
26. 3.94	Birmingham City	(a)	0 1		Pears	Fleming	Liburd	Pollock	Vickers
29. 3.94	Grimsby Town	(a)	1 1	Pollock	Pears	Fleming	Liburd	Pollock	Vickers
2. 4.94	Nottingham For	(h)	2 2	Pollock 2	Pears	Fleming	Liburd*	Pollock	Vickers
4. 4.94	Tranmere Rov	(a)	0 4		Pears	Fleming	Winnie	Pollock	Vickers
9. 4.94	Oxford United	(h)	2 1	Moore, Wilkinson	Pears	Fleming	Liburd	Pollock*	Vickers
16. 4.94	Portsmouth	(h)	0 2		Pears	Fleming	Liburd	Pollock	Vickers
19. 4.94	Charlton Ath	(h)	2 0	Moore, Hendrie	Pears	Fleming	Liburd	Pollock	Vickers
23. 4.94	Bolton Wand	(a)	1 4	Wilkinson	Pears	Fleming	Liburd	Pollock	Vickers

1993–94
Division 1

6	7	8	9	10	11	12	Crowd
Whyte	Hendrie	Hignett*	Wilkinson	Mustoe	Moore	Fleming	9.392
Whyte	Hendrie	Hignett	Wilkinson	Mustoe	Moore		15,168
Whyte	Hendrie	Hignett	Wilkinson	Mustoe	Moore	Fleming	10,597
Whyte	Hendrie	Hignett*	Wilkinson	Mustoe	Moore	Fleming	21,061
Whyte	Hendrie	Hignett	Wilkinson	Mustoe	Moore		6,495
Whyte	Hendrie	Hignett	Wilkinson	Mustoe*	Moore	Wright	13,189
Whyte	Hendrie	Hignett**	Wilkinson	Mustoe	Moore	Fleming/Kavanagh	12,487
Whyte*	Fleming	Hignett	Wilkinson	Mustoe	Moore	Kavanagh	15,766
Whyte	Hendrie*	Hignett	Wilkinson	Mustoe	Moore	Fleming	11,871
Whyte	Hendrie	Hignett*	Wilkinson	Mustoe	Moore	Kavanagh	13,801
Whyte	Hendrie	Hignett	Wilkinson	Mustoe	Moore		7,582
Whyte	Hendrie	Hignett	Wilkinson	Mustoe	Moore		12,772
Whyte	Hendrie	Hignett	Wilkinson	Mustoe	Moore	Kavanagh	6,686
Whyte	Hendrie	Hignett	Wilkinson	Mustoe	Moore		10,704
Whyte	Fleming	Kavanagh	Wilkinson	Johnson	Hignett		12,503
Whyte	Kavanagh*	Hignett	Wilkinson**	Mustoe	Moore	Barron/Illman	9,687
Whyte	Kavanagh*	Hignett	Stamp*	Peake	Moore	Morris/Forrester	6,828
Whyte	Stamp	Hignett	Wilkinson	Peake	Moore	Vickers	8,441
Whyte	Peake	Hignett	Wilkinson	Mustoe	Moore	Hendrie/Gannon	13,777
Whyte*	Gannon	Kavanagh**	Wilkinson	Peake	Moore	Johnson/Todd	7,869
Whyte	Gannon	Pollock	Wilkinson	Peake	Moore		26,901
Whyte	Gannon	Pollock	Wilkinson	Peake	Moore		12,351
Vickers	Gannon	Pollock	Wilkinson	Peake	Moore		5,763
Vickers	Mustoe	Gannon	Wilkinson	Peake	Moore		10,441
Vickers	Stamp*	Peake	Wilkinson	Mustoe	Moore	Hignett	16,473
Vickers	Kavanagh	Hignett	Wilkinson	Peake	Moore		8,089
Whyte	Wright	Hignett	Wilkinson	Mustoe	Moore		6,286
Whyte	Wright	Hignett*	Wilkinson	Mustoe	Moore	Kavanagh	7,020
Whyte	Stamp	Hendrie	Wilkinson	Mustoe	Moore*	Wright	14,716
Whyte	Hendrie	Mustoe	Wilkinson	Peake	Moore	Wright/Mohan	12,092
Whyte	Hendrie	Mustoe	Wilkinson	Peake	Moore		6,741
Whyte	Hendrie	Mustoe*	Wilkinson	Peake	Moore**	Wright/Hignett	16,116
Whyte	Hendrie	Mustoe	Wilkinson	Peake	Moore		7,378
Whyte	Hendrie*	Mustoe	Wilkinson	Peake	Moore	Wright	10,516
Whyte	Pollock	Hignett	Wilkinson	Peake	Moore		12,811
Whyte	Mustoe*	Hignett	Wilkinson	Peake	Moore	Wright	12,409
Whyte	Stamp	Hignett	Wilkinson	Peake	Moore		5,709
Whyte	Hendrie	Wright	Wilkinson	Peake	Moore	Mohan	17,056
Whyte	Hendrie	Wright	Wilkinson	Peake	Moore*	Mohan/Stamp	8,225
Whyte	Hendrie	Wright	Wilkinson	Peake	Moore	Stamp	8,586
Whyte	Hendrie	Wright*	Wilkinson	Peake	Moore	Hignett	10,041
Whyte	Hendrie	Stamp	Wilkinson	Peake	Moore*	Hignett	6,982
Whyte	Hendrie	Stamp	Wilkinson	Peake	Moore*	Wright	9,220

1993–94

Division 1

Date	Opposition		Result	Scorers	1	2	3	4	5
26. 4.94	Barnsley	(h)	5 0	Taggart (og), Pollock 2, Wilkinson 2 (1 pen)	Pears	Fleming	Liburd	Pollock	Vickers
1. 5.94	Crystal Palace	(h)	2 3	Liburd, Wilkinson	Pears	Fleming	Liburd	Pollock	Vickers
8. 5.94	Charlton Ath	(a)	5 2	Wilkinson, Hendrie 3, Pollock	Pears	Fleming	Todd	Pollock	Vickers

FA Cup

Date	Opposition		Result	Scorers	1	2	3	4	5
8. 1.94	Cardiff City	(a)	2 2	Wilkinson, Moore	Pears	Fleming	Liburd	Mustoe	Mohan
19. 1.94	Cardiff City	(h)	1 2*	Kavanagh	Pears	Fleming	Liburd	Pollock	Mohan

League Cup

Date	Opposition		Result	Scorers	1	2	3	4	5
21. 9.93	Brighton & HA	(h)	5 0	Hignett 4, Hendrie	Pears	Morris	Liburd	Pollock	Mohan
5.10.93	Brighton & HA	(a)	3 1	Wilkinson, Hignett, Hendrie	Pears	Morris*	Liburd	Stamp	Mohan
27.10.93	Sheffield Wed	(h)	1 1	Hendrie	Pears	Morris	Liburd	Fleming	Mohan
10.11.93	Sheffield Wed	(a)	1 2	Mustoe	Pears	Fleming	Liburd	Mustoe	Mohan

Anglo-Italian Cup

Date	Opposition		Result	Scorers	1	2	3	4	5
31. 8.93	Grimsby Town	(a)	1 2	Hendrie	Pears	Morris*	Barness	Mustoe	Mohan
7. 9.93	Barnsley	(h)	3 0	Hendrie, Wilkinson 2 (1 pen)	Pears	Fleming	Liburd	Pollock	Mohan
12.10.93	Pisa	(a)	1 3	Hendrie	Collett	Fleming	Liburd	Todd	Mohan
16.11.93	Ancona	(h)	0 0		Collett	Fleming	Liburd	Gannon*	Mohan
24.11.93	Ascoli	(a)	0 3		Collett	Fleming	Liburd	Barron	Mohan
22.12.93	Brescia	(h)	0 1		Pears	Todd*	Liburd	Mustoe	Mohan

1994–95

Division 1

Date	Opposition		Result	Scorers	1	2	3	4	5
13. 9.94	Burnley	(h)	2 0	Hendrie 2	Miller	Cox	Fleming	Vickers	Pearson
20. 9.94	Southend Utd	(a)	2 0	Hendrie 2	Miller	Cox	Fleming	Vickers	Pearson
27. 9.94	Bolton Wand	(h)	1 0	Wilkinson	Miller	Cox	Fleming	Vickers	Pearson
31. 8.94	Derby County	(a)	1 0	Blackmore	Miller	Cox	Fleming	Vickers	Pearson
3. 9.94	Watford	(a)	1 1	Blackmore	Miller	Cox	Fleming	Whyte	Pearson
11. 9.94	Sunderland	(h)	2 2	Moore, Pearson	Miller	Cox	Fleming	Vickers	Pearson
14. 9.94	West Brom	(h)	2 1	Mustoe, Hignett (pen)	Miller	Cox	Fleming	Vickers	Pearson**
17. 9.94	Port Vale	(a)	1 2	Pollock	Pears	Cox	Fleming	Vickers	Whyte
24. 9.94	Bristol City	(a)	1 0	Hendrie	Pears	Cox	Fleming	Vickers	Whyte
1.10.94	Millwall	(h)	3 0	Wilkinson, Hendrie, OG	Pears	Cox	Fleming	Vickers	Whyte
8.10.94	Tranmere Rovers	(h)	0 1		Pears	Cox	Fleming	Vickers	Whyte
15.10.94	Luton Town	(a)	1 5	Whyte	Pears	Cox	Fleming	Vickers	Whyte
23.10.94	Portsmouth	(a)	0 0		Miller	Cox	Fleming	Vickers	Whyte
29.10.94	Swindon Town	(h)	3 1	Cox, Wilkinson, Hendrie	Miller	Cox	Fleming	Vickers	Whyte

1993–94

Division 1

6	7	8	9	10	11	12	Crowd	
Todd	Hendrie	Mustoe	Wilkinson	Peake	Wright		6,368	
Whyte	Hendrie	Mustoe	Wilkinson	Peake	Wright		8,638	
Whyte*	Hendrie	Mustoe*	Wilkinson	Peake	Wright	Mohan/Kavanagh	8,905	

FA Cup

6	7	8	9	10	11	12	Crowd	
Vickers	Pollock	Stamp	Wilkinson	Peake	Moore		13,750	round 3
Vickers	Mustoe	Hignett	Wilkinson	Peake	Kavanagh	Whyte	10,769	round 3r

League Cup

6	7	8	9	10	11	12	Crowd	
Whyte	Hendrie	Hignett	Wilkinson	Mustoe	Moore		5,651	round 2/1
Whyte	Hendrie	Hignett	Wilkinson	Mustoe	Moore**	Todd/Fleming	2074	round 2/2
Whyte	Hendrie	Hignett	Wilkinson	Mustoe	Moore		14,765	round 3
Barron	Kavanagh*	Hignett	Stamp	Peake	Moore	Illman	19,482	round 3r

Anglo-Italian Cup

6	7	8	9	10	11	12	Crowd	
Whyte	Fleming	Kavanagh	Wilkinson	Hendrie	Wright	Hignett/Pollock	996	preliminary
Whyte	Hendrie	Hignett	Wilkinson	Mustoe*	Moore**	Stamp/Wright	5,173	preliminary
Whyte	Hignett	Kavanagh	Hendrie	Mustoe	Illman*	Taylor	500	Inter Group B
Whyte	Illman	Hignett	Kavanagh	Peake	Moore	Barron	2,985	Inter Group B
Peake	Stamp	Hignett*	Kavanagh	Mustoe	Illman*	Moore/Johnson	1,200	Inter Group B
Whyte	Gannon	Kavanagh	Wilkinson	Peake	Moore**	Barron/Illman	1,633	Inter Group B

1994–95

Division 1

6	7	8	9	10	11	12	Crowd
Blackmore	Robson	Pollock	Wilkinson	Hendrie	Moore		23,343
Blackmore	Robson	Pollock	Wilkinson	Hendrie	Moore		6,722
Blackmore	Robson	Pollock*	Wilkinson	Hendrie	Moore	Mustoe*	19,570
Blackmore*	Robson	Pollock	Wilkinson	Hendrie	Moore	Mustoe*	14,659
Blackmore	Robson	Pollock	Wilkinson	Hendrie	Moore		9,478
Blackmore*	Robson	Pollock	Wilkinson	Hendrie	Moore	Hignett*	19,578
Hignett	Robson*	Pollock	Wilkinson	Hendrie	Moore	Mustoe*/Blackmore**	14,878
Hignett	Mustoe	Pollock	Wilkinson	Hendrie	Moore		10,313
Hignett	Mustoe	Pollock	Wilkinson	Hendrie	Moore		8,642
Blackmore	Mustoe	Pollock	Wilkinson	Hendrie	Hignett*	Moreno*	17,229
Blackmore*	Mustoe	Pollock	Wilkinson	Hendrie	Hignett	Moreno*	18,497
Blackmore	Hignett	Pollock	Wilkinson	Hendrie	Wright*	Kavanagh*	8,412
Blackmore	Todd	Pollock	Wilkinson	Hendrie	Moreno*	Hignett*	7,281
Blackmore	Todd	Pollock	Wilkinson	Hendrie	Moore*	Hignett*	17,328

1994–95

Division 1

Date	Opposition		Result	Scorers	1	2	3	4	5
1.11.94	Oldham Athletic	(h)	2 1	Moore, Hignett	Miller	Cox	Fleming	Vickers	Whyte
5.11.94	Grimsby Town	(a)	1 2	Hignett (pen)	Miller	Cox	Blackmore	Vickers	Whyte
20.11.94	Wolves	(h)	1 0	Hendrie	Miller	Cox	Morris	Vickers	Whyte
26.11.94	Charlton Ath	(a)	2 0	Hendrie, Pollock	Miller	Cox	Morris	Vickers	Whyte
3.12.94	Portsmouth	(h)	4 0	Wilkinson 2, Hignett 2	Miller	Cox	Morris	Vickers	Whyte
6.12.94	Reading	(a)	1 1	Wilkinson (pen)	Miller	Cox	Morris	Vickers	Whyte
10.12.94	Southend Utd	(h)	1 2	Hendrie	Miller	Morris	Whyte	Vickers	Pearson
18.12.94	Burnley	(a)	3 0	Hendrie 3	Miller	Cox	Fleming	Vickers	Whyte
26.12.94	Sheffield United	(a)	1 1	Hignett	Miller	Cox	Fleming	Vickers	Whyte
28.12.94	Notts County	(h)	2 1	Pearson, Hignett	Miller	Cox*	Fleming	Mustoe	Whyte
31.12.94	Stoke City	(a)	1 1	Vickers	Miller	Morris	Fleming	Vickers	Pearson
15. 1.95	Swindon Town	(a)	1 2	Hignett	Miller	Morris	Fleming	Vickers	Pearson
21. 1.95	Grimsby Town	(h)	1 1	Mustoe	Miller	Morris	Fleming	Vickers	Pearson*
4. 2.95	Reading	(h)	0 1		Miller	Morris	Whyte	Vickers	Pearson
18. 2.95	Charlton Ath	(h)	1 0	Fuchs	Miller	Morris	Whyte	Vickers	Pearson
21. 2.95	Wolves	(a)	2 0	Vickers, Fuchs	Miller	Morris	Whyte	Vickers	Pearson
26. 2.95	Millwall	(a)	0 0		Miller	Morris	Whyte	Vickers	Pearson
4. 3.95	Bristol City	(h)	3 0	Fuchs 3	Miller	Cox	Whyte	Vickers*	Pearson
7. 3.95	Watford	(h)	2 0	Mustoe, Fuchs	Miller	Cox	Whyte	Vickers	Pearson
11. 3.95	Bolton Wand	(a)	0 1		Miller	Cox	Whyte	Vickers	Pearson
14. 3.95	Barnsley	(h)	1 1	Moreno	Miller	Cox	Whyte	Vickers	Pearson
18. 3.95	Derby County	(h)	2 4	Pollock, Fuchs	Miller	Cox	O'Halloran*	Vickers	Pearson
21. 3.95	Sunderland	(a)	1 0	Pollock	Miller	Cox	Whyte	Vickers	Pearson
26. 3.95	Port Vale	(h)	3 0	Robson, Vickers, Fuchs	Miller	Cox	Whyte	Vickers	Pearson
1. 4.95	West Brom	(a)	3 1	Pollock, og, Moore	Miller	Cox	Whyte	Vickers	Anderson
5. 4.95	Oldham Athletic	(a)	0 1		Miller	Cox	Whyte	Vickers	Pearson
8. 4.95	Stoke City	(h)	2 1	Pearson, Moore	Miller	Cox*	Whyte	Vickers	Pearson
15. 4.95	Notts County	(a)	1 1	Fuchs	Miller	Cox	Whyte	Vickers	Pearson
17. 4.95	Sheffield United	(h)	1 1	Fjortoft	Miller	Cox	Whyte	Vickers	Pearson
22. 4.95	Barnsley	(a)	1 1	Fjortoft	Miller	Cox	Morris	Vickers	Anderson
30. 4.95	Luton Town	(h)	2 1	Hendrie 2	Miller	Cox	Whyte	Vickers	Pearson
7. 5.95	Tranmere Rov	(a)	1 1	Fjortoft	Miller	Cox	Morris	Vickers	Pearson

1994–95

Division 1

6	7	8	9	10	11	12	Crowd
Blackmore*	Todd	Pollock	Wilkinson	Hendrie	Moore	Hignett*	15,929
Todd	Hignett	Pollock	Wilkinson	Hendrie	Moore		8,488
Mustoe	Hignett	Pollock	Wilkinson*	Hendrie	Moore	Blackmore*	19,953
Pearson	Mustoe	Pollock	Wilkinson	Hendrie	Hignett		10,019
Mustoe	Hignett	Pollock	Wilkinson	Hendrie*	Moore	Moreno*	17,185
Pearson	Hignett*	Pollock	Wilkinson	Hendrie	Mustoe	Moore*	10,301
Mustoe	Cox	Todd*	Wilkinson	Hendrie	Moore	Blackmore***/ Moreno****	16,843
Pearson	Robson	Mustoe	Wilkinson	Hendrie	Moore		12,049
Pearson	Robson	Kavanagh	Wilkinson	Hendrie*	Moore	Hignett*	20,963
Pearson	Hignett	Pollock	Wilkinson	Hendrie	Moore	Morris*	21,558
Mustoe	Robson	Pollock	Wilkinson	Hendrie	Hignett		15,914
Whyte	Mustoe	Pollock	Hignett	Hendrie	Moore*	Kavanagh*	8,888
Mustoe	Blackmore	Pollock	Wilkinson	Hendrie	Hignett	Moore*	15,360
Mustoe	Hignett*	Pollock**	Wilkinson	Hendrie	Moore	Robson**/Fuchs*	17,982
Blackmore	Robson	Pollock	Fuchs	Mustoe	Moore		16,301
Blackmore	Robson	Pollock	Fuchs	Mustoe	Moore		26,611
Blackmore	Robson**	Pollock*	Fuchs	Mustoe	Moore	Cox*/Wilkinson**	7,247
Blackmore	Robson	Moreno	Fuchs**	Mustoe	Moore	Wilkinson**/Hignett*	17,371
Blackmore	Pollock	Moreno	Fuchs	Mustoe	Moore		16,630
Blackmore**	Robson*	Pollock	Fuchs	Mustoe	Hendrie	Moreno*/Stamp**	18,370
Mustoe	Hignett*	Pollock	Fuchs**	Moreno	Moore	Hendrie*	19,655
Mustoe	Robson	Pollock	Fuchs	Hendrie	Moore	Moreno	18,163
Mustoe	Robson	Pollock	Fuchs	Hendrie	Moore		16,501
Blackmore	Robson	Pollock	Fuchs	Hendrie	Moore*	Moreno*	17,401
Blackmore	Robson	Pollock	Fuchs	Fjortoft	Moore		20,256
Blackmore	Robson*	Pollock	Fuchs	Fjortoft	Moore	Hignett*	11,024
Kavanagh	Hignett	Pollock	Fjortoft	Hendrie	Moore**	Moreno**/Blackmore*	20,867
Kavanagh	Hignett**	Pollock	Fjortoft	Moreno*	Hendrie	Fuchs*/Stamp**	9,377
Blackmore	Kavanagh	Pollock	Fuchs	Fjortoft	Moore*	Hendrie*	23,225
Blackmore	Kavanagh	Pollock	Fjortoft	Hendrie	Moore		11,711
Blackmore	Robson	Pollock	Fjortoft	Hendrie	Moore		23,903
Whyte	Stamp	Liddle	Fjortoft	Hendrie*	Moreno	Freestone	16,377

1994–95

FA Cup

Date	Opposition		Result	Scorers	1	2	3	4	5
7. 3.95	Swansea City	(a)	1 1	Moore	Miller	Morris	Fleming	Vickers	Pearson
21. 3.95	Swansea City	(h)	1 2	Hendrie	Miller	Morris	Fleming	Vickers	Pearson

League Cup

					1	2	3	4	5
20. 9.94	Scarborough	(a)	4 1	Mustoe, Pollock, Hendrie, Moore	Pears	Cox	Fleming	Vickers	Whyte
27. 9.94	Scarborough	(h)	4 1	Wilkinson 3, Hignett	Pears	Morris	Fleming	Vickers*	Whyte
26.10.94	Aston Villa	(a)	0 1		Miller	Cox	Fleming	Vickers	Whyte

Anglo-Italian Cup

					1	2	3	4	5
24. 8.94	Piacenza	(h)	0 0		Miller	Morris	Taylor	Vickers	Todd
5.10.94	Cesena	(h)	1 1	Moreno	Pears	Morris	Taylor	Barron	Whyte
18.10.94	Udinese	(a)	0 0		Miller	Fleming	Taylor	Cox*	Vickers
15.11.94	Ancona	(a)	1 3	Morris	Roberts	Morris	Byrne	Liddle	Barron

1995–96

Premier

Date	Opposition		Result	Scorers	1	2	3	4	5
19. 8.95	Arsenal	(a)	1 1	Barmby	Miller	Cox	Morris	Vickers	Pearson
26. 8.95	Chelsea	(h)	2 0	Hignett, Fjortoft	Miller	Cox	Morris	Vickers	Pearson
30. 8.95	Newcastle Utd	(a)	0 1		Miller	Cox	Morris	Vickers	Pearson
9. 9.95	Bolton Wand	(a)	1 1	Hignett	Walsh	Cox	Morris	Vickers	Pearson
12. 9.95	Southampton	(h)	0 0		Walsh	Cox	Morris	Vickers	Pearson
16. 9.95	Coventry City	(h)	2 1	Vickers, Fjortoft	Walsh	Cox	Morris	Vickers	Pearson
23. 9.95	Manchester City	(a)	1 0	Barmby	Walsh	Cox	Morris	Vickers	Pearson
30. 9.95	Blackburn Rov	(h)	2 0	Barmby, Hignett	Walsh	Cox	Morris	Vickers	Pearson
15.10.95	Sheffield Wed	(a)	1 0	Hignett (pen)	Walsh	Cox	Morris	Vickers	Pearson
21.10.95	QPR	(h)	1 0	Hignett (pen)	Walsh	Cox	Morris	Vickers	Pearson
28.10.95	Manchester Utd	(a)	0 2		Walsh	Cox	Morris*	Vickers	Pearson
4.10.95	Leeds United	(h)	1 1	Fjortoft	Walsh	Liddle	Morris	Vickers	Pearson
18.10.95	Wimbledon	(a)	0 0		Walsh	Cox	Morris	Vickers	Pearson
21.10.95	Tottenham Hot	(h)	0 1		Walsh	Cox	Morris	Vickers	Pearson
25.10.95	Liverpool	(h)	2 1	Cox, Barmby	Walsh	Cox	Morris	Vickers	Pearson
2.12.95	QPR	(a)	1 1	Morris	Walsh	Cox	Morris	Vickers	Pearson
9.12.95	Manchester City	(h)	4 1	Barmby 2, Stamp, Juninho	Walsh	Cox	Liddle	Vickers	Pearson
16.12.95	Blackburn Rov	(a)	0 1		Walsh	Cox	Fleming	Vickers	Pearson
23.12.95	West Ham Utd	(h)	4 2	Cox, Morris, Hendrie, Fjortoft	Walsh	Cox	Morris	Vickers	Pearson
26.12.95	Everton	(a)	0 4		Walsh	Cox	Fleming	Vickers	Pearson
30.12.95	Nottingham For	(a)	0 1		Walsh	Cox	Fleming	Vickers	Pearson

1994–95

FA Cup

6	7	8	9	10		11	12		Crowd	
Whyte*	Mustoe	Pollock	Wilkinson	Hendrie		Hignett	Moore*		8,407	round 3
Mustoe	**Hignett**	**Pollock**	**Wilkinson**	**Hendrie**		**Moore***	**Kavanagh**		**13,940**	**round 3r**

League Cup

Hignett	Mustoe	Pollock	Wilkinson	Hendrie		Moore*	Wright*		4,751	round 2/1
Hignett	**Mustoe**	**Pollock**	**Wilkinson**	**Moreno**		**Wright**	**Cox***		**7,739**	**round 2/2**
Blackmore	Todd*	Pollock	Wilkinson	Hendrie		Moore	Hignett*		19,524	round 3

Anglo-Italian Cup

Whyte	**Stamp***	**Pollock****	**Hignett**	**Mustoe**		**Wright**	**Cox*/Wilkinson****		**5,348**
Todd	**Stamp**	**Kavanagh**	**Moreno**	**Blackmore**		**Wright**			**3,273**
Liddle	Stamp	Kavanagh	Moreno	Todd		Wright	Barron*		300
White	Stamp	O'Halloran	Moreno*	Mustoe**		Wright	Norton**/Richardson*		1,500

1995–96

Premier

Whyte	Barmby	Pollock*	Fjortoft	Mustoe	Hignett	Whelan*		37,308
Whyte	**Barmby**	**Pollock**	**Fjortoft**	**Mustoe**	**Hignett**			**28,286**
Whyte	Barmby	Pollock	Fjortoft	Mustoe	Hignett*	Moreno*		36,438
Whyte	Barmby	Pollock	Fjortoft	Mustoe	Hignett			18,376
Whyte	**Barmby**	**Pollock**	**Fjortoft**	**Mustoe**	**Hignett**			**29,188**
Whyte	**Barmby**	**Pollock**	**Fjortoft**	**Mustoe**	**Hignett**			**27,882**
Whyte	Barmby	Pollock	Fjortoft	Mustoe	Hignett			25,865
Whyte	**Barmby**	**Pollock**	**Fjortoft**	**Mustoe**	**Hignett**			**29,462**
Whyte	Barmby	Pollock	Fjortoft*	Mustoe	Hignett	Hendrie		21,177
Whyte*	**Barmby**	**Pollock**	**Fjortoft**	**Mustoe**	**Hignett****	**Hendrie*/Whelan***		**29,293**
Whelan	Barmby	Pollock	Fjortoft**	Mustoe	Hignett	Moore*/Moreno**		36,850
Juninho**	**Barmby**	**Pollock**	**Fjortoft**	**Mustoe***	**Hignett**	**Moore*/Moreno****		**29,467**
Juninho	Barmby	Pollock	Fjortoft	Stamp	Liddle			13,780
Juninho	**Barmby**	**Pollock***	**Fjortoft****	**Stamp**	**Liddle**	**Robson*/Moreno****		**29,487**
Liddle	**Barmby**	**Pollock**	**Fjortoft**	**Stamp**	**Juninho**			**29,390**
Liddle	Barmby	Pollock	Moreno	Juninho*	Stamp	Hignett*		17,546
Whyte	**Barmby**	**Pollock**	**Fjortoft**	**Juninho**	**Stamp**			**29,469**
Whyte	Barmby	Liddle	Fjortoft*	Juninho	Stamp	Hendrie		27,996
Whyte	**Hendrie**	**Pollock**	**Fjortoft**	**Juninho**	**Robson**			**28,640**
Whyte*	Hendrie	Pollock	Fjortoft	Juninho**	Liddle	Morris*(***)Moore***/ Moreno**		40,091
Liddle	Hendrie	Pollock	Moore	Juninho	Blackmore			27,027

1995–96

Premier

Date	Opposition		Result	Scorers	1	2	3	4	5
1. 1.96	Aston Villa	(h)	0 2		Walsh	Cox	Fleming*	Vickers	Pearson**
13. 1.96	Arsenal	(h)	2 3	Juninho, Stamp	Walsh	Liddle	Blackmore	Vickers	Pearson
20. 1.96	Southampton	(a)	1 2	Barmby	Walsh	Cox	Morris	Vickers	Pearson
4. 2.96	Chelsea	(a)	0 5		Walsh	Cox	Morris	Vickers	Pearson
10. 2.96	Newcastle Utd	(h)	1 2	Beresford (og)	Walsh	Cox*	Morris	Vickers	Pearson
17. 2.96	Bolton Wand	(h)	1 4	Pollock	Walsh	Cox	Morris	Vickers	Pearson*
24. 2.96	Coventry City	(a)	0 0		Walsh	Cox	Fleming	Vickers	Whyte
2. 3.96	Everton	(h)	0 2		Walsh	Cox	Fleming	Barron	Whyte
9. 3.96	West Ham Utd	(a)	0 2		Walsh	Morris***	Fleming	Cox	Pearson
16. 3.96	Nottingham For	(h)	1 1	Mustoe	Walsh	Cox	Fleming	Branco	Pearson
19. 3.96	Aston Villa	(a)	0 0		Walsh	Cox	Fleming	Branco**	Pearson
30. 3.96	Leeds United	(a)	1 0	Kavanagh (pen)	Walsh	Cox	Fleming	Whelan	Pearson
5. 4.96	Sheffield Wed	(h)	3 1	Fjortoft 2, Freestone	Walsh	Fleming	Branco	Vickers	Pearson
8. 4.96	Tottenham	(a)	1 1	Whelan	Miller	Cox	Fleming	Whelan	Pearson
13. 4.96	Wimbledon	(h)	1 2	Fleming	Miller	Cox	Fleming	Vickers	Pearson
27. 4.96	Liverpool	(a)	0 1		Miller	Cox	Branco	Vickers	Pearson*
5. 5.96	Manchester Utd	(a)	0 3		Walsh	Cox	Branco**	Vickers	Pearson

FA Cup

Date	Opposition		Result	Scorers	1	2	3	4	5
6. 1.96	Notts County	(a)	2 1	Pollock, Barmby	Walsh	Liddle	Fleming*	Vickers	Pearson
7. 2.96	Wimbledon	(h)	0 0		Walsh	Cox	Morris	Vickers	Pearson
13. 2.96	Wimbledon	(a)	0 1		Walsh	Cox*	Morris	Vickers	Pearson

League Cup

Date	Opposition		Result	Scorers	1	2	3	4	5
20. 9.95	Rotherham Utd	(h)	2 1	Mustoe, Fjortoft	Walsh	Cox	Morris	Vickers	Whelan
3.10.95	Rotherham Utd	(a)	1 0	Vickers	Walsh	Cox*	Whelan	Vickers	Pearson
25.10.95	Crystal Palace	(a)	2 2	Barmby, Hignett	Walsh	Cox	Morris	Vickers	Pearson
8.11.95	Crystal Palace	(h)	2 0	Hignett, Fjortoft	Walsh	Liddle	Morris	Vickers	Pearson
29.11.95	Birmingham City	(h)	0 0		Walsh	Cox	Morris	Vickers	Pearson
20.12.95	Birmingham City	(a)	0 2		Walsh	Cox	Fleming*	Vickers	Pearson

1995–96

Premier

6	7	8	9	10	11	12	Crowd
Liddle	Hendrie***	Pollock	Moreno	Juninho	Stamp	Moore*/Whelan**/Blackmore***	28,523
Whelan	Barmby	Pollock*	Fjortoft	Juninho	Stamp	Moore*	29,359
Whelan	Barmby	Blackmore	Wilkinson	Moore**	Stamp*	Hignett**/O'Halloran*	15,151
Liddle	Barmby	Blackmore	Fjortoft*	Hignett	O'Halloran	Wilkinson*	21,060
Whelan	Barmby	Pollock	Wilkinson	Juninho**	Stamp*	Hignett**/Liddle*	30,011
Whelan***	Barmby	Pollock	Fjortoft	Hignett	O'Halloran**	Whyte*/Hendrie**/Moore***	29,354
Whelan	Barmby	Pollock	Fjortoft	Kavanagh	Mustoe		18,810
Hignett*	Barmby	Moore	Fjortoft	Kavanagh**	Mustoe	Hendrie**/Branco*	29,809
Whyte	Barmby	Hignett**	Fjortoft*	Kavanagh	Mustoe	Hendrie*/Juninho**/Branco***	23,850
Whyte	Barmby	Pollock	Hendrie	Juninho	Mustoe		29,392
Whyte	Barmby	Pollock	Hendrie	Juninho*	Mustoe	Kavanagh**/Hignett	29,933
Whyte	Barmby	Pollock	Hendrie	Kavanagh	Mustoe		31,778
Whyte	Freestone**	Kavanagh*	Fjortoft	Juninho	Mustoe	Hignett*/Campbell**	29,791
Whyte	Freestone	Moore	Hignett	Juninho	Mustoe*	Summerbell**	32,036
Whelan	Barmby	Pollock	Kavanagh*	Juninho	Mustoe	Freestone*	29,192
Whyte	Barmby	Pollock	Campbell**	Juninho	Stamp	Fjortoft**/Whelan*	40,782
Whyte	Barmby	Pollock*	Fjortoft	Juninho	Mustoe	Moore*/Stamp**	29,921

FA Cup

6	7	8	9	10	11	12	Crowd	
Whelan	Barmby**	Pollock	Wilkinson	Juninho	Robson	Moreno**/Stamp*	12,621	round 3
Whelan	Barmby	Pollock	Wilkinson	Juninho*	O'Halloran	Freestone*	28,915	round 4
Whelan	Barmby	Pollock	Wilkinson	Juninho	O'Halloran	Hignett*	5,220	round 4r

League Cup

6	7	8	9	10	11	12	Crowd	
Whyte	Barmby	Pollock	Fjortoft	Mustoe	Moreno		13,280	round 2/1
Whyte	Barmby	Pollock	Fjortoft	Mustoe	Hignett	Liddle*	6,867	round 2/2
Whelan	Barmby	Pollock	Fjortoft**	Mustoe	Hignett*	Hendrie**/Moore*	11,873	round 3
Moore	Robson	Pollock	Fjortoft	Moreno	Hignett*	Blackmore*	16,150	round 3 r
Liddle	Barmby	Pollock	Fjortoft*	Juninho	Stamp	Hignett*	28,031	round 4
Whyte	Hendrie	Pollock	Fjortoft	Juninho	Stamp	Moore*	19,898	round 4r

Player	Birthplace	Birthdate	From	Fee	To	Fee	Now
Anderson V	Nottingham	29. 8.56	Barnsley '94	Free			Assistant Manager
Arnold I	Durham City	4. 7.72	Professional '90		Scarborough '92	Free	Player Kettering
Baird I	Rotherham	1. 4.72	Leeds United '90	£500,000	Hearts '91	£350,000	Player Plymouth
Barham M	Folkestone	12. 7.62	Huddersfield Town '88	Free	Released '89	Free	Retired Norwich
Barmby N	Hull	11. 2.74	Spurs '95	£5.25 million	Everton '96	£5.75 million	Player Everton
Barness A	Lewisham	25. 2.72	Chelsea '93	Loan			Player Charlton
Barron M	Chester-le-street	22.12.74	Professional				Player Middlesbrough
Beagrie P	Middlesbrough	28.11.65	Juniors '83		Sheffield United '86	Free	Player Manchester City
Beck M	Arhus	12. 5.73	Fortuna Cologne '96	Free			Player Middlesbrough
Blackmore C	Neath	23. 9.64	Manchester United '94	Free			Player Middlesbrough
Branco	Bage	4. 4.64	Internacional				Player Middlesbrough
Brennan M	Rossendale	4.10.65	Ipswich '88	£350,000	Manchester City '90	£500,000	Player Oldham
Burke M	Solihull	12. 2.69	Aston Villa '87	£50,000	Wolves '90	£25,000	Player Fortuna Sittard
Byrne W	Dublin	9. 2.77	Professional '94		Stoke '96	Free	Player Darlington
Campbell A	Middlesbrough	18. 4.79	Professional '96				Player Middlesbrough
Coleman S	Worksop	13. 3.68	Mansfield '89	£500,000	Derby '91	£300,000	Player Bolton
Collett A	Middlesbrough	23.10.73	Juniors '90		Bristol Rovers '95	£50,000	Player Bristol Rovers
Comfort A	Aldershot	8.12.64	Orient '89	£175,000	Retired injury '90		Chaplain Leyton Orient
Cook M	Scarborough	15.10.61	Darlington '85	£5,000	Scarborough '86	£15,000	Player Whitby
Cooper C	Sedgefield	28. 2.67	Juniors '84		Millwall '91	£300,000	Player Nottingham Forest
Corden S	Eston	9.1.67	Juniors '83		Retired injury '87		Player Northern League
Cox N	Scunthorpe	8.10.71	Aston Villa '94	£1 million			Player Middlesbrough
Coyle R	Glasgow	19. 8.61	Celtic '87	Free	Rochdale '87	Free	Player Raith Rovers
Currie D	Stockton	27.11.62	Professional '82		Darlington '86	Free	Player Carlisle
Davenport P	Birkenhead	24. 3.61	Manchester United '88	£700,000	Sunderland '90	£300,000	Player/Coach Southport
Dibble A	Cwmbran	8. 5.65	Manchester City '91	Loan			Player Manchester City
Emerson	Rio de Janeiro	12. 4.72	Porto '96	£4 million			Player Middlesbrough
Falconer W	Aberdeen	5.4.66	Watford '91	£300,000	Sheffield United '93	£300,000	Player Motherwell
Fjortoft J	Aalesund	10.1.67	Swindon '95	£1.3 million			Player Middlesbrough
Fleming C	Manchester	8.10.68	St Patricks '91	£50,000			Player Middlesbrough
Forrester P	Edinburgh	3.11.72	Professional '93		Released '94	Free	Player Berwick Rangers
Freestone C	Nottingham	4. 9.71	Arnold Town '94	£15,000			Player Middlesbrough
Fuchs U	Kaiserslautern	23. 7.66	Kaiserslautern '95	Loan			Player Bielefeld
Gannon J	Wimbledon	18.12.66	Sheffield United '93	Loan			Player Rotherham
Gill G	Middlesbrough	28.11.64	Professional '82	Loan	Darlington '89	Free	Radio Reporter
Gittens J	Moseley	22. 1.64	Southampton '92	£200,000	Released '93	Free	Player Portsmouth
Glover D	Birmingham	29.12.63	Aston Villa '87	£40,000	Port Vale '89	£200,000	Player Port Vale
Hamilton G	Glasgow	27.12.65	Professional '83		Retired injury '92		Coach in USA
Heard P	Hull	17. 3.60	Newcastle United	£5,000	Hull City '86	Free	
Hendrie J	Lennoxtown	24.10.63	Leeds '90	£550,000	Barnsley '96	£250,000	Player Barnsley
Hewitt J	Aberdeen	9. 2.63	Celtic '91	Loan			
Hignett C	Whiston	12. 1.70	Crewe '92	£500,000			Player Middlesbrough
Hodgson D	Gateshead	1.11.60	Norwich '87	Loan			Football Agent
Horne B	Billericay	5.11.67	Millwall '92	Loan			Non-league Player
Illman N	Doncaster	29. 4.75	Professional '93		Released '94	Free	
Ironside I	Sheffield	8. 3.64	Scarborough '91	£80,000	Stockport County '92	Free	Player Scarborough
Johnson I	Sunderland	1. 9.75	Juniors '93		Bradford City '94	Free	Non-league Player
Juninho	São Paulo	22. 2.73	São Paulo '95	£4.75 million			Player Middlesbrough
Kamara C	Middlesbrough	25.12.57	Luton Town '93	Loan			Manager Bradford
Kavanagh G	Dublin	2.12.73	Home Farm '91	Free	Stoke City	£500,000	Player Stoke City
Kernaghan A	Otley	25. 4.67	Professional '95		Manchester City '93	£1.6 million	Player Manchester City
Kerr P	Portsmouth	9. 6.64	Aston Villa '87	£50,000	Millwall '91	£125,000	Financial consultant
Kite P	Bristol	26.10.62	Southampton '86	Loan			Player Bristol City
Laws B	Wallsend	14.10.64	Huddersfield Town '85	£30,000	Nottingham Forest '88	£120,000	
Liburd R	Nottingham	29. 9.73	Eastwood Town '93	£20,000	Bradford City '94	£150,000	Player Bradford
Liddle C	Chester-le-street	21.10.71	Blyth Spartans	Free			Player Middlesbrough
McAndrew A	Lanark	11. 4.56	Chelsea '84	Free	Darlington '86	Free	Youth Coach Aston Villa
McGee O	Middlesbrough	29. 4.70	Professional '88		Leicester '91	Free	Player Guisborough Town
McManus E	Limavady	14.11.50	Bradford City '86	Loan			
Marshall D	Jamaica	3.10.63	Plymouth Argyle '93	Loan			Player Luton Town
Marwood B	Seaham Harbour	5. 2.63	Sheffield United '91	Loan			PFA representative

PLAYERS A–Z 1985–96

Player	Birthplace	Birthdate	From	Fee	To	Fee	Now
Miller A	Epping	29. 3.70	Arsenal '94	£425,000			Player Middlesbrough
Mohan N	Middlesbrough	6.10.70	Professional '87		Leicester '91	£200,000	Player Bradford
Moore A	Dublin	25.11.74	Rivermount '92	Free			Player Middlesbrough
Moreno J	Santa Cruz	19. 1.74	FC Blooming '94	£250,000	Washington United	£100,000	Player Washington Utd
Morris C	Newquay	24.12.63	Celtic '92	£600,000			Player Middlesbrough
Mowbray A	Saltburn	22.11.63	Professional '81		Celtic '91	£1 million	Player Ipswich
Mustoe R	Oxford	28. 8.68	Oxford '90	£375,000			Player Middlesbrough
Nattrass I	Fishburn	12.12.52	Newcastle United '79	£475,000	Retired '86		Business, Durham area
Norton P	Middlesbrough	15.10.75	Professional '93		Freed '95		Non-league Player
O'Halloran K	Dublin	10.11.75	Cherry Orchard '94	Free			Player Middlesbrough
Oliver M	Middlesbrough	2. 8.75	Professional '93		Stockport '95	£15,000	Player Darlington
O'Riordan D	Dublin	14. 5.57	Carlisle United '85	£50,000	Grimsby Town '86	Free	Coaching
Pallister G	Ramsgate	30. 6.65	Billingham Town '84	Free	Manchester Utd '89	£2.3 million	Player Manchester United
Parkinson G	Thornaby	10. 1.68	Everton '86	Free	Bolton Wanderers '93	Free	Player Burnley
Payton A	Burnley	3.10.67	Hull City '91	£750,000	Celtic '92	£600,000 (swap)	Player Huddersfield Town
Peake A	Market Harboro.	1.11.61	Charlton Athletic '91	£150,000	Retired '94		Policeman Leicester
Pears S	Brandon	22. 1.62	Manchester United '85	£80,000	Liverpool '95	Free	Player Hartlepool
Pearson N	Nottingham	21. 8.63	Sheffield Wednesday '94	£750,000			Player Middlesbrough
Phillips J	Bolton	8. 2.66	Oxford United '90	£250,000	Bolton Wanderers '93	£250,000	Player Bolton Wanderers
Pollock J	Stockton	16. 2.74	Professional Dec '91		Osasuna '96	Free	Player Osasuna
Poole K	Bromsgrove	21. 7.63	Aston Villa '87	Exchange	Leicester City '91	Free	Player Leicester City
Proctor M	Middlesbrough	30. 1.61	Sheffield Wednesday '89	£300,000	Released May '93	Free	MFC academy work
Proudlock P	Hartlepool	25.10.65	Hartlepool '86	£25,000	Carlisle United '89	Free	Player Gateshead
Putney T	Harold Hill	11. 2.61	Ipswich Town '89	£300,000	Watford '91	£100,000	London stockbroker
Ravanelli F	Perugia	11.12.68	Juventus '96	£7 million			Player Middlesbrough
Richardson P	Durham	22. 7.77	Professional				Player Middlesbrough
Ripley S	Middlesbrough	20.11.67	Apprentice '85		Blackburn '92	£1.3million	Player Blackburn
Roberts A	Newcastle	8.12.64	Professional '82		Darlington '85	Free	
Roberts B	Bishop Auckland	22. 6.75	Professional '92				Player Middlesbrough
Robson B	Witton Gilbert	11. 1.57	Manchester United '94	Free			Player/Manager M'bro
Rowell G	Seaham	6. 6.57	Norwich City '85	£25,000	Brighton '86	Free	Sports sales in Burnley
Russell M	Dublin	27. 4.67	Scarborough '90	£100,000	Portadown '91	Free	
Senior T	Dorchester	28.11.61	Watford '88	£200,000	Reading '88	£100,000	Coach Dorchester
Shannon R	Bellshill	20. 4.66	Dundee 18. 9.61	Loan			
Slaven B	Paisley	13.11.60	Albion Rovers '85	£25,000	Port Vale '93	Free	Retired Middlesbrough
Spriggs S	Doncaster	16. 2.56	Cambridge United '87		refused contract '87		Cambridge Business
Stamp P	Middlesbrough	12.12.75	Professional '93				Player Middlesbrough
Stephens A	Liverpool	19. 5.54	Bristol Rovers '85	£20,000	Carlisle United '87	Free	Lives on Teesside
Summerbell M	Durham	30.10.76	Professional '94				Player Middlesbrough
Taylor M	Saltburn	8.11.74	Professional '92		Darlington '95	Free	Player Fulham
Todd A	Derby	21. 9.74	Professional '93		Bolton Wanderers '95	£250,000	Player Bolton
Turnbull L	Stockton	27. 9.67	Professional '85		Aston Villa '87		Player Scunthorpe
Vickers S	Bishop Auckland	13.10.67	Tranmere '93	£700,000			Player Middlesbrough
Walsh C	Hamilton	22. 7.62	Charlton '91	Loan			Player Charlton
Walsh G	Wigan	21. 3.67	Manchester United '95	£500,000			Player Middlesbrough
Ward P	Sedgefield	15. 9.63	Professional '82		Darlington '85	Free	
Wark J	Glasgow	4. 8.57	Ipswich Town '90	£100,000	Ipswich July '91	Free	Player Ipswich Town
Whelan P	Stockport	7. 3.72	Ipswich Town '95	£300,000			Player Middlesbrough
White A	Darlington	22. 3.76	Professional				Player Middlesbrough
Whyte D	Glasgow	31. 8 68	Celtic '92	£900,000			Player Middlesbrough
Wilkinson P	Louth	30.10.64	Watford '91	£500,000	Barnsley '96	Free	Player Barnsley
Winnie D	Glasgow	26.10.66	Aberdeen '93	Loan			Player Aberdeen
Wright T	Fife	10. 1.66	Leicester '92	£650,000	Bradford '95	Free	Player Bradford
Young M	Chester-le-street		Newcastle '91	Free	Released '92	Free	Halfords, Newcastle

APPENDIX 3
APPEARANCES AND GOALSCORERS 1985–96
(Figures up to end 1995–96 season)

Player	League Apps	League Goals	FA Cup Apps	FA Cup Goals	League Cup Apps	League Cup Goals	Other Comps Apps	Other Comps Goals	Total Apps	Total Goals
V Anderson	2	0	0	0	0	0	0	0	2	0
I Arnold.	0(3)	0	0	0	0	0	10(1)	0	10(4)	0
I Baird.	60(3)	19	3	1	5	1	2	1	70(3)	22
M Barham	3(1)	0	0	0	0	0	0	0	3(1)	0
N Barmby	32	7	3	1	4	1	0	0	39	9
A Barness	0	0	0	0	0	0	1	0	1	0
M Barron	1	0	0	0	0	0	4(1)	0	5(1)	0
P Beagrie	21(4)	1	0	0	1	0	1(1)	0	23(5)	1
C Blackmore . . .	30(5)	2	0	0	1(1)	0	1(1)	0	32(6)	2
Branco.	5(2)	0	0	0	0	0	0	0	5(2)	0
M Brennan	61(4)	6	4	0	6	0	8	1	79(4)	7
M Burke	32(25)	6	2(1)	0	3	0	2(1)	0	39(27)	6
W Byrne	0	0	0	0	0	0	1	0	1	0
A Campbell	2	0	0	0	0	0	0	0	2	0
S Coleman	51(4)	2	5	0	0	0	8	1	64(4)	3
A Collett	2	0	0	0	0	0	3	0	5	0
A Comfort.	15	2	0	0	3	1	3	0	21	3
M Cook.	3(3)	0	0	0	0	0	1(1)	0	4(4)	0
C Cooper.	273(5)	6	13	0	18	0	15(1)	3	319(6)	9
S Corden	1	0	0	0	0	0	0	0	1	0
N Cox.	74(1)	3	2	0	7(1)	0	1(1)	0	85(3)	3
R Coyle.	1(2)	0	0(1)	0	0	0	1(1)	0	2(3)	0
D Currie	21(5)	4	0(1)	0	2	1	2	0	25(6)	5
P Davenport . . .	53(6)	7	4	0	2	0	7(1)	1	66(7)	8
A Dibble	19	0	0	0	0	0	0	0	19	0
W Falconer	47(6)	10	3	2	2(1)	0	0	0	52(7)	12
J Fjortoft	35(1)	9	0	0	6	2	0	0	41(1)	11
C Fleming	113(11)	1	8	0	8(1)	0	7(1)	0	136(13)	1
P Forrester.	0	0	0	0	0	0	0	0	0	0
C Freestone	1(2)	1	0(1)	0	0	0	0	0	2(3)	1
U Fuchs.	0	0	0	0	0	0	0	0	0	0
J Gannon.	7	0	0	0	0	0	2	0	9	0
G Gill	51(6)	2	4(1)	0	5(1)	0	6(1)	0	66(9)	2
J Gittens	22(3)	1	1	0	0(1)	0	0	0	23(4)	1
D Glover	44(6)	5	5	0	4	0	3	2	56(6)	7
G Hamilton	149(4)	20	9	1	11	1	11(1)	1	180(5)	23
P Heard.	25(2)	2	1	0	0	0	2	0	28	2
J Hendrie.	181(16)	42	11(3)	2	20	6	4	3	216(19)	52
J Hewitt.	0(2)	0	0	0	0	0	0	0	0(2)	0
C Hignett	88(19)	22	3(1)	0	10(1)	7	5(1)	0	126(22)	29
D Hodgson	2	0	0	0	0	0	0	0	2	0
B Horne.	3(1)	0	0	0	0	0	0	0	3(1)	0
N Illman	0(1)	0	0	0	0	0	1(4)	0	1(5)	0
I Ironside.	12(1)	0	0	2	2	0	0	0	14(1)	0
I Johnson.	1(1)	0	0	0	0	0	1	0	2(1)	0
Juninho.	20(1)	2	3	0	2	0	0	0	27(1)	2
C Kamara	3(2)	0	0	0	0	0	0	0	3(2)	0
G Kavanagh. . . .	20(15)	3	2(2)	1	1(1)	0	7	0	30(18)	4
A Kernaghan . . .	174(41)	15	8(4)	3	22(7)	1	12(1)	2	216(41)	21
P Kerr	124(11)	13	9(2)	3	10	1	9(3)	1	152(16)	18
P Kite	2	0	0	0	0	0	0	0	2	0
B Laws	92(5)	11	8(1)	0	6(1)	2	5	0	111(14)	13
R Liburd	41	0	2	0	4	0	5	0	52	0
C Liddle	12(2)	0	1	0	1(1)	0	2	0	16(3)	0
A McAndrew. . .	34	2	1	0	2	0	2	0	39	2
O McGee.	18(3)	1	0(1)	0	0(1)	0	3(3)	0	21(8)	1
E McManus	2	0	0	0	0	0	0	0	2	0

APPEARANCES AND GOALSCORERS 1985–96

Player	League Apps	League Goals	FA Cup Apps	FA Cup Goals	League Cup Apps	League Cup Goals	Other Comps Apps	Other Comps Goals	Total Apps	Total Goals
D Marshall	0(3)	0	0	0	0	0	0	0	0(3)	0
B Marwood	3	0	0	0	1	0	0	0	4	0
A Miller.......	47	0	2	0	1	0	2	0	52	0
N Mohan	89(9)	4	9(1)	0	11	0	6	0	115(10)	4
A Moore	81(9)	15	2(1)	2	7(2)	1	4	0	94(12)	18
J Moreno......	8(13)	1	0(1)	0	3(2)	0	3	1	14(15)	2
C Morris	73(5)	3	6	0	10	0	4	1	93(5)	4
A Mowbray....	247	22	15	1	24	2	18	0	304	25
R Mustoe	170(10)	13	10	0	24(1)	7	11	1	215(11)	21
I Nattrass	19	0	4	0	0	0	1	0	24	0
P Norton......	0	0	0	0	0	0	0(1)	0	0(1)	0
K O'Halloran...	3(1)	0	2	0	0	0	1	0	6(1)	0
M Oliver......	0	0	0	0	0	0	0(1)	0	0(1)	0
D O'Riordan ...	41	2	1	1	2	0	2	1	46	4
G Pallister	156	5	10	1	10	1	9	0	185	7
G Parkinson...	198(8)	5	17	1	20	1	15	0	250(8)	7
A Payton	8(11)	3	1(3)	0	0	0	0	0	9(14)	3
A Peake.......	81(3)	1	9	0	2	0	3	0	95(3)	1
S Pears........	331	0	23	0	32	0	24	0	410	0
N Pearson	69	3	5	0	5	0	0	0	79	3
J Phillips	139	6	10	0	16	0	3	1	168	7
J Pollock	142(11)	16	13(1)	1	17(2)	1	4(1)	0	176(15)	18
K Poole	34	0	0(1)	0	4	0	2	0	40(1)	0
M Proctor	101(18)	6	5(3)	0	7(2)	0	9(1)	0	132(24)	6
P Proudlock....	2(3)	0	0	0	0	0	1(1)	2	3(4)	2
T Putney	45(3)	1	2	0	5	0	3	0	55(3)	1
P Richardson ...	0	0	0	0	0	0	0(1)	0	0(1)	0
S Ripley.......	280(38)	26	17	2	21	5	15(1)	2	333(39)	35
A Roberts	1	0	0	0	1	0	0	0	2	0
B Roberts	0	0	0	0	0	0	1	0	1	0
B Robson......	23(1)	1	1	0	0	0	0	0	24(1)	1
G Rowell......	27	10	1	0	3	2	1	0	32	12
M Russell	10(1)	2	0	0	2	0	0	0	12(1)	2
T Senior.......	9(1)	2	0	0	1	0	0	0	10(1)	2
R Shannon.....	0(1)	0	0	0	1	0	0	0	1(1)	0
B Slaven.......	286(21)	118	16(3)	4	26(2)	10	21	12	349(26)	144
S Spriggs	3	0	0	0	0	0	0	0	3	0
P Stamp.......	20(4)	2	3	0	2	0	5(1)	0	30(4)	2
A Stephens.....	71(7)	22	3	0	8(1)	1	3	2	82(8)	28
M Summerbell..	0(1)	0	0	0	0	0	0	0	0(1)	0
M Taylor......	0	0	0	0	0	0	0(1)	0	0(1)	0
A Todd	7	0	0	0	1(1)	0	5	0	13(1)	0
L Turnbull.....	8(8)	4	0	0	0(1)	0	1(1)	1	9(10)	5
S Vickers	101	7	7	0	9	1	2	0	120	8
C Walsh	10(3)	1	1	0	0	0	0	0	11(3)	1
G Walsh	31	0	3	0	6	0	0	0	40	0
P Ward	3	0	0	0	2	0	0	0	5	0
J Wark	31(1)	2	2	0	5	0	1	0	39(1)	2
P Whelan......	9(5)	1	3	0	2	0	0	0	14(5)	1
A White.......	0	0	0	0	0	0	1	0	1	0
D Whyte	135(1)	2	2	0	11	0	8	0	156(1)	2
P Wilkinson....	157(5)	48	14	5	16	8	5(1)	4	192(5)	65
D Winnie......	1	0	0	0	0	0	0	0	1	0
T Wright	44(7)	5	3	1	3(1)	0	6	0	57(8)	6
M Young......	0(1)	0	0	0	0	0	0(1)	0	0(2)	0

(Figures in brackets show substitute appearances)

APPENDIX 4

DISMISSALS

The following players were sent off while playing for Middlesbrough FC during the decade 1985–96.

Player	Opposition	Venue	Date
Archie Stephens	Sunderland	Roker Park	22.10.85
Gary Pallister	Shrewsbury Town	Gay Meadow	3. 5.86
David Hodgson	Bristol City	Ayresome Park	7. 3.87
Dean Glover	Sunderland	Roker Park	18. 8.87
Gary Parkinson	Plymouth Argyle	Home Park	2.11.87
Stuart Ripley	Leeds United	Elland Road	28.12.87
Colin Cooper	Ipswich Town	Portman Road	23. 4.88
Peter Davenport	Southampton	The Dell	14. 1.89
John Hendrie	Sunderland	Ayresome Park	28. 9.91
Stuart Ripley	Bristol Rovers	Twerton Park	5.10.91
Jimmy Phillips	Southend United	Roots Hall	14. 3.92
Nicky Mohan	Wolves	Molineux	2. 5.92
Willie Falconer	Southampton	Ayresome Park	26. 1.93
Alan Kernaghan	Everton	Ayresome Park	10. 4.93
Jamie Pollock	Cardiff City	Ayresome Park	19. 1.94
Derek Whyte	Millwall	New Den	24.10.93
Richard Liburd	Charlton Athletic	Ayresome Park	16. 4.94
Robbie Mustoe	Reading	Elm Park	6.12.94
Curtis Fleming	Swindon Town	County Ground	15. 1.95
Uwe Fuchs	Sheffield United	Ayresome Park	17. 4.95
Derek Whyte	Blackburn Rovers	Ewood Park	16.12.95
Alan Moore	Arsenal	Cellnet Riverside Stadium	13. 1.96
Phil Whelan	Southampton	The Dell	20. 1.96

APPENDIX 5

SEASON TICKET HOLDERS

DIRECTORS' BOX
Mr Eason
Enconofreight
Mr Walker
Taylor Woodrow

DISABLED HOME
Mr C.A Allen
Mr Arnison
Mr M.B Brown
Mr R.P.B Brown
Mr A.F Frank
Mr M.J.H Harvey
Mr B.K.H Holloway
Mr D.M Marshall
Mr B.P Paul
Mr J.R Robinson
Mr J.S Stirland
Mr T.T Thompson

EAST STAND LOWER
Mr A J Abbott
Mr G Abbott
Mr R.A Adam
Mr W.A Adam
MISS E J Adamson
MR J W Adamson
MR K J Adamson
Mr T.D. Adamson
MRS M A Adamson
MSTR M K Adamson
Miss V.A Agar
MR D AGAR
Mstr M Agar
MSTR R.D AGAR
MSTR C Ainsworth
Mr M.A Aisbitt
Mr R.A Aithwaite
MR A J Aitken
Mr W.A Alderson
Mstr J.A Aldus
MR R Allan
MR G Allday
MSTR P G Allday
Mr C.A Allen
Mr P.A Allen
Mr P.R.A Allen
Miss C L Allison
Mr J Allison
Mr M.L.A Andrews
Mr M.S.A Andrews
Mr D.P.A Appleby
Mr P.A Appleby
Mr S.G.A Appleby
Miss C.A Appleton
MISS S L Appleton
Mrs D.A Appleton
Mstr M.A.A Appleton
MR A Appleyard
MR S W Appleyard
MSTR D Appleyard
MR J Arger
MRS P M Arger
MR P Armes
Mr P.A Armes
MSTR L M Armes
Mr G.A Armistead
Mstr M.A Armistead
Mr M.J.A Armstrong
MISS S L Ashley
MR S Ashley
MR T Ashley
MSTR L Ashley
MSTR M Ashley
MSTR P Ashley
Mrs J.A Atkins
Miss C.L.A Atkinson
MISS J L Atkinson
Mr B.A Atkinson
MR D J Atkinson
MR M Atkinson
MR N Atkinson
MR N J Atkinson
MRS S M Atkinson
MSTR J M Atkinson
MSTR M Atkinson
Miss S.A Atterton
Mr I.A Atterton
Miss C Bage
Mr P Bage
Mr S Bage
Mr N Bailey

Mr T Bailey
Mstr A W Bailey
MSTR T.W Bailey
Miss G.B Bainbridge
Mr R.B Bainbridge
Mr S.B.B Bainbridge
Mstr G.S.B Bainbridge
Mr M Baines
MR R Baines
MSTR A Baines
Mstr J Baines
Mr A.J Baird
Mstr P.A Baird
Mrs I.B Baker
Mstr R.A Baker
Mr D.B Ball
Mrs A.B Ball
Ball Valve UK Ltd
Mr W.B Banks
Mrs K.B Banks
MR S Barber
MSTR P L Barber
Mr R Barclay
Mstr M J Barclay
MR C Bargewell
MSTR A D Bargewell
MSTR P Bargewell
Mr M.B Barker
Mstr C.N.B Barker
Mr Barnes
Mr M.S.B Barnes
MR A Barnett
Mr G.B Barnett
Mr P.B Barnett
MISS L D Barthram
MR J H Barthram
Mr A.B Bassett
Mr G.B Bassett
MRS Y Bate
Mr R.B Bates
Mstr D.J.B Bates
Mr C.S.B Batey
Mr L.T.B Batey
Mstr L.D.B Batey
Mstr S.A.B Batey
Mr S.B Battram
Mstr D.B Battram
MR S Baxter
MR R M Beadnall
Mr W.A Beadnall
Mr S.B Bean
Mr K.B Bedwell
Mstr J.B Bedwell
Mstr S.B Bedwell
Mr M. Beedle
Mr C.B Beever
Mstr M.B Beever
Mr E.B Beevers
Mstr P Beevers
Miss A Bell
Mr A.A.B Bell
Mr J Bell
MR R G Bell
Mr R.B Bell
Mstr C.B Bell
Mstr S.B Bell
MR G A Bennett
Mr I.B Bennett
MR G Bent
MRS Bent
Miss H.M. Bentley
MR J A Bentley
MR M Bentley
MR J Berry
Mr P B Best
Mr D.B Besterfield
Miss E Betts
Mr J.W. Beveridge
Mr M.B Bickerton
Miss C.E.B Bigerstaff
Mr J.A.B Bigerstaff
Mrs H.E.B Bigerstaff
Mstr D.J.B Bigerstaff
Miss L Bingham
Mr D Bingham
Mr J S Bingham
Mr K.J.B Binks
MRS J Birrell
MR R Birtwhistle
MSTR D Birtwhistle
MSTR M P Birtwhistle
MR T Bishop

Mr W Blackburn
Mr P.G.B Blackmore
Mr R.W.B Blackmore
Mstr M.G.B Blackmore
Mrs N.B Blackwood
Mstr R.B Blackwood
Mr B Blades
Miss K.B Blakey
Mr P.D.B Blakey
Mstr C.B Blockley
MR Blyth
MSTR G A Blyth
MR M Boanas
MRS M Boanas
MSTR D Boanas
MSTR P Boanas
MR R Boardman
MSTR D Boardman
MSTR R M Boardman
MR F BOINTON
Mstr K Bonas
Mr D.B Bond
Mstr P.B Bond
Miss M.B Boocock
Mr D.B Boocock
Mr R Booth
Mstr R.P.B Booth
Mrs S M Bourne
Miss N.M Bowe
Mr E.N.B Bowe
Mrs M.B Bowe
Mstr A.J.B Bowe
Mstr M.A.B Bowe
Mr R.B Bowen
Mr R Bowens
Mr F.P.B Boyd
Miss S.B Boydell
Mr P.J.B Boydell
Ms J.B Boydell
Mstr J.W.B Boydell
Mstr T.A.B Boydell
MSTR M J Boyt
Mr M Brabanski
Mstr D Brabanski
Mr I.B Bradford
Mstr M.B Bradford
Mstr S.B Bradford
MISS A C Bradley
MISS C A Bradley
MISS R L Bradley
Mr Bradley
MR P Bradley
MISS H Braithwaite
MR I Braithwaite
Miss K.B Bray
Mr P.B Bray
Mrs E.B Bray
Mstr G.D.B Bray
Miss K Breen
Mr M.M. Brennan
Mstr G.T Brennan
Mr R.B Brion
Mr J Brittain
Mr D.W.B Broadbent
Mr J.W.B Broadbent
Mstr M.B Broadbent
Mstr N.B Broadbent
Mstr P.D.B Broadbent
MSTR C Brodie
MSTR P Brodie
Mstr D.B Brodrick
Mr C P Brooks
Mrs C Brooks
Mstr C G Brooks
Mstr S Brooks
MISS S M Brown
MR Brown
MR BROWN
Mr D Brown
Mr D.J.B Brown
MR G Brown
Mr I.D.B Brown
MR J Brown
Mr P.L.B Brown
Mr R.J.B Brown
MR W.A BROWN
MRS C Brown
MSTR A Brown
Mstr P.J.B Brown
Mr M.A.B Brudenell
Mstr K.M.B Brudenell
Mstr P.A.B Brudenell

Mr P.W.B Brunton
MR T Brunton
Mstr C Brunton
Mstr P.A.B Brunton
Mr S.T. Bruton
MR L Buck
Mr P.G Buckby
Mstr B.P Buckby
MSTR J A Buckton
Mstr M.P.B Buckworth
Miss C.A Budd
Mr D Budd
MR T Buist
MR Bullock
Mr A.B Bullock
Mr F G Bullock
MR L Bullock
Mr N A Bullock
Mrs J Bullock
MSTR A J Bullock
MISS E.C Bunting
MR J Burke
Mr M.B Burke
MR T H Burke
MSTR P Burke
Mstr P.M.B Burke
MSTR S Burke
Mr L.R.B Burn
Mstr A.B Burn
Mstr T.B Burn
Mr J Burns
BURTON
MSTR G Burton
MR G Butcher
MSTR D I Butcher
Mr S T Butters
Mr K.P.B Byrne
Mr P.B Byrne
Mstr K.B Byrne
Mstr C Cairnes
Mr P.C Cairney
MR A Callan
MRS K Callan
MSTR P Callan
MSTR P callan
Mr P.C.C Calvert
Mr W.C.C Calvert
MSTR P Campbell
MSTR S Campell
Mr A P Cant
Mstr C J Cant
Mstr J.P Card
Mr A.P.C Cargill
MR M F Carling
Mr M.C Carman
Mr T.C Carney
Mstr D.C Carney
Mr G. Carr
Mr J.R.C Carr
MR E R Carrick
Mr J.P.C Carroll
MR P Carroll
MSTR A E Carroll
Mstr F Carroll
Mr J.W Carson
Mstr W.J Carson
Mr D. Carter
Mr D.J.C Carter
Mr M.R Carter
Mr W.C Carter
MSTR M.G Carter
Mstr P.J.C Carter
Mstr R.D.C Carter
MR C Carvello
MR J Carvello
Miss C Casey
Miss R.C Casey
Miss S.C Casey
Mr P.C Casey
MR B.A Casson
Mr L Casson
MR N Casson
Mr G.C Caster
Mr P.C Cattermole
Mstr A.C Cattermole
Mr M Chamberlain
Mr R M Chamberlain
Mstr D S R Chamberlain
Mr J.W.C Chambers
Miss C Chapman
Miss C.C Chapman

Mr N.K.C Chapman
Mr T.W.C Chapman
Mstr C.S.C Chapman
Mstr K.C Chapman
Mr D.C Charlton
Mstr D.C Charlton
MR A Charville
MSTR W Charville
MR A Chillmaid
MRS Y Chillmaid
MSTR D Chillmaid
MSTR P Chillmaid
MISS M Chilton
MR D M Chubb
MR M Chubb
Mr A.C Church
Mr S.C Church
MR G W Clark
MR T Clark
Mr T.E.C Clark
Mstr J.N.C Clark
MSTR N G W Clark
Mr C.C Clarke
Mr D.L.C Clarke
Mr P.A.T Clarke
MR R Clarke
Mr R.C Clarke
MR S Clarke
Mstr L.C Clarke
Mstr N.C Clarke
Mr V.S.C Clement
Mstr P Clement
MSTR D Clements
Mr J.J.C Clifford
Mr Close
Mr K Close
Mr M.C Close
Mr P Close
Mrs E Close
Mstr D.J.C Close
Mstr J Close
Mstr L.M.C Close
Mstr N Close
Mr C.A Coates
Miss A.L.C Coates
Mr M.B.C Coates
Mstr M.L.C Coates
MR P Cobb
Mstr S J Cobb
Miss T.C Cochrane
Mr J.R.C Cochrane
Mrs J.C Cochrane
Mstr M.C Cochrane
Mr D Cockerill
Mrs C Cockerill
Mstr C D Cockerill
Miss G Cockfield
Mr H Cockfield
Mr R.B.C Codling
Mr A J Colclough
Mr B Colclough
Mr G J Colclough
Mr L. Colclough
Mstr J. Colclough
Miss E Cole
MR A Colefield
MSTR A C Coleman
MR S Collings
MRS M Collings
MSTR P Collings
MR C Collins
Mr P.C Collins
Mr R.C Collins
Mr W.G.C Collins
Mstr P.C Collins
Mstr R.C Collins
MR T Colvin
Mstr A.J.C Conlin
Mstr M.A.C Conlin
Mrs J.C Conlin
Mstr P.J.C Conlon
MISS T J Connor
MR D M Connor
Miss T.C Conroy
Mr G.A.C Conroy
Mrs C.M.C Conroy
MR C J Conway
Mr M.C Conyard
MR E.J.C Cook
Mr Cook
Mr G.J. Cook
Mr J Cook
Mr W Cook

Mrs D.A.C Cook
Mstr Cook
Mstr G.D.C Cook
Mstr S.J Cook
MR A Cooke
Mr N.C Cooper
Mr R N Cooper
Mr C.C Cope
Mr J.C Cope
Mr P.A.C Cope
Mr S.J.C Cope
Mr D.C Corbyn
MR A D Corner
MR A B Cossey
MR I A Cossey
MR RE Cossey
MSTR A A Cossey
Mr M.C Cottle
Mstr G.M.C Cottle
Mr E.C Coulson
MR R Coulson
MSTR A Coulson
Mr R. Coupe
Mstr R.D. Coupe
Mr C Coupland
Mr P Coupland
COVERDALE
MR COVERDALE
MR R.C Cowell
Mstr J.R.C Cowell
Mr B.S.C Cowen
Mr E.S.C Cowen
Mr J.N.C Cowen
Mstr C.J.C Cowen
Mr J A Cowley
Mstr A Cowley
Mr S Cox
B. Cranny
Mr G. Cranny
Mstr B. Cranny
Mr A Crawford
Mr M.C Crocker
MR C.M.C Crocker
MR CROCKETT
Mstr G. Crockett
Mstr G.C Crosby
Mstr M.S.C Crosby
MISS K A Crossen
MR J A Crossen
Mr D.C Crossman
Mrs H.C Crossman
MR J Cuff
MR S Cuff
Mstr G.N.D Cuff
MR H.W. Cummings
Mrs S.H. Cummings
Mr N M Cunningham
Mstr C N Cunningham
MR R E Curry
Mr A Curtis
Mstr L A Curtis
MISS N Cutts
MR C Cutts
Mr C Cutts
MR D Cutts
MRS L Cutts
MISS L Daggett
Mr M.D Dahms
Mr P.D Dahms
Mrs B.D Dahms
MR A Dale
MR S.H.W DALE
Mr G N Dales
Miss J Daley
Mr E Daley
MR M Daley
Mstr C.D Daley
MSTR M Daley
Mstr T Daley
Mr S Dalgleish
MRS P Dalgleish
MISS V Dalton
Mr W.D Dalton
MRS M P Dalton
Mr S.B.D Danby
Mstr I.D Danby
Mstr J.D Danby
MR M J Daniels
Mr N.A.D Daniels
Mstr I.R.D Daniels
MISS L M Darbey
MR A B Darbey
MRS G J Darbey
Mr R.D Dargue

Mr M.G.D Davie
Miss Davies
Mr Davies
Mr A.D Davies
MR C Davies
Mr I.D Davies
Mr M.D Davies
MSTR A Davies
Mstr M.D Davies
Mstr M.J.D Davies
MR J Dawson
MR P J Dawson
Mr P.D Dawson
MRS J L Dawson
MSTR M A Dawson
MSTR P J Dawson
MR M J Dean
MSTR C Dean
Mstr C.D Dearlove
Mr A.D Degnan
Mr D.D Degnan
MR H Denham
MS M Denham
Mr J.D Dennis
Mstr S.D Dennis
MSTR C A Dent
DR W.R Desira
MISS F.H Desira
MISS N.L Desira
MRS E.A Desira
Miss C.D Devine
Miss R.L Dick
Mrs V Dick
MISS C Dickinson
MISS M Dickinson
MR Dickinson
MR G Dickinson
Mr K.D Dickinson
MRS V Dickinson
MSTR A D Dickons
MSTR C L Dickons
Miss V.J.D Dixon
Mr Dixon
Mr A.D Dixon
Mr C Dixon
MR D Dixon
Mr E.D.D Dixon
Mr I.M.D Dixon
MR J A Dixon
MR K Dixon
Mstr G.N.D Dixon
Mstr L.J.D Dixon
MSTR N A Dixon
Mr M E Dobson
RE Dobson
Mr J.D Docherty
Mr T.D Docherty
Ms D.D Docherty
Mstr A.D Docherty
Mstr C.D Docherty
Miss L.D Dodd
Mr P.D Dodd
Mr C.D Dodds
Mstr C Dodds
Miss S.D Dodgson
Mrs A.D Dodgson
Mstr A.P.D Dodson
Mr C Donkin
Mstr S.J.M Donkin
MISS A Doogan
MISS L Doogan
MISS S Doogan
MR J Doogan
Mr D.J Doogan
Mstr M Dorgan
Mr W Douthwayte
Mr M.A.D Dover
Mr S Doyle
Mstr S Doyle
Mr W. Dreher
MR D Drinkhall
MISS L.R Driver
MR M.J Driver
MSTR A.S Driver
Miss E Drummond
Mr D Drummond
Mstr A Drummond
Mr M Drury
MR E Duckling
MSTR C.J Duckling
MR G.D Duffy
Mr M.D Duffy

DOOM TO BOOM

Mr P.D Duffy
Mrs M Duffy
Mstr J.D Duffy
MR I Duncan
MSTR B Duncan
MR G Dunford
Mr D.M.D Dunkerley
Mr B.D Dunning
MR J Dunning
Mstr A.D Dunning
Mstr C.D Dunning
MR R Durent
MR P.S Dwyer
MSTR S.L Dwyer
Mrs G Dyer
Mstr S B Dyer
Mr S.R.E Eckersley
Mstr S.E Eckersley
Mr K.E Eddleston
Mstr M.R.E Eddleston
MR S.W Eddon
Mstr C Eddon
MSTR L Eddon
Mstr D.G.E Edgecombe
MSTR L M Edwards
MR D D Eggleston
MSTR T Eggleston
Mr M.E Eland
Mrs D.E Elder
Mstr D.E Elders
MR S.D Elliott
Mstr B.W Elliott
MSTR C Elliott
Mstr M Elliott
MISS N K Ellis
MR B Ellis
MR R Ellis
Mrs L.E Ellis
MSTR ELLIS
Mstr D.E Ellis
Mstr G.L.E Ellis
Mstr T.E Ellis
MISS M V Ellison
MR T W Ellison
MR R J Ellyatt
MSTR D P Ellyatt
Mr N.J.E Elstob
Mstr R.A.E Elstob
Mrs J.E Elwick
Mstr R.J.E Elwick
Mstr S.E Elwick
Mr B Emmerson
Mr D. Emms
Mr R Emms
Mstr D.C. Emms
Mstr J.R. Emms
Mr A.E.E Evans
MR K P Evans
Mr P.D.E Evans
Mr R.E Evans
Mr M.E Evans
MR S Everson
Mstr J Everson
Mr A.H. Ezard
Mr N.F. Fairless
Mr N.J. Fairless
MR G R Faulkner
Mr H.F Fawcett
Mr J.F.F Fawcett
Mr T.F Fawcett
Miss J.M.F Fearon
Mr P.F Fearon
Mrs J.F Fearon
Mstr J.P.F Fearon
Mstr J.F Featham
MR K M Feeney
MR S M Feeney
Mr B.P.F Finn
Mr P.F Finn
Mr P.J.F Finn
Mstr M.A.F Finn
MR M Fiske
Mr A.R.F Fitzhugh
Mr R.J.F Fitzhugh
MR J G Flanagan
MRS C.A FLANAGAN
MSTR A Flanagan
MSTR W.F FLANAGAN
Miss S J Flavell
MR T D Flavell
Mrs K M Flavell
Mstr T Flavell
MSTR M Flemming
MISS M Flemming
Mr K.F Fletcher
Mr N.F Fletcher
Mstr J.J.F Fletcher
Mr M.T.F Foley
Mstr M.J.F Foley

Miss L Forbes
Miss S Forbes
Mr R J Forbes
MR I Forrest
MR S.J Forrest
MR D Forrest
MR J V Forster
MR P W Forster
MSTR P M Forster
MSTR S P Forster
Miss J Foster
MR Foster
MR A Foster
Mr M.F Foster
MSTR P Fountain
MR J E Fowell
Miss B.J Fowler
Mr A D Fowler
Mr C.E.F Fowler
MR D C Fowler
Mr D J Fowler
MR J Fowler
Mrs K.J Fowler
MSTR A J Fowler
Mr P Fox
Mstr D J Fox
Mr B.F Frankland
Mr R.F Frankland
Mstr A.F Frankland
Mstr W.F Frankland
MISS S French
Mr B.T Frewin
MR L Frewin
MR D Fryett
MR Z Gaines
MR C Galbraith
Miss J.G Gale
Mr C.G Gale
Mr M.G.G Gale
Mstr T.C.G Gale
Mr B.G Gallagher
Mstr D.G Gallagher
Mr M Galloway
Mr P.G. Galloway
MISS J L Gamble
MR P Gamble
MRS E Gamble
Mr S.G Gamlin
Mstr M.G Gamlin
MR A M Garbutt
MR K Garbutt
MSTR D Garbutt
Miss S J Gardner
Mr G K Gardner
MR J A Garrod
MRS J A Garrod
MSTR G W Garrod
Mr P.G Garton
Mstr P.G Garton
Miss R.E.G Gatiss
Mr D.A.G Gatiss
Mr D.G Gatiss
Mr D Gettings
Mstr J.H Gettings
Mr I.M.G Gibson
Mr M.G Gibson
Mr T.B.G Gibson
Mstr J.P.G Gibson
MRS H.S Gilbert
MSTR A Gilbert
MSTR J Gilbert
MSTR P Gilbert
Mr D.W.G Gill
Mr S.G Gillow
MR A Gilmore
MR I D Gilmore
MSTR J Girvin
MR R Gladders
Mr T.W.G Glasper
Mrs F.G Glasper
Mstr S.G Glasper
MISS L Glass
MR G Glass
MRS W A Glass
Mr R.J.G Glover
Mstr P.S.R Glover
MR M Godfrey
Mr M Good
Mrs P Good
Mstr J.M Good
MR A Goodman
MSTR C P Goodman
MSTR M A Goodman
Mr G C Goodwin
MISS S GORDEN
Mstr P. Gordon
Mr D.M.G Gosney
MRS GOSNEY

MR D A Gott
Mr J.A.G Gott
Mr T.J Gowland
MR A Grace
MSTR P Grace
MR P Grafton
MSTR D Grafton
Mr B. Graham
Mr I.S.G Graham
Mstr B.J. Graham
Mstr R.G Graham
Mstr S.G Graham
Mstr T.M. Graham
Miss D.G Grainger
Miss S Grainger
Mr M.G Grainger
MR P.R GRAINGER
Mr S.P.G Grant
Mstr D.N.G Grant
Miss D.M.G Grant
Mr R.G Gratton
Mr G A Gray
Mrs K Gray
Mstr D.P.G Grayson
MR B Green
MR N Green
Mr K.G Greenwood
MR C J Gregg
MR F Gregg
Miss K Gregory
MR P.D Gregory
Mr S.G Gregory
Mrs W.G Gregory
MSTR S.P Gregory
Miss C Griffiths
MR GRIFFITHS
Mr D.G Griffiths
Mr J.G Griffiths
Mr P Griffiths
Mstr J Griffiths
Mstr L.G Griffiths
Mr K. Groves
Mstr K. Groves
Mr M Gutcher
Mstr L Gutcher
Mr M.G Guymer
Mrs A.M.G Guymer
MR P Hadlet
MSTR T.P Hadlet
Mr A.D.H Haley
Mr P.F.H Haley
Miss R.H Hall
MR A Hall
MR C A Hall
MR D.J Hall
MR G S Hall
MR K HALL
Mr R Hall
MSTR D Hall
Mstr G.N.H Hall
MSTR M L Hall
MSTR S Hall
MSTR J Hamilton
Mstr R.J.H Hamilton
Mr M.A.H Hammond
MR P Hammond
MSTR A W Hammond
MSTR W Hammond
Mrs J.H Hampson
Miss C.H Hancock
Mr J Hanratty
Mstr J.J. Hanratty
MSTR C J Hansen
MR F J Hanson
Mr I. Harbron
Mstr C. Harbron
Mr A.H Harburn
Mr C.C.H Harcourt
Mstr M.C.H Harcourt
Mr P.H Harding
Mr J.H Hardman
M L Hards
Mr J.H Hardy
Mr M Hardy
Mr R Hardy
Mstr A Hardy
Miss R Hare
Mr D Hare
Mr D.H. Hargreaves
MISS J K Harker
Mr P Harker
MRS A Harker
MSTR A D Harker
MR Harnby
Mr A V Harper
MR A Harrington
MSTR M Harrington
MSTR S Harrington

MR J Harriott
MR S Harriott
Mr D.J Harris
Mr I Harris
Mstr D.R Harris
MR Harrison
MR A Harrison
Mr F.W.H Harrison
Mr P.H Harrison
MR R M Harrison
MSTR L R Harrison
Mstr P.P.H Harrison
Mr C.H Harston
Mstr C.D.H Harston
Mstr M.C.H Harston
MR C Hart
MR R Hart
Mrs Y Hart
Mstr A.R Hart
Mstr J Hart
MSTR R Hart
Mstr C Hartshorn
MR S Hatfield
MSTR J Hatfield
Mr H. Hawes
Mstr P.J. Hawes
MR T Hawman
MSTR D J Hawman
Mstr C. Hawthorne
MR G Hawxwell
Mr G Hazard
MSTR D Hazard
Mstr D.H Headlam
Mr G.H Heaney
Mr M.J.H Hearn
MRS HEARN
Mstr D Hearn
Mstr D.J.H Hearn
Mstr S.A.H Hearn
MR R.M Hebbron
Mrs D.M Hebbron
MSTR E.R Hebbron
MSTR R W Hebbron
Miss E.C.H Hedley
Miss K.M.H Hedley
Mr S.J.W Helm
Mr D.H Henderson
Mr J.W. Henry
MSTR S.D HENRY
Mr D.H Henwood
Mr J.H Hepworth
Mstr S.H Hermon
Mr C.F Heron
Mstr P.M Heron
MR Heslehurst
Mr D.H Heslehurst
MR A Heslehurst
Mr J.D. Heslin
Mstr L.R. Hewitt
MISS E High
MR S High
Mr R Highmoor
Mr B.H Hill
MR D R Hill
MR J L Hill
Mr K.H Hill
Mstr J.D.H Hill
Mstr J.H Hill
MSTR JW Hill
Mr P Hilton
Miss P Hind
Mr E. Hindmarsh
Mstr M. Hindmarsh
MR A Hislop
Miss L E Hobson
MR T Hobson
Mstr T A Hobson
Mr D.H Hockney
Mstr M.H Hockney
MSTR A HODGKISS
Mr J.H Hodgson
Mstr R.A.H Hodgson
Mstr R.J.H Hodgson
Mr T L Hogarth
Mr I Hoggart
Mr P Hoggart
MSTR D Hoggart
MSTR M Hoggart
Mr M.H Holian
Mr M C Holley
Mrs L E Holley
Mrs J.H Hollingworth
Miss A.H Holmes
Mr C.V Holmes
MR G Holmes
Mr G Holmes
MS K Holmes
MSTR M Holmes
MR K S Holt
MSTR P Holt

Mr R.N.H Homer
Mstr M.R.H Homer
MR HOPE
Mrs A Hope
Mr R.H Horn
Mr R.H Housley
MR A.D Howe
Mr M Howell
MR R M Howes
MSTR M.R Howes
Mr R.H Huck
MISS L Huddlestone
MISS J E Hudson
Mr J E Hudson
MRS P V Hudson
Mr L Hughes
Mr M.E.H Hughes
Mr R.H Hughes
Mr R.T Hughes
MSTR C J Hughes
MSTR G Hughes
MSTR J Hughes
Mstr M.D.H Hughes
MR M W Hugill
MRS J L Hugill
Mr P.W.H Hulbert
Mstr C.E.H Hulbert
Mstr M.J.H Hulbert
MR A Hulse
MSTR A Hulse
MISS C J Humphery
MRS E Humphrey
Mr R.W.H Hunter
Mr M.J.H Hunter
Mstr R.A.H Hunter
Mr B. Huntley
Mstr G. Huntley
MR J L Hunton
Mr R.H Hunton
MSTR D J Hunton
Mr L.H Hurst
Mstr C.D.H Hurst
MR K Husband
MR R Husband
Mr P.H Huskinson
MISS J Hutchcraft
MR S Hutchcraft
Mr K.H Hutchinson
Mr P.H Hutton
Miss A.H Hynes
Miss R.H Hynes
Miss S.J.I Ibbetson
Mstr M.I Igo
Mstr C.I Iles
Mr C.J.I Iley
Mr D.J.I Iley
Mr J.R.I Iley
Mstr D.R.I Iley
Mstr P.J.I Iley
Mr C.I Illingworth
Mstr G.I Illingworth
Mstr R.M.I Illingworth
MR G P Ingham
MR L Inman
Mr J Irwin
Mstr C.J.I Irwin
MR P Iseton
MR R Iseton
MR P.A JACKSON
Mr R Jackson
MR S Jackson
Mr S.J Jackson
Mrs K Jackson
MRS S Jackson
MSTR A Jackson
Mstr A R Jackson
MSTR C Jackson
Mstr G J Jackson
Mstr L A Jackson
Mr A.J Jahan
Mstr J.J Jahan
Miss L.J James
MISS R E James
MR A James
MR J James
MSTR A James
Miss J.J Jameson
Mr J.J Jameson
Mr A.B.J Jamieson
MSTR D Jamieson
Mr J.P Jaye
Mr I.C. Jeffrey
Mstr P.I. Jeffrey
Mr D.J.J Jenkinson
Mrs M.J Jenkinson
Mstr G.W.J Jenkinson
MR T.L Jennison
MSTR P Jennison
MR P Jevons

Mr T.J. Jinks
Mstr T.M. Jinks
Miss C Johnson
Miss J.J Johnson
MR A Johnson
Mr A.J. Johnson
Mr B Johnson
MR G M Johnson
Mr I Johnson
MR J Johnson
Mr P.J Johnson
Mr R.J Johnson
MR S Johnson
Mr S.J Johnson
Mr T.J Johnson
Mr S Johnson
MSTR B M Johnson
Mstr C P Johnson
Mstr C.J Johnson
MSTR M A Johnson
Mstr M.J Johnson
MISS A Johnston
MR G Johnston
Mr I G Johnston
MR P A Johnston
Mr S Johnston
MRS D C Johnston
MSTR B Johnson
Miss A.M Johnstone
Miss K.J Johnstone
Miss S.J Johnstone
Mr A.J Johnstone
Mr M Johnstone
MR S Jolly
MISS C A Jones
MISS H R Jones
Miss N.J Jones
Mr D.J Jones
Mr E.J Jones
MR G Jones
Mr G. Jones
Mr I.R.J Jones
Mr N.J Jones
MR P Jones
MR P A Jones
MR R Jones
MRS A Jones
Mr S.J.J Jones
Mr T. Jones
Mrs G Jones
Mstr A.C.J Jones
Mstr A.D.J Jones
MSTR C Jones
MSTR L Jones
Mstr S. Jones
MR T Jordan
Miss H.J Joss
Mr G.J Joss
MR G Judd
Mr R.J Judd
Mr D.J Julian
Ms J.K Kay
Mr C.K Kaye
MR K Kaye
Mr D.G.K Kearsley
Mr G.F.K Kearsley
Mr S A Keery
Mstr I. Keery
Miss J.K Kelleher
Miss N.J.K Kelleher
Mr P.J.K Kelleher
Miss M Kelly
Mr P Kelly
MR/MSTR Kelly
Mstr M Kelly
MR D Kermode
Mstr G J Kermode
Mstr K.K.M Kerr-Morgan
Mstr D.J.K Kett
MR G A Kidd
MR K H Kidd
D R King
Miss D.A.K King
MISS R L King
MISS S J King
Mr R.A.K King
Mr A.K King
Mr M.K Kirby
Mstr D.K Kirby
Mstr R.K Kirby
MR M Kirk
MR M J Kirk
MSTR O M Kirk
Mr B Kirkbride
Mr J.K Kirkbride
Mstr J.A.K Kirkbride
Mstr P.A.K Kirkbride
Mrs S.K Kirton

Mstr M.K Kirton
MSTR P.R KIRWAN
MR T Kitching
Mstr T Kitching
Mr J.T. Konya
Mstr N. Konya
KUMAR
Mr A.W.L Lake
Mr R.W.L Lake
Mstr M.A.L Lake
Mstr M.R.L Laker
Miss A M Lamb
MR R Lamb
MISS V J Lamballe
MR P Lamballe
Miss R Lambert
Mr C.L Lambert
Mr P Lambert
Mrs E Lambert
Mrs J.L Lambert
Mstr C.W.L Lambert
MISS LANCASTER
MR A Lancaster
MRS E Lancaster
Ms J.L Lancaster
MSTR I Lancaster
Mstr P.L Lancaster
Mr G D Lane
Mr D.W.L Langstaff
Mrs S.M.L Langstaff
Mstr A.L Langstaff
Mr K Larkin
Mstr G Larkin
Mstr P Larkin
Mr P Latham
Mstr A Latham
Mstr S Latham
Mr A.M.L Law
Mr I.D.L Lawson
Mr J.A.L Lawson
MR A Lawther
MSTR A M Lawther
MSTR S Lawther
MISS D.A Lawton
MISS J.F Lawton
Mr A.L Lawton
MR G.R Lawton
Mr J Lax
MISS N Leach
MR M Leach
MR S Leach
Mr C.M. Leahy
Mr C.M.L Leahy
Mr J.L.L Learman
Mr S.J.L Learman
Mstr A.B.L Learman
MR W Learmonth
MR Lee
MR S.D Lee
Mstr M.P. Legg
MR T A Lenehan
Mr D.L Leng
Mr H.L Leng
MR S D Leng
MSTR P J Leng
Mr D.R. Lettin
Mr J.L Leyden
Mstr D.L Leyden
MR A Liddle
MR R F Lillie
MSTR J J Lillie
MSTR R F Lillie
MR F.G Limon
Mrs R.L Limon
MSTR J Little
M J Littler
MR M Littler
Mr P.L Livingstone
MSTR A Lond
Mr S.L Longmire
Mstr R.L Longmire
MR LONGSTAFF
MSTR LONGSTAFF
Mr A.L Lonsdale
Mstr J.L Lonsdale
Mr J.G Louden
Mr P.L Louden
Mr A. Lough
Mr S.T. Lough
Mr G.L Loughborough
Mstr J.G.L Loughborough
Miss B.L Loughran
Mr K. Love
Mstr A.R. Love
Mstr C.L Love
Mr I.M MacFarlane
MR N Mack
Mrs M.M Mackey
Mstr S.M Mackey

MR J Mackin
MR P Mackin
Mr D.K.M Macro
Miss N.M Maguder
Mr A.M Maguder
Mstr A Mallaby
MRS V Mallen
Mstr C Mandiville
Mr A.M Mannering
Mrs D.M Mannering
Mstr P.M Mannering
Mr B.M Mannion
Mstr B.M Mannion
MANSFIELD
MR G Mansfield
MR C Mapplebeck
Miss L Marlborough
MR D Marlborough
Mr J.M Marlborough
MR N Marlborough
MISS C J Marley
Mr Marley
Mr A Marley
MR A Marley
MR B S Marley
Mr I.R.M Marshall
Mstr A.D.M Marshall
MASTER G Martin
MR C Martin
MR M Martin
Mrs M Martin
Mstr A.M Martin
Mstr G.D.M Martin
Miss K.L.M Marwood
MR Marwood
Mr A.E.M Marwood
Mr Mason
Mr D Mason
Mr F.M Mason
Mr P.J.M Mason
Mstr C.D.M Mason
Mstr R D Mason
Miss D.L.M Matthews
MR P MATTHEWS
Mr R L Matthews
Mr T.M Matthews
Mrs C.P.M Matthews
MSTR N Matthews
MR K Mawston
MR G Maxwell
Mr J.M Maxwell
Mr P.M Maxwell
Mr T.P.M Maxwell
Mstr D.M Maxwell
Mr M.D.M May
MR K R Maynard
MSTR P J Maynard
Mr M.R Mayo
Miss E.M McBride
Mrs T McBride
MR A McCabe
Miss G M McCallay
Miss G.M McCallay
MR A.J McCann
Miss L M McCarrick
Mr N C McCarrick
Mstr C I McCarrick
Miss K.M McCarthy
MRS P McCRUM
Mr B.M McCullagh
Mstr P.M.M McCullagh
Mr D. McCulloch
Mr T. McCulloch
Mstr C. McCulloch
Mstr S. McCulloch
Mr A.M McDermott
Mstr P.M McDermott
Mr S.J. McDonagh
MR S J McDougall
Mr V.M McFee
Mrs M.M McFee
MISS V H McGarth
MRS A McGarth
J.R McGee
MISS K L McGee
MR J P McGee
MR K McGee
Mstr J.M McGlynn
MR P G McGough
MR P C McGowan
MRS E.M McGowan
MSTR M P McGowan
Miss C.M McGreal
Mr M.M McGreal
Mstr D.M.M McGreal
Mstr McGurk
MR J P McHale
MRS L M McHale
MCILHERON
Miss H McIlheron
Mr G McIntosh
MR S McIntosh
MSTR G McIntosh
Mr V.A.M McIntyre
Mrs M.P.M McIntyre
MSTR J L McKenna
Mr I. McKenzie
Mstr D.I. McKenzie
Miss A M McKinley
Miss D.E.M McKinley
Mr J McKinley
Mr N McKinley
Mrs M H McKinley
Mstr C.J Mckinley
Mstr M.M Mckinley
Miss R McLaine
Mr I.M McLean
Mr K McLean
Mstr J.A.M McLean
Mr D.M McMahon
Mr T.M McMahon
Mrs L.M McMahon
Mstr A.M McMahon
Mstr R.M McMahon
Mr S.M McNicholas
Mr J McParland
MR S McPartland
MSTR D J McReynolds
MR D McTiernan
MR G McTiernan
Mr K.M McTiernan
Mr M.M McTiernan
Mr D.M Medley
MR J M Meehan
Mr M.M Meehan
MSTR D M Meehan
MSTR S J Meehan
Miss C Meggeson
MR A Melvin
MSTR A Melvin
MSTR L Melvin
MR E Merrington
Mr C Metcalfe
MR S P Metcalfe
Mr U Metti
Mstr A Metti
MASTER Middleton
Miss EM Middleton
MR Middleton
Mr & Mrs P&C
Middleton
Mr AE Middleton
Mr P.M Middleton
Mstr D Middleton
MSTR S.M Midgley
Mr S.J.M Milburn
Mr T.M.M Milburn
Mrs S.H.M Milburn
Miss A.M Mitchell
MR MITCHELL
Mr G.M Mitchell
Mr W.M Mitchell
MSTR MITCHELL
MSTR J Mitchell
MR M J Mitchinson
MR P.W MITCHINSON
MSTR J M Mitchinson
Mstr S J Mitchinson
Miss L.M Moloney
Mr K.M Moloney
Mstr S.K.M Moloney
Mstr D Monks
MISS R Moody
MR MOODY
MR K Moody
C Moore
MISS C L Moore
MISS H Moore
MISS J Moore
MISS S Moore
MR A T Moore
Mr B.H.M Moore
Mr J.H.R Moore
Mr P.R.M Moore
MR R W Moore
Mrs S.V.M Moore
Mstr G.P.M Moore
Mstr P.C.M Moore
Mstr S.L.M Moore
Mr K Morgan
MR S Morgan
MSTR A Morgan
MSTR S MORLEY
Mr T. Morphet
Mstr B. Morphett
Mr G.M Morren
Mr P.S.M Morren
Mstr I.P.M Morren
MR A J Morris
Mr G.A.M Morris
Mr W Morris
MSTR C Morris
Mstr L J Morris
MSTR SJ Morrison
Mr F M Morrissey
Mrs L M Morrissey
Mr A Mortimer
Mr J Mortimer
Mstr S.C. Morton
Mr T.M Mothersill
Mstr C.P.M Mothersill
Mstr D.P.M Mothersill
Mstr M.A.M Motley
Mstr A.M Moutrey
MR Moxham
Mr G.M Mudd
Mr S J Mullen
MR T Mullen
Mrs H Mullen
MSTR C J Mullen
Mr C.M Mullins
Mr G.M Mullins
Mr P.M Mullins
Mrs M.M Mullins
Mr J Mulpetre
MR G Mulroy
Mr J.M Mulroy
Mr G W Mundy
MR K Munford
MR R Munford
MR T Munkley
MR K Munroe
Mr K.O.M Murphy
Mstr A.J.M Murphy
Mstr A.S.M Murphy
MR W.C Murrish
MSTR D.C Murrish
MSTR P.W Murrish
MR T Musicka
MSTR C Musicka
MR A NATH
T NATH
Mr D.H. Neale
Mrs B Neale
MR R Neilson
MSTR J C Neilson
Mr P S Nellist
MISS K Nelson
MR S Nelson
MRS E Nelson
MASTER L M Newbold
Mr J. Newbold
Mrs H NEWBOLD
MSTR K.J NEWBOLD
Mstr K.J. Newbold
MISS G Newbould
Mr M P Newbould
DR M E Newton
Miss S Newton
Mr C.E.N Newton
MR J.R Newton
Mr M. Newton
Mrs K. Newton
MSTR D Newton
MSTR M.J Newton
MSTR S J Newton
MSTR S.J Newton
MR K NICHOL
Mstr J Nichol
Mr J.R.N Nicholas
Mstr L.O.N Nicholas
MR D Nichols
MR I D Nichols
MR NICHOLSON
MR S Nicholson
MRS NICHOLSON
MR S G Nobbs
MSTR M Nobbs
MRS C Nolsan
MISS S M Norgan
MR S R Northend
Mr G Nugent
Mr P.W.N Nugent
MR A J O'BRIEN
MR D O'BRIEN
Mr S.O O'Connor
Mstr A.O.O'Hara
Mr M.O O'Hara
Mr S.O O'Hara
MR J O'Keefe
MR J.P O'Keefe
MISS J O'Reilly
MR P O'Reilly
MR K O'Riordan
MR M O'Riordan
MR N J O'Riordan
Mstr M J O'Riordan
Mr P.O O'Rourke
Mstr D.O O'Rourke
Miss C Ogden
Mr P.A Ogden
Mr D J Oliver
Mr M T Oliver
Mr N.O Oliver
Mrs E.O Opie
Mr S.O Ord
Mstr M.L.O Osbourne
Mstr N.G.O Osbourne
Mr J.V.O Ovington
Mrs F.A.O Ovington
MR T Owens
MSTR D Owens
MISS J L Owst
MR D K Owst
MSTR J M Owst
MR C M Oxley
MSTR M A Oxley
MR M V Pagan
MR P Page
MRS J Page
MSTR J Page
R Page
Mr S.P Paley
MR W J Palmer
Mrs A.P Palmer
Mrs M.P Palmer
Mstr C.P Palmer
MSTR G.M Palmer
MISS G Parker
Mr D Parker
Ms A.M.P Parkinson
Mr J.P Patterson
Mrs H.P Patterson
Mstr G.P Patterson
MR D Pattison
MSTR D J Pattison
Mr D.W.P Paylor
MR S J Paylor
MSTR A J Paylor
MR A PEACOCK
Mr C.P Peacock
Mr J.R.P Pearce
Mrs M.P Pearce
Mstr A.P Pearce
Miss K Pearson
Miss K.L.P Pearson
Mr G.R.P Pearson
Mr J Pearson
MR W A Pearson
Mrs H.E.P Pearson
MSTR M Pearson
Miss R Peat
MR H Peat
Mr S Peat
Mstr A Peat
Mr G.P Pennick
MR M Pennick
MR S Pennick
MSTR A Pennick
Mstr A.F.P Pennick
MSTR S D Pennick
MR P J Peterson
MSTR M J Peterson
Miss K L Peverell
Mr R A Peverell
Mstr M A Peverell
Mr D.P Phillips
Mr W.F Phillips
MSTR A C Phillips
Mstr R.P. Phillips
Mstr T.W. Phillips
R G Phillips
Miss H.L.P Phoenix
Mrs S.M.P Phoenix
MR B Pickering
Mr C.A.C Pickover
Mstr A.J.P Pickover
Mr P.H.P Pierce
Mstr P.P Pierce
Mstr S.P Pierce
Mr D.P Pierre
Mr J Pierre
Mr S Pierre
MR A Piggott
MR G Piggott
Mstr K Piggott
P Piggott
Mr H Pilot
Mstr R Pilot
MR C Pinkney
Mr D.J.P Pinkney
MR J R Pinkney
MRS PINKNEY
Mstr C J Pinkney
Mstr J D Pinkney
Mstr M.J. Pinkney
MR I Pirnie
Mr L.J.P Pisani
Mstr P.R.P Pisani
Miss K.P Porter
Mr E.W.P Porter
Mr M.P Porter
Mstr B.P Porter
Mstr D.L.P Porter
Miss D.M.P Portland
Mr A.D.P Portland
Miss M.P Pounder
Miss N.P Pounder
Mr S.P Pounder
MR G Povey
Miss S.P Pratt
Mr C.P. Pratt
Mr K.P Pratt
Mr R.P Pratt
Mstr N.J.P Pratt
Mr T Preston
MSTR P.R Preston
MR A Price
Mr D.J.P Price
MR I Price
MR J I Price
MSTR A Price
Mstr M.D.P Price
Mstr M.G. Priestley
MR D H Pringle
MSTR P I Pringle
Mr C.J.P Pritchard
Mstr D.J.P Pritchard
Mr T Probert
Mstr J.M.P Proud
Mr K.P Proudler
Miss E.L.P Pryde
Mr R.W.P Pryde
Mstr K.R.P Pryde
Mr D.J.P Purvis
Mr D.P Purvis
MR W J Purvis
Mr K.P Pybus
Mr R.P Pybus
Mr M D Quigley
Ms C Raine
Mstr P Rainsley
Mr D.K. Ramsey
MR G Randall
Mr P Randall
MR G S Rayner
MR S J Rayner
MR S P Rea
MSTR M S Rea
MSTR S Read
Mr B.R Readman
Mstr M Readman
MR M Reay
MRS C Reay
MR REDMAN
MR D M Reed
MR J.W Reed
Mr S.G.R Reed
Mstr C.S.R Reed
MSTR J Reed
MSTR S Reed
Mr A.F.R Reeve
Mr N.R Reeve
Mr F.R Regan
Mr A.P.R Reid
Mrs B.R Reid
Mstr J.W.R Reid
Mstr P S Reilly
Mstr T Reilly
Mr D.A.N Reubens
MISS C J Rhind
MISS K A Rhind
MSTR T J Rhind
Mr M.R Rice
Mstr A.R Rice
MR S J Rich
MISS A Richards
Miss L.E. Richards
MR G T Richards
Mr S Richards
Mr TWP Richards
B M Richardson
MISS D Richardson
MISS E Richardson
MISS S Richardson
Mr D.K.R Richardson
Mr F.C.R Richardson
MR R J Richardson
MRS L Richardson
Mrs M.R Richardson
MSTR D Richardson
Mstr P.R Richmond
MASTER J Rickard
MSTR C Rickard
MR A G Rickman
Mr N.R Rickwood
Mstr W.E.R Rickwood
Mr J.D.R Ridsdale
Mstr S.T.R Ridsdale
Mstr J.M.R Rielly
MISS T Rigg
Mstr S.R Rigg
MR RIORDAN
MR Ripley
MR M Roberts
MISS L Robinson
MISS P Robinson
Mr C.L Robinson
MR G Robinson
Mr I.R Robinson
MR J Robinson
Mr J.R Robinson
MR M Robinson
Mr N.A.R Robinson
Mr R.R Robinson
Mr S.J.R Robinson
Mrs F.R Robinson
Mrs J M Robinson
MRS L Robinson
Mrs M Robinson
MSTR Robinson
Mstr A Robinson
MSTR C Robinson
MSTR D Robinson
MSTR I Robinson
Mstr J.L.R Robinson
Mstr K.A. Robinson
MSTR M Robinson
Mstr S Robinson
Mstr S A Robinson
Mr A.E.R Robson
MR C Robson
Mr J P Robson
Mr T.R Robson
Mstr P Robson
MSTR S Robson
PC Roddam
MR I S Rodger
MSTR W A Rodger
MR H Rodgers
MRS J Rodgers
Mstr R.R Rodgers
MR A J Rogers
Mr J.P. Rogers
Mr T.J. Rogers
MSTR M A Rogers
MR G R Roper
MSTR S Roper
Mr S. Rowden
Mstr C Rowe
Mstr J.P.R Rowe
Mr P.M.R Rowland
Mr P.R Rowland
Mstr S.R Rowland
MISS Rowlands
Mr S.R Rowling
Mr C.E.R Rowney
Mr P.R Rugg
Mstr D.R Rugg
Mr J.R Rusinek
Mr N.A Russ
Mr C.R Russell
MR A Rutherford
MISS H L Ryalls
MR A Ryalls
MR D S Ryalls
MISS S Ryan
Mr K Ryan
Mrs C Ryan
Mr D.R Ryder
MR J Sadler
Mr R.R.S Sadler
MSTR D Sadler
MSTR V Sadler
MSTR D Salah
Mr I.S Samson
Mstr M.S Samson
Mr A J Sanders
MISS C L Sanderson
Miss R Sanderson
Mr B.E.S Sanderson
Mr G D Sanderson
Mr M Sanderson
MR M Sanderson
Mr R.S Sanderson
Mrs H Sanderson
MSTR M J Sanderson
Miss A L Sandrawich
Miss C Sandrawich
Mr M.S Sands
Mstr M.S Sands
Mr J.S Sanson
Mstr K.S Sanson
MR T Sargent
MSTR L G A Sargent
Mr A L Savage
MR M Scaife
Mrs J.B.S Scaife
MSTR C Scaife
Mstr C.D.R Scaife
Mr D.C.S Schumm
Mr K.S Scoby
Mr L Scoby
Mrs Mrs Scoby
Mrs T.S Scoby
Miss Scotland
Mr Scotland
Mr D.L.S Scott
MR J Scott
Mr L. Scott
Mr S Scott
Mr T.S Scott
MR W P Scott
Ms L.S Scott
Mstr C.S Scott
MSTR D P Scott
Mstr J Scott
MSTR M Scott
Mstr P.A. Scott
MR P A Seaman
MSTR S A Seaman
MR S Secker
Mr S Sedgewick
Mr W Sedgwick
Mr S.S Senyurek
Mr J.S Serginson
Mstr J L Shadbolt
Miss A Shann
Miss G Shann
Mr D.S Shannon
MR J Shannon
Mr C.M.S Sharkey
Mr D.N.S Sharp
MR J J Sharp
Mr J.S Sharp
Mr M.S Sharp
Miss K.V. Shaw
Mr S.S Shaw
Mrs P. Shaw
Miss C.S Shea
Mr T.S Shea
Mrs A.S Shea
Mstr A.S Shea
Mstr M.S Shea
Miss J E Shepherd
Mrs W Shepherd
MR A Sherris
MR L Sherris
MRS A Sherris
Mr P.S Shipton
Mr H.S Shore
Miss L Short
Miss L.A Short
Mr R.S Short
Mrs L Short
Mstr J Short
Mstr S.A.S Short
Mstr A Shroufi
Mstr O.S Shroufi
MR J P Sigsworth
Mr M.S Sigsworth
MRS G A Sigsworth
MSTR L A Sigsworth
Mr S.S Simmons
Mstr N.T.S Simmons
Miss A.S Simpson
Miss C.K.S Simpson
Mr B Simpson
Mr C.S Simpson
MR G K Simpson
MR S.S Simpson
Mrs B.S Simpson
Mstr C M Simpson
Mstr D.J.S Simpson
MSTR P Simpson
Mr G.B.S Sinclair
Mr P J Sinclair
Mstr A J Sinclair
Mstr J M Sinclair
Mstr N.S Sinclair
Mstr P.S Sinclair
Mr C.J. Singer
MR S Sizer
Miss L.A.S Skelton
MR D P Skelton
Mr D.S Skelton
MR P J Skelton
Mr D. Skidmore
Mstr C. Skidmore
Mstr G. Skidmore
MSTR D Skilbeck
MR J G Skinn
MR J Skipp

DOOM TO BOOM

MR K Skipp
MR P Skipp
Miss S Smales
Mr A D Smales
Mrs P Smaling
Mstr R Smaling
Mr A.E.S Small
Mstr A.M.S Small
Mr D W Smart
Mstr D W Smart
Miss L.R.S Smiles
Mr N.S Smiles
Mstr B.R.S Smiles
Mr C Smiley
Mstr C Smiley
Mstr D A Smiley
C A Smith
K R Smith
Miss D.M.S Smith
Miss S.S Smith
MR SMITH
Mr A Smith
Mr A.M.S Smith
Mr G D Smith
Mr G.S Smith
MR J Smith
Mr J Smith
Mr J.S Smith
MR K A Smith
Mr L.S Smith
MR M A Smith
Mr N.T.S Smith
Mr P.S Smith
Mr R.S Smith
MR S Smith
Mr T.S Smith
Mrs A.S Smith
Mrs J A Smith
Mrs M Smith
MRS T Smith
Mstr A Smith
Mstr A C Smith
Mstr A.S Smith
MSTR C Smith
Mstr C Smith
Mstr D Smith
Mstr L F Smith
Mstr N G Smith
Mstr R.S Smith
Mstr S.S Smith
P Smith
Mr I.M.S Smitheringale
MR M C Smurthwaite
MISS K J Snowden
MASTER M A Solan
MR A G Southall
Mr R Southall
MSTR R SOUTHALL
G Southworth
L A Southworth
Mr W.L.S Spedding
Mstr A.W.S Spedding
Mr G Spence
Mrs H Spence
Mstr C Spence
Mstr M Spence
Mr D.S Spenceley
Mr M.S Spiller
CANNON SPORTS
Miss E.S Springhall
Mr M.S Springhall
Mr P.A. Squires
Mr M.S Stage
MR K Stainthorpe
MSTR L Stainthorpe
Mstr P Stainthorpe
MR P Stalker
MSTR A J Stalker
Mr M.S Stallard
MR D Starling
MR J Starling
Mr D Staton
Mstr P Staton
Miss E.L Steel
Mr J.S Steel
Mr E.W. Stephens
Miss A.R.S Stephenson
Miss P.S Stephenson
Mr D.J.S Stephenson
Mr G.S Stephenson
Mrs E.S Stephenson
Mstr G.S Stephenson
Mstr M.S Stephenson
MR D Stevens
Mr G Stevens
Mr G Stevenson
MR R G Stevenson
Mr M.D.S Stewart
Mrs V.S Stewart

Mstr D.T.S Stewart
Mr A E Stobbs
Mr A S Stobbs
Mr M.J.S Stobbs
Mstr D Stobbs
MR D Stockburn
Mr C.J.S Stockwell
MSTR M J Stockwell
Mr P.M.S Stoddart
Mr M.J.S Stone
Mrs V.E.S Stone
Mstr M.E.S Stone
Mr A.S Stonehouse
Mr G.N.S Stonehouse
Mstr G.S Stonehouse
Mstr P.S Stoneman
Mstr J Stones
MR K STOREY
Mr J.S Storr
Mstr M.J.S Storr
MR J A Storrie
MR J Stott
MR M A Stracey
Mr J.D.S Struth
Mr A J Suffell
Mr A.S Suggitt
Mr M.B.S Summerbell
MR W Sutherland
MSTR A Sutherland
Ms K.S Swainson
Mstr M.S Swainson
Miss S.A.S Swales
MR Swales
MR A Swales
Mr J.A.S Sweeney
Mstr R.J.S Sweeney
MR N Swinburne
Mr T.S Swinburne
Mstr J Swinburne
Mr S.W.S Sykes
Mstr M.D.S Sykes
MASTER J Taggart
MR P R Taggart
MISS H Tait
MR A Tait
MR D Tait
Mr S.T Tait
Mr E.T Talbot
MRS E Talbot
Mstr S.T Talbot
MR D Tate
MR J.E. Tate
MSTR P Tate
A.J. Tattersfield
Mr D Tattersfield
MR TAYLOR
Mr E.T Taylor
Mr J M Taylor
MR M A Taylor
Mr P.T Taylor
Mr R.W.T Taylor
Mr S Taylor
MSTR TAYLOR
Mstr J Taylor
Mstr M.D.T Taylor
Mstr M.I.T Taylor
Mstr M.T Taylor
Mstr P.T Taylor
MSTR M J Teasdale
Mr A.R.T Templeton
MSTR A Templeton
MISS K Tennant
MR J Tennant
MR K Tennant
MR L E Tennant
Mr P.J.T Tennant
Mr N.M.T Terry
Mr P.T Terry
MRS P Theaker
MISS B Thompson
MR A L Thompson
Mr A.T Thompson
Mr E Thompson
Mr J.F.T Thompson
Mr J.T Thompson
Mr M Thompson
MR N Thompson
Mr N.T Thompson
Mr R.T Thompson
Mrs C. Thompson
MRS L Thompson
Mrs M.T Thompson
MSTR A Thompson
Mstr B. Thompson
MSTR J Thompson
MstrJ.T. Thompson
Mstr P.T Thompson
Mr I.T Thomson
Miss C L Thorman

Mstr J F Thorman
Miss L Thorpe
Mr K Thorpe
Mstr C Thorpe
MR T E Thurlwell
Mstr M Tibbet
Miss A Tibbett
Mr J. Tibbett
Mr J.C. Tibbett
Mr A.F.T Tidy
Mr G.K.T Tindall
Mr J.T Tindall
Mstr A.T Tindall
Mrs S.T Tinney
Mr K.T Tiplady
Mstr P.T Tiplady
TODD
Mr V.T Tonner
Mrs L.T Tonner
Miss C.L.T Tooke
Miss G.E.T Tooke
Mr P.T Tooke
Mr D.T Topham
Mr P.D.T Topham
MR S.A Trainor
MSTR S Trainor
MR B Tranter
Mr K Tranter
MR S T R Tranter
MSTR L N R Tranter
Mstr S Tranter
Mr J.T Trattles
Mstr A.T Trattles
Mstr P. Trenholm
Miss N Trigg
Mr P Trigg
Mr J.T Truscott
MSTR M J Tuck
MASTER TURNER
MASTER C.J Turner
Miss K.T Turner
MISS V L Turner
Mr I.T Turner
MR K M Turner
MRS B Turner
MRS J Turner
Mr G.J.T Turton
Miss C.L.A Turver
MR A N J Turver
Mr J.N.T Turver
Mrs P.T Turver
Mr J Tyzack
Miss H.U Umpleby
MR P Umpleby
Mrs D.U Umpleby
MSTR J R Umpleby
MSTR J V Umpleby
Mstr J.U Umpleby
MR R K Upton
MSTR C Upton
MSTR M Upton
Mstr S.U Usher
MR Usherwood
MSTR P A Varley
Mr P.R.V Vaughan
Mstr M.P.V Vaughan
Mr D.P.V Veazey
Mstr L.J.V Veazey
Mstr M.A.V Veazey
Mr L.V Vickers
Mstr P J Vickers
MR D F Vickerson
Mr G Vipond
Mr J Vipond
Mr W.A Waines
Mrs G.M Waines
Mr J.W Waite
Mr S.W Wales
Mstr K.R.W Wales
Miss H.W Walker
Mr A.W Walker
Mr C.J.W Walker
Mr G R Walker
Mr J.E.W Walker
Mr M.A.W Walker
Mr M.J.W Walker
Mr P.A Walker
MR S K Walker
Mr S.W Walker
MRS C Walker
Mrs K.W Walker
MSTR A Walker
Mstr C.J.W Walker
Mstr J G Walker
Mstr J.W Walker
Mstr M.A Walker
Mstr M.W Walker
MSTR N Walker
Mstr P.W Walker

Mstr R J Walker
MSTR I. Walkington
MR J Wall
MR L.W Wall
Mstr S.W Wall
Mstr P.W Walls
Mr J.P.W Walmsley
Mstr D A Walmsley
MR M Walters
MSTR S S Walters
MR M Walton
Mr S.A.W Walton
Mstr S.T.W Walton
Mrs M.W Wanless
Mr JP Ward
Mr P S Ward
Mr S Ward
Mr V Ward
Mstr I.S Ward
Mstr JA Ward
Mstr P Ward
Mr D.G. Wardell
Mr E D Wardell
Mrs B Wardell
Mstr M.P.W Warrior
Mstr P Warrior
Mr K.W Wass
Mr P.E.W Wass
Mstr P.F.W Wass
Miss K.W Waters
Mr D.W Waters
Mr G.W Waters
MR H Waters
Mrs J.W Waters
Mstr M.D.W Waters
Mstr M.W Waters
Miss E.J.W Watson
Mr A.W Watson
MR G Watson
Mr G.W Watson
Mr J Watson
MR J A Watson
Mr J.E.W Watson
MR K T Watson
Mr P.A.W Watson
Mr S.A.W Watson
MSTR B J Watson
Mstr C.A.W Watson
MSTR G A Watson
MISS K Watt
MR N Watt
MSTR A Watt
MISS L Wears
MR M Wears
MR F S Weatherall
MRS A E Weatherall
Mstr C A Weatherall
MR D.J Weatherell
Mr D.W Webb
Mstr A.D.W Webb
Mstr R.B.W Webb
MR Webster
Mr A Welburn
Mstr M Welburn
Miss R.S. Wellfare
MISS L Wells
MR G Wells
Mr D.N.W Wem
Mrs S.M.W Wem
Mstr M.T.W Wem
Mstr S.M.W Wem
MR C West
Mrs E.W Wharry
Mr P Whatmore
MSTR J.P.Whatmore
Mr D.W Wheeler
MR A White
Mr A.W White
MR B M White
Mr C White
Mr G R White
MR M White
Mr M A White
Mr M.P.W White
Mr M.W White
Mstr M D White
Ms M.W Whitehead
Mstr N.W Whitehead
Mr D.W Whitehouse
Mstr M.W Whitehouse
MR D E Whitfield
MR E G Whitfield
MR P C Whitfield
MRS C Whitfield
MSTR M R Whitfield
Mr S.D Whittingham
MR S Whyman
Mr G. Wigham

MISS N Wiles
Mstr A J Wilkins
MR H Wilkinson
Mr B.W Williams
MR D Williams
Mr D.W Williams
Mr G.D. Williams
Mr G.W Williams
Mr J.W Williams
MR O Williams
Mr P Williams
Mr S D Williams
Mrs I.W Williams
Mstr D.G. Williams
Mstr L.W Williams
Mstr M.D.W Williams
Mstr P Williams
Mstr S.W Williams
Mr S. Williamson
MRS S Williamson
Mstr T. Williamson
MISS C E Willoughby
MR D Willoughby
Wilson
J Wilson
K Wilson
MASTER JPW WILSON
Miss L C Wilson
Miss T.W Wilson
MR A Wilson
Mr A.W Wilson
MR B Wilson
Mr D A Wilson
Mr H A Wilson
MR J J Wilson
Mr J K Wilson
Mr K.W Wilson
MR R Wilson
Mr S Wilson
Mr S A Wilson
Mr WJW WILSON
MRS J Wilson
MSTR C WILSON
Mstr C.M.W Wilson
Mstr D.A Wilson
Mstr S Wilson
Mstr S K Wilson
Mstr S T Wilson
Mr R Winter
Mr R.W Winter
Mr L.D.W Winward
Mstr D.I.W Winward
Mr C.W Wood
Mr I.P. Wood
Mr J. Wood
Mr J.W.W Wood
Mr P. Wood
Mstr C. Wood
Mstr D.C.W Wood
Mstr G.J.W Wood
MSTR D N Woodcock
Mr M.W Woodgate
MISS H Woodhouse
MISS S Woodhouse
MR R Woodhouse
MRS M Woodhouse
MISS C A Woods
Mr A.C.W Wootton
MR P Wootton
MRS V Wootton
Mr A.W Wormald
Mr J. Wrigglesworth
Mstr T. Wrigglesworth
Master Wright
Mr R W Wright
Mr S.W Wright
Mr T.W Wright
MRS A.M WRIGHT
Mstr C.S.W Wright
Mstr K.W Wright
Mstr M Wright
MR A Yeo
Mr M.Y York
MR P York
Mr S.J.Y York
MR Yorke
Mr A.Y Young
Mr B Young
Mr M Young
Mr M.Y Young
Mstr A.Y Young
Mstr J.M.Y Young
Mstr K YOUNG
MSTR S Young
Mr J.Y Yuille
Ms C.Y Yuille

EAST STAND UPPER

MRS V.A. Abbas
Mr D.E.A Abbott
Miss L. Abel
Mr J B Abel
Mr R J Abel
Mrs K A Abel
Mstr P J Abel
Mr N P Abercrombie
MR P Ableson
Miss J.S Ackerley
MR A Ackerley
MR G Ackerley
MR H Ackerley
Mr M.A Ackerley
Mr N.A Adair
MR Adams
Mr D S Adams
Mr P.A. Adams
Mr P.D. Adams
Mr S J Adams
MRS E Adams
Mstr T.A Adams
Mr M.A Addison
Mr P. Affleck
MISS L.E AGAR
MR C Agar
Mr E.O Agar
Mr M Agar
MSTR M Agar
MR R Ainscough
Miss J.G. Akerman
Mr S.A Alder
MR G Alderson
Mr R.A Alderson
Mr T.A Alderson
MSTR C I Alderson
MR D.J Alderson
Mstr J.C.A Alderton
MR G Aldus
Mr J.W.A Alexander
MR B Allan
Mr J R Allan
MR P Allan
MR R Allan
MRS J A Allan
Mr N.J.A Allcock
MR D Allen
Mr H Allen
Mr P. Allen
Mr T.J.A Allen
Mstr S.A Allen
Mr V.A Allenby
Miss L.D.A Allison
MR D Allison
Mr D J Allison
Mr J Allison
Mr M J Allison
Mr T Allison
Mr D.J. Almond
Mr I Almond
Mr M.A Amos
Mrs B.J.A Amos
Mr D.C.A Anderson
Mr N Anderson
Mr C.P.A Andrew
MR A Angel
MRS I Angel
MR M.A Angell
MR L G Angouin
MR H Antill
MR D Appleby
Mr D. Appleby
MR G Appleby
Mr H.N. Appleby
MR N Appleby
MR P APPLEBY
MR A Appleton
Mr D K Appleton
MR K Appleton
Mr W.A Appleton
MISS A Appleyard
Miss K.A. Appleyard
MR G Appleyard
Mr J. Appleyard
MR S Appleyard
Mrs D.S. Appleyard
Mr A.Y Archer
Mr P.J.A Archer
MSTR J C Archer
MR G Archibald
MR K A Archibald
Mr S.A Arkless
MR Armstrong
MR A J Armstrong
Mr D Armstrong
MR H Armstrong
Mr J.A Armstrong
Mr M.R.A Armstrong
Mr A.D. Arnold
MR M C Arnold

MSTR R A Arnold
MR M.A. Aronson
MR J G Ash
MSTR G E J Ash
Miss C.A Ashley
Ashstead Plant Co
Mr S H Askew
Mstr G P Askew
MR S Aspery
KEITH THOMAS ASSOCIATES
MR B Astbury
Mr A.R.A Atherton
MISS E Atkins
MR D Atkins
Dr C J Atkinson
Mr A Atkinson
MR C J Atkinson
MR C.G.A Atkinson
Mr D.B.A Atkinson
MR G Atkinson
MR J A Atkinson
Mr M R Atkinson
Mr M.A Atkinson
Mr M.J.A Atkinson
Mr M.P.A Atkinson
Mr N M Atkinson
Mr P.A Atkinson
Mr R A Atkinson
MR S Atkinson
MR S A Atkinson
Mr T.J.A Atkinson
Mrs J Atkinson
MSTR J C Atkinson
Mstr M A Atkinson
Mstr M.E.A Atkinson
Mstr T D Atkinson
Mr M R Axe
MR D A Axford
Mr M.L.A Axton
Mr P.T.B Bacon
MISS J Bage
MR A Bage
MR M Bage
Mr B. Bagley
Mr A Bailey
Mr K.D.B Bailey
Mr L Bailey
MR P Bailey
Mr P Bailey
Mr R B Bailey
Mr S.L.B Bailey
Mrs C E Bailey
Mstr P.T.B Bailey
Miss A.B Bainbridge
MR A J Bainbridge
Mr A.M. Bainbridge
Mstr R.B Bainbridge
Baines
MR Baines
Mr J Baghul
MISS S J Baker
Mr B Baker
Mr D.B Baker
Mr J.B Baker
Mr K Baker
MR P Baker
Mr S.P.B Baker
Mr P.P. Banks
Mr B.B Barber
Mr G Barber
Mr G.A.B Barber
Mr P.B Barber
MR A Barker
Mr A. Barker
Mr A.J.B Barker
MR C L Barker
Mr S.B Barker
MSTR G Barker
Mr R.J.B Barnes
MR I Barraclough
MR M G Barras
Mr M J Barry
Mr R.S.W Barry
Mr A Bartley
Mr C.C.B Bartliff
Mr A Bashford
Mr J P Bashford
MR M G Bashford
Mr M.N.B Bashford
MSTR S G Bashford
Mr N.C.B Batchelor
Mr S.R Bateman
MR C Bates
Mr D.B Bates
Mr P.B Bates
Mr M.B Baty
MR E Baxter
Mr P J Baxtram

MR A.C Bayles
MR J.F Bayles
Mr A.B Baynes
Mr M.B Beadnall
Mr P.B Beadnall
MR C BEADNELL
MRS S Beagrie
Mr T.B Beagrie
MR W Beagrie
Mstr D.J.B Beagrie
Mr G.B Beales
Mr C.B Bearman
Ms K.B Bearman
Mr A Beattie
MR A D Beaumont
Mr A.J.B Beaumont
Mr L.B Beaumont
MR B W Beaver
MRS J Beaver
Mr P.B Beedle
MR D Begley
Mr A.B Belden
Mr N.B Belford
Mr Bell
MR A.L Bell
MR C BELL
Mr G D Bell
MR J Bell
MR J A Bell
Mr J. Bell
Mr J.L.B Bell
Mr R Bell
Mr S.B Bell
Mr S.P.B Bell
Mr T. Bell
Mr T.l.B Bell
Mr W D Bell
Mstr C G Bell
MR W Bellerby
Mr D.J.B Bellett
Mr C.M. Belshaw
Mr J.H.B Belshaw
Mrs V. Belshaw
Mr J.B Belt
MR K Bennet
MR A Bennett
MR A.M Bennett
Mr A.R.B Bennett
Mr J Bennett
Mr P A Bennett
MR S.P Bennett
Mr H.B Bennetts
Mr G.M.B Bennington
Mr N D Bennington
Mrs G D Bennington
Mr A.P. Bennison
MR T BENOLIEL
Miss L.J.B Bentley
Mr J Bentley
MR L A Bentley
Mr M M Bentley
MR P Bentley
MR M Benton
Mr G.S.B Bernard
Mr W.I.B Bernard
Mr R.M.B Berriman
Mr A.B Best
Mr C.B Bettinson
P Bevington
Mr A.B Bezance
MR A Bickham
MR D R Bickham
MRS Bickham
MR A Biggs
Mr M.R. Bigley
Mr S.R.B Bilton
Miss H A Binks
Mr Binks
Mr D.B Binks
Mr J.B Binks
Mr R.B Binks
Mr S.B Binks
Mrs S.A.B Binks
Mr J Birch
Mr P Birch
Mrs P Birch
MR S Bird
Mr I D Birdsey
Mr D.A.B Birkett
Mr H.B Birtwhistle
Mstr C.B Birtwhistle
Mr J.H.W Bishop
Mr S.B Bishop
Mr D.B Bivens
Mr D.B Blackburn
Mr G.B Blackburn
Mr L.B Blackburn
Mrs S.B Blackburn
Mr C.B Blackett

Mr J.B Blackett
Mrs M.B Blackett
Mr P.G.B Blackler
MR G P Bladwin
MR C S Blake
Mr D.S.B Blake
MR T Blake
Mstr S.A.B Blake
MR A Blakemore
Mr A Blakey
Mr G Blakey
Mr W.B Blakey
Mr G.J.B Bland
Mr R.B Bland
Mrs M.R.B Bland
Mstr D.B Bland
Mstr M.B Bland
MR W Blenkinsop
Mr J Blenkiron
MR BLIGH
Mr D Blount
Mr D.A.B Blyth
MR T Blyth
MR G B Boates
MR P.G Bodo
MR S.l. Bodo
MRS P Boldison
Mr G.B Bolton
Mr G.M.B Bolton
Mr J.B Bolton
MR N D Bond
MR K Bone
Mr T.D.B Bonner
MR M Booth
Mr A.E.B Bourne
Mr T. Bourne
MR D Bouttell
Mr K.B Bouttell
MR M Bouttell
MR H Boville
Mr G.D.B Bowden
Mr R.D.B Bowden
Mr P.R Bowers
MR C Bowes
Mr C.A.B Bowler
Mr M.B Boyer
Mrs J.R.B Boyer
Mstr R.L.B Boyer
MR Boyes
MR D Boyes
Mr R.J.B Boyes
MRS L Boyes
Miss M.A. Boyle
Mr B.J.B Boyle
MR C Boyle
Mr O Boyle
MR P.E Boyle
Mr S.R.B Boyle
MR M D Brack
Mr P.B Brack
Mr D. Bradley
Mr F A Bradley
Mr M T Bradley
Mr R.B Bradley
Mrs M T Bradley
MR J Brady
Mr J M Brady
MR P Brady
MR S Brady
MR S E Brady
Mrs T Bramley
Mr A Branson
MR M.R Breedon
MR N Brewer
MRS J M Brewer
Mr G Bridge
Mr Briggs
Mr J.G.B Britton
Mr A.B Broadbent
Mr P A Brockett
Miss D.B Brodie
MR D Brodie
MR L J Van Den Broecke
Mr G. Brogden
Mr F.M.B Bromham
Mr G.A.B Bromham
Mr A Brook
Mr S.A.B Brook
MR A BROOKS
MR D Brooks
Mr P Brooks
MRS S Broom
MR W O Broom
Mr P.B Brothwold
Mr A Brown
MR A R Brown
MR A T Brown
MR A.E Brown
Mr A.J.B Brown

MR C Brown
MR C.A Brown
Mr C.D.B Brown
MR D A Brown
Mr D.B Brown
Mr D.W.B Brown
MR G S Brown
Mr G. Brown
Mr G.C.B Brown
Mr J.B Brown
MR J.G Brown
Mr K.P Brown
Mr M Brown
Mr N.E.B Brown
Mr N.J.B Brown
MR P Brown
MR P S Brown
MR R Brown
Mr S Brown
Mr S.P.B Brown
Mr T.W.B Brown
MR W A Brown
Mrs K.E.B Brown
Mr D.J.B Brownbridge
Mr N.B Browne
Mr A J Browning
Mr C.P.B Brownlee
MR P Brownlee
Mr D.R.B Bruce
Mr R.S.B Bruce
Mrs C.M.B Bruce
MR A D Brudenell
Mr D. Brundall
Mr A.B Brunskill
Mr K Brunskill
Mstr B A Brunskill
Mr F Brunton
Mr L A Brunton
MR D Bryan
MR N J Bryan
MSTR J Bryan
Mr D.B. Buchanan
Mrs J.B. Buchanan
BUCKLEY
A H ATKINSON
BUILDERS
Mr R.R. Bull
MR P D Bullen
MR R M Bullen
Miss S.J.B Bullock
Mr A.J.B Bullock
MR B Bullock
Mr J.W.B Bullock
Mr M Bullock
Mr M.B Bullock
Mr M.K.B Bullock
Mr S.B Bullock
MSTR J Bullock
Mstr M S Bulman
Mr B.D. Bulpitt
Mr R Bulpitt
MR A.E Bunn
Mr G.R.B Bunn
Mr K.W. Bunn
Mr S.B Bunn
Mr T J Bunn
Mstr D.K. Bunn
Mr G E Burke
MR P M Burke
Mrs S Burke
MSTR C Burke
Mr M Burn
A BURNISTON
N.R BURNISTON
MR J F Burns
Mr N.B Burns
Mr P.B Burns
Mstr J.B Burns
Mr A.B Burridge
MR P.F Burton
MR D Bushby
MR M A Bushby
Mr R.J.B Butcher
Mr J Butler
Mr K R Butler
Mr L.B Butler
Mr R Butler
MR W.J Butler
Mr I.B Butterwick
Mr K Buxton
Mr R.B Buxton
Mr C.J.B Byrne
MR J Byrne
Mr H.V.B Bywater
Mrs J.S.B Bywater
MR J Cadman
Mr J.P.C Cain
Mr M.C Cain
Mr S.C Cairne

Mr K J Cairns
Mr P. Cairns
Mr T Cairns
MR C Callaghan
Mr G.C Callaghan
Mr P.C.C Callaghan
Mr I Callender
MR G Calvert
Mr S.C Calvert
Mr T Calvert
MR G B Cameron
MR D Camp
MR A Campbell
Mr D.C Campbell
Mr G.C Campbell
Mr J D Campbell
Mr M.C Campbell
MR S Campbell
Mr S.M Campbell
Mstr G.C Campbell
MR CAMPLIN
MR H J Cann
MR R Canning
Mr P.A Cannon
Mr A.C Carbert
Mr I C Carlisle
Mr W. Carlisle
Mr M.C Carman
Mr R.C Carman
Mr L.E.C Carmen
MR D.A Carnaby
MR M.J Carnaby
Mr K.C Carney
Mstr M.C Carney
MISS K Carolan
Mr A. Carr
MR D A Carr
Mr D. Carr
Mr I.C Carr
Mr J Carr
Mr D.C Carrigan
Mr J.C.C Carrigan
Mr M.T.C Carrigan
Mr S.C Carruthers
Miss M.C.C Carswell
Mr D.G.C Carswell
Mrs C.C Carswell
Mr K.C Carter
Mr M.R.C Carter
Mr R. Carter
Mrs A Carter
MR K Cartmell
MR D W Carvello
Miss L.E Carver
Mr J. Cass
Mr B.J.C Cassidy
Mr C.J.C Caswell
MR J P Caswell
MR L H Caswell
MISS J Catchpole
MR D Catchpole
Mr J L Catchpole
Mr E.C Cave
MR K E Caygill
Mr A Chadwick
Mr N M Chaffey
Mr G Chamberlain
Mr J Chamberlain
Mr R F Chamberlin
Mr D. Chambers
Mr G. Chambers
Mr I.C Chambers
Mr J.K. Chambers
Mr. M. Chambers
MR P W Chambers
Mr A.M. Champion
Mr J.P.C Chan
MR B Chapman
Mr B R Chapman
Mr C Chapman
MR D Chapman
Mr D Chapman
Mr J.A. Chapman
Mr K Chapman
MR P Chapman
Mr C Charlton
Mr P.A.C Charlton
Mstr J Charlton
Mr P.C Chaytor
Mr R.C Chaytor
Mr C Cheesbrough
Mr S.A.C Chesney
Mr P.S Chisem
Mrs K.A. Chisem
Mr J.D.C Chisholm
MR A M T Christon
Mr A.P.C Christy
Mr P.E.C Chudley
Mr J.W.C Church

Mr M.C Church
MR M J Cimmermann
Mr J. Clamp
MR P Clamp
MR M Clancey
MISS A Clapton
Mr G.L.C Clapton
Mr M.C Clapton
G J Clark
Mr A S CLark
Mr D H Clark
MR G Clark
MR G.E Clark
MR H.C Clark
Mr I.C Clark
MR J G Clark
MR I. A Clark
Mr L. Clark
MR M Clark
MR R Clark
Mr S.J.C Clark
MR W Clark
MR G Clarke
Mr G.F.C Clarke
MR M J Clarke
MR S Clarke
Mr S.C Clarke
Mr F.P Clarkson
MR G P Clarkson
MR I Clarkson
Mr P E Claxton
MR G Clay
Mr P.C Clayton
Mr R P Clayton
Mr R. Clennett
MISS C Clifft
Mr E.F.C Clift
Dr G Clixby
Miss L.J Clixby
Mr Clocherty
MR J L Close
Mr S Close
Mr S.M Close
MR W M Close
Mr D Clyburn
MR D Coates
Mr D J Coates
Mrs C A Coates
MR W Coatsworth
MR A J Cobbold
Mr I Cobby
J Cochrane
Mr G.C Cochrane
Mr M.C Cockburn
Mr G.R.C Cockerill
MR M Cole
Mrs L.C Cole
Mstr P.M.C Cole
MR D P Coleman
MR G Coleman
Mr R.J.C Collier
Miss J.M. Colligon
MR Collins
Mr C.A.C Collins
MR P Collins
Mr R.A.C Collins
MR S A Collins
Mr T.C Collins
MSTR Collins
Mr DFSJ Collis
Mr J.F.C Colmer
John Holmes Motor
Company
MR P.C Compton
Mr D.C Conlin
MR I Conlin
Mr G.J.R Connolly
Mr J Connor
MR P Connor
MR P G Connors
Miss T Conroy
Mr A Conroy
Mr A E Conroy
Mr I.S.C Conroy
Mr S.C Conroy
Mstr L.C Conroy
Mr G.C Conway
Miss S Cook
MR Cook
MR A M Cook
Mr A.C Cook
Mr D.C Cook
Mr E Cook
Mr E.C Cook
Mr G.C Cook
MR I F Cook
Mr J.C Cook
Mr S Cook
Mr S A Cook

Mr S.C Cook
Miss A Cooke
MR COOKE
Mr R.C Cooke
Mr P Cooling
Mr D.T.C Coombes
Mrs P.J.C Coombes
MISS S Cooper
Mr C.C Cooper
MR G Cooper
Mr G.A.C Cooper
Mr G.C Cooper
Mr J G Cooper
Mr J.C Cooper
Mr M.D.C Cooper
Mr N.C Cooper
Mr P.D Cooper
MR T Cooper
Mstr A.W.C Cooper
Mstr D.C Cooper
Mr P.C Copeland
Mr R.C Copley
Mr J Coppinger
Mr K.C Coppinger
Mr A.D. Cordiner
MR N Corking
Mr P Corking
Mr K.C Corner
MR M Corner
MR I Cornfield
MR G Cornick
Mr G.R.C Cornwell
Mr T. Cossins
Mrs L. Cossins
MR G R Cotts
Mr D.C Cotty
Mrs C.M.C Cotty
Mr R.C Coulson
MR G G Court
MR N G Court
Mstr L.J.C Court
Mr E.C Coverdale
MR M J Cowan
Mr D.C Cowe
MR N Cowell
Mr R H Cowell
Mr D.J.C Cowen
MR S Cowen
MR M A Cowley
MR COX
Mr M.K Cox
Mr S Cox
Mr W Coyle
MR A Crabbe
Mstr D Crabbe
Mr A.B.C Craddy
Mr I.C Craddy
Mr A.D.C Craggs
MR D Craggs
Mr M.C Craggs
MRS B Craggs
MR CRAIG
Mr I.C Craig
Mr P.C Craig
Mr A Crandon
Mr D.E.C Crane
Mr S.R.C Crane
Mr G.N.C Crass
Mr A.N.C Craven
Mr D A Crawford
Mr L.C Crawford
Mstr C J Crawley
Miss S.C Crilly
Mr B.C Crilly
Mr D.C Crinion
Mr P.D.C Crinion
MR S Croasdale
Mr C.C Croce
MR S Crocker
Mr M.J.C Crofts
MR CROLLA
Mr S.J.C Crone
Mr D.J.C Cronin
Mr M. Cronin
Mr M.J. Cronin
Mstr P.A. Cronin
Mstr P.A. Cronin
MISS F J Crooks
MR P Crooks
Mr P.C Crooks
Mstr C.C Crooks
Mstr N.C Crooks
MR A W Crosby
MR D Crosby
Mr J.H. Crosby
MR P Crosby
MRS W.A Croshaw
Miss A.C Crossling
Mr J.C Crossling
MR A Crossman

MR A A Crow
Mr M. Crow
Mr B.A. Crusher
Mr R.C Crust
Mr M.R.C Csorba
MR D Cubbin
MR R Cuffe
Mr M A Cummings
MR P A Cummins
Mr F.C Cunningham
Mr G.D.C Cunningham
MR P J Cunningham
Mstr C.C Cunningham
Mr I.S.C Curry
Mr A.G.C Curtis
MR J Curtis
MR J M Curtis
Mr N.C Curtis
Miss M Cuthbert
Mr C D Cuthbert
MRS S Cuthbert
MRS S A Cuthbert
Mr R.C Czarnecki
Mr S Dack
Mr B T Daggett
Mrs L B Daggett
Mr A J Dale
MR D Dale
Mr L.D.D Dale
Mr M Dale
Mrs E Dale
Mstr M J Dale
Mstr S Dale
Mr. M. Dales
Mr A B Daley
MR J T Daley
MR T Daley
Mr N.D Dalrymple
Mr G.W.D Dalton
MR I.A Dalton
Mr N.A.D Dalton
Mr G Daly
MS P Danby
MR M Daniel
Mr P.D Daniel
MR RD Daniel
MRS H Daniel
Darbyshire
Mr J P Darbyshire
MR A Darcy
MR B DARCY
MR D DARCY
MSTR R A Darcy
MR M W Darwin
Mr N Darwin
Rev G.M.D Dasey
Mr C.J Davey
MR P Davey
Mr P.S.D Davey
MR C Davidson
MR K Davidson
MR N R Davidson
Mr P.G.D Davidson
MR R Davidson
Mr R.D Davidson
I Davies
MISS M Davies
Mr G.D Davies
Mr H. Davies
Mr I.S.D Davies
MR M Davies
Mr M.A. Davies
Mr P Davies
Mr P.D Davies
MR S Davies
Mr T.D Davies
Mrs A. Davies
MR J P Davis
Mr M.D Davis
Mr W.K.D Davis
Mrs L Davis
Mr A.J.D Davison
Mr L.D Davison
Mr P.J.D Davison
Ms E.L.D Davison
Mstr P.A.D Davison
Miss J.D Dawson
MR B Dawson
Mr J.W Dawson
MR M Dawson
MR N Dawson
Mr N R Dawson
Mr N.D Dawson
MR P Dawson
Mr P J Dawson
MR R Dawson
Mrs D J Dawson
Mrs I Dawson
Mr G.D Day

Mr I.M.D Day	MR W Dryden	MR R Evans	Mr D P Forbes	Mr P.G Geldard	Mr F Gowland	Mr R. Hall
Mr J.B.D Day	MR DRYSDALE	Mr R.E Evans	MR Ford	MR M D Gelder	MR M Gowland	Mr R.W.H Hall
Mstr N.D Day	MR M K Duck	Mr T.E Evans	Mr A.E.F Ford	Mstr L Gelder	MRS M Gowland	MR S D Hall
Mr A.T.D Daynes	Mr M.K.D Duck	Mr T.M.E Evans	Mr C.F Ford	Ms B.G Gell	MR D Graham	Mr T.G.H Hall
Mr C Deaton	Mr R Duck	Ms S.E Evans	Mr R P Ford	MISS J Gendle	Mr I Graham	Mr W.R.H Hall
Miss S H Dedman	Mr M.G.D Duffey	MR M Everton	Mr N Forrest	MR A Gendle	MR K I Graham	MSTR C Hall
Mr C G Dedman	Mr J Duffield	MR A Evetts	MR M Forrestal	Mr A Gent	MR L Graham	Mstr K.H Hall
Mrs M A Dedman	Mr P Duffield	MR C Evetts	J Forster	MR B Gent	MR M.J Graham	Mstr M.S.H Hall
Mr R Defty	Mr C.P.D Duffy	MRS L Evetts	Mr C.S.F Forster	MR C Gent	MR P Graham	Miss V.H Hamilton
Mrs A M Defty	Mr J.D Duffy	Mr B.E Exelby	Mr G Forster	MR G Gent	Mr S.G Graham	MR D Hamilton
MR M.W Dell	Mr P.S.D Duffy	Interlink Express	MR J Forster	Mr G Gent	MRS D H Graham	Mr I.H Hamilton
Mr W.J Dell	Miss R A Duke	Mr D Eynon	Mr J Forster	Mr H.G George	Mrs M Graham	Mr J.R.H Hamilton
MR P Denham	Miss S A Duke	Mr S Eynon	Mr J.W.F Forster	Mr P.G George	Mstr E.J Graham	MR K Hamilton
Mr S. Denham	Mr B A Duke	Mr I Eyre	Mr M.F Forster	Mr C.J.G Geraghty	Mr D.G Grainger	Mr K.H Hamilton
Ms C.D Denham	Mr E.D Dumphy	Mr D.L. Fairbridge	Mr S.F Forster	Mr A Gerdard	Mr J.D.G Grainger	Mr M Hamilton
Mr I.J.D Dennis	Mr T.D Dumphy	Mr D.W. Fairbridge	Miss L.E.F Foster	MR D Gibb	Mr C.R.G Gray	Mr R.H Hamilton
MR M C Dent	MR J P Dunbar	Fairless	MR C Foster	MR N Gibb	Mr M.G Gray	MRS S Hamilton
Mr P.D Dent	Mr J.M.D Dunbar	MR D Fallows	Mr C.J.F Foster	MR G Giblin	MR S Gray	Mr F Hand
MSTR S Dent	Miss E.J. Dunn	Mr R.F Farbridge	MR D Foster	Miss J.A.G Gibson	MR E A Greaves	K. Hanley
MR J M T Devitt	Mr T.M Dunn	Mr N.F Farley	Mr K.F Foster	Miss N.A.G Gibson	MR J Greaves	Mr Hanley
Mr P.D Dewings	MRS A Dunn	MR B P FARLEY	Mr M P Foster	Mr D Gibson	GREEN	Mr J.H Hanley
MR Dhand	Miss S. Dunnigan	Mr D Farnaby	Mr M R Foster	Mr E S Gibson	Miss J S Green	Mr C.F.H Hanlon
Mr N.G.D Dibble	Mr J.D. Dunnigan	Mr S.R. Farnaby	Mr M.F Foster	Mr F Gibson	Mr G Green	MR J.S Hanna
Miss A.D Dickens	Miss C.L.D Dunning	MR F Farndale	Mr R.F Foster	MR G Gibson	Mr J.G Green	HANNAH
Mr J.A.D Dickens	Mr C.D Dunning	Mr P Farndale	MR S Foster	Mr J.T.G Gibson	Mr M. Green	Mr J.J Hannan
MR S Dickson	MR D Dunning	Mr K Farr	Mstr A.J.F Foster	Mr K.G Gibson	Mr M.A. Green	Mr D.H Hanratty
Mr M.J.D Dietz	Mr G.S.D Dunning	Mr M Farr	Mstr M D Foster	Mr M.G Gibson	Mr R Green	Mr F G Hanratty
Mstr J.M.D Dietz	MR A Durant	Mr A.S.F Farrell	Mstr S.K Foster	MR N GIBSON	Mr R.D.G Green	MR I R Hansell
Miss C Ditchburn	Mr B.D Durant	Mr M J Farrell	Mr L.F Fothergill	Mr P R Gibson	Mr S.G Green	Mr N Hansom
MR L Ditchburn	Mr C.D Durham	Mr J Farrer	Mr C.F Fountain	Mr T D Gibson	Mr S.J.G Green	Mr C.H Hanson
Mrs J Ditchburn	Mr P.L Durrant	MR C Fawcett	Mr A.J.F Fox	MR W Gibson	Mrs J.G Green	MR D Hanson
MR P D Dix	Mrs H.J Durrant	MR D Fawcett	Mr D.G.F Fox	Mr G.G Giles	Mr S.G Greening	MR E Hanson
MR A Dixon	Mstr M.T Durrant	MR K J Fawcourt	Mr D.F Fox	Mr R I Giles	MR K Greenley	MR M A Hanson
Mr A.D Dixon	MR D Dykes	Mr B.F Fawdon	Mr G.F.F Fox	Mr T.M.G Gilgallon	Mr D.G Greenock	MSTR M.W Hanson
MR C D Dixon	Corze North East	Mr N.G Fawdon	Mr I.A.F Fox	Mr A.G Gill	Mr J Greenslade	MISS K Haplin
MR C H Dixon	MR K A Easton	Mr S.M.F Feasey	MR K B Fox	MR B Gill	MR D Greensmith	MR HARDING
MR D S Dixon	Mr V.F. Eckerman	Mstr B.F Feasey	MR P R Fox	Mr C.G Gill	Mr J.A.G Greenwood	Mr I Harding
Mr J.R.D Dixon	MR Eddy	Mstr S.F Feasey	Mr P.E. Fox	MR D R Gill	Mr D Greer	Mrs D.H Harding
MR M Dixon	Mr N.E Eden	MR FEATHERSTONE	Mr P.F Fox	Mr I Gill	MR J Gregory	MR E T Hardy
Mr P.M.D Dixon	Mr T.E Eden	MR A.D FEENAN	Mr S.M.F Fox	Mr K.G Gill	Mr J.S.G Gregory	Mr J.H Hardy
MR S Dixon	Mr I.E Edge	Mr P Feeney	Mr T.P.F Fox	Mr P.G Gill	MR S Gregory	Mr K Hardy
Mr S.D Dixon	Mr W.M.E Edmond	Mr L.F Fegan	MISS C Foy	Mr T.G Gill	Mr B.G Gregson	Mr M.D.H Hardy
MR G Dobindson	Mr W.R.E Edmond	MSTR C FEGAN	MR C Foy	MR M I Gillen	Mr J.G Gretton	Mr J Hargan
Miss S.J.D Dobson	Mrs H.C.E Edmond	MR M J Fellowes	Mr S.F Foy	MR J A Gills	Mstr J.J.G Gretton	Mr A.M. Harker
Mr A M Dobson	Mstr E.D.E Edmond	Mr T.H.F Fenton	Mr M.F France	MRS T A Gillson	Mr P A Griffin	Mr D.J.H Harkin
Mr D Dobson	Miss J Edwards	MR J P Fenwick	Mr T.F Frank	S Gillson	MISS T.L Griffiths	Mr J. Harland
MR K Dobson	Mr G.E Edwards	Mr A.F Ferguson	Mr N Frankish	Mr A Gilmore	MR C J Griffiths	Mr K J Harland
Mr N.M.D Dobson	MR N Edwards	Mr I.M.F Ferguson	Mr G.F Frankland	Miss S.A.G Ginty	MR C P Griffiths	Mr K.D. Harland
Mr S P Dobson	Mr P.A.E Edwards	Mr K Ferguson	Mstr J.F Frankland	Mrs S.G Ginty	Mr D Griffiths	Mr K Harper
Mr J.D Docherty	MR A J Eland	Mr L Ferguson	Mr D.F Franks	Miss S.A.G Girling	Mr D.G Griffiths	Mr A.M.H Harriman
Mrs M.D Docherty	Mr S.E Elerick	Mrs A Ferguson	Mr M.F Franks	Mstr E.M.G Gjertsen	MR G J Griffiths	Mr J. Harrington
Mr A.G.D Dodds	Mrs S.P.E Elkin	Mrs K.A.F Ferguson	Mrs C.F Franks	Mstr F.T.A Gjertsen	MR GA Griffiths	MR A Harris
Mr H.D Dodds	MR P Ellershaw	Mrs W.F Ferguson	MISS A Fraser	MR D Glasper	Mr M.S.G Griffiths	Mr C J Harris
Mr J H Dodds	MSTR D Ellershaw	Mr A.F Ferri	Mr P.F Freary	Mr D.G Glazebrook	MR N.D Griffiths	MR C P Harris
MR S C Dodds	Mr L.B.E Ellerton	MR B J Ferris	Mr R.F Freeman	Mr S.P.G Gledhill	MR S C Griffiths	Mr G.H Harris
Mr G.D Dodsworth	Mr M.L.E Ellerton	Mr M.D.F Ferris	Mr T.P.F Freer	Mr S.G Gleeson	Mr J.F.G Grimes	Mr G.R.H Harris
Mr J.J.D Dodsworth	MR R A Ellerton	MR A D Fewtrell	Mr E.F French	Mr R.P.G Glindon	Mr R.G Grimes	MR P Harris
Mstr P D Dolan	MR ELLIOTT	Mr C L W Field	Mr J.J French	Mr I Glover	Ms A.G Grimes	Mr P A Harris
Mr M.J.D Donaghy	Mr A.B.E Elliott	MR F Field	MR T French	Mr P.N.G Glover	Mr A.G Groom	Mr P.H Harris
MISS D L Donaldson	MR M Elliott	MR M Field	Mr K J Frew	MR D Gniadek	Mr D.J. Grover	MR R Harris
Mr J.D Donaldson	MSTR D.M ELLIOTT	MR P Finch	Mr I Fryer	MR B S Godfrey	Mr M. Grover	Mr R A Harris
Mr J.G.D Donaldson	Mr F.J Ellis	MR I Fines	MR J F Fryer	Mr C.G Godfrey	Mr M.G Grubb	MSTR P Harris
MR M S Donaldson	MR H Ellis	Mr T. Finlay	Mr K M Fryer	MR I S Godfrey	Mr I.G Grunwell	Mr A Harrison
MR P F Donaldson	MR P G Ellis	Mr P.F Finn	MR N S Fryer	Mr D.G Golding	GUNN	Mr B.T.H Harrison
Mr T.J.D Donaldson	Mr P.E Ellis	Mr C Finney	Mr A.F Fryett	Mr P Goldsmith	Mr D.G Gunn	MR C D Harrison
Mstr J.H.D Donaldson	Mr P.W.E Ellis	A Firman	Mr P.R.F Fryett	Mr K Goldthorpe	Mr S.P.G Gunn	Mr E A Harrison
MISS S B Donnelly	Mr S.E Ellis	MR M P R Firman	Mr D. Furber	Mr B W Goodall	Mr V.G Gunn	Mr G.H Harrison
Mr C.D Donnelly	Ms J.E Ellis	Mr B.M.F Fisher	MR C Gadd	Mr J J Goodall	Mrs K J Gunn	MR J Harrison
MR F J Donnelly	Mstr C.G.E Ellis	Mr G.F Fisher	Mr D P Gaffney	Mr L Goodall	Mrs M.G Gunn	Mr J A Harrison
MR J Donnelly	Mstr M.E Ellis	Mr G.H.F Fisher	Mr S.M.G Galbraith	Mrs M. Goodall	Mr C.G Gustafsson	Mr J.F.H Harrison
MR M Donnelly	Mstr P R Ellis	Mr M.G.F Fisher	Mr S P Gale	Mr G.G Goodchild	Mr S.G Guy	MR K Harrison
Mr M.D Donnelly	Miss Ellison	Mr I Fishpool	Mr Galey	Mr I.G Goodchild	Mr M Guzmics	Mr K.H Harrison
MR N Donnelly	MR R Ellison	Mr J.F Fitzgibbon	Mr L.N. Gallagher	Mr S.G Goodman	MR J M Hackett	MR M C Harrison
Mr S Donnelly	MR L Ellwood	Mr A.F Fitzpatrick	Mr P.C.G Gallagher	Mr S Goodridge	MR K P Hackett	Mr P Harrison
Mstr G.D Donnelly	Mr D.E Elrick	MSTR CM Fitzsimmons	MRS K Gallagher	MR S.F GOODWILL	Mr G.J.H Hackney	Mr P.E Harrison
J Donovan	Mr D.E Elsdon	Mr S.M.F Flaherty	MRS J M Gallet	MSTR J A Goodwill	MR A Haddow	Mr R.W.H Harrison
MR M D Donovan	Mstr P.J.E Elsdon	Mr G Flanagan	Mr A.E.G Gamesby	Mr M Goodwin	Mr R.J.H Haddow	MR S D Harrison
Mr K.D Doody	Mr B Emmerson	Mr B.F Flannigan	Mr P.G Gamesby	Mr R.C.G Goodwin	MR K Hagan	Mr S.C.H Harrison
Mrs A Doody	Mr D Emmerson	Mr D.F Flannigan	MR A Garbutt	MR GORDON	Mr J.H.H Hagen	MSTR P Harrison
Mr D.J. Douglas	MR D R Emmerson	Mr J.D.F Flannigan	MR C Garbutt	MR M D Gordon	Mr M.A.H Haigh	Mr G A Harrow
MR M Douglas	MR J C Emmerson	Mrs T.F Flannigan	MR C J Garbutt	Mr M.B.G Gordon	Mr C.B.H Hale	Mr A Hart
MSTR L.M Douglas	Mr N.J.E Emmerson	Mr T.R. Fleetham	Mr D.G Garbutt	Mr M.J.G Gordon	Mr S.P. Hale	Mr C.H Hart
MR L J Dove	Mr P.E English	Miss J Fletcher	Mr K.G Garbutt	Mstr D.S.G Gordon	MR I M Haley	Mr D.H Hart
Miss J A Dowson	Mr S English	MR A W Fletcher	Mr T. Garbutt	MSTR S E Gordon	MRS P A Haley	Mr M.O.H Hart
MR A Dowson	Mstr A S English	MR C Fletcher	MR B J Gard	MR K B Gorman	MISS D Hall	MR P D Hart
MR G Dowson	Mr M Essery	MR D R Fletcher	MR P Gardner	MRS A J Gorman	MISS J.L Hall	Mr W.J.H Hart
Mr H C Dowson	H H Evans	Mr K.F Fletcher	Mr A.G Garnett	Mr A.I Gornall	MR B Hall	Mr F.H Hartnett
Mr M.K. Dowson	Miss H.E Evans	MR W E Fletcher	Mr S.C.G Garratt	MR R Gornall	Mr B A Hall	MR A J Harvey
MR N Dowson	Miss T.E Evans	MSTR C A Fletcher	Mr R.A.G Garrens	MR P Gotheridge	Mr B.H Hall	MR I R Harvey
MRS K Dowson	MR Evans	MR N J Flinn	Mr J Garrett	GOTT	MR D Hall	Mr D.H Haskins
Mr P Drew	MR A H Evans	Mr K.G.F Flint	MR F H Garton	Miss L.A.G Gott	Mr D.H Hall	Miss J.H Hatton
Mr D Drinkel	Mr B Evans	Mr S.J.F Flint	MR N F Garton	Mr M.S.G Gott	MR J Hall	MR J.P HAWKINS
MRS D A Drinkhall	Mr B.E Evans	Mstr D.K.F Flint	Mr J.M.G Gaskin	Mr N.G Gott	Mr J R Hall	MR S A Hawkins
MR R C Driscoll	MR I Evans	Mstr M.J.F Flint	Mr D.G Gatenby	Mr D.M.G Goult	Mr J.H.H Hall	MR C Hay
MR S Driscoll	MR J W Evans	Mstr N.G.F Flintoff	MR R Gaunt	Mr E W R Goult	Mr K.H Hall	Mr W.H Hayes
MR M Drury	Mr J.E Evans	Mr G.F Flinton	Mr K Geddes	Mr J L Goult	Mr M.R. Hall	Mrs P Hayes
MR C J Dryden	MR K Evans	Mr M P Flynn	Mr M Geddes	Mr M.A.G Goult	MR N A Hall	MISS F Haywood
Mr E.D Dryden	MR M Evans	Mr A Fodden	Mr C.G Gee	Mr R.J.P Gowan	Mr P C Hall	
MR S E Dryden	Mr M Evans	MR M Foden		MR D A Gowing		

MR J D Haywood
MSTR M Haywood
M Headlam
MRS C L Headlam
MR J.C Headley
Mr H.S.H Healy
Mr I.J.H Heard
Mr A Heath
Mr A.J.H Heath
Mr D.H Heath
Mr J Heath
Mr M.H Heath
MR B Hebbron
MR J Hebbron
MSTR G Hebbron
MSTR M A Hebron
Mr P.W Helm
Mr D.G.H Hembury
Mr A.H Henderson
MR B K Henderson
Mr D.H Henderson
Mr G Henderson
MR I Henderson
MR I C Henderson
MR I.C Henderson
Mr I.C.H Henderson
MR M Henderson
Mr M A Henderson
Mr N.A.H Henderson
MR R Henderson
Mr R Henderson
MRS E Henderson
Mr I Henderson-Thynne
Mr C.P.H Henry
Mr P.D.H Henry
MR C A Hepworth
Mr J.P.H Hepworth
MRS B G Hepworth
Mr J.R.H Herbert
Mr T.J.H Herbert
Mstr A.J.H Herbert
MR P Herman
MR A Herrington
Mr T.H Herron
Mr Heselton
MR S Heslehurst
Mr B.H Heslop
MR P K Heslop
MR R W Heslop
MR D Hetherington
MR S R Hetherington
Mr G.H Heward
Mr I.D.H Hewitson
Mr I.R.H Hewitson
Hewitt
Mr C.D.H Hewitt
MR G Hewitt
Mr J.P Hewitt
Mr P.E.H Hewitt
Mr M.J. Hey
Mrs E. Hey
Mrs J.H Heywood
Mr S.H Hibberd
MR N A Hickford
Mrs M.H Hide
Mstr A S Hide
MR J D Higgins
Mr S.H Highfield
Mr S.H Hildon
MISS S A Hill
Mr A.H Hill
MR B Hill
MSTR B E Hill
Mr C Hill
Mr C.J. Hill
Mr I.J.H Hill
Mr J Hill
Mr J.D.H Hill
MR M Hill
MR N Hill
MR N J Hill
Mr S.B.H Hill
Mr S.S.H Hill
MRS J A Hill
Mrs J.A.H Hill
Mr P Hills
Mr A P Hilton
Mr B.A. Hind
Mr Hobson
Mr B Hobson
MR M A S Hobson
Mr G.G.H Hodds
Mr I.G.H Hodds
MR D E Hodge
MR A J Hodgkinson
MISS S Hodgson
MR A Hodgson
Mr C S Hodgson
Mr C.OL.H Hodgson

Mr D.H Hodgson
MR E Hodgson
MR G Hodgson
Mr I.H Hodgson
Mr M.H Hodgson
Mr P Hodgson
Mrs T.M. Hodgson
MSTR C J Hodgson
PM Hodgson
MR D Hogg
MR S M Hogg
MR A P Hogson
MR C G Hoilloway
MASTER D M Holden
Mr G Holden
Mstr S.H Holden
Miss J.V.H Holland
Mr R.H Holland
Mr K.R.H Holliday
Mr C. Hollifield
MR S.M Hollifield
Mr A R Holligon
MR B Hollingworth
MR M Hollingworth
MSTR D Hollingworth
MR M Holloway
MISS HOLMES
MR A J Holmes
MR D HOLMES
MR D.H Holmes
MR L S Holmes
MR M Holmes
MR W G Holmes
Mr E.T.H Holroyd
Ms J.A.H Holroyd
Mr B.D.H Holsey
Mr I.D.H Holtby
MR HOLTON
MR I Homer
Mr M.H Homer
MR R Homer
MR G A Honeyman
MR P Honeyman
Mr S R Honeyman
Mr A.H Hooker
Mr T.B. Hope
MR D Hopson
Mr M.H Horn
Mr J Horner
Mr R.H Horner
Mr P Hornsby
MRS HORNSBY
Mr M.A.H Horrigan
Mr J.O.H Horsburgh
Mrs D.A.H Hough
MR G Houghton
MR D J House
MR S D house
MR P Housley
Mr G.H Howard
Mr A.J.H Howe
Mr I.H Howe
Mr G.R.H Howes
Mr G.H Howsden
Mrs M.H Howsden
Mr I.H Hoy
MR A Hoyle
Mr G Huby
MR D Huddleston
MR C Hudson
MR D HUDSON
Mr D.H Hudson
MR J Hudson
Mr J B Hudson
MR P C Hudson
Mrs J.H Hudson
MSTR P J Hudson
S HUDSON
Miss L Hughes
PM Hughes
Mr K.H Hughes
Mr P.H Hughes
MR J.D HUGILL
MR S Hugill
Mr I G Huitson
Mr J.H Huitson
Mr R Huitson
Mstr C R Huitson
Mr R.W.H Hull
MR R V Hulse
Mr A.J.H Humble
Mr K.H Humble
MR S J Hume
MR G M Humpherys
Humpherys
MR S Humphreys
Mr C Hunt
Mr C.T.H Hunt
Mr G.H Hunt
Mr J Hunt

Mr P.H Hunt
Mrs A Hunt
Mr D.H Hunter
MR I Hunter
Mr J Hunter
Mr M J Hunter
MR T J Hunter
Mr T.A.H Hunter
MRS J M Hunter
Ms N.M.H Hunter
MR C P Hurd
MR C Hurndall
Mr S.H Hurndall
MR D Hurst
MR A Hussain
MR Hutchinson
Mr B. Hutchinson
Mr S. Hutchinson
Mr T.H Hutchinson
Mr J P Hutson
Mr M.C.H Hutton
Mstr C.H Hutton
Mr D Hyde
MR A I'Anson
Mr A.I Ibitson
Mr P.E.I Ibitson
Mrs G.I Ibitson
Mstr J.M.I Ibitson
Mstr T.A.I Ibitson
Mr D Iceton
MR N.C Iceton
Mr J.A.I Igoe
MR A T Illingworth
Mr G.L.I Ingleby
Mr J.I Ingledew
Mr S.I Ingram
Mstr D.I Innerd
Mr D.A.I Innes
Mrs B.A.I Innes
MRS J Instone
Mr P.T.I Ironside
Mr R.J.I Irving
Mr A.R. Irwin
Mr P.I Irwin
Mr P Ivison
JEGS Co Ltd
Miss K R Jackson
Mr B Jackson
Mr D E Jackson
Mr D. Jackson
Mr I R Jackson
Mr J M Jackson
MR R Jackson
Mrs J.J Jackson
Mstr Jackson
Mr M.P.J Jakolins
Mr B.J. James
Mr P.B.J James
MR T.P James
Mr R.P.J January
Mrs K.T.J January
Mr D.J Jefferson
Mr I.D.J Jefferson
MR M R Jefferson
Ms N.J Jenkins
Mr M.J Jenkinson
Mr M.A.J Jinks
MR T M Joel
Mr D I Joel-Chilton
Dr I.F.J John
Mr S Johns
Mrs J Johns
MR Johnson
Mr A.J Johnson
Mr B.J Johnson
Mr C.P.J Johnson
Mr C.W.J Johnson
MR D Johnson
Mr G Johnson
Mr G.J Johnson
Mr G.R.J Johnson
Mr I.J Johnson
Mr J.J Johnson
MR M Johnson
Mr M.J Johnson
MR P Johnson
Mr R Johnson
MR S M Johnson
MR S R Johnson
Mr S.J Johnson
Mr W Johnson
Mr. Johnson
MRS Johnson
Mrs D.R. Johnson
MISS F Johnston
MISS H Johnston
MR A M Johnston
MR P Johnston

MR W Johnston
Mr M Johnston
Mr P Johnstone
Mr S.E. Johnstone
Mrs M.A. Johnstone
Mstr R.E. Johnstone
Miss W Jones
MR A Jones
Mr A.J Jones
MR B Jones
Mr C.J Jones
MR D Jones
MR D P Jones
Mr D.J Jones
MR E Jones
MR F Jones
MR J Jones
Mr J A Jones
Mr N.A.J Jones
Mr N.G.J Jones
Mr N.S.J Jones
MR P Jones
Mr P H Jones
Mr S Jones
Mr S D Jones
Mr S.J Jones
MRS E M Jones
Mstr S.C.J Jones
Mr D.J Jordan
Mr S. Joyce
MR K Julian
MR L S Kandola
MR J kane
Mr R.K Karlsson
MRS J Kashou
Mr D P Kaufman
MR B.D Kaufmann
Mr A Kay
MR J Kay
MR S Kayley
MRS M Kayley
MR Keavney
G Keenan
MR C T Keenan
MR C Keightley
MR M Keightley
Mr A.J.K Kelly
MR B.J Kelly
Mr J.K Kelly
Mr M Kelly
Mr P.K Kelly
Mr V.K Kelly
MR A J Kemp
Mr M R Kendal
MR S J Kendrew
MISS C L Kennedy
Mr M.K Kennedy
Mr P.G.K Kennedy
MR R Kennedy
Mr R.K Kennedy
Mr S.K Kennedy
Mstr S.T.K Kennedy
MR B Kent
MR I.D KENT
MR J.E KENT
Mr M.R.K Kent
MSTR M.E KENT
MSTR P.D KENT
MR D H Kenworthy
Mr P. Kermode
MR S Kernan
MRS P Kernan
Mr D Kerr
MISS S Kettlewell
MR B J Kettlewell
Mr P.G.K Key
Mr A.K Khan
Mr A.K Kiddle
Miss H Kidger
Mr H Kidger
Mstr S.K Killen
Mr J.K Kilvington
MR D King
MR G King
Mr G King
MR M King
Mr R King
Mr T.J.K King
MR I Kinloch
Mr B.K Kirby
Mr D.E Kirby
Mr M.J.K Kirby
D Kirkbride
Mr B Kirkbride
MR M A Kirkbride
Mr P.K Kirkbride
MR A Kirton
Mr Kitchen
MR G D Knaggs

Mr I.G.K Knaggs
Miss J.L.K Knapper
Mr M.G.K Knapper
Mr A Kneeshaw
Mr B Kneeshaw
Mrs P Kneeshaw
Mr D.K Knight
Mr J.B. Knight
Mstr D Knight
Mr G.W.K Knights
Mr R.J Knights
Mr R Knowels
MR A Knowles
MR D M Knowles
MR P A Knowles
MR P M Koeppl
Mr B.K Kossick
Mr G.K Kossick
Mr D.L Lacey
Mr C.J. Lackenby
Mr Mr. Lackenby
Mr N.E. Lackenby
Mr J.P.L Laden
Mr M.I. Laden
Mr P.L Laden
Mr A.L Lagan
Mr G.L Lamb
MR D M Lambert
MR J D Lambert
Mr S D Lambert
MRS M J Lambert
<R G Lambton
MR A Lambton
MR J R Lambton
MRS C M Lambton
MR C Lamming
Mr G.L Lamming
MR M Lamport
MR A Lancaster
Mr B.L Lancaster
MR N A Lancaster
MR P A Lancaster
MRS C Lancaster
Mstr C.L Lancaster
MR B Land
Mr S.L Land
Mrs P.I. Land
MR A Lane
Mrs P.C.L Langston
Mr D.M Lannon
Mr M.L Lanyi
Mr S Lapworth
Mr R.L Larder
MRS M Large
Mr A.L Larkin
Mr A.M.L Larkin
MR C J Larkin
MR P R Larkin
MRS M Larkin
Mrs S.L Larkin
Mr M B Larry
K Latus
Mr M J Lavan
MR P Laverick
MR A.L Lavery
Mr I Lavery
MR J Lavery
MRS K Lavery
Mr B Laville
Mr C.R.L Laville
Mr G.L Laville
Mr W.A.L Laville
Miss K.L Law
Mr C.T.L Law
Mstr D.L Law
Mstr J.L Law
Mstr S.L Law
MSTR T.S Lawlor
Ms F.L Lawson
Mr I.L Layton
Mr J. Layton
MR B LAZENBY
Mr I.L Lazenby
Mr K.L Lazenby
Mr M Lazenby
Mrs I.H.L Lazenby
Mr A.L Leach
Mr J.E.L Leach
Mr P Leach
Mr P J Leach
Mstr J.D.L Leach
Mr J.I. Leadbitter
Mr P.J.L Leadbitter
Mr A Leake
Mr G.L Leatherland
Mr W.J.L Ledbetter

Mr A.T.L Ledsham
Mr M.T.L Lee
MR W M Lee
MR W S Lee
Miss J.L Leech
Mr C.B.L Leech
Mr C.L Leech
Mr B.W.L Leeks
Mr J.C.L Leeks
Mr D.L Leen
Mrs S.L Leen
Mr A.L Lees
Mr R.G.L Lees
MR A L Legg
Mr K.L Legg
MISS A D Leng
Mr A.M.L Leng
MR S Lennon
Mr G Lenton
Mr S Lenton
MR D J Lewis
Mr I.L Lewis
MR R Lewis
MR S Lewis
MR A Leyshon
Mr B T Leyshon
MR J E Leyshon
MSTR K Leyshon
Mstr M B Leyshon
Mr J K Libbey
Mr K.L Libbey
Mrs M V Libbey
Mr P.I.L Libbey
Mr R.L Liddle
Mr S.L Liddle
Miss A.L Lightfoot
Mr J.L Lightfoot
Mr G.L Lilley
Mr K.L Lilley
Mr J Lillystone
Mr D.P.L Lincoln
Mr D J Lindley
Mrs J Lindley
Mr J.W.L Lindsay
Mstr A.J.L Lindsay
Mr M.L Lindsey
MR M Lines
Mr M.L Ling
MR G A Linton
Mr R.G.L Linton
Mr G.L Lister
Mr K.W.L Little
MR P R Littlewood
MR B D Livesey
Mr M.J.L Livesey
MR M Livingstone
Mr G.L Lloyd
Mr M. Lloyd
Mr T.L Loborik
Mr D C Lockwood
Mr P.D.L Lockwood
MR C Lofthouse
Mr D Lofthouse
Mr G Lofthouse
Mr R Lofthouse
Mstr C.J Lofthouse
Mr D.P. Lofts
MR J P Lofts
MR P G Lofts
J Logan
Mr D Long
MR B Longstaff
MR C C Longstaff
MR D Longstaff
Mr P J Longstaff
MSTR M Longstaff
Mr J.L.L Lonsdale
MR C.S.L Lord
Mrs LL Lord
Mr J Loughram
MR A Loughran
MR M Loughran
MR P Loughran
Mr S.L Loughran
Mr T Loughran
Mrs M.L Loughran
Mstr A.L Loughran
MR J P Louth
MR A Lowe
Mr A J Lowe
Mr J.L Lowe
Mr K.L Lowe
Mr P Lowe
Mstr D.L Lowe
MR R N Lower
MR G E Lowes
Mr I.W.L Lowes
MR J R Lowes
Mr W.L.L Lowes

MR A.J Lowther
Alan Brown Eng Ltd
Gene & Sons Ltd
John Nixon Ltd
Mr P.I. Luke
Mr A.J.L Lumley
MR D Lumley
Mr K.I. Lumley
Mr S.L Lumley
MR M J Lynas
MR R A P Lynch
Mr W P Lynch
Mr H Lyons
Mr M Lyons
MB Rewinds Ltd
MR P D Macadie
MR J MacDonald
MR Mack
MR S Mack
Mr J.W.M MacSween
Mr T.J.M Maggs
MR D Magson
Mr P.M Magson
MR S P Magson
Mr F.M Maguire
Miss D.I. Maher
Mr D.J. Mahoney
MR A J Main
Mr M R Main
Mrs S J Main
Mstr D R Main
MR I Mallon
MR A.D Malone
Mr K.M Malone
MR P.J Maloney
Mr G.M Maloy
Mr J.M Maloy
Mr N.M Maloy
Mr G R Malyon
Mr P.M.M Manders
MR D.R Mann
Mr J Manning
Mr P. Manrow
Mr G.M. Mansfield
Mr A Mapp
Mr C.M Mapplebeck
Mr A Markham
MR G J Marlbrough
Mr D.M Marley
Mr E.M Marquis
Mr L.M Marr
Mstr B J Marr
Mr C.D.M Marron
MR I A Marron
Mr J.D.M Marron
Mr N.D.M Marron
Mr R.I.M Marron
Mr M.M Marsay
Mr I Marsh
MR P Marsh
Mstr J Marsh
Mr D.M Marshall
Mr J T Marshall
Mr S.L.M Marshall
Mr W Marshall
Mrs P. Marshall
SERCK MARSTON
MR A Martin
Mr D.M Martin
Mr I.D.M Martin
Mr J.M Martin
MR W Martin
Mr W O Martin
Mrs C.M. Martin
Mr P.M.D Martin-Dixon
Mr S.M Marwood
MISS Mason
Mr B Mason
MR D Mason
MR D.G Mason
Mr J E Mason
Mr J J Mason
Mr J.M Mason
MR K Mason
Mr S.M Mason
Mr A.M Massey
Ms S.M Massey
MR P Mather
Mr R.S Mather
MR I Matson
Mr D Matterson
Ms Z.L.M Matthewman
Mr S.M Matthews
MR G Maud
Mr A.M Maude
Mr S.I.M Maude
Mr J.P.M Maughan
Mr A G May
MR K May

Mr M.W.M May
Mr N.P.M May
MR R May
Mrs M May
Mr D.M Maycroft
Mr R.J.M Maycroft
Mr P.A.M Maynard
MR S H Maynard
Miss H.B.M McAndrew
Mr R.M McAndrew
Mr J McArther
Mr C.M.M McAuley
MR G McBean
MR K McBride
Mr A.M McCabe
MR B D McCabe
MR D McCabe
Mr K.P.M McCabe
Mr O.M McCabe
Mr P.A.M McCabe
Mr P.M McCabe
MSTR G McCabe
Mr R.J.M McCallion
MR M McCann
MR J McCarthy
MR R.A McCarthy
MR M McCartney
MR B.D MCCAULEY
Mr C.I. McCleod
Mr C.M McCluskey
Mr P. McCluskey
Mr A.S.M McCombie
Mr G.S.M McCombie
Mr A.M McCormick
Mr G.M McCormick
MR K McCormick
Mr S.M McCormick
Mr D.J.M McCune
Mrs T.M.M McCutcheon
Mr J.M McDermott
Mr K.M McDermott
Mr McDermottroe
Mr K McDermottroe
Mr J.G.M McDonagh
Mr I A McDonald
Mr I.J. McDonald
MR S J McDonald
Mr J P McElvaney
Mr J.M McFadden
Mr C.T McFadzean
Mr R.S Mcfadzean
MRS M.E McFadzean
Mr V McFee
MR P A McGarth
MR J.G McGee
Mstr L.S.M McGee
MR P McGloin
Mr P McGlynn
Mr T.M McGlynn
Miss E.M McGough
MISS R McGough
MR J M McGough
Mr T.M McGough
Mr P. McGrath
Mr E.M McGreevy
Mr G.M McGreevy
Mrs C.M McGreevy
Mrs J.M McGreevy
Mstr M.M McGreevy
Mr D.W.M McGregor
MR S McGuill
Mr D.J.M McIlveen
Mr R.A.M McIlveen
MR P McInnes
Mr G.M McIntyre
MR P McIntyre
Mr C.M McKenna
Mr P.M McKenna
Mr C.O McKeown
Mstr M.R McKeown
MR McLachlan
Mr P.N.M McLaren
Mr T.M McLaughlin
MR G McLay
MR McLEAN
Mr A.M McLean
Mr G McLean
Mr S.M McLean
MRS T J McLone
MR A J McLoughlin
MRS S L McLoughlin
Mr I A McLure
Miss G McMahon
Miss J.M McMahon
Mr A McMahon
MR D.G McMahon
Mr J.T.M McMann

Mr P.E.M McMann
MR G McManus
T MCMANUS
Miss C M McMenamin
Mr A McMenamin
Mr N McMenamin
Mr D.M McMillan
MR A McMordie
Mr P.E.M McMurdo
Mstr J.P.M McMurdo
Mr J.M McNally
MR I McNaughton
MSTR I McNaughton
MR C.W McNeill
Miss C.B McNicholas
Mr A McNicholas
MR S McNicholas
MR P F McNicholl
Mr S.D.M McNiff
Mr G.M McNulty
Mr M.J. McNulty
Mr S.P.M McNulty
Mr K.A. McPartland
G.M McPherson
Mr P.M McPhillips
MR McQuade
MR A.S McQUADE
Mr B.A.M McQuade
Mr J J McQuade
MR S McQuade
Mr S McQuade
Mr J.M McReynolds
Mr R.M McWilliam
Mr A.E.M Mead
MSTR P Meadley
Mr J.M Meek
Mr N.M Meek
Mr R.M Meek
Mr G.D.M Mendum
MR R MENZIES
MISS J V Merriman
Mr B. Merritt
Mrs S.F. Merritt
Miss M.M Mescus
Mr P.M Metcalfe
MR T Metcalfe
Mr M.M Mett
MR S G Micklewright
Mr S.M Micklewright
Mr R.M Middleton
MRS J M Middleton
Mr G.J.M Milburn
Mr J.M Milburn
Mr M.J.M Milburn
Mr R W Milburn
MR S D Milburn
Mr A.M Millard
MR J Miller
Mr N A Miller
Mr G. Mills
MR T C Mills
Mr A.M Millward
Mr N.M Millward
MR G Milner
Mr A. Minto
MR B Minto
MR A Mitchell
MR D G Mitchell
Mr D.M Mitchell
MR R J Mitchell
Mr B.M Mitchinson
Mr K Mitchinson
Mr K.M Mitchinson
Mr M.M Mitchinson
Mr R.M Mitchinson
Mrs S.M Mitchinson
Mstr C.M Mitchinson
Mstr N.M Mitchinson
MR G S Mitford
Mr S.G.M Mitford
Mr A Mogie
Mr P.A Mogie
Mr I.M Mohan
Mr E Moir
Mr C Mondal
Mr J.G.M Monkhouse
Mr G.M Monkhouse
Mr D.L.M Montague
Mrs A.M.M Montague
Miss K.M Moody
MR K Newbury
J Moore
Mr D Moore
MR D Moore
Mr D. Moore

MR D.J Moore
Mr D.M Moore
Mr M.M Moore
MR N Moore
Mr P.M Moore
MR R Moore
Mr R Moore
Mr R.W.M Moore
Mr S.C.M Moore
Mr R.P.M Moorsom
Miss S J Morgan
Miss S.L.M Morgan
Mr A.M Morgan
Mr B.M Morgan
MR D Morgan
MR L Morgan
Mr S.M Morgan
MR W Morgan
Mrs J.L.M Morgan
Mr G.M Morland
Mr S.M Morland
MR C Morren
MR MORRIS
MR A M Morris
Mr A.J.M Morris
Mr A.M Morris
Mr J.P.M Morris
Mr P.M Morrison
Mr J.M Morrissey
Mr R.M Morrissey
Mstr J.P.M Morrissey
MT P Morritt
MR R Morrow
MR K MORSHEAD
MRS J.M MORSHEAD
Mstr A Morshead
MR G Morton
Mr G.M Morton
Mr M.M Morton
Mstr D.J. Morton
Mr P.R.M Motson
Mr D Mottram
Mstr G Mottram
Miss Mower
Mr A.M Mower
Mstr S.M Mower
Mr C.M Mudd
Mr S.M Mudd
Mr P.M Muir
Mr A.R.M Muirhead
Mr J.M Muirhead
Mr S.J.M Muirhead
MSTR D Mukherjee
Mr P.F Mulligan
MR I Mundell
MR P Mundell
MISS N J Mundy
MRS C Mundy
MR N A Murnane
Mr I.P.M Murphy
MR L K Murphy
Mr L.M Murphy
Mr P.M Murphy
Mr T.G.M Murphy
MR L Murray
Mr S.P.M Murray
Miss R.M Myers
Mr B.M Myers
MR G Myers
MR S Myers
Mr T R Myers
MR T S Myers
MR W Myers
MR M P Nash
MSTR P A Nash
Mr P.T.N Naylor
Mr P.D.N Nayman
Mstr P.N Nayman
MR Neal
Mstr Neal
Mr D.N Neale
MR G Neasham
Mr P.O.N Nedley
MR M T Neeson
Mr D.N Neil
Mstr A.N Neil
MR T W Nellis
Mr M.T.N Nellis
Mr S.I.N Nelson
Mstr D.J.N Nelson
Mr P.A. Nevitt
MR W Newbould
MR I Newbury
MR A Nicholas
MISS C L Nichols
Miss B Nicholson
MISS D Nicholson

MR A J Nicholson
Mr B Nicholson
Mr C.L.N Nicholson
Mr G.E.N Nicholson
Mr H Nicholson
MR J Nicholson
Mr J T Nicholson
Mr J.L.R Nicholson
Mr W.N Nicholson
MRS E M Nicholson
Mrs I Nicholson
Mstr C Nicholson
Mstr C.J.N Nicholson
MR G Nixon
John Nixon Ltd
Mr M.N Nixon
Mr E.A.N Nobbs
MR B Noble
Mr B.A.N Noble
Mr M.N Noble
Mr S.N Noble
MRS P Noble
Mstr C.N Noble
MR K R Noctor
Mr C.N Nolan
Mr J.L.N Norman
MR L G Norman
MR R Norman
Mr A.N Norman
Mr N.N Norrie
Mr G.A Norris
Mstr S Norris
Northern Landlords
MR G E Norton
MR P.M Norton
Miss E Noteyoung
Nutime Ltd
MR G O'Brien
Mr K.O. O'Brien
Mr M.R.O O'Brien
MR P J O'Brien
MR P K O'Brien
MR M O'Byrne
Mr C.O O'Connor
Mr J O'Donnell
Mr K O'Donnell
Mr K.O O'Donnell
Mr M.V.O O'Donnell
Mr N.O O'Donnell
Mr P.P.O O'Donnell
Mr K.O O'Donoghue
MR M O'Donoghue
Mstr S O'Donoghue
MSTR S O'Farrell
MR T E O'Gara
Mstr P.O O'Hagan
Mr C.O O'Hara
Mstr C.O O'Kelly
Miss M.C.O O'Neil
Mr J.P.O O'Neil
Mr G G O'Neill
Mr M.O O'Neill
Mr P.J. O'Neill
Mstr C.O O'Neill
MASTER K O'Rourke
MR P O'Rourke
Mr P O'Rourke
Mr J.O Oakes
Mrs S.O Oakes
Miss Oakley
MISS M M Oakley
Mr Oakley
Mr C Oakley
Mr G Oakley
Mr I.O Oakley
Mr J Oakley
Mr M.B.O Oakley
Mr S.I.O Oakley
Mr E Oglesby
Mstr L A Oglesby
Mr I.O Oliver
MR P Oliver
Mr R Oliver
MRS C Oliver
Mr K.O Orange
MISS K Ord
MR A Ord
MR M Ord
MR S Ormesby
Mr S.O Orourke
Mr C.G Orpen
MRS J.D Orpen
Mr K.O Orton
MR S Osbaldeston
MR B G Oswell
MSTR M J Oswell
Mr J A Otter
Mr A.O Overfield
Mr E.O Overton

Mrs P.O Overton
Mr P.O Ovington
Mr B.O Owen
Mr N.O Owen
Mr S.O Owen
MR Owens
MR A Ä Öwens
Mr C.R.O Owens
Mr J.R Owens
Mr M Owens
G J Pacey
J Pacey
MR B Pacitto
MR M Pacitto
Mr M.A.P Pacitto
MR M J Padfield
Mr M.J.P Page
MR K Pallister
Mr R. Pallister
Mrs D.P Pallister
MR Palmer
Mr C.J.L Palmer
Mr F Palmer
MR G Palmer
MR S Palmer
Mr Parker
MR B Parker
MR G Parker
Mr J A Parker
Mr J. Parker
Mr J.S.P Parker
Mrs P.P Parker
Mstr R.P Parker
Mr B.P Parkes
Mr I.M.P Parkes
Mr D.P Parkin
MR K Parkin
Mr S.P Parkin
Mr P.P Parkinson
Mr S A Parnaby
MR I Parsons
Mr P.D.P Parsons
Mr B.J.P Partlett
MR M Passman
Mr T.P Patchett
Mr J.A.S Patience
Mr M.P Patterson
Mstr S.P Patterson
Mr Pattison
MR M Pattison
MR T Pattison
Mr S.P Patton
Mstr K.P Patton
Mr A.P Payne
Mr S.P Payne
MR A J Peacock
Mr D J Peacock
Mr G.P Peacock
MR M Peacock
Mr M.A.P Peacock
MR N Peacock
MR S M Peacock
MR T Peacock
Mr A J Pear
Mrs C Mazencieux Pear
MW J W Pearce
Mr S.R.P Pearce
MR Pearson
Mr Pearson
Mr A.P Pearson
Mr B.R.P Pearson
MR C Pearson
Mr C Pearson
Mr F.P Pearson
MR G A Pearson
Mr I.P Pearson
Mr J Pearson
MR J A Pearson
MR J W Pearson
MR M Pearson
Mr M. Pearson
Mr S.P Pearson
MR D F Peat
MR S Peat
Mr F Peel
Mr J.C.P Peel
MR R A Peel
Mstr J Peel
Mstr P Peel
Mr N Peggs
Mr M.J.P Peirson
Mr R.I.P Peirson
Mr J.P Pendlington
MR M Pennick
Mr A.P Pennington
Mr K.P Pepper
Mr P.M.P Perkin
MR A.J. PERKINS
Mr D.A.P Perry

MR M E Perry
Mr D.J.P Phillips
Mr D.P Phillips
Mr M.P Phillips
MR N Phillips
MR S Phillips
MR M G Philpott
Mr C.P Pickard
Mr J.E.P Pickard
Miss V.L Pigg
Mr J.K.P Pigg
Mstr J.R.P Pigg
S Pinnell
Mrs S.E.P Pipes
Mr A.R.P Pixton
PLANT
MR K PLlews
Mr J.A.P Plummer
Mr A Plunkett
Mr S Plunkett
MR J M Poole
MSTR D M Poole
Mr J.P Porrit
Mr C Porritt
MR M Postgate
Mr N. Potter
Mr S.B. Potter
MRS C.M Potter
MR A E Potts
MR C Potts
MR D E Potts
Mr D.A.P Pountney
Mstr G D Pountain
Miss J Povey
Mr A J Povey
Mr D.L.P Powell
Powerstream
MR L T Powles
Mr K.A Pratt
MR S Pratt
MR T J Prest
MR N Preston
MSTR L Preston
MR B Price
Mr E.A. Price
Mr G.G.P Price
Mr E.R.P Priddy
Mr M.P Priest
Mr T Priest
Mr A.P Pringle
IMAGE PRINT
Mr B.J.P Prior
MSTR S P Pritchard
MR T H Profitt
MR C Prosser
MR R W Proud
MR S D Pryke
MR A Purcell
Mr R.P Purcifer
Mr J.D.P Purdy
D Purvis
J Purvis
MR M Pyle
Mr S Pyle
Mr A.Q Quain
Mr J Quain
Mr I.Q Quick
Mr D.R. Quigley
MR G W Quine
Mr B.J.Q Quinn
Mr K Quinn
Mr M.Q Quinn
Mr P. Quinn
Mr P.T.Q Quinn
MR S J Quinn
MR S T Quinn
Mr D.N.R Raby
MRS Y Radcliffe
Mr M.J.R Radigan
MR P A Radigan
Mr O.R Radstrom
Mr A.R Rafferty
Mr P.R Ragan
Mr C Raistrick
Mr A Ramsay
Mr L Ramsay
Mr M.R Ramsdale
Mr S.R Ramsdale
Mstr M.R Ramsdale
Mr D.R Ramshaw
Mr M Randal
MR D Randall
MR MR RANDALL
Mr G.R Ranson

MR I D Ratcliffe
Mr S.R Ratcliffe
Mr I.R.R Rathbone
Mr M.D.R Rathbone
Mr P.R Rawden
Mr J.M.R Ray
MR P Ray
Mr P.M.R Ray
Mr R.E.R Ray
Mr M Rayner
Mr M. Rayner
Mr M.J.R Rayner
MR P A Rayner
MR P L Rayner
Mr K.R Readman
MR L Readman
MR R Readman
MRS C A Readman
MSTR L Readman
Mr G M Reap
MR P Reason
Mr R Reason
Mr N.R Reay
Mstr D.S.R Redman
Mr M.R Redshaw
Mr A.R Reed
Mr A Rees
Mr D.R Rees
Mr G.M. Rees
Mr S Rees
Mstr D Rees
Miss C.D.R Reeve
Mr B.A.R Reeve
Mr J.R Regan
Mr A.E.M Regan
Mr R Regan
MR C Reid
Mr P Reidy
Mr P.G.R Renwick
MR G Reynolds
Mr G.R Reynolds
MR M G Reynolds
MR R P Reynolds
MSTR T E Reynolds
Mr C.A.R Richards
MR D A Richards
Mr D A L Richards
Mr G Richards
Mr I.R Richards
Mr L.W.R Richards
Mr P.R Richards
Miss L.R Richardson
Mr C.R Richardson
Mr F.R Richardson
Mr G Richardson
Mr J Richardson
Mr J.R Richardson
Mr L.B.R Richardson
Mr L.R. Richardson
Mr M Richardson
Mr N.R Richardson
MR P J Richardson
Mr R.P Richardson
MSTR D Richardson
Mr S.J.R Richarson
Mrs F J Rickaby
MR J J Ricketts
Mr R.D.R Riddiough
MR N Rider
Mr P. Rider
Mrs J. Rider
MR A Ridgway
MRS J Ridgway
Miss L E Ridley
Mr A D C Ridley
Mr D.A.R Ridley
Mr G.R Ridley
Mrs J M Ridley
Mstr M.R Ridley
MR M A Ridsdale
A N Riley
Mr A J Riley
Mr A.R Riley
MR M J Riley
Mr M.T.R Riley
Mr P.R Riley
Mr T.R Riley
Mstr J.R Riley
S B Riley
MR M H Riordan
MR A M Ritchie
MR L Ritchie
MR J Rober
MISS L S Roberts
MISS T Roberts
Mr D.W Roberts
MR I.R Roberts
Mr L.E.D. Roberts
Mr N.P.R Roberts
Mr P.R Roberts

APPENDIX 5

Mr R.R Roberts
Mrs J.R Roberts
Mstr P.M.R Roberts
MR J Robertson
MR N A Robertson
Miss D.R Robinson
MISS H Robinson
Miss L.K. Robinson
MR A L Robinson
Mr A.R Robinson
MR B Robinson
MR C K Robinson
Mr C.R Robinson
Mr D Robinson
Mr D.M.R Robinson
Mr D.R Robinson
MR F E Robinson
Mr G.B.R Robinson
Mr G.R Robinson
MR I Robinson
MR I M Robinson
MR J Robinson
Mr J.R Robinson
MR K Robinson
MR K.E Robinson
Mr K.J. Robinson
MR M J Robinson
MR M W Robinson
Mr M.A.R Robinson
MR P N Robinson
MR P.A Robinson
Mr P.D.R Robinson
Mr S.D.R Robinson
Mr S.R Robinson
MR T Robinson
Mr W.J.R Robinson
Mrs A.R Robinson
MRS L Robinson
MSTR C W Robinson
Mstr G.R Robinson
MR A J Robson
MR A.G Robson
Mr B.E. Robson
Mr C Robson
MR D.S ROBSON
MR E Robson
Mr H.R Robson
MR J Robson
Mr M.I. Robson
Mr P.R Robson
MR R ROBSON
MR S.E Robson
Mr T Robson
Mr W.R Robson
MR M E Rodger
MR RODGERS
MR D Rodgers
Mr F. Rodgers
Mr S Rodgers
MR J Roffey
MRS S M Roffey
Mr G W Rogers
MR N Rogers
Mr M. Rollings
MR J.D.N Roper
MR C Rose
MR D H J Rose
Mr J.R Rose
Mr M.R Rose
Mr R.R Rose
Miss D.E.R Ross
Mr A Ross
Mr D.A.R Ross
Mr G Ross
MR J Ross
Mr P.R Ross
Mrs L Ross
Mstr I.P.R Ross
Mstr P.D.R Ross
Mr J.D. Rosser
MISS H C Routh
Mr M.R Rowbotham
Mr B.R Rowcroft
MR A R Rowe
MR D Rowe
Mr K.A. Rowe
MR T Rowe
Miss F.R Rowland
Mr J.R Rowland
Mr B.R Rowlands
Mrs B.R Rowlands
Mr G.R Rowling
Mr K.R Roy
MR M A Ruane
Mr P.G.R Rudd
MR Rudland
MR J Rush
Mr J Rush
S Rush

Miss R.R Rusinek
Mr S.A.R Rusinek
Mr Rusk
MR A Russell
Mr A Russell
Mr B.J.R Russell
MR C Russell
Mr J.R Russell
Mr S.R Russell
Mr W.R Russell
Mstr P.R Russell
Mr G.R Ryan
MR M Ryan
SR Engineering
Mrs C L Saddington-
Smith
Mr G. Sadler
Safebond Ltd
MR A Saiger
MISS N Salah
Mr L.S Salmon
MR S D Salmon
MR Salter
Mr J.S Salter
Mr K.S Salter
Mr N Samuel
Mr M.S Samuels
Mstr J.S Samuels
Miss N Sands
Mr R Sandwell
Mstr M J Sandwell
MR T W Sangster
Mr D.I.S Sargeant
MR T Sargeant
Mr P.S Saunders
Mr S.J.S Saunders
MRS I Saunders
Mr B.T.S Savage
Mr J.R.S Savage
Mr P J Savage
Mr S.S Saville
SAWNEY
Mr N.S Sayers
Mr D. Scafton
MR N Scaife
Mr G.S Scarth
Mr J.S Schmidt
Mr N Schneider
Mstr P.S Scollett
Miss L.S Scotcher
Mr I.K.S Scotcher
MISS G.I Scott
Mr D B Scott
MR J.S Scott
Mr K.S Scott
Mr S Scott
MR T Scott
MR W G Scott
MRS C Scott
Mr P.S Scrimgour
Mr J.S Sealey
DR S SEARSON
Mr D.S Secker
MR SELL
Mr M.A.S Sell
Mr A.L.S Selmer
MR G Senior
Mr K.S Senior
MSTR P G Senior
Mr C.G.S Serino
Mr R.S Serino
MR P Sermon
Mr P.S Sermon
P.S Sermon
MR B Sexton
Mr T.S Sexton
MR J B Seymour
MR S A Seymour
Mr G.L.S Shackleton
Mr M.S Shackleton
Mr R.S Shakeshaft
Mr D.S Shannon
Mr A.S Sharp
Mr D.S Sharp
Mr M.C.S Sharp
Miss H Sharples
Mr A Sharples
MR S Sharples
MR B Shaw
Mr D.J.S Shaw
Mr G.S Shaw
Mr M.S Shaw
Mr P Shaw
Mr P.J.S Shaw
MRS V M Shaw
Mr P A Shayler
Mr D Shea
MRS S Shea
Mr A.P.S Sheffield

MR C J Shenton
MR D Shepherd
Mr K.L Shepherd
Mstr A.S Shepherd
Mstr C.J.S Shepherd
Mr G Shepherdson
Mr M.S Sheridan
Mr T.W. Sherrington
MISS C E Sherwood
MR C Sherwood
MR G Sherwood
Mr H.S Sherwood
MR M Sherwood
Mr M.C.S Sherwood
Mr J M Shields
Mr M Shildrick
MR A A Short
MRS T E Short
Shorttle
Miss M.A.S Shout
Miss S Shutt
Mr A Shutt
Mr C C Sibley
Mr P.F Sibley
Mr R M Sibley
Mstr G Sibley
Mr K.S Sickling
MISS G Siddle
MR H Siddle
Mr D.R.S Sidgwick
MR K Sidwick
MR E Silk
MR K Silk
MRS A Silk
MR G SILLETT
Mr G Sim
MR P.G Simcox
Mr D.J.S Simmonds
Mr P Simon
Mstr O Simon
Miss Simpson
Miss E.S Simpson
MR C Simpson
Mr C Simpson
Mr C.D.S Simpson
Mr D Simpson
Mr D.J Simpson
Mr D.S Simpson
Mr G E Simpson
Mr G H Simpson
Mr G.I.S Simpson
Mr H.E.S Simpson
Mr H.S Simpson
Mr I.R.S Simpson
Mr M.S Simpson
MR P Simpson
Mr S Simpson
Mr W.S Simpson
MRS H Simpson
Mrs J.S Simpson
MSTR C Simpson
Mr A.G.S Sinclair
Mr A.S Sinclair
Mr B.F.S Sinclair
Mr J.S Sinclair
Mr N.S Sinclair
MR R Sinclair
MR S Singh
Mr P.W.S Sinton
Mr N Skeldon
Mr G.R.S Skelton
MR G.W Skidmore
MSTR K Skidmore
Mr G.W.S Skinn
Mr J Slade
Mr P Slade
Mr J.W.S Slater
Mr R.W Slater
Mr W.J Slater
Mr J.R. Slee
Mr W.J.S Sleight
Mr S.J.S Sleightholme
Mr M.J.S Small
Mr D.N.S Smallwood
Mr M.S Smethurst
Mr J Smiddy
Mr S.J.S Smiles
Miss A.S Smith
MISS D Smith
Miss G.L.S Smith
MISS J Smith
Mr A.M. Smith
Mr A.S Smith
Mr B Smith
Mr B J Smith
Mr B L Smith
Mr C.M. Smith
Mr D Smith
Mr D A Smith

Mr D.G. Smith
MR D.J Smith
MR D.J Smith
Mr DJR Smith
Mr G Smith
MR G Smith
Mr G Smith
MR G Smith
Mr G P Smith
Mr G.R.S Smith
Mr G.S Smith
Mr I Smith
Mr J T Smith
MR J W Smith
Mr J.B.S Smith
Mr J.K Smith
Mr J.M.S Smith
Mr J.T.S Smith
MR K M Smith
Mr K.S Smith
Mr L.J.S Smith
Mr L.S Smith
MR M A Smith
Mr M.L Smith
Mr M.R.J Smith
Mr M.S Smith
Mr M.V.S Smith
Mr P J C Smith
MR R Smith
MR R A Smith
Mr R.S Smith
Mr S J Smith
MR S.B Smith
Mr S.R.S Smith
Mr T.S Smith
Mrs E.S Smith
Ms T Smith
MSTR A D Smith
Mstr C Smith
Mstr M.J.S Smith
Mr J.A.S Smithard
Mr L Smitheman
Mr A.S Smitherman
MR J M Smitherman
Mr J.S Smithson
Mr W.A Smithson
Mr M.J. Smulders
Mr R.S Snaith
Mr T.A.S Snaith
Mstr S A Snaith
K Snowdon
Mr G Soloman
MR A.J Solomon
MR P Solomon
MRS B Solomon
MRS S A Southern
Mr G.S Sowerby
MR M A Sowerby
MR J A Spark
Mr D.J Sparrow
Mrs J Sparrow
Mr J.S Spayne
MR P Speight
Spence
MR P M Spence
Mr W.S Spence
Mr M.D.S Spencer
MR T Spencer
MR D Spruce
MR S Spruce
MR Stableforth
MR R I Staines
Mr C.S Stainsby
Mr M.S Stainsby
MR N R Stainthorpe
Mr P.S Stainthorpe
MR M Stamp
Mr G.S Stamper
Mr R.S Stamper
Mr G Stanway
MSTR J L Stanway
Mr A P Staples
MR R M Stark
Mr M.A.S Stather
Mr R.A.S Stather
MR E W Stead
Mr G.S Steel
Mstr J.S Steel
Dr G.W.S Stephen
Mr R I Stephen
MR B Stephenson
MR C Stephenson
MR D M Stephenson
MR D R Stephenson
MR H M R Stephenson
MR K Stephenson
MR M Stephenson
MR R A Stephenson

MRS I Stephenson
MRS S Stephenson
A STEVENSON
MR A Stevenson
MR A D Stevenson
MR D M Stevenson
MR G Stevenson
Mr J.S Stevenson
MR M Stevenson
Mr M.J.S Stevenson
Mr M.S Stevenson
MR P.D Stevenson
Mr P.S Stevenson
Ms K.S Stevenson
Mr P.S Stewart
Mr A B Stirzaker
Mr G.S Stirzaker
Mr G.W.S Stockburn
Mstr M.S Stockburn
Mr A.R Stokeld
MR K Stokeld
Mr S.C Stokeld
Mr D.W.S Stoker
Mr M Stoker
Miss J.R.S Stone
MR J A Stone
Mr K.E.S Stone
Mr D.P.S Stonehouse
Mr J.D Stonehouse
MRS J Stonehouse
MR A.M. Storey
MR G Storr
MR S J Story
Auston Stroud & Co
Mr D.S Stout
Mr D Strickland
MR M Stuart
MR W Stuart
Mstr M.S Stubbings
MR D R Stubleuy
MSTR J D Stubley
MSTR R J Stubley
Mr M J Sturdy
Mr L A Suggett
Mr P Suggett
MR A Suggitt
Mr A.S Sullivan
Mr L.S Sullivan
MSTR J Summerfield
MR S Summerfield
Mr R.P Sunley
Mr G Sutherland
Mr J Sutherland
Mrs J Sutherland
MR D N Sutherst
MR A N Swainston
Mr J A Swainston
Mr R.J.S Swales
MR R.L. SWALWELL
MR E A Swan
MR M I Swan
Mr D.R.S Swatman
Mr M.E.J. Sweeney
Mstr T.E. Sweeney
Mr G.N.S Sweeting
Mr T.S Sweeting
Dr. A. Sykes
MR M.D Symmonds
MR G.J Tait
MR A G Talbot
Mr B Tanfield
Mr J.W.T Tarren
Mr P.J.T Tarren
MR N Tarry
Mr A.D.T Tate
MR K Tate
Ms R.T Tate
Mstr S.T Tate
MR M.D Tattersdill
MR Tattersfield
MR Taylor
MR A J Taylor
MR B Taylor
Mr B. Taylor
MR G Taylor
Mr J Taylor
MR J Taylor
MR J T Taylor
Mr J.M.T Taylor
Mr K.J.R. Taylor
MR P B TAYLOR
Mr R Taylor
MR R J Taylor
MRS S M Taylor
Mr W.B.T Taylor
Mrs A Taylor
MSTR M TAYLOR
Mstr P.M.T Taylor
Mr D Teasdale

Mr G.K.T Teece
Mr G.T Teesdale
Mr V.T Teesdale
Ms C.L.T Teesdale
Dr R.G.J Telfer
Mr J O Telfer
Mr J.G.T Telfer
Mrs J.A.T Telfer
Mr A.T Tempestoso
MR M Temple
MSTR P Tenke
Miss A R Terry
Mr C J Terry
Mr N.T Thacker
Mr S Thirkle
Mr H.F.T Thirsk
Miss S Thistlethwaite
Mr G Thistlethwaite
MR G B Thistlethwaite
MR D Thom
MR B Thomas
Mr C Thomas
MR G W Thomas
Mr L.T Thomas
MR P A Thomas
MR S Thomas
MSTR D J Thomas
Dr D.T Thomas
MR A Thompson
Mr A Thompson
MR D Thompson
Mr D. Thompson
MR G R Thompson
Mr G.M.T Thompson
Mr G.T Thompson
Mr H J Thompson
MR J R Thompson
Mr J. Thompson
Mr J.T Thompson
Mr K Thompson
Mr K.T Thompson
Mr L.T Thompson
Mr N.A.T Thompson
Mr P Thompson
Mr P A Thompson
Mr P.T Thompson
Mr R Thompson
Mr R G Thompson
Mr R.M.T Thompson
Mr S P Thompson
MR S R Thompson
Mrs J.C.T Thompson
Mrs S Thompson
Mstr D.G.T Thompson
MSTR M S Thompson
Mstr S P Thompson
Mr D.H.T Thomson
Mrs O.T Thomson
MR P Thornburn
Mr A.T Thorne
MR C J Thornton
Mr D.S.T Thornton
MR G Thornton
Mr P Thornton
MS S Thorp
Miss A.T Thwaites
Miss S.T Thwaites
Mrs H.M.T Tibbett
MR R Tickner
Mr L Tinney
Mr P.T.B Tiplady
Mr D.M.T Titchmarsh
MR C D Todd
Mr J Todd
Mr J.T Todd
Mr R.T Todd
Mr S.C.T Todd
Mr V.R. Todd
Mrs A Todd
Mstr I Todd
MR D F Tomasetti
Mr J.T Tombs
Mr W. Tomlinson
Mrs K. Tomlinson
Miss K.E.T Tonge
Miss S.L.T Tonge
Mr M.T Tonge
Mrs A.T Tonge
MR D Tongue
Mr F Tonkin
Mr P.T Toogood
Mr J.T Topping
Mr G.M.T Towers
Mr S.T Towers
MR G Towes
Mr S.W.T Townsend
Mr L Trainor
MRS E M Trattles
Mr G.L Tremain

Mr H.T Trewhitt
MR D Trewick
MR W Trewick
MSTR N W Trewick
Mr F.T Trodden
Mr J.A.T Trodden
Mr D.M.T Trollope
Mr K.E.T Trollope
Mr M.T Trotter
Mr G Truefitt
MR C J Tucker
Mr N.P. Tucker
MR A TULLOCK
MR R TULLOCK
MRS S A Tullock
Mr J.T Turley
Mr M.P Turnbull
MR A Turner
Mr A.J.T Turner
Mr C.T Turner
MR D H Turner
MR G Turner
Mr G Turner
Mr G.T Turner
MR J A Turner
MR J W Turner
Mr J.E.T Turner
Mr L.T Turner
MR M Turner
MR R Turner
MR S A Turner
Mstr M.R Turner
Mr P Turton
Mr D.T Tweddle
Mr D.A. Twigg
MR G B Tyreman
Mr J.P. Tyson
Mr M A Underwood
Mr R Underwood
MR N P Upton
MSTR C F Upton
Mr S.U Urwin
MR M Vaithianathar
Mr A.V Vallely
MR K P Vallely
MRS S M Vallely
Dr C.V Vamplew
MR T.J.V Vamplew
MR R Vasey
R Vasey
Mr A Vasiliou
MR B VAUGHAN
Mr B T Vaughan
Mr C.V Vaughan
MR I G Vaughan
Mr M.V Vaughan
MR P VAUGHAN
MR S Vaughan
Mr C.G.V Vaux
Mstr A.J.V Vaux
Mr S.V Veacock
Mr J.I. Veacock
Mr A.V Venners
Mr R.V Vernon
Mr D.V Verrill
Mr K.V Vester
Mr P.V Vester
Mr A.V Vickers
Mr S.V Vickers
MR P Vinter
MR D I Virr
MRS A Virr
MISS J.A Waddell
MR Waddup
Mr J Wade
Mrs S.W Wade
MR S Wadlow
MR C J Wain
Mr R. Waines
MR B Waite
Mr K.W Waites
MR G Wakes
Mr M.W Wakes
MR N R Waldock
MSTR S Waldow
MR G Wales
Miss J Walker
MISS S Walker
MR A Walker
Mr A Walker
Mr A.W Walker
MR B Walker
MR C Walker
Mr C.B.W Walker
Mr C.W Walker
MR D Walker
Mr G.H.W Walker
Mr I.R Walker

215

Mr K.D.W Walker
Mr K.W Walker
MR. M J Walker
Mr M.J.W Walker
MR N Walker
Mr N Walker
MR P M Walker
Mr R. Walker
Mr S Walker
Mr S.A.W Walker
Mr S.C.W Walker
Mr S.R. Walker
Mr S.W Walker
Mr T S Walker
Mr W A Walker
Mrs A.W Walker
MRS J Walker
MRS K J Walker
MSTR C A Walker
MSTR M C Walker
MR A R Wallace
Mr A.W Waller
Mrs M.W Waller
Mr I.W Wallis
Mr S.R.W Wallis
Mr G.W Walpole
MR E A Walsh
Mr F.W Walsh
MR J Walsh
Mr J.M. Walsh
Mr S.W Walsh
MR G K Walters
Mr M P Walters
Miss J.E.W Walton
Mr A.E.W Walton
Mr D W Walton
Mr K H Walton
MR M D Walton
Mr S. Walton
Mr A.M Wanless
Mr A.P.W Wanless
Mr D.W Wanless
Ms M.W Warbarton
Mr A.J.W Warburton
Mr A.W Warburton
Mr C.B Warburton
MR J Warburton
Mrs P.M Warburton
MR A E Ward
Mr A.W Ward
Mr C.W Ward
MR D Ward
Mr D Ward
Mr D.S. Ward
Mr G Ward
Mr H.G.W Ward
MR J J Ward
Mr P.W Ward
MR S Ward
Mr W.W Ward
Mrs J.W Ward
MSTR M Ward
Mr D.J.W Wardell
MR H Wardell
MR P Wardell
Mr P T Wardell
Mr W. Wardell
Mr E.W Wardhaugh
Miss K Wardle
Mr K J Wardle
MR L Wardle
Mr D.W Warnock
Mr R.D.W Warnock
Mr G.W Warr
MR B G Warren
Mr M.A.W Warriner
MR A Warwick
Mr J.P.W Warwick
Mr A Waters
MR C Waters
Mr C Waters
Mr M Waters
Mrs P Waters
Mstr J WATERS
MR A Watson
MR A.R Watson
Mr AW WATSON
Mr C M Watson
Mr F.P.W Watson
Mr G.W Watson
Mr J.G. Watson
Mr M.C. Watson
Mr M.D.W Watson
Mr N.W Watson
Mr P.W Watson
MRS D Watson
Mstr C.W Watson
Mstr M.A.W Watson
MSTR MR Watson

Mr N.L Wattis
Mr C.E. Watts
Mr G.W Watts
MR J.K Watts
Mr M.A.W Watts
Mr M.R. Watts
Mrs V Weallans
Mr Wears
MR P Weatherall
Mr J M Weatherill
Mr J.H.W Weatherill
MR R Weatheritt
Mr J.W Webb
Mr K.J. Webb
Mr M.W Webb
MR R.J Webb
MR S R Webb
Mr S.W Webb
Mstr S.C. Webb
Mr S.W Webley
MR C R Webster
Mrs J.C.W Wedgewood
Mstr M J Wedgewood
MSTR S J Wedgewood
Mrs A.W Weedon
Mr M T Weir
MR D Welch
Mr R P Welch
Mr N.P.W Welford
Mr P.F.W Welford
MR A Wells
MR A J Wells
MR P Welsh
Mr T.M Welsh
Mrs E Welsh
Mr J.P.W Wentworth
Mr S.M.W Wentworth
Mr D.W Wesson
Mr P.E.W Wesson
Mr H.W West
Mr I. West
Mr P West
Mr R.W West
Mr T.W Westwick
Mr J.B. Wharry
Mr S.M. Wharry
Mr J. Whatmore
Mr J.A. Whatmore
MRS B Wheatheritt
MR L Wheatley
Mr P N Wheatley
Mr P.W Wheatley
Mr S.G.W Wheatley
Mr R E Wheeler
Mr T A Wheeler
Mr F.M.W Whelan
Mr F.W Whelan
MR P Whelan
Mr P.J.W Whelan
Mr J D Wheldon
Mr M H Wheldon
Mr G.P.W Whisker
Miss LVMW White
MR A G White
Mr A.W White
MR B White
MR C White
Mr E White
Mr G M White
Mr J White
MR J White
Mr J.L.W White
MR M White
Mr M.W White
Mr R.W White
Mrs D.W White
Mstr C.J.W White
Miss D.M.W Whitehead
MISS J Whitehead
MR D J Whitehead
Mr S.A.W Whitehead
Mstr C.A.W Whitehead
Mr P.A.W Whitehouse
Mr P.F.W Whitehouse
Mr D. Whiteside
MR F E Whitfield
MR F T Whitfield
Mr G. Whitside
MR J E Whittaker
MSTR J E Whittaker
Mr J.W Whittingham
Mrs E.W Whittingham
MR A Whitwell
Mrs K Whyman
Mstr R Whyman
Mr C.C.W Wild
Wilkinson
Miss C Wilkinson

Miss E G Wilkinson
Miss R.W Wilkinson
Mr A. Wilkinson
MR G Wilkinson
Mr G.A.W Wilkinson
Mr I.J. Wilkinson
Mr J R Wilkinson
MR M B Wilkinson
MR M.I WILKINSON
Mr R.N.W Wilkinson
Mr R.W.S Wilkinson
MR S P Wilkinson
Mr S W Wilkinson
Mr T.W Wilkinson
Mrs D.W Wilkinson
MR W P Willers
MSTR D Willers
MSTR M Willers
Miss S J Williams
Mr D.A.W Williams
Mr E.W Williams
MR G Williams
Mr I.W Williams
Mr J.W Williams
Mr L.E.W Williams
MR N Williams
Mr R.D.W Williams
Mr R.W Williams
Mr S.A.W Williams
Mstr P.W Williams
Mr D Willis
Mr K.W Willis
MR A Wilson
Mr A.W Wilson
Mr B.W Wilson
MR D Wilson
MR D A Wilson
Mr D.L.W Wilson
Mr D.M.W Wilson
Mr G.W Wilson
MR J Wilson
Mr J Wilson
Mr J.L.W Wilson
Mr J.W Wilson
MR M Wilson
Mr M.A. Wilson
Mr M.J.W Wilson
MR P J Wilson
MR P.L Wilson
Mr S Wilson
MR S Wilson
MRS E Wilson
Mrs G.W Wilson
Mrs P.W Wilson
MSTR A.P Wilson
MSTR D Wilson
Mstr S.M.W Wilson
Mr J Wiltshire
Mr M J Wiltshire
MR A Windross
MR WINK
Mr P.W Wink
Mrs E. Winkcup
MR A Winn
MR Winspear
Mr D.W Winspear
Mr I Winspear
Mr M.W Winspear
Mr P.W Winspear
Miss S Winstone
Mr M Winstone
MSTR C M Winter
Wistech PLC
MR P Woddier
MR A D Wood
MR B Wood
Mr D.W Wood
Mr J.C.W Wood
Mr L.W Wood
Mr S Wood
Mr T.W Wood
MS J Wood
Mstr C.w Wood
MSTR N Wood
MSTR P Wood
MR A Woodard
MR D Woodhouse
MR K Woodhouse
Mr M Woodhouse
MR R Woodhouse
Mr C.D.W Woods
Mr D.E.W Woods
Mr I.W Woods
Mr M.W Woods
Mr P. Woodward
Mr W. Woodward
MISS C A Wooff
MR C A Wooff
Mr S.W Wooler

Mr Worton
Mr M Worton
MR R Worton
Mr R.W Worton
Mr C.W Wray
Mr M.W Wray
MISS M Wright
MR C B Wright
MR G Wright
MR L Wright
Mr L.R.W Wright
Mr M.W Wright
MR T.A Wright
Mr W Wright
Mr W T Wright
Stripe n Write
R.H Xerox
MR E J Yare
Mr F.C. York
Mr I.Y York
Mr J A York
Mr L.R. York
Mr M. York
MR A Young
Mr A.Y Young
MR C P Young
Mr C.A.Y Young
MR G Young
MR G P Young
Mr I.W Young
MR J Young
MR M Young
Mr M.L Young
Mr P.J.Y Young
Mr S Young
Mr S.C.Y Young
MR T Young
Mrs D.M Young
Mstr S.P.S Young
MR A Zielinski

EXECUTIVE BOX
I.C.I. Chemicals
SES Engineering
Bulkhaul Ltd
Cresstale Ltd
Tees Dock Yard Ltd
Redpath Eng. Ltd
Royal Mail

NORTH EAST CORNER
Mr M.J. Abbott
Mr M.I.A Ackerley
Mstr A A Adams
Mr A.M.A Adamson
Miss P.A.A Aitken
Mr G.D.A Allen
Mr L.J.A Allen
MSTR J P Allen
Mr S.A Allendale
Mr W.C.P Allendale
Miss P Allinson
Mr M Allinson
Mr M.J.A Anderson
Mr A.A.B Appleton-Brown
Mstr A Appleyard
Mr C Arbon
Mr C.R Arbon
MR D Arbon
Mr D.R Arbon
Mr P Arbon
Mr A.A Archer
Mr R Ash
Mr B.A.A Aspery
Mr S L Atkins
Miss R Atkinson
Mr A Atkinson
Mr B Atkinson
Mr D.G.A Atkinson
MR M Atkinson
MR M J Atkinson
Mr N.A Atkinson
Mstr A Atkinson
Mstr S A Atkinson
Mr G. Aungiers
Mr J. Aungiers
Mr J.G.A Austick
Mr N.A Austick
MR B Bainbridge
S Bainbridge
Mr C P Bakewell
MR C Banks
MRS J M Banks
MISS J Bareham
Mr S Barker
Mr S.A.B Barnett
Mr S.B Barron
Mrs M.B Barron

Miss D.J.B Barry
Mr P J Barry
Mr K.M.B Bateman
Mstr M.W.B Bateman
MS J D Battram
Mr P.J.B Beattie
Mrs H.B Beck
MR Beddard
MR J K Beddard
Mr A Bedi
Mr D J Beedle
Mr M.T.B Beeforth
MR JD BELL
Mr D.A.B Bennett
Mr I.K.B Benoliel
Mr J.S.B Bentley
Mstr I.B Bentley
Mstr D.B Berry
Mr A S Bewick
Mstr A Bianco
Mr D Bishop
MSTR D I Black
MR T Blackburn
MR G Blades
Mr T Blanchard
Mr K.B Blewitt
Mstr C.B Blewitt
Mstr S Bloor
Mr P Blyth
Mstr M.B Boldison
Mr D Bower
MR P D Bowering
MISS K Boyle
MR A Boyle
Mstr C Bozeate
MSTR J Bradford
Mr B.H.B Bradley
MR A J Bragg
Mstr M J Brooke
Mstr P M Brooke
J D Brown
M Brown
Miss J Brown
Mr A Brown
MR A.B Brown
Mr G.B Brown
Mr G.N Brown
Mr L M Brown
Mstr A.J.B Brown
Mr J.G.B Brown
Mstr S.P.B Brown
Mrs S.M. Brownridge
Mstr R.A. Brownridge
Mr D.W.B Bruce
Mstr P.D.B Bruce
Mr G S Buckle
Mr R.J.B Buckle
Mr S.B Buckle
Mstr S.P.B Buckle
Mr J Buckton
MRS L Bunbar
Mr J Bunting
Mr D.B Bunyan
Mstr R.D B Bunyan
Mr L.M.B Burke
MSTR Burke
MR S.J BURNS
MSTR S BURNS
Mr R.S.B Burton
Mrs B.A.B Burton
Mstr P.B Bussey
Mr G.C Cable
Mr L.C Cain
MISS P J Carmichael
MR E J Carmichael
Mrs K.C Casey
Mstr M.C Casey
Mr P Casterton
Miss L.M.C Catterson
Mr J.S.C Catterson
Mr T.J.C Chamberlain
Mr D.S Chape
Mr I R Chape
A.K Chapman
MR N Chapman
Miss J.C Charlton
Mr E.J Charlton
Mrs S.C Charlton
Mr P Chilton
Mstr G Chilton
Mstr J Christie
Mr P.A.C Churchill
Mstr C.C Churchill
Mstr J.A.C Churchill
Mr J.C Cimmerman
Mstr J.C Cimmerman
Mr R.W.C Clapham
Mr D.C Clark

Mr D.T.C Clark
MR J A Clark
Mr K.C Clark
Mr M D Clark
MR S Clark
MR G R Clarke
MSTR J D Clarke
Mr M J Close
Mr D.C Coates
Mstr M.C Coates
Miss R Cockerill
Mr R Cockerill
Mstr S Cocks
Mr S.M. Coleman
Miss L.S.C Colley
Mr J.C Colley
Mr M.P.C Colley
Mr P.C Collins
Mstr P.C Collins
Miss J.A.C Collinson
Mr A.J.C Collinson
Mr A.R.C Collinson
MISS L Colpitts
Mr L.C Connor
Mstr L Connor
Conway
F Conway
MASTER CONWAY
Mr K Cook
Mstr A M Cook
Mstr L Cook
Mstr T Cook
Mr B.C Cooper
Mstr G.C Corkain
A W Corner
M.T Corner
R M Corner
Mr M.C Cornforth
Mr A.J.C Corrigan
Mstr R K Corrigill
Mr C.J.C Cotton
Mr T.H.C Coulton
Mrs J.C Coulton
MR M.A CREEDON
Mr D.I Cropper
Miss M.C Cross
MR A Cross
Mr A.J.C Cross
Mr J.C Cross
Mstr D.C Cross
Mstr K.C Culley
Mstr D.J.C Cunningham
MR D T Currie
Mr J.A Currie
Mr J J Cuthbert
MR C Daggett
MSTR A Daggett
MSTR M Daggett
Mr A Dales
Mstr A Dales
Mstr C Dales
Mstr B J Dancey
Mr J.C Daniels
MSTR A.J Daniels
Mr P.A Davie
Miss A.D Davies
Miss L.D Davies
Mr E.D Davies
Mr P.D Davies
Mstr M.J Davies
Mr S.D Davis
Mstr M.L.D Davison
Mr D.P.D Day
Mr M.R.D Day
Mr E.V.D Dean
Mstr P.M.D Dean
MR M A Dearlove
Mr T.M Deeks
Mr J B Dennis
Mr M.D Dennison
Mr G Devine
MISS W Dingwall
Mr M J Dingwall
Mstr D.P.D Dinning
MR L Dixon
Mr L Dixon
Mstr B Dobson
MR P A Dodds
Mr D.D Dolan
Mr G.H. Dolan
Mr D.D Donovan
Mr R Douglas
MR S Dowse
Mstr T.D Dowse
Mr J.W.D Dudley
Mr A J C Dudley-Wood
DUFFIELD

J M Duffy
Miss J Duffy
Mr M.D Duffy
Mr P.T.D Duffy
Mr D W Duley
Mr P.D Duncan
Mstr J.D Duncan
Mr J P Dunn
Mr K Dunn
Mrs C.D Dye
Mstr M.J.D Dye
Mr P R Eccles
Mrs D Eccles
MR A Edwards
MR D Edwards
Mr D.E Edwards
MSTR R A Edwards
Mr M.E Elliott
Mr P.W. Elliott
Mstr R.J. Elliott
Mr G.J. Ellis
MR J A Emmerson
Mr C.E Endrodi
MR R Englioh
Mr T Fairhurst
Mstr J Fairhurst
Mr M.F Farley
Mr G.A.F Farrel
Mstr R.G.F Farrel
Mr J.G.F Farrell
MR A H Fawcett
MR P A Fawcett
MRS S A Fawdon
S G Fawdon
MISS L Fields
MSTR A S Fields
Mstr G.F Fields
Mstr S Fields
Mstr T S Fields
Miss S.F Fisher
Mr D.F Fisher
Mstr M.F Fisher
Miss A Fishlock
Mr D Fishlock
Miss M.A. Fitzpatrick
Mr A.C.F Fletcher
MR D T Fletcher
Mstr D.J.P Fletcher
Mr J Flintham
MR J Floyd
Mr M.G.F Forbes
Mrs W.F Forbes
Mstr J.G.F Forbes
Miss B M Ford
Mr A Ford
Mstr A Ford
Mr D Foreman
Mr N.F Forrester
Mr A.F Forster
Mr L.S Forth
MR D W Foster
Mr I.F Foster
Mrs A Fowell
Mstr R Fowell
Mr P.F Fox
J Francis
Mr T Frank
Mstr D.J. Frank
Mr R H Frankland
Miss R Franks
Mr I.S.F Freeman
Mstr L.F Fuller
Mr A.G Gallagher
Mr M.J.G Gallon
Mstr A.J.G Gallon
Mr A.G Garrens
Mstr A.M.G Geddes
Mr S Gee
Mstr R M Gething
Mr A.P.G Gettings
Mr A S Gibbon
Mr D Gibbon
MISS G Gibson
Mr A J Gibson
Mr C Gibson
Mr D.G Gibson
Mr J C Gibson
Mr T B Gibson
MR W Gibson
MRS A Gibson
MRS P A Gibson
MSTR A Gibson
Mr K Gilbey
Mstr M.G Gilbey
Mr N.G Gilhespie
Mstr M.G Goldsworthy
Mr C.G Goodchild
MR K Goodchild
Mr P Goodchild

APPENDIX 5

MSTR J K Goodchild
MSTR J P Goodchild
MSTR P Goodchild
Mr D.G Goodings
Mstr C.G Goodings
Mr D.G Goodrum
Mr M.J.G Goodrum
P Gowland
Mastr M J Graham
Miss S A Graham
Mr Graham
MR C A Graham
Mr D I Graham
Mr D.G Graham
Mr P.V.G Graham
Mstr P Graham
MR A Grainger
Mr M.G Grayson
Mr R.E.G Green
MR T Green
Mr S.C.G Greenfield
Mr T E Greenfield
Mr D J Grimes
Mr A Guest
MR D J Gunn
MR J W Gunn
Mr P Gunn
Mr W H Gustar
MR J Haggarth
Mstr R Haggarth
MISS N.J Hall
Miss T.L.H Hall
Mr D.H Hall
MR G A Hall
Mr G.A.H Hall
Mr G.S.H Hall
Mr J.R.H Hall
Mr L.A.H Hall
Mr C.E. Hallam
Mr D Hampton
Mstr S.H Hampton
Mr R.P. Hancock
Mr A.J. Hanratty
HARDMAN
MR T Hardman
Mr B.D.H Hardy
Mr D Harland
MSTR C Harrington
HARRISON
Miss H Harrison
Miss S.H Harrison
MR A G Harrison
Mr C.J.M Harrison
MR P A Harrison
Mr R Harrison
Mr R.H Harrison
Mr S.H Harrison
Mr P.H Hart
Mr S.H Hartas
Mr T Hartley
MSTR J Hatch
MR A Hay
Mr G.H Hay
Mr C Hayden
MR A HAYES
Mr M.H Heaney
MISS K Hearn
Mr W.H Hearn
Mstr C.H Hearn
V Hearn
Mr K.H Heath
Miss J. Heathcote
Mr P.H.H Hebbron
Mstr P.M.H Hebbron
MSTR A C Heilds
Mr C.H Helm
Ms D.H Helm
Miss A R Henderson
Mr A.K.H Herbert
Mrs L.J.H Herbert
Mr M.H Heslehurst
MR T Heslehurst
Mr B.H Heward
C R M Hields
MSTR D A Hirlam
Mr M.H Hirst
Mstr J.H Hirst
Mr A Hiscocks
Mr A D Hodges
Mr D Hodges
Mrs H G Hodges
Mstr M P Hodges
MR D Hodgson
Mr S.H Hodgson
B Hodson
MR K Hogg
Mr S.J.H Hollifield
Mr D.H Holmes
Mr S.J.H Holroyd

Mr K.H Holt
Mstr K.H Holt
Mr A.M.H Honneyman
Mr K J Hooper
Mr C.H.H Hopkin
Mr T.H Hopper
Mstr N J Hopper
Mr A Horner
Mstr J Horner
Mstr S Horner
Mr M Hotson
Mstr D Hotson
Mr S W Houliston
MR Hudson
Mr M.H Hudson
Mstr M I Hume
Mstr P Hume
Mstr L.A Hunter
Mr A. Hussain
MR I Hutchinson
Mr S.M.H Hutchinson
Mr M P Imeson
Mstr M.J. Inman
Mr P.I Irvine
Mstr J.P.I Irvine
Mr G.I Irving
MSTR C JAMES
MISS G K Jessop
MR M Johnosn
MR D S Johnson
Mr D.J Johnson
Mr M.A.J Johnson
MR A Johnston
Mr T.J Johnston
Mr D.W.J Jones
Mr J.K.J Jones
Mr N Jones
MR W Jones
Mstr C.J Jones
MR J.S Kane
Mr S.D.K Kane
MISS P Kay
MR A Kay
Mstr J.K Kay
Mstr L. Kay
Mr S Kell
MISS R Kelly
Mr A. Kelly
MR B A Kelly
MR C Kelly
Mr J. Kelly
Mstr J Kelly
Mstr T Kelly
S Kelly
T P Kelly
MR K Kennedy
Mr S.T.K Kent
Mr T.T.K Kent
Mr L King
Mr P King
Mr M.K Kirkbride
MR P.A Kirkwood
Miss C.M.K Knowles
Mrs E.M.K Knowles
Mr S. Konya
Mr A.L Laird
Mr K.R.L Lamb
Mr D H Lambert
Mr D.N Langthorne
Mstr J.J Langthorne
Mr R A Large
Mr S.J.L Lavelle
MR B Laverick
Mr P.L Lawrence
Mstr J.L Lawrence
Mr A.J.L Lawson
Mr J Leach
MR D Leen
Mr D.L Lees
Mrs H.L Lees
Mr K Legg
MISS S J Leggett
MR J P Leggett
D.L. Leng
J D Leng
Mr E.L Lewis
Mr D.L Liddle
Miss R A Lilleker
MR B Lilleker
MR D B lilleker
Mstr J Lillystone
MR D W Lipthorpe
MSTR D L Lipthorpe
Miss K A Little
MISS S Little
Mr A Little
MR P Lloyd
MR J M Lofthouse
J M Longster

Mstr G.L Loram
Mstr A.M Lowney
Mr C.L Lynn
Mr J.L Lyth
Mr M.M MacDonald
Mr R.M Mack
Mr S.D. Macpherson
MR G.J MAJOROS
Ms M.E Mallon
Mr S.J. Malyon
MR K MANNION
Mr D March
Mr J.K.M Marchant
Mr S Marron
Miss J Marshall
Mr B Marshall
Mr R Marshall
MARTIN
Miss M Martin
MR J Martin
Mr P Martin
Mstr J Martin
Mr D.J.M Matthews
Mr M Matthews
Mr N McAndrew
Mr S McAndrew
MSTR D McAndrew
MR P McCabe
Mr L.M McCallum
Mr S.M McCallum
Ms M.M McCallum
MCCARTEN
Mccarthy
Mr J E McCarthy
MR K McCarthy
Mr K.M McCarthy
Mr P A McCarthy
Mr J McCarty
Mr S. McCulloch
MR G McElvaney
MR J McElvaney
MSTR G McElvaney
MR M.L McGahon
MR D McGee
MR J A McGee
MR J T McGee
Mr M J McGee
MR P McGee
MRS D C McGee
MSTR A M McGee
MSTR P McGee
MR S McGlade
MR M McGuiness
Mr D J McGuire
Mr P McHugh
Mr L.M McIlroy
Mstr A.M McIlroy
Mr D McKinley
Miss M P McLean
Mr J Mclean
Mr M P McLean
Mr P McLean
Mr W K McLean
Mstr I P McLean
Mstr P McLean
Mstr S McLean
Mstr T J McLean
Mr G.M McNally
Mr K McNaughton
Mstr G.K. McNaughton
Ms E.M.M McNicholas
MISS C L McNicholl
MR T McNicholl
MSTR P McNicholl
Mr P.J.M McNulty
Mr P.M McNulty
Mr J McPike
Mr J.M McPike
C McSorley
J McSorley
Miss J.M Melling
Mr R.M Melling
Mstr P.M Melling
MR A M Melton
Mr W.M Merryweather
Mr N Meynell
MR A Middleton
MSTR R Middleton
Mr S.M Mitchell
MR P MOLLOY
Miss L.H Monkhouse
MR M Monkhouse
Miss H.M Moore
MR A Moore
Mr D.M Moore
MR G Moore
MR G C Moore
MSTR J Moore
MSTR J E A Moore

Miss C. Morley
Mr D.M Morris
MISS L Morrison
Miss J.M Morton
Miss M.M Muncaster
MURDOCH
Mr A Murdoch
Mr D Murdoch
Mr S.P Murgatroyd
Mr A.T Murphy
Mr T.D. Murphy
Mr N.A. Murphy
Mr T Myer
Mrs S Myer
Mr L.N Naylor
Mstr P.N Naylor
MSTR M G J Neasham
Mr M.S. Newton
NIXON
Mr J.N.V Nixon
MR M Nixon
Mr P.N Nixon
Mr G Nolan
Mr M.J.N Nolan
MR A Norman
Mr A G Norster
MISS L. Nugent
MR P Nugent
Mr P.F.N Nugent
Mstr J.E.N Nugent
Mr B.O O'Keeffe
Mstr A.O O'Keeffe
MR J O'NEIL
Mr F.O O'Neill
Mr N.P Oberon
Mr S. Oliver
ONEILL
Mr M Overend
Mr A.O Oyston
Miss C.O Ozelton
Miss L.O Ozelton
Mr J.O Ozelton
Mr J.P Paget
Mstr A.J.P Paget
Mr A J Palmer
Mr M J Palmer
Mr P W Palmer
Mr R J Palmer
Miss E Parker
Miss J. Parker
Miss L Parker
Mr R Parker
MR S Parker
Mr D.E.P Parkes
MR A Parvin
Mr S.N.P Parvin
Miss R Patrick
Mstr A Patrick
Miss C.L.P Pawass
MR B J Payne
O J Payne
Miss N.K. Peacock
MR B Peacock
MR J P Peacock
Mr J T Peacock
Mr J.A.P Peacock
MR S Peacock
Mrs L. Peacock
MRS Y Peacock
Mstr T.N. Peacock
Mr J.L. Pearce
Mr N C Peary
Mstr D J Peary
Mstr M T Peary
Mstr S.C.P Peat
Mr M Pennick
Mstr D.M Pennick
Mr P.P Perkin
MR N Peterson
Mr R T Pick
Mr S.P Pickering
Mstr D.P Pickering
MR M Pierce
MR Platts
Mstr C.P Poole
MR C Porritt
Mr J.E PORTER
Miss V Powell
Mr L Price
Mr N.P Pringle
MR B A Prout
Mr J.R. Pulman
MR A PURVIS
MISS C F M Race
Mr R Ragusa
Miss S Rand
Mr M Rand
Mr JA Randall
Mstr C J Randall

MISS S J Read
MR R Read
Mrs M.R Reader
READMAN
Mr P.A. Readman
REDDMAN
Mr J Reed
Mstr C Reed
Mr D.R Reeder
REGENT
Mr P.R Renwick
Mr M Rhucroft
Mrs S.J Richards
Miss D Richardson
Mr D P Richardson
MR G.S. Richardson
MR N Richardson
Miss K.R Rickard
MR J M Ridgen
Mr P.R Ridley
Mr W.R.R Ridley
Mr C.K. Rigby
Mr K. Rigby
Mr M.R Riley
MR R ROBERTS
Mr M.A.R Roberts
Mr P.D.R Roberts
I Robertson
Mr D.J.R Robinson
Mr M.R Robinson
Mr S J Robinson
Mr W J Robinson
Mrs P.R Robinson
MR D Robson
Mr G M Robson
Miss K.R Rowntree
Mr K.R Rowntree
Mr S Rowntree
Miss C.R Rudd
Mr J.R Rudd
Mstr A.R Rudd
Mr P. Ruse
Mr P Rusk
Mr S.R Russell
Mstr B.R Russell
Miss N Rutter
Mr K Rutter
Mr D.M.S Salmon
Mstr C Samson
MR M Saunders
Mrs R Saunders
MR I Sayer
MR L M Sayer
Mr A.C.S Sayers
Mr D.S Sayers
Mr M.D.S Scott
MSTR K S Scott
Mr P.S Sellers
Mr I A Serginson
Mr R A Serginson
Mstr M R Serginson
Mr J A Shaughnessy
Mr D.S Shaw
Mr P.S Shepherd
Mrs L.S Shepherd
Mstr A.S Shepherd
Mr G Sigsworth
MRS C A Sigsworth
MSTR P A Sigsworth
SIMPSON
MISS H M Simpson
MR D J Simpson
Mr D J Simpson
Mr J Simpson
Mr M Simpson
Mrs J Simpson
Mr P.S Simpson
P Sissan
P Sisson
Mr R.S Skinner
MR J Skjelhaug
MR M W Slattery
Mr N Slavin
MR P Smailes
Mr J J Smallwood
Mr R.J. Smeeton
Mr A.G.S Smith
MR B M Smith
Mr D Smith
Mr D.S Smith
Mr G N Smith
MR G W Smith
Mr K.S Smith
Mr M Smith
Mr R A Smith
MSTR L T Smith
Mstr R.S Smith
Mstr S Smith
MR J Smitheringale

MISS K A Snowden
MISS V M Snowden
MR K J Snowden
MSTR J K Snowden
Mr D.J. Solly
MR D Spellman
MR J Spellman
MR A Spence
Mr M.S Spender
Mstr C.S Spender
Mr A.P Stangoe
MSTR D.A Stangoe
Mstr D.P Stangoe
Mr A.S Steedman
MR C Steffenson
MISS M Stephenson
Mr C.P. Stephenson
Mstr L.D Stephenson
Mstr M P Stephenson
Mr N R Stinson
Mstr G J Stinson
L Stirland
Miss D.C.S Stockton
Mstr D.J.N. Stockton
Mstr N.S Stockton
Mstr S.S Stockton
Mr A.S Stokes
MR D.R Stokes
Mstr M.J.S Stokes
MSTR P Stokes
MR J P Stone
Mstr P J Storey
Mr G.D.S Struthers
MR D Stubbs
MR J Stubbs
Mr M Stuckey
Mr M R A Stuckey
Mstr S M Stuckey
Mr A.M.S Sturdy
MR G Sudron
MSTR R Sudron
Mstr D.S Suggett
Mr G Sunley
Mr J Sunley
Mstr L Sunley
MR W Sutcliffe
MSTR A Sutcliffe
Mr S.S Sutherby
Mstr K.S Sutherby
Mr P Sutherland
Mr G I Swatman
Mr K. Sweeney
MR G.R Sweetman
Mstr M Sweetman
Mr C A Sykes
MR D Sykes
Miss V. Szucs
TB North East
Landlords
Mr S.L. Takacs
Mr A.D. Tandy
Mr D.T Tate
Mstr D.T Tate
Mstr W.T Tate
Mr D.M Taylor
Mr G.J.T Taylor
Mr P.T Taylor
MR R TAYLOR
Mr S J Taylor
MR S T Taylor
Mstr T.E.T Taylor
Mr N.W.T Teasdale
Mr N.W.T Temple
Mr I Tennant
Mr A Thom
Mr E Thomas
Mr E E Thomas
Mr L Thomas
Mr S Thomas
Mr W Thomas
MRS R Thomas
MSTR B Thomas
Mstr S Thomas
Miss E.T Thompson
Miss V.A.T Thompson
Mr Thompson
Mr A Thompson
Mr D.T Thompson
Mr I.R.T Thompson
Mr J Thompson
Mr N Thompson
Mr N.J.T Thompson
Mr N.T Thompson
Mr P.T Thompson
MR R Thompson
Mr S.T Thompson
MRS D Thornburn
MR A J Thorne

MSTR A J Thorne
Mr D Thornton
Miss L.A.T Thrower
Mr C.T Thrower
Mstr J.T Thrower
Mr G Todd
Mr N.T Todd
Mstr C. Todd
Mstr D.N.T Todd
Miss E.M.T Toland
Mr K.T Toland
Mr P.T Toland
Mr L.A Tose
Mr R.W Tose
Mrs S Tose
Mr R Towse
D Trodden
M Trodden
Miss J.T Tucker
Mr G.P.T Tucker
Mr A.W. Tunney
MR D J Turley
MR D V Turley
Mr J. Twiddle
Mr G Usherwood
Mr P.A.V Vallender
Mrs C.V Vallender
Mr Vasey
MISS S J Vickers
Mr L Vigilante
Mr J.H.V Vigors
MR J Waid
MR J D Walker
Mr K Walker
Mr M.A.W Walker
Mr S.W Walker
Mr I A Wallace
Mr M.R.W Wallis
Mr T.W.W Wallis
Mr D Walton
Miss D.C Ward
MR A Ward
Mr S.A.W Ward
Mstr S.L.W Ward
MSTR L S Wardell
MR J Wardle
MR J I Waterson
Mr H.W Watkins
MISS K Watson
Miss S.W Watson
MR A Watson
Mr D Watson
Mr K.W Watson
Mr S.W Watson
MSTR J C T Watson
Mr D.W Weedy
Mr S.J.W Weighell
MISS C Welburn
MISS P Welburn
G A Welch
MISS P J Welch
Miss L Weldrake
MR M Weldrake
MR M Wells
Ms A.W Wells
Mstr A.W Wells
Mr W.W Wesson
Mstr G.W Wesson
MSTR G J Westwood
MR J S Whaley
MR T Whaley
Miss L.J.W Wheeldon
Mr N.W Wheldon
Mr D.A.W White
Mstr C.W White
MR S Whitlock
Mr S Whyman
MR K Wickham
Miss M Wieczorek
Mstr D Wieczorek
Mr M.A.W Wild
Mr S.W Wild
A Wililiams
Mr G.W Wilkinson
Mr J Wilkinson
Mr N.W Wilkinson
Mr R A Wilkinson
Mstr C A Wilkinson
Mstr D.W Wilkinson
Mstr J Wilkinson
Mstr N Wilkinson
F Williams
MR A Williams
Mr N Williams
Mr R.W Willoughby
Mr C M Wilson
MR P Wilson
Miss E.K.W Wing

Mr M.W Wing
Mstr G.R.W Wing
Mr D.W Wiseman
Mr L.W Withers
Mstr C.A.T Withers
Mstr T.A.W Withers
Miss L Woodier
Miss V Woodier
Mr P.J.W Woodier
Mr S Woodier
Mstr A.W Woodier
Mstr L.W Woodier
Mstr J P Woodworth
Mr I Wright
Mr I.W Wright
Mrs B Wright
Mstr A Wright
Mr A.Y Yates
Mr N J Yates
Mstr M Youll
Mr M Young
Mr M.K.Y Young
Mstr A.Y Young
Mstr N Young
Mr R.Y Yoxall

NORTH STAND
Mr M.A Abbott
Mr P.A Abel
Mr D Adams
Mr M.A Adams
Mr D. Adamson
MR M.I ADAMSON
Mr M.I.A Adamson
P. Adamson
Mr E Addison
MR S D Addison
MSTR R.P Addison
Mr N.A Ahitan
Mrs A.A Ahmed
Mstr S.J.A Aithwaite
MR S T Alcock
Mr J.K.A Alderton
MR S G Aldridge
MSTR G C Aldridge
MR D Alexander
MR S Alexander
Mr S.C.A Algie
Mr S Ali
MR D Alker
MR K Allan
MSTR D Allan
Mr L S Allcock
Mr D.A Allen
Mr D.K.A Allen
MR T M Allen
MR W Allen
Mstr J.A Allen
Mrs B Allenby
MS S Allick
Miss D.M.A Allinson
MR D A Allinson
Mr D A Allinson
MR G Allinson
Mr L.A Allinson
Mr T.A Allinson
Miss D.J.A Allison
Miss L.J.A Allison
Mr M.A Allison
MR S C Allison
Mr S.A Allison
Mstr P Allison
Mr G.A Allport
MR M Allport
Almond
Mr J.A Amer
MR N Amer
MR K Andelin
Mr S.K.A Andelin
Mr C Anderson
Mr C J Anderson
MR G E Anderson
Mr G.R.A Anderson
MR N.W Anderson
Mr R.J.A Anderson
MSTR D P Anderson
MR C Andrews
Mr G.A Angel
MR P Angel
MRS A Angel
Mr R.A Angell
Mr J.A Angus
Mr K.J.A Angus
Mr M.A Angus
Mr M C Ankers
MR R Ankers
MSTR R.J Antill
MISS E K Appleby
MR M Appleby

MR T S Appleby
Mr A.A Applegarth
Mr L M Applegarth
MR M Applegate
Miss A.A Appleton
MR B Appleton
MR D Appleton
MR K Appleton
Mr M.A.A Appleton
Mr M.D.A Appleton
Mr N.C. Appleton
Mstr A.A Appleton
Mr T.A Appleyard
Mr G A Archer
Mr T.A Archer
MSTR P Archer
MR P.L.A Arkley
MR M Armatage
MR N Armes
Mstr P Armes
Mr Armstrong
Mr G Armstrong
Mr I.D.A Armstrong
Mr K.A Armstrong
Mr M Armstrong
MR S Armstrong
Mstr N.A.A Armstrong
Mr S.P.A Arnold
Mstr A.P.A Arnold
Mstr C Arthur
Mr I.A Ascroft
Mr D.A Ashbridge
MR C Ashcroft
Mr J.A Ashcroft
MR S.L Ashley
Miss B.A.A Ashton
MISS J.N ASKINS
Mr M.A Askins
Mr S.A Askins
Miss D.A Atkinson
Mr A.L. Atkinson
Mr C.A Atkinson
Mr J Atkinson
MR J Atkinson
MR K Atkinson
Mr M.A Atkinson
Mr M.I.A Atkinson
Mr P.A Atkinson
Mr P.R.A Atkinson
Mr R Atkinson
Mr R.D.A Atkinson
MR S H Atkinson
Mr S.J.A Atkinson
Mrs M.A.A Atkinson
Mr J.R.A Attwood
MSTR S P Auckland
Mr G A Austick
Mr J D Austick
Mr M.R.A Auty
Mstr D.O.A Axtell
MR M AYRE
Mr S.A Ayre
Mr J.A Azam
Mr K.A Azam
Mr M.A Azam
Mr N Aziz
Mr A.B Backhouse
MSTR K Bacon
Mr Bailey
Mr B Bailey
Mr G.B Bailey
Mr H.L.B Bailey
MR M Bailey
Mr M.A Bailey
MR N M Bailey
MRS A J Bailey
Mstr A.M. Bailey
Miss T.B Bainbridge
Mr Bainbridge
MR G Bainbridge
Mr C. Baines
Mr C.B Baines
MR N C Baines
Mr J.B Baird
MR A Baker
Mr D.B Baker
MR N E Baker
MRS J E Baker
MSTR M Baker
Mr P. Bakes
Mr K.B Baldwin
MR G.R BALL
MR N Ball
Mr S.B Ball
V Ball
MSTR C J Balmer
MSTR I M Balmer
Mr S J Balnaves
MR G M Bandeira

MR M I Banks
MR D Bannister
MR R Bannister
Mr A.L.B Barber
MR D Barber
Mr R.A.B Barber
MR S Barber
Mr G Barfoot
Miss L.B Barker
Mr C.B Barker
Mr D. Barker
Mr J.H.B Barker
MR K Barker
Mr R.B Barker
Mr M.B Barley
MISS J barlow
Mr C Barlow
Mr D.B Barlow
Mr J Barlow
Mr J.B Barlow
Mr P.A.B Barlow
MRS S Barlow
Mstr J.K.B Barlow
Mr R.P Barnard
Miss J.B Barnes
Mr A.M.B Barnes
MR N Barnes
Mstr P.B Barnes
Mr S M Barraclough
Mstr A P Barraclough
MR C N Barras
MSTR A P Barras
Miss N.B Barrett
MR BARROW
MR M Bartholemew
Mr D Bartholomew
MR C D Bartle
MSTR C M Bartlett
Mr A Bartley
Mr K.B Bartley
Mrs J.T.B Bartley
MSTR C Bartram
MSTR J Bartram
MSTR L Bartram
MR K Barugh
MR S K Barugh
Mr A.J.B Barwick
Mstr C Basford
Mstr M Bashford
Mr A.W.B Bass
Mr G.J.B Bass
MR G Batchelor
Mr O. Batchelor
Mr G.B Bateman
MR L Bateman
Mr P Bateman
MSTR R Bateman
BATES
Mr J Bates
Mr J.B Bates
Mr S.B Battle
Mr J.B Batty
Mr M. Batty
Mr M.A.B Baxtrem
MR R Bayles
Mr S.G. Beach
MR J D Beadle
Mr R.G.B Beadle
MR A R Beamson
MR C J Beamson
MR R Beamson
MR S Beamson
Mr A R Beane
Mr S.B Bearne
MR D N Beattie
MSTR S Beattie
Mr N.T.B Beaumont
MR I D Beaver
MRS A Beaver
MR BECK
Miss J.L.B Beckett
MR J D Beckett
Mr K Beckett
MR S J Beckett
MR BECKLEY
Mr J.P. Beckley
Mr M.P. Beckley
Mr P. Beckley
Mr A.D Beddard
Mr M.B Bedford
Mr M.J.B Bedford
Mr S Bedwell
MR W Beeby
Mr M.B Beecher
MR J P Begley
Miss K.L.B Bell
Mr A.P. Bell
MR G Bell
Mr J Bell

Mr J F Bell
Mr J.D.B Bell
Mr M.B Bell
Mr M.P.B Bell
Mr N Bell
Mr P Bell
MR S Bell
Mr S.B Bell
Mrs M.L.B Bell
Mstr C Bell
MSTR C.H Bell
MSTR R bell
MSTR S Bell
MISS H Bellerby
Miss J.L.B Bellerby
Mr B.B Bellerby
Mr I J Bellerby
MR J C Bellerby
Mr W. Bellerby
Miss E.M.B Belt
Mrs J.M.B Belt
Mr N.R Bendelow
MR G J Bennett
Mr G.B Bennett
Mr K.D.B Bennett
MR M BENNETT
Mr M.B Bennett
MSTR S Bennett
MR S R Bennington
Mr D.B Bennison
MSTR N M Bensley
Mr M.B Benson
Mr N.J.S Benson
MSTR M Benson
MR J H Benstead
Miss C.L.B Bentley
Mr C.B Bentley
Mr H.B Bentley
Mr S.B Bentley
Mstr D.B Bentley
Ms D.B Benton
Mr A Berkley
MISS E Berkovits
MR F L Berkovits
MRS C A Berkovits
Miss J.B Berrey
Mr G.B Berrey
Mr C.B Berry
Mr P Berry
MR D Bertram
Mr P.J.B Best
MR S Betteridge
Mr W.D.B Betts
Mr B.R.B Beulah
MR J.P Bibby
Mr M Bickley
Mstr J.J. Biggs
MR I.J Billing
MR L Billon
MR S.T Billon
MR L Bilton
MR S L Bilton
Mrs A.B Bilton
MR E Binns
Mr K.J Binns
Mr A.S.B Bint
MR G Birch
MSTR P S Birch
MR BIRCHALL
MR L Birchall
Miss R.L.B Bird
MR Bird
Mr A Bird
Mr A Bird
Mr D Bird
MR I Bird
Mr R J Bird
Mr R.B Birkby
Mr P A Birkett
Mr S.B Birt
MR C A Bishop
MSTR C A Bishop
MSTR N R Bishop
Mr S.B Bishoprick
Mr S.B Bivens
Mr I.W. Black
MR M Blackburn
MR N Blackburn
Mr P Blackburn
MR R E Blackburn
MR R.A.A BLACKBURN
Mrs B.B Blackburn
MSTR M R Blackburn
MR G.A Blackman
MSTR J BLACKMAN
Mr A.N.B Blackwood
MR C Blackwood
Mr M.W.B Blackwood
Mr K.B Blair

Mr K.J. Blair
Mr S.B Blair
Mr I Blakeman
MR W.B BLAKEY
MR Blamire
Mr S.J.B Bland
MSTR J Bland
MR O J Blaney
Mstr C.B Blenkinsop
Mr R.H. Blood
MR D. Bloomfield
Mstr D Bloomfield
Mr A J Blowman
Mr B M Boal
Mr R.B Boal
MR BOARDMAN
MR J C Boardman
MSTR P R Boardman
MSTR S M Boardman
Mr R.B Boase
Mr A.B Boddy
Mr C Boddy
Mr D Boddy
Mr J A Boddy
Mr P.B Boddy
MR S Boddy
Mr B Boettger
Mrs L.B Boettger
MR J Bognar
Mr A Bolan
MR R Boldison
MSTR G Boldison
Mr M J Bollands
Mr t.W. Bolton
Miss H.E.B Bone
MR S Bone
Mr D.N.B Bonnington
Mr A.G.B Boocock
MR S A Bookless
Miss G.A.B Boon
Mr J.R.I. Booth
MSTR J Boothby
MR A.M. Booton
Mr P Borg
MR A M Borley
MR A.W Bosomworth
MR I Bosomworth
MSTR C.A Bosomworth
MR P Bostock
Mr S.B Bostock
Mr A Boughey
Mr A.N.B Bourne
Mr I.R.B Bourne
Mr J Bourne
Mr J.P.B Bourne
Mr S H Bourne
MISS S Bowden
MR E Bowden
Mr Bowen
MR P Bowen
Mr T.B Bowen
Mr S L Bower
MR G Bowes
Mr J Bowes
Mstr M.B Bowes
MS V Bowker
MR A G Bowman
Mstr G.B Bowman
Mr C Boyd
MR M Boyd
Miss L.B Boyes
Mr J.R.B Boyle
Mr J.B Bracchi
MR A G Brack
Mr J.D.B Bradley
Mr J.M.B Bradley
MR K A Bradley
MR K R Bradley
Mrs K.J.B Bradley
Mr J.B Bradshaw
Mr K.B Bradshaw
Mstr Bradshaw
Mstr D.B Bradwell
Mr P.B Brady
Mr S.J.B Braid
Mr G.B Braithwaite
MR M S Braithwaite
Mr M.A.B Braithwaite
Mr L.J.B Bramley
MSTR L J Brannan
MSTR S J Brannan
Mr L.B Bratt
Mstr D.B Bratt
MR N BRAY
Mr G Brayfield
Mstr M.J. Brazier
MISS S.A BRECKON
MR A P Breckon

MR D R Breckon
MR G Breckon
Mr A C Breslin
Mr M.B Brette
MR Briggs
Mr J Briggs
Mr S Briggs
Mrs J.A Briggs
Mr R Brighton
Mr R.A.B Brine
Mr N. Brinsley
Mr S.G.B Brittain
Mr A.B Broadhurst
Mr A.J. Broadley
Mr C Broadley
Mr A Brockbank
Mr A Brocklesby
Mr G Brocklesby
Mr D.B Brodie
Mr A.M.B Brodrick
Mr S.P.B Brodrick
Mr D.B Bromage
Mrs J.B Bromage
MR T BROMFIELD
MISS N Brooks
MR BROOKS
MR C Brooks
MR P B Brooks
Mr S G Brooks
Mstr D.A.B Brooks
MR I Broom
MR J.W Broomfield
Mr I.B Broomhead
MR L Broomhead
Mr S.P.B Brotton
Mr N.E. Broughton
A Brown
MASTER S Brown
Miss C Brown
Miss E Brown
MISS T Brown
MR A Brown
Mr A Brown
MR A M Brown
MR A P Brown
Mr C Brown
Mr D.A.B Brown
Mr D.B Brown
Mr D.F.B Brown
Mr D.W. Brown
MR F Brown
Mr G.B Brown
Mr H Brown
Mr J Brown
Mr J D Brown
Mr J.B Brown
Mr K Brown
Mr K.B Brown
Mr K.D.B Brown
MR M A Brown
Mr M. Brown
MR P Brown
Mr P.B Brown
Mr R.B Brown
Mr S.B Brown
Mr S.F.B Brown
Mr S.G.B Brown
Mr S.R.B Brown
Mstr A.R.B Brown
Mstr B Brown
MSTR C D Brown
Mstr D Brown
Mstr K. Brown
Mstr N.B Brown
Mr D. Bruce
MR M J Bruce
Mr N Brundall
Mr R.B Brundenell
Mr P.S.B Brundle
Miss C.L.B Brunskill
Mr A.P.B Brunton
Mr M.A.B Bryan
Mstr C.S Bryan
Mr A.R.B Bryce
MSTR S D Bryne
Mr A.W Bryson
MR N J Buchanan
Mr S.G.B Buck
MR C Buckingham
Ms S Buckingham
Mr P.B Buckton
Miss H Budd
Mr M.H.S Bull
Mr R.B Bull
Mr R.B Bullen
MR B Bullock

Mr G.B Bullock
MR J Bullock
Mr L.B Bullock
MR M Bullock
MR S Bullock
Mstr J Bulman
MR K Bulmer
Mr D.B Bunn
Mr M.B Bunn
Mr R Bunn
Mstr D.B Bunn
Mr P.A. Bunting
MR J Burdon
Mstr J Burham
MSTR A Burke
MSTR G Burluraux
MR N Burnell
MSTR P M Burnett
Mr K Burnham
Mr A.S.B Burns
Mr D.B Burns
Mr M.B Burns
MSTR A Burns
Mr A Burnside
MR Burnup
Miss S L Burr
MR S.W Burridge
Mr J.B Burrows
Mr J.J.B Burrows
MSTR S G Burrows
MR A Burt
MR C Burt
Mr G.B Burt
MR H N Burt
MR J A Burt
Mstr A.B Burt
Mr G E Burton
Mr I.B Burton
Mr M Burton
Mr P.A.B Burton
Mr J.B Bustfield
Mr C.B Butcher
Mr G.H.B Butcher
MR R W Butler
Mstr A Butler
Mr M Butt
Mr A.B Butterfield
Mr C.B Butters
MR N Buxon
Mr G.J. Buxton
Mr S.B Buxton
Mr G.N.D. Byass
Master K.B Byles
MR Byles
Mr A.B Byles
Mr A.D.B Bylett
Mr J.H.B Bylett
MSTR G J Bylett
MR M Byran
Mr G.B Bytheway
Mr R.A.B Bytheway
Mstr T. Bywater
MR C CAHILL
MR A Cairnie
MR J Cairns
MR M R CAIRNS
Mr J Caisley
Mr A.C Callaby
Mr J.J.C Callaby
MR S Callaby
Mr J.C Callaghan
MR N Callaghan
MR S Callaghan
Miss C.P.C Callan
Mr A.C Calvert
Mr P Calvert
Mstr A D T Calvert
MR L Cameron
Mr A Campbell
Mr G Campbell
MR P M Campbell
MR S Campbell
MR W C Campbell
Mstr I.M.C Campbell
MR S CAMPLIN
MR P Cann
MSTR J Cann
Mr S.C Canney
MISS K E Canning
MSTR P I Canning
MR A Cantwell
MR A Capel
MR K Capel
Miss C.C Capocci
MR I.R.C Carlton
Mr P Carney
MRS J A Carney
MR A J Carr

APPENDIX 5

Mr D P Carr
Mr J.G.C Carr
MR D.I. Carrick
Mr A.C Carroll
Miss S Carter
Mr A R Carter
Mr A.J.C Carter
Mr A.R. Carter
Mr D.C Carter
Mr D.J.C Carter
Mr I.R.C Carter
MR J G Carter
Mr J.P.C Carter
MR P V Carter
Mr P.J.C Carter
Mr R. Carter
Mr S. Carter
Mr S.C Carter
Mrs L.S.C Carter
MSTR C N Carter
Mstr L T Carter
MSTR P A Carter
Mr W.C Cartman
Miss R.C Cartwright
Mr P.A.C Cartwright
Mr T.C Carvell
Mr M.C Casey
Mstr K.C Casey
Mr D.C Cass
Mr M W Cass
MR D Caster
MSTR C A Caster
MR C M Catchpole
Mr D.J. Catron
Mr A Catterson
MR A Catterson
Mr R.C Cawthorne
Mr N.C Caygill
Mr D.A.C Cessford
Mr S E Chaffer
Mr J Chambers
Mr P. Chambers
Mstr J.A.C Chambers
Mr A.C Chaplin
Mr S.C Chaplin
MISS A Chapman
Miss I.D. Chapman
MISS L G Chapman
Miss L.H.C Chapman
MR C Chapman
Mr C.S.C Chapman
MR N R Chapman
MR P F Chapman
Mr P.A.C Chapman
Mr S.B.C Chapman
Mstr D.C.C Chapman
MSTR P A Charles
Mr A.C Charlton
Mr G.C Charlton
Mr A.J. Charnock
Mr P.D.C Charnock
Mr B.M.C Chesser
Mr A M Chillmaid
Mr J.D.C Chilton
Mr P.L.C Chilton
Mrs J.C Chilton
MR P Chilver
Miss K Chilvers
Mr M Chilvers
Mr I.G.C Chinnock
Mr S.C Chittenden
Mr H.T.K Chohan
Mr A.P. Chown
Mr A.R. Chown
MR P C Chrisman
Mr D.C Christie
Mr S.C Christie
Mr D Christon
Mrs T Christon
Mr I.P.C Church
Mr I J Clacherty
MR D Clare
Mr D.B. Clare
Mr I.A.C Clare
Miss N.L.C Clark
MR A J Clark
Mr A.J.C Clark
Mr C.S. Clark
Mr D Clark
MR G Clark
MR G A Clark
Mr G.C Clark
MR G.G. Clark
Mr L. Clark
Mr P A Clark
Mr P.E.C. Clark
MR Q A Clark
MR S Clark
Mr S.D.C Clark

Mrs I. J Clark
Mstr S.C Clark
Mr M.G. Clarke
Mr N.T.C Clarke
Mr R Clarke
MR S Clasper
Mr A.C Claxton
Mr A.C Clay
MR A W Claypole
Mr N.M.C Cleary
Mr D.T.W Cleasby
MR J P Cleasby
MR M Cleasby
Mr N.C Cleasby
Mr N.D.C Cleasby
MR A Clements
Mr M.P.C Clements
Mr T.B.C Clements
MSTR G I Clements
MR I Clemmit
Mr M.C.C Clemmit
Mr R.M.C Clews
Mr J.J.C Clifford
Mr D Close
Mr J Clydesdale
Mr C Coates
Mr J.C Coates
Mr J.S Coates
MR K A Coates
Mr N.C Coates
Mr R Coates
Mr S Coates
MR D Cobb
Mr G Cobb
MR M.G Cobb
Mr G A Cobbold
MR M A Cochrane
MR M D Cochrane
MR S.M Cochrane
Mr S Cockburn
MR I.D Cockerill
Mr M.W.C Cockerill
Mr D.C Codd
Mr G.C Codd
Mstr A.D.C Codd
MR A P Cogan
Mr C.C Cole
Mr p.a Cole
Mr S.C Cole
Miss J.L.C Coleby
Ms J.C Coleby
Mstr P.J.C Coleby
MR M Coleman
Mr P.R.C Coleman
Mr S.C Coleman
Mr Collett
Mstr Collett
Mr G Collier
Mr L Collier
MR COLLINS
MR P C Collins
MR S Collins
Mr Cone
Miss J.A.C Cones
MR G J Congdon
MR M G Congdon
MSTR D J Congdon
Mr D.N.C Conley
Mr I.C Conley
Mr P.B.C Conley
Mr D Conlin
Mr N.J.C Connelly
Mr N.P.C Connelly
Mr P Connelly
MISS J L Connor
Mr M.D.C Connor
Mr C.C Connorton
MR F Connorton
Mr G.C Connorton
Mr M.C Connorton
Mstr P.C Connorton
CONROY
Mr G.J. Conroy
Mr M.C Conroy
Mr M.J.C Conroy
Mr P.C Conroy
Mstr G. Conroy
Mr B.C Constable
Mrs A.C Constable
Miss C Conway
Mr A.C Conway
MR P Conway
MRS KJ CONWAY
Mstr P.R.C Conway
Mr D.C Cook
Mr E.C Cook
MR G Cook
Mr G Cook
Mr M.C Cook

Mr M.J.C Cook
MR N H Cook
MR P A Cook
MR P K Cook
MR R Cook
Mr W.F.C Cook
MRS J Cook
MSTR A B Cook
Mstr A D Cook
Mr J.R.C Cooke
Mr C.C Cookson
MR COOPER
Mr G Cooper
Mr M J Cooper
Mr M.E.C Cooper
MR P E Cooper
Mr P.C Cooper
Mr S Cooper
Mr S. Cooper
Mr S.J.C Cooper
MR S.R Cope
Mr A M Corbett
Mr J.A.C Corcoran
Mr R.N.C Corden
Mr D.C Corfield
MR M Corley
Mr R.C Corner
Miss L.J.C Cornfield
Mr C.C Cornfield
G Cornforth
MISS E.A Cornforth
MISS V.E Cornforth
Mr A.J.C Cornforth
MR M J Cornforth
MSTR M Cornforth
Ms S K Cornwell
Mr P.A. Corrigan
Mr P.C Corrigan
Mr C Cory
Mr P.M.C Cosgrave
Mr D.G.C Coston
Mr A.M. Cotter
Mr P.M. Cotter
Mr A.L Cottrell
Mr M.C Cotty
Mr B Couch
MISS G Coulson
MR A J Coulson
Mr M.J. Coulson
Mr J. Coulthard
Mr J.A. Coulthard
Mstr M.G. Coulthard
Mr K.T.C Counter
Mr G.M.T Coupe
Mr R.J Covell
Miss J.C Coverdale
Mr N.C Coverdale
Mstr I.C Coverdale
Miss D.C Cowell
Mstr S.M.C Cowell
MR I A Cowton
MR A J Cox
Mr G.P.C Cox
MR J Cox
Mr J.C Cox
Mr M.J.C Cox
Mr M.T.C Cox
MRS C A Cox
Ms K.J.C Coxon
MR G W Craggs
MR I Craggs
Mr J.C Craggy
Mr P.C Craggy
Mr P M Cramer
MR S Cramer
MR S Crank
MR T Crank
Mr P. Crannage
Mr J.C Cranston
MR T Cranston
Mr K.C Craven
MR L P Craven
Miss D Crawford
Miss K Crawford
Mr N Crawford
MR S J Creaser
MISS M C Creedon
Mr A R Crofts
MR M P Crones
Miss D E Cronin
MR Crooks
MR M Crooks
MR D W Crosby
Miss E.L Cross
Mr A Cross
MR K Cross
Mr K.B Cross
Mr R.A.C Cross
MR S Cross

Miss L.C Crossley
Mr J.B. Crossley
Mr M.C Crossley
MR J A Crossman
Mr P.A.C Crossman
MR G A Crow
Mr L.C Crow
Mstr J.C Crow
Mr A.C Crowe
Mr P.A Crozier
Mstr P.B Crozier
Mr G.C Cruickshank
Mr J.A. Cruickshank
MR J.H Cubbin
Mr P.L. Cuff
Mrs K.A Cuff
MR A Cullen
Mr C.C Cullen
Mr G S Culley
Mstr C.D.C Culley
MSTR S Culley
MR G Cummings
MR G Cummins
Mr M.J.C Cummins
MRS CUMMINS
Mstr D.A.C Cummins
MR L D Curry
MSTR D Curry
MISS L J Curtis
MR A.C Curtis
Mr L J Cuthbert
Mr P. Cuthbert
Mr N Cuthbertson
MR I Cutler
Mr J.C Cutler
MRS M Cutler
Mr B.C Cutter
Mr A Czifra
Mr K Daggett
MSTR J Daglish
Mstr L.A.D Dalby
Mr M.D.D Dale
Mr P.D Dale
Mr C.D Dales
Mr J.D Dales
MR L A Dales
Mr M.J.D Dales
Mr O. Dales
MR R M Dales
Mr R.P.D Dales
Mr A Daley
Mr A.P.D Daley
Mr K.D Dalglish
Mstr S.J. Dalkin
Mr G Dalton
MR L Daly
Miss T.A.D Dalziel
Mstr T.D Daniel
MSTR DANIEL
Mr P R Daniels
Mstr P Daniels
Mstr S Daniels
Mr M.D Danilowicz
MSTR J M Darbey
MR E Darby
Mr M.E.D Darby
MR T Darby
Mstr P.D Dark
Mr D.D Darlington
MR D.M Darragh
MR D. Darroch
MR I M Date
MR M J Date
Mr A. Davey
Mr B.H.D Davey
Mr R.J.D Davey
Miss N.A.D Davidson
Mr A Davidson
MR P R D Davidson
Mr R Davidson
MR T Davidson
Miss J.D Davies
MR A C Davies
Mr D.D Davies
Mr G Davies
Mr G.D Davies
Mr G.R.D Davies
Mr I Davies
Mr J Davies
MR M B Davies
MR M G Davies
Mr P.R.D Davies
MR S Davies
Mr S.D Davies
MR T Davies
MSTR A I Davies
Mstr C.D Davies
Mstr G Davies

Mstr L.S.D Davies
Mr J.D Davis
Mr N.W.D Davis
Mr D J Davison
MR M Davison
Mr S Davison
MR M Davy
Miss A.D Dawson
Mr A.D Dawson
Mr G Dawson
Mr K. Dawson
Mr M Dawson
Mr M.D Dawson
Mr N.D.D Dawson
Mr P. Dawson
Mr R.J.D Dawson
Mstr M.D Dawson
Mr J.L.D Dea
MISS L J Deakin
MR S A Deakin
MRS D Deakin
Mr A.K. Deamer
Mr C. Dean
MSTR A.D Deane
Mr J B Dedman
Mr G.D Demoily
Mr R.D Dennis
Mr S.J. Dennis
MSTR C M Dennis
Mr S.D Dent
Mr J Dick
MR G D Dickens
MR R Dickens
MSTR P R Dickens
Mr N.D Dickinson
Mr D.J.D Dickson
Mr R.J.D Dickson
MR S C Dinsdale
Mr A.L Distasi
Mrs N.E Distasi
MR A A Ditta
Mr A.D Ditta
MASTER A.J Dixon
Mr D.A.D Dixon
Mr J Dixon
Mr L R Dixon
Mr M.A.D Dixon
Mr M.J.D Dixon
Mr O.M.D Dixon
Mr P.D Dixon
Mr P.J. Dixon
MR S Dixon
Mrs A.D Dixon
Mstr A.G.D Dixon
Mstr S.D Dixon
Mr M.D Doab
Mr C.D Dobbs
MSTR J Dobbs
Mr M.D Dobing
Mr C.W.D Dobinson
Mr A I Dobson
Mr P.D Docherty
Mr Dodds
Mr C.J.D Dodds
Mr J.D Dodds
Mr K.D Dodds
Mr P.A.D Dodds
Mr S.D Dodds
Mr T.D Dodds
Mr T.C.H. Doggett
Mstr T.J.E. Doggett
MR D A Doherty
Mr J.A.D Doi
Mstr N.D. Dolan
MR F J Donaghy
Mr K.M.D Donald
Mr R.I.D Donald
Mr M.I.D Donaldson
Mr R P Donaldson
Mr S Donaldson
Mr A.D Donkin
Mr M T Donnelly
Mr N A Donnelly
MSTR C Donnelly
MR J Donovan
Mstr S Donovan
Mstr R P Doolan
MR B Doublett
Mr I.P.S. Doublett
Mr M.P.D Doublett
MR S Doublett
Mr V.J.D Doublett
Mr E.J.D Dougan
Mr K.D Doughney
MR B Douglas
Mr D.D Douglas
Mr G.D Douglas
Mr J.S.D Douglas
Mr A.J.D Downer

Mr D.C.D Downey
Mr G.D Downing
Mr J.W.D Downing
Mr S Downing
Miss C M Dowson
Mr B.D Dowson
MR S Dowson
MR A Doyle
MR J Doyle
Mr M.D Drake
Mr W. Draper
MR S DRAYCOTT
Mr M.D Drinkel
Mr G.K.D Drinkhall
Mr P.D Drinkhall
MR J A Driver
Mr K.D Droniuk
Mr R.D Drummond
MR A Drury
Mr A. Dryden
Mr A S Dudley
Mr A.J.D Dudman
Mr I.P.E Duffew
Mr A J Duffield
MR D DUFFIELD
MR D A Duffield
Mr J.R.D Duffield
MSTR S Duffield
Miss A.D.D Duffy
Mr J.M.D Duffy
Mr K.D Duffy
MR O M Duffy
MR P J Duffy
Mstr C.G.D Duffy
Mr J.M Duggan
Mstr L.J.D Dunbar
MR A Duncan
Mr A.G.D Duncan
Mr S R Duncan
MR P A Dunford
MSTR D J Dunford
MSTR S T Dunford
Mr A.K.D Dunn
Mr A.M.D Dunn
MR C R Dunn
Mr J.M.D Dunn
Mr R Dunn
MR R J Dunn
Mr R.D Dunn
MSTR J M Dunn
Mstr S.D Dunn
Mr M.D Dunne
Mr P.A. Dunnett
Mr C Dunning
MR S M Durant
MR S Durham
Mr T M Durkin
Mstr P.M. Durston
Mr S.D Dyer
Mr W.A.D Dymond
MISS E J H Dyson
Mr A.N. Dyson
MR P J Dyson
D.J. Eadington
MISS E Eadington
MR A Eadington
Eagle Supplies
Mr F.E Eanor
Mr P J Earl
Mr R.E Earl
Mr S.P.E Earley
MR EASBY
Mr P.E Easby
MR A Easton
Mr G.E Eastwood
Mr S.E Eastwood
Mr Ebon
MR J.S EBISON
Mstr C.E Eccles
Mr M.A.E Eddon
Miss C J Eddy
Miss E M Eddy
MR C Eddy
MSTR C Eden
MSTR H Eden
MASTER D W Edgar
MR G.D Edmends
Mr A.E Edon
Mr R.E Edon
MR S Edon
Mstr D.E Edon
Mr C.T.E Edwards
Mr D.E Edwards
Mr P.E Edwards
Mr S.A. Edwards
Mr W.E Edwards
Mrs E.E. Edwards

Mr G P Eeles
Mr J.L. Elcoat
MR I Elcoate
MR J Elder
Mr M.J.E Elder
Mstr A.E Elder
Mr S.L.E Elderfield
Mr P.D.E Eldredge
MISS L M Ellerton
MISS ELLIOTT
MISS T.A ELLIOTT
MR ELLIOTT
Mr A.B.E Elliott
MR M Elliott
Mr R J Elliott
MR S Elliott
Mr S.D.E Elliott
MR S.S Elliott
MR ELLIS
Mr S.E Ellis
Mr A G Ellison
Mr C M Ellison
Mr D.E Elstob
Mr A S Elston
Mr M.E Elston
Mr M.E Emmerson
MSTR D J Emmett
Mr N Empson
Mr P Empson
MR J Enderwick
MR J Eneerwick
Mr A.S.E English
Mr B.E English
Mr S.A.E English
MSTR K English
Mr D W Errington
MR J Espin
MR C Etherington
MR D Etherington
MRS J Etherington
Mr A.E Evans
MR C Evans
Mr C.W.E Evans
MR D M Evans
Mr D. Evans
Mr G Evans
Mr J.E Evans
Mr K Evans
Mr M.R.E Evans
MR N J T Evans
Mr P.E Evans
Mr R Evans
Mstr C J Evans
Mr P.E Evendew
Mr S.H.E Ewart
MR S Exley
Mr S.E Eyeington
Mr S.J.E Eyre
Mr S.D.F Fairbank
Mr A.S.F Fairbank
Mstr M Fairburn
Mr S.P.F Falconer
Mstr A.J.F Falconer
MR P Faloona
Mr A.D.F Farrell
Mr J.F Farrell
Mr A.J.F Farrell
MISS A Farrow
MR D C R Farrow
Mr P.F Farrow
Mr L.S.F Farthing
Mr N.S.F Farthing
MR D J Fasey
MR K C Faulks
MISS L M Fawcett
Mr B.F Fawcett
Mr L.S.F Fawcett
Mr L.S.F Fawcett
MR P Fawcett
Mstr D.F Fawcett
Mr M.D.F Feasey
Mr J Featham
Miss R Featherstone
Mr G Featherstone
Mr J M Featherstone
Mr L.N Featherstone
Mstr P.A.F Featonby
Mr S Felgate
Miss C.E.F Fell
Mr D Fellows
Mstr G Fellows
Mr C.F Fenwick
Mr S.F Fenwick
Mstr A.F Fenwick
Mr J.L. Ferguson
MR E FERGUSON
Mr W. Ferguson
MSTR M FERGUSON

219

Mr M.F Fern
Mr A Ferrier
Mr B. Fielding
Mstr L Fields
Miss S L Finn
Mr G.F Finn
Mr M. Finn
Mr P.F Finn
MR S Finn
MR M Finnegan
MISS V FIONDA
Mr I.F Fionda
MR P FIONDA
MR I.J Fish
Mr N.P.F Fishburn
MR L Fisher
MSTR A J Fitt
Mr G.F Fitzgerald
Mr L.F Fitzgerald
MR M Fitzpatrick
Mr S.F Flanders
Mr D.J.F Flandin
Mr J.D.F Fleet
Mr G Fleetham
Mstr A Fleetham
Mr D.F Fleming
Mr N W Fleming
Mr T.F Fleming
Mr D.J Fletcher
Mr M.F Fletcher
Mr N.F Fletcher
Mr S.F Fletcher
Mr S.N. Fletcher
Mr H.L.F Flewker
Mr J.F Flewker
Mr K.F Flint
Mr N.F Flint
Mr P.F Flint
Mr S Flintoff
Mr P.F Flowerdew
MR B Flynn
Mr G.F Flynn
MSTR C D Flynn
MSTR N T Flynn
MR K M Fogg
MR E Foley
Mr S. Forbes
MISS L C Ford
MR C T Ford
MR D B Foreman
Mr M Foreman
Mrs J Foreman
Mr J.F Forgan
Mr M.F Forma
Mr M L Forrester
Mrs A.V.F Forshaw
Mr D.F Forster
Mr J A Forster
MR M Forster
Mr P.A Forster
MR R Forster
Mr R.F Forster
Mr A.F Forsyth
MR D Fortune
Mr A.G.F Foster
MR N Foster
MR P FOSTER
Mr P.J.F Foster
MR S Foster
MR A Fothergill
MR G Fotheringham
MR S Fotheringham
MSTR S Fotheringham
MSTR K Fountain
MISS D Fowler
MR D Fowler
Mr H.W. Fowler
MR R C Fowler
Miss K S Fox
MR C Fox
Mr D Fox
MISS A France
Mr K J France
MR J.E Francis
Mr D Frank
Mr R.E Frank
Mr S Frank
MR G E Frankland
MR K Frankland
Miss J Franklin
Mr D.H.F Franklin
MR G M Fraser
Mr K.F Fraser
MR M Fraser
MR R C Frater
MR R S Frater
Mr N S Freeman
MSTR A Freer
Mr K.F Frelich

Mrs C.F Frelich
MR A J French
Mr M.N.F French
Mr S French
MR S A French
Mr C.F Frewin
Mr C.F Frost
Mr D.F Frost
Mr M.W.F Frost
Mr N I Frost
MR P Frost
Mr S.F Frost
Mr E.D.F Fryer
Mr M J Fryer
Mr M.J.F Fryer
MR Fryett
MR D Fryett
MR D R Fyfe
Mr G.G Gabriel
MSTR D J Gaffney
Mr D.G.G Gall
Mstr C.J.G Gall
MR N Gallagher
MR P M Gallagher
MR R Gallagher
Mr S.R.G Gallagher
MR T Gallagher
Mr B.W Gallon
MISS T A Galloway
Mr C Galloway
Mr G Galloway
Mr G.G Galloway
Mr S.G Galloway
Mstr S.P.G Galloway
Mstr W.J.G Galloway
MSTR S J Gamesby
Mr A.G Garbutt
MR P M Garbutt
MR S E Garbutt
Mr S.G Garbutt
Mstr A.G Garbutt
MR J.N GARDNER
Mr D.G Gargett
MR D Garnsey
Mr S.G Garnsey
Mr J S Garratt
Mr N Garrett
MR B J Garthwaite
MSTR M J Garthwaite
Mr A Gatiss
Mr D Gatiss
Mr M Gatiss
Mr J. Gaunt
GAVAGHAN
MR J Gawthorpe
Mr A.J.G Gaynor
Mr M.P.G Gaynor
Mr J.D.G Gent
Mr P C Gent
Mr D J Gentle
Mr A.G Gerhard
Mr S.G Gettings
Mr R.G Gibb
MSTR A.P Gibbon
Mr I.G Gibbons
Mr G.G Gibbs
MR M Gibbs
Mr M.G Gibbs
Mr S.G Gibbs
Mr A.G Gibson
Mr A.J.G Gibson
Mr C.G Gibson
MR G N Gibson
Mr J Gibson
MR M Gibson
MR P Gibson
MSTR P A Gibson
MSTR S P Gibson
Mstr M.J.G Gidney
MISS J.E. Gilbert
Mr P.G Gilbert
Mr M.J.G Gilbey
Mr M.R.G Gilbey
Mr J.D.G Gilby
MR Gilhespie
MISS P.T Gilhooley
MR A P Gilhooley
Mr A.J.G Gill
Mr J.R.G Gill
MR R A Gill
Mr C.G Gillespie
MR N K Gittus
Mr M Glasgow
Mr W B Glasgow
Mr N.G Glasper
Mrs A.G Gledhill
Mr B.G Glenton
Mr S Godfrey
Mstr L Godfrey

Mr K.G Goldby
MR D Golightly
Mr R.G Golightly
MR A G Golloway
MR S Gomm
MR S Gooch
MR D Good
Mr G Good
Mr L P Good
MR E Goodall
Mr L.B.G Goodchild
Mr S.G Goodhall
Mr T.G.G Goodhall
MR K.R Gooding
Mr G.R.G Goodman
MR N Goodridge
GOODSELL
MSTR S M Goodsell
Mr A.G Goodwill
Mr M Goodyear
MR P M Goodyear
MISS S Gordon
Mr D.A.G Gordon
MR J Gordon
Mr J.B.G Gordon
Miss C Gorman
MR C Gorman
Mr R Gorman
MR S T M Gorman
MRS J Gorman
Mstr M Gorman
MR P J Gosling
Mr D.M.G Gosney
Mr K.R. Gott
Mr S.G Gouldthorp
Mrs J.G Gouldthorp
MR G J Grabham
Mr A Graham
MR A O Graham
Mr C.R.G Graham
Mr D.A. Graham
MR G Graham
Mr G Graham
MR J R Graham
Mr P.G Graham
Mr S.G Graham
Mr T Graham
Mstr A Graham
Mr A.G Grainge
Mr J B Grainge
Mrs S.M.G Grainge
MR A Grainger
Mr S.J. Grainger
Mstr C.D.G Grange
Mstr K Grange
MR M D Grant
Mr S.G Granville
MSTR A Granville
Mr J. Grassham
Master Gray
MISS M Gray
MISS R Gray
Mr A.G Gray
Mr D Gray
Mr D L Gray
MR L.G Gray
MR M Gray
Mr M.G Gray
Mr P A Gray
MR T GRAY
MR T Gray
Mstr B.G Gray
Mstr D.A.G Gray
Mstr D.G Gray
MR D.A Greaves
Mr J.T.G Greaves
MR A Green
MR A J Green
Mr A.J.G Green
MR D Green
Mr G.A.G Green
Mr J.G Green
Mr P.A Green
Mr P.G Green
Mr S Green
Mr S.G Green
MR T J Green
Mstr C.G Green
Mstr D.G Green
Mstr M.A Green
MSTR T M Green
MR H Greenan
Mr L.G Greenhough
Mrs L.G Greening
Mr J.G Greensitt
MR B T Greenway
MR A Greenwell
MR P Greenwell
MR A GREENWOOD

MR D GREENWOOD
Mr S Gregory
Mrs R Gregory
Mr P.M.G Grief
Mr A Grieff
Mr R.T.G Griffin
Mr S.K.G Griffin
Mr C Griffiths
MR L Griffiths
Mr M.G Griffiths
MR P.M Griffiths
MR T J W Griffiths
Mr T.E.G Griffiths
Mr W Griffiths
Mr M.G Grimes
Mr R N Grimwood
MR N Groom
Mr A.J.G Grosvenor
Mr J C Grover
Mr G M Groves
GRUBB
Mr S.D.G Guilfoyle
Miss C.E. Gunn
MR R Gunn
MRS S Gunn
MR D.R Gutteridge
MR M.J Gutteridge
Mr A J Guy
Mr A.P. Guy
Mr D Guzmics
Mr S Hadman
Mr G.D.H Hagen
Mr L.H Haggath
Mr M.H Haggath
Mr R.H Haggath
Miss J.H Haigh
MR A Haigh
Mr C.H Haigh
Mstr M.H Haigh
Mr D.J. Hails
MSTR K J Haith
MR R Hale
MR R J Hales
MR A M Haley
Mrs A.T.H Haley
Mr A.I.H Hall
Mr B Hall
Mr G.H Hall
Mr J.J.H Hall
MR M Hall
MR M C Hall
Mr M.G. Hall
Mr R. Hall
Mr S Hall
Mr S.T.H Hall
Mrs S.H Hall
MSTR C Hall
R Hall
Mr I.G.H Hamblett
Mr K.J.H Hamill
Mrs E.A.H Hamill
Mstr D.J.H Hamill
Mr H H A Hamilton
Mr R.N Hamilton
Mr S D Hamilton
Mr W.T Hamm
MR L Hammersley
MR MR Hammond
Mr P.J.H Hampson
Mr T.B.H Hampton
Mr A Hancock
Mr D.J.H Hancock
Mr P. Hancock
Miss R Hand
Mr A.P Hand
Mr B.P Hand
Mr D Hand
Mr F D Hand
Mr J Hand
Mstr C.J.H Hand
Mstr D Hand
Mstr I Hand
Mstr M.H Hand
Mr P.A Handley
MR M.T HANLEY
MR A D Hanlon
Miss E Hannaford
MR D G Hannaford
Mr D.H Hannah
Mstr J.H Hannah
Mr A J Hanratty
Mr J.R.H Hanratty
Mr S A Hanratty
MISS M Hanson
Mr Harbron
Mstr P.H Harcourt
MR K Hardesty
Miss Z Harding
MR D F Harding

MR F G Harding
Mr J.R.H Harding
Mr M.H Harding
MR S Harding
MR G Hardman
Mr B.P.H Hards
Mr A.D.H Hardwick
Mr A.J.H Hardwick
MISS E Hardy
MISS J.E Hardy
MR C.R Hardy
MR D M Hardy
MR G K Hardy
Mr J.J.H Hardy
Mr M. Hardy
MR P Hardy
MR R N Hardy
MR T Hardy
Mr G.H Harkin
Mr K.H Harkin
Mr D.J.H Harland
MR K Harland
Mr P.H Harland
Mr R.C.H Harland
Mstr P.R.H Harland
Mr G.H Harper
Mstr J.M Harper
Mr A.M.H Harrington
Mr J.R.H Harrington
MR P Harrington
MR T Harrington
Mstr J.S.H Harrington
Mstr M.R.H Harrington
Miss S.L.H Harris
Mr A.J.H Harris
Mr C.H Harris
MR G Harris
Mr J.H Harris
MR M Harris
Mr M H Harris
MR M R Harris
Mr M.H Harris
MR P G Harris
Mr P.P.H Harris
Mr S.D.H Harris
Mr S.H Harris
Mstr S.P.H Harris
MISS A Harrison
MISS C Harrison
MR A Harrison
Mr A.H Harrison
Mr D Harrison
MR H Harrison
Mr I. Harrison
MR K Harrison
MR K W Harrison
Mr L.H Harrison
MR M Harrison
Mr M. Harrison
Mr M.K.H Harrison
Mr P. Harrison
MR R Harrison
Mr R Harrison
Mr S J Harrison
MR S P Harrison
MR S R Harrison
MSTR J Harrison
Mstr R Harrison
MRS J Harriss
Mr M.W.H Harsley
Mstr S.W.H Harsley
Mr A.H Hart
Mr F Hart
Mr J.W.H Hart
Mr M Hart
MR M T Hart
Mstr G.H Hart
MR M.L Hartas
Mr S.P.H Harte
Mr A S Hartley
Mr M.A. Hartley
Mr N J Hartley
Mr S.M.H Hartley
Mr T G Hartness
Mr A.C. Hartshore
MR A R Harvey
Mr F.H Harvey
MR L.J Harvey
Mr M.D.H Harvey
MR M J Haslam
MR G J Hassell
MR M P Hastings-Long
MR R.C Hatfield
MR S P Hatfield
Mr C.H Hatton
MR C Haverson

Mr K.M.H Haverson
MSTR B Haverson
Mr G.H Hawkins
MR G M Hawksworth
Mr Haye
MR A Hayes
Mr J Hayes
Mr A.H Head
MR C Head
Mr J.D.H Head
MSTR C T Head
MR J.L.C Headlam
MR M P Headlam
Mr M.H Heagney
Mr D Heald
MR S Heald
MR S E Heald
MRS C Heald
Mr P A Healey
Mr S.A. Healey
MR K J Healy
MRS J.E Healy
MR K Harland
MR M S Heatherington
Mr M.J.H Heatley
Mr S J Heawood
MR M Heighton
MISS D Helm
MR A Helm
MR D Helm
Mr M.P Helm
Miss A.H Helyer
MR HELYER
MR A J Hemer
Mr M Hemblade
Mr A.H Hemmingway
Master S.S Henderson
Mr B.J.H Henderson
Mr J.K.H Henderson
Mr M.S.H Henderson
Mr P.W.H Henderson
Mr S.J.H Henderson
Mrs L.A.H Henderson
Miss G.H.T Henderson-Thynne
Miss K.H.T Henderson-Thynne
MR D Henderson-Thynne
Mstr S.H.T Henderson-Thynne
Mr N HENELAN
MR T Henry
Mr J.T.H Henwood
MR D B Hepburn
Mr K Hepplewhite
MSTR M Herrell
MR D K Herrfield
MR G N Herron
Mr N Herron
MR S Heseltine
Mr W.J.H Heseltine
Mr G.P.H Heselton
Mr J Heslop
Mr J.H Heslop
Mr M A Heslop
Mr P.H Heslop
Mr E Hesp
W G Hesse
Mr A Hesse
MR T Hetherington
Miss K Heward
MR C W Hewison
MR S Hewison
Mr A C Hewit
Mr D.H Hewitson
Mr A.H Hewitt
Mr D.T.H Hewitt
MR L Hewitt
MR P Hewitt
Mrs J.H Hewitt
Mrs C.A.H Hewlett
Mr G.T.H Hewling
Mr A.H Hewson
MR T R Hickes
MR M Hierons
Mr D.J Higgins
Mr G S Higgins
Mr S.H Highfield
Mr B.H Hill
Mr C.J.H Hill
Mr D.W.H Hill
Mr G J Hill
MR M E Hill
MR P B Hill
MR R hill
Mr S.H Hill
Mstr A.H Hill

Mstr S.H Hill
MR M Hillerby
MR P Hillerby
MR T Hillerby
MSTR S Hillerby
Mr R.I. Hills
Mstr R.H Hills
Mr J.N.H Hilton
MISS H.J Hind
Mr W.C.H Hingley
Mr W.L.H Hingley
Mr J Hirst
Mr A Hislop
Mr S.J.H Hislop
Mr J.H Hitchcock
Mstr D.J.H Hitchen
Mr B Hoare
Mstr C.H Hobaiter
Mr P.H Hobbs
Mr C.M.H Hobday
Mstr C.A.H Hobday
Mr K T Hobson
MR M Hobson
MISS A Hockney
MR M Hockney
MR M A Hockney
Miss C.H Hodgson
MR Hodgson
Mr A D Hodgson
Mr A.C. Hodgson
Mr A.F.H Hodgson
Mr A.H Hodgson
MR B.T Hodgson
Mr D A Hodgson
Mr G.A.H Hodgson
Mr M. Hodgson
Mr P Hodgson
MR S P Hodgson
MR T G Hodgson
Mr T.S.H Hodgson
Mstr M Hodgson
MSTR O R Hodgson
Miss S Hogg
Mr C.H Hogg
Mr S R Hogg
Mr S.J.H Hold
Mr D Holden
MR S R Holdsworth
MR N G Holgate
Miss J.H Hollas
Mr D.M.H Holley
Miss J Holliday
Mr S.H Holliday
Mr S Holloway
Mr Holmes
Mr A.H Holmes
MR C P Holmes
Mr D Holmes
MR D Holmes
MR G Holmes
Mr J.H Holmes
Mr L.B.H Holmes
Mr L.H Holmes
MR P A Holmes
MR P C Holmes
Mr P L Holmes
Mr P.H Holmes
Mr R.H Holmes
Mr T.H Holmes
Mstr J.H Holt
Mr J.H Homan
Mr M.H Homan
Mstr L S Homer
Mr R Honeyman
Mrs J Honeyman
Miss C.H Hood
Mr G.H Hood
Mr I.J.H Hooker
MR A Hookey
Mr A.J.H Hope
Mr S.H Hopkins
MSTR L A Hopper
MR P C Hopps
MSTR W Hopps
Mr C.H Hopson
Mr M.S.H Hopson
MR P Hopson
MSTR A Hopson
Mstr D.I.H Hopson
Mstr J.H Horne
MR C Horner
Mr D.J.H Horner
MR P Horner
MR B Hornsby
Mr N F Horsfall
MR A Horsman

Mr A.H Horton
Mr H.H Horton
MR J S Hosie
Mr P.H Hoskins
Mstr B.T.H Hoskins
Mr M.H Hough
Mr S.H Housley
Mr P.H How
Mrs M.H How
Mr A.H Howard
MR S.J Howard
Mr R.N.H Howart
Mrs A.A.H Howart
Mr C.R.H Howe
MR D J Howe
Mr D.H Howe
Mr S.A.H Howe
Mstr L.D.H Howe
Miss J.H Howes
Mr L.H Howes
Mr N Howes
MR D C Howgill
MR N R Howgill
Mr D.H Hoy
Mr I.H Hoy
MR B.A Hubbard
MR J D Hubbard
MSTR C Hubbard
Mr T.H Hudson
Mstr R.H Hudson
MISS A Hughes
MR A.T Hughes
Mr C Hughes
MR D Hughes
MR G Hughes
MR J Hughes
Mr M.A Hughes
Mr P Hughes
MR G E Hughff
MR J C Hughff
MSTR G A Hughff
MR D L Hugill
MR I Hugill
MR K Hugill
MR S HUGILL
MSTR P Hugill
Mr P.H Huitson
MR D Hume
Miss S.N. Humphreys
Mr A.R.H Humphreys
Miss E G Hunneysett
MR P A Hunnysett
Mr L.H Hunt
Mr S Hunt
MSTR M Hunt
Miss R.A.H Hunter
MR B Hunter
Mr C Hunter
MR G Hunter
Mr K T Hunter
MR P Hunter
Mr S.J.H Hunter
Mr S.R.H Hunter
MSTR A G Hunter
Mstr C.A.H Hunter
MSTR R Hunter
Mr D.H Hurn
Mr N.D.H Hurren
Mr P.H Hurren
Mr R.H Hurren
Mr J. Hurst
Mr R J Hurst
Mr S Hurst
Mr N.H Husband
Miss H.H Huskinson
MR G Huskinson
Mr G.D.H Huskinson
Mstr J.H Huskinson
Miss K.H Hutchinson
Mr A.J Hutchinson
MR B Hutchinson
MR B N Hutchinson
MR C Hutchinson
Mr J.M.H Hutchinson
Mr N.G.H Hutchinson
Mr P S Hutchinson
Mr P.H Hutchinson
MR S Hutchinson
Mstr A.L Hutchinson
MSTR J Hutchinson
Mr C.D.H Hutton
Mr D.H Hutton
Mstr C.R.H Hutton
Mr M P I'Anson
MISS F Iceton
Mr J.A.I ICETON
Mr P.I Iceton
Mstr N.J Iceton
MISS J Iley

Mr D Iley
Mr S.I Iley
MR W Iley
MR D.P Illingworth
Mr J.I Ingham
MR S Ingham
MSTR S Ingham
Mr K. Ingledew
Mr M Ingledew
MR A Ings
Mstr M.J. Inman
Mr A.R.I Innes
MR M J Instone
Mstr R P Instone
Mr P Ireland
MR T.J Irvine
Mr L.I Irving
Mr K.W.I Irwin
MR C Iveson
Mr D.I Iveson
Ivison
Miss K Ivison
Mr A Ivison
Mstr A Ivison
Miss K A Jackson
MR Jackson
MR B Jackson
Mr C Jackson
Mr D Jackson
Mr D.R.J Jackson
MR G.D Jackson
MR G.D.J Jackson
MR M Jackson
Mr M.J Jackson
Mr P A Jackson
Mr P R Jackson
Mr P.G Jackson
Mr P.J Jackson
Mr R.M.J Jackson
MR S C Jackson
Mr S.P.J Jackson
Mr T Jackson
Mrs L Jackson
Mstr P.B Jackson
Mr A.J.J Jaffray
MR P Jaffray
MRS J Jaffray
Mr H James
Mr L.J James
Mr P.J James
Mr S James
Mstr S.J James
Mr A.D. Jameson
Mr B.J Jameson
Mr P.J Jameson
MSTR M.A JAMESON
MSTR N.E JAMESON
MR J Jamieson
Mr M Jamieson
Mr A.D Jardine
Mr J.P.J Jarvis
MSTR G C Jarvis
Mr A.J Jasinek
Mr P.R.J Jeffels
Mr C.J Jefferies
MR N M Jefferson
Mr N.J Jefferson
Mr W.V.J Jefferson
MR R Jeffery
Mr Jeffery
MR JEFFREY
Mr C.G Jeffrey
MR E W Jeffrey
Mr O.J Jeffrey
Mr C.J Jenkins
MR G Jenkins
MR J Jenkins
Mr M.P Jenkins
Mstr S.D.J Jenney
MR K Jennings
Mrs L.H. Jewkes
Mr B.J Jinks
MR M R Jinks
Mr D Job
Mr M.J.J Jobling
Mr R.J Jobling
Mstr P.R.J Jobling
Mr G.J John
Mstr D.J John
MR C Johns
Mr G.J Johns
MR K Johns
Mr P.R.J Johns
MSTR R Johns
MR A Johnson
MR A M Johnson

Mr A.J Johnson
MR B Johnson
Mr C M Johnson
Mr D Johnson
Mr G P Johnson
Mr H.J Johnson
Mr K Johnson
MR K E Johnson
Mr M.J Johnson
Mr M.K.J Johnson
MR N T Johnson
Mr P.A.J Johnson
Mr R Johnson
MR S N Johnson
Mr W.J Johnson
Mrs L.P.J Johnson
Mr G Johnston
MR K Johnston
Mstr A.J Johnston
MR A Johnstone
MSTR G Johnstone
MR Joly
JONES
MR A Jones
Mr A Jones
MR A J Jones
MR A.P Jones
Mr C M Jones
MR C.A Jones
MR D Jones
Mr D.A.J Jones
Mr D.J Jones
Mr E.J Jones
MR G Jones
Mr J.J Jones
Mr K.J Jones
MR M Jones
MR M E Jones
Mr M.E.J Jones
MR P J Jones
Mr P.J Jones
Mr P.J.J Jones
Mr R Jones
MR R E Jones
MR S Jones
MR S J Jones
Mr S W Jones
Mr W.H.J Jones
MSTR A Jones
MSTR M Jones
MSTR M.S.J Jones
MSTR P Jones
MSTR P R Jones
Mstr P.A.J Jones
Mstr P.B Jones
MISS K Jordan
Miss N.J Jordan
Mr A.J Jowers
MR A E Jowsey
Mr N.W.J Jowsey
MR M Joynes
Mr P.D.J Judd
MR D Julian
Mr T Walker Junior
Mr B Kane
Mr J Kane
MR M.J Kane
MR M Kavanagh
Mr S.K Kavanagh
Mstr S.K Kavanagh
Miss C M Kay
MISS K Kay
MISS R C Kay
MR C Kay
Mr G Kay
MR J Kay
Mr P.C.N Kay
Mr R.T.K Kay
Mr S Kay
MRS D Kay
MRS F Kay
S Kay
Mr G.K Keagle
MISS V.M Kearton
Mstr P.A Keating
Mr T.K Keay
MSTR KEAY
Mr C. Keebie
Mr C.J. Keebie
Mstr S.K Keegan
Mstr M.G.K Keeley
Mr A Keelty
Mr A Kell
MR B Kell
MSTR R.B Kell
MR B.M KELLEHER
MSTR L.M KELLEHER
Mr M P Kelley
Mstr D.M.K Kelley

Miss J.L.K Kelly
Mr A.D.K Kelly
Mr D.I.K Kelly
Mr J.P.K Kelly
Mr M.I.K Kelly
Mr M.P Kelly
MR P Kelly
Mr S B Kelly
Mr S.M Kelly
Mstr P.M.K Kelly
Mr C.K Kemp
Mr M Kemp
Miss L J Kennedy
MR G D Kennedy
MSTR A Kennedy
MSTR J Kennedy
Mr M.A.K Kent
Mr S.D.K Kent
Mr J.M.K Kenyon
D Kerr
MISS A Kerr
MR C Kerr
MSTR M.I Kerr
MSTR R.N Kerr
Mr C.C. Kerridge
Mr R. Kerridge
MSTR J H Kerridge
MR I Kerwin
Mr L.K Ketteringham
Mr T.K Ketteringham
MR.J Keynon
KHAN
Kidd
MR G T Kidd
MR I Kidd
Mr P A Kidd
MSTR A Kiddell
MR A Kidner
MSTR S Kidson
Mr A J Kindleysides
Miss J.K King
Mr A King
Mr B.J.K King
MR D F King
MR G P King
Mr J.K King
MR K King
MR M A King
Mr M.D.K King
Mr N King
Mr P M King
Mr R King
Mrs C King
Mstr C J King
Mstr J.E. King
Mr J Kirby
Mr P.K Kirby
MR S G Kirby
Mstr G.P.K Kirby
MSTR S Kirby
MR A Kirk
MR A.D Kirkbride
Mr C.M.K Kirkby
MR A Kirkham
MR N Kirkham
Mr R.J. Kirkwood
MR P Kirtley
MSTR D Kirtley
Mstr L.K Kirtley
Mr G.K Kirton
Mr T N Kirton
MRS P Kirton
MR C P Kish
Mr J A Kish
Mstr D Kitchen
Mr J M Kitching
Mr L.D. Kitching
Mr S.K Klincke
Mr B Knaggs
Mr D.K Kneeshaw
Mr D C Knight
Mr J.H.K Knight
Mr C G Knights
Mstr D.C.T. Knowles
MR P.N Koeppl
Mr J.H.K Kotch
Mr I.M.K Kraus
Mr P.W.K Kraus
Mr P Kulcsar
Mr V Kuvelker
Mr W G Kyle
Mr M.J. Labron
MR J Lacey
Mr M.G Lacey
Mr R.L Lacey
Mr S.J Lacey
MR D Lackenby
MR S Lackenby
MR D Laing

MR N Lake
MR P Lake
MSTR N J Lakeman
Miss A M Lamb
Mr G.A.L Lamb
Mr T Lamb
MR P Lambert
MR P J Lambert
Mstr G L Lambert
MSTR R P Lambert
Mr N.J. Lambson
Mstr G.L Lamming
MISS C Lanagan
MR P Lanagan
Mr T.L Lancaster
Mstr A. Lancaster
MSTR D Landin
MR A.L Lane
MR M Lane
Mr S.L Lane
Mr W.L Lane
Mrs E.A.L Lane
Ms P.L Lane
MSTR C Lane
Mstr J.L Lane
MR S Langford
Mstr S P Langshaw
MR P E Langstaff
MR A Lannon
Mr M.L Lappin
Mr K.L Large
Mr B.P. Larkin
Mr J Larkin
Mr M. Larkin
Mr R.L Larkman
Mrs W Larry
Mr I.D.L Larsen
MR J D Lavander
MSTR D Lavander
MSTR D S Lavander
Mr S.V.R Lavender
Mr A.M.I Laverick
Mr J.M. Laverick
Mr M Laverick
Mr P.L Laverick
MR S K Laverick
MISS K Lavery
MR B lavery
MRS C Lavery
Mstr S.L. Law
MR M W Lawrence
Mr M.A.L Lawrence
MR Lawrie
Miss A.L Laws
MR D Lawson
Mr D.L Lawson
MR I D Lawson
Mr I P Lawson
Mr M.L Lawson
Mrs P. Lawson
Mstr J.A.L Lawton
MR W Lax
Mr C.A.L Layton
Mstr D.I.L Layton
Mr A.L Lazenby
Mr J Lazenby
Mr S.L. Lazenby
MR J Leach
MR K R Leach
Mr S.L Leadbeater
Mr J Leadley
MRS L Leadley
MR J A Leafe
MSTR D Leafe
MISS J Leahy
Mr A.L Leahy
MR J Ledger
Ms J.E Ledwon
MR J Lee
Mr P.E.L Lee
MRS S Lee
MSTR S Lee
Mr B.L Leeson
Mr M.L Leeson
Mr B.L.L Lefevre
Mr D.W.I Legg
Mr J.L Legg
MR M Leggett
S.K Leggett
MR D Leighton
MR I Leighton
MR D Leisham
MSTR A Leisham
MR R Leishman
Miss K.M. Leitch
MR R Lennard
MR M Lennox
MR P Lennox
MR S Lennox

Mr C.S.L Lester
MR D Lester
Mr M.L Lethbridge
Mr M.L Levitt
MR J D Lewis
Mr P.L Lewis
Mr R.T.L Lewis
MSTR C J Lewis
Miss H.E.L Lickess
MR M J Liddle
Mstr M.D.I Liddle
Mstr S.T.L Liddle
MR J Liggett
Mr C.L Lilley
MR S F Lillie
Mr J K Linberg
Mr C.E.L Lindberg
MR J R Lindberg
Mstr C.L Lindberg
Miss V.L Lindridge
Mr M.P.L Lindridge
MR S B Lindsay
Mr N.B.L Lines
Miss J.M. Ling
Mr J Lings
Mrs T M Lings
MISS A LINKLATER
MR D W Linklater
MR S Linley
Mr D.L Linton
MR S P List
Mr D.L Lister
Mr G Lister
Mr G.J Lister
MR J J Lithgo
MISS K E Little
Mr P. Little
Mr D.A. Littlefair
Mr T.W. Littlefair
MR M R Littlemore
Mr J.L Liversidge
S.L Livingston
MISS J Livingstone
Miss N. Livingstone
Mr A.L Livingstone
Mr F.L Livingstone
Mrs S.L Livingstone
MSTR M Livingstone
Mr A.R. Llewellyn
Mr D.J.L Llewellyn
Mr N.L Llewellyn
Mr T.L Lloyd
Mr M Lochrane
Mstr J H Lochrane
Miss J.L.L Lochrie
MISS N J Lochrie
MR A Lochrie
Mr I.S.L Lochrie
MR P Lochrie
Mr S.L Lochrie
Miss Z Locke
Mr T Locke
Ms P Locke
Mr A.L Locker
Mr D.J.L Locker
MR P W Lockett
Lockey
Mr A.L Lockhead
Mr B.D.L Lockney
MSTR A Lockwood
MSTR M Lockwood
Mstr N. Lockwood
Mr M Lofthouse
Mr M R Lofthouse
Mr P.L Lofts
MR J S P Loftus
Mr A.J.L Lombard
Mr P.R.L Long
MR I Longsdale
Mr D.A.L Longstaff
Mr G.L Longstaff
MR J P Longstaff
Mr J.L Longstaff
Mr A.J.L Loraine
Mr M.J.L Loraine
Mr D.L Lord
Mstr S.L Lord
MR D G Loughborough
MSTR G Loughborough
Mr A.L Loughran
Mr K.C.L Loughran
Mr A Lovatt
MR LOW
Miss K.F.A Lowe
MISS P Lowe
MR K C Lowery
Mr P Lowery
Mstr A S Lowery
Mr R.C.L Lowes

Miss E.L.L Lownsbrough
Mr D.M Lownsbrough
Mrs S.L Lownsbrough
Mr D.L Lucas
MR G M Luck
MR P J Luck
Mr S Ludley
Mr C.B.L Luke
Mr P.B.L Luke
MR A W Lumb
Mr D.L Lumb
Ms K.L.L Lumley
MR N S Lund
Mr J.M. Lyden
MR P Lynam
Mr B Lynas
MR C P Lynas
Mr P W Lynas
MR R M Lynas
MR R.S Lynas
Mr A.J.L Lynch
MR P Lynch
MR R M Lynch
Mr S.L Lynch
MSTR A D Lynch
MSTR M S Lynch
MSTR S G Lyon
Mr D Lyonette
MR Lyth
Mr J.W.L Lyth
MR P L Lyth
MR N Macaulay
MR S.N MacDermid
MR R S Macdonald
MR A J Macgregor
Mr I. MacGregor
MR M Macgregor
MR P MacGREGOR
MR R H MacGREGOR
Mr E.J.M Mack
MR P Mack
MR C J Mackay
MR I Mackay
MR W J Mackay
MSTR M Mackay
Mr C.W.M Mackey
MR P Mackey
MR R Mackey
MR R.M Mackey
Mr S Mackey
Mstr R.J.M Mackey
MR A Mackin
Mr R Mackin
Mr S Mackin
MR S P Mackin
Mr C.M MacKinnon
Mr N.M MacPherson
MR I D Madden
MISS N Maguder
MR M J Maguire
MS D M Maguire
Mr P.W.M Maidstone
Mr G.M Mains
MSTR B Mains
Mr C S Makin
MR C M Mallaby
Mr D.M.M Mallaby
Mr N.M Mallaby
MR R Mallaby
MR R.L.M Mallory
Mr J S Maloney
Mr G.J.M Manders
Mr M.M Manders
Mr W.M Manders
Mstr D.M Manging
Miss L.J.M Mann
Mr L.M Mann
Mr P J Manns
Mstr I K Manns
Mr A.E.M Mansell
MR P Manton
MSTR C P Manton
MSTR P D Manton
MR S A Mapplebeck
MSTR E J Mapplebeck
MSTR N R Mapplebeck
Mr A.M March
MR G L Marley
D. Marples
MR I Marr
Mr P.D.M Marr
Mr S.J. Marr
Mrs A.M Marr
MR C Marram
MR C Marron
MR J Marron
MR J R Marron
MR K Marsahall
Mr A.J.M Marsay

Mr K.T.M Marsay
MR S MARSAY
Mr H.L Marsden
Mr M.J.E Marsden
Mr P.M Marsh
Miss C.M Marshall
Mr A Marshall
MR A.P Marshall
Mr G Marshall
Mr M.W Marshall
Mr S. Marshall
Mr S.M Marshall
MR B J Martin
Mr C.M Martin
Mr P.D.M Martin
Mrs J.M Martin
MSTR D Martin
Mr A. Mash
MR Mason
Mr B.P.M Mason
Mr C N Mason
MR D J Mason
Mr D.M Mason
MR G MASON
Mr G.M Mason
Mr L Mason
Mr M.M Mason
Mr R Mason
MR S C Mason
Mr S.M Mason
Mstr D Mason
Mr J.M Masterman
Mr C D Matthews
MR J MATTHEWS
Mr J M Matthews
Mr L.R. Matthews
Mr N.M Matthews
Mr R Matthews
MR R Matthews
MR W.E MATTHEWS
Mrs M.M Matthews
Mstr S M Matthews
Mr D.S.M Maude
Mr K.S.M Maude
Mr J Maughan
Mr J.M Maughan
MR P D Maughan
Mr R.M Maughan
Mr A.C.M Mawson
Mr A.J.M Mawson
Mr J.C.M Mawson
Mr M J Mawson
Mr M S Mawson
MISS K J Mawston
Mr R. Maxwell
MR A L May
Mr P J May
MR W May
Mr P.A. Mayes
Mrs A.J. Mayes
MSTR A T Mayhew
Mr W.M Mazzey
Mr J.M Mcaskill
MR A G McAuliffe
MR G McAuliffe
MRS J McAuliffe
MR G McAvoy
MRS C J McAvoy
MSTR P McAvoy
Mr D McCabe
MR P McCabe
MSTR P McCabe
MR J H McCable
Mr D A McCallan
Mr J.M McCann
Mrs D.M McCann
MR M McCardle
MR A McCarrick
Mr D.M McCarthy
Mr N A McCarthy
MR P McCarthy
Mr P.A.M McCarthy
Mr P.W.M McCarthy
Mr K McCartin
Mr D.W.M McCauley
Mr M.S.M McCauley
Mr I.M McClelland
Mstr C McClennan
MR P McClure
MASTER P McCluskey
MR J P McCluskey
MR P A McCluskey
MSTR P A McCluskey
MR J McConnell
MR M McConnell
Miss R.M McCormack
Mr J.C.M McCormack
Mstr S.M McCormack
MISS L E McCormick

MR McCormick
MR T McCormick
MR F McCoy
MSTR E McCoy
Mr W.M McCreesh
D McCULLAGH
MR S McCulloch
Mrs E.M McCulloch
Mr E G McCulloch
Mr A.M McDermott
MSTR K McDermott
MR S McDermottroe
MR A McDonald
Mr C.T.M McDonald
Mr J J McDonald
Mr K.M McDonald
Mr M.R.M McDonald
Mr N McDonald
MSTR A W J McDonald
Mr A.M McDonough
Mr J McDonough
Mr L.D.M McDonough
Mr T.A.M McDonough
Mr McDougall
Mstr M.W. McElvaney
Mr M.M McFadden
Miss M.M McFarlane
Mstr M.M McFarlane
Mstr S.M McFarlane
Mr L. McFaul
Mr B.M McFee
MR K McGarrity
Mr M.K.M McGeary
Mr M.D.M McGee
Mr P McGee
Mr W.J.M McGee
Mstr E McGee
Miss D.M McGhee
Mr R.M McGillicuddy
Mstr S.M McGillicuddy
Mstr A McGinley
MR D.A MCGLADDERY
MR G.M MCGLAD-DERY
MSTR D.P MCGLAD-DERY
MSTR N.J MCGLAD-DERY
Mstr A.J. McGlade
MR I.J McGlone
Mr D.M McGoohan
MISS G McGough
Mr I.M McGough
MR M P McGough
MSTR A McGough
MSTR M McGough
MR J P McGovern
Mr J.C.M McGovern
Mr P. McGovern
Mr S.J.M McGovern
MRS C McGovern
MR A D McGowan
Mr D.A.M McGowan
MR P T McGravey
MSTR M P McGravey
Mr A. McGuigan
MR A McGuiness
Mstr P McGuinness
MR P McGuire
Mr T.P McGuire
Mr D.M McKay
Mr G.M McKeown
Mr A.M McKeown
Mr S.M McKeown
Mr I McKereth
Mr G McKinlay
MR A McKinnon
MR D McKittrick
MRS S McLauchlan
MR C Mclean
MR G.M McLean
Mr K.M McLean
MR L Mclean
MSTR D McLean
MSTR S McLean
MR D R A McLeod
Mr L. McLoughan
MR B McLoughlin
MR M McLoughlin
MR A S McLurg
MISS H McMahon
MR B McMahon
Mr J.M McMahon
Mr N.R.M McMahon
Mr I.S McMann
Mr M.M McMann
Ms M.M McMillan
MR D McMullen
MR D.W McMullen

MR D McNally
MR L J McNally
Mr B.M McNamara
Miss E.L.M McNeil
Mr C.M McNeil
Mr M.T.M McNeil
Mr S.M.M McNeil
Mrs C.M McNeil
MR McNeilly
MSTR A J McNichol
MISS C McNicholas
Mr M.M McNulty
Mr K.P MConnell
MR C T McPartland
MR K McPartland
MR G McPhail
MR I McPoland
Mr S.M McQuillan
Mr K.J.M McTaggart
Mstr C.M McVeigh
Mr A.M Mead
Mr D.A.M Mead
Mr R.M Mead
Mr D.M Meadows
Mr J Meager
Miss K.M Medd
Mr G.M Medd
MR J Mee
Miss K.E.M Meek
Mr B.J.M Meek
Mr C.R.M Meek
MR P C Meekings
Mr J.P.M Melling
Miss C.L.M Mellor
Mstr D.P.M Mellor
MR M D Mendoza
Mr C. Mendum
Mr J.A.M Mendum
Mr J.M Mennell
Mrs J.M Mennell
MR Menzies
MR G Mercer
MR M A Meredith
MR P Meredith
MSTR C D Meskill
Mr N.A.M Metcalf
MR A.J Metcalfe
MR S Metcalfe
MR M Meynell
MR R Middlemas
Mr K.M Middlemiss
Mr D Middleton
Mr D.M Middleton
Mr M.W.M Middleton
Mr P Middleton
Mstr J.D.M Middleton
Mstr M Middleton
Mr S.C.M Millar
MR B Miller
MR G Miller
MR I G Miller
MR I S Miller
MR P B Miller
Mr C.A.M Millington
Mr D Millington
Mr M J Millington
MR A D Mills
Mr I Mills
Mr K.M Mills
MR M.J Mills
Mstr C Mills
Mr A.G.M Millward
Mr D Millward
Mr K.M Millward
Mr R.S.M Millward
Mr S.L.M Millward
Mstr S.M Millward
MSTR A J Milne
Mr S.M Milner
MSTR J Milner
Mr G Minford
Mr G.S. Minikin
Mr C.J.M Minnighan
MR A T Mitchell
MR R G H Mitchell
Mstr A.R Mitchell
MR R Moffoot
Mr B A Mohan
Mr C. Mohan
Mr F.M Mohan
Mr M.M Molloy
Mstr Moloney
MR J Monaco
MSTR C Monaco
Mr H.M Monaghan
Mr I.J. Monkhouse
Miss A J Monks
Mr P.M Monks

Mr N Monty
MRS L Moody
MSTR D M Moody
MR D Moon
MR P H Mooney
Miss S.A.M Moore
Mr D B G Moore
Mr H.M Moore
Mr J.M Moore
Mr K.R. Moore
Mr M.J.M Moore
Mr P A Moore
Mr S Moore
Mr S.M Moore
Mr W.M Moore
Mstr K.M Moore
MR T Moran
Mr A Morgan
Mr C.M Morgan
Mr D.A.M Morgan
Mr F.M Morgan
Mr G Morgan
Mr P.M Morgan
Mr R.W.M Morgan
Mr K.T.M Morley
Mr M.K.J Morley
MR S R Morley
Mr J.M Morning
Mr M.C.M Morrell
MR D.N Morren
MR K MORREN
MSTR A MORREN
Mr R.J.M Morrill
Mr C.J.M Morris
MR L Morris
Mr M.I.M Morris
Mr P Morris
Mr S Morris
Mrs D P Morris
MSTR P N Morris
Mstr P.M Morris
Mr D.M Morrison
Mr G.A.M Morrison
MR I B Morrison
Mr M.M Morrison
Mr P.A.M Morrison
Mstr D.M Morrison
Mr S.E.M. Morrison-Peacock
Mstr A.M Morrissey
MR A Morrow
Mr B Morrow
Mr S.M Morte
Mr J Morten
MSTR K Morten
MR T Mortimer
MR A Morton
Mr P Moses
Mr P Moss
Mr A.K.M Mount
Mr T J Mountain
MR P MOYLAN
Mstr C.M Mozley
Mr A.D.M Mudd
Mr A Muddiman
Mr J Muddiman
MR Muir
MR MULDOON
Mr D Mulholland
MR S P Mulholland
Mr F.M Mullen
Mr P D Mullen
Miss D M Mullins
MR L D Mullins
Mr P.M Mullins
Mr G Mulvaney
Mr D.M Murdoch
MR C S Murphy
Mr D Murphy
Mr G Murphy
Mr K Murphy
Mr M A Murphy
Mr P.E.M Murphy
Mr P.G. Murphy
Mr S Murphy
Mr S.M Murphy
Mstr A Murphy
MSTR B Murphy
Mr A. Murray
Mr B Murray
Mr C. Murray
Mr D.M Murray
Mr J.M Murray
Mr M.I.M Murray
Mr P.R.M Murray
Mrs K L Murray
Mstr D.M Murray
Mr G Musgrave

Mr L Musson
Mr S Musson
Mr S.J.P. Musson
Mr S.M Mustard
MISS J Myers
MR E Myers
Mr P A Myers
Mstr D Myers
Mstr c Mylan
Mr B.N Naisbitt
MR M Nassau
Mr M.N Nawaz
MR A G Naylor
Mr J.N Naylor
Mr M.D.N Naylor
Mr B.J.N Neal
Mr D M Neal
MASTER NEALE
Miss T A Neil
MR D Nellist
MR S Nellist
MSTR C Nellist
Mr I.C.N Nelson
MR S Nelson
Mstr C.N Nelson
MSTR S P Nelson
MR D.A Nesbitt
MR Nevison
Mr D.N Newbould
MR B J Newman
Mr J M Newman
Mr P S Newman
Mr A.N Newton
Mr J Newton
Mr P.N Newton
Mr S.N Newton
MSTR C E Newton
MSTR C J Newton
Mr C.W.N Nichol
MR T J Nichol
Mr K.N Nicholas
Mr W.N Nicholas
MSTR J.P NICHOLAS
MR S Nicholls
Mr G.N Nicholls
MR R A Nichols
Miss L.N Nicholson
Mr C.J.N Nicholson
MR D Nicholson
Mr D J Nicholson
MR F Nicholson
Mr L.N Nicholson
Mr J.R.N Nicholson
Mr R Nicholson
Mr D.N Nixon
Mr H.N Nixon
Mr K Nixon
MR P M Nixon
MR S J Nixon
MSTR S.J Nixon
MR C. Noble
Mr C.N Noble
Mr K.N Noble
Mr T. Noble
Mr D.N Nolan
Mr J.D Nolan
Mr M L Nolan
Mr A.C.N Norman
Mr B.L. Norman
Mr P Norman
Mr S. Norman
Mstr J.A.N Norman
Mr P.G.N Norminton
Mr D Norris
Miss A Norton
Mr M R Norton
Mr M.J.N Noteyoung
Mr K Nudd
Mr S.M. Nugent
MSTR G.J Nugent
Mr E.R.N Nunn
Mr S.R.N Nunn
Mr M.K. Nurk
MISS M D O'Brien
MISS S N C O'Brien
Mr C.R.O O'Brien
Mr G.O O'Brien
Mr J.O O'Brien
Miss J.A.O O'Brien
MR C C O'CONNOR
Mr B.O O'Connor
Mr D.O O'Connor
MR L O'CONNOR
Mr M.A.O O'Connor
Mr R.J.O O'Connor
Mr R.O O'Connor
Mr T.F.P O'Connor

MSTR J C O'Donnel
Mr A O'Donnell
Mr D.J.O O'Hagan
Mstr M.O O'Hara
Mr K J O'Keefe
Mrs L A O'Keefe
MR C J O'Neil
MR G P O'Neil
Mr M.O O'Neil
Mstr L C O'Neil
MR A O'Neill
MR C O'Neill
MR M J O'Neill
Mr M.O O'Neill
Mr P O'Neill
Mr P.O O'Neill
Mr S C O'Neill
Mstr M.O O'Neill
Mr C.O O'Rourke
Mr N.F.O O'Rourke
Mstr C.O O'Rourke
Mstr M.J O'Rourke
MR N O'Brien
MR A.C O'Donnell
Mr M.O Oakes
MSTR M.D Obern
Mr K.O Ogleby
MR S J Oglesby
Mr C.O Old
MR G Old
MR D A Oliver
Mr D.O Oliver
MR E Oliver
Mr G Oliver
Mr M.R Oliver
Mr R.I.O Oliver
Mr R.O Oliver
Mstr A.O Oliver
Mr J Olley
MR S Olley
Mr J.D Ollis
Mr S Ollis
Mr P.A.O Olone
Mr S. Ord.
MR D M Ormesby
Mr S.O Orritt
Mr A.W.O Osborne
MR G Osborne
MR J A Osborne
MR M A Osborne
MR P D Osborne
MR S Osborne
MRS J Osborne
Mr J.V.O Outhwaite
Mr A.J.O Overton
Mr L.M. Ovington
MR B Owen
MR K Owens
Mr N.J.O Owens
MR P J Oxby
MR D Oxley
Mr G Oxley
MR P Oxley
Packer
MR A J Paczynski
Mr C.N.P Padgett
Mr A Page
Mr D.P Paget
Mstr K.L.P Pain
Mr R.E.P Painter
Mstr J A Paleschi
MR A Pallagi
MR J Pallister
Mr J.C.P Pallister
Mr K.P Palm
MR G L Palmer
MRS K Palmer
MRS A Pape
Mrs L.P Pape
MSTR B Pape
Mr K.L. Parish
MR M PARISH
MR PARK
Mr A.S. Park
Mr S.J. Park
Mr W.J.P Park
Mstr C.P Park
Mr A.S.P Parker
Mr C.L.P Parker
MR D Parker
Mr D.P Parker
Mr F.W.P Parker
MR J Parker
Mr K A Parker
MR N J Parker
MR S Parker
MSTR C Parker
Mstr F.T.P Parker

Mr A.P Parkes
Mr M.P Parkes
Mr S.P Parkes
Mr M.S.P Parkin
Mr R.D.P Parkin
Mstr I.S.P Parks
Mstr P.P Parks
MR M A Parnaby
Mr R.J.P Parnaby
MR C J Parrott
MR E Parry
Mr G.R Parry
Mr L.W.P Parry
MSTR K.P Parry
MISS K L Parsons
MR A I Parsons
MR D Partington
MRS J Partington
MR A Partleton
Mr A J Parvin
Mr J.P Patchett
MR D J Paterson
Mr P.P Paterson
MR A D Patterson
MR C Patterson
MR G Patterson
Mr G.P Patterson
Mr L.G. Patterson
MR R M Patterson
Mr R.D.P Patterson
Mr P.P Pattinson
Mr D Patton
Mr A Patton
MR G N Patton
MR I Patton
Mstr M Patton
Mr A.P Paul
MR K Paul
MR A J Paxton
Mr A.P Paylor
MR J Paylor
MSTR S D Paylor
Mr D.P Payne
MR G W Payne
MR W H Payne
Mr A.B.P Peacock
Mr A.J.P Peacock
Mr B Peacock
MR D Peacock
MR D.H Peacock
Mr G Peacock
Mr I.P Peacock
Mr J R Peacock
MR M Peacock
MR M A Peacock
Mr P.A.P Peacock
Mr P.P Peacock
MR R Peacock
Mr S.P Peacock
Mr S.P.P Peacock
Mr T.I.P Peacock
MSTR J M Peacock
Mstr M.S.P Peacock
MR S Peake
MR J Pearce
Mrs A.P Pearce
Miss R.K.P Pearey
Mr S.P Pearey
Mstr B.J.P Pearey
MR I R Pearley
MISS C L Pearson
MISS J A Pearson
Miss R.P Pearson
Mr Pearson
MR A J E Pearson
Mr B.R.P Pearson
MR C Pearson
Mr C.G.P Pearson
MR D Pearson
Mr D.J.P Pearson
Mr D.P Pearson
MR J Pearson
MR M Pearson
Mr M.A.P Pearson
Mr M.J.P Pearson
Mr S Pearson
MR S R Pearson
Mrs J.P Pearson
Mstr A Pearson
MSTR J M Pearson
Mstr N Pearson
Miss A.P Peart
Mr D.P Peart
MR S Pease
Mr L.C.P Peckitt
Mr G.A.P Peel
Mr L.J.P Peel
MR M Peel
Mr R.F. Peevor

APPENDIX 5

Mr S.P Peggs
Mr I.L.P Peirson
Mr R J Peirson
Mr D.G. Pell
Mr M.D.P Pell
Mstr J.M. Pell
Mr M.E Pelling
MR S Pendlington
Mr M.P Pengilley
Mr C.P Penketh
Miss V Pennick
Miss S E Pennock
Mr D T Pennock
Mstr S J Pennock
MR M G Perks
MRS S Perks
Mr R.M.P Perrie
MR J.T Perrott
MSTR J Perrott
Mr M.P Peters
MR M Petford
Mr G.A.P Peverley
Mr A.D.P Phelps
Mr B.P Phillips
Mr C.P Phillips
MR D H Phillips
Mr E.C.P Phillips
Mr J.P Phillips
Mr M.P Phillips
Mstr G.J.P Phillips
Mstr G.M.P Phoenix
MR S Pickard
Mr S.P Pickard
Miss J.P Picken
Mr A.J.P Pickering
Mr D R Pickering
Mr E.P Pickering
Mr J.G.P Pickering
Mr P.A.P Pickering
MR G Pickup
MR M J Pickup
MR S Pickup
MASTER PIDGEON
Mr G Pidgeon
Mr G.P Pierce
MR G.F Pierre
MR K E Pierson
Mr A M Pinchbeck
Mr N. Pinder
Mr R Pink
MR S R Pinkney
Mr S.P Pirrie
Mr D.K Place
MR D Plank
MR I Plank
Mr K J Plant
Mstr M.P Plant
Mr L.J. Pledger
MISS A Pletts
MRS C M Pletts
Mr J.J.P Plews
MR M Plews
Miss J. Poad
Miss H Polasek
Mr D Polasek
MR C E Pollitt
MR I C Pollitt
Mr I.C. Pollitt
Mr T.P Pollock
MISS C L Poole
Mr G P Poole
MR L P Poole
Mr M.P Poole
MR K Pooley
MR M Pooley
MSTR P Popple
MR A Porch
MR S A Porch
MR I Porley
MR K Porley
Mr J.P Porritt
Mr K.P Porritt
Mr S G Porritt
Mr S.J.P Porritt
MSTR D R Porritt
MSTR I Porritt
MSTR M E Porritt
Mr C R Portas
Mr D Portas
Mr M.D.P Portas
Mstr T R Portas
MR C Porteous
Mr D.M.P Porteous
Mr I.P Porter
Mr D.P Potter
MR M Potter
Mr M P Potter
Mr S.D.P Potter
Mstr C.P Potter

MR M.J Pottinger
Miss V J Potts
Mr B Potts
Mr P B Potts
Mstr M J Potts
Mr C Poulter
Mr R.P Pounder
MR S Pounder
Mstr N.R.P Pounder
Mr K.P Povey
Mr N.A.P Povey
MASTER G E Powell
MR D W Powell
MR J Powell
MR J.M Powell
Mr L.D.P Powell
Mr S.J Powell
Mstr L Powell
Mstr L.A Powell
Mstr S Powell
Mstr C.P Power
Mr M.P Powls
MSTR D Powner
MSTR S Powner
Mr R Pratt
MR S Pratt
MR G PRESGRAVE
MR D Preston
Mr C.M.P Price
MR D Price
Mr F J Price
MR G Price
Mr S.P Price
Mstr P R Price
Miss J. Prichard
MR R Priddy
Mr A.E.P Pritchard
Mrs L.E.P Pritchard
Mstr P.K.P Pritchard
Mr W Prosser
Mr D Proud
MSTR M Proud
MR B.R PROVAN
MR M Pryce
Mr J.P Pryke
Mstr L Pugalin
Mr M.P Pugalis
Miss C.M.P Pugh
Mr B Pugh
MR J Pugh
Mr S C Pugh
Mr J.P Pulling
Mstr J.W.P Pulling
Mstr R.J.P Pulling
Mstr S.R.P Purcifer
Mr S.P Purkis
Miss A.J.P Purvis
Miss V.L.P Putson
Mr A.N.P Putson
Mr B.M.P Putson
MR D Putson
Mr C.P Pyle
Mr A Quinn
Mr R Quinn
Miss S.R Raby
Mr J.B.R Raby
MR P Raby
Mstr C.A.R Raby
Mstr M Raby
MR A B Race
MR S Race
Mr K.R Raddigan
MR S Raddigan
Mr F.R Ragan
Mr D.R Raine
Mr G.J.R Raine
Mr P D Raine
Mr P.N.R Raine
Mr S.R Raine
Mr N.R Raitano
MR MA Raitino
Mr D Ralph
Mr P.N.R Ralston
Mr J.M.R Ramm
Mstr A.L.R Ramsay
MR M Ramsdale
MR P Ramsdale
MR A Randall
Mr C.P. Rathbone
Mr G.D. Rawden
Mr W.H.R Rawlings
Mr D J Raybould
Mr B.P.R Rayner
Mr P.M.R Rayner
Mr S.R Rayner
Mr G.M.R Raynor
Mstr D C Raynor
Miss T.M.R Rayson
MR W.P Rayson

MR R Rea
MR T M Rea
MR V Rea
Mr A.R Readman
Mr M.R Readman
Mrs A.R Readman
MR D Reaney
MR P Reason
MR D Reay
Mr P. Redling
Mr Redman
MR J E Redman
MR B Reed
Mr D Reed
MR G Reed
MR M Reed
MR N Reed
Mstr D.M.R Reed
MSTR N Reed
Mr B.R Rees
MR C Rees
Mr L.R Rees
Mr J.R Reeve
MR J N Reeves
Mr M.J Reeves
Mr K.R Regan
MR M Reiblein
MSTR C Reiblein
Mr P.R Reidy
Mstr S Relph
MR P A Remmer
Mr L.R Revely
Mstr C.E.R Revely
MR M Rhea
Mr T.J.R Rhoden
MR N Rhodes
Mr A J Rhucroft
Mr C D Rhucroft
Mr M J Rhucroft
Mr M.D Rice
Mr A.R Richards
Mr D. Richards
Mr D.R Richards
Mr I.K.R Richards
Mr K.D.P Richards
Mr M E J Richards
MR P Richards
Mr P.D.R Richards
Mr Richardson
Mr A.B.R Richardson
Mr A.R Richardson
Mr B.J.R Richardson
MR C Richardson
Mr C.R Richardson
Mr D Richardson
Mr G.B.R Richardson
Mr J.R Richardson
Mr K.R Richardson
MR L R Richardson
Mr M.R Richardson
Mr P J Richardson
MR P.A. Richardson
Mr P.H.R Richardson
Mr R A Richardson
MR T Richardson
MRS T Richardson
MSTR M Richardson
MSTR M.A. Richardson
MSTR N Richardson
MSTR R Richardson
MR J A Riches
MSTR G A Riches
MR M.P Richie
Mr M J Richings
Mr J.R Richmond
MR C Rickaby
Mr K.G.R Rickards
Mr M. Riddle
Mstr P.J. Riddle
Mr C.J.R Rider
Mr R.R Rider
MR N O Ridgway
Miss S.R Ridley
Mr J.D Ridley
Mr S.R Ridley
Mr G Ridsdale
Mr G.E.R Ridsdale
Mr P.A.R Ridsdale
MR J J Riley
Mr R.M.R Riley
Mr M.R Ripley
MR S Ripley
Mstr R.R Ripley
Mr L.J.R Risker
MSTR A Ritchie
Mr C.R Roach
MR A Roberts
Mr C J Roberts
Mr G.R Roberts

Mr I Roberts
Mr I.R Roberts
MR J Roberts
Mr J. Roberts
Mr M Roberts
MR P Roberts
Mr P.G.R Roberts
Mr P.R Roberts
Mr S B Roberts
Mr S.R Roberts
Mstr S M Roberts
Mr Robertson
Mr A.W.R Robertson
Mr J.M.F Robertson
Mr S.R Robertson
MASTER D.N Robinson
Miss J.R Robinson
Miss K.L.R Robinson
Mr A.S.R Robinson
MR D P Robinson
Mr D P Robinson
Mr D.P Robinson
Mr E.R Robinson
MR G L Robinson
MR H Robinson
MR J Robinson
MR J B Robinson
Mr J L Robinson
MR K A Robinson
MR K B Robinson
Mr K M Robinson
Mr K.R Robinson
Mr M Robinson
Mr M D Robinson
MR M P Robinson
Mr M.J.B. Robinson
Mr N Robinson
Mr N.D.R Robinson
MR P Robinson
Mr P Robinson
Mr P.T.R Robinson
MR R ROBINSON
MR S J Robinson
Mr S.W.R Robinson
MR T P Robinson
Mr V G Robinson
MRS J J Robinson
Ms M.R Robinson
Mstr A.B.R Robinson
Mstr B Robinson
MSTR C J Robinson
Mstr C.R Robinson
MSTR D Robinson
MSTR P Robinson
Mstr S.K. Robinson
Mr A Robson
Mr A. Robson
MR C Robson
MR D N Robson
Mr G Robson
MR G Robson
MR I.J Robson
Mr I.L.R Robson
MR J D Robson
Mr M.S.R Robson
MSTR P Robson
MR P J Robson
MR R K Robson
MSTR S Robson
Mr G J Roche
Mr D.R Rock
MR C M Rodgers
MR P J Rodgers
Mr T.J.R Rodgers
Mr B.R Rodgerson
Mr A.L.R Rogers
Mr E.W.R Rogers
Mr P.R Rogers
Mstr N.W.R Rogers
Miss S.R Rogerson
Mr C Rolfe
MR Rooney
MR D Rooney
Mr K.R Rooney
Mr M.R Rooney
MR W R Rooney
MR J R Roper
Mr P.R Roper
Mr S.R Roper
Mstr P.S.R Roper
MISS A Rose
MR S Rose
Mr M.S.R Rosemurgey
Mr A Ross
Mstr D.R Roth
MR A J Rothwell
Mr S.R Rouse
Mr P.R Routh
Mr P.R Routledge

Mstr S.P.R Rovardi
Mr D J Rowbottom
Mr C.R Rowe
MR K Rowe
Mr J. Rowney
Mr P.R Rowney
Mr J.R Rudd
Mr K D Rudd
Mr S Rudd
Mr S.R Rudd
Mstr J.R Rudd
Mr A.G.R Ruddick
Mr M.E.R Ruddick
Miss L Ruff
Mr N.J.R Ruff
Mstr M.R Ruff
Mstr C.R Rugg
MR A Ruisnek
RUSSELL
Mr A.D.R Russell
Mr H.J. Russell
MR M Russell
Mr M P Russell
MR N Russell
MR P Russell
Mr S.J Russell
MSTR S W Russell
Mr A. Rutherford
MR J J Rutherford
Miss E.R Rutland
Mr G.A.R Rutland
Mr P.R Rutland
Mrs B.A.R Rutland
Mr Mr Rutley
Mr A.R Ryan
MR G Ryan
Mr J.R Ryan
Mr N.A.R Ryan
MR M H Rymer
Mr T.G.S Sabey
Mr A.S Sadler
Mr K Sadler
Mr M.W.S Sadler
MSTR S Sadler]
MR C Sainsbury
Mr M.S Sainsbury
MR L Salmon
MR P Salter
Mr J.S Salvati
MR M Sancto
MR SANDBACH
Mr C.S Sandbach
Mr D.C Sandbach
Mr C.S Sanders
MR M.W.S Sanders
MR S Sanders
MR G SANDERSON
MR P G Sanderson
Mr C.S Sandford
Mrs V.J.S Sandford
MR P.A Sargeant
MSTR S Saunders
MR G Savage
MR R Savage
MSTR R Savage
MR K Savill
MR S A Savory
Mr F.A.S Sawdon
Mr M.J Sawyer
Mr P.G.S Sawyer
MR A J Sayer
Mr Mr. Sayers
MR P S Sayers
Mr A.W.J Scaife
MR M.J Scales
Mr M Scanlan
MISS H SCOTT
Mr C.P.S Scott
Mr C.S Scott
MR D Scott
Mr D G Scott
Mr D. Scott
Mr G. Scott
Mr J.J.S Scott
Mr M.D.S Scott
MR W M Scott
Mstr A.J.S Scott
MSTR C M Scott
MSTR S Scott
MR Scuffmam
Mr D. Scuillion
Mr L.S Scurr
Mr B.J.S Seaman
MR N A Seaman
MSTR A P Seaman
Mr M.S Seddon
Mr K.S Sedgwick
MR S.J Sedgwick
MR S.N Seed

Mr G.S Seetree
Mr J Segell
MR J Sellers
MR N Sellstorm
MR T Walker Senior
Mr D.S Serginson
Mr A.S Serrechia
Mr A.J. Severn
Mr Sexton
MR K Shackleton
Mr J.S Shakeshaft
Mr J.D.S Sharkey
Mr B.S Sharp
Mr J.S Sharp
Mr C.A.S Sharpe
MR M P Sharpe
Mstr A.C. Sharpe
Mr B.S.S Sharratt
Mr C.G.S Shaw
Mr H.W.S Shaw
MR I R Shaw
MR J Shaw
MR M Shaw
Mr R.A. Shaw
Mr R.A.S Shaw
Mstr A.S Shaw
Mstr M.S Shaw
Mstr T A Shaw
Mr S.S Sheard
MR R P Sheavills
MR M.J Sheffield
MR C P Shepard
Mr J.W.S Shepherd
Mr C.R.S Sheridan
MR D.A SHERIDAN
MR J Sherrington
Mr K.S Sherrington
MR A.K Sherwood
Mr A Shield
Mr N Shield
Mr G.R.S Shields
MR J Shields
Mr P.S Shields
Mr Shildrick
Mr M A Shilham
MR B Shipley
MSTR J M Shipley
Miss S.S Short
Mstr G.S Short
MSTR K.L SHORT
Mr A.P.S Shutt
Mr C.P. Sibson
Mr D.M. Sibson
MR G Siddle
MR A S Sidgwick
Mr P R Sidgwick
Mr G Silcox
MR D K Silk
MR B.F SILL
MSTR B SILL
Mstr J Silvester
Mr N.S Simmons
Mr Simms
MR A Simms
Mrs J E Simms
Mr S.A.S Simpkin
Mr P Simpkins
Dr D.S.S Simpson
Miss B.S Simpson
MR B Simpson
MR C Simpson
Mr C.R.S Simpson
Mr D. Simpson
Mr I C Simpson
Mr L.A.S Simpson
Mr M. Simpson
Mr M.J.S Simpson
Mr M.S Simpson
MR P A Simpson
Mr P.S Simpson
Mr R.S Simpson
Mr S.J.S Simpson
Mr W.T.S Simpson
Mrs S.S Simpson
Mstr D.S Simpson
MSTR J Simpson
Mstr K Simpson
MSTR M. Simpson
MR Sinclair
Mr G.J. Sinclair
Mr J.B. Sinclair
Mr G.B. Singh
MR B Skeldon
MISS K Skelton
MISS R C Skidmore
MR K Skidmore
MR M J Skidmore
MR T J Skilbeck
Mr P.S Skipper
Mr T.S Skjeklhaug

Mr M A Slack
Mr M Slavin
Mr Slingsby
MR P J Slingsby
Mr C Smart
Mr C.I.S Smeaton
Mr A.S Smee
Mrs L.S Smee
Mstr C.S Smee
Mr J.S Smelt
MR D Smiddy
Smith
Miss C A Smith
Miss C.S Smith
Miss M.J.S Smith
MISS N J Smith
Miss R Smith
Miss T.L.S Smith
MR SMITH
MR Smith
Mr A Smith
Mr A K Smith
Mr A.S Smith
Mr B.S Smith
Mr C.S Smith
MR D Smith
Mr D Smith
MR D Smith
Mr D N Smith
MR D R Smith
Mr D.S Smith
Mr E D Smith
MR J Smith
MR J C Smith
Mr J.S Smith
MR J.W Smith
MR K Smith
Mr K.P.S Smith
MR M P Smith
Mr M.A. Smith
Mr N.S Smith
MR P Smith
Mr P Smith
MR P A Smith
MR P A Smith
Mr P.L.S Smith
MR R Smith
Mr R.A.S Smith
Mr R.F.S Smith
Mr R.M.S Smith
MR S Smith
MR S E Smith
Mr S.J.S Smith
Mr S.S Smith
MR T Smith
Mr T E Smith
Mr T.S Smith
Mr W.A.S Smith
Mr W.R Smith
MRS J J Smith
Mrs M.P.S Smith
Mrs T.W. Smith
Mstr A Smith
MSTR B.W SMITH
Mstr G.A.S Smith
MSTR M L Smith
Mstr N R Smith
Mstr W.P.D. Smith
Wasteneys Smith
Mr D.S Smithies
Mr C.J.S Smithson
Mr N.S Smithson
MR S Smithson
MISS E.L Smurthwaite
MR I Smurthwaite
MR J Smurthwaite
MR M Smurthwaite
Mr A. Snowdon
Mstr A.S Sobey
Mr D Southern
Mr G.I.J Southgate
Mr I.S Southgate
D Sowerby
Mr M.S Sowerby
MASTER L T Spargo
MASTER R D Spargo
MR G A Sparrow
MR R Sparrow
Mr J Speight
Mr A.G.S Spence
MR D J Spence
Mr D.A.S Spence
Mr D.S Spence
MR K Spence
MR M Spence
MR R T Spence
Mrs Spence
Mr D.S Spenceley

MISS H Spencer
Mr C.S Spencer
Mr I.A.S Spencer
MR J SPENCER
Miss E.M.S Spensley
Mr R.J. Spevins
MR R J Spoor
Mr A.S Sprigg
Ms A.S Sprigg
Mr A.S Sproston
Mr N.S Squires
Mr B N Stainforth
Mr S. Stairmand
Mr S.A.S Stanton
Mr J.C.S Stapley
MR P Starovla
Mr A.S Staton
MR G Staton
Mr M.S Stead
MR C Steel
Mstr A.E.S Steel
Mstr J.S Steel
Mstr A.S Stelmach
STEPHENS
Mr J.S Stephens
Mr A.R.G. Stephenson
MR C Stephenson
Mr C.M.S Stephenson
MR D Stephenson
Mr F.R.S Stephenson
Mr G.S Stephenson
MR H Stephenson
Mr J.B Stephenson
Mr J.P.S Stephenson
Mr J.R.S Stephenson
Mr K.R.S Stephenson
Mr M.A.S Stephenson
Mr M.J.S Stephenson
Mr M.S Stephenson
Mr N E B Stephenson
Mr P A Stephenson
Mr P E B Stephenson
MR P S Stephenson
Mr P.S Stephenson
MSTR J Stephenson
Mstr J.R.S Stephenson
MSTR P Stephenson
MR T Sterling
MR C J Stevens
Mr D.J.S Stevens
Mr P P Stevens
MISS E Stevenson
Miss G Stevenson
Mr M R Stevenson
Mstr A.G. Stevenson
Mr D.J.S Stewart
Mr J.S Stewart
Mr M.A.S Stewart
MSTR G.J Stewart
MR Stimpson
Mr G.I.S Stinchcombe
Mr D.M. Stinchcombe
Mr A. Stinton
Mr M.J.S Stinton
MR D Strickland
Mr N.S Stirk
Mr S.S Stirk
Mr I Stirman
MR B Stobbs
MR T Stock
MR STOCKBURN
MR K J Stockill
Mr K.S Stockill
Miss L.S Stockton
MR L.B.S Stockton
Mr M.J.S Stockwell
Mstr J Stoddard
Mr M Stokeld
Mr D A Stokes
Mr H.S Stokes
Mstr K.S Stokes
MR J Stone
MR P T Stone
Mr C.L.S Stonehouse
Mr J.S Stonehouse
Mr P Storey
Mrs S.S Story
MR D Stott
Mr M.I Stott
Mr L.M.S Strachan
Mstr C.B.S Strachan
Mr D A Strafford
Miss K. Strangeways
Mstr M.G.S Straughan
MR STRAW
Mr C.G. Street
MR P Strike
MSTR C Strike
MR P Strophair

Mr D.S Stuart
Mr B Stubbs
MR Stubbs Stubbs
Mr D.A. Sturdy
Mr F Sturdy
Mr K.S Sturdy
Mrs K Sturdy
Mstr D J Sturdy
Mr G.S Stuttard
Mstr C.J.S Stuttard
Mr P.J.H Styan
Mr M S Sudron
Mr P.S Sullivan
Mr R.J.S Sullivan
MR T Sullivan
Mr T.S Sullivan
Mr G.S Summerfield
Mr J.S Summerhill
MR A W Summerson
MR G Summerson
MR P W Sunley
Mr A.R.S Sutcliffe
MR G Sutcliffe
Mr S.J.S Sutherland
MR J.A Suttill
MR M.R Suttill
Mr P.G.S Swainston
Mr K.A.S Swales
Mstr J Swales
Mstr L.S Swales
MSTR A J Swalwell
Mstr D.J.S Swan
Mr P.S Swinburne
Mr J R S Swindale
Mr A.P.S Swindon
Mr C Swinnerton
MR G Swinnerton
Mr G Swinnerton
Mstr J Swinnerton
MISS S Sykes
Mr P.D Sykes
Miss E Symmonds
Miss H Symmonds
MR H Symmonds
Mstr G.T Taggart
Mstr M.T Taggart
MISS R.J Tait
Mr I.T Tait
MR J M Tait
Mr J.W.T Tait
MR S.J Tait
Mstr A.J.T Tait
Mr G.H.J Talbot
Mr S.H.T Tallon
MR C.J Tarran
Mr P.S Tash
MISS A Taylor
MR D Taylor
Mr D.A.T Taylor
Mr E.T Taylor
MR G E Taylor
Mr G.J Taylor
Mr G.T Taylor
Mr I Taylor
MR I D Taylor
MR J Taylor
Mr J.C.T Taylor
Mr J.W. Taylor
MR M R Taylor
Mr M.T Taylor
Mr N.T Taylor
Mr W.J.T Taylor
Mstr J.A.T Taylor
Miss E.T Taylorson
Mr D.W.T Taylorson
MR R Taylorson
Teeside Power
Coating Ltd
MR PF TEMPERTON
Mr S.T Tempestoso
Mr G D Templeman
MR S D Theaker
Mr J.J.T Thirsk
Mr A Thistlewaite
Miss N.J.T Thomas
Miss S.G.T Thomas
MR A D Thomas
Mr A.T. Thomas
Mr A.W.T Thomas
MR B Thomas
Mr B.T Thomas
Mr D. Thomas
Mr D.T Thomas
Mr G.J.T Thomas
Mr G.T Thomas
Mr I Thomas
Mr J Thomas
Mr M.T Thomas
MSTR A P Thomas

Mstr C D A Thomas
MSTR P.J Thomas
Miss J.T Thompson
MR A Thompson
Mr A S Thompson
Mr A.T Thompson
Mr B Thompson
Mr B.T Thompson
Mr C.N.T Thompson
Mr C.T Thompson
MR D G Thompson
MR G W Thompson
Mr G.T Thompson
Mr I.T Thompson
MR J P Thompson
Mr J.P.T Thompson
Mr K.T Thompson
Mr M Thompson
Mr M.P.T Thompson
Mr M.T Thompson
MR P M Thompson
Mr R Thompson
MR R.K THOMPSON
Mr R.M.T Thompson
Mr R.T Thompson
Mr S Thompson
Mrs B.E.T Thompson
Mrs G.A.T Thompson
Mstr A.T Thompson
MSTR C Thompson
MSTR D Thompson
MSTR M Thompson
Mstr P Thompson
Mr P.T.S Thompson-Smee
MR I H Thomson
Miss S.J.T Thorndike
MR J Thornhill
Mr S Thornton
Miss T.T Thorpe
Mr C Thorpe
MR I A Threadgill
MR M Threadgill
MR K Thurlow
MR P Thurlow
Mr R.J.T Thurlow
MSTR P A Thurlow
Mr J W Thurston
Mr S.T Thurston
Mrs S.M.T Thwaites
Mr P.J. Tickle
Mstr A Tickle
Mstr D.P Tickle
MR M Tierney
MR D Tiffney
MSTR A K Tiffney
MSTR S Tighe
Mr M.J.T Tilling
Mrs L.K.T Tilling
Mstr B.M.T Tilling
Mstr J.D.T Tilling
Mstr S.D.T Tilling
Mr A.T Timmiss
MR B A Tinkler
Mr D.T.T Tinkler
MR I Tinkler
MR J Tinkler
MISS L Tinney
MR Tinsley
Mr A.T Tippey
MR G Todd
Mr G.A Todd
Mr S.T Todd
Mr I. Tombs
Mr D Tomlinson
Mr I.R. Tomlinson
Mr S.T Tonkiss
Mr M.T Tooke
Mr N.T Tooke
MR C Tosh
MR D Tosh
MR R G Tosh
MR S.J Tosh
Miss A.M.T Toth
MR TOTH
Mr B.T Toth
Mr P.A.T Toulson
Miss E.A Towell
Mr E.T Towell
MR M.J Towell
Mr C.T Towers
Mr D.T Towers
MR I J Towers
MR J Towers
Mr M.T Townsend
MR P Townsend
MSTR A P Townsend
MSTR B Towse
Mr T S Train
MRS D Train

Mr D.T Tranter
Mr S.J Trattles
MR TRAYER
MR D.J Traylor
Mr S Traynor
MR D J Trebble
Mr B.A. Tregonning
Mr G.T Tregonning
Mr W. Tremholm
Mr M A Trett
Mr M.J.T Trewin
Mr J.A.T Trodden
Mr M.T Trotter
Mr S.T Trotter
Mr R.F.T Trowsdale
MR J Truscott
Mr P.T Truscott
MR N Tucker
Mr P. Tucker
MSTR J P Tunley
Mr J.P. Tunney
MSTR C Tupling
Mr G.T Tupman
Mr N.A.T Turnbull
MR S Turnbull
Mrs B Turnbull
Mstr S.J Turnbull
MISS Turner
MR Turner
Mr B.T Turner
MR G Turner
MR G J Turner
Mr K.E.T Turner
Mr M L Turner
MR N Turner
Mr P.G.T Turner
Mr P.T Turner
MRS M Turner
MSTR Turner
MSTR G Turner
MSTR G.J Turner
Mr D.J.T Tweddle
Mr M.T Tweddle
Mr S Tweddle
MR M D Twiby
Mr S.C.T Twomey
Mr G.W.T Tye
Mr M.T Tyerman
MISS C Tyreman
Mr K.C.T Tyreman
Mr C A Tyzack
Mr M D Tyzack
MR A K Unsworth
Mr S.T.U Urwin
Mr D.U Usher
MR S M Vallely
MR J Vamplew
MISS L.A Vanzeller
MR I Vart
Mr P. Vart
Mr T Vasey
Mr J.V Vaughan
Mr J.S.V Veitch
Mr P.S.V Veitch
Mr S.S.V Veitch
Mr D.K. Ventress
MR J Verrill
MR S J Verrill
Mr B Vickers
Mr B.R Vickers
Mr C.E.V Vickers
Mr R A Vickers
Mr R.V Vickers
Mstr R.B. Vickers
MR VIGILANTE
Mr P.V Vikebo
Mstr D.P Vikebo
Mr I VILNITIS
MR M Vincent
Mr C.V Vinter
MR A Vipond
Mr T.V Vipond
MSTR D J Vipond
MR H Vokes
MR P A Vokes
MR WADE
MR C Wade
MRS A E Wade
MR P WADROP
MSTR S J WADROP
Mr D.W Waines
Mr A Wainwright
MR Waite
Mr D Waite
Mr J.W Waite
Mr M R Waite
MRS E Waite
MSTR B Wake
MR P K Waldby

Mr R.C.W Walden
Miss R.W Walker
MR Walker
MR C Walker
MR C S Walker
Mr C.W Walker
Mr D Walker
MR D Walker
Mr D.W Walker
Mr E Walker
MR G R J Walker
Mr G.L.W Walker
Mr I.P.W Walker
Mr J A Walker
Mr J.A. Walker
Mr J.W. Walker
MR M Walker
Mr M.A Walker
Mr M.W Walker
MR P Walker
MR P B Walker
Mr P.A.W Walker
Mr P.W Walker
MR R Walker
Mr R.J Walker
Mr R.J. Walker
Mr S J Walker
Mr S.W Walker
Mr T.C.W Walker
MR W Walker
Mrs J.C.W Walker
Ms J.L.W Walker
MSTR D Walker
Mstr J.W Walker
MSTR L Walker
Mr C.G.W Wallace
MR G H Wallace
Mr I.C.W Wallace
Mstr S.C.W Wallace
MR Waller
Mr D Waller
Mr D.M. Waller
Mr E. Waller
Mr J Waller
Mr P R Waller
MRS N K Waller
Mstr D Waller
Mstr S.G Waller
MR J D Wallis
Miss J.W Walsh
Miss S.W Walsh
Mr A.W Walsh
Mr W.D.W Walsh
Mrs J.W Walsh
Mr G.W Walter
Mstr G.W Walters
MSTR P M Walters
Mr A.I. Walton
Mr P Walton
Mstr R.J.W Walton
Miss C.M.W Wanless
Mr I.W Wanless
Mr N.W Wanless
Mr W G Warburton
MR B Ward
Mr G Ward
Mr I G Ward
Mr K Ward
Mr K.J.W Ward
Mr M. Ward
MR C A Wardle
Mr L. Wardle
Mr R.A. Wardle
Mstr M.A. Wardle
MR C J Warren
Mstr N.W Warren
Mr M.F.W Warrior
Mr G.C.M. Warters
Mr S.W Warwick
Mr J.W Waterhouse
MR K Waterhouse
Mr G.L. Waters
Mr J.L Waters
Mr M.R.W Waters
Mr T.W Waters
Mr A Watkins
Mr D.L. Watkins
Mr G.A.W Watkins
Mrs D.W Watkins
Miss E.W Watson
MISS N Watson
MR Watson
Mr A Watson
Mr A J Watson
Mr B Watson
Mr C.W Watson
Mr D.W Watson
Mr F Watson
Mr F Watson

Mr F.R.W Watson
MR K J Watson
Mr M Watson
MR M J Watson
MR P Watson
Mr P.W Watson
Mstr Watson
MSTR D Watson
MSTR D J Watson
MSTR D S Watson
Mr D.W Watt
MSTR L Wattis
Mr D.H.W Watts
MR M F Watts
Miss K.W Weall
MR S J Wearmouth
Mr S.C. Wearne
Mr I. Weatherall
MR M.S WEATHERALL
Mstr M.D Weatherall
MR R Weatherhead
MR M W Weatherill
Mr I.W Webb
Mr M.W Webb
Mr N.D.W Webb
Mr K.J.W Webber
Mr Webster
Mr C.W Webster
MR P Webster
Mr S P Webster
Mstr C S Webster
MRS M Weedal
MRS J Weedall
MISS H K Weighell
MR M H Weightman
Mr D.W Welch
Mr J.D Welch
Mr M.W Welch
MR A Weldon
MSTR C Weldon
MR C Welford
MR D WELFORD
Mr P.W Welford
MR A Wells
Mr B.M Wells
MR L D Wells
Mr S.W Wells
Mr Welsh
Mr C.H. Welsh
Mr J.D Welsh
MR R Welsh
Miss L A Wennington
Mr D W Wennington
MR A J Wentworth
MR T W Weschenfelder
Mr K.W Wesson
MR D R West
Mr E.W West
MR M J West
MR R.S.W West
MR S G West
Mr K.D. Westcough
Mstr S.J. Westcough
Mr C.W Westwood
MRS S L Wetherill
Mstr P.G Whaley
MR P Whatmore
Mrs W.W Whatmore
Mstr G.W Whatmore
Mstr R Whatmore
Mr D.W Whelan
Mr M. Whetter
MR WHINYATES
Miss S. White
Miss V.A.W White
MR A G White
Mr B.W White
Mr G.W White
Mr L.W White
Mr K White
Mr M.W White
MR P S White
Mr P.A.W White
MR P.W White
Mr R R W White
Mr S.W White
MRS B White
Mrs T.M.W White
Mr K.W Whitehead
Mr D J Whiteway
Mr F Whitfield
MR P Whitfield
Mr J E Whitney
Mr A.P.W Whittaker
Mr E.J.W Whittaker
Mr G Whittingham
Mr S Whittle
MISS L M Whitton

MR T R Whitton
MR P Whitwick
Mr A.W Whorlton
MR S Whorlton
Mr D.E.C Whyborne
MR WHYMAN
MR K WHYMAN
MR M J Wieghell
Mr J.R.W Wigmore
MR N Wilcock
MSTR D J Wilcock
MR S.M WILCOX
MRS C WILCOX
MR B Wild
Mr J.W Wild
MSTR S Wild
MR P G Wilde
MR W K Wilde
MRS R Wilde
Mr P.W Wilford
Mrs S.E.W Wilford
Mstr N.W Wilford
Mstr S.W Wilford
MSTR L Wilkes
Miss R.L.W Wilkin
Mr Wilkinson
MR A D Wilkinson
Mr B.W Wilkinson
MR D P Wilkinson
Mr D.W Wilkinson
MR G A Wilkinson
Mr I.G.W Wilkinson
Mr I.W Wilkinson
Mr J.D.W Wilkinson
MR K Wilkinson
Mr K L Wilkinson
Mr M.F.W Wilkinson
MR P.R Wilkinson
Mr R Wilkinson
Mr S.R.W Wilkinson
Mstr M.P.W Wilkinson
Mstr S.W Wilkinson
Mr A.G.W Wilks
MISS A L Willey
MR P D Willey
MSTR G M Willey
MR WILLIAMS
MR A R Williams
Mr A.M.W Williams
Mr C Williams
Mr E.W Williams
MR G D Williams
MR J Williams
Mr K P Williams
MR L Williams
Mr L.D.W Williams
Mr L.P.W Williams
Mr M Williams
Mr M.R.J Williams
MR P Williams
Mr P.A Williams
Mr P.R.W Williams
Mr R.J.W Williams
MR S J Williams
Mr S.W Williams
Mr T.W Williams
MR W Williams
MSTR L J Williams
Mstr L.A Williams
MSTR S A Williams
Mstr S.A Williams
Mr A.J.W Williamson
MR B V Williamson
Mr G. Williamson
MR W K Willis
Mr M.J.W Willis
MRS S Willis
Mr C.P.W Willoughby
Mr J.A.W Willoughby
Mr J.M.W Willoughby
Mr J.P.W Willoughby
Mr M.N.W Willoughby
Dr B M Wilson
MISS Wilson
Miss S Wilson
MISS T J Wilson
MR WILSON
MR A Wilson
MR A M Wilson
Mr B Wilson
Mr B.M Wilson
Mr C Wilson
Mr C.W Wilson
Mr D Wilson
MR D.A Wilson
Mr D.M. Wilson
MR G Wilson

Mr H.S.W Wilson
Mr I.W Wilson
MR J WILSON
Mr J.A.W Wilson
Mr J.W Wilson
Mr L.V. Wilson
MR M Wilson
MR N Wilson
Mr P Wilson
MR P G Wilson
Mr P.W Wilson
MR R J Wilson
MR R L Wilson
Mr R.J.W Wilson
MRS S Wilson
Mr S.A.W Wilson
Mr S.D.W Wilson
Mr S.W Wilson
MRS P Wilson
Mstr A.W Wilson
Mstr B J Wilson
MSTR D Wilson
Mstr D T Wilson
MSTR J Wilson
Mstr R.M.W Wilson
MR D Wimble
Mr D.A. Windross
MSTR A J Windross
Miss C Wing
MR A P Wing
MR A.P Wing
MR C J Winnard
Mr Wintersgill
Mr C.A.W Winthrop
MR D Wiper
Mr P.W Wise
MR M A Witham
MR A D Witterick
MISS K Womack
MR D Womack
MSTR L Womack
Mr A.P.W Wood
Mr A.S.W Wood
MR C I Wood
MR G Wood
MR G L Wood
Mr H.G. Wood
MR J Wood
Mr M.W Wood
MSTR S M Wood
Mr S.W Woodacre
Mstr J.W Woodacre
MR I Woodard
MR A Woodhouse
Mr P Woodhouse
Mr C.F.W Woodward
Mr C.L.W Woodward
Mr R.A.W Woof
Mr R.W Woof
Mr A.C.W Worley
Mr A.J.W Worsnop
Mr P.R.W Worton
Mr R.W Worton
Mr W.G.W Worton
Mrs B.W Worton
MR WRAY
MR B Wray
MSTR C.T Wray
MR N Wren
MSTR P Wrigglesworth
Mr A.J.W Wright
Mr C Wright
MR C Wright
Mr C M Wright
Mr D.W Wright
Mr I Wright
Mr J.W. Wright
MR M Wright
Mr M.W Wright
MR S Wright
MR S.D Wright
Mr S.T. Wright
MSTR P A Wright
Mr I Wrightson
M S Wyatt
Mr A.W Wyatt
Mr P.W Wynn
MR R K Yale
Mr C. Yare
Mrs J. Yare
Mstr K. Yare
MR B Yates
MR J.R Yates
MR K.J Yates
MR P Yates
Mr D.Y Yeates
Mr N Yorke
J A Young
Master A M Young

Miss E L Young
MR A Young
MR C.A Young
Mr C.Y Young
Mr D Young
MR J Young
Mr K Young
Mr K.R Young
Mr K.Y Young
Mr M.Y Young
MR R A Young
Mr S D Young
Mr S.J.Y Young
MR P Zaino
Mr D.J.Z Zimmerman
Mstr C.J.Z Zimmerman

SOUTH EAST CORNER
Mr A.A Abbott
Miss B.A Adams
MR J Ainley
Mr D.R. Aitken
Mr T.A Allan
MR J J J Allen
MR M.R Allen
MSTR C Allen
Mr S.P. Allison
MR A Allport
Mr M Andrews
Mr S.A Ankers
MRS O Ankers
Mr M.J.A Ansboro
Mstr M.D.A Ansboro
Mr A B Antill
Mr D.A Armstrong
Mr J.A Armstrong
Mr J.D.A Armstrong
MRS K Armstrong
Mr N.A Atkinson
Mr P Atkinson
Mrs E Atkinson
Mr G.A Aveling
Mr M.S.A Ayre
MR M E Bache
MR E Bailey
Miss C Baillie
Mr B.B Bainbridge
Mr A. Baines
Mr S. Baines
Mstr D.B Baister
Mr C.B Baker
MR L Banks
MR T.K Bareham
MRS C Bareham
Mr A.N.B Barker
Mr J.B Barker
Mr A.B Barker
Mstr A.B Barker
Mr K.B Barkley
Mr A D Barlow
Mr N Barlow
Mr R F Barlow
Mrs G C Barlow
Mstr S A Barlow
Mstr T L Barlow
Mr K. Barnes
R M Barnes
MRS K E Barry
MR L Bartle
D Basham
Mr K Bashford
Bass Taverns
G M Baxter
Mr S.B Baxter
MISS S Beaumont
Mr N.B Beck
Mrs A.B Beck
Mr R Beedle
Miss M Bell
Mr D.R.B Bell
Mr R.A.B Bell
Mr K Bellamy
Miss G.L.B Best
Mr J.J.B Best
Mr M.C.B Best
Mr T.B Bird
Mstr T.B Bird
Mr J.J.B Birtill
MR B J O Blackett
MR S W Blackett
MSTR H R W Blackett
Mr L.B Blades
Mrs A Blades
MR A Blair
Mr A.J.B Blair
Mr C Blair
Mr S D Blair
MRS B Blair
Mr A.R.B Blake

Mr M.B Blake
Mr N.F.B Bland
Mr M.D Blaney
Mr P.A. Blythe
MR P Boothby
MRS C Boothby
Mr L.T.B Bowes
MR J M Bowman
MR R Bowman
MSTR C Bowman
MR I Bowstead
A Boynes
D C Boynes
J W Boynes
Miss K.A.B Bradford
Mr L.C.L. Bramley
Miss J.B Brannigan
Miss L.B Bratt
Mr G.B.B Bratt
MR I D Brickman
MR C Brights
Mr G.D.B Broadley
Mr L.B Broadley
Mr A Brooks
Mr P G Brooks
Mr A.B Brown
Mr A.G. Brown
Mr C.J. Brown
Mr I Brown
MR M Brown
Mr R Brown
Mr R.G.P. Brown
Mr R J Brown
Mr T.B Brown
Mrs K J Brown
Mrs M.S Brown
Mstr J S N Brown
MR P J Brudenell
MRS P L Brudenell
Mr G.B Brunskill
MR G J Buckle
Mstr C.B Bunn
Mr P A Burke
Mrs I.B Burke
Mr W. Burniston
K Burton
Mr D.B Burton
MR G G Butler
MR E Butterfield
MR M Butterfield
Mr G.R.B Buxton
CTS Northern Ltd
Miss S Cadwallader
Mr M Cadwallader
Mr P.C Campbell
Capper Engineering
Mr J.C Cardwell
Mstr B.C Cardwell
Mr E Carr
Mr W T Carter
Mrs M M Carter
Mstr D R Carter
Mstr A.T.C Caswell
Mr C.C Catterick
Mr D.C Causier
Mr N.C Cave
Mr P A Cawley
MR D.T Chadwick
Mr J.C Chambers
Mr T D Chambers
MR W Chape
Mrs A.C Chaplin
Mr P.C Chapman
Mr S.C Chapman
Miss K.L.C Charlton
Mr D.C.C Charlton
Mr G.C Charville
Mr P Chillmaid
Mr N.R. Cholmondeley
MR P Chow
MR J Clark
MR R J Clark
Ms S.C Clarke
Mr E G Clarkson
Mr S E Clarkson
Mr A Clayton
Mr G.C Cleeton
Mr M Clements
Mr R.C Clemmons
Mr H.C Coaker
MR K M Coaker
Mrs E.A.C Cocks
MR I J Coghlan
Miss N.C Colbeck
Mr L.C Coleman
K.W Gillbrook Tech.
College
Mr P.D. Colley

Mr E.J Collingwood
Mstr O.G Collingwood
Mr I Collinson
MR J W Collinson
MR N Collinson
MR B Conley
Mr S.B.C Connell
MISS J Conway
Mr C.C Conway
MR M.J Conway
MRS M Conway
Mr G.C Conyard
MR M B Cook
Mr P.A.C Cook
Mr P.D.C Coombes
Mr A.J Cooper
Mr C J Cooper
Mr R.C Cooper
Mr S Cooper
Mrs J Cooper
Mstr A Cooper
Mstr J.C Cooper
Mr P.K.C Corker
Miss A.L Corner
Mr E Corner
Mr J L Couling
Mr A.G.C Coulton
MRS H Covell
Mrs E.M. Cowell
MR C Craggs
Mr J Craggs
MR P Craggs
Mr N.R.C Craig
Mr M Crame
Mr I.C Craster
Mr T.C Crinion
Mstr J.C Crinion
Mr T Crompton
Mrs B Crompton
Mr N.D.C Cronin
Mr N Crosby
Miss H.E.C Crossen
Mr J.M.C Crossen
MR S.A CROWE
Mr K.C Cruz
Mr C Cullen
Mrs P Cummins
MR D Curry
MR P.S Curry
MSTR G.M Curry
Mr G Cuthbert
Mrs G Cuthbert
Mstr B.T Cuthbert
Mstr G.E Cuthbert
MR A.D Cutler
Mr C Dale
Mr N.D Daly
Mr D.D Danby
Mr W Danby
Mstr S.W.D Danby
Mstr S.K.D Danieli
MR DARGUE
MR A A Dargue
Miss K Darragh
Mrs B Davey
Mstr S Davey
Miss J.D Davies
Miss S.D Davies
Mr A.E Davies
MR J Davies
Mr J Davies
Mr J.M Davies
Mr S.D Davies
MR B Davison
MSTR C.T Davison
Mr S Dawson
MR J Day
MR P Day
Mr B.R.P. Dea
Mstr P.J.D Dea
Mr M.D Deeley
MISS N DELUCE
MR N DELUCE
Mr L Dennis
Mr A.D Dent
Mr M.D Dent
Mstr P T Derbyshire
Mr J.M.D Devlin
Mr D Dewhurst
MR A Ditchburn
Mr P Ditchburn
MRS J Ditchburn
Mr F.D Dobson
Miss L.D.D Dodsworth
Mr G.D Downey
MR K Downie
MR M Doyle
Mr C L Driver
MR K W Druery

Mr N.W. Ducking
Mr N.D Duffield
Mr S.J.E Duffy
EM Construction Co Ltd
Mr D.J Eames
MISS M Earl
D East
S A East
Mr B.D.E Eaton
Mr T.E Eaton
Mrs L.E Eaton
Mr P R Eccles
MR A Edwards
Mr J.T.E Elders
MR M Ellerby
MR B.D ELLIS
Mr D J Ellis
MR L Etherington
MR G Evans
MR W Evans
Mr M Farndale
Mrs S Farndale
Miss J.F Farrell
Miss N.F Farrell
Mr C.F Farrell
Mr Fearns
MR S Featherstone
MR S A Featherstone
Mr T.F Featherstone
Mr J.P.F Ferrie
Mr R A Field
MSTR M R Finegan
Mr C.A.F Finn
Mr C.M.F Finn
Mr M.J.F Finn
MR P A Finn
Mrs P.F Finn
Mr K Finnisan
MR G.D Fisher
Mr A Fishlock
MR P Fitzgerald
Mr G.F Fixter
Mstr A.F Flanders
MR G.W Fleet
Mr S.F Fletcher
Mr J Flutter
D Ford
MR J R Ford
R Ford
Mr J.F Forsythe
MR M B Foster
MSTR D D Foster
Mstr M.J.F Foster
Mr F.F Fothergill
Mr I Frank
Mrs S Frank
Mr L.F Freer
Miss R M Fryett
Mr R M Fryett
Mr K.J.G Galloway
Mstr S.K.G Galloway
Mr M.P.G Gamblin
MISS A.E Gamesby
MR S Gamesby
Ms Y.M.G Gamesby
MR M E Gappy
MR M J Gappy
Mr D.G Garbutt
Mstr A.G Garbutt
Mr A.G Gardner
Mr P S Gardner
Mr A.G Gaunt
T George
Mr G A Gibbin
MR T Gibson
Mrs M.G Gibson
Mr S.K.G Gilday
Mr J.T.G Gill
MR S Gill
Mrs A.L.G Gill
Mr P Gilmore
Mr P Godfrey
Mr D Goodchild
Mr D.G Goodman
Mr P.G Goodman
Mr J C Goodwin
Mr N G Goodwin
Mr N.A.G Goodwin
Mrs P.E.G Goodwin
Mstr B.G Goodwin
Mstr C.G Goodwin
Dr I.A Gordon
MR D Gordon
MR I A Gordon
Mrs A.G Gosnay
Mr L M Goult
MR A Graham
Mr C.I. Graham

Mr J.G Graham
Mr R I Graham
Mr T Grainger
Mr S.J.G Grant
J A Gray
Mr Gray
MR D A Gray
MR D J Gray
Mr D.T.G Gray
Mr S.C.G Gray
N S Gray
MR D A Grayson
Mr A Green
Mr C Green
Mr K Green
Mr R Green
Griffiths
Mr D.G Griffiths
Mr T.W.G Griffiths
Mrs M.G Griffiths
MR A D Hall
Mr B.H Hall
Mr G.H Hall
MR V Hall
Mrs E.H Hall
MR Halliday
D E Hamilton
MSTR D Hamilton
MSTR K Hamilton
Mr I.H Harding
Mstr R.H Harding
MR A P Hare
Mr C.R.H Harper
MR DJ HARPER
Mr A Harris
Mr D Harris
MR P Harris
Mr E.A Harrison
Mr G.J.H Harrison
Mr J.W Harrison
Mr S Harrison
Mr T.H Harrison
Mrs S.M.H Harrison
MR A P Harvey
MR P T Harvey
M HATFIELD
Mr M G Hawes
MR G D Hawke
HAWKINS
Mr P.M.H Hayden
Mstr M.P.H Hayden
Mr R.J.H Hayes
Mr M.T.H Helm
Mr A.H Henderson
Mr P Henderson
Mr K.H Henry
Mr N.H Henson
Mr K.G.H Heppenstall
Mr C.H Heslop
Mr D.H Hetherington
Mr J.H Hewitt
MR R F Hickey
MR D HIGGET
MSTR C HIGGETT
MR G Higham
MSTR R Higham
MR T Hill
Mr P.H Hindhaugh
MR S Hirst
Mr S.W Hitchen
Mrs H.H Hitchen
MR HOAD
Mr M.C.H Hobday
Mrs D.H Hobday
Mr P. Hobson
MR S Hobson
MR G A Hodgson
A Hoe
Mr J Hollifield
Mr A.B Holligon
Dr J Hollins
Mr B A Holmes
MR J Holmes
Mr R Holmes
MR P Holyoake
Mr J D Honeyman
Mstr J Honeyman
C J Hopson
MR A M Hopton
MR J Hopton
MR BL Hornby
Mr T Horton
Mstr A Horton
Mr A.H Howard
Mr D.H Howard
Mrs B.H. Howard
MR N A Howell

Mr R. Howes
MR T.R Howes
MISS A Hoyland
Mr A.R.H Huggins
Mr D.J.H Hughes
Mr M.H Hulse
MR T R Humphreys
Mr E. Hunter
Mr L.H Hunter
Mr M.H Hussain
MR R Hutchcraft
MSTR T D Hutchcraft
Jackson
MR A Jackson
Mr B.P.C Jackson
Mr D.J Jackson
Mr L Jackson
Mr W.J Jackson
Mr W.J Jackson Snr
Mrs R.J Jackson
MSTR C.A Jackson
Mr B.J Jaffray
Mstr T.J Jaffray
Mr P.J.A Jagels
Mr I.P. James
R Jardine
Mr M.J Jenkins
MR P Jennings
MR P Johns
DR D J Johnson
J Johnson
MR M Johnson
MR R Johnson
Miss A.M.J Jones
MR M Jones
Mr S Jones
MSTR J Jones
Mr F. Jowsey
Mr G Kay
Mr J Kay
Kaye
Mr B.K Keen
D Kell
J C Kell
Mr C.D.K Kelly
MR D M Kelly
Mr W. Kemp
Mrs I. Kemp
Mr D.K Kennedy
Mr M M Kenworthy
Mr D. Kidd
Mr L. Kidd
Miss E King
MR D J King
Mr D.I.K King
Mr T V King
Mr V King
J Kirk
Mr M Kirk
Mr S Kirton
Mr M.K Kiss
G Knight
I Knight
MR N J Knott
MR A I Knox
Mstr P.K Kreczak
MISS M lakey
Mr C.L Lamb
Mr D.G.L Lamb
Miss S.L Lambert
Miss S.M Lamming
Mr J Lamming
Mr G I Lamplough
Mr I Lamplough
MR M Landers
Mr M.L Landers
Mr D.L Lane
Mr D Lawn
Mstr D Lawn
Mstr P Lawn
MSTR S Lawton
Mr P.L Layton
Mr J.L Leach
MR J J Leahy
MR A S Learmonth
Mr M.A.L Lee
MR Legg
Mr P.J.L Lempiere
Mstr R.J.L Lempriere
Mr S.A.L Lenaghan
Mr S.C Leng
Mr D.A.L Leonard
Mr D Lett
Mr S.J.L Lever
MR C Lewis
Mr S Little
Mr J A Littlefair
Mr S.B Lochrie
MR M A Locker

DOOM TO BOOM

LOUGHRAN
Mr E P Loughran
Mrs D J Loughran
MISS A Lowe
Ms A.L Lowe
Mstr J C Lowe
Mr R.L Lowes
Mr B.L Loy
Miss Lynas
Mr G.T.L Lynas
Mr E Lynn
Mr P.D Lynn
MR A L Lyth
MR G Macalees
MRS V Macalees
Mr B.M Mackin
Mr J.M Mackin
Mr P.J.M Mackin
MR S Maguire
Mr G Maher
MR M Maloney
Mstr L T Maloney
Mstr P T Maloney
MR C A Mark
MISS B Marr
Miss L.M Marron
Mrs P.J.M Marron
Mr D.P.M Marshall
C.J MARTIN
L MARTIN
MR D.G Martin
Mr J.M Martin
MR N.D Martin
Mr P P Martin
Mrs M MARTIN
Mstr G.B.M Martin
Mstr G.J.M Martin
Mstr S Marwood
MISS K Mason
Mr A. Mason
MR M Mason
MRS G M Mason
MSTR M T Mason
MR C Masterson
MRS J Masterson
Mr K. Maurice
MR J McCabe
Mr T.J.M McCabe
Mr J.H.M McCall
MR M McCletchie
MR T L McCue
MSTR J E McCue
Mr N.B.M McCutcheon
Mstr S.M McCutcheon
MR C McDermott
MR P T McDonagh
MR A E McDonnell
MR G McDonnell
Mr A.J.M McDonough
MR G McElvaney
Mr G.A.M McFee
Mr P.A.M McFee
MR M L McGloin
Mr K.M McGregor
Mr B.M McGrother
MR D R McIntyre
Mr J.M McKewan
MISS I McLane
Mr B McLaughlin
Mstr M.B. McLaughlin
Mr P.M McLinn
Mr C.M McManus
Mr D.M McNeill
Mr J.M McNicholas
Mr A.W.M McNinch
Mr B.A.M McNinch
Miss C McPhee
Miss H L McPhee
Mr J R McPhee
Miss S McQueeney
Mrs B McQueeney
Mstr I McQueeney
MISS D McShannon
Mr P.M McTiernan
MR W J Mellor
Mrs E.M Metcalfe
MISS B E Midcalf
Mr C.M Middleton
Miss S Milnes
Mr G.M Mitchell
Mr G Molloy
Mr C.M Monty
Miss K.M Moore
Mr A.M Moore
MR G R Moore
MR J Moore
Mr R.M Moore
MRS J Moore
Mstr A.M Moore

MR G Morte
D Mortlock
MR D Motson
MR S Motson
MR A Mullen
Mrs W.M Mullins
Mstr R.R.M Mullins
Mr A.M.M Murphy
MR R Murphy
MRS J Murphy
Mrs L.N Murphy
MRS P Murphy
MSTR MURPHY
MSTR T Murphy
P.B Murphy
Mr C.W.M Murray
Mr S.M Myers
MSTR S Myers
MR T P Narey
Mr P Neesam
Newby
Miss A Newton
Mr P.R.N Newton
Mstr A.J.N Newton
MR J Nicholson
Mr J.R.N Nicholson
MR K Norton
MR J W O'Brien
Mr J.O O'Brien
Mr J.P.A O'Brien
MR A O'Connor
MSTR D O'Connor
Mr M O'Donnell
Mr B.J. O'Hagan
Mr J.O O'Hara
Mr C O'Malley
MISS N L O'Neil
MR A J O'Neil
MR M O'Neil
MR D O'Neil
MRS S O'Neil
Mr M.O O'Rourke
MR A Office
MISS F M Oliver
Mr N.G.O Oliver
Miss F Osborne
Mr C Osborne
Mr E Osborne
Mrs L Osborne
MR T A Ovington
MRS S Ovington
Mr C Pallent
Mr I Pallent
Mr N.P Pallent
MR L Palliser
Mr G.P Pallister
Mrs J.A.P Palmer
Mr B Pape
Mr J F Pape
MR J W Parker
Mr N.P Parker
G Parkes
Mr J Parkin
MR D.G Parry
MR K A Parry
Mr J Parsons
Mr D.M Pattison
Mstr J.W Pattison
MISS L.K Peacock
Mr G.D.P Peacock
Mr J.P Peacock
Mr W Pearson
MR M Pennick
MRS J Pennick
MR J E Perciual
MR T Phillips
Mr J Phipps
Mr J.P Phipps
Miss L.J Pickering
Mr A Pickering
Mr F Pickering
MR J A Pickering
MR A Pierre
Mr S.P Pierre
MR M Pitman
Mr S Plummer
MR J W Pollard
MR L Pollard
POOLE
Mr A Poole
Mr M Poole
Mstr G.P Poole
Mr K J Power
Mr D. Presgrave
Mr J.P Preston
MR A Price
MR J Price
Mr R Price
Mr S.J.P Price

Mstr A Price
MR B Procter
MR G B Pyle
MRS R K Pyle
J L Pyne
Mr S Quigley
Mstr M.W.Q Quigley
Mr R Ramsey
Mr C.R Ranson
Mr J. Raper
Mr S.J.E. Raper
Mr C.R Redman
Mrs P.R Redman
J A REED
Rees
Mr Rees
MR G Reilly
Mr I Reynolds
MR R Rich
MR S Rich
MR M Richards
MSTR A Richards
Miss H.R Richardson
Mr K.R Richardson
Mr M.W.R Richardson
Mstr S.R Richardson
Mr D Richmond
Mr I Richmond
Mr M Richmond
MR J M Riddiough
MR M C Riddiough
Mr S.P Rigg
G RILEY
MR RIPLEY
MR B Roberts
Mr J.M.R Roberts
Mr M.D.R Roberts
MR S Roberts
Mstr C Roberts
MSTR S Roberts
Mr R.R Robertson
Mrs E.R Robertson
D R Robinson
Miss D.R Robinson
MR Robinson
MR A Robinson
Mr M.G.R Robinson
MR S A Robinson
Mstr M.R Robson
Mr G.P Rogers
MR G Ronald
MRS S Ronald
Mstr M.S.R Rooney
MISS L Rothwell
Mr M W Routledge
C Rowbotham
Mr W.R Rowe
Mr R P Rowntree
Mstr J O Rowntree
Mstr N J Rowntree
MR S Rpberts
Miss K.R Rudd
Mr J.R Rugg
Mstr G.J.R Rugg
Mr C Rumsey
Mstr C C Rumsey
Mrs B Rush
Mstr M Rush
MSTR J Russell
Mr I M Russon
Mr G Ryan
Mstr S Ryan
Mr P.S Saager
Mr G S Sadler
Mr R.S Samson
Mstr L.R.S Samson
Mr A G Sanderson
Mstr D G Sanderson
Mr D.S Saul
Mrs M.J Saunders
Mr B Sayer
Mrs S Sayer
Mr M.T.S Scarlett
Mr R P Schofield
Mr I Scott
Mr P W Scott
Mr R Scott
Mr T Scott
MSTR S Scott
Miss L Screen
Mr A Screen
Mstr J Screen
Mstr M Screen
Mr M Secret
Mstr J Secret
Miss R Sharif
MISS S Sharrock
MR J V Shaw
MR P Shaw

Mr W.B.S Shaw
Mr P.R.S Shayler
MR H Shepherd
MR S Shepherd
Mr L.S Sheppard
Mr A Shutt
Mr C P Shutt
Mstr M A Shutt
MISS L Sidgwick
MISS A Sigsworth
Mr D.S Simblet
MR C Simpson
MR R Simpson
Mr S. Simpson
MR W Simpson
Mrs J. Simpson
Mstr A.S Simpson
Mstr D Simpson
Mr D Sinnott
Mr p Sinnott
Mr P.A. Sinnott
Mr A.E.S Slater
Mr P.S Sleightholm
Mr A Smailes
Mr M G Smailes
Mr P A Smailes
MR D Small
Mr G.S Smiley
Mr I.S Smiley
J P Smith
MISS K Smith
Miss M P Smith
Mr A.D.S Smith
MR B Smith
Mr C.S Smith
Mr D.J Smith
MR G Smith
Mr G Smith
MR J R Smith
MR K Smith
Mr K.E Smith
MR L.D Smith
MR M J Smith
MR R Smith
Mr R.J Smith
Mr R.S Smith
MRS M M Smith
Mrs M.S Smith
MSTR P N Smith
Mstr R J Smith
MR B Smurthwaite
Mr D.S Smurthwaite
Mr H Smurthwaite
Mr M.S Smurthwaite
Mrs L Smurthwaite
Mrs L.S Smurthwaite
MR B Snook
Mstr J Snook
Mr C.S Snowball
Mr C.I.S Solomon
Mr A Somerset
MR A Sowa
Mr M.S.S Spayne
Mr G D Spence
Mr J Starling
Mr R D Stead
MR P Stephenson
Miss H.M Stevens
Mr F Stevenson
MR I R Stewart
MISS E Stonehouse
Mr M Stonehouse
MR P Stonehouse
Mrs J Stonehouse
MSTR C Stonehouse
MSTR M.A Stonehouse
Mr B.S Storey
Mr I Storey
Mstr J P Storey
Mstr M I Storey
MR G STOTT
Mr D Strange
Stuart
MR J Sturdy
Mr T.S Styles
Mr G.S Sullivan
Mr P.D.S Sullivan
Mr D J Swash
R J Swift
Mstr M Symmonds
MR S Tarren
J Tate
Ms C Tate
Taylor
C Taylor
MISS M.G Taylor
MR TAYLOR
Mr A.T Taylor
Mr D.T Taylor

Mr M A Taylor
MSTR TAYLOR
Mstr M.T Taylor
Mstr W.T Taylor
Mr B.T Teasdale
Miss L.A.T Tebay
Mr H.T Thomas
Mr P.A.T Thomas
MR R L Thomas
MRS J Thomas
MSTR THOMAS
Mr J.A.E Thompson
Mr M Thompson
MR N A Thompson
Mr P Thompson
MR R J Thompson
MR S G Thompson
MRS C M Thompson
MRS J Thomson
D Thornton
Mr A Thornton
Mr C.T Thornton
Mrs T.T Thornton
Mr G Thrower
Mr M.P.T Thurlbeck
Mr P.E.T Thurlbeck
Mr N. Tighe
Mr L.E.J Tilley
Mr L.S Tilley
MR S Tipper
MISS R Toase
Mr D.T Towell
Mr M Trodden
K Tuck
Mr P A Tunney
MR M Turley
Mr S.R.T Turner
Mstr D Tuttle
MR B Tweddell
MR J Tweddell
Mr C Twiby
Miss E.J. Vaughan
Mr R Vickers
MRS T M Vickers
Mr D.V Vipond
Mstr C.V Vipond
Mstr J.V Vipond
MISS J Waites
MR G A Wake
MR A Walker
Mr D.W Walker
Mr G.J.W Walker
Mr I.W Walker
Mr M.W Walker
Mr P.J.W Walker
Mr P.W Walker
Mr A.J.W Walker
Mstr T Walker
Mr P.J.W Wallace
Mr S C Wallace
Mr S.J.W Wallace
S.J WALLACE
MR S Wallinger
MR G Walsh
Miss J.D Walton
Miss S Walton
Mr L.D.W Walton
Mrs D Walton
Mr A C Wanless
Mr N.K.F. Wanless
Mr D.W Warburton
Miss S Ward
Miss S E Ward
Mr B.W Ward
Mr D Ward
MR D Ward
Mr D S Ward
Mr G Ward
Mstr D.L.W Ward
Mstr M.J.W Ward
Mr D Warwick
Mr J W Warwick
Mr A.W Waters
Mr P.W Waters
Ms J.W Waters
Mstr M.P.W Waters
Mr G.D. Watson
MR R Watson
Mstr C.L. Watson
Mr P.L. Weatherston
Mr J.R.W Webster
MR N Welford
MR S West
Mr S.J.W Whalley
MR Wharton
Mr G.J.W Wheatley
Mstr J Wheatley

Mstr M Wheatley
Mr R.W Wheeler
MR T Whelan
MRS J Whelan
MRS M Whelan
Mr G.M.G Whisker
Mr M Whisson
Mrs L Whisson
MS D.L Whitcher
Mr D T White
Mr J R White
Mr M J White
Mr M.E.W Whitfield
Mr P.W Whitfield
MR G H Wilberforce
MRS B Wilberforce
Miss K Wilde
Mr G Wilkinson
Mr N Wilkinson
MRS S Wilkinson
Mr A Williams
MR K A Williams
MR L M Williams
Mr W G Williams
Mr C.W Williamson
Miss K Willmore
Mr M Willmore
Miss G.L.W Wilson
MISS N Wilson
MR A A Wilson
Mr D Wilson
Mr D.J.W Wilson
Mr M. Wilson
Mr N.W Wilson
Mr P.G.W Wilson
MRS A Wilson
MRS M Wilson
Mstr A P Wilson
Mr S.W Wise
Mr A.W Witham
MR C Witherley
MR S Wolfenden
Miss V A Wood
Miss V L Wood
Mr C.W Wood
Mr M Wood
Mr P.A Wood
Mr S.W Wood
Mrs C A Wood
Mr D Woodhouse
MR R Woodhouse
MSTR B Woodhouse
Mr T.F. Worland
MR H Wrigglesworth
MR O Wright
Mr P. Wright
Mr S Wright
Mrs S.M. Wright
Mr J Wylie
Mr A.R.Y Youngs
Mr S Zipfell

SOUTH STAND
Mr P Ableson
Mstr M.W Ableson
Mr C.A Adams
Mr M.A Adams
Mrs A.A Adams
MR D.J Addison
MSTR L Akerman
Mr R.M.A Al-Ridha
Mstr A.N.A Aldick
Mstr T.S.A Aldick
Mr C Alewood
MISS K Allen
Miss M A R Allen
Mrs G Allen
Mstr C.A Allen
MR M Allinson
Miss M.A Anderson
Mr P.A.N Anderson
Mrs C.A Anderson
Miss K E Archard
Mrs S J Archard
Mstr M.P.A Arnold
Mstr P.N.A Arnold
Miss C.L.A Ascough
Mr K.A Ashbridge
Mstr D.J.A Ashbridge
Mstr A.K.A Ashby
Mr J.G. Askins
Mr J.K. Askins
Mr K.A Aspery
Miss L Atkinson
Mr J Atkinson
Mstr S Atkinson
MR G R Auckland
MRS L M Auckland
Mstr D A Auckland

Mstr J G Auckland
Mr M Axford
MR C Azemar
MR D Azemar
Mr E.F.B Backhouse
Mstr A M BAILEY
MR C Barclay
MSTR D E Barclay
MR F Barker
MSTR R Barker
MSTR D.L Barnes
Mr N Barnnan
Mr R.B Barrett
Mstr R.A.B Barrett
Mr C K Barwick
Mr D.T Bashford
Mstr J.T Bashford
Mstr J Bates
Mr J.M Batty
Mr K.J Batty
Mstr A.B Baxtremen
MSTR R Beadnall
Miss H.J.B Bean
Mr F.B Bean
Mr K.M.B Bean
Mrs K.E.B Bean
Miss S J Beattie
MR L Beavis
Mstr P Becks
L Bell
Mr C.I.B Bell
MR D W Bell
Mr M.B Bell
Mr P.H.B Bell
MR S J Bell
MR S R Bell
Mr H Bennett
Mr K Bennett
Mrs M.B Bennett
Mstr M.C Bennett
Miss K Bermingham
Mr M Bermingham
Mstr S Bermingham
Mstr D A Bezance
Mr J H Bircham
Mr K.B Bishop
Mstr J.B Bishop
Mr I.B Bisset
Mstr D.B Bisset
Mstr L.B Blackburn
MR A Blackmore
MSTR M Blackmore
Mr J.T.B Blakeman
Mr M Bloomfield
Mstr A Bloomfield
MR K Blott
MR D Boddy
Miss H Bollands
Mr G Bollands
Mstr P Bollands
Mr I Boon
Mstr W.B Botham
Mr G.J.B Bothwell
Mstr G.W.B Bothwell
Mr G.P.B Bowater
Mr J. Bowes
Mr S.B Bowes
Mstr J. Bowes
Mstr S.T.B Bowes
MR G Boyce
MR D P Boyd
Mr G.B Brackenborough
Mr M.B Brackenborough
Mr A Bradbury
Miss E M Bradley
Mr J Bradley
Mstr S J J Bradley
Mr A.R. Brady
Mstr T.G.β Brady
Miss A Braithwaite
Mr A Braithwaite
MR C Braithwaite
Mr D Braithwaite
Mr R Braithwaite
MSTR D Braithwaite
Mstr J Braithwaite
MR A Brettle
MRS E Brettle
MSTR G Brettle
MRS H.M Brighty
Mstr S.B Britain
MR J Broadbent
MSTR P A Broadbent
Mr A.E.B Brodrick
Mr R.S.B Brodrick
Mstr C.B Brodrick
Mstr D.S.B Brodrick
Mstr J.B Brodrick
MSTR Brogden

MR N J Broome
MRS A Broome
Miss J Brown
Mr A Brown
Mr D Brown
Mr J Brown
Mr M.B Brown
Mr R Brown
Mrs M Brown
Mstr C Brown
Mstr D Brown
Mstr G.B Brown
Mstr P.B Brown
MR P.J Browne
Mr A D Brownlee
Miss C.B Brudenel
Miss K.B Brudenell
Mrs G.B Brudenell
MRS R Brudenell
Mr R.B Brumpton
Mstr J.B Brumpton
Mr A.P Bunn
Mstr W.J.B Bunn
MSTR P A Burgess
MR G G Burke
MSTR J A Burke
MR J Burkhart
MR P H Burkhart
MSTR J Burkhart
MR R Burn
MR G Burns
Mr S.B Burns
MSTR D Burns
MSTR R Burns
Mr D.J Burton
Mr P M Burton
Mstr J.L Burton
R Butcher
S Butcher
MISS A L Butler
Mr B.B Butler
MRS S Butler
MSTR A J Butler
Mstr D.B.B Butler
C Butterworth
MR L Butterworth
MR P Butterworth
MRS S Butterworth
MR P.R Bye
MSTR B Bye
MSTR M.G Bye
MSTR N Bye
Miss L.E.C Calvert
Mr D.S.C Calvert
Mrs R.C.C Calvert
Mstr A.S Calvert
Mstr G.J.C Calvert
MR S W Campbell
Mr S.C Campbell
Mstr M.C Campbell
Mr A.C Cane
Mr C.C Cane
Mr R.C Cane
Mrs A Cannon
Mr D.C Carass
Mrs K.C Carass
Mstr A.C Carass
Mstr R.C Carass
Mr J.T.C Carbert
Mr J Carey
Mstr D Carey
MISS F Carman
H L Carr
Miss E.L Carr
Miss K J Carr
Mr E Carson
MR C D Carter
MR E Carter
Mr K.C Carter
Mr P.N.C Carter
Mstr A J Carter
MR P M B Cass
A Cassidy
MR D Cassidy
Mr M.L.C Casson
MR S Caster
MSTR A P Caster
Mstr R.I.C Caster
Cattermole
Mr C.C Catterson
Mrs L.M.C Catterson
Mstr J D Catterson
Mstr L.G.T Catterson
Mstr S.A.C Catterson
MR D Catton
MR L Catton
Mstr A.C Caveney
Mr N Cawthorne

Mr J.L.C Chantrell
Mr J.C Chapman
Mstr J Chapman
Mstr M Chapman
Mr J.C Charlton
Mrs M.V.C Charlton
Mstr J.D.C Charlton
Miss J.E.C Chatterton
Miss S.L.C Chatterton
Mr G.C Chatterton
Mr R.C Chatterton
MISS N L Cheung
MR B Cheung
Dr S.A Chilton
Mstr P.W Chilton
Mr R Cholmondeley
Mstr D M Cholmondeley
Mstr P Christen
Mr C Clark
MR M R Clark
Mstr D.K Clark
Mstr R A Clark
MR H Coakley
MSTR P Coakley
Mr M.C Cocker
Miss S I. Collins
Mrs L Collins
Mstr B.C Collins
Mr T.H Coltman
Mr M.C.C Compitus
Mstr S M Conlin
Mr C Connelly
mr M J Connelly
MR R Conroy
Mr G Conway
Mstr D Conway
Mr D Cook
Ms L.C Cook
MR B Cooper
MSTR A Cooper
MSTR D Cooper
MSTR S Cooper
Miss E.C Coppinger
Miss K.C Coppinger
Mr M.C Coppinger
Miss C Corcoran
Mrs L Corcoran
Mr P. Cornfoot
Mstr S.R. Cornfoot
Miss A Costello
Miss C.C Couhig
MR M Couhig
MR A G COULTHARD
Mstr D.K.M Coulthard
Mr K Cowl
Mstr C Cowl
MR M Coyle
MSTR A Coyle
MSTR M Coyle
Miss J.C Craggs
Mr D.C Craggs
Mr M.C Craggs
Mr N.S.C Craggs
Mr P.C Craggs
Mstr D.C Craggs
Miss L.M.C Creedon
Mr A Crilley
Mstr S Crilley
Ms A.J.C Croft
Mstr J.L.C Croft
MR P W Crookes
MSTR M J Crookes
Mstr M.J.C Crooks
MR J.P Cullen
Mr P.A. Cummings
Mr B Cummins
Mr J.B Cummins
Mr M Cummins
Mstr C Cummins
Mr D P Curran
Mstr P Curran
Mstr A Curtis
MR K M Dale
Mr I.D Dales
Mrs A.D Dales
Mr P.K.D Dasey
Mstr E.P.D Dasey
Mstr J.J.D Dasey
MISS K Davies
Mr F Davison
Mr G Davison
Mstr J Davison
Mr B Dawson
Mr K Dawson
Mr K.D Day
Mrs J.D Day
Mstr R.D Day
MISS C Dickens
MRS I Dickens

MRS M Dickens
Mr J Dickson
MR P Dillon
MSTR M Dillon
G J Dinsdale
J Dinsdale
MR G Dinsdale
Mr B.S.D Ditchburn
Dixon
MR A E Dixon
MR D Dixon
Mr D J Dixon
MR S J Dixon
MR W G Dixon
MSTR C J Dixon
MSTR P S Dixon
Mr P Dobby
Mstr A.D Dobby
Mr L.D Doble
Mstr L.D Doble
Mr I Dolan
Mr K.M. Dolan
Mr P.J. Donoghue
Mrs P Donoghue
Mstr P.J. Donoghue
A J Donsdale
K M Donsdale
MRS L Donsdale
S W Dosdale
MR R E Dove
Mr T.J.D Dove
Mstr D.D Dove
Mr A Dowd
Mstr J Dowd
MSTR M W Downie
MR M M Downing
Mr A.D Dowson
Mr K.J.D Dowson
Mr J Doyle
Mstr B Doyle
Mr K.D Drury
Mr M.K.D Drury
Ms S.D Drury
Mstr A.D Drury
S Drury
D K Dryden
Mr J Dryden
Mr K Dryden
MR L Dryden
MR H Duffield
Mr A.C.D Duffy
MR J Duffy
Mr K.C.D Duffy
MR M Duffy
MRS J Duffy
Mstr A.M.D Duffy
Mstr C.K.D Duffy
MRS S J Duggan
Mstr J Duggan
MR M N Dunford
T J Dunford
MRS S Dunk
Mstr R M Dunn
Miss L.J.D Durham
Mr J.D Durham
Mstr A.G Durham
Mrs J.S.D Durham
Mrs M.D Durham
Mstr J.S.D Durham
MSTR M K Durkin
MR K Dyson
MR E Eastham
Mr I.E Eastham
Mstr N.E Eastham
Mstr J Ebbs
Mrs V.E Eddleston
Miss L Edwards
Mr G Edwards
Mstr P.C.E Ellerton
MR A Ellis
MR J C Ellis
MR J M Ellis
MR M Ellis
Mr R.D.E Ellis
MRS H Ellis
MSTR D Ellis
MSTR N J Ellis
Mrs S.E Elsdon
Miss S.E Elwick
Mr R.E Elwick
Mstr M.E Elwick
MISS S A Emmerson
MR A D Emmerson
MR D A Emmerson
MSTR M P Emmerson
Miss K Empson
Mrs JL Empson
Mr S.D Eyre
Mrs K.J Eyre
Mstr J.E Eyre

Mstr T.S Eyre
MISS C.L Fagan
MR B D Fagan
Mr a Faloona
Miss H Farmer
Miss L Farmer
Mr D Farmer
Mrs L Farmer
Mstr N Farmer
Mr J W G Farries
Mr P J Farries
MR C J Fawcett
Mstr R.F Fawcett
Mr k J Featherstone
MISS R A Field
MRS L Field
MSTR G D Field
Mr B.F Fields
Mstr S.F Fields
Mr B.T.F Finn
Mr T.W.F Firbank
Mstr R.F Firbank
Mr M.L Fisher
Mstr M.M.F Fitzgibbon
MR P Flanagan
Mr G.M.F Fleming
Mr A.K Fletcher
Mstr A.M.F Fletcher
Mstr C.J.F Fletcher
Mstr M.D Fletcher
Miss S.F Flett
MR N J Flight
MR T N J Flight
Mr D.F Foley
Mr P Ford
Mr S Ford
A Foreman
Mr J.S.K Foreman
SK Foreman
MR A Forgan
Mr B Forster
Mr J.F Forster
Mstr J.F Forster
Mr D.J Fowler
Miss N.F.F Fox
Mr P.C.F Fox
Mr G Frame
Mstr J G Frame
MR C Frankland
MSTR C Frankland
MSTR L Frankland
Miss A.M.F Franklin
Miss L.M.F Franklin
Mr R.F Franklin
Mrs P.F Franks
Mr S Fraser
Mstr K S Fraser
Mr S Frost
Mstr S M Frost
Mr R.M Furness
Mstr S Furness
Mr L.G Gaffney
MR A Gamble
Mr P.M.G Gamble
Mstr A.G Gamble
MSTR D Gamble
MSTR M Gamble
MR R.J Garbutt
Mrs A Garbutt
K T Gardiner
MR K F Gardiner
Mr P.A.G Garland
Mstr A.G Garland
Mstr S A Garrett
Mr L Gibson
Mr T.G Gibson
MR A.J Gill
Miss L.A. Gilmour
Mr C.A. Gilmour
Mstr L.E. Gilmour
Mr K.G Glazebrook
Mstr C.J.G Glazebrook
Mstr M.G.G Glazebrook
MISS L Glover
MR B Glover
Mr B Gobson
Mr P Gobson
MR G.D Gofton
MSTR M.D Gofton
Miss M Goldsack
Mr S Goldsack
Mstr A Goldsack
MISS I. Good
MR M Good
MR P A Good
Miss T.G Goodwin
Mr A.G Goodwin
Mstr P.G Goodwin
Master S.M Gordon

Mr D Gordon
Mr S.M Gordon
Mstr Gordon
Miss L Gosnay
Mr J Gosnay
Mr M Gosnay
Mr W Gowing
Mstr T Gowing
MR L Graham
MRS J Graham
MSTR L Graham
Mrs C Grant
Mstr R Grant
Mr D.W Gray
Mr D.W Gray
Miss G.G Greco
Mr T.G Greco
Mstr A.G Greco
Miss A.E Green
Miss R.G Green
Mr C.W.G Green
Mr S.G Green
Mstr A Green
Mr N T Greenfield
Mstr S T Greenfield
MSTR A Grey
Miss Z J Griffiths
Mr P Y Griffiths
MR A Grounds
MSTR J Grounds
Mr B.A.G Gunn
Mr G.H Hadman
Mstr S.H Hadman
Mr A. Halfpenny
Mr R. Halfpenny
MR J Hall
Mr J Hall
Mr N Hall
MR R W Hall
MRS A Hall
Mstr A D Hall
MSTR A T Hall
Mstr J Hall
Mrs M.M.H Hallet
MR S Hamilton
MSTR A.L Hamilton
MISS J.C Hamilton
Mrs M Hancock
MR C Hand
MR D Hand
MRS L Hand
MR N Hand
Mr A.H Hannah
Mr B Hannah
Mr J.H Hansen
Mrs E.D.H Hansen
Mr D.H Harding
Mr M.H Hardman
Miss R Hardy
Mr K G Hardy
Mr C.R.H Hare
Mr D Harkess
Mr T.W. Harper
Miss S.H Harrington
Mr J.H Harrington
Mrs S. Harrington
Mstr M.H Harrington
Mstr N.S. Harrington
Miss L.H Harris
Mr C.P.H Harris
Mr K.H Harris
Mr M Harris
Mr N.H Harris
Mstr L.D.H Harris
Mstr S Harris
A Harrison
J Harrison
Master R.P Harrison
Miss E J Harrison
Miss K R Harrison
Mr E L F Harrison
MSTR D Harrison
R Harrison
Miss K.L.H Hart
MR D Hart
Mr D.H Hart
MR F Hart
MR J Hart
Mr J.F.H Hart
MR K J Hart
MR N Hart
Mr S.H Hart
MRS P Hart
MSTR J Hart
Mr Harvey
MR L Harvey
Mr C J A Harvison
Mr P J Harvison
Mr G Hatton

Mstr D W Hatton
MSTR G L Hatton
Mstr R J Hatton
Miss L Haveron
Mr J Haveron
Mstr L Haveron
A J Haycroft
Mr G Hayes
Mr M Hayes
Mr R Hayes
Mstr M Hayes
Miss V Hazlett
MR J J Hazlett
Mr J Healy
Mstr R.J Healy
Mstr C I Heatley
Mr M Hebb
J. Henderson
Mr H.H Heslop
Mstr L J Hewitson
MR C Hill
Mr G.S.H Hill
Mstr M.H Hill
MR I C Hinde
Mr E.H Hindson
Miss K.L.H Hipkins
Mr K Hoar
Mr P Hoar
MRS S A Hodge
MR I Hodgson
Mr I.J.H Hodgson
MSTR S A Hodgson
MR E.A HOLDEN
MSTR M.A HOLDEN
MR D Holmes
Mstr M.H Holmes
Mr C.J Hornby
Mr J Hornby
Mstr J.D Hornby
MSTR R J Hornby
Miss A.L.H Horncastle
MISS L M Horne
MR R M Horne
MR K J Horner
Mstr P Housley
MSTR A.L Howdon
<R A S Howdon
MR P S Howdon
MR B Howe
MSTR N L Howe
Mr K.G Hudson
Mstr C.D Hudson
Ms A.H.C Hudson-Calvert
Miss D Hughes
Mr A Hughes
MR J Hughes
Mr J.F Hughes
Mr K Hughes
MR L Hughes
Mr P.A Hughes
MR R Hughes
Mrs C Hughes
Mstr T.M Hughes
Mr A.H Hugill
Mrs S.H Hugill
MSTR A J Hume
Mr A.W. Hunt
Mr D Hunt
Mr S G Hunter
MISS V Husband
MISS L.E Huskinson
MISS L.J Huskinson
MR K Huskinson
MSTR S.K Huskinson
L R Hutchinson
Mr I Hutchinson
MR P Hutchinson
Mr R Hutchinson
MR R.S Hutchinson
Mrs S.M Hutchinson
Mstr I.J.H Hutchinson
MSTR M.I Hutchinson
Mstr P.M.H Hutchinson
MSTR S.H Hutchinson
J P Hyndman
Mr C Ibitson
Mr J.E Ibitson
Miss S. Iley
Miss D A Ing
Mstr C K Ing
Mr E.I Ingleden
Mr A Ingledew
Mrs M.I Ingledew
MRS L Irving
MRS R Irving
MSTR J R Irving
Mr J Ives
Mr Jack
Mr D Jack

MR A Jackson
Mr E Jackson
Mr G Jackson
Mr G.H.J Jackson
Mr N Jackson
Mstr D Jackson
MSTR S Jackson
K James
Mr R James
Mrs J James
Mr C Jameson
MISS R Jarvis
MISS A Jeffels
MRS A Jeffels
MRS M H Jefferies
MRS M H Jeffries
Mr D.J Jenkins
Mr M Jennings
Mr R.J Jewett
Ms M.J Jewitt
Miss E Johnson
Mr Johnson
Mr D Johnson
Mr D.S.J Johnson
Mr N.J Johnson
Mstr A D Johnson
Mstr D Johnson
Mr I.J Johnston
Mstr I.J Johnston
Miss R L Jones
Mr C.J Jones
Mr G.J Jones
Mr L.J Jones
Mr P.J Jones
Mrs J.J Jones
Mrs M.J Jones
Mstr C.J.J Jones
Mstr D.J.J Jones
Mstr E.J Jones
Mstr M.J Jones
Mr T.J Jordan
Mstr S.J Jordan
Miss C.J Jowett
Mrs J.J Jowett
MSTR MT Joyce
MISS S E Jubb
MRS M E Jubb
MSTR M H Jubb
Mr T.D. Judd
KAMARA
C L Kay
Mr A.W.K Keen-
Mr D H Kennedy
Mstr N J Kennedy
Miss H.E.K Kennington
Mr D.G.K Kennington
MSTR J.M Kent
Mr D Kilburn
Mstr M D G Kilburn
Mr N.K Kill
Mr N.K Kill
MR D J Killington
MSTR J Killington
MSTR S D Killington
Mr D.A. Kilvington
Mstr A. Kilvington
MISS L K King
MR P King
Mr S King
MSTR M D King
KIRKBY
Miss L M Kirkham
Mrs M.E Knapton
Mstr J Knapton
Mr S Knight
P Knowles
MR J.F Kokarevis
Mstr P Kreczak
Mr S.J.K Kubaj
MR S Lairlow
Mr I Lambert
Mr P Lancaster
Mstr P G Lancaster
Mr T.B North East Landlords
MISS H Lane
Mr D Lane
Mr J.L. Lane
Mr P Lappin
MR A Latheron
MRS B Latheron
Mstr D Latheron
MISS A Laverick
MR A Laverick
Mr J I Lawrence
Mr J Leahy
Mstr M Leahy

Mr N.R.L Learman	MISS N McCulloch	Mstr K.J.N Naylor	Mr J.J.P Pockington	Mr R Rutter	Mr D.S Sparrow	P M Trodden
Miss K.L.L Leatherland	MR D McCulloch	Mr M.H.N Nelson	MRS L Pogue	Mr S Rutter	Mr M.S Sparrow	Mr G Tucker
Mr G.L Leatherland	MSTR P McCulloch	Mstr J.R.N Nelson	MSTR R Pogue	Mr L.S Salvati	Mstr S.S Sparrow	Mr J E Tucker
L Lee	Mr P.M McDonough	Mr J Newbold	MSTR S Pogue	Mstr M.S Salvati	Mstr D Spaven	Mrs A Tucker
Mstr C.L Lee	Mstr A.M McDonough	Mr D.N Newlove	Mr A.R Pollock	Mstr S.S Salvati	Mr K.S Speck	Miss H.E.T Tunnicliffe
Mstr M Lee	RJM I.R.M McDonough	Miss E Newton	Mr J.A Pollock	Mr J Sanders	MRS L Spencer	Mrs N.T Tunnicliffe
A J Legg	Miss C.E.M McElvaney	Miss K.N Newton	Mr J H Polson	Mstr M J Sanders	MSTR S.B Spencer	Mstr P.A.T Tunnicliffe
MISS J C Legg	Mr M.M McElvaney	Miss R Newton	Mr R J Polson	Mr D.S Sands	Mstr R.J.S Stacey	Mr P.J.T Turley
Miss S.J.L Legg	Mr I.M McGlade	Mr G Newton	Mr L.D. Porritt	MR B Scaife	Rev J.N.S Stacey	E Turnball
Mr J.M.L Legg	Mstr M.M McGrogan	Mr K.N Newton	Mr R. Porritt	MSTR M Scaife	MR Stainsby	MISS L M Turnbull
MR T Legg	Miss J McKenna	Mr M.N Newton	Mr D Portas	Scott	D G Stainthorpe	MR G Turnbull
Mstr C.J.L Legg	MR J A McKeown	MR D Nicholson	Mstr J Portas	Miss A.L Scott	MR G D Stainthorpe	Mr J Turnbull
MR D Lewis	MSTR D McKeown	MSTR D Nicholson	Mstr S.P Portas	Miss L Scott	Mr N.L.S Starling	Mr M Turnbull
MR G Lewis	MSTR S McKeown	Mr D J Nimmo	MR D Porteous	Mr I R Scott	Mr K Stebulitis	Mrs E F Turnbull
Mr K.A.L Lewis	Miss A.M McLean	MR J P Nimmo	Mstr C Potts	Mr K Scott	Miss M.S Stephens	Mstr J Turnbull
Mrs J.R.L Lewis	Mr B.L.M McLean	Mr J.N Nixon	Mr D Powell	Mr R.W.S Scott	MR M Stephenson	MSTR L C Turner
Mstr A.J.M Lewis	Mrs M.M McLean	MR M Nolan	Mstr A.P Powell	Mstr A T Scott	MSTR S Stephenson	Mr R.S.T Turnpenney
Mstr M.P.L Lewis	Mstr C.M McLean	MR P.R Nolan	Miss C.J.P Power	Mstr M J Scott	Mr P.A Stevens	Mstr O.P.T Turnpenney
Mstr G Liddle	Mr C.S.M McLeary	MSTR C Nolan	Mr K.J.P Power	Mstr N.S Scott	Mr C.P Stevens	Mr R Twist
Mr R J Lidster	Mstr J.M McLeary	Miss K.N Noon	Mr A.J.P Power	MSTR T Scott	Miss L Stockport	Mrs A Twist
Mstr P Lidster	MR M McMahan	Mr B.N Noon	Mr M.G Pratt	Mr A.D.S Scrimgour	Mr A Stockport	MR P D Umpleby
Mstr P Lightfoot	MISS R McMahon	Miss J.N Norrie	Mstr M Pratt	MR P Seaton	Mr T Stockport	Mr A.V Vanloo
Mr P Lillie	MISS K A McManus	Mr K. Norrie	MSTR J Prest	MR P Severs	MSTR B J Stockwell	Mstr P.V Vanloo
Mrs S Lillie	Mr K.M McManus	Mr P.M.N Norris	Mr A Price	Miss K.M.S Seymour	Miss C Stonehouse	Mr M.J Vaughan
Mr A.H Lin	Mr G McMullen	Mrs E Norris	Mstr L Price	Mr C.S Seymour	Mr R M Stonehouse	Mstr J.V Vaughan
MR A List	Miss R.M McNamee	Mstr S Norris	MR A D Prior	Mr G.S Seymour	MSTR K C Strachan	Mstr P.M Vaughan
Mr s.l Livesey	Ms M.M McNamee	Mr J Noteyoung	MSTR R A Prior	Mstr A.P.S Seymour	MISS Strange	Miss A.L.V Veitch
Mr V.I. Livesey	Mr D.M McNeill	Mr P Noteyoung	Mr J.P Prosho	Mstr J.S Seymour	MR Strange	Mr D.V Veitch
Mstr T.L Livesey	Miss H McTaggart	MRS J Nottingham	Mstr J.P Prosho	Miss J Shail	MSTR Strange	Mr J.V Verduro
Mr J.L Llewellyn	Miss J McTaggart	MR S O'Brian	Miss C Prosser	Mrs B Shail	MR J.W Sturdy	Miss K Vickers
Mrs B.L Llewellyn	Mr S.J. McTaggart	MSTR D O'Neill	MSTR D J Purdy	Mr B Sharpe	MSTR B Sturdy	Mr D Vickers
MR J Lloyd	MR L McVay	MSTR T A O'Neill	Miss L A Pyrah	Mr B.J Sharpe	Mr C.W Suddes	Mr J Vickers
MRS J Lloyd	Miss V.L.M Meadows	Mstr P B Olszowski	Mr A Pyrah	MISS D Sharples	Mstr R.I.S Suddes	Mrs C Vickers
MR M Van Loo	Miss G O'Rourke	Mr G Ord	K.J Quinn	MSTR K Sharples	Mr E.M.S Summerfield	Mstr A Vickers
Mr R Lowes	Mrs C.M Meadows	Mstr A Ord	MR QUINN	Mr A.E.S Shaw	Mstr K Sumners	Mstr J Vickers
Mstr J Lowes	Mstr L.W.M Meadows	Miss J Ovington	MSTR QUINN	Mr S.C.S Shaw	Mstr S Sumners	MSTR W J Vickers
Miss S.L Lumley	Mstr D.J.M Mellon	Mr R Owen	Mstr W.R Raby	MR T M Shaw	Miss J.S Surrey	Mstr D Waites
Mstr G.L Lumley	Mstr M.M Mellon	M Owens	MSTR J D Raistrick	Mstr W.G.S Shaw	Mrs R.S Surrey	Mstr C.R Waites
Mstr P.J.L Lunnon	Mstr M.J.M Mellor	MR N Oxley	Mr I Rankin	Mstr J Sheperd	Mstr T.S Surrey	Mstr L.L Waites
Mr J G Lynch	Mr D J W Melville	MRS R Oxley	Mrs M Ratcliff	Mr D.H Shepherd	MRS D SUSCENS	E L Walker
Mr T Lynch	Mstr S D T Melville	Miss M Pain	Mr M Rathbone	Mrs M.E Shepherd	Mr P.S Swainson	J R Walker
Mstr D Lynch	Mr A.W.M Metcalfe	Mstr A Pain	Mstr P Rathbone	Mr P.S Shildrick	MR J C Swales	Miss K Walker
Mstr P.A.L Lynch	MR G Metcalfe	Mr C.P Pallister	Mr A Ray	MR H Short	MR T A Swales	Miss L.C.W Walker
Mr P.J.M Mableson	Mr K.M Metcalfe	Mr J Pallister	Mstr C D Redmond	Mrs E.S Short	Miss C Swarbrick	MISS N Walker
Mstr C.J.M Mableson	Mstr C.M Metcalfe	Mstr M Pallister	Mr S A Reed	Mstr D.S Short	Mstr J.F. Swarbrick	Mr C.W Walker
Mr I M Mack	Mstr L.A.M Metcalfe	Mstr R.P Pallister	Mstr D M Reed	Mstr G Shotton	MR M A Syrett	MR D Walker
Mstr Mack	MSTR R J Metcalfe	Mr R A Parker	Mstr L D Reed	Mr J.S Siddaway	MR A.H Tait	Mr D J Walker
Mstr A.N.M Mack	Mr A.S.M Meynell	Mr R.I.P Parker	Mr J.A Reeve	Mstr S Siddaway	Mr C J Tait	Mr K Walker
Mstr C.E.M Mack	Mstr G.J.M Meynell	Mrs S E Parker	Mr S Regan	MISS K Simmons	Mr M W Tait	Mrs W.M.W Walker
Mr P Mackell	Mrs J.M Middleton	Mstr R A Parker	Mstr C.R Renahan	MISS S Simmons	Mr N Tait	Mstr C.G.W Walker
Mr J.K.M MacKenzie	Miss R.M Milburn	Mstr S T Parker	Mr P Renton	MR J Simmons	MR M Tamblingson	Mstr D.A.W Walker
Mstr A.K.M MacKenzie	Mr A.M Milburn	Mr J.A Parry	Mstr M Renton	Mr A J Simms	Miss R Taylor	Mstr J Walker
Mstr C.M Madden	Mr R.F.M Mitchell	MSTR M Parry	MR I J Reynard	Mr D.A.S Simpson	Mr G.E.T Taylor	Mstr P Walker
Mstr C.T.M Maggs	Mr M Mitford	Mr D Passmore	MSTR D J Reynard	Mr H.S Simpson	Mr J. Taylor	WALLACE
Miss V A Mahon	Mr T Mitford	Mr G Passmore	Miss L.R Reynolds	MR L A Simpson	Mr J.W.T Taylor	Mr C Wallace
Mr M A Mahon	Mrs J R Mitford	Mr G M Patchett	Mr R.R Reynolds	MRS P Simpson	Mr T.T Taylor	MR S E Wallace
Mstr J P Mahon	Mrs T Mitford	W Patterson	Mr J Rhind	Mstr C.D.S Simpson	Mrs H Taylor	Mstr D Wallace
Mr G.M Mallam	MR C Mohan	Pattison	Mr D Rice	Mr R Singh	MSTR D Taylor	Mstr D.W Wallace
Mstr B.M Mallam	MR F Mohan	G Pattison	Mrs J Rice	Mstr R Singh	Mstr D Teasdale	MSTR S R Wallace
Mr J P Malone	Mr C.L.M Moloney	Mr I Pattison	Mstr S.A Rice	Mstr C.S Skidmore	Mr J Telford	MR R Wallis
MRS B J Malone	Miss R Moon	Mr T.P Pattison	Mr D.R Richardson	Mstr C.E.S Slasor	Mstr R Telford	MR M.J Walsh
MRS V Malone	Mr R.M Moore	MR J.E Patton	Mrs E.R Richardson	Master S.R Slater	MR W A Thackray	Mr P.W Walsh
Mr M Malowey	Mstr D.M Moore	Mr D R Paul	Mstr A.R Richardson	Mr R.W Slater	Mr S P Theaker	Miss S M Walton
MISS C A Mann	Mr D.P Moorfoot	Mr B.P Paxton	Mstr C.R Richardson	Miss J Sledge	Mstr A S Theaker	Mr A M Walton
MR A Mann	Mstr J Moorfoot	Mstr N Payne	MR E.P Riley	Mr J.S Slee	MR P.A THOMAS	Mstr J Walton
MR S Marlborough	MR D.R Morgan	Mr M.P Pearce	MISS D Ritchie	Miss N.S Smales	Mstr A.R.T Thomas	Mstr S G Walton
Miss S.E.M Marley	MR E Morgan	Miss A G Pearson	MR B Ritchie	Miss R.S Smales	Mstr D.T Thomas	MR A Ward
Mr I.M Marley	Mr M Morgan	Miss R.S.P Pearson	MSTR A R Roberts	Mr A.P.S Smales	Mr C.T Thompson	Mr M. Ward
Mrs C Marley	Mr N Morgan	Mr A.P Pearson	Mr R.R Robertson	Miss C Smaling	Mr D W Thompson	MSTR A Ward
Mstr C Marley	MR P.L Morgan	Mr J.C.P Pearson	Mr A Robinson	Miss C.L. Small	Mr J D B Thompson	Mstr M. Ward
Mr K.J.M Marlow	Mr S Morgan	Mr K.P Pearson	Mr B Robinson	Mr S.R. Small	MR K Thompson	R G Ward
Miss S.K. Marr	Miss A Morrison	Mr P.P Pearson	Mr D J Robinson	Mr T.R. Small	Mr S Thompson	Mr A.W Wardle
MR E Marr	Mr K Morrison	Mr T.P Pearson	Mr G.A Robinson	Mr D.S Smallwood	MRS L Thompson	Mstr M.W Wardle
MR K Marr	Mr P Morrison	Mstr J.P Pearson	Mr M Robinson	Mstr A.R.S Smallwood	MRS Y Thompson	Mstr A.P.W Warriner
MR A Martin	Mr Mousa	Mr G Peat	Mr P.R Robinson	Miss C.J. Smith	Mstr A S Thompson	Mstr E.J.W Warriner
MSTR L Martin	Mr Moyle	Mr J.D.P Peel	Mstr C Robinson	Miss K Smith	Mstr A.T Thompson	Mstr T.W Warwick
MSTR C Massey	Mr G.W.M Mudd	Mr J.A.P Pennick	Mstr C.R Robinson	Miss L L Smith	MSTR G Thompson	Mr M Wase
Mrs L.A.M Maude	Mrs L.M Mudd	Mstr J.A.P Perry	Mstr J.I Robinson	Miss R.S Smith	Mstr N D Thompson	Mstr C Wase
Mr J.P Maynard	Mstr I.A.M Mudd	Mr G.P Phillips	MR A J Robson	Mr A.L. Smith	Mstr R.I Thompson	Mr D Watcham
MISS J S McAndrew	Mstr P.V.M Mudd	Mr T Phoenix	Mr J.D Robson	Mr D M Smith	MSTR R.S Thompson	Mr M Waterson
MR A McAndrew	Mr R.M Muldowney	Mrs S Pierce	Mr K.R Robson	Mr G P Smith	MISS R.L Thurwell	MISS M J Watson
MR K McAndrew	Mrs D.M Muldowney	Mr S.J Pilkington	MR S Robson	Mr H.S Smith	MR R Thurwell	MR A M Watson
MRS K M McAndrew	Mstr C.M Muldowney	Mstr J.D Pilkington	Mstr A.R Robson	MR P Smith	MRS J.A Thurwell	MR B R Watson
MSTR C McAndrew	Mr J M Mulgrew	Miss H.L.P Pinkham	Mstr D P Robson	Mr P.S Smith	Miss V E Thwaites	Mstr C Watson
Mr K McArthur	Mstr D J Mulgrew	Mr A.J.P Pinkham	Mstr J.D Robson	Mr R D Smith	MISS R Tinkler	Mstr K Watson
Miss L.M McCann	Mstr S Mulgrew	Mr N.W.P Pinkham	Mstr L.R Robson	Mr S.R.S Smith	MR G Tinkler	MSTR M Watson
Mr G.M McCann	MR G.J Murphy	Mr J.P Piper	Mstr B.R Roffey	Mrs L Smith	MRS P Tinkler	Mr N Watts
Mstr A.M McCann	Mr M.M Murphy	Mr M Piper	MSTR L.D Rogers	Mrs L.N. Smith	MR K Tiplady	Mstr A Watts
Mstr J.M McCann	MR P.C Murphy	MSTR D Piper	MR C Rose	Mr V.S Smith	MRS P Tiplady	Mr C.W Weatherall
MISS L McCarthy	Miss K A Murray	Mr D Pitt	Mstr M.J.R Rose	Mstr G.P.S Smith	Mr G.T Tombs	Mstr J.W Weatherall
Mr T McCarthy	MR C S Murray	Mstr T.D Pitt	Miss N R Nowcroft	Mstr J.S Smith	MR N Topham	MISS A Weatherley
MSTR D R McCarthy	MR R W Murray		Mrs J.R Rudd	Mstr L Smith	TORR	MR P J Weatherley
MSTR G T McCarthy	Mr S Murray		Mstr C.R Rudd	Mstr M J Smith	Mr D.W Torr	MR S B Weatherley
Mr I. McCartney	Mrs E R Murray		Mstr M.R Rudd	Mstr M.A.S Smith	MR A.W Tott	MR K Webb
Mstr L. McCartney	MSTR M A Murray		Miss A L Ruddock	Mstr P.S Smith	Mr J Tott	MR W Webb
Mstr R. McCartney	Mstr T J Murray		Mstr S A Ruddock	Mstr R.T. Smith	MR M A Trainor	MRS K Webb
Mstr J McCauley	Mstr P.M.M Murrell		A Russell	Mr P Solan	MSTR P A Trenholme-Horner	MSTR W Webb
Mstr M McCauley	MR C Nayham		Rutledge	MR A Spacey		Mr A.W Weeks
Mstr A.M McCue	Mr J.W Naylor		L Rutledge			Mr M.W Weeks

APPENDIX 5

Mstr J A Weeks
Mstr J C Weeks
Mstr T A Weeks
Mr L.W.W Welburn
MISS B C Wells
MR A Wells
Mr J Wells
Mr S.E.W Wells
S J Wells
Miss D.L Welsh
Mr R.G.W Welsh
Mrs J.W Welsh
Mstr R.J.W Wensley
Mr J Wesson
Mstr M.J Wesson
Mstr D West
MR L Wharfe
MSTR L J Wharfe
B A Whatmore
MR P Whatmore
Mr A.E. Wheadon
Mstr B.A. Wheadon
MR S J Wheatley
Mr T.W Whelan
Mstr A.T.W Whelan
Mr C.M. White
Mr G.J. White
Mstr D.J. White
Mr D Whitehead
Mr R Whitehead
Mstr D D Whitehead
Mstr G Whitehead
Mr A.W Whitfield
Mr C.J.W Whitfield
Mr E.W Whitfield
Mstr D.C.W Whitfield
Mstr I.W Whitfield
Mstr N.W Whitfield
Mr K.W Whitley
MISS J A Whittle
MR J L Whittle
MSTR L A Whittle
MR G W Widdowfield
MSTR P G Widdowfield
MSTR S J Widdowfield
Mr P A Wild
Miss F.M.W Wilkinson
Miss H.L.W Wilkinson
Miss J.W Wilkinson
Miss R.A.W Wilkinson
Mr E.H Wilkinson
MR T G D Wilkinson
Mrs C.W Wilkinson
Mrs F.A.W Wilkinson
MSTR A N Wilkinson
Mstr M.H Wilkinson
MSTR S S Wilkinson
Mr J Willet
J Williams
Miss S L Williams
Mr D Williams
MR G N Williams
MR K J Williams
Mr K.J.W Williams
Mr M.W Williams
Mr R.G Williams
Mstr B Williams
Mstr J Williams
Mstr M.W Williams
Mstr N.M.K Williams
Mr A.W Willis
MSTR A Willis
G.W Wilson
L.J.W Wilson
Miss H Wilson
Miss M.L.W Wilson
Miss P.L.W Wilson
MISS V J WILSON
Mr A Wilson
Mr C J Wilson
Mr C.A.W Wilson
Mr D.W Wilson
Mr H Wilson
Mr J.K.W Wilson
Mr M Wilson
Mr T.J.W Wilson
Mrs J Wilson
MRS P Wilson
Mstr A T Wilson
Mstr J Wilson
Mstr J Wilson
Mstr M.L.W Wilson
Mstr P Wilson
MSTR S I Wilson
Mr J Windross
Mstr J.J Windross
Mr S.G.W Wing
Mstr F.L.W Wing
MISS T L Wood

Mr A.W Wood
Mr M Wood
MR RF Wood
Mrs R Wood
MSTR A Wood
Mstr G.J.A Wood
Mstr S Wood
T Wood
Mr D.P.W Woodhouse
Mrs L.K.W Woodhouse
Mstr D.J.W Woodhouse
Mstr J.D.W Woodhouse
MSTR R Woodhouse
Mr Woods
Mr N.W Woodward
Miss LA Worton
DK Wray
Mr K Wray
Mr NL Wray
C A Wright
MISS A L Wright
MR C Wright
Mr J.W Wright
Mr P S Wright
Mr R.W Wright
Mrs H.W Wright
Mstr A.W Wright
Mstr C Wright
Mstr D.W Wright
MSTR G Wright
Mstr S P Wright
Mstr S.R.W Wright
MR J Wyatt
MISS CF Yates
Mr P.A.Y Yates
Mstr M.C.Y Yates
Mr D.G. Yellow
Mr M. Yellow
MR A Young
MSTR M J Young

WEST STAND LOWER
Mr C.A Abell
Mstr C.A Abell
MR G.A Adams
Mr K.A Adams
Mstr N.A Adams
Mstr R.B.A Adams
Mr K Adamson
Mstr M A Adamson
Miss A.A Addison
Mr P.A Addison
Miss S Akerman
Mr D Akerman
Mstr M Akerman
Mr C.A Alderson
Mr S Alderson
Mstr P.A Alderson
Mr J.A Alderton
MSTR K R Alderton
Miss T Aldus
MR M Aldus
Mr R.A Allan
Mstr K.D.A Allan
MISS M Allen
MR B S Allen
Mr M.A Allen
MRS Allen
Mstr S.A Allen
Mr M.E.A Allenby
Mr R.E.A Allenby
Mr R.W.H Allenby
Mr I.A Allinson
MR R Allinson
Mstr M.G.A Allinson
Mstr M.J.A Allinson
Mr N.A Allison
Mr R.A Allison
Mrs A.A Allison
Mrs C.A.A Allison
MR A R ALTON
MSTR P A Alton
MR F Anderson
MRS M Anderson
MSTR J Anderson
MR K Angel
MSTR D.R Angus
Mr D.A Ankers
Mr M.A Ankers
Mstr C.A Ankers
Mstr M.A Ankers
Miss H.S. Antill
Mrs M. Antill
MR Appleton
MR B Appleton
MR J Appleton
MR M R Appleton
Mr P.A Appleton

Mr T.A.A Appleton
MRS L.A Appleton
MSTR A M Appleton
MSTR D Appleton
MSTR J.B Appleton
MR A Araf
Miss J. Archer
Mr J.A Archer
Mstr L.A Archer
Mr R Arkinson
Mr G.A Armes
MSTR D Armson
MR H Armstrong
MR J Armstrong
MR J A Armstrong
Mr J.V. Armstrong
Mr P.A Armstrong
Mr T. Armstrong
Mrs E.M. Armstrong
Mstr J.J. Armstrong
Mr D.B.A Aspin
MISS H J Atkinson
MISS J Atkinson
Miss J.A Atkinson
Miss N.A Atkinson
MR A R Atkinson
Mr B Atkinson
Mr J G Atkinson
MR M Atkinson
MR M L Atkinson
Mr S.A Atkinson
Mrs F.D.A Atkinson
MRS T Atkinson
MSTR C J Atkinson
Mstr P Atkinson
Mr R.G.A Attwood
MR M Ayers
MR A.A Ayre
MR T Ayre
MSTR A Ayre
MSTR M Ayre
Mr G.B Bailey
Mrs A.B Bailey
Miss J Baillie
Mr A.B Bainbridge
MR S J Baines
Miss C.M. Baird
Miss S Baird
Mr R. Baird
Mstr P Baird
MR A G Baker
MR C Baker
Mr C.R.B Baker
MR J Baker
Mr R Baker
Mr R.F.B Baker
Mr S.A.B Baker
Mr T.C.B Baker
Mstr J C J Baker
Mstr L.B Ball
MR A Balls
Mr I.T.B Bambro
Mr C.B Bamlett
Mr J.B Bamlett
Ms C.B Bamlett
Mstr C.B Bamlett
MR C Banks
Miss D F Barker
MR A Barker
MISS C Barnes
MR J Barnes
Mr J.B Barnes
MRS Barnes
Mstr J.J.B Barnes
Mr R Barrigan
Mstr C.H.S Barrigan
Mstr D.P.S Barrigan
Mstr H R S Barrigan
Mstr A.J.B Barry
Mr R.J.B Barton
Mstr M.B Barton
Mr J.B Barwick
MR L V Bateman
MR T W Bateman
MSTR P Bates
MR P E Bath
MSTR M Bath
MR T Batkin
Mr D.B Baverstock
Mrs P.B Baverstock
Ms L.B Baverstock
Mstr G.B Baverstock
Mr P J Bavin
Mr W.J. Bavin
MSTR D Baxter
MR J D Bayes
MSTR A.D Bayes
MR D Bayles
MR K.B Bayles
MR N Bayles

Mr P.K.B Bayley
Mstr M.G.B Bayley
Mstr P.K.B Bayley
Mr R.A.B Bean
Mstr P.N.B Bean
Mr C.N. Beardmore
Mstr R Becket
Mr J.F Beckett
MRS H Beckley
MSTR M A Beckley
MR G W Beddard
Mrs A.E.B Beddard
MR C Beevers
MISS G Bell
Miss H.B Bell
MISS M Bell
MR A Bell
MR A R Bell
MR C G Bell
Mr C.J. Bell
MR D H Bell
MR D J Bell
Mr D.G. Bell
Mr D.R Bell
MR J T Bell
Mr M.B Bell
MR S Bell
MRS B Bell
Mrs M.L Bell
MRS R H Bell
Mstr A Bell
Mstr C.P Bell
Mstr J.D.B Bell
MSTR L Bell
MSTR N W Bell
MSTR R Bell
MSTR R J Bell
MSTR R L Bell
MSTR S J Bell
Mr J.J.B Belmont
Mr A.L. Bendall
MR S Bendall
Miss S Bennett
Mr D Bennett
MR P E Bennett
MSTR C Bennett
Mstr I Bennett
Mstr S.B Bennett
Mr W.B Bennison
Mr R.C. Benton
Mr S.B Benton
Mstr S.C. Benton
MRS J Bettinson
Mstr L Bettinson
Mr N.B Bill
Mstr D.N.B Bill
MR G A Billington
MR G M Billington
Mr G T Billington
MR D H Bilton
Mstr P.B Bird
Mstr D.K.B Birdsall
Mstr R.O.B Birdsall
Mr A.B Bishop
Mstr C.B Bishop
Mstr T.B Bivens
MR L Blackburn
Mr M W Blackburn
Mr R.B Blackburn
Mstr I M Blackburn
Mstr L Blackburn
Mstr M.B Blackburn
MSTR P BLACKBURN
Mstr D.J.B Blackley
Mr B Blacklidge
Mstr A J Blacklidge
Mr W.G Blacklock
Miss T A Blackwell
Mr K Blackwell
MSTR I F Blair
MR M Blenkey
Mr J.C Blenkinsop
Mrs S.B Blewitt
Mstr A.D.B Blewitt
MISS D M Bligh
MR J C Bligh
MR P J Bligh
Mstr L.B Blockley
Mstr M.B Blockley
P.B Blockley
Mr J.R. Bloom
MSTR BLOOM
Miss S.L.B Blount
Mr C.W.B Blount
Mr J.E.B Blowman
Mstr J.E.B Blowman
Mr J K Boden
Mr K.B Boden
Mr K.D.B Boden

MR A Bollen
Miss G.B Boon
Mr P.B Boon
Mstr D.B Boon
Mr P.B Booth
Mstr C.M.B Booth
Mstr C.P.B Booth
Mr L.B Boothby
Mr T.A.B Boothroyd
Mr M. Borzomato
Mrs A.M.B Bostock
Mr S.A.B Bould
Mstr M.B Bould
MR J Bowden
MSTR R Bowden
Miss C Bowdler
Mr C Bowdler
Mr P M Bowdler
MSTR J R Bowen
Miss M.B Bowes
Mr D.B Bowes
Mrs S.B Bowes
Mstr D.B Bowes
Mr I.B Bowley
Mstr D.B Bowley
Mr J.S.B Bowmaker
Mstr D.J.J Bowmaker
Mr P.E.B Bowmer
Mr V.E.B Bowmer
Mr D.J.B Bowstead
Mstr A.D.B Bowstead
Mr J.A.B Bradbury
Mr R.N.B Bradbury
Mr T.S.B Bradley
Mstr T.G.W Whiteford Bradley
Mr S R Brady
MR E Braim
MASTER BRAITHWAITE
Mr N. Braithwaite
MR R H Braithwaite
MR Brakewell
MR D Braney
MR L Braney
Mr I.A.B Breckon
Mr M.E.B Breckon
Mr P.A.B Breckon
Mrs M.R.B Breckon
Mr C J Breen
MR J H Brennan
MSTR M J Brennan
MSTR M Bridgett
Mr S.P.B Brisley
MISS J Briston
MISS J E Briston
MISS L Briston
MR C M Briston
MR G Briston
Mstr D.S. Brittain
Mr A.M. Brook
Miss H.B Brooks
Mr F.J. Brooks
Mr I.W. Brooks
Mr J J Brooks
MR M Brooks
Mr M.J.B Brooks
Mrs P.B Brooks
MSTR G Brooks
Mstr S.B Brooks
Mr S W Broughton
Mr W G Broughton
MASTER P.R Brown
Miss S.B Brown
MR BROWN
MR A Brown
Mr G.B Brown
MR H Brown
Mr I.R.B Brown
Mr J.W.B Brown
MR K Brown
MR K N Brown
Mr N.B Brown
Mr P.F.B Brown
Mr P.J.B Brown
Mr R.B Brown
MR S Brown
Mrs C.B Brown
Mrs D.L.B Brown
MS B BROWN
MSTR A K Brown
Mstr B.B Brown
MSTR D M Brown
Mstr J.W.B Brown
Mstr M.B Brown
Mstr P.B Brown
MR K A Bullen
Mr D Bunn
Mr G.B Bunn

Mstr A.B Bunn
Mstr C.B Bunn
Mstr J Bunn
Mr P.J.B Bunnett
Miss M. Bunting
Mr R. Bunting
MSTR E Bunting
MR P Burke
Mstr M.B Burke
Mr P.J.B Burleigh
Mstr R.J.B Burleigh
MSTR BURNIP
MISS J A Burns
Mr R Burns
MRS C Burns
MRS M F. Burns
Mstr A Burns
Mr J.B Burrell
Mr J.I.B Burrell
MASTER M Burton
Miss K.E.B Burton
Mr C.B Burton
Mr K.D.B Burton
MR N Burton
Mstr A.K.B Burton
MR D Busfield
MSTR C Busfield
Mr I.B Butler
Miss A.L.B Buttery
Mr S.J.B Buttery
Mstr C.J.B Buttery
MR P P Byrnes
MSTR L Bythway
MR A Caddy
MSTR P Caddy
Mr C.D.C Cairns
Mr J.D.C Cairns
MR J R Calder
Mr P Caley
Mr F. Callaghan
Mr E.C.C Calvert
MR R Calvert
Mr J.C Campbell
Mr T Canty
Mrs V Canty
Miss S Cappleman
Mr D.M. Cappleman
Mstr T.M. Cappleman
Mr C J Cardwell
Mstr P.K.C Cardwell
Mstr S.G.C Cardwell
Mr P.C Carey
Mrs E.C Carey
Mstr J.A.C Carey
Mstr J.D.C Carey
Mr L.C Carless
Mr V.C Carless
Mr M.C Carlin
MST M CARLIN
MR L Carlton
MSTR M L Carlton
Mstr S Carlyon
MSTR S Carney
MSTR S P Carrington
D Carter
MISS D Carter
MISS H Carter
MR D P Carter
MR G A Carter
MR S Carter
MRS M E Carter
MSTR A M Carter
MSTR D A Carter
Mr B.J.C Cartwright
Mr S.C Cartwright
Ms S.C Cartwright
Mstr J.C Cartwright
Mstr M.C Cartwright
MISS Casey
MSTR Casey
Mr M Cass
MSTR A Cass
MR E.D. Casson
Mstr J Casson
MSTR G Cattermole
Mstr G.C Cattermole
MR T E Caygill
Mr P.S.C Chambers
MSTR B Chambers
Miss E.J.C Chapman
Mr A.C Chapman
MR D.J Chapman
Mr M.C Chapman
MR S H Chapman
MSTR J Chapman
Mstr S Chapman
MSTR S R Chapman
Mstr S.D.C Chapman

MR D.J CHARLESWORTH
Mr D.N Cheesebrough
Mstr M.R Cheesebrough
Mr D Chillmaid
Mstr M.S Chorlton
Miss E.L Christie
Mr B.M Christie
MR E Christie
Mr J.S.C Christie
Mstr N.R Christie
Mr S.B.C Christopherson
MR Ciancio
MSTR Ciancio
MR D Clancy
MISS E Clapham
MSTR S J Clapham
Miss K.M Clark
Miss R.C Clark
Mr A Clark
MR E M Clark
Mr J.J.C Clark
Mr R.H.C Clark
MR T J Clark
Mrs V.M.C Clark
Mstr A.C Clark
Mstr D.C Clark
Mstr I.C Clark
Mstr P.C Clark
MSTR S M Clark
MISS L A Clarke
MR H Clarke
Mstr J Clarke
Mstr T Clarke
Mr D.C Clarkson
Mstr R.J.C Clarkson
Mr J Clayton
Mstr M.C Clayton
Mstr S.C Clayton
Miss S Clennan
Mr C Clennan
Mrs J Clennan
Mr C.C Close
Mstr S.C Close
Mr J Clough
MASTER L D Coates
MR B Coates
MR J Codling
Mr R.C Codling
MSTR J I Codling
Mr C. Colbeck
Mstr S. Colbeck
MISS R.L Cole
MR J.I. Cole
MRS V Cole
Mrs W.C Coleby
Mr P.M.C Coleman
MR P Colley
MSTR T M Colley
Mr M.C Colligan
MSTR M Colligan
MSTR S Colligan
MR J Collingan
MISS S Collins
MR G Collins
MR H Collins
MR J R Collins
Mstr A Collins
MSTR A Collins
MSTR L A Collins
Mstr M.I.C Collins
Mrs B.A.C Collinson
Mstr J.E.C Collinson
Mr L.J.C Colllingwood
Mr T.C Connell
Miss S A Connolly
Mr M Connolly
Mstr T M Connolly
Mr P Connors
Mstr E Connors
Mr J.C Connorton
Mr M.J.C Connorton
MR MR Connorton
MR P Connorton
MR S J Connorton
MSTR D R Connorton
MR W R Constantine
MSTR W Constantine
Mr CONWAY
Mr P.A.C Conway
Mr T.B.C Conway
MR Cook
Mr H.C Cook
Mr M.C Cook
Mr P.J.C Cook
Mstr G Cook
MSTR M Cook
Mr C.E.C Cooke

MR D Cooke
Mr G.W.C Cooke
Mr P.C Cooke
MSTR N Cooke
Mstr C.C Cookson
Mr A.C Cooper
Mr D.E.C Cooper
Mr S.C Cooper
Mstr N.D.C Cooper
Mr J.J. Copeland
MR J R Coppack
MSTR D J Coppack
MSTR R S Coppack
Mr J.E.C Corbett
CORR
Mr N.C Cottle
Mr B.P Coulton
Mr P.A Coulton
MR A J Counsell
MR D J Counsell
Mstr N.C Court
Mr N. Cowen
Mrs G.C Cowen
Miss L.C Cowley
Miss N.C Cowley
Mr K.C Cowley
Mstr N.C Cox
MR G Coxon
MSTR C A Coxon
Mr B.C Coyle
Mr G.C.C Coyle
Mr J.T.C Coyle
MR A Craig
Mr A.C Craig
Mr H.J.C Craig
Mr P.C Craig
Mstr G.C Craig
Mr I.J.C Craven
Mr J.C Craven
Mr I.B. Crawford
MR C J Cree
MR J C Cree
MSTR J M Cree
MSTR L C Cree
MSTR S A Cree
MR G J Cripps
MSTR P J Cripps
MR A Croft
MSTR M.A Croft
MR F H Crombie
MSTR A J Crombie
MR J Crooks
MR D N Cummings
MR W A Cummings
MSTR A D Cummings
MSTR M W Cummings
MR C Cunningham
MR J C Cunningham
MSTR A Cunningham
MSTR P Cunningham
Mr E.C Curran
Mr T. Curran
Mstr A.C Curran
MR D Curtis
MR S Curtis
Mr S.C Curwen
Miss H.E.C Cuthbert
Mrs C.C Cuthbert
Mstr S.J.C Cuthbert
Mr L.C Cuthbertson
MSTR P Dalby
MISS S H Dale
MR J Dale
Mr K Dale
MR P Dale
Mr R J Dale
MSTR J A Dale
MSTR N I Dale
MR J R Dales
MR I Dalgarno
MSTR L Dalgarno
Mr L.M.D Dalrymple
MR B Dalton
Miss A M Daly
Mr B.D Daly
V Daly
Mr G.D Dalziell
Mrs I.F.D Dalziell
MRS M E Daniels
MR DARBYSHIRE
MRS Darbyshire
MR D.M Dargue
MR M Dargue
MSTR J.W Dargue
MSTR S J Dargue
Mrs J.M. Darnley
MSTR P Davaston
MR A P Davey
MRS R Davey

MSTR A Davey
Mr I.A.D Davidson
Mr K Davidson
MR P Davidson
MSTR D A Davidson
Mstr D M Davidson
Mstr J.E.J Davidson
Miss A.D Davies
Mr Davies
Mr G Davies
Mr J.D Davies
MR K Davies
MR P L DAVIES
Mr S.D Davies
Mstr G.D Davies
MSTR L Davies
Mstr O.D Davies
Mrs L Davis
MR J A Davison
MRS B Davison
Mr B.J. Day
Mr D.D Dean
Mr N.D Dean
MR S Dean
Mstr B Dean
MSTR C S D Dean
MR S.D Deaton
MR B J Deenan
MR E DEER
MRS J Dell
The Dene School
MR G Deprez
Mr R.D Deprez
Miss K.D Devlin
Mr A.D Devlin
MRS D Dew
Miss E Dewings
Mr N Dewings
MSTR B R Dey
MR D Dickens
Mr M.L.D Dickins
Mr A.D Dickinson
MR G Dickinson
MR M Dickinson
Mstr L.D Dickinson
Mr A.H.D Dilcock
Miss H Dinsdale
Mr M Dinsdale
MR W Dinsdale
MR Dixon
MR B Dixon
MR K J Dixon
Mstr D.S.D Dixon
MSTR J.B Dixon
MR R Dobby
Miss C.D Dobson
Mr F.R.D Dobson
Mstr D Dobson
Mstr L.D Dodds
MR D Dodgson
Mr T.L.D Dodsworth
Mrs A.D Dodsworth
Mr D.D Doherty
Mstr R.D Doherty
MR DOLAN
Mr I.D Dolan
Mr J.D Dolan
Mstr M.D Dolan
MR DONACHIE
Mr Donaghue
MR P R Donaghy
Mr P.D Donaghy
MRS J Donaghy
MSTR S R Donaghy
Miss L.D Donnelly
MR M Donnelly
Mr R.G Donnelly
Mrs C.A.D Donnelly
Mr D.D Donovan
Mrs H.D Donovan
Mstr D.P. Donovan
Mr N.D Douglas
MSTR C Douglas
Miss S.D Douglass
Mr J.D Douglass
Mr L.D Douglass
Mrs A.D Douglass
Mstr P.D Douglass
Mrs P.D Douthwaite
Mr A.D Dowden
Mr J.A.D Dowden
Mstr J.D.D Dowden
MR M A Downes
MSTR R M Downes
MSTR A Downey

MSTR S Downey
Mr D. Dowson
Mrs K.M. Dowson
Mstr A.M. Dowson
Mstr S.D. Dowson
Mstr S.P. Dowson
MR A Doyle
Mr B.D Doyle
MR J Doyle
MR R E Doyle
Mstr G.T.D Doyle
Mr C.D Dresser
Mr P.D Dresser
Mstr G.D Dresser
Miss L Dring
Miss S.L. Dring
MISS L.A Drummond
Mr K.P.D Drummond
MR L Drummond
MR P S Drummond
Mrs D.D Drummond
MRS G P Drummond
MR K Dryden
MSTR C Dryden
Miss H.I..D Duffy
Miss] H.M.D Duffy
Mr J.F.D Duffy
Mr K.J.D Duffy
Mr M.D Duffy
Mstr G.D Duffy
Mstr J.D Duffy
MR D Duggan
Miss S.M.D Duncan
Mr D.K.D Duncan
MR W Dunford
Miss H.J.D Dunlop
Mr G.M.D Dunlop
Mstr I.J.D Dunlop
Mr G.D Dunn
Mr J.D Dunn
MR M Dunn
Mr R. Dunn
Mr S.J.D Dunn
MR A J Dyball
MSTR A J Dyball
Mr D.M.D Dyson
Mr G.E Earl
Mr W.E Earl
Mstr S.E Earl
Mr J.R.E Earley
Mr P.W. Earnshaw
Mrs E.V. Earnshaw
MSTR S J Eastwick
MISS A J Eastwood
MRS N A Eastwood
Miss L.E Eaton
Mr I.J.E Eddie
MASTER R Edemenson
MR C Edemenson
MR M Edemenson
Mr A.E Edwards
Mr B.E Edwards
Mr J.I.E Edwards
Mr E.M. Edwardson
MR J K Edwardson
MR S J Edwardson
Mr P G Elders
MSTR P Eldrett
MR I Elgey
MISS C.H Ellingsen
MR B Ellingsen
Mr G.V.E Elliott
MR M D Ellis
Mr S M Ellis
Mrs J.E Elsdon
MR B Emmerson
MR G Emmett
MSTR P G Emmett
Mr G.E Emms
Mstr A.I.E Emms
Mstr C.J.E Emms
MR A.E Errickson
Mr N.E Errickson
Mstr R.E Errickson
Mr K.E Errikson
Miss C.L.E Evans
Miss R. Evans
Mr C.S.E Evans
Mr M Evans
Mr P.E Evans
Mstr M.E Evans
Mstr M.W.A. Evans
MR A K Everitt
MRS B Everitt
L Evison
MSTR G Fagan
Mr M.F Fancourt
Mstr M.F Fancourt
MISS R I. Farley

MR D W Farley
Mr A J Farquharson
MRS K Farren
MR G E Farrington
Mr R Farrow
Mstr J Farrow
Mr M.F Fascia
Mrs P.F Fascia
Mr A.F Fawcett
Mr P Fawcett
Mr R.F Fawcett
Mr H.F Fawcett
Mstr P B Fawcett
MSTR M S Fawdon
MSTR J R Featherstone
Mr D.A. Feeney
Mr A.C.F Felgate
Mstr S.A.F Felgate
Miss L.H.F Fell
Mr H.W.F Fell
Mr M H Fennon
Mr N J Fenwick
MR S Fenwick
Mstr S A Fenwick
Mstr S L Fenwick
MR A Ferguson
Mr A Ferguson
Mr J.F Ferguson
Mrs A.F Ferguson
Mrs Y Ferguson
Mstr D M Ferguson
Mstr G D Ferguson
Mr R.J.F Field
Mstr R.F Field
Mr D.D.F Fieldhouse
Mr D.F Fieldhouse
Mr P Findley
MISS K Fines
MR B Fines
MR J D Firth
MSTR D W Firth
MSTR N J Firth
Mr P.F Fisher
Mr W.F Fisher
Mrs D.F Fisher
Mstr J.F Fisher
Mr J.F Fitzpatrick
Mr R.F Fitzpatrick
Mstr R.F Fitzpatrick
Mr D Fletcher
MR E Fletcher
MR R Fletcher
MR W Fletcher
Mstr M Fletcher
Mr E.J.F Flett
Mr J Flett
Mr S.F Flett
MR G Flewker-Barker
MR I Flewker-Barker
MSTR S Flewker-Barker
MR R D Flunder
MR S Flunder
MSTR L S J Flunder
MSTR R J Flunder
MISS S.A Flynn
MR D Flynn
Mr E T Flynn
MR M V Flynn
MR R A Flynn
MR S P Flynn
Mrs V.F Flynn
MSTR J Flynn
MSTR J.J Flynn
MSTR S L Flynn
Mr J.S. Ford
Mr K.F Ford
Mstr S.J. Ford
Mr D J Fordyce
Mr T A Fordyce
Mrs S D Fordyce
MR S H Forrest
MSTR J S Forrest
Mr P.F Forrester
MR R Forster
Miss K.F Foster
Mr A.F Foster
Mr J.F Foster
Miss H.F Fox
MR A Fox
Mr I.F Fox
Mr R.D.F Fox
Mr W.H Fox
Mrs H Fox
Mr W.T Francis
Mr Frank
Mrs J Frank
Miss L.F Frankland
Mstr S.F Frankland
Miss L Fraser
Mr I.C.F Fraser

Mr K.F Fraser
Mrs L Fraser
Mr J R French
Mr J.F French
Mr M.J.F French
MR R J French
Mstr S.J.F French
Mstr M Fretter
Miss E J Fryett
Mr G.P.G Gaffney
MSTR D Galasso
Miss K.A.G Gale
MISS A Gallacher
MR H Gallacher
Mr D.E. Gallagher
MR K Gallagher
Mr W G Gallagher
Mrs M. Gallagher
MR M Gallaher
Mr I Galloway
Mstr S Galloway
Mr I. Gamble
Mr K. Gamble
Mstr P.M. Gamble
Mr R.R.G Garbutt
MR T D Garbutt
Mr J.G Garcia
Mr J.G Garcia
MR A R Gardiner
Mr G.W Gardner
MISS GARLAND
MR GARLAND
MRS GARLAND
MR S J Garncarek
MSTR J Garncarek
MSTR P Garncarek
Mr J Garry
Mstr J.R Garry
Miss J.M. Gaskarth
Mr A.R. Gaskgarth
Mr C.G Gavillet
MR W N Gee
Mr G.J.G Gell
Mstr O.W.G Gell
Miss A.E.G Gibson
Miss J M Gibson
Miss L.D.G Gibson
Mr C Gibson
Mrs G M Gibson
Mstr R M Gibson
Mr E.G Gildersleeve
Mr P.G Gildersleeve
Mr D Gill
Mr D W Gill
MR H Gill
MR J Gill
Mr J.R.G Gill
Mr L. Gill
MR N Gill
Mr R.D Gill
MRS C J Gill
Mrs E. Gill
Mrs M.A Gill
Mrs S.E. Gill
Mr A.J Gill
Mstr C.G Gill
MSTR M Gill
Mstr M C Gill
Mstr P D Gill
Mstr S J Gill
Mr T.G Gilmour
MR G Gladders
MRS D Gladders
Miss G.L.G Glazzard
MSTR A Glover
Mr D.G Glynn
Mstr M.G Glynn
MR R Godley
MRS J Godley
MR R.V Golden
MSTR D.J Golden
Mr C.C. Goldsbrough
Mrs D.J. Goldsbrough
Mr J R Goodison
Mr S.R. Goodman
MR M Goodwill
MSTR I Goodwill
Miss S.L.G Goodwin
Mr J.W.G Goodwin
Mrs B.G Goodwin
Mstr G.J.G Goodwin
Miss R.E.G Gordon
Mr D.G Gordon
Mr D.J Gordon
Mr K.G Gordon
Mr L.A Gordon
Mr T.J.G Gordon
Mstr J.L. Gordon
Mstr R.K Gordon

MR V Gough
MR M R Goult
Ms C.G Goult
Mr F.G Gowland
MR L Grace
GRAHAM
Miss M. Graham
MR A J Graham
Mr H.L.G Graham
MR I M Graham
Mr K R Graham
MR L Graham
Mr M.D. Graham
Mrs C.G Graham
Mrs G. Graham
Mstr A Graham
Mstr M Graham
Mr Grainger
Mr B.G Grainger
MR J B Grainger
Miss V J Grange
Mr D. Grant
MR P Grant
Mr P.G Grassie
MR I Graves
Mr S.A.G Graves
Mrs J.G Graves
Miss E.G Gray
MISS J GRAY
Mr J Gray
Mr K P Gray
Mr K.G Gray
Mrs M.G Gray
MSTR D J Gray
MISS M Green
MR GREEN
MR A J Green
MR C Green
Mr C.J. Green
Mr M.G Green
Mr M.S.G Green
Mr R.G.G Green
Mstr A.G Green
MSTR A Green
MSTR S A Green
MR A E Greening
MR P Greening
MR W Greening
MRS D E Greening
MSTR B P Greening
MSTR J GREENING
MISS H C Greenmon
MR B Greenmon
MR H Greenmon
MRS P J Greenmon
Mrs D.G Greensitt
MR N Greenwell
MR B.J Greenwood
MR J Greenwood
MR P Greenwood
Mr J.S.G Greggs
Mr A.J.G Gregory
Mstr A.C.G Gregory
Mr E.G Grief
Mr W.E.G Grief
Mstr A.G Grier
Miss L.G Griffiths
Mr A. Griffiths
Mr G.G Griffiths
Mr H D Griffiths
Mr M Griffiths
Mstr D Griffiths
MR B Grimes
Mstr J.G Grimley
Mr J.A.G Groat
Mr J.H.G Groat
Mr I.G Groves
Mstr C.G Groves
Mr A.D.G Guillaume
Mr D.A.G Gullon
Mr T.G Guy
MR H Hadfield
Mr K. Hadley
MR S C Hadley
Mstr A Hagan
MR T Haigh
Mr K.H Hair
Mstr G.P.H Hair
Mr M.R.H Halfpenny
Mr R.W.H Halfpenny
MR A Hall
Mr D Hall
Mr D.J Hall
Mr F Hall
Mr G S Hall
MR J W Hall
Mr M J Hall
MR M R Hall

MR S Hall
Mr T.J.H Hall
MRS H Hall
Mrs P.H Hall
Mrs S B Hall
MSTR A A Hall
Mstr C Hall
Mstr J A Hall
Mstr M J Hall
MSTR R A J Hall
Mstr R.A.H Hall
Mstr L. Hallet
MR D Halliday
MR Hamill
MR M Hamilton
Mrs J.H Hamilton
MSTR B Hamilton
MSTR M Hamilton
MISS B C Hammill
MR A G Hammond
MR D KL Hammond
MR G Hammond
MISS C Hanley
Mr D.H Hanley
MR P Hanley
Mr K. Hannan
Mstr D. Hannan
MR M Hanratty
MSTR M Hanratty
Mr J.H Hansell
MR D G Hardwick
Mstr C Hardwick
MSTR P J Hardy
Mstr A.H Hargate
Miss K.P Harker
MR C.R Harker
Mr J.J.H Harker
MR B Harland
Mr W.J.H Harnett
MISS K Harper
MR F Harper
Mr K.H Harper
MRS S L Harper
MSTR G Harper
Mstr S D Harper
MISS H Harrington
Miss K Harrington
MR K Harrington
MSTR R Harrington
MISS H Harris
MR D Harris
MR M W Harris
MR P Harris
Mstr A. Harris
MSTR J Harris
MSTR L A Harris
MSTR S Harris
Mr J.H Harrison
MR K S Harrison
Mr R.A.H Harrison
Mr S. Harrison
Mstr L.H Harrison
Mstr M.H Harrison
Mstr R.P.H Harrison
MSTR S.R Harrison
Mr K.A.H Harrow
MRS P A Hartas
MSTR C W Hartas
Mr D.O.H Hartley
MR S.A Hartley
MRS A Hartley
Mstr L.J.H Hartley
MR D.L Harton
MSTR D.J Harton
MSTR M Harton
MRS J Hartshorne
MR M Haslock
MSTR P Haslock
Mr L Hatfield
MR M Hatfield
MR R Hatfield
Mstr D Hatfield
Mstr S Hatfield
Mr D.H Hatton
MR R Hatton
Mstr A.H Hatton
Mr A.H Haverson
MRS J Haverson
MR Haye
Miss L.H Hayes
Mr M.H Hayes
Mrs S. Hayes
Mstr M.H Hayes
Mr C.R.H Head
Mr W. Head
Mstr C.T.H Head
MISS HEALD
MISS N Heald
Miss R.C.H Healey

Mr M.G.H Healey
Mr B.H Healy
MASTER J Heather
Mr B.H Heaton
Mstr G.B.H Heaton
Mrs C Hebbron
MSTR G Heerin
MR D Heightley
Mr N.H Helyer
Mstr M.H Helyer
MR I Henderson
MSTR A Henderson
AJ HENMAN
MR S A Henman
Miss A Henry
Miss J Henry
MR L S S Henwood
Mr L.A. Henwood
MR S F Henwood
Mstr D.H Hepple
Mstr W Herbert
Mr G.H Heritage
Mstr D.H Heritage
Dr D.H Heseltine
MR M Heseltine
Mstr N.H Heseltine
Mstr T.D.H Heseltine
Mr J.R. Hesketh
Mstr J.M. Hesketh
Mstr M.G. Hesketh
Mstr P.I.H Heslehurt
MR HESLOP
Miss C.A.H Heward
Mr R.T.H Heward
Mstr A.H Heward
Mstr M.H Heward
Mr R.J.H Hewgill
Miss J Hey
MR HICKSON
MSTR D C Hide
MSTR S Higgins
Mr G.H Higgs
Miss L.M.H Hill
MR Hill
MR A Hill
Mr C Hill
Mr D.H Hill
MR F Hill
MR G Hill
MR G.M Hill
Mr J.C. Hill
Mr N W Hill
Mr R.H Hill
MSTR C Hill
MSTR C N Hill
Mstr C.S.H Hill
Mstr M J Hill
Mstr R.C. Hill
Miss K.D.H Hillerby
Mr D.H Hillerby
MR D Hills
MSTR P Hills
MR HIMSWORTH
Mstr R J Himsworth
Mr J.H Hinton
Mstr P.J.H Hinton
MISS R E Hitchinson
Mr H Hoar
MR A Hodge
MR J Hodge
MRS J Hodge
MSTR R Hodge
Mr P.H Hodgers
Mrs N.H Hodgers
Mstr D.J.H Hodgers
MSTR DJ HODGERS
MISS E L Hodgson
MR A N Hodgson
Mr K.H Hodgson
Mr L Hodgson
MR P M Hodgson
MR T E Hodgson
Mstr B E Hodgson
Mstr C G Hodgson
MSTR J P Hodgson
MSTR T J Hodgson
Mrs R.H Hogg
Mr D.A.H Hoggarth
Mstr A.H Hoggarth
MR H Holden
MR M Holden
MR S Holden
MSTR T Holden
MSTR C Holley
Mr P W Holliday
MR G D Hollingsworth
MSTR D G Hollingsworth
MASTER M J Holloway
MR C Holloway

M.D Holly
MR D.R Holly
Mr P.H Holmes
MR R W Holmes
MSTR S Holmes
Mr D W Holtham
Mr S D Holtham
Mstr P J Holtham
MISS G L Homer
Mr A.D Homer
MR S P Homer
MR A E Honeyman
Mr D.H Honeyman
MR M Honeyman
MSTR C Honeyman
Mr N.H Hood
Mr P.H Hood
Mr R Hood
Mstr D.H Hood
Mstr D.M.H Hood
Mstr J.R. Hood
Mr P.D.H Hope
Mstr I.J.H Hope
Miss R.A.H Hopkins
Mr C.W.H Hopkins
Miss V.H Hopper
MR M W Hopper
Mr M.G Hopper
MR S Hopper
Mrs P.B Hopper
MSTR R W Hopper
Mstr S.M Hopper
Mr H.H Hornby
MSTR C J Horne
MSTR J Horseman
Mstr D. Horsley
Miss L Houghton
Mr N Houghton
Mrs C A Houghton
Mr P. Ransdale House
MRS J Howard
MSTR S J P Howell
MISS G L Howes
MISS M J Howes
MR M Howes
MR R Howes
Mrs D.H Howes
Ms C.J.H Howes
Mr A.H Howlett
Mstr D.H Howlett
Mstr A Howling
MASTER J V Hoyland
Miss L.M.H Hudson
Mr A Hudson
Mr D.H Hudson
Mr E.J.A Hudson
Mrs P.M.H Hudson
MSTR G Hudson
Mstr S Hudson
MR Huggins
Mr E.H Hughes
Mr J.T.H Hughes
Mr L.H Hughes
MR M T Hughes
Mr M.H Hughes
Mrs E.H Hughes
Mstr A.J.H Hughes
Mstr M.T.H Hughes
MR G Hugill
MSTR A Hugill
MSTR M G Hugill
MR HUME
Miss J.A Hunter
Miss K L Hunter
Mr A Hunter
Mr C.K.H Hunter
Mr G.H. Hunter
Mr P Hunter
MR W M Hunter
Mstr M.P. Hunter
MR S Huntley
MSTR M Huntley
MSTR J Husband
Miss R.H Hutchinson
Miss S.J.H Hutchinson
Mr A.H Hutchinson
Mr G.H Hutchinson
Mr J.G.H Hutchinson
Mr S.H Hutchinson
MSTR B J Hutchinson
HYNES
Mr K.H Hynes
Mstr D.H Hynes
Mstr J.H Hynes
MSTR A N I'Anson
MSTR M C I'Anson
MSTR K Ianson
MSTR T Illingworth
Mr C.C.I Ingoe

Mstr C.J.I Ingoe
Mstr C.P.I Ingoe
MR A M Ingram
MR K Instone
Mr W C Instone
MSTR L Instone
Miss J Ireland
Mr A R Ireland
MR T Ireson
Mstr S.I Irvine
Mr P.A.I Irwin
MR A Isbell
MSTR S.A Isbell
Mr G.K. Jaab
Mr Jackson
Mr M.J Jackson
Mr R.T.J Jackson
Mrs S.J Jacobs
Mstr A.J Jacobs
Mstr G.J Jacobs
Mr S.G Jameison
James
MR JAMES
Mr A.J James
MR B James
MR B.L James
Mr G James
MR J E James
MR K James
Mr S.J James
Mr W A James
Mstr B James
Mstr D A James
MSTR L K James
Mr G.D Jamieson
Mr H.E Jamieson
Mr M Jamieson
Mrs E.A Jamieson
Mstr L.P. Janes
MR G P Jaworski
Mrs A.J Jefferson
Mstr D.J.J Jeffles
Mstr S.J Jepson
MISS A Jerrison
Mr A.M. jobson
Mstr M.C. Jobson
Mrs G.E. Joel
MISS S L Johns
Mr A P Johns
Mr W.E.J Johns
MRS E Johns
Mrs M.P.J Johns
Miss L E Johnson
Miss H Johnson
Miss S.J Johnson
MR B E Johnson
Mr B.J Johnson
Mr J.M. Johnson
Mr N.J Johnson
Mr R.T. Johnson
Mrs B.A. Johnson
Mrs B.J Johnson
Mstr C.J Johnson
Mstr M.N.J Johnson
Mstr P.J Johnson
Mr M.J Johnston
Mr S Johnston
Miss C.M Johnstone
B A Jones
G W Jones
MISS H L Jones
Mr A Jones
MR E C Jones
Mr G.M.J Jones
Mr M.G.J Jones
MR P Jones
MR R Jones
MR R E Jones
Mr R.E.J Jones
Mr S. Jones
Mr T.M.J Jones
Mrs S.M.J Jones
Mstr C.M. Jones
MSTR E A Jones
MSTR G C Jones
Mstr G.T.J Jones
Mstr K.J Jones
MR P V Jordison
MR P W Jordon
Mr G.J Jowett
Mstr A.J Jowett
Mr D Joynes
Mr P Joynes
Mr F.L. Kane
Miss E. Kay
Miss L Kay
Mr J. Kay
Mstr P J Kay
MR Kearton

Miss J.K Keegan
MISS M Keegan
MISS T Keegan
Mr J.K Keegan
Mrs E.K Keegan
Mr A.C.K Keeley
Ms E.K Keeley
MR A Keen
Mr A Keightley-Smith
MSTR J Keightley-Smith
Mr N Kelley
Mr J P Kelly
Mr M Kelly
MR S J Kelly
Mr T.N Kelly
Mrs R M Kelly
Mr M.S.K Kemp
Mstr P M Kemp
MR D J Kendall
Mstr R.M.K Kendall
Miss E.A.K Kennedy
Mr D.M.K Kennedy
Mr R.S.K Kennedy
Mrs A.K Kennedy
Mstr J.S.K Kennedy
MISS C.M Kennerley
MISS J.J Kennerley
MR V.A Kennerley
MISS A C Kennington
MISS H M Kent
MISS N J Kent
MR A Kent
Mr P.K Kent
MR KENYON
MSTR KENYON
Mr G.K Keogh
Mr J.K Kerr
Mrs S.K Kerr
Mstr A.K Kerr
Mstr J.K Kerr
Mr R.N.K Kerruish
Mr M.K Kerruish
MSTR M Keyworth
Miss A Khair
Mrs C.A.K Kidner
MR J L Kilpatrick
MR K Kilpatrick
MSTR J J Kilpatrick
Mr T C King
Mrs C King
Mstr D A King
Mstr K V King
MRS S kirby
MR D Kirk
MR P Kirkbride
Mstr K W Kirtley
Mr F.K Kitching
Mr D.K Knight
Mr D. Knights
Mstr A.C. Knights
Miss A.K Knott
Mr A.K Knott
MR J Knott
Mr K Knott
Mrs J Knott
Mrs S.K Knott
Mstr M C Knott
MSTR S Knott
Mr A. Knox
Mrs M. Knox
Mstr A. Knox
Mstr A Labonte
Mstr P.L Laidler
Mr K.L Laing
MR C Laird
Mr D.L Laird
Mstr G.L Laird
Mr J M Lakeman
Mstr T W Lakeman
Mr L.L Lakin
MR J Lambert
Mr J.L Lambert
Mr R.L Lambert
MR S Lambert
MSTR A Lambert
MSTR D Lambert
Mstr S.R.L Lambert
MR G A Landers
MSTR T M Landers
MR N Langford
MISS J Langstaff
MR T Langstaff
MSTR C Langstaff
Mr S.G.F. Larsson
MSTR R Laville
Mr G Law
Mr J Law
Mr S Law
Mrs S Law

Mstr M.J.L Lawrance
Mr G.L Lawrence
Mr M Lawrence
Mrs J A Lawrence
Mstr M Lawrence
MR D Lawson
MR S Lawson
Mrs M.A Lax
Mstr P.J Lax
Mrs B.K.L Layburn
Mr G Leatherland
Mstr P Leatherland
K Lee
MISS A Lee
MISS C Lee
MR B Lee
Mr G.W.L Lee
Mr M Lee
Mr M.L Lee
Mr S.M Lee
Mr W.T.L Lee
Mrs M.L Lee
Mstr S.D.L Lee
MR M J J Leech
Mr C.P.L Leeming
Mr N Lees
Mstr J Lees-Edmondson
Mr M.L Legg
Mr P Leibrick
MRS J Leibrick
MASTER D Leigh
MASTER N Leigh
MR K Leigh
MSTR D Leigh
MSTR P Leigh
Mr F.L Leighton
Mstr M Lemmon
MR F Lenaghen
Mr J Leonard
MISS M Leslie
MR C J Leslie
MR P Leslie
MRS J Leslie
MR E Lesson
Mr C.V.L Levenson
Mstr J.G Lever
MR A Lewis
Mrs J Lewis
Mstr K.M.L Lickess
MR A Liddell
MR D Liddell
MRS E Liddell
MSTR N Liddell
MR J A Liddle
MISS C Lightfoot
Miss J.L Lightfoot
MR J Lightfoot
Mstr K.M Liley
Mr J.E.L Lilley
Mr I.D.L Lilleystone-
MR C Lillystone
Mstr D Lillystone
MSTR M Lillystone
Mr W Linacre
Mstr W Linacre
Mr A.L Lincoln
MSTR W C Lincoln
MR A Lindberg
MR D Lindberg
Mr K S Lindo
Mr K T Lindo
Mrs D Lindo
MR G.L Lindridge
MSTR A C Lindridge
Mr R.M.L Lindsay
Mr I.R.L Linklater
Mstr J.R.I Linklater
MR A D Linton
Mr D.L Linton
Mstr A.L Linton
MR W P List
Mstr D T List
Mr D.J.L Little
Mstr R.L Little
M J Littlefair
MR G Littler
Mr P.J. Livingston
MR A Livingstone
MR J Livingstone
Mr J.L Llewellyn
Miss H.J.L Locke
Mr C Lofthouse
Mr P Lofthouse
MISS J Logan
MR B Logan
Mr M.L Logan
Miss S.L Logue
Mr A.V.L Logue
Mr R.I Long

Mstr A Long
Mstr M Long
MSTR C LONGHORN
Mr P.L Longstaff
Mrs R.L Longstaff
MR F Longthorne
Mr J.P.L Longwill
Mr S.J.L Longwill
G Loughran
MSTR J Loughran
MSTR P Loughran
Mr M Love
Mstr Love
Mstr R Love
Mr M.L Lovell
MR Lowe
Mr G. Lowe
Mr I.L Lowe
Miss L.L Lowery
Mr M.L Lowery
Ms J.L Lowery
Miss D.I.L Lunn
MR R W Lupton
Miss A.L Lynch
Miss S.J.L Lynch
Mr C.L Lynch
Mr L Lynch
MR M Lynch
Mrs D Lynch
Mstr D.L Lynch
Mr J Lyth
Mr R Lyth
Mrs M Lyth
Mr D.M Macaulay
Mstr D.T.M Macaulay
MR C W MacFarlane
MR D MacFarlane
MSTR A D MacFarlane
Mr N.M Macgregor
Mr D.P. Mack
Mr Mr Mack
Mr N Mackin
Mstr L Mackin
Mr L Mackrell
MSTR D R MacManus
MRS C A Madeley
MSTR E W Madeley
MSTR J A Madeley
MR Mahan
Mr K.D.M Mahan
Mstr D.K.M Mahan
Mr D.P.M Mahoney
Miss M C Makin
MR G A Makin
Mr J.R.M Malcolm
Mrs R.F.M Malcolm
Mr T Malkin
Mr K Mallon
Mstr J Malone
Mr R Mannion
MR P.G.M Mannix
Mstr R.P.M Mannix
Miss L. Mansfield
Mr A. Mansfield
Mr C Mansfield
Mr K.M Mansfield
Mr M. Mansfield
Mstr C Mansfield
MSTR S Manson
MSTR R Mapplebeck
MR H MARDON
Mr T.S.M Marlow
Mstr D.S.M Marlow
MSTR P Marquis
Mr J.M Marsay
Mrs S.M.M Marsay
MSTR J.L Marshall
Mr A.M.M Marston
MISS L.C Martin
Mr D.S. Martin
Mr D.T Martin
Mr H Martin
Mstr A. Martin
MSTR J Martin
Mstr R.S. Martin
MRS A Martinez
MRS C Martinez
MSTR D C Martinez
Mr D Mason
MR E Mason
Mr J.S. Mason
MR S Mason
Mstr I.S. Mason
Mr D Masterman
Mr D.M Masterman
Miss L. Masters
Mr W. Masters
Mstr D Masters
Mstr P Masters

Mr M Mathews
Miss G.M Matthews
Mr I Matthews
MR R G Matthews
D Maude
M D Maude
Mstr G.M Mawson
Mr J A May
Mr K A May
Mstr J.R.M Mayo
MR McAdams
Mstr T McAvoy
MRS M McBRIDE
Mr P.M McCabe
Mr S.J McCabe
Mstr K McCabe
Mstr R.A McCabe
Mstr A McCarten
MR J.C McCarthy
MISS J McCaskill
MR J McCaskill
Mr J.M.M McCollin
Mstr S.M McCollin
Mr J.A.M McConnell
Mstr S.M.M McConnell
Mr D.E McCormick
Mr F.D.M McCormick
Mrs I.M McCormick
Ms J.M McCormick
MR N McCourt
Mr J McCoy
MR M McDermott
Mr M McDermott
Mstr P McDermott
MISS C McDonald
MISS S McDonald
MR I McDonald
MSTR M J McDonald
Mr M. McDonnell
Mr K.S.M McElvaney
Mstr A.M McElvaney
Miss V.L.M McGee
Mr A McGee
MR L M McGee
Mr J.M McGee
Mr T.J.M McGee
Mstr C McGee
Mstr C McGlade
Mr D McGlade
Miss R McGloin
Mr D McGloin
Mr F M McGloin
Mstr L McGloin
Mr M.M McGoff
Mr M McGough
MR C McGowan
MR M McGowan
Mr M C McGowan
MSTR M R McGowan
MRS W McGrath
Miss A.M McGuire
Miss K.M McGuire
Mr J.M McGuire
Mstr K.M McGuire
Mstr L.M McGuire
Miss E.L.M McGurk
MR K McGurk
Mr P.F.M McGurk
MRS L MCGURK
Mr S.M McIntyre
Mr A S McKee
Mrs J A McKee
Mrs J M McKee
Mstr D L McKee
Mstr M S McKee
Miss S.M McKenna
Mr M.A.M McKenna
Mr D.M McLaren
Mr J.T McLaughlan
Mstr M McLaughlan
Mstr T Mclaughlan
MR C McLean
MR S McLean
Mr S.W McLean
MSTR C J McLean
Mr I McLintock
Mr R McLintock
Mstr P T McLintock
MSTR N J McLoughlin
Miss H. McMahon
MR D McMahon
Ms. S. McMahon
Mstr S. McMahon
MR A E McManus
Mstr P McNamara
Miss H.M McNeil
Mr C.M McNeil
Mr W.M McNeil

Mstr D.M McNeil
Mr M.M McNeill
Mr S McNicholas
Mstr K.A.M McNicholas
Mstr M McNicholas
Miss R.C.M McPartland
Mr P.M McPartland
Mstr J.N.M McPartland
Mr J.L.M McPherson
MR D McTiernan
MSTR M E McTiernan
Mr T.M McVey
Mr E J Meaburn
Mstr C A Meaburn
MR A W Mead
MRS J T Mead
MR E Measor
Miss P Medley
Mr R Medley
Mr S Medley
Mstr M Medley
Miss K J Meehan
Mr N L Meehan
Mrs B J Meehan
Mstr J D Meehan
MEERES
MSTR D P Meeres
MISS H.J Meikle
MISS S.A Meikle
MR K.B Meikle
Mrs J.M. Mellon
Mstr J. Mellon
MRS H Mellor
DR J R Melrose
MSTR J P Melrose
MR P Menzies
MRS A C Menzies
Mr A.M Mercer
Mstr M Mercer
MR J.W Merry
Mr J.M Metcalfe
Mrs E Metcalfe
Mr Mr Micallef
Mr C.M Middleton
Miss B.M Milburn
Mr B.M Milburn
Mr J.M Milburn
Mstr C.M Milburn
MR A Miles
Mr S.J.M Miles
Mstr C.S.M Miles
Mstr D.J.M Miles
MSTR P Miles
MRS S Milestone
MSTR G Milestone
Mstr G.M Miller
Mr M.R.M Millman
Mr S.J.M Millman
Mr G.M Millward
MRS A Millward
Mstr A.A.M Millward
Mstr G.M Millward
Mr A.M Milner
Mr J.M Minto
Mr A.M Mitchell
MR K Mitchell
Mr L.M Mitchell
MR M W L Mitchell
Mr P.F.M Mitchell
MR W Mitchell
MSTR A Mitchell
MRS MITCHISON
Mr D.J.M Moffatt
Mr D Mohan
MR J Mohan
MSTR D Mohan
Mr D.M Moloney
Mstr K.M Moloney
MR MONKS
MR C Moody
Mstr N.J.M Moody
Miss L.J.M Moore
Miss V.M Moore
Mr C.M Moore
Mr D.J.M Moore
Mrs L.M.M Moore
Mstr N.J.M Moore
Mstr R.M Moore
Mr J.M Moorhead
Mstr A.M Moorhead
MSTR F Moran
Mr S Moreham
Mr C.J. Morgan
MR R Morgan
Miss K Morris
Mr D Morris
Mr P Morris
Mr P.H. Morris
Mstr C.M Morris

MR C Morrish
Mr R.M Morrison
Mrs W.M Moses
Mstr B.M Moses
MR R G Moss
MSTR R J Moss
MR Muir
MR D Muir
Mr D E Muir
Mstr E Muir
Mstr M.W Mulcaster
MISS E A Mullins
MR T E Mulroy
MR T Mulvey
MR G Munck
MSTR J Munck
MR L Mundy
MR D F Munroe
MR F H A Munroe
Mr A.W.M Murdoch
Mrs C.M Murdoch
Mstr A.M Murdoch
Mstr C.I.M Murdoch
Miss J. Murphy
Mr D.R.M Murphy
Mr R.J. Murphy
Mstr D Murphy
Miss L.A.M Murray
Mr M.D.M Murray
Mr R.M Muscroft
Ms S.M Muscroft
Mr C.M Myers
Mr L.M Myers
Mr B Mc Naramara
Mr J.N Nassau
Mstr L.G.N Nassau
Mstr C. Neal
Mrs M.E. Neale
Mr J.N Nellist
MR B L Nelson
MR C J Nelson
MR M H Nelson
Mr J M Nertney
Mrs M M Nertney
Mstr M.N Nettleton
Mr D.N Newsam
Mstr S.N Newsam
Mstr E.A. Newsam
MASTER A D Nicholson
MISS L Nicholson
MR D M Nicholson
MR J Nicholson
Mr S.A.N Nicholson
Mr S.N Nicholson
MRS J Nicholson
MR R R Nightingale
MR S Nimmo
MSTR A Nimmo
MSTR R Nimmo
MR M Nixon
MR P Nixon
Mr Nobbs
MR R Noble
MRS J M Noble
MSTR R Noble
Mstr K.R.N Nodding
Mr A Nolan
Mr B.N Norland
Mstr C.N Norlund
Mr A Norman
Mrs S Norman
MR J H Norris
Mr J C Northway
Mstr C J Northway
Ms C.A.N Nussey
MR C O'Brien
Mr G O'Brien
Mr J.O O'Brien
MR K O'Brien
Mr M.O O'Brien
MR S O'Brien
Mr T.O O'Brien
MSTR D O'Brien
Mstr D O'Brien
Mstr D.J O'Brien
Mstr D.O O'Brien
Mstr M.J.G O'Brien
MR D O'Connor
MR G O'Connor
Mr M O'Donoghue
Mr J.P.O O'Farrell
Mstr M.J.O O'Farrell
Mstr L.O O'Gorman
MISS K M O'Hara
MISS L A O'Hara
MRS J M O'Hara
Mr F O'Hare
Mr S O'Hare

MR A O'Malley
MR A J O'Malley
MR I O'Neil
MR R J O'Neil
Mr D.O O'Neill
MR K O'Neill
Mstr A.O O'Neill
Mr D.O Oakley
Mr G.S.O Ogden
Mr A R Oliver
Mr J A Oliver
Mr M.J.O Oliver
Mr P.O Oliver
Mr R Oliver
Mrs A Oliver
Miss E.O Olszowski
Miss H.M.O Olszowski
Mr A.J.O Olszowski
MISS E Oram
MR J.T. Ord
Mr R.M.O Ord
MR S Ormston
Miss R Osbaldeston
Mr J Osbaldeston
MR T.J Outterside
MSTR D.M Outterside
Mr A Owen
Mr C Owen
Mr P Oxley
MR J W Oyston
MSTR M J Oyston
MISS R E Pacy
MR M C Pacy
Mr D.P Palfreeman
Mstr J.M.P Palfreeman
MR A J Pape
MR J F Pape
Mr J Pardoe
Mr G.P Parker
MR T Parker
Mstr T Parker
MR S Parkes
Mstr D.M.P Parkes
MSTR S Parkes
MRS H Parkinson
Mr J.R.P Parnaby
Mstr D.J.P Parnaby
MR D E Parr
Mstr C E Parr
Miss L.P Parry
Mr B.P Parry
Mr D.T.P Parry
Mstr T.P Parry
Miss K.L.P Parsons
Mr M.D.P Parsons
Mstr D.M.P Parsons
MISS L Partridge
MR L Partridge
MISS K Parvin
MISS G Patterson
Mstr J.R. Patterson
Miss A J Patton
Mrs R Patton
Miss M.L. Payne
Mr A B Payne
Mr B Payne
Mstr C Payne
Mr T R Peacock
Pearce
MR PEARCE
Mr D.P Pearce
MSTR M Pearce
Mstr N.D.P Pearce
Mr A.P Pearson
Mstr D.P Pearson
Mstr N.P Pearson
Mr C.J.P Pederson
Mr J.J.P Pederson
MR PEEBLES
MR R Pell
MISS L Pennington
MR D Pennington
Mr D J Pennington
MR J Pennington
MR J T Pennington
MR L T Pennington
MRS G Pennington
MSTR I Pennington
Mr L.P Perkins
MISS K.L Petch
MR J.P Petch
MSTR J.P Petch
MR J Petty
Mr R.P Peverell
Mr S.P Phelps
Mstr P Phelps
Mstr S J Phelps
Mr D.G.P Phillips

MR H H Phillips
Mstr H.C.P Pickett
Mstr I.C.A Pickett
Mr S Pickles
MR J L Piggott
MSTR D J Piggott
Mstr P Pinkney
Miss V J Plane
Mr J H Plane
Mstr M S Plane
Mr J.P Platts
Mstr M.P Platts
Mr C.P Pletts
Mr A.P Plews
MR L Pollitt
MISS J Poole
MR J W Poole
MR L Poole
MR B Popple
Mr J.D.P Porritt
Mstr D.P Porritt
Miss J.P Porteous
Miss L.J.P Porteous
Mr E.P Porteous
Mrs L. Porteous
Mr S.P Porter
Mstr L.P Porter
MR K Postgate
Mrs C.R Postlethwaite
Mr B.F Postlethwaite
Mr I.T Postlethwaite
Mr D.H.J. Potter
Mr I.P Potts
Miss H.N.A Power
Miss S.E.S Power
Mr D.A.P Power
Mr D.J.P Pratt
Mr T W Prest
Miss N.M.P Price
Mr C Price
Mr D Price
MR G R Price
Mstr S Price
Mr P.P Pringle
Mstr A.P Pringle
Mstr T.P Pringle
Mr M Procter
Mstr P Procter
Mr E V Protheroe
Mr G.P Proudman
Mstr A.P Proudman
Mstr D.P Proudman
Mstr M.P Proudman
Miss N.D.P Prouse
Mr D.C.P Prouse
Mr S.J.P Prouse
Mstr R.D.P Prouse
Mstr R Puckrin
Mr G.R.P Pugh
Mr S.P Purvis
Mstr W.P Purvis
MR M.J PYLE
Mr R.Q Quinn
Mstr J.Q Quinn
MR A Raby
MR S Raby
MRS I D Raby
Mr P.R Radics
MR G Railton
Miss C.L Ramsay
Miss E.J Ramsay
Mr S.G Ramsay
Mrs C Ramsay
Mstr L Randall
Mr E Rathmell
MR Rawson
MISS L A Raybould
MR J Raybould
MRS L Raybould
MISS L J Rea
MR A Rea
Mstr S J Rea
MISS A Read
MSTR C Read
Mr H.R Readman
MR I Readman
Mr P Readman
MRS M Readman
Mr T.W.R Reap
Mr D Reay
Mr J.R Redfearn
Mr P Redfearn
MSTR L Redfearn
Mstr P.R Redford
MR A G Redshaw
MSTR B Redshaw
MR P E Reed
MRS M E Reed
MSTR S.P Reed
Mstr P.R Regan

Mr A.S.R Regent
MR R T Reid
Mr T Reilly
MR J.J Reney
MR M Reney
Mr L.R Reynolds
MR D.F Rhatigan
Mr C.R Rhodes
Mr M Rhucroft
Mrs L C Rhucroft
Mr H.R Rice
Mstr M.A.R Rice
Miss P.R Richards
Mr Richards
Mr C.R Richards
Mr D.R Richards
Mr M.R Richards
MR R Richards
MR W Richards
Mrs A.R Richards
MRS R Richards
MSTR A Richards
Miss D.R Richardson
Mr J.V. Richardson
Mr P.R Richardson
Mr S Richardson
Mr W.R Richardson
Mrs C.R Richardson
Mstr G.R Richardson
Mstr S.R Richardson
MASTER D A Richie
MASTER M R Richie
MR P Richie
Mr K T Richmond
MR C Riddle
MR C Riddle
Mstr A. Rider
MR G J Ridler
Mstr J P Rigall
MR D Rigby
MR J L Riggall
MR J S Riggall
MR P J Riggall
MR J S Riley
MR S Riley
E V Risker
MR H.R Robbins
Mrs W.R Roberts
Ms M.J.R Roberts
MR N ROBINS
MSTR A M Robins
MISS C Robinson
MISS L Robinson
Mr A.J. Robinson
Mr B R Robinson
Mr B.R Robinson
MR C Robinson
MR D A Robinson
MR H.H Robinson
Mr H.R Robinson
MR I Robinson
MR J R Robinson
MR M Robinson
Mr O.R Robinson
Mr P Robinson
MR P E Robinson
MR S Robinson
Mr S.R Robinson
Mrs D C Robinson
MSTR A Robinson
MSTR A R Robinson
Mstr A.J.R Robinson
Mstr C.R Robinson
Mstr M.P.R Robinson
Mstr P D Robinson
Mstr P M Robinson
Mstr P.A.R Robinson
Mstr R C Robinson
MSTR T Robinson
C M L Robson
C O L Robson
MR ROBSON
Mr B.L.R Robson
MR D J Robson
MR I Robson
MR J S Robson
MR K J Robson
MR L Robson
Mstr A C Robson
Mstr J.A.R Robson
MSTR M J Robson
S Robson
MR S.A Roche
MSTR A Roche
MR S P Rodgers
MSTR M Rodgers
MRS M Roe
MR W ROGERS

MSTR P R Rogers
MSTR R ROGERS
Mr H.R Ross
Mr R. Ross
Mr R.R Ross
Mstr M. Ross
Mstr M.I.R Ross
Mstr R.R Ross
MSTR M Ross
Mstr M.R Routledge
Mr A.R Rowland
Mr C.K. Rowland
MR S K Rowland
MSTR D S Rowland
Mr J.L.R Rowland
Mr J Rowlands
Mr P J Rowlands
Mr Rowlinson
Mr C.R Rowney
Mr n.r Rowney
Mstr S.N.R Rowney
MR G J Rowntree
Mr R Rowntree
MSTR M Rowntree
Mr E.J.R Roxburgh
Mr M.E.R Roxburgh
Mr C.R Roxby
MISS J Ruane
MISS S Ruane
MR M Ruane
Mr D.R Rudd
MISS K E Ruddick
Mr J R Ruse
Mstr J M Ruse
Mstr M G Ruse
MR B J Rush
MSTR M Rush
Mr P J Rushby
Mstr S G Rushby
Mstr V.R.R Rushton
Mr A.R Rutherford
Mr C.R Rutherford
MR W M Rutherford
MSTR P M Rutherford
MISS S E Rutledge
Mstr M.R Ryan
MR B Ryder
MR D B Ryder
Mr M Salmon
Mr N.S Salmon
Mstr E M Salmon
Mstr S Salmon
Mr M.J.S Salt
Mr T.S Salter
Mstr M.R. Salvati
Mr D Salvin
Mstr A.C.S Salvin
Mstr G Salvin
Mstr P.D.S Salvin
Miss M Samuels
Mr C.M. Samuels
R Sands
MR J Saunders
Mr P.R. Saunders
Mstr C P Saunders
Mstr M L Saunders
Mr A C Savage
Mstr T C Savage
MR P.D Sawyer
MSTR D.J Sawyer
Mr S.H. Sayer
MSTR J Sayer
Mr E.W.S Sayers
Mrs M.S Sayers
Mr A Scholfield
Miss H.L.S Scotson
Mr M W Scotson
Mr J.F.S Scotson
MSTR S A Scotson
Scott
MR D A Scott
Mr E.W. Scott
MR G Scott
Mr M.W.S Scott
MR S J V Scott
MR W R Scott
Mr J. Scott
MSTR C Scott
Mstr C.M.S Scott
MSTR G Scott
Dr E.G. Scovell
Mstr P.R. Scovell
MR J.H.S Scrivens
Mstr A.G.S Scrivens
Mstr O.T.S Scrivens
Mr J.E.D Scully
Mr J.S Scully
Mr A.S Seaman
Mr K.S Seaman

Mstr S.S Seaman
Miss A.L.S Sedgwick
Mr A.L.S Sedgwick
Mstr J.J.S Sedgwick
Mr G.S Sevier
Mrs C L Seymour
Mstr M T Seymour
Miss M.S Shannon
Mr P.A.S Shannon
Mrs P.S Shannon
Mr G H Sharp
MR M Sharp
MSTR S P Sharp
MR B Shaw
MR M Shaw
Mr M.I Shaw
Mr A.P.S Shea
Mr D.P.S Shea
Mr T.S Shea
Mstr M.J.S Shea
MR A Sheekey
MR N F Sheekey
Mrs H.S Sheperd
Miss F.L.S Shepherd
MISS K.M Shepherd
Mr J.W.S Shepherd
Mr K.S Shepherd
Mrs L G Shepherd
Mstr J.A.S Shepherd
MSTR M.J Shepherd
Miss C.L Sherwood
MR I F Sherwood
MSTR M J Sherwood
Mstr W Sherwood
Mr J M Shipley
Mr T Shipley
Mstr J E Shipley
Mstr T J Shipley
Miss Z. Shipp
Mstr W H Short
Mstr M.J.S Sigsworth
Mr R Sildre
Miss S.K.S Simcox
Mr C.S Simcox
Mr R A Simcox
Mrs T.J.S Simcox
Mstr G.C.S Simcox
MISS I. M Simpson
MR B M Simpson
MR G Simpson
MR M R Simpson
Mr M.E.S Simpson
MR M J Simpson
Mr P.S Simpson
MR W P Simpson
MSTR G Simpson
MSTR R T Simpson
MISS J A Sims
MR C J Sims
MR R J Sims
Mr S A Sims
Mstr M A Sims
Mstr P J Sims
Mrs J. Sivills
Mstr G. Sivills
MR P J Sizer
MSTR A W Sizer
Mr L.S Skelton
Mr W.S Skelton
MSTR I S Skene
MSTR J A Skene
Mr T.J.S Skipper
Mstr M.J.S Skipper
Mr D.R.S Skipsey
Mr R.S Skipsey
Mrs F.A.S Skipsey
Miss B.S Slater
Mr P.S Slater
MR J Small
Mstr A C Smallwood
MSTR D Smee
MISS A L Smith
Miss A.E.M. Smith
MISS L M Smith
Mr A.M Smith
Mr A.S Smith
Mr D Smith
MR D M Smith
MR G Smith
Mr G L Smith
Mr G.R.S Smith
Mr G.S Smith
MR J M B Smith
Mr J R Smith
Mr J W Smith
Mr M.A. Smith
Mr M.S Smith
Mr R.W.S Smith
Mr S.S Smith

Mr T Smith
Mr T.S Smith
MR V J Smith
MR W Smith
Mr W.D.S Smith
Mr W.M Smith
Mrs J.R.S Smith
MRS L M Smith
Mrs L.S Smith
MS A Smith
Mstr A.D.S Smith
Mstr A.M.S Smith
Mstr C.J. Smith
MSTR G Smith
Mstr G.J Smith
Mstr J.S Smith
MSTR K A Smith
Mstr L.P.S Smith
Mstr P.W Smith
Miss C.S Smitheringale
Miss J.S Smitheringale
Miss M.A.S Smitheringale
Mr J.G.S Smitheringale
Mr M.S Smitheringale
Mstr M.A.S Staintheringale
Mstr S.S Smitheringale
Mr G Smithies
Mstr L G Smithies
MR B.A Smithson
MSTR A Smithson
Miss M Snaith
Mr R.J. Soeakman
MR S Sohoo
Miss J.K.S Souter
MR A C Souter
MR S Souter
Mrs K.S Souter
Mstr G Souter
MSTR M Souter
Mr A.S South
Mr D.E.S South
Mr P.S South
Miss A.J.S Southcote
Mr D.C.S Southcote
Mstr L.D.S Southcote
MR J Sparks
MR S.R Speck
Mr D Spence
MR H Spencer
Mr L Spreadbury
MR P Spreadbury
Mstr L Spreadbury
Mrs A.E.S Stainthorpe
MR C Stanley
MSTR D Steer
Miss L M Stelling
Mr M J Stelling
Mr A.P.S Stenson
Mr M.P.S Stenson
MISS J Stephenson
MISS J E Stephenson
MISS S A Stephenson
MR A Stephenson
MRS A Stephenson
MSTR J Stevens
Mr G.S Stevenson
MR H Stevenson
Mr I R Stewart
Mstr D I Stewart
MR K Stiles
MRS M Stiles
MSTR J P Stiles
MRS L Stobbs
Mr K.S Stockdale
MSTR T C Stockdale
Mstr J Stocks
Miss S.S Stockton
Mr G.S Stockton
Mr M.S Stockton
Mr R.S Stockton
Ms A.S Stoddart
Mstr J Stoddart
MR D Stokes
MR K Stokes
MR T A Stolweather
Mstr L S Stolweather
Miss S.L.S Stonehouse
MR A A Stonehouse
Mr G.P.S Stonehouse
Mr J.S Stonehouse
Mrs W.S Stonehouse
Mstr M.P.S Stonehouse
Mstr S.P.J Stonehouse
Mr M.S Storey
Mr P G Storey
Mr P.C.S Storey
Mr T W Storey
Mstr C.C.S Storey
Mstr M J Storey

Mstr R.P.S Storey
Mr P Sturdy
Mstr P Sturdy
Miss C.L.S Sturman
Mr E.A.S Sturman
Mstr T.E.S Sturman
Mrs D Suckling
Mr J.E.S Sudlow
Mstr S.W.S Sudlow
MR G Sudron
MR K Sullivan
Mrs P.S Summers
Mr I.S Sutcliffe
Mrs L.S Sutcliffe
Mr D.S Sutherland
Mr K.S Swain
Mstr A.W.S Swain
Mstr E.J.S Swain
MR A E Swalwell
Mr N Swash
MISS L E Sykes
Miss L.S Sykes
MR J Sykes
Mr N.S Sykes
MRS A Sykes
MSTR J Sykes
Mstr T.S Sykes
Mr P.S Szuszkewicz
Mr T.T Talbot
Miss M.T Tate
MR A Tate
MR D Tate
Mr R.T Tate
Mr C.T Taylor
Mr J.T Taylor
Mr M.C.T Taylor
Mr M.J.T Taylor
Mr M.P.T Taylor
Mr P.A.T Taylor
MSTR B W Hoy Taylor
Mstr C.A. Taylor
Mstr D.M.T Taylor
Mr J.M.T Templeman
Mstr S.J.T Templeman
MR W Tennent
Miss S.E.T Thomas
MR Thomas
MR G K Thomas
MR M Thomas
MR M.C.T Thomas
Mr P.A Thomas
MRS B I Thomas
Mstr G.W.T Thomas
Mstr S.T Thomas
Miss A.R Thompson
Miss N.C.T Thompson
Mr A.T Thompson
Mr B.T Thompson
Mr D. Thompson
Mr D.W.T Thompson
Mr G Thompson
MR I R Thompson
MR J Thompson
Mr L Thompson
Mr M.T Thompson
MRS C Thompson
Mrs P.F.T Thompson
MSTR A Thompson
MSTR P J Thompson
MSTR S.M Thompson
Mstr S.T Thompson
MSTR M L Thornton
Mr R.F.T Thurlwell
MR P G Tibbett
MSTR C W Tibbett
MISS M A Tilley
MR J Tilley
MR K Tillotson
MSTR P A Tillotson
Timber Cleveland
Mstr M D Tingle
MR T Todd
Miss S. Tombling
Mstr S.P. Tombling
Mr S.T Tombs
Mr R.T Tomlin
MISS l Toole
MR M D Toole
Mr M.J.T Tosh
Mrs M.T Tosh
Mr C.E.T Toulson
Mstr A.J.T Toulson
MSTR S.K.T Toulson
Mr P.T Towse
Mr J.T Tracey
Mr G.T Tranter
MR P Tranter
MSTR L M Tranter

Mr A M Trapp
Miss L.T Travis
Mr N.T Travis
Mr J.T Trigg
Miss L.L.T Trillo
Mr S.L.T Trillo
Mstr C.S.T Trillo
MR T Trollope
MSTR P M Trollope
MR A C Trowsdale
Mr C Tudor
Mr J Tudor
MISS A Tunney
MRS D E Tunney
MSTR R Tunney
Mr I Turford
Mr K.J Turland
Mstr D.C Turland
Miss L Turnbull
Mr R G Turnbull
Mstr R G Turnbull
Miss A D Turner
Miss A.L.T Turner
Mr A.T Turner
Mr M.T Turner
Mrs J.R.M Turner
Mstr I.T Turner
Mstr S.J Turner
Mstr D.M.T Tutill
Mstr P.A.T Tutill
Mr R.J.T Tweddle
MSTR J Tweedle
Mr K.U Underdown
Mr B.V Varah
MISS K.L. VAUGHAN
Mstr D.V Veazey
MISS J Vickers
MR G A Vickers
Mr J.A Vickers
Mr K.V Vickers
Mr R.T.V Vickers
Mstr D.V Vickers
Mstr M.V Vickers
MR M Waddleton
MR J Waid
MRS C Waid
Mr M.J.W Waine
Mstr D.S.W Waine
Miss E. Walker
MR Walker
Mr A.W Walker
MR F.A. Walker
Mr F.C.W Walker
Mr F.M.W Walker
MR G.W Walker
Mr J.G Walker
Mr J.G.W Walker
Mr M Walker
Mr T W Walker
MRS S.E. Walker
Mstr A M WALKER
MSTR C R Walker
Mstr L M Walker
Mstr L.M.W Walker
MSTR M J Walker
MISS S M Wall
Mr S Wall
Miss J.A.W Wallace
Mr I. Wallace
Mstr A.C. Wallace
Mstr G.J. Wallace
Mstr J.R. Wallace
MR B Waller
MStr S Waller
MSTR T Waller
MR G Walls
MR M Walmsely
MSTR S J Walmsley
Mr K.W Walpole
Mr R.W Walpole
Miss D. Walsh
Mr R Walt
Miss K.W Walton
Mrs B.W Walton
Mr R Wanless
Miss K.W Ward
Mr S.T Ward
Miss S.J.W Ward
MR WARD
Mr Ward
Mr K L Ward
Mr P.T.W Ward
MRS Ward
MR S Warden
MSTR R Warden
Mr D.C.W Wardle
Mstr S.W Wardle
MR M Wardman
Mr P R Warner
Mr A.W Warnock

Miss L Waters
Miss V.J.W Waters
MR Waters
Mr D.W Waters
Mr G Waters
Mr G.W Waters
Mr H.W Waters
MR J Waters
Mr J.W Waterson
MISS S Watson
Mr C.J.W Watson
Mr C.W Watson
Mr H.W Watson
Mr I W Watson
MR R Watson
MR T Watson
MRS D Watson
Mrs S.W Watson
MSTR A I Watson
MSTR G Watson
Mstr S.O.W Watson
Mr F Watts
MR G H Watts
MR P Watts
Mr R Watts
MRS J Watts
Mstr A Watts
Miss K Waugh
Mr G Waugh
Mrs G Waugh
Mstr G Waugh
Miss L Wayhill
Mr G.W. Webb
Mr M Webb
Miss T.W Webley
MISS E M Webster
Miss M.W Webster
MR D Webster
MR J M Webster
Mr S.W Webster
MR T I Webster
MR J.W WEIR
MRS J Weir
MSTR M Weir
Mr I R Welch
Mstr L.J.W Wells
Mr D.W Welsh
Mr G.R.W Wem
Mrs M.I.W Wem
Mr J. Weschenfelder
Mstr R. Weschenfelder
MISS S J West
Mr C.W. West
MR D West
MR E L West
MR M West
Mr M.W Whalley
Mr R.M.W Whalley
MR J I Wharry
MRS J Wharry
MSTR C Wharry
Mrs M.J.W Wheater
Mstr D.J.W Wheater
MR M C Wheather
Miss E Whelan
MR A Whelan
MRS M Whelan
MSTR P Whelan
Mstr P Whelan
Mr B.W Whitaker
MR C White
MR F W White
Mr J.W White
Mr M.M.W White
MR P White
Ms E.W White
MSTR A M White
Mstr C.W. White
Mstr D.B.W White
Mstr G White
MSTR J P White
Mstr N.W White
Miss K.W.D White-Davies
Miss L Whitecross
Mr P Whitecross
Mrs S Whitecross
Mstr M Whitecross
Ms J.W Whiteford
Miss E Whitehead
Miss K.L.W Whitehead
Miss J Whitehead
MR J H Whitehead
Mrs C.W.D Whitehead
MSTR M A Whitehead
Mstr R.W Whitehouse
MISS J Whitehouse
MSTR L Whitehouse
Mr T.W Whitfield
Miss K.W Whitham

Miss S.W Whitham
Mr S.K.W Whitham
Mr F.W Whittingham
MR J Whittingham
MR I.D Whittle
MSTR A J Whittle
MISS T Whitwell
MR J Whitwell
Mstr R Whitwell
Mstr M R Whyman
Mr R.M.W Whyte
Mstr M.A.W Whyte
WICKS
Mr D.A. Widd
Mstr S.A. Widd
Mr M.C.W Wigham
Mr S.I.R Wilcox
Mstr A.I. Wilcox
Mstr S.M Wilcox
Mrs W.W Wiles
MISS C A Wiley
MR R Wiley
Miss H. Wilkinson
Miss M Wilkinson
Miss P.W Wilkinson
Mr C. Wilkinson
MR D R Wilkinson
Mr M.F.W Wilkinson
Mr P.W Wilkinson
Mr R.K.W Wilkinson
Mr R.P.W Wilkinson
MR S Wilkinson
Mrs J.W Wilkinson
Mstr J Wilkinson
MSTR J.F Wilkinson
Mstr S.P.W Wilkinson
MR V William
MISS R Williams
MR D Williams
Mr E.W Williams
Mr R Williams
Miss G Williamson
MR M R Williamson
MSTR J J Williamson
Mrs D.E.W Willis
Mrs P Willis
Mstr C Willis
Mstr J.I.W Willis
Mstr L Willis
MASTER C D Wilson
Mr A M Wilson
Mr A.W Wilson
Mr B.W Wilson
MR D J Wilson
Mr G. Wilson
Mr M.L.W Wilson
Mr N.W Wilson
MR R Wilson
Mr W H Wilson
Mstr A D Wilson
Mstr A N Wilson
MSTR J J Wilson
Mstr J.A.W Wilson
MSTR M Wilson
MSTR S C Wilson
Mstr S.J. Wilson
Mstr S.J. Wilson
Mstr S.W Wilson
MR J F Windsor
MR C D Wing
Mr B.W Winnard
MR S Winskill
Mr L.W Winter
MSTR C R Winter
Mr Mr Winterschladen
Mstr J B Winterschladen
Mr G.S.W Winton
MASTER I Wise
MASTER R G Wise
MSTR G Wise
Miss Miss Wood
MR C A Wood
Mr C.W Wood
Mr E. Wood
Mr H.H.W Wood
Mr M.J.W Wood
Mr P.H.W Wood
Mr V.W Wood
Mrs S. Wood
Mstr C.D.W Wood
Mstr C.J.W Wood
Mstr D. Wood
Mstr K.J.W Wood
Mr M.W Woodall
Mrs J.S.W Woodall
Mstr E.J.W Woodall
Mstr J.M.W Woodall
Mr J.M.W Woodcock
MR D A Woodgate

Mr C Woodhouse
Mstr C Woodhouse
Mstr D Woodhouse
Mr J T Woodier
Mstr L J Woodier
MR A.T Woods
Mr G.R.W Woods
Mstr R.W Woods
Mr H.W Worthy
Mstr S.W Worthy
MISS K.L WRATHMALL
MSTR G Wrathmall
Mr H.W Wray
Miss A.V. Wright
MR D E Wright
Mr I.W.W Wright
Mr J.M.W Wright
Mr M.J. Wright
Mr T.V.W Wright
Mrs T M Wright
Mstr G.W Wright
Mstr K.W Wright
Mstr W.J.W Wyatt
Mr D.W Wyatt
MSTR S.D Wyke
MR A Wylie
MSTR P K Wylie
M Yare
MR Yare
Mr Yates
Mrs J.M.Y Yates
Mr D.J.Y Yendall
Mstr M.D.Y Yendall
MSTR J York
MR Young
MR F Young
MR P Young
MR P N Young
Mr S.V.Y Young
Mr T.Y Young
Mrs M Young
MSTR A N Young

WEST STAND UPPER
Mr D.A Abrook
Access Ind
Mr P.S.J Acheson
MISS J Ackroyd
MRS M A Ackroyd
MR A J Adam
MR J L Adam
Mr J A Adams
MISS G P Adamson
MR F L Adamson
Mr G.A Addison
Mr M J Addison
Mr N R Addison
Mr G.A Addy
MISS C S Affleck
Mr B.E.A Agar
Mrs L.A Agar
MR E Ainscoe
MR R Ainscoe
Mr S.A Ainsley
Mr E.A Airey
MR J Airey
MR N Airey
MRS D Airey
MSTR D P Airey
Mr K.A Aitchison
Mr C.A Aitkin
Mr R. Akien
Mr D Alcock
MR G Alcock
Mrs M Alcock
Mr I J Alderson
Mr M.A Alderson
Mr P.M Aldis
Mr N.M.A Aldridge
Mrs A.M.A Aldridge
P Aldridge
Mr C.N.A Alexander
Mr J.R.A Alexander
Mr R.P.A Alexander
Mrs J.A Alexander
Mrs K.J.A Alexander
Miss L.H Allan
Mr D.J Allan
Mr K.J.A Allan
MR D J Allanson
Mr Allen
MR A Allen
MR E Allen
Mr George Allinson
MR J H Allinson
Mr M.E Alsop
Mr N Alt
MR P Amer

MR M Amos
MR C Anderson
MR I R Anderson
MR K.A Anderson
Mr L.A Anderson
MR M K Anderson
MR P K Anderson
Mr R.C Anderson
Mr R Andrew
Mr R Andrew
Mr R.I. Andrew
Mr R.M. Andrew
Mr C.A Andrews
Mr K.A Andrews
MR G ANGEL
Mr G.A.A Angell
Mr A Angus
MISS C Annal
MR J.S Annal
Apex Electrical Distribution
Miss L Appleton
MR Appleton
Mr G. Appleton
MR I Appleton
Mr K.C. Apps
Mr M Arceri
Mr P Arceri
Mr V Arceri
J.E. ARCHIBALD
MR T ARMES
Mr S.J. Armitt
Miss S Armstrong
Mr A.A Armstrong
Mr H.A Armstrong
MR R Armstrong
MR R S Armstrong
MRS D Armstrong
Mstr H.A Armstrong
Mr D.A Arnott
Mr J.A Arnott
Mr T.A Arnott
Mr Artley
Mr G.A Artley
Mr D.A Ashman
Mr J B Ashman
Mr C.A Ashton
Mr D.A Ashton
MRS B C Askey
MR A M Askins
Assistance Technica Ltd
Mr T.A Atherton
Mr J.A Atkinson
Mr N.R.A Atkinson
Mr R Atkinson
Atlas Parcels
Mr A.A Attwood
Mr R.A Atwood
Autocarriers Ltd
MR R Axtell
Miss R.A. Ayers
RC Ayres Ltd
MR C Ayres
MR T W Ayres
BHK (UK) Ltd
MR G.J Bache
Mr J.B Baggott
MR J K Bailey
MR M Bailey
Mr A.B Bainbridge
Mr C.B Bainbridge
MR J Bainbridge
Mr M J Bainbridge
MR R Bainbridge
Mr T D Baker
Mr S.B Baksh
Mr R.B Baldwin
Mr A.B Ball
Mr M.B Ball
Mr S D Ball
MR J J Bamlett
Mr I.B Banks
Mr D.A.B Barker
Mr S.J.B Barker
Mr D.C.B Barlow
MISS A Barnard
Mr N.L.B Barnbrook
Mr E.R Barnes
Mr P Barnes
Mr M.J Barrett
Mr D.A. Barron
MR D Barry
MR S Barton
MRS C E Barton
Mr P.B Bashir
Mr J Basnett
MR D BASSETT
MR D Bates
MR G Bates

Bass Breweries
MR M Battista
Mr D Batty
Mr A Baxter
Mr M Baxter
MR P Baxtrem
Miss L.B.B Bayne
Mr C.B Beadnall
Mr G.B Beadnall
Mr H.B Beadnall
Mstr D.B Beadnall
MR C F Beal
MR H Beal
MR J Beal
Mr G.B Beales
MR B Beall
Mr B Bean
MR C B Bean
Mrs K.B Bean
Mr A Beattie
Mr R Beattie
Mstr S Beattie
Mr P Beckett
MR C C Beckwith
MRS P A Beckwith
Beckside Properties
Mr D.B Beddard
Dr S S Bedi
Mr V A Bedi
Mrs M E Bedi
Mr D. Bell
Mr G.B Bell
Mr M.B Bell
Mr K.B Bellamy
Mr P.J.B Bellamy
Bells Stores
Mr J A Benfield
Mr A Bennett
Mr J W Bennett
Mr R.B Bennett
Dr B.R.B Bennison
Mr T. Bensley
Mr M.B Benson
Mr M.D.B Benson
Mr A.P Bentley
Mr A.M.B Berry
Mr S.M.B Berry
Mr N Bhandany
Mr R Bhandany
Dr J.B Bharier
MR D Bibb
Mr A.B Bicknell
Mr C.B Bicknell
Mr A.B Biesterfield
Biffa Waste Services
Mr C Bilton
MR R K Bilton
Mr J.C.B Binge
Mr D Bingham
Mr F R Bingham
Mr P Binks
Miss A.J Birch
MR C Bird
Mr P.G. Bird
Mr A.D.B Birks
Mr D.J.B Birks
BKE Ltd
D P Black
MR B BLACKBURN
Mr C. Blackburn
Mr G.B Blackburn
Mr K M Blackburn
Mr M Blackburn
Mr T.W.B Blackburn
Mr C Blackett
Mr D.B Blackett
MISS A Blackwell
MISS B Blackwell
MR M Blackwell
MR T Blackwell
MSTR T Blackwell
Mr G.D.B Bladen
MR R Blair
MR G A Blakemore
Mr M.A.B Blakey
MRS A Blakey
MR BLAND
Mr C.B Bland
MRS L BLAND
MSTR BLAND
Mr P.B Bliwert
MR S P Bliwert
Mr B.B Bloomfield
Mr D.A.B Bloomfield
MR E Blott
MR T J Blows
Mr N.B Blyth
Mr P. Blyth
BOC Gases

Mr Janet Boddy
MR K Boddy
Boddy Thomas & Pacitto
Mrs A.J.B Boddy
G. Bolam Foods Ltd
MR W Bolland
Mr G.B Bollands
Mr P.S.B Bollands
MR P Bonar
Mr P.A.B Bond
Mr W K Bond
MR B H Bonnard
Mr D.B Booth
Mr J G Booth
MR N Booth
Mr T.W.B Booth
Mr G.B Boothby
Mr A Boothroyd
MR C Booty
MRS H Borland
MR A Borsumato
Mr A Boston
MR E Bostwick
Mr K M Boughey
Mr Bourne
Mr J.R. Bourne
Mrs J.A. Bourne
Mr M.B Bowater
MR D Bowes
Mr J Bowes
MR P.E Bowles
MRS A.M Bowles
MR K Bowmaker
Mr J.I.B Bowman
Mr J.P. Bowman
Mr M J Boyd
Mr A Boyes
BP Bulkhaul Ltd
Mr S.B Brace
Mr C.N Braddock
MR A J Bradley
MRS M Bradley
MR J Bradshaw
MR T Braithwaite
MSTR D Braithwaite
Mr P.A.B Bramley
Mr T.C.B Brand
Brand Papers
Mr D.W.V Branfoot
MR C Brannigan
MR D Brannigan
MRS A Brannigan
Mr F.B Bratt
MR M A Brazell
Mr M.C Breckon
Mrs J.A Breckon
Mr P.J.B Brenan
Mr P.B Brennan
Mr S.M.B Brennan
Mr J.B Brentnall
Mr A. Brereton
Mrs J. Brereton
MR D I Bridgewood
MRS D Bridgewood
Mr B M Bridson
Miss M Briggs
Mr P Briggs
Mr K Brigham
Miss M Britton
MR A P Broderick
Mr D Brook
MR A Brooke
Mr J.B Brookes
Mr J.F.B Brookes
Mr T.B Brophy
Miss Brown
Mr Brown
MR Brown
MR A M Brown
Mr A.G. Brown
MR A.L. Brown
Mr B.B Brown
Mr C.B Brown
MR D R Brown
Francis Brown Ltd
Mr D.R.C Brown
Mr P Brown
Mr P.B Brown
MR R Brown
Mr R.B Brown
Mr S.J. Brown
Mrs E. Brown
MRS M E Brown
MRS R Brown
MR A Brownbridge
MR D S Brownless
Mr A.J.B Bruce
Mr R.B Bryan
Mr C.J.B Buchanan

Mr J P Buck
A. Buckler Haulage
MR R M Buckley
Mr N Bulman
Mr K.B Bulmer
Mr A.G.B Bunting
Mr E Burniston
MR R Burns
James Burrell Ltd
G.M. Burton & Co Ltd
MR J E Burton
MR R P Burton
Mr D.B Busfield
MR V F Bushell
MR K T Butler
Mr R.M.B Butler
Mr W J Butler
MR W.J Butler
Mr D T Butta
MR D N Butters
MRS I Butters
Mr L Buttery
Mrs M Buttery
Mr D.B Bye
Mr J.B Bye
Mr C.A.B Byrne
MR P Byrne
Mr D.B Byrnes
MR G Cain
Mr M.S.C Cairnie
Mr G.C Caligari
MR A M Callaghan
MR P A Callaghan
MR A Campbell
Mr A.J. Campbell
MR I W Campbell
MRS J Campbell
MRS R M Campbell
Cameron Brewery
MISS E CANNELL
Mr K.J.C Cannings
Mrs A Cannon
Cape Industrial Services
Capper Pipe Services
Mr D Card
MR G J Cardwell
MRS K A Cardwell
Mr P.A.C Carey
MR M Carley
Mr D Carling
Mr D.C Carling
Mr D.W.C Carling
Carlsberg Tetley
MR Carney
Mr J.C Carr
Mr K.C Carr
Mr S.G.C Carr
Mr S.C Carroll
Mr A.C Carter
Eric Carter Car Sales
Mr J.C Carter
Mr M.C Carter
Mr N.C Carter
MR R Carter
Mr S.C Carter
Mrs J.G.E Carter
Carter Steel Ltd
Mr B.H.C Carver
Mr A D Casson
Mr L.C Casson
MR D Castor
MSTR MR Castor
Mr J Catterson
Century Windows
Mr A.J.C Chadwick
Mr C.C Chambers
Mr P.C Chambers
Mr R.E.C Chaney
MR C Chapman
Mr D.C Chapman
Mr D.J.C Chapman
Mr E.C Chapman
MR J Chapman
Mr J.C Chapman
Mr T.M.C Chapman
MR I Charlton
MR I S Charlton
MR T Charville
MRS G A Charville
MR R Chatterton
MR R Chatto
Mr M.W.C Cheall
Mrs D.M.C Cheall
D A D.A. Cheeseborough
Mrs S.J. Cheesebrough
MR S Chesworth
MR S Chesworth
Mr T Chesworth
Chieftain Insulation

MR J Chilton
Miss A.J.C Chipchase
Mr M.J.C Chipchase
Mr M Choinski
Dr I.C Chorlton
Mr R.C Chown
Ms A.C Chown
Mr G.C Christison
Mr A.C Chung
Mr E Church
CIS Northern
Mr B.C Clare
Mrs T.C Clare
Mr D Clark
Mr G.C Clark
MR J Clark
Mr K.C Clark
MR P A Clark
MSTR R D Clark
MR Clarke
Mr J.L.C Clarke
Mr K.C Clarke
Mr G.C Clarkson
Mr R.M.C Clarkson
Clarkson Bros and Casper
Mr B.D.C Claybrook
Mr D.C Claybrook
MISS A Claypole
MR J Claypole
MR D Clayton
Mr L.C Clayton
Mr R.C Clayton
Mr Cleminson
Mrs Cleminson
Cleveland Potash
Mr P.W.C Clifford
Mr S.C Clifford
MR D Clingo
R H Close
Mr M Closs
Mr K.B. Clough
Mr K. Coates
Mr R.C Cochrane
Mr P.S. Cocker
Mr J Cockfield
Mr C.C Cocks
Mr M.C Cocks
MR J H Code
Mr E.C Cody
Mr I.T.C Colclough
Cold Tec Refrigeration
MR D J Cole
Mr J.C Cole
Mr S.C Cole
Mr G F Coleman
Mr J.C Coleman
Mr K.C Coleman
MR M P Coleman
Mr M.C Coleman
MR V Coleman
Mr A.E.C Coles
Mrs M.J Coles
Mr W.P.C Colgan
Mr C.L.C Collantine
Mrs J Colley
Mr D.W.C Collier
MR D Collighan
Mr R Colling
Mstr T Colling
Mr G.A. Collingwood
MR W B Collingworth
MR S A Collins
Mr C Collinson
Mr G Colvin
Mr P.C Comasky
Mr A.P Compitus
Miss H.C Connelly
Mr D.C Connelly
Mr J.A.C Connelly
Mr J.B.C Connelly
Mr K.A.C Connelly
Mr R.C Connelly
Mr R.P.C Connelly
Rev R W Connelly
MR S Connor
Mr T Connor
Mr A.P.C Conorton
Mr G.R.C Conroy
Mr M.C Conway
Mr P.C Conway
Mr P.D.C Conway
Mr S.C Conway
Mrs M.C Conway
Mr Bruce Cook
Mr C.G.C Cook
Mr I.T.C Cook
MR J Cook
Mr N.C Cook
MR P M Cook

MR P.C Cook
Mrs J.C Cook
Mr A Cooke
Mr B Cooke
Mr D Cooke
Mr D.K.C Coombes
Miss M.J.C Cooper
Miss N.A.C Cooper
MR A Cooper
Mr A.J.C Cooper
MR P Cooper
Mr R.A.C Cooper
Compass Royston Group Travel
MR G J Copeland
MR A E Corbett
DR P Cornes
Mr A.C Cornforth
Mr C.P.C Cornforth
Mr J.A.C Cornforth
Corrigan
MR R Corrigan
MR D J Cosgrove
Mr S Cosgrove
Mr T Cosgrove
MR J E Cowan
Mr I G Cowie
Cowie BMW
MR N Cowley
MR P E Cowley
W Cowley
MR R Cowperthwaite
MRS C Cowperthwaite
Mr B.C Cox
MR R Cox
Mrs D.M.C Cox
Mr A Craig
Mr R Crake
Mr M.J. Crandon
Mr P.M.C Craster
Mr R.C Craster
Mr P Crawford
Mr R.C Crichton
Mr I.G.C Crocker
Miss R E Croft
Cromwell Tools
Mr W.B.C Cronin
Mr S W Crooks
Mr K.C Crosby
Crosling Ltd
MR D Crow
MR G.W Crow
MR M A Crowe
MR T M Crowe
Crutes Solicitors
MR A Crutchley
Cumbrian Ind
MR B Cummings
Mr C.C Cummings
Mr D.I.C Cummings
Mr I.C Currie
MR G Curry
Mr A.C Custance
Mr A.C Cuthbert
Mr K.C Cuthbert
Mr L Cuthbert
Mr P Cuthbert
DYJ Contracts
Mr C.D Dakin
Mr K Dale
MR R G Daniel
Mr C.D Daniels
Mr H.D Daniels
Mr T.D Daniels
MR D Dankin
MR T Dankin
Mr L Dar
Mr M M Dar
MR DARBYSHIRE
MR N A Darbyshire
MR J G Darcy
Darlington Building Society
Mr P.M.D Dasey
DAV Engineering & Marine
Mr D W Davey
Mr J Davey
John Davey Ltd
Mr L Davey
MR I David
MISS H Davidson

MR C Davidson
MR I W Davidson
MR N Davidson
Mr S.G.D Davidson
MR T A Davidson
MRS S Davidson
DAVIDSONS
DR A Davies
MISS C M Davies
MR A Davies
MR G Davies
Mr I.W.D Davies
MR J Davies
Mr L.D Davies
Mr M J Davies
Mr M.R.H Davies
Mr N.M Davies
MR P Davies
MR R G Davies
Mrs S.E.D Davies
MR I Davis
Mr H J Davison
Mr I.J Davison
Mr J Davison
Mr M.P.D Davison
Mr M.P.D Davison
Mr S.C.D Davison
MR T J H Davison
Mr R. Dawson
MRS A Dawson
A.V. Dawson Ltd
C Day
MR DAY
Mr A Day
Mr R.D Daykin
Mrs J.D Daykin
Mr N.C.D Dean
MR R Dean
Mr R Defty
Mr D.R.D Demoily
Christopher Denney
Mr I.D Dennis
Mr M.D Dennis
Mr C.M.D Dent
MR I A Dent
Mr B.D Desmond
Mr S.B.D Dick
DICKENS
MR J Dickson
MR M C Dismore
MR G Ditchburn
MR S Ditchburn
Mr A.D Dixon
MR J Dixon-Barker
Mr P.D Dobbin
MR R Dobbin
Doberman & Horsman
Mr M.D Dobson
Mr R.D Dobson
Mr K.W.D Dodds
Mr P. Dodds
Mr N.J.D Dodsworth
Mstr C.J.D Dodsworth
Dr J.C.D Doherty
Mr P.J.D Doherty
Mr S.M.D Doherty
Mstr R.P.D Doherty
Mr P Dolan
MR P A Dolan
DAVE DONACHIE
Mr D.D Donaldson
MR S Donnelly
MRS C Donnelly
Mr A.I.D Dotchin
Mr T.D Doughty
Mr H.D Douglas
Mr E R Douglass
J.T. Dove Ltd
MR J A Dowd
Mr L.J Downs
MRS J Downs
Mrs J Downs
Mr A.D Dowson
Mr A.W.D Dowson
MR M Doyle
MRS T A Doyle
Mr F.D Draycott
Mr R.M Draycott
MR J R Drennan
Mr G Driscoll
Mr D A Drumm
MR J K Drury
MR M Drury
Mr M.D Drury
Mr P.D Drury
MR R Ducker
Mr A Duckling

MR C E Duckling
MR I Duffield
MRS DUFFIELD
MR B Duffy
MR P Duffy
Mr C.J. Duggan
MR J W Duncan
Mr C.A.D Dunleavy
Miss N.J Dunn
Mr B.G.D Dunn
Mr D S Dunn
Mr J I Dunn
Mr K Dunn
Mr R Dunn
Mr P.R. Dunnakey
Mr R. Dunnakey
Mr P J Dunne
Mr B. Dunnill
MR P Dunning
MR J.R Dunwell
MASTER R J Durham
MR W R Durrant
Mr K.R.D Dutton
Mr M.D Dutton
Mr P.L.K Dutton
Mr K.D Dwyer
Eagle Supplies
Eagle Welding
Mr Easby
Mr S.E Easby
MR J Eason
Mr S Eason
MR S EASTBURY
MR P Eastwood
Mr P.E Eccles
MR G EDGAR
MR P.E Edmondson
MR R Edmundson
Mr G.E Edon
Miss K.A.E Edwards
Mr B.E Edwards
Mr D.E Edwards
MR M R Edwards
Mr P.B.E Edwards
Mr P.E Edwards
Mr R Edwards
Mrs B.E Edwards
Mr M J Eeles
MISS D.J Egerton
MR A Elliott
MR F H Elliott
MR G ELLIOTT
Mr M.E Elliott
MR C J Ellis
MR S J Ellis
Ellis & Everard
MR ELSDON
MR ELSTOB
ELSTONE ENGINEERING
Mr N.E Emmerson
MR R Emmerson
MR S Emmerson
MR M England
Mr J G Etheridge
Mr A.E Evans
Mr D.E Evans
Ms A.M.E Eves
W. Eves & Co
Mr A.D.E Ewart
Mr J.E Ewart
Eyecatch Teesside
MR A Eyles
Mr B.F Fagan
Mr R.F Fagan
Mrs J.M.F Fagan
MR M Fairbank
MR S Fairbank
MISS H M Fairest
MR J Fairest
MR J B Farley
MR M S Farley
Mr R.P.F Farnham
Mr C.F Farrar
Mr P.C.F Farrer
MR M Farroll
MRS E Farroll
MR V S W Farrow
Mr G Fawcett
Mr H Fawcett
Mr J Fawcett
MRS S Featherstone
MR C Fee
MR F P Feenan
MR B Fenwick
Mr D.F Ferguson
MR J Field
Mr P Fields
Mrs C Fields

Mr A.M.D. Fisher
MR I M Fisher
MR M C Fisher
MR R S Fitzpatrick
MRS J Flavell
MR J Fleming
MR M Fleming
MR J A Fletcher
MR M J Fletcher
Mr R.K.F Fletcher
Mr William Fletcher
Mrs M.J.F Fletcher
Mr G.C.F Flintoft
Mr P.G. Flintoft
MR C Foley
MR I J Ford
MR J Ford
Mr K S Ford
Mr J.N.F Fordham
Mr J.W.F Fordham
Mr M Forrester
Mr H Forster
Mr A Foster
Mr M.F Foster
Mr M.D.F Fothergill
Mr P.J.F Foulkes
A Fountain
Fox Advertising
Mr M.F Fox
Mr M.J.F Fox
MR J Foxton
MR D Frank
MR B French
MR D J French
MR D W French
Mr J French
Mr N French
Mstr C D French
Mr S.F Frost
Mr P.F Fry
Mr J S Furness
Mr K Gains
Mr D.A.G Gallagher
MR J T Gallagher
Mr J.K.G Gallagher
MR M Gallagher
REV F.G. Gallagher
Mr S.R. Ganguly
Mr CJ Gant
MR R D Garbutt
Miss A.M.G Gard
MR N Gardener
MR G Garnett
MR J S Garnett
Mr R Garry
MRS J Garry
Miss M.G Garthwaite
Mr A.G Gash
MR G Gash
MR GATENBY
Mr C.G Gates
Mr A.R. Gaunt
Mr B. Gaunt
Mr M.G Gaynor
Mr T.P.G Gaynor
Mstr J.G Gaynor
Gazelle Transport Ltd
MR J T Gentry
MR A R Gibb
MR K G Gibb
Mr K.G Gibb
Mr S.J.G Gibb
MR Gibbons
MR GIBBONS
MRS Gibbons
Mr R.W Gibbs
MR J Gibson
Mr N.G Gibson
Mr P.H.G Gibson
MR R Gibson
MISS R Gifford
MR J Gifford
MR C Gilbert
MR J Gilbert
MR J Gill
Mr J R Gill
Mr N.G Gill
MRS F B Gill
Mr A.G Gillow
Mr J H Ginty
MR G Gittus
Mr B.G Gladwin
Glamal Engineering
Mr N.G Glasper
Mrs L.J.G Glasper
Mr B W Glaves
Mr J W Glaves
Mr J.G Glover
Mr M.R.G Glover

MR A Godfrey
MR J Godfrey
MR I Gofton
MRS Gofton
Mr E Goldstraw
MISS A B Gollogly
Mr E.A. Goodhall
Goodswens Solicitors
C N Goodwin
MR I D Gordon
MR M Gordon
Mrs A Goring
Miss L J Gorman
Mrs J Gorman
MR P Gorthorpe
MR W Gorthorpe
Faithful Gould
Mr M W Gould
Mr P.J.G Gourlay
Mr R.P.G Gourlay
MISS J D Govan
Mr D.G Govan
Mr P.G Govan
MR Gowland
Mr G.G Gowland
MR M Gowland
Mr M.J.G Grace
Ms T.M.G Grace
Mr M.G Grady
MR Graham
Mr A D Graham
Mr A.P.G Graham
Mr C.G Graham
MR D Graham
MR D J Graham
Mr I.J. Graham
MR J R Graham
Mr R.F. Graham
Mr W.G Graham
MRS Graham
MRS A O Graham
Graham & Waites
MR J.M Grainge
Mr F.G Grainger
Grange Eng
Miss L.G Grant
Mr D.G Grant
Mr G.G Grant
Mr I L Granville
MR J Granville
Mr P.G Graves
MR C A Gray
MR M Gray
MR R Gray
Mr Grayson
Mr G.G Grayson
Mr K Grayson
MR R K Grayson
MR J W Grayson
MRS M D Grayston
Mr A Green
MR A S Green
Mr B.G Green
Mr I Green
Mr J P Green
Mr J.A.G Green
Mr M.G Green
MR P Green
Mr P Green
MR P T Green
Dr J.R.G Greenaway
Mr R.R.G Greenaway
Greenham Trading Ltd
MR M Greenup
Mr M.G Greenup
Miss H.L.G Greenwell
Mr D.G Greenwood
Mrs S.M.G Greenwood
MR D Greer
MR N M T Gregory
MR A K Greig
MR G Greig
MR K Greig
Mr W.A.G Grey
MR R Grier
Mr T.G Griffin
MR A J Griffiths
Mr P.A Griffiths
Mr P.G Griffiths
Mr R P Griffiths
MR V Griffiths
Mrs P Griffiths
Mr C.G Griveson
MR GROSVENOR
Mr D.G Guest
Mr M Guest
Miss C.E. Gunn
Mr M.G Gutteridge
MR E Guy

MR A Hailstone
Halifax Building Society
Mr Hall
MR A Hall
Mr A.H Hall
Mr D. Hall
Mr D.G.H Hall
Mr J E Hall
MR K Hall
Mr L.J.H Hall
Mr Leslie Hall
Mr R.H Hall
Mrs S.H Hall
MR J Hallett
MR S J Hallett
Mr Hamilton
Mr D.L. Hamilton
MR J.B Hamilton
MR N Hamilton
MR S J Hammond
MR J J Hampton
MR J S Hannon
Mr J C Hanson
Mr P Hanson
Mr G C Harbottle
Mstr M Harbottle
Mr A.H Harding
MR S J Harding
Mrs M.K.H Harding
Hardware Supply
Mr F.H Harker
MR N Harker
Mr P.R Harker
Mr S.H Harker
MR W Harker
E Harland
Mr D Harland
Mr J Harland
Mstr P.J Harland
Dr J.J.H Harley
Mstr J.A.H Harley
Mstr J.M.H Harley
Mstr J.P.H Harley
P. Harnett
Mr D Harper
Mr K.H Harper
mr M A Harper
Mr L.A. Harriman
Mr K.H Harrington
Mr A.H Harris
MR G Harris
Mr G.H Harris
Mr J.H Harris
MR S Harris
Mr W Harris
Miss J.M.H Harrison
Miss L.H Harrison
Mr Harrison
Mr A Harrison
MR A I Harrison
Mr D.J.H Harrison
Mr E Harrison
MR G Harrison
Mr H.G.H Harrison
Mr J.J Harrison
MR L Harrison
Mr M W Harrison
Mr N.H Harrison
MR S Harrison
Mr S.P.H Harrison
Mrs A Harrison
Mrs H.L. Harrison
Mrs L.H Harrison
Ms E.H Harrison
Mr A.D.H Harrow
Mstr A.J.H Harrow
MR M Hart
Mr T J Hart
Mstr J P Hart
MR Hartas
MR R Hartas
Mr W.J Hartley
MR P Hartshorn
Mr J.D.H Hatfield
John Hatfield and Sons
MR G T Hathaway
Hautin Ltd
Mr T W Havelock
Mr R.B.H Haw
MR A Hawkins
Mr D.J.H Hawkins
MR L N Hawkins
MR N Hawkins
Mr Hayes
Mr C Hayes
Mr T.H Hazell
Mr G B Heaney
MR E Heap
Mr A Hearn

Mr A.T Hebbron
Mr A.T.H Hebbron
Mr J.E.H Hebbron
Mrs A.T.H Heffernan
MR J W Heightley
Mr P.G Hellings
Mr B.H Helyer
Mrs G.H Helyer
Hemlington Social Club
Mr D Henderson
Mrs L Henderson
Mr C.H Henry
Mr G T Henry
Mr P D Henry
Mr S P Henry
Mr W Henry
MR B Hepburn
Mr J.P.H Hepworth
Mr S.C.H Hepworth
Hermgrove (M&I) Ltd
Hertel UK Ltd
Mr G.H Heslehurst
MR B A Heslop
MR J W Heslop
Mr J B Hewitson
Mr A.J.H Hickman
Mr P J Hide
Mr A J Higgins
MR B J Higgins
Mr N A Higgins
Mr A.H Hill
Mr B.L.H Hill
MR D Hill
Mr D Hill
Mr D.H Hill
Mr G Hill
Mr G.P.H Hill
Mr L Hill
Mr P.D.H Hill
Mr R.A.H Hill
Mrs J Hill
Mrs V.H Hill
Williamson Hill
Mr S Hillary
Mr N J Hills
Mrs C J Hills
Hindmarsh
Mr C.J. Hinds
Mr C.G.H Hingley
Mr A.H Hirst
Mr S.H Hirst
Mr T.H Hirst
Hoban
Mrs V.R.H Hobson
Mr B.H Hodgkinson
Mr M.H Hodgkinson
Mr N.H Hodgkinson
MR S Hodgkinson
Mr B.H Hodgson
MR C Hodgson
Mr C.J.H Hodgson
MR D Hodgson
Mr G.H Hodgson
MR I R Hodgson
Mr J.R.H Hodgson
Mr W.H Hodgson
Mr I Hogarth
MR D Hoggarth
Mr J.R.H Hoggarth
Mr S.E.H Hoggarth
Mrs E.A.H Hoggarth
Mr C Holden
MR R S Holden
Mr W.H Holden
Mrs E.H Holden
Mr D Holdsworth
K. Holme Engineering
Mr D Holmes
Mr T.D.H Holmes
MRS P Holt
MR G W Holyfield
Mrs D.H Homer
Mr P.S.H Honeyman
Mr E Honeywell
Mr E.H Honeywell
MR H M Hood
Mr M.A.H Hood
Mr J.D.H Hook
MR HOPKINSON
Mr J.F.H Horkan
Mr A W Hornby
Mr J Horsley
Mr P Horton
Mr J R Hough
MR S Howard
MSTR J C Howard
MR I J Howden
MR T H Howe
Mr J.S.H Hoyland

Mr P.M.H Hubbard
MR B Hudson
MR D J Hudson
Mr J.D.H Hudson
Mr M.H Hudson
MR A Hughes
MR E Hughes
Mr M.S.H Hughes
Mr S.A.H Hughes
Mr S.D.E Hughes
Mr D Hull
Mrs D I Hull
MR S Humble
Mrs C.H.M Humphreys-Middleton
Mr E.J Humphries
Mrs J Humphries
J.P HUNTER
Mr C Hunter
MR D N G Hunter
Mr J.H Hunter
Mr L. Hunter
Mr T.A Hunter
MR A Hunton
MISS C Hurst
Mr B G Hurst
MR G Hurst
Mr J.H Hurst
MR R Hurst
MR P A Husband
Mr D A Hutchins
Mr R.S. Hutchinson
Mrs H.M. Hutchinson
HW Associates Ltd
MR A H Hyams
Hydro Polymers Ltd
Mr M Idle
MR R M W Idle
ICI Chemicals
ICI Eutech
ICI Wilton Site
MR F Inganni
IND & MARINE HYDRAULICS
Mr I Ingleden
Mr K.I Inman
Mrs A.I Inman
Mstr N.I Inman
Mr M.J.I Innes
Mr L.I Instone
MR J Irvine
Mr B. Irwin
Mr M. Irwin
MR K J Isley
Mr S.I Ismail
MR I.D.I Ithurralde
Mr B.J Jackson
Mr D A Jackson
Mr M.J Jackson
MR P M Jackson
Mr P.M.J Jackson
Mr S Jackson
Mr W.E.J Jackson
Mrs A Jackson
Mrs A.J Jackson
Mrs J.J Jackson
MSTR K M Jackson
MR M E Jacobson
Dr E.A James
Miss S.L James
Mr A.C.J James
Dr M J Jasztal
Mrs J Y Jasztal
Mr D. Jelly
Mr G.C.J Jenney
MR I Jennings
Mr J F Jennings
Mr M.J Jessup
Mr R.C.J Joel
Miss C.L.J Johns
Mr S.G.J Johns
K.M JENNINGS JOHN-SON
MR C L Johnson
Mr E R D Johnson
Mr J K Johnson
Mr N Johnson
Mrs J Johnson
Mrs K Johnson
Mr N. Johnston
Mr D.E.J Johnstone
MR G Johnstone
Miss C Jones
Mr B.J Jones
MR C. Jones
Mr C. Jones
Mr D.T.J Jones
Mr E.G.J Jones
MR G P Jones

Mr M.J Jones
MR P.B Jones
Mr RAY JONES
Mr S J Jones
Mr W Jones
Mrs H N Jones
Mrs J A Jones
Mstr B.J Jones
Mr K.L.J Joss
Mr R.I.J Joss
Mr S D Joynes
Mr AJ Kavanagh
Mr F W Kay
MR J Kay
Mr M.K Kay
Mr G.O.K Keegan
A M Keen
Miss J.K Keenan
Mr M.K Keenan
Mr Tom Keenan
Mr D.K Keetley
MR A.M KELLERMAN
Mr I.J.K Kelly
MR P Kelly
Mr P Kelly
Ms J.K Kelsey
Miss J. Kemp
Mr G.R. Kemp
Mr B.K Kendrick
Lionweld Kennedy
Mr J M Kennedy
MR P Kent
Mr J. Kerr
Mr A.G.K Kerry
Miss S.K Kettlewell
Mr C.K Kettlewell
Mr E.J. Kettlewell
Mr S.K Key
Mr T.K Key
MR P A Kicks
Mr I.J.K Kidson
K Kilvington
MR M Kilvington
M J Kimmings
Miss V King
MR KING
Mr G.W King
Mr J.A. Kirk
Mrs S.J.K Kirk
MR M Kirkbride
Mr M.K Kirkbright
Mr S.K Kirkbright
MR J D Kirton
MR P Kirwan
Mr A.K Kitching
MR T Kitching
Mr W.K Kitching
Mr G.E. Knaggs
Mr R.J.K Knaggs
C Knight
E Knight
Mr M S Kokri
Mr D.G.L Laidler
Mrs L.L Laidler
MR E J Lake
MSTR A J Lake
Miss K.L Lamb
Mr D.L Lamb
DR J Lamballe
Mrs D Lamballe
Lancaster & Winter
Mr J.L Lane
MR A Larkin
MR S Larkin
MRS M Larkin
Mr Laroche
Mr T.L Larry
Mr E.A.L Larsen
MR M Laver
MR T Lavery
Mrs S M Lawrence
MRS E Lawson
MR K.L Layburn
Mr K.S.L Leavesley
MR T Lee
Mr P T Leech
MR Leen
Mr D.L Legg
Mr T Legg
Mr M.L Leneham
Mr J E Lenihan
MR B Leonard
MR V J Leonard
MRS P Leonard
Leven Bridge Eng
MR K Levett
G N Lewin
Mr A.G.L Lewis
MR J L Lewis
Mr A.J.L Lewis

Mr B Lewis
Mr G Lewis
Mr J.B.L Lewis
MR K Lewis
Mr M.J.L Lewis
Mr M.L Lewis
Mr T A Lewis
MRS M R Lewis
Lex Vehicle Leasing
MR D S Libby
Mr R Liddle
Mr C Lightfoot
Mr K Lightfoot
MR P M Lince
MR T F Lince
MR B V Lincoln
Linden Group Ltd
MR LINDSAY
Mr S.J.L Lindsay
Mr R J Lines
Linkman Tankers
AW Linpac Insulation
MR W H Lings
Mr H.L Lippiatt
Mr G Lipthorpe
MR D A Lister
MR D H Lister
MR J M Lister
MR T Lister
MRS J Lister
Mr S.J.L Lithgo
Mrs B.L Lithgo
Mr J Little
Mrs R Little
Mr A.E Littlefair
Mr A.L Littlewood
MR R D Llewellyn
Mr A.J.L Lloyd
Mr C.L Lloyd
Mr E.L LLoyd
MR J G Lloyd
Kevin Lloyd Ltd
MRS L A M Lloyd
Mr R.L Lobley
MR A LOBORIK
Mr D.L Lodge
MR B Logan
MR J M Long
MR S P Long
MR D Longstaff
Mr G Longstaff
MR B Longster
MR G S Longworth
MR S J Longworth
MR M Lonsdale
MR R.L.L Lonsdale
MR B Love
Mr M.S. Love
Mr R.M. Love
Mre L Love
Mstr E.J. Love
SENIOR B Love
Mr A.L Lowe
Mr M.A.L Lowe
Mr S Lowe
Mr M.L Lowther
Mr J.P.L Lupton
MR A Lynch
MR P Lynch
MRS R Lynch
MR R LYNN
Miss V.L Lyons
Mr N.L Lyons
Mr P.L Lyons
Mr F.R.L Lyth
MF Sealing Systems
MK Northern Electric
MM Olympic Chevin
MP Storage
Mr A.M MacDonald
Mr B.K.M MacDonald
MR E R Mack
Mr K. MacKenzie
MR A Mackey
MR N A Mackey
MR A Mackie
Mr S.C.M Maddren
MR N A Maguire
Mr A E Maidstone
Mr M.E. Maidstone
Mainstream Eng
MR W C Mair
Miss K.M Malcolm
Mr A.M Malcolm
Mrs C Malcolm
Mr S.A Malik
MR D Maloney
MR E Maloney

MR A M W Maltby
Mr F.G.M Maltby
MR K G Maltby
Mr D.M Manders
Mr D.R.M Manning
Mr N.M Mannion
Mr P.M Mannix
MR E Marlborough
Mr M Marley
Marlows Foods
Miss J.M Marron
Mr G.M Marron
MR R W Marsden
MR W Marsden
MR B Marshall
Mr J Marshall
MR W B Marshall
MRS A Marshall
Mrs M Marshall
Miss T.C.M Martin
Mr C.M Martin
Mr S Martin
MR A Martino
MRS N Martino
Mastercopy Ltd
Mr T.M Mason
Mr S.M Masri
Mr R.J.M Mather
Mr M.C.M Matson
Miss D.M Matthews
MR D G Matthews
MR J K Matthews
MRS J.L Matthews
Mr S.D.M Maude
Mr M.M Mawson
Mr K.M May
Mr A.M McArthur
Mr K.M McBride
Mstr J M McBride
Mr P A McCairns
Mr D.J.M McCall-Smith
Mr M.M McCarron
MISS D.L McCarthy
Mr B.R.M McCarthy
Mr D.J.M McCarthy
Mr M McCarthy
Mr S.M McCarthy
Mr P.M McClure
MR P S McCormick
MR R J McCormick
Mr J.M McCourt
Mrs V McCourt
MR K J McCue
MR C P McDermott
Mr J.M McDermott
Mr R.P.M McDermott
MR M A G McDonagh
Mr J.M McElroy
MR A McElvaney
MSTR K McEwan
Mr L McGee
G&H McGill Ltd
MR M G McGlade
MR N McGloin
MR G McGough
Mr N. McGowan
Mr P.M McGowan
Mr P.M McGowran
Mr B.K.M McGowron
Dr J.J.M McGrath
Mr A.D.M McGregor
Mr W.M McGregor
MR M J McGrogan
MR M McGuinness
MR M P McGuinness
Mrs A.M.G McGuinness
Mstr C.M McGuinness
Mstr J.M McGuinness
Mr I.J.M McIntosh
MR M P McIntosh
Rev J McKeever
Mr J.G.M McKenny
Mr K.M McKimm
Mr N.A.M McLaren
Mr P R McLaren
Mr A.M McLay
Mr B.M McLay
Mr D.G.M McLay
Miss P.M McLean
Mr S McLean
Miss J. McLedd
Mr F.M McLellan
Mr I McLeod
MR P J McLone
Mr P McLoughlin
MR M J McMahon
Mr C.E.M McManus
MR N.C McMaster
MR McNamee

MR I McNaughton
Mr M.M McNay
Mr N.M McNay
Mr S.M.M McNeil
Mr C.M McNeill
Mr S.M McNeill
Mr P.M McNichol
Miss C Mcnulty
MR D McNulty
MR M.Q MCPARLAND
Mr M.J.M McPartland
MR A D McPherson
MR D P Medd
Mr J.M Medd
Mr J.I.M Megson
MR J.P Meir
Mr P.T Meir
Mr T.E Meir
Mr H.M Melling
Mrs M.M Melling
Mr D.M Mellon
Mr P.M Mellon
Mr N. Mellors
Melton Building
Mr M.M Mendum
MR J K Metcalf
Master A.M Metcalfe
Miss C Metcalfe
MR A Metcalfe
MR D Metcalfe
Mr D.S.M Metcalfe
Mr S.C.G Metcalfe
Mr M Meynell
Mr P Meynell
Mr E.M Middleton
Mr N.M Middleton
Mr D.W.M Milburn
MR M Milburn
MRS M P Milburn
Mr D.V.M Miller
MR J Miller
Mr M Millett
MR D C Millins
Mr C.R Mills
Mr D.M Mills
MR G Mills
Mr J.B.M Mills
Mr M Mills
Mrs S.M Mills
Mr B P Mitchell
Mr D Mitchell
Mr G.M Mitchell
Mr I.M Mitchell
Mr J Mitchell
MR J C Mitchell
Mr J.A.M Mitchell
MR K Mitchell
MR M Mohan
Shelagh Molley
MR F A Monaghan
MR P F Monaghan
Mr C. Monehen
MR A D Montague
MR P J Montellier
MR G Moodie
MR T I Moodie
Moody
Mr A Moody
Mr G Moody
Mr I Moody
Mr L.J.M Moody
Mrs J Moody
MR C Moore
MR D P Moore
Mr D.M Moore
Mr E Moore
MR A G Moore
Mr M.P.M Moore
Mr P S Moore
MR R J Moore
Mr R.M Moore
MR W P Moore
Mrs C.A.M Moore
Mr J Moran
Mr D Moreton
MRS S B Moreton
Mr J.M Morgan
MR J Morley
MR K Morley
MR P R Morlock
Mr P.J.M Morren
Mr H.M Morris
MORRISON
MR M Morrison
MR C Morton
MR J.W Morton
Miss J.M Moses
Mrs H.M Moses
MISS M S Mosley

Mr P Mosley
Mr R.M Moss
Mr T.M Moss
Mr K.M Mothersill
Mrs D.M Mothersill
Morgan Moore Eng
MR M Moy
Mr H Mucklow
Mr Mudd
Mr K.M Mudd
MR W S Mudd
Mr G T Mulholland
Mr J Mulholland
Mr K. Mulholland
MR P Mulholland
MSTR S Mulholland
Mr G.M Mundy
MR I Murphy
Mr J.H.M Murphy
MR P Murphy
Mr R.M Murphy
Mr A.M Murray
Mr J.H.M Murray
Mr J.M Murray
Mr R.M Murray
Mrs M.M Murray
MSTR D Murray
Mr J.P.M Mutter
Mr M.J.A Mutter
Mr B.M Myers
Mr G.M Myers
Ms C.N Narbrough
MR B Narey
MR P Narey
Mr G.N Naughton
Mr C Neil
Mr E Neil
Mstr C Neil
Mr D.W.N Nelson
MR L Nelson
Mr D.N Nesbitt
Mr T.D.N Nesbitt
Mr M Neville
Mrs S Neville
H. Newbould Ltd
Newcastle Breweries Ltd
Mr J.A.N Newhouse
MR P J Newhouse
Mr M Newman
Mr Nichol
Mr J.N Nicholls
Mr P.R.N Nicholls
MR A N Nichols
MR S J Nichols
Mr A S Nicholson
MR G Nicholson
Mr J.N Nicholson
Mr R.N Nicholson
Miss E Nisbet
Mr D Nisbet
Mr J Nisbet
Mrs V Nisbet
MR Nixon
Mr J K Nixon
Mr P.N.N Nixon
MRS Nixon
Mstr S.N Nixon
MR C Noble
MR M Noble
Mr D.M. Noddings
MR P A Norman
Mr E. Norminton
Nothern Landlords
Northern Machine Tools
Northfield International
Mr G.N Norton
MR M D Norton
MSTR D E Norton
Norton Cleaning Services
Mr I.W Nunn
Mr M.O O'Brien
Mr P O'Brien
MR P.D O'Brien
Mr G W O'Donnell
MR O'Hagan
MR O'HARA
FATHER D O'Neill
MR O'Neill
MR J O'Neill
MR T O'Neill
MR O'Riordan
MR C J Oakes
OBC Shipping Ltd
MISS D Oliver
MISS P Oliver
Mr J.W.O Oliver
Mr S.E.O Oliver
Mr G Olvanhill
Onetran Ltd

Mr B.O Orton
Mr L.E.O Osbourne
Mr L.O Osbourne
Mr A J Oswin
Mr C.O Ottolini
MR T.B Outhwaite
MRS M Outhwaite
Mr D Outwaite
MISS C A Owen
MR R.J Owen
MR K Oxley
Pace Financial Services
Mr R.P Padget
Mr M.D Pagel
Mr D.L.P Painter
Mr G.A.P Painter
Mr J.D. Paling
Mr D.P Palleschi
Mr J Pallister
MSTR F Pallister
MR A M Palmer
MR D R Palmer
Mr J Palmer
Mr J Palmer
Panda Supplies
MR L A Pankhurst
Mr D.P Papaioannou
Mr B.P Park
Mr J.R. Park
Park Electrical
MR A J Parker
Mr G.P Parker
Mr N.P Parker
Mr D.J. Parkes
Mrs L. Parkes
Miss R.M. Parkin
MR PARKIN
Mr J.R. Parkin
MR Parks
MSTR Parks
MR K R Parnaby
MR L Parnell
J.P. Joseph Parr Ltd
Parson & Crosland
Mr A.P Parsons
MR J W Parsons
Mr NAP Partnership
MR B J Paterson
Pathwedge 87 Ltd
MR N Patterson
Mr R.N.P Patterson
Mr P.P Pattison
Pattison Decoration
Mr A.P Patton
Mr G.J.P Patton
Mstr D.S.P Patton
Mr C. Payne
MR D Payne
Mr G. Payne
Mr M Payne
MR Peacock
Mr D.A.P Peacock
Mr F. Peacock
Mr J R Peacock
MR N Peacock
Mr A J Peaker
Mr C.J Peaker
Mr M. Peaker
E Pearsall
MRS D W Pearsall
Miss J.P Pearson
Mr A.P Pearson
MR A P Pearson
MR D R Pearson
Mr D.P Pearson
Mr G Pearson
MR I Pearson
Mr J.R.P Pearson
MR S M Pearson
Mrs J.M.P Pearson
Mrs P A Pearson
MR D J Peart
MR I E Pease
Mr M.J.P Peevor
J D Pelmar
MR S Pelmar
Mr K.P Pemberton
Mr D Penman
Mr V F Pennick
Mr P.R Pennock
Miss Peppert
MR D Percy
MR L Percy
Mr S R Percy
MR W Percy
Mr F.W.P Perfitt
MR D Perkins

MR L Perkins
Mr R.P Perry
Mstr D.P Perry
MR W B Philips
MR Phillips
MR K Phillips
Mr K.P Phillips
MR P.D Phillips
Mrs M.K.P Phillips
Phillips Petroleum Products
Mr D.J Pickersgill
Mr G.M Pickersgill
Mr G.P Pilkington
Mr S.A.E. Pilley
Mr D.L.P Pinchbeck
Mr D.P Pinder
Mr A Pinkney
Mr J Pipe
Mr J.M.P Pirie
Mr A.P Plant
Mr G.A.P Plant
Mr Pledger
Mr D Plews
Mr M A Plews
Miss A Pollard
Mr A C Pollard
Mr D.P Poole
Mr J.D.P Poole
Mrs A.P Poole
Mr I. Pooley
Mr R.D.P Pooley
Mr E Porritt
Mr K.P Portas
Mr G.S.P Porteous
Mr C.N.P Porter
Mr R A Porter
Mr R.P Porter
Mr M.A.P Poskitt
Mr S.J.P Poskitt
Mr L.P Postgate
Cleveland Potash
Mr B.G. Potter
Mr L.O.P Potter
Mr S.A.P Fountain
Mr A Powell
Mr A.P Powell
Mr M Powell
Mr M.P Powell
Mrs J Powell
Mstr C Powell
Mstr S Powell
Mr Enron Power
Mr A.D.P Pratt
Mr D.W.P Pratt
Presentation Plastics
Mr Falcon Press
MR A V Prest
MR S A Prest
Mr A.P Preston
Mr C.P Preston
MR W Pretty
Mr W.G.P Pretty
Mr C.P Price
Mr D S Priddy
Mr D.P Priestley
Mr G Priestley
Mr W.P Priestley
MR G Priiestley
Priory Social Club
MR D J Procter
MR N B Procter
Mr J Prosser
Mr W.J Proud
Mr N.P Prudom
Dr I J Pryde
Mr A. Pugh
Miss A.J.P Purnell
Mr D.P Purnell
MR M S Quinn
RAOB Club
MR RACE
Mr A.L.R Race
Race for Furniture
Mr S.R Radics
Mrs V.R Radics
Mr C.R Raine
MR P W Raisbeck
Mr R Ramsay-Connell
Mr MWR Ramshaw
Mr W Ramshaw
MR T RAWDEN
Mr A.L.R Rayson
Mrs J R Rayson
Mr V.T Rea
MR G P Read
READMAN

Mr G.R Readman
MR J P Readman
MR P D Readman
Mr W G Readman
MR W G READMAN
W.G. Readman
MR M J Reaney
MR J P Redding
Mr P W Redding
Mr D W Redpath
Miss K Reed
MR G D Reed
MR J Reed
Mrs I.R Reed
MR J Reeve
MR C Reeves
Mr N.R Reeves
NIA Refractories
Mr K.R Regan
Mr V.R Regan
Mrs P.R Regan
Mr N Reid
MISS C Relph
MR C Relph
MR S Relph
Mr D Reynolds
MR J K Reynolds
Mrs J.A Reynolds
Mr S.R Rhodes
Mr A.M.R Rice
MR D Richards
J & R M Richardson
Miss J Richardson
Miss S.R Richardson
Mr A.R Richardson
MR B Richardson
Mr C.R Richardson
MR D J Richardson
Mr D.R Richardson
Mr G.R Richardson
John Richardson Construction Ltd
Mr J.F.R Richardson
Mr K.F.R Richardson
Mr K.R.R Richardson
MR S A Richardson
Mrs A.R Richardson
Mrs K.R Richardson
Mr D Richman
Mr A.R Richmond
MR J Richmond
MR J M Ridgen
Mr R.O.R Ridsdale
Mr P Riley
MR P A Riley
Mr S.P.R Riley
Mrs B Riley
Mr S.R Ripley
MR C Rivers
Riverside Foods (NE) Ltd
Miss A Rix
Mr R W Rix
P&O Roadtanks
Mr W H Robbins
MR A. Roberts
MR D Roberts
Mr P.D Roberts
Robins North Ltd
ROBINSON
MR Robinson
Mr A.M.R Robinson
Mr C.R Robinson
MR D W Robinson
Mr D.C.R Robinson
Mr D.G.R Robinson
Mr F.M.R Robinson
MR I.A Robinson
Mr J A Robinson
Mr K Robinson
MR K N Robinson
Mr L. ROBINSON
MR M J Robinson
MR R Robinson
MR R E Robinson
MR S Robinson
MR S C Robinson
MR T.W Robinson
Mr W.J.R Robinson
Mrs M.R Robinson
Mstr A Robinson
Mstr M Robinson
MR M A Roboson
Mr Robson
Mr G Robson
Mr K.H.R Robson
Mr Punch Robson
Mrs Robson

MRS J Robson
MR G F Roddam
MR C A Rogers
Mr G.R Rogers
MR M Rogers
Mr P.R Rogers
Mr T.R Rooke
Mr A.R Rose
WILLETT ROSS
Miss C.C.R Rossi
Mr J.R Rossi
Mr G Rothwell
MR P Rowe
Roxby Eng
MR A Rowlands
MR D Ruff
MR G W Rumins
Mr N.A.R Russel
MR E Russell
Mr J.E. Russell
MR E Rutherford
Miss L.S Sadler
Mr D.J.S Sadler
Sadler Tankers
Safehire (Plant) Ltd
MR SALMON
MR S G Salway
Miss I.S Sams
Mr B. Sanderson
MR I Sanderson
Miss C.S Saul
Mr I.S Saul
Mr N.S Sayers
MR J.C Scandrett
MRS J C Scandrett
MR D Scott
Mr D.J.S Scott
Mr E.E.S Scott
MR G Scott
MR J Scott
Mr J.H.S Scott
Mr J.S Scott
Mr L.J.S Scott
Mr M Scott
MR P A Scott
Mr P.H.S Scott
Mr C.A.S Scott
Mr A.S Scotter
Mr B. Scullion
MR B J Scurr
Mr N.S Seaman
Mr P Seaman
Mr A.S Seaton
Mr J Seed
Mr B.E.S Sellers
Miss J.M Selwyn
MR G Selwyn
MR S Selwyn
Mr F.S Serplus
Mr R G Sewell
MR P Shann
Mr J F Sharpe
Mr G.T.S Shaw
MR J Shaw
MR M Shaw
Mr M Shaw
MR P Shaw
Mrs J L Shaw
Mr A. Shell
Mr D Sheperd
MR Shepherd
Mr I.S Sheraton
Mrs B.M.S Sheraton
MR W Shields
MR D Short
Mr J.M.S Short
WILLETT Short
Mr P.F.S Short
Mrs M.S Short
Mstr S.S Short
Miss L.E.M. Shuttleworth
Mr K.M. Shuttleworth
MR L Sidgwick
Mr M.N.S Sidwell
Mrs D.S Sidwell
Mr K.S Sigsworth
Mr A.S Simmons
Mr N.S Simmons
Mr S.C.S Simmons
Mr B.S Simon
Mr R.S Simons
MR A Simpson
MR A W Simpson
MR D Simpson
MR P E Simpson
Dr P J Sinclair

APPENDIX 5

Mr I Sinclair
Mr N.A.S Sinclair
Mr R.J.S Sinclair
Mr R.S Sinclair
MR T Sirila
Mr C Sixton
Mr C P Skeldon
Mr C.K.S Skelton
Mrs M.S Skelton
Mr R.P.S Skilbeck
MR W Skitt
Mr R.S Smales
MR L Small
MR D M Smallwood
Mr D.S Smart
Mr G Smiles
A P Smith
Miss C.A.K Smith
MISS E A Smith
Miss E C Smith
Miss H M Smith
MR A Smith
MR A H Smith
Mr A.C.S Smith
Mr A.W.S Smith
Mr B.S Smith
MR C Smith
Mr C A Smith
MR C F Smith
MR C S J Smith
Mr C.D.S Smith
Mr D Smith
Mr D.R Smith
Mr D.R.S Smith
Mr D.S Smith
MR D.W Smith
Mr G Smith
Mr G.H. Smith
Mr I T Smith
Mr I.M.S Smith
Mr J R R Smith
Mr J.B.S Smith
Mr J.C.S Smith
Mr J.G.F Smith
Mr J.S Smith
Mr K.W.S Smith
MR L Smith
MR M Smith
MR M.G Smith
Mr M.H.S Smith
Mr Mr Smith
Mr N Smith
Mr P Smith
MR P A Smith
Mr P.A Smith
MR R Smith
MR R E Smith
Mr R.S Smith
Mr S.M.S Smith
Mr T. Smith
Mr V.S Smith
MR W R Smith
Mr W.S Smith
Mrs D.J. Smith
Mrs S C A Smith
Mrs S.S Smith
Ms C.S Smith
P A Smith
Mr G.S Smitheringale
Mr G.S Smithson
Mrs V.M.S Smithson
MR C Snell
Mr MR Sonley
Mr C.J.S Southall
Mr G.B.S Southam
Mr J.I.S Sowerby
Mr D Spears
Mr J.A.S Speck
Mr K.S Speck
MR J SPEIGHT
Mr J Spence

MR J Spence
Mr I.S Spencer
Mr T.S Spensley
MR A F Spiller
Mr S.J.S Spoerry
Mr K.S Spring
Mr P.R.S Sprott
Stakis Casinos
Stanland Group
Mr S.C.S Staples
MR P Stapley
MR G Staton
Mr G.L.S Staton
Mr R.R.S Stebbings
Mr K.S Steel
Mr M A Steel
Steel North Tooling
MR STEPHENSON
MR A A Stephenson
MR A J Stephenson
Mr F.N. Stephenson
MR J Stephenson
MR J F Stephenson
MR J.F Stephenson
Mr J.R.S Stephenson
Mr K.S Stephenson
MR P C Stephenson
Mr P.S Stephenson
MRS STEPHENSON
Mrs M.P. Stephenson
Mr S.W. Stevenson
Mr P.W.S Steward
Mstr R.M.S Steward
Mr M Stewart
MR M Stewart
Mr W.N.S Stewart
Mrs S.J.S Stewart
Mr B Stobbs
MR R Stobbs
MR C Stockdale
MR P Stockdale
Stockton Engraving Co
Mr G T Stokeld
MR M A Stokeld
MSTR A A Stokeld
Mstr J B Stokeld
Miss S.A.S Stonehouse
Mr J.M.S Stonehouse
Mr Stones
Mr T Stones
MR R W Storey
MR K Storr
MR A Stoves
MRS D Stoves
Mr P.S Stowe
MRS A Strangeways
MR J D Straughan
Mr N.S Strong
MR W.S Stuart
Mr G.L Studholme
Mr R Studholme
Mr Stuttard
Mr T.S Suffell
Mr Summerfield
Mr J.C.S Summersgill
Mr R Sutton
MR Swainston
MR C Swainston
MSTR Swainston
MR B Swales
MR T Swales
MRS S Swales
MR E Swan
MRS B Swan
G. Sweeney Ltd
MRS J Sweeney
MSTR J.M Sweeney
Mr N Sweeting
Mr R.T. Sweeting
MR N A Sweetman
Mr J.N.S Swinbank

Mr G D Swinton
Andrew Sykes Ltd
MR G SYKES
MR I Symington
TB North East Landlords
MR R Tanfield
MR S Tanfield
Mr W.T Tarren
MR G I Tate
John Tate & Co
Mr K.T Tayloe
MR A Taylor
Mr A R Taylor
MR B Taylor
Mr C.D.T Taylor
Mr D Taylor
Mr D.T Taylor
Mr J A Taylor
Mr J F Taylor
MR M W Taylor
Mr M. Taylor
Mr M.T Taylor
MR R Taylor
Mr S.T Taylor
Mr T.C.T Taylor
MRS A Taylor
MRS J Taylor
Mrs S.T Taylor
Mstr C Taylor
Team Eng (UK) Ltd
Teeside Insurance
MR P N Telfer
Mr M.A.T Templeman
Mr E.S.T Tennant
Mr R.T Tennant
Mr T.T Theakston
Mr G.T Thirkell
MR J.T Thirling
MISS Thomas
Mr A.B.T Thomas
Mr A.F. Thomas
MR D Thomas
MR P H Thomas
Mr R Thomas
Mr S. Thomas
Mr S.T Thomas
Mr A.P.T Thompson
Mr A.T Thompson
MR B Thompson
Mr M Thompson
Mr M.T Thompson
Mr N.F.T Thompson
Mr N.T Thompson
Mr S.J Thompson
MR W Thompson
Mrs C.T Thompson
MSTR A Thompson
M J Thomson
Thornaby Social &
Welfare Club
MR M A Thornton
MR S Thornton
Mr R.T Thorpe
Mr R.T Thorpes
MR P Thwaite
MSTR M A Thwaite
Mr J N Tiffen
Mr K Tiffen
T.L. Lifting Ltd
THE TIGER
Mr C.P. Tighe
CEC Time
Mr P.G.W Tindale
MR A J Tinkler
MISS S Todd
Mr G P Todd
MR R Todd
MR S Todd
MR K.S TOMBS
Mr K.T Towse
Mrs B.T Towse

MR I Tracey
MISS A Trant
Mr T.T Tranter
Trapezium Transport
Trattles & Rushforth Ltd
Mr S.J.T Trigg
Miss C.L.T Trotter
Mr P.M.T Trotter
MR C Tuck
Mr M.A Tuck
MR R Tuck
Mr K.R.T Tulip
MR B J Tully
MR T M Tunney
Mr M.A.T Turnbull
MR R Turnbull
MR A Turner
MR C Turner
MR J Turner
Mr J.C.T Turner
MR M N Turner
MR N Turner
Mr W R Turner
Mrs E Turner
Mr D J Turnock
MR H Turton
Mr H Turton
Mr W.S.D Turton
Mr P Tutill
Mr R.T Tweddle
Mr S.T Tweddle
Mrs D.A.T Tye
Ms A.T Tye
Mr G.S.T Tyerman
Ms E.T Tyerman
Miss L.V.T Tyler
Mr D.T Tyler
MR M D Tyreman
Tyne TeesLeyland
MR P Tyrie
Mr K.T Tyrrell
Mr P.A.T Tyrrell
Mr L Underwood
Mr M Upton
Mr B.M.U Usher
Miss A.V Vallely
Mrs D.V Vallely
Ms C.V Vanham
D Varely
K Varley
MR H C Varley
MR R A Varley
Mr N R Vaughan
MR K VAUX
Mr R.V Vaux
Mr G. Veazey
Mrs J. Veazey
MR R Vickers
Mr S.V Vickers
Mr M.V Vigilante
Mr A. Wadding
MR M J Wadding
Mr P. Wadding
Mr L.W.W Waddington
Mr W.W Waddington
Mr D.R.W Waddleton
Mr J.W Wade
MR D Wadsworth
Mr C. Wainwright
Mrs D. Wainwright
MR B Waite
Mr R.W Waite
MR S Waite
MRS J Waite
Mr H.W Waites
MR N Waites
Mr S.W Waites
MR G P Wake
MR K Wakefield
MR T J Waldron
Mr C.W Walford

Mr D.W Walford
Mr J.W Walford
MR A Walker
Mr A M Walker
Mr J.M.W Walker
Mr J.S Walker
Mr J.W Walker
MR P Walker
Mr P.A. Walker
Mr P.W Walker
MR S J Walker
Mrs D.A.W Walker
MSTR L J Walker
Mstr S M Walker
Mr D.W Wallace
MR R.J Wallace
Mr R.W Wallin
Mr A.W Wallis
Mr D.G. Wallis
Mr A J Walls
Mr B Walls
MISS C Walters
Mr A.W Walton
Mr C J Walton
Mr F Walton
MR N Walton
MR R Walton
Mrs Fern Walton
MRS M Walton
MSTR D Walton
MISS K Ward
MR Ward
MR A F Ward
MR F Ward
MR G J Ward
Mr H.W Ward
Mr J.R. Ward
MR T A Ward
MRS J Ward
Mr M.D.W Warne
Mr P.L.W Warren
Mr P.G.W Wastnedge
Mr N Waterfield
Watson Associates
Miss E.A.W Watson
Mr A. Watson
Mr C.F.W Watson
Mr C.J.W Watson
Mr C.M.W Watson
MR J M Watson
Mr P.W Watson
Mr R.W Watson
MR T G Watson
MR W E Watson
Mrs Y.W Watson
WATSON WOOD-
HOUSE
Mr J.W Wattis
Mr T.B.W Wattis
MR A Wayman
MR C Wayman
MR J Wayman
MSTR C Wayman
Mr M.D.W Weall
MR G P Weatherald
Mr J. Weatherill
Mr J.L. Weatherill
Miss N.M.W Weatherston
Mr A.I.W Weatherston
Ms M.C.W Weatherston
Mr P.W Webb
Mrs K.W Webb
Mr N.W Webster

MR P Webster
Mr R.A Wedlake
Mrs J.P Wedlake
Miss A M Weeks
Mrs J Weeks
Weir Eng
Mr B Welburn
Mr M.W Welch
Mr S.W Weldon
Mr B.W Wells
Mr G W Wells
Mr N.W Wells
Mr P.A.W Wells
Mrs C.W Wells
Mr I Welsh
Mr P Welsh
Mr P.W Welsh
Mr S.A.W Wentworth
Miss G.L.W West
Mr T.D.W West
Mr G Weston
Mr D.J.W Whaley
Mr M.W Whaley
Mrs M.W Whaley
Mrs M.W Whatley
MR D M Wheatley
Mr L Wheatley
MR D Wheetman
MR T Wheetman
MR P Whelerton
MR R Whelerton
MR S Wheelerton
MRS W Wheelerton
Mr B.J. White
MR D White
Mr D.W White
MR P White
Mrs L.W White
MR A Whitfield
Mr D Whitfield & Young
Mr J.W Whitfield
MR N Whitfield
Mr N. Whitfield
MR R Whitfield
Mr A.J.W Whitham
Mr C.J.W Whitlam
MR I Whitney
Mr D.W Whittaker
WHITTLE
MR M Whittle
MR R.G Wight
Mr P E Wigley
MSTR P Wilcock
MR D Wild
Mr J R Wildon
Mrs B Wildon
Mr B.W Wiles
Mr C.A Wiles
MR D Wiles
Mr P.R.W Wiles
Mr S.R.W Wiles
MR P Wilkes
MR S Wilkes
Miss H.W Wilkin
Mr C.J Wilkinson
Mr J P Wilkinson
Mr K.J.W Wilkinson
Mr N J Wilkinson
Mr P.W Wilkinson
MR D P Willett
MR P Willett
Mr B.W Williams
Mr C Williams
Mr D.W Williams
Mr E Williams
MR G Williams
Mr G.W Williams
MR H Williams
MR I Williams
Mr P.W Williams

Mr S Williams
MR S Williams
Mr S.G.W Williams
Mrs J Williams
Mr A Williamson
Mr D Williamson
MR M Williamson
Mr K Willis
Mr D G Wills
MISS H Wilson
Mr A Wilson
MR C A Wilson
Mr C.G.W Wilson
Mr C.M.W Wilson
MR D Wilson
Mr D Wilson
Mr D.W Wilson
Mr H Wilson
Mr I Wilson
MR J Wilson
Mr M Wilson
Mr P Wilson
MR P J Wilson
Mr P.W Wilson
MR R Wilson
Mr S Wilson
MR T Wilson
Mr T.W Wilson
Mrs C.W Wilson
MRS D Wilson
Mrs L Wilson
Wilton Eng. Serv. Ltd.
Mr S.J.W Winfield
Mr D.W Winter
Mr S.W.W Winter
Mr D Wise
Miss E.L.W Wishlade
Mr P.W Wishlade
Mstr B.P.W Wishlade
Mr D Witton
Mr G B Womack
Mr D.W Wood
MR H C Wood
Mr J.R.W Wood
MR P WOOD
Mr A.W.W Woodgate
Mr J.S.W Woodgate
MR A Woodhouse
Mr J A Woolhouse
MR WOOTON
Mr K.A.W Worley
Mr D Wormald
Mr Worrall
MR D Worton
Miss E.J Wray
MR A J Wright
Mr D.W Wright
Mr G.P. Wright
Mr H.W Wright
Mr J.P.W Wright
Mr P J Wright
Mr P.W Wright
Wright & Co
Miss N.M. Wrightson
Mstr G.T. Wrightson
Mstr P.J. Wrightson
Mr K.C.W Wulder
MR D S Yates
Mr K M Yates
Mr R.Y Yeoman
Mr R.Y Yeomans
Mr R.A.Y York
MR Young
Mr C.J.Y Young
MR K Young
Mr D.Y Younger
Mr S.Y Younger
MR G D YOUNGS
Mr P.D.Y Youngs
MR R E Yuille